EMPLOYMENT LAW

WITHDRAWN

EMPLOYMENT LAW

Gillian Phillips MA (Cantab), LLM, Solicitor, Part-time Judge,
Employment Tribunals

Karen Scott LLB, LLM, Solicitor, Part-time Judge,
Employment Tribunals

Published by

College of Law Publishing,
Braboeuf Manor, Portsmouth Road, St Catherines, Guildford GU3 1HA

British Library Cataloguing-in-Publication Data

A catalogue record for this book is available from the British Library.

ISBN 978 1 909176 22 5

Typeset by Style Photosetting Ltd, Mayfield, East Sussex

Printed in Great Britain by Polestar Wheatons, Exeter

Preface

This book has been written primarily for students of the Employment Law and Practice elective on the Legal Practice Course. It covers a number of important areas of individual employment law, although it does not deal with trade union law or collective agreements.

For the sake of brevity, the masculine pronoun is used to include the feminine.

The law is stated as at 1 October 2012, although some later developments have been referred to where possible.

We express our thanks to the many previous authors and contributors to this book. In particular, we would like to thank Peter Rumbelow, for all his sterling efforts over the years. We would also like to express our thanks to Jo Bingham, Cathryn Glover, Penny Hayhurst, Coral Hill, Christopher Morris, Christine Taylor, Laurie Toczek, Debbie Woods, Janet Wright, Christine Pashley and the rest of the Employment Law team at the College of Law for their comments on the previous editions of this book. Though we benefitted enormously from their advice, all errors are strictly of our own making. Thanks too to John Moore of Bevan Brittan LLP.

Thanks as always to David Stott for his help and guidance.

GILLIAN PHILLIPS
KAREN SCOTT

Contents

Table of Cases

D

H

Table of Statutes

Table of Secondary Legislation and Codes of Practice

Introductory Note

The renaming of the Department of Trade and Industry

In June 2009, the Department for Business, Enterprise and Regulatory Reform (DBERR) (the former Department of Trade and Industry (DTI)) became the Department for Business, Innovation and Skills (BIS) (www.bis.gov.uk). A number of the websites referred to in this book were originally DTI/DBERR websites. The authors have endeavoured to change web addresses where necessary; in most instances, however, pre-existing DTI/DBERR website addresses remain operative and will automatically redirect the user to the correct web page. References to the DTI/DBERR are retained where relevant for historical purposes.

European developments

Working time

Talks on a revised Working Time Directive have been ongoing since the European Commission issued a proposal for its amendment in September 2004. This proposal followed two Court of Justice (ECJ) judgments: *Sindicato de Medicos de Asistencia Publica (SiMAP) v Conselleria de Sanidad y Consumo de la Generalidad Valenciana* (Case C-303/98) [2000] ECR I-7963 and *Landeshauptstadt Kiel v Norbert Jaeger* (Case C-151/02) [2003] ECR I-8389, which were regarded by a number of national governments as giving too lax an interpretation to the Directive.

In SiMAP, a Spanish court referred five questions to the European Court of Justice for a preliminary ruling on the interpretation of the Directive. The court wished to know, *inter alia*, whether time spent by doctors on-call, either at medical centres or under a contact system, should be regarded as 'working time' and therefore whether that time should be included in the calculation of working hours for the purposes of the 48-hour maximum weekly working time. The ECJ ruled that 'time spent on-call by doctors in primary health care teams must be regarded in its entirety as working time and, where appropriate as overtime, within the meaning of Directive 93/104 if they are required to be at the health centre'. If they merely had to be contactable at all times when on-call, only time linked to the actual provision of primary health care services must be regarded as 'working time'. In *Jaeger*, Dr Jaeger, a hospital doctor, carried out a number of periods of on-call duty each month, where he stayed at the clinic (he had a room with a bed in the hospital) and was called upon to carry out his professional duties as need arose. The ECJ held that the Directive must be interpreted as meaning that on-call duty performed by a doctor where he is required to be physically present in the hospital must be regarded as constituting working time in its totality for the purposes of the Directive, even where the person concerned is permitted to rest at his place of work during the period when his services are not required. Periods when the doctor was on-call but not working should not be treated as rest periods, and compensatory rest periods must immediately follow the periods worked.

The EU's talks focused on two key issues arising out of the SiMAP and *Jaeger* cases: an individual's right to opt out of the 48-hour working week, and whether time spent on call is counted as working time. In mid-September 2008, the Council of the European Union, after lengthy and difficult negotiations, reached an agreement on amendments to the Directive. To amend the Directive there must be agreement between the Member States (represented by 'The 'Council', of ministers from each Member State) and the European Parliament. The European Parliament did not support the proposed amendments and in December 2008 voted for considerable amendments of its own, including the phasing out of the opt-out provisions over three years and for the entire period of on-call time, including any inactive part, to count as working time. A period of intense negotiation (known as conciliation) followed, but on 27 April 2009 the negotiations failed. It was agreed that as the European Parliament and Member States were unable to resolve their long-standing differences over whether to retain the opt-out or not, there was no point in continuing the negotiations.

Following the failure of the previous efforts to revise the Directive, the Commission moved to the second-stage consultation with EU-level social partners on 21 December 2010. It had concluded from responses to the first consultation, and from its own examination of the Directive's implementation, that 'changes to the current working time rules are urgently needed'. The second-stage consultation document asked for the social partners' (workers and employers' representatives) views on two options for revision of the Directive:

- a focused review, dealing only with the issues of on-call time and compensatory rest;
- a comprehensive review, dealing with a wider range of matters highlighted by the social partners in their responses to the first consultation, including the individual opt-out from the Directive's 48-hour maximum working week.

In November 2011, the EU-level social partners indicated that they would enter into talks to revise the Directive. Under the process provided for by Article 155 of the Treaty on the Functioning of the European Union (TFEU), they had nine months in which to negotiate an agreement. In August 2012 the deadline was extended to December 2012.

In May 2011, the UK Government published plans to amend the Working Time Regulations 1998 in order to resolve uncertainty following a series of European and UK judgments on the rights of workers who are unable to take holiday due to sickness. In essence, the Government is proposing that annual leave may be carried over to the next leave year in circumstances where leave cannot be taken at the scheduled time due to sickness, or where the employee is sick during scheduled annual leave. More uncertainty exists following the ECJ decision, *KHS AG v Schulte* (Case C-214/10), which held that the EU Working Time Directive does not require unlimited accumulation of holiday when a worker has been on sickness absence for several years. The ECJ said that a 15-month 'carry over period' was lawful. The Government's firm proposals are still awaited. It is yet to publish a response to its consultation.

Data protection

In January 2012, the European Commission published proposals for a comprehensive reform of the EU Data Protection Directive (95/46/EC). The main aim is to remove inconsistencies created by Member States having implemented the Directive in different ways. The Commission proposes a general data protection Regulation. The proposals also attempt to reflect the rapid advances in technology since the Directive first came into effect. Any proposals will need to be approved by the Member States and ratified by the European Parliament. It is unlikely that the proposal will be in force before 2015.

Equal treatment

Following the coming into force of the EC Directive on conditions for temporary (agency) workers (Directive 2008/104/EC) on 5 December 2008, the Agency Workers Regulations 2010 came into force at the beginning of October 2011, providing agency workers with the right to equal treatment as to basic employment and working conditions (working time, overtime, holidays, public holidays and pay) compared with their directly-recruited counterparts after 12 weeks in a job. Agency workers started to acquire these rights from 24 December 2011. BIS has published Guidance on the Agency Workers Regulations, available at http://www.bis.gov.uk/assets/biscore/employment-matters/docs/a/11-949-agency-workers-regulations-guidance.pdf.

Family rights

The EU Parental Leave Directive (2010/18/EU), which was adopted by the EU Council of Ministers in March 2010, increased the amount of (unpaid) parental leave from 13 to 18 weeks. BIS has indicated that implementation will take place in March 2013.

UK developments

Responsibility for employment law is spread across a number of different government departments, including the Department for Work and Pensions, BIS, the Ministry of Justice and the Home Office.

On 23 December 2011, the Secretary of State for Business, Vince Cable, announced a series of 'radical reforms to the employment law system'. The main ones are summarised below and will be developed in more detail at appropriate places in the main text. The impetus for reform seems to be underpinned by three main tenets – cutting costs, reducing the risk of paying compensation and reducing the time taken up by employment disputes. BIS said there were more than 236,000 tribunal claims in 2010, a 56% increase on 2009. It estimated that businesses spent on average nearly £4,000 to defend themselves against a claim. The main changes announced related to:

- increasing the qualifying period for bringing an employment tribunal claim from one year to two for employees who start work with an employer on or after 6 April 2012 (see **Chapter 3**) – it is estimated that this will reduce the number of claims by between 3,700 and 4,700 (this change was introduced in April 2012)
- charging a fee for the lodging and continuing of a tribunal claim (see below and **Chapter 6**)
- introducing the concept of 'protected conversations' between an employer and an employee which could not be given in evidence to a tribunal (see **Chapter 6**)
- a root-and-branch review of the Tribunal Rules (see below)
- a 'simpler, quicker and clearer' dismissal process, which may include amendments to the Acas Code of Practice
- reducing the consultation period for collective redundancies (see **Chapter 4**)
- changing the rules concerning the transfer of undertakings.

On 14 September 2012, Mr Cable announced a package of reforms. Some of the proposals are discussed below.

The Enterprise and Regulatory Reform Bill

The Government has included a number of provisions in the Enterprise and Regulatory Reform Bill, which was introduced into Parliament on 23 May 2012. These include:

- the introduction of a scheme whereby employment disputes will have to go to Acas for mandatory pre-claim conciliation before they can go to an employment tribunal
- the introduction of protected conversations to cover termination settlement discussions
- the introduction of a discretionary power for employment tribunals to impose financial penalties on employers who lose cases. The level of penalty would be half of the total award made by the tribunal, with a minimum threshold of £100 and a maximum of £5,000 where there are 'aggravating factors'. The penalty would be reduced by 50% if paid within 21 days
- the power to vary the statutory upper limit on the compensatory award in unfair dismissal cases (consultation will close on 23 November 2012)
- closing a 'loophole' in the Public Interest Disclosure Act 1998 on whistleblowing that allows employees to claim that 'blowing the whistle' about a breach of their own employment contract is a protected disclosure. The Bill provides for protection to be restricted to disclosures that are 'in the public interest'. See **5.5.5** below.

In October 2012 at the Conservative Party Conference, the Chancellor of the Exchequer announced a plan to create a new type of employment contract called an owner-employee contract, which would enable employees to exchange some of their employment rights for shares in the company they work for. The Government intends to launch a consultation process on this, which it is hoped will clarify a number of practical concerns about how the proposal will work.

Family rights

In April 2010, the Equality and Human Rights Commission (EHRC) published 'Working better', a report calling for significant changes to the statutory maternity, paternity and parental rights regime (see **Chapter 14**). The report stated that the UK's current parental leave policies were the worst in Europe and that its statutory framework did not reflect 21st century family life. The report called for fundamental changes so that both mothers and fathers are provided with greater support in bringing up children. The report proposes a move, over three stages and in 10 years, towards more 'gender neutral' parental rights, including the removal of any length of service eligibility requirements, a shift to statutory maternity pay payable for 26 weeks at 90% of salary and a new 52-week period of parental leave with four months for the mother and four for the father and the remainder to be taken by either parent, to be available until the child is 5 years old. The current parental leave policies reportedly cost the Government £2.07 billion a year; the EHRC estimates that these changes will cost a further £5.26 billion a year.

The Government issued its 'Modern Workplaces Consultation' on 16 May 2011 (www.bis.gov.uk/Consultations). The consultation sought views on:

- a new system of flexible parental leave which would allow mothers and fathers to share leave, and give parents and employers greater choice about how leave is taken;
- how to extend the right to flexible working to all employees, not just those with children under 17 (or 18 for parents of disabled children);
- changes to the Working Time Regulations as a result of European cases about the interaction of annual leave and sick leave. The proposal is to amend the Working Time Regulations so that when a worker falls ill during planned annual leave, annual leave entitlements can be rescheduled and carried over to the next leave year. The proposal is to limit the amount of carried-over holiday for sickness absence to the four weeks' compulsory paid leave that is available under the Working Time Directive, ie the employee would lose the extra 1.6 weeks he receives under the UK's Working Time Regulations. The Government is also considering proposals to allow employers to 'buy out' that extra 1.6 weeks; and
- tackling unequal pay through requiring employers who lose an employment tribunal case on equal pay to carry out a pay audit.

The Government response to the Modern Workplaces Consultation was due to be published early in 2012, but at the time of writing had still not appeared. However, the proposal to introduce a new system of flexible, shared parental leave from 2015 was included in the Queen's Speech to Parliament on 9 May 2012, which confirmed that that will be included in a forthcoming Children and Families Bill (not yet published).

Pensions

From October 2012, employers in Great Britain are required to enrol eligible workers automatically into a workplace pension scheme. The new duties will be implemented over a four-year period, with larger employers being affected first.

Employment tribunals

On 27 January 2011, BIS began a consultation on reforms to the employment tribunal system, 'Resolving Workplace Disputes: A Consultation' (www.bis.gov.uk/Consultations). The consultation closed in April 2011. This came against a background of a continued rise in the number of employment tribunal claims. In the year to 31 March 1998, there were just over 80,000 claims. For the year to 31 March 2010, there were 236,100 claims.

The Government announced its response to the consultation in November 2011. The following changes have now been implemented:

- increasing the qualifying period for unfair dismissal to two years with effect from April 2012
- changes to costs and deposit orders
- Employment Judges sit alone in unfair dismissal cases
- witness statements are no longer read out but are taken as read.

See **Chapter 6** for more details.

Fees

The Lord Chancellor has the power, under s 42 of the Tribunals, Courts and Enforcement Act 2007, to introduce fees in certain tribunals, which could include employment tribunals and the Employment Appeal Tribunal (EAT). However, since their inception in 1964, taking claims to employment tribunals (or appealing to the EAT) has been free of charge to users and funded entirely by the taxpayer. In the financial year 2010/11, the employment tribunals received 218,100 claims and 2,048 appeals were made to the EAT at a total cost to the taxpayer of £84.2 million.

In early 2011, the Government announced its intention, as part of the 'Resolving Workplace Disputes' consultation (http://www.bis.gov.uk/Consultations/resolving-workplace-disputes), to introduce fee-charging into employment tribunals as part of a series of wider reforms 'to support and encourage early resolution of workplace disputes and in order to transfer some of the cost burden from the taxpayer to the users of the system'. The Institute of Employment Rights (IER) (see www.ier.org.uk) has pointed out the unfairness of fee charging, referring to Ministry of Justice research in 2009, which found that 12 months after judgment, 31% of claimants had not been paid at all. Although the system has since been improved, the number of unpaid tribunal awards and Acas settlements remains high. The IER argue that the introduction of fees could mean that significant numbers of claimants who win their cases end up suffering a net loss. So the Government's assertion that the cost will be 'ultimately borne by the party who caused the system to be used' may not be a fair or accurate conclusion to draw.

On 14 December 2011, the Ministry of Justice published a Consultation Paper entitled 'Charging Fees in Employment Tribunals and the Employment Appeal Tribunal' (CP22/2011). The consultation ran until March 2012. The consultation sought views on two alternative fee-charging structures for the employment tribunals (and one proposed structure for the EAT). Option 1 for the employment tribunal proposed that there should be a two-stage charging system, with stage one at issue (payable at the time of lodging the claim by the party who makes the claim to an employment tribunal (or appeal)) and, for those claims proceeding to hearing, a second fee payable before the hearing. The fees proposed ranged form £150 to £250, depending on the type of claim and stage in the proceedings. Further fees were also proposed for certain specified applications that might be made after a claim had been accepted (eg setting aside a default judgment). Option 2 proposed:

(a)   that there should be only one main charging point for fees, at issue of claim stage, plus further fees for certain specified applications that might be made after a claim had been accepted;

(b)   that the level of fees should vary depending on the nature of the claim made (reflecting the likely level of resources used by claims of this nature) and the value of the claim, and for multiple claims, the number of people in the claim;

(c)   that if the claimant chooses to seek an award over the threshold of £30,000, a higher fee is payable irrespective of the nature of the claim.

The HM Courts and Tribunals Service (HMCTS) fee remission system for civil courts in England and Wales would be applied to the employment tribunals fee structure across the whole of the UK, to protect access to justice for those who cannot afford to pay the full fee or who can only afford make a contribution to it.

The Ministry of Justice's Response was published on 13 July 2012. A total of 140 responses were received to the consultation. This included 25 from unions and other organisations representing the views of employees, 29 from legal groups and solicitors, 31 responses from business, 25 on behalf of advisory and equality groups, and 30 from other interested parties and individuals. Claimants and groups representing their interests came out as strongly opposed to the principle of charging fees (primarily on the basis that they would deter claimants from making claims and that it was unfair that claimants were being asked to pay the majority of fees, particularly given the perceived financial inequality of employee versus employer). Many responses disagreed with both options presented in the consultation. Business respondents generally supported both options, with a tendency towards favouring Option 2. Overall, there was little consensus on the key issues, but respondents overall seemed to prefer a two-stage fee, believing that it offered a second opportunity to encourage parties to consider settlement. The proposed HMCTS civil courts remission system was criticised by both business and claimant groups. Business thought it was too generous and did not take into account savings or recent payments of lump sums to employees. Claimant groups argued it was too complicated, would not protect as many individuals as suggested and was not generous enough. Following the consultation, the Government decided not to pursue Option 2. In respect of employment tribunals, the Government decided to introduce the Option 1 fee structure in the latter half of 2013, with some amendments to the level of fees proposed in the consultation.

The Government also decided to adopt the proposal to extend the HMCTS civil courts remission system to protect access to justice in employment tribunals and the EAT for those who cannot afford to pay the fees. The Government is going to undertake a review of remissions as part of a wider review required for the introduction of Universal Credit. The review will aim to produce a single remissions system for courts and tribunals which is simpler to use, more cost-efficient and better targeted to ensure that those who can afford to pay fees do so, while continuing to provide access to the courts and tribunal system to those who cannot.

The actual amount of the fee will depend on the nature of the claim. 'Level 1' claims, which cover disputes over matters such as unauthorised deductions from wages and a failure to pay a redundancy payment, will attract a fee of £160 when the claim is issued and a further £230 prior to hearing, ie a potential total of £390. 'Level 2' claims, including discrimination, equal pay and unfair dismissal, will attract an issue fee of £250 and a hearing fee of £950, making a possible total of £1,200. Employers will not be required to pay a fee to file a response. Fees for employers will be possible once a claim has been issued; for example, they will be required to pay to issue a counterclaim in a contract claim or to make a review application. If a case goes to the EAT, the party who decides to appeal must pay £400 to lodge the appeal and a further £1,200 for a hearing.

Tribunal Rules

In November 2011, the Government commissioned Mr Justice Underhill to lead a Working Group to conduct the review of the rules of procedure governing employment tribunal proceedings. The terms of reference were:

(a)   cases to be managed in a way that is proportionate to the nature of the issues involved, with the importance of saving expense considered throughout;

(b)   proceedings to be handled quickly and efficiently, with an emphasis on helping proceedings to resolve themselves otherwise than through judicial determination at hearings, and dealing robustly and, so far as appropriate, consistently with cases where they appear to have little or no reasonable prospect of success, with a view to fairness for all parties and the tribunal and its resources;

(c)   rules to be both simple and simply expressed, in particular given the significant proportion of unrepresented parties using employment tribunals;

(d)   proceedings to have as much certainty as the nature of particular case allows, and that in particular –

    (i)   like cases are treated alike (with as much use made of standardised orders and directions as possible, building on the good work already developed around Case Management Discussion agendas),

    (ii)   rules are exercised, and orders are made, in a manner that is consistent, so far as appropriate, across Great Britain (backed, where necessary and appropriate, by relevant and published practice directions).

The review was due to be completed by the end of April 2012. Although the time table slipped a little, at the end of June 2012 Mr Justice Underhill wrote to the Government attaching a draft set of new Rules that the Group recommended should be made in place of the current rules. The new Rules are less than half the length of the old. Mr Justice Underhill says that this has been achieved 'not only by more succinct wording but also by leaving out many rules that simply prescribe administrative practice and by leaving some general case-management discretions unglossed'. The proposed draft rules were published in July 2012 and consultation will close on 23 November 2012.

See **Chapter 6** for a more detailed account of the main proposed changes.

Immigration

The Government is currently consulting on limiting the opportunities for non-EU workers to stay permanently in the UK. At present, skilled workers (Tier 2) could normally expect to be granted indefinite leave to remain if they complete five continuous years in the UK, have confirmation of continuing employment and have passed certain English tests. One proposal is that such 'general assumptions' would be removed and admission at the outset would be on a temporary basis.

Other matters

Transfer of Undertaking (Protection of Employment) Regulations 2006

The Government has been consulting on the effectiveness of the Transfer of Undertakings (Protection of Employment) Regulations 2006 – in particular, whether the rules are unnecessarily 'gold-plated' and bureaucratic. The closing date for responses was 31 January 2012. The Government published its response in September 2012.

Collective redundancy consultation

The Government has published a Consultation Paper recommending making changes to the rules on collective redundancy consultation, in particular shortening the minimum periods of consultation for large establishments (over 100 employees) from 90 days to 45 or 30 days. It has also proposed issuing a new, non-statutory code of practice on how to conduct consultations. The consultation closed on 19 September 2012. Any changes arising are likely to be implemented in Spring 2013.

General

For some years now, there have been common commencement dates for the introduction of employment policy. The two dates for commencement of domestic employment law for which

BIS has responsibility are 6 April and 1 October of each year. BIS publishes an annual statement of forthcoming employment legislation every January. An e-mail alert system is also available on the BIS website.

The Employment Tribunal Annual Statistics for 2011–12 were published in July 2012 (http://www.justice.gov.uk). The statistics show that between 2010–11 and 2011–12 there was a 15% fall in accepted claims to employment tribunals (the number of receipts (claims) was 218,000 in 2010–11 and 186,300 in 2011–12). This was primarily due to a large fall in multiple claims (ie claims involving two or more claimants).

Of the total number of jurisdictional (as opposed to individual) claims, 31% were for unfair dismissal, breach of contract and redundancy, 29% related to working-time claims and 16% were for unauthorised deductions. Of the jurisdictional claims disposed of, 27% were withdrawn, 33% were Acas-conciliated settlements, 27% were disposed of at hearing (12% were successful at tribunal) and 13% were struck out. Of all claims presented, 8% of unfair dismissal claims, 22% of redundancy pay claims, 17% of working time claims, 2% of sex discrimination claims, 3% of race discrimination claims and 3% of sexual orientation claims were successful at hearing.

Of unfair dismissal cases upheld, reinstatement or re-engagement orders were made in five (out of 5,100) cases. The maximum unfair dismissal award was £173,408, the median award was £4,560 and the average award was £9,133. In race discrimination cases, the maximum award was £4,445,023, the median award was £5,256 and the average award was £102,259. In sex discrimination cases, the maximum award was £89,700, the median award was £6,746 and the average award was £9,940. In disability discrimination cases, the maximum award was £390,871, the median award was £8,928 and the average award was £22,183. Costs were awarded to claimants in 116 cases and to respondents in 1,295 cases. The median costs award was £500. Costs awards of over £10,000 resulted in 48 cases. The highest costs award was £36,446.

In 2011–12 the EAT received 2,217 appeals, and 560 appeals were disposed of at a full hearing.

Reference resources

Useful information for employees may be found at www.direct.gov.uk. The site contains guidance on a number of employment matters, such as starting a new job, pay, employment contracts, work and families, discrimination and redundancy. The site also contains a link to 'TIGER' (Tailored Interactive Guidance on Employment Rights), which provides interactive guidance on flexible working and maternity rights too.

The EHRC has sections on its website (www.equalityhumanrights.com) containing guidance on all aspects of discrimination. The website also contains past publications and reports governing disability, gender and race.

The Acas website (www.acas.org.uk) provides a series of online publications (for example, advisory booklets on redundancy and stress, handbooks on the new statutory dispute resolution procedures, and leaflets on topics such as flexible working and holiday pay). It also offers a range of e-learning courses.

A number of law firms with employment law practices provide a range of publications and guidance on their websites.

Table of Abbreviations

Statutes and statutory instruments

APLR 2010	Additional Paternity Leave Regulations 2010
COSHH 1999	Control of Substances Hazardous to Health Regulations 1999
DDA 1995	Disability Discrimination Act 1995
DDA(A)R 2003	Disability Discrimination Act 1995 (Amendment) Regulations 2003
DPA 1998	Data Protection Act 1998
EA 2002	Employment Act 2002
EA(DR)R 2004	Employment Act 2002 (Dispute Resolution) Regulations 2004
EE(A)R 2006	Employment Equality (Age) Regulations 2006
EE(RB)R 2003	Employment Equality (Religion or Belief) Regulations 2003
EE(SO)R 2003	Employment Equality (Sexual Orientation) Regulations 2003
EPA 1970	Equal Pay Act 1970
EP(C)A 1978	Employment Protection (Consolidation) Act 1978
ERA 1996	Employment Rights Act 1996
ERA 1999	Employment Relations Act 1999
ETA 1996	Employment Tribunals Act 1996
ET(CRP)R 2004	Employment Tribunals (Constitution and Rules of Procedure) Regulations 2004
HRA 1998	Human Rights Act 1998
HSCER 1996	Health and Safety (Consultation with Employees) Regulations 1996
HSWA 1974	Health and Safety at Work etc Act 1974
HS(YP)R 1997	Health and Safety (Young Persons) Regulations 1997
ICE Regulations	Information and Consultation of Employees Regulations 2004
ITEPA 2003	Income Tax (Earnings and Pensions) Act 2003
MHOR 1992	Manual Handling Operations Regulations 1992
MHSWR 1992 and 1999	Management of Health and Safety at Work Regulations 1992 and 1999
MPL(A)R 2002	Maternity and Parental Leave (Amendment) Regulations 2002
MPLPAL(A)R 2006	Maternity and Parental Leave etc and Paternity and Adoption Leave (Amendment) Regulations 2006
MPLR 1999	Maternity and Parental Leave etc Regulations 1999
NAWR 1989	Noise at Work Regulations 1989
NMWA 1998	National Minimum Wage Act 1998
PALR 2002	Paternity and Adoption Leave Regulations 2002
PIDA 1998	Public Interest Disclosure Act 1998
PUWER 1998	Provision and Use of Work Equipment Regulations 1998
RIPA 2000	Regulation of Investigatory Powers Act 2000
RRA 1976	Race Relations Act 1976
RRA(A)R 2003	Race Relations Act 1976 (Amendment) Regulations 2003
SDA 1975	Sex Discrimination Act 1975
SM(S)R 1992	Supply of Machinery (Safety) Regulations 1992
TULR(C)A 1992	Trade Union and Labour Relations (Consolidation) Act 1992
W(HSW)R 1992	Workplace (Health, Safety and Welfare) Regulations 1992

Employment case reports

ICR	Industrial Cases Reports
IRLR	Industrial Relations Law Reports

Other abbreviations

AAL	additional adoption leave
Acas	Advisory, Conciliation and Arbitration Service
ACOP	Approved Code of Practice
AML	additional maternity leave
APL	additional paternity leave
APP	additional paternity pay
BIS	Department for Business, Innovation and Skills
BRE	Better Regulation Executive
CEHR	Commission for Equality and Human Rights
COET	Central Office of the Employment Tribunals
CRE	Commission for Racial Equality
DDPs	disciplinary and dismissal procedures
DfWP	Department for Work and Pensions
DLA	disability living allowance
DRC	Disability Rights Commission
DTI	Department of Trade and Industry
EAT	Employment Appeal Tribunal
ECtHR	European Court of Human Rights
ECJ	European Court of Justice
EDT	effective date of termination (of employment)
EHRC	Equality and Human Rights Commission
EOC	Equal Opportunities Commission
EP	European Parliament
ETO	economic, technical or organisational (reason for dismissal on transfer of an undertaking)
EWC	expected week of childbirth
GOQ	genuine occupational qualification (in relation to sex or race discrimination)
GOR	genuine occupational requirement
GPs	grievance procedures
HMRC	HM Revenue and Customs
HSC	Health and Safety Commission
HSE	Health and Safety Executive
MA	maternity allowance
NJC	National Joint Council for Local Authorities' Administrative, Professional, Technical and Clerical Services
NMW	national minimum wage
NRA	normal retiring age
OAL	ordinary adoption leave
OML	ordinary maternity leave
OPL	ordinary paternity leave
PAYE	Pay As You Earn (in relation to Schedule E Income Tax)
PILON	payment in lieu of notice
PHR	pre-hearing review
ROET	Regional Office of the Employment Tribunals
RRO	restricted reporting order
S2P	Second State Pension Scheme
SAP	statutory adoption pay
SERPS	State Earnings Related Pension Scheme
SMP	statutory maternity pay
SOSR	some other substantial reason
SPP	statutory paternity pay
WHO	World Health Organisation

THE CONTRACT OF EMPLOYMENT

LEARNING OUTCOMES

After reading this chapter you will be able to:

- understand and explain the differences between an employee and a worker, and identify which statutory rights apply to which
- understand and explain the difference between a written statement of terms and an employment contract
- identify statutory restrictions on the freedom to contract
- understand how implied terms operate in an employment contract
- list the key terms that *must* be included in a written statement of terms/contract of employment
- list the key additional terms that *may* be included in a written contract of employment, and understand the importance of and the enforceability of restrictive covenants
- understand how the protection of wages legislation works
- understand the Working Time Regulations
- advise as to the enforceability of post-termination duties.

1.1 INTRODUCTION

Employment law in the UK derives from various sources – not only common law and statute, but also codes of practice and European Union (EU) law. In recent years, EU legislation has had a particularly significant influence, in terms both of legislation and judgments of the Court of Justice (ECJ). Further, quite separately, decisions of the European Court of Human Rights (ECtHR, in Strasbourg) have influenced its development. This book will attempt to explain the impact and effect of all these areas on UK employment law. The main emphasis of this book is on individual employment rights – that is to say, the law that relates to employers and their employees and workers. There is very little commentary on collective areas of labour law such as trade unions, but these areas are touched upon where relevant.

1.2   BACKGROUND

Set out below is a summary of the main sources of employment law and their relevance.

1.2.1   Common law

Prior to the enactment of legislation affecting the relationship of employer and employee, the obligations each owed to the other were largely governed by the law of contract. Case law developed as the courts were called upon to interpret express contractual provisions, and to determine the nature and extent of implied contractual rights and duties. Case law has also developed on the interpretation of statutory provisions, many of which depend on the concept of 'reasonableness'.

This book considers reports of decisions reached by the UK courts and by the employment tribunals, as both forums can be used to determine issues of employment law. Judgments of the ECJ and ECtHR are also referred to, where relevant.

1.2.1.1   Employment tribunals

Employment tribunals have jurisdiction (through statute) to hear claims arising out of breaches of most aspects of the employment relationship, for example unfair dismissal, wrongful dismissal, redundancy payments, discrimination claims, equal pay claims and protection of wages claims (see **6.2.1** for further details). Tribunals also have jurisdiction to hear some claims by workers (eg, claims under the protection of wages legislation – see **1.10** below – and discrimination claims). For the distinction between a worker and an employee, see s 230 of the Employment Rights Act 1996 and **1.3** below.

1.2.1.2   The Employment Appeal Tribunal

The Employment Appeal Tribunal (EAT) hears appeals on questions of law from an employment tribunal. Its decisions are binding on employment tribunals. An appeal from the EAT lies to the Court of Appeal and from there to the Supreme Court.

1.2.1.3   The civil courts

In addition to the appellate function of the civil courts, the High Court and county court can hear breach of contract claims (eg wrongful dismissal) (see **Chapter 2**). Further, the civil courts can grant injunctive relief (eg where a restraint of trade clause has been breached, see **1.8.7.1**).

Note that the last House of Lords hearings took place in July 2009. The House of Lords has been replaced by the Supreme Court.

1.2.2   Legislation

The Industrial Relations Act 1971 attempted for the first time to introduce a comprehensive regulatory framework for all aspects of employment law, from collective bargaining to individual rights. Prior to this, employment issues had had to be dealt with in the common law courts under the common law. There were no special provisions or protections. There were no concepts of fairness – an employer was free to dismiss an employee as long as it did so in a contractually correct manner. The 1971 Act introduced the right to complain of 'unfair' dismissal. The majority of individual rights were consolidated, first in the Employment Protection (Consolidation) Act 1978 (EP(C)A 1978) and most recently in the Employment Rights Act 1996 (ERA 1996). The ERA 1996 was amended by the Employment Relations Acts

1999 and 2004 (ERA 1999 and 2004), the Employment Act 2002 (EA 2002) and the Work and Families Act 2006.

The Trade Union and Labour Relations (Consolidation) Act 1992 (TULR(C)A 1992), as amended by the Trade Union Reform and Employment Rights Act 1993 and the ERA 1999, consolidated all statute law containing trade union and group provisions. In the field of equal pay and discrimination, the Equal Pay Act 1970 (EPA 1970), the Sex Discrimination Act 1975 (SDA 1975), the Race Relations Act 1976 (RRA 1976) and the Disability Discrimination Act 1995 (DDA 1995) have all been repealed and replaced by the provisions of the Equality Act 2010 (see **Chapter 8**).

In addition to statutes there is a plethora of delegated legislation regulating employment law (much of it driven by EU law – see **1.2.4**) which will be referred to where relevant.

1.2.3 Codes of practice

A code of practice is not legally binding and is intended to give guidance to employers on good employment practices. It may, however, be used in evidence. For example, the Advisory, Conciliation and Arbitration Service (Acas) Code of Practice on Discipline and Grievance is often referred to by tribunals (see **Chapter 5**).

1.2.4 European Union law

Following the passing of the European Communities Act 1972 (which became effective on 1 January 1973), the UK joined the European Community and ceded sovereignty on areas covered by EC law, such as some employment and discrimination laws, to the EC. The two principal sources of EC law were the EC Treaty of 1957 (the Treaty of Rome) and the Treaty on European Union of 1992 (the Maastricht Treaty).

The EC Treaty was renamed the Treaty on the Functioning of the European Union (TFEU) when the Treaty of Lisbon came into force on 1 December 2009. All references to the 'Community' are changed to the 'Union'. All references in this book are to the new TFEU but, where readers need to know the original (EEC) or previous (EC) numbering, we include that information. This information is needed to make sense of older case law. The Court of Justice of the European Union (the CJEU) is an umbrella term which refers collectively to the Court of Justice (ECJ), the General Court and the Civil Service Tribunal. Most of the case law referred to in this book comes from the ECJ.

This section looks very briefly at how some particular provisions that are important in the context of employment law have been applied to give remedies in English courts and tribunals.

1.2.4.1 Treaty provisions and Regulations

Provisions of EU treaties and EU Regulations which give clear, precise and unconditional rights to individuals may be directly enforced in English courts because they have direct applicability (see *Van Gend en Loos v Nederlandse Administratie der Belastingen* (Case 26/62) [1963] ECR 1). One important example is Article 157 TFEU (ex Article 119 EEC/141 EC), which provides that 'Each Member State shall ... [maintain] the application of the principle that men and women should receive equal pay for equal work or work of equal value'.

In the case of *Barber v Guardian Royal Exchange Assurance Group* (Case C-262/88) [1990] 2 All ER 660, Article 157 TFEU was applied directly in favour of a man in order to entitle him to the same benefits as a woman under an occupational pension scheme. The scheme was discriminatory as it permitted women to receive a pension from age 50, but men only from age 55. Article 157 TFEU was applied despite the fact that different retiring ages in pension schemes were apparently permitted under the SDA 1975 and the EPA 1970. In equal work cases, Article 157 TFEU is directly effective and overrides inconsistent national law.

1.2.4.2 Directives

A Directive is secondary EU legislation. It is not directly applicable, as it must be implemented by national legislation. However, if a Directive gives clear, precise and unconditional rights to an individual, and the State fails to implement it at all or to implement it properly within the stipulated time frame, the individual has a right to rely on the Directive directly against the State or an emanation of the State.

This means that Directives that have not been properly implemented in the UK may be directly enforced, but only by employees of the State or of an emanation of the State. In *Marshall v Southampton and South West Hampshire AHA* [1986] QB 401, a female former employee of the Area Health Authority was able to rely on the Equal Treatment Directive 76/207 in order to challenge contractual retirement ages which discriminated on the grounds of sex. A challenge was possible in this case only because the Area Health Authority was found to be an emanation of the State; Ms Marshall would not have been able to rely directly on the Directive if she had been employed in the private sector. (However, see *Kucukdeveci v Swedex GmbH & Co KG* (Case C-555/07) where the general principle of non-discrimination on grounds of age was given effect between individuals by the ECJ.)

The ECJ, in *Impact v Ministry for Agriculture and Food (Ireland)* (Case C-268/06) [2008] IRLR 552, confirmed that public sector employees can bring such claims in employment tribunals as well as in the national courts.

1.2.4.3 Interpretation of national legislation

Employees who cannot rely on direct effect, for example if they work in the private sector, may seek to enforce rights conferred by EU Directives which have not been properly implemented by asking the UK courts to interpret UK legislation in the light of the EU Directive (indirect effect).

Section 2(4) of the European Communities Act 1972 provides that 'any enactment passed or to be passed ... shall be construed and have effect subject to [EU law]'. Where UK legislation has been passed to implement an EU Directive, the English courts have interpreted the UK legislation so as to comply with EU law. For example, in *Litster v Forth Dry Dock & Engineering Co Ltd* [1989] IRLR 161 (see **7.2.2.3**), the House of Lords (now Supreme Court) put a very strained interpretation on the Transfer of Undertakings (Protection of Employment) Regulations 1981 in order to make the Regulations comply with the Acquired Rights Directive 77/187 which they were intended to implement. The ECJ held in *Marleasing SA v La Comercial Internacional de Alimentacion SA* [1990] ECR I-4135 that national courts must 'as far as possible' interpret national law in light of EU law, irrespective of whether the national law was adopted before or after the Directive in question. In *Webb v EMO Air Cargo (UK) Ltd* [1993] IRLR 27, the House of Lords followed *Marleasing* and stated that

> it is for a UK court to construe domestic legislation ... so as to accord with the interpretation of [a] Directive as laid down by the European Court, if that can be done without distorting the meaning of the domestic legislation.

1.2.4.4 Action against the State

If the State fails to implement a Directive at all (or incorrectly), an employee who is affected might be able to bring a claim against the State for damages under the principle in *Francovich (Andrea) and Bonifaci (Danila) v Italy* (Cases C-6 and 9/90) [1992] IRLR 84.

1.2.5 Human Rights Act 1998

The Human Rights Act 1998 (HRA 1998) came into force on 2 October 2000. Courts and tribunals in the UK now have to interpret national law in the light of the rights contained in the European Convention for the Protection of Human Rights and Fundamental Freedoms ('the Convention'), and where this is not possible, the High Court is empowered to declare such law incompatible with Convention rights. Employees of public authorities have a direct cause of action against their employer under the Act for contravention of the Act (see **Chapter 15**).

1.2.6 Immigration, Asylum and Nationality Act 2006

Section 15 of the Immigration, Asylum and Nationality Act 2006 provides that an employer who employs a person subject to immigration control who does not have the right to take employment, shall be guilty of a civil offence. The Act allows employers to avoid a civil penalty if they have carried out specific document checks before they employ the employee. The Act also makes it a criminal offence knowingly to employ someone who has no permission to work in the UK (s 21).

All UK citizens have the right to work in the UK. Citizens of the European Economic Area (EEA) also have the right to work in the UK subject to proving that they have such citizenship. Otherwise, no one has the right to work in the UK unless they are granted the right to work by the Home Office – generally by a visa. Asylum seekers can apply for permission to work if they have waited more than 12 months for a decision from the Home Office. All asylum seekers who apply for permission to work from 9 September 2010 are restricted to national shortage occupations. Students, if studying at foundation degree level or above, can work part time during terms, for no more than 20 hours a week. Students, if studying below foundation degree level, can work part time during terms, for no more than 10 hours a week.

Dismissal of an employee on the basis that he does not have the right to work in the UK may involve a consideration of issues relating to whether he has contravened a statutory enactment (ERA 1996, s 98(2)(d)), some other substantial reason and illegality (see **1.2.7** and **Chapter 5** below), as well as discrimination (see **Chapter 8** onwards).

Readers should log on to the Home Office UK Border Agency website (http://bia.homeoffice.gov.uk) for further detailed guidance (see also **8.4.1**).

1.2.7 Illegality

An employee whose contract is illegal may be prevented from asserting both his contractual and statutory rights (see **5.2.2.4** regarding statutory rights). If employers effectively are allowed to recover compensation for their illegal actions, that would be contrary to public policy (see, eg, *Hounga v Allen* [2012] IRLR 685).

1.3 THE RELATIONSHIP OF EMPLOYER AND EMPLOYEE

1.3.1 Introduction

Not all persons who perform work for others are employees, ie employed under a contract of service (a name derived from the old-fashioned terminology of master and servant). Some are workers (see **1.3.3**) and some are truly independent contractors who work under a contract *for services*. In marginal cases, it may be difficult to distinguish a contract of service from a contract for services.

The difference is important in practice because, for example, only employees are entitled to redundancy payments or to present a claim of unfair dismissal. Further, there are different income tax regimes. Employees pay income tax which is deducted at source under the PAYE scheme, whereas independent contractors pay income tax under a different regime. There are also differences in National Insurance contributions and entitlement to benefits.

Certain employment-related rights, such as discrimination, are not limited to employees and, increasingly, protections are being applied to 'workers' rather than the more narrow 'employee'. The term 'worker' includes employees but is wider (see ERA 1996, s 230(3)). It can be difficult to distinguish between a worker and an employee, and between a worker and those who are to be regarded as carrying on a business (see *Byrne Brothers (Formwork) Ltd v Baird* [2002] IRLR 96 for a discussion) (see below at **1.3.3**).

1.3.2 Employee

Section 230(1) of the ERA 1996 defines an employee as 'an individual who ... works under ... a contract of employment'. Section 230(2) defines contract of employment as 'a contract of service ... whether express or implied, and (if it is express) whether oral or in writing'. Over the years, the courts have formulated a variety of tests to identify the existence of a contract of service. These tests have included the 'control' test (see, eg, *Yewens v Noakes* (1880) 6 QBD 530); the 'integration' test (see, eg, *Stevenson Jordan & Harrson Ltd v McDonald and Evans* [1952] 1 TLR 101); and the 'economic reality' test (see, eg, *Market Investigations Ltd v Minister of Social Security* [1969] 2 QB 173). Currently in favour is the 'multiple factor' test advocated by McKenna J in *Ready Mixed Concrete (South East) Ltd v Minister of Pensions and National Insurance* [1968] 1 All ER 433).

McKenna J stated that a contract of service existed if three conditions were fulfilled:

(a)   the servant agrees that, in consideration of a wage or other remuneration, he will provide his own work and skill in the performance of some service for his master (mutuality of obligation, ie to provide work and personally do the work);

(b)   the servant agrees, expressly or impliedly, that in the performance of that service he will be subject to the other's control in a sufficient degree to make that other master (control);

(c)   the other provisions of the contract are consistent with its being a contract of service.

Freedom to do a job by one's own hands or by another's is inconsistent with a contract of service, though a limited or occasional power of delegation may not be. (These principles were recently confirmed by the Supreme Court in *Autoclenz Ltd v Belcher* [2011] UKSC 41.)

When, if at all, might an express agreement be challenged? This was considered by the Supreme Court in *Autoclenz Ltd v Belcher* (above). The Court of Appeal, in its judgment ([2010] IRLR 70), set out the circumstances in which courts can look behind the express terms of the parties' agreement. The EAT had held that the 20 car valets who worked for Autoclenz at its premises in Derbyshire were not employees but were workers within the meaning of s 230(3) of the ERA 1996. The Court of Appeal disagreed. The terms of the agreement between Autoclenz and the valets provided that:

(a)   there was no obligation on the valets to perform any work or for Autoclenz to provide it;

(b)   the valets' services would be engaged from time to time;

(c)   the valets could arrange for a substitute to carry out their valeting duties; and

(d)   the valets paid their own tax and had to purchase their own insurance, uniforms and materials.

However, according to the Court of Appeal, the above terms did not accurately reflect the relationship between the parties:

(a)   the valets were required to notify Autoclenz whether or not they would be turning up for work; and

(b)   whilst there existed a substitution clause, the valets would not, in practice, be permitted to send a substitute in their place and were expected to turn up and provide services in person.

The Court of Appeal, upholding the Employment Judge's decision at first instance, held that the valets were employees. The Court said that tribunals should focus on the actual legal obligations of the parties rather than merely relying on the written terms of an agreement when determining what kind of employment relationship existed. The fact that Autoclenz described the valets as workers and not employees was not conclusive. The tribunal has to consider whether or not the words represent the actual legal obligations of the parties. The Court of Appeal said it was not necessary to find any deliberate intention to deceive. The written terms are always the starting point, but where an issue is raised the tribunal must ask if the parties ever realistically intended or envisaged that its terms would be carried out as written.

The Supreme Court agreed with the Court of Appeal that the individual valets were not self-employed subcontractors and, although it was not necessary for the claims for minimum wage and holiday which only necessitated a finding that the valets were workers, it also upheld the finding that they were 'employees'. The Supreme Court held the real situation trumped what was written in the contract. It was not necessary for the valets to prove a 'sham', in the sense that the parties intended to mislead HM Revenue and Customs. The fact that the employer had written a 'substitution clause' into the contracts did not reflect the reality, as everyone expected the valets to carry out their duties personally. The essential question was: What was the true nature of the agreement between the parties? That *might* be what is written down, but was not necessarily so.

See also *Protectacoat Firthglow Ltd v Szilagyi* [2009] EWCA Civ 98. There is a helpful review of the legal distinctions between a contract of service and a contract for services in *Drake v Ipsos Mori UK Ltd* (UKEAT/0604/11).

1.3.2.1   Case law

Mutuality

The courts draw a distinction between mutuality on the one hand (which is necessary for there to be a contract at all) and, where there is a contract, the nature of that contract. That will be determined by the *nature* of the mutual obligations: mutual obligations on the employee to work personally for another, and on the employer to pay for the work. It is useful to repeat part of Elias J's judgment in *Stephenson v Delphi Diesel Systems Ltd* [2003] ICR 471:

11   The significance of mutuality is that it determines whether there is a contact in existence at all. The significance of control is that it determines whether, if there a contract in place, it can properly be classified as a contract of service, rather than some other kind of contract.

12   The issue of whether there is a contract at all arises most frequently in situations where a person works for an employer, but only on a casual basis from time to time. It is often necessary then to show that the contract continues to exist in the gaps between the periods of employment. Cases frequently have had to decide whether there is an over-arching contract or what is sometimes called an 'umbrella contract' which remains in existence even when the individual concerned is not working. It is in that context in particular that courts have emphasised the need to demonstrate some mutuality of obligation between the parties but, as I have indicated, all that is being done is to say that there must be something from which a contract can properly be inferred. Without some mutuality, amounting to what is sometimes called the 'irreducible minimum of obligation', no contract exists.

13   The question of mutuality of obligation, however, poses no difficulties during the period when the individual is actually working. For the period of such employment a contract must, in our view, clearly exist. For that duration the individual clearly undertakes to work and the employer in turn undertakes to pay for the work done. This is so, even if the contract is terminable on either side at will. Unless and until the power to terminate is exercised, these mutual obligations (to work on the one hand and to be paid on the other) will continue to exist and will provide the fundamental mutual obligations.

14   The issue whether the employed person is required to accept work if offered, or whether the employer is obliged to offer work if available is irrelevant to the question whether a contract exists at all during the period when the work is actually performed. The only question then is whether ... the contractual relationship which does exist is one of a contract of service or not [ie, is there control and a contract to work personally and no other terms inconsistent with a contract of service?].

In *St Ives Plymouth Ltd v Haggerty* (UKEAT/0107/08), the EAT upheld the tribunal's decision that a casual worker was an employee and that there was a sufficient mutuality of obligation in the gaps when no work was performed to infer the existence of a contract of employment. Although there was no obligation upon the casual worker to accept offers of work, the tribunal was persuaded that, had she persistently declined offers of work, her name would have been removed from the list of casuals. Equally, although there was no guaranteed minimum amount of work, the claimant had an expectation that she would be offered a reasonable amount of work. On that basis, the EAT held that the tribunal had been entitled to find that there was an 'overarching' contract because there was sufficient mutuality of obligation.

In *Cornwall County Council v Prater* [2006] EWCA Civ 102, the Court of Appeal upheld the EAT's decision that there was sufficient mutuality of obligation during each assignment carried out by a teacher while the individual contracts were in force. During each assignment there was an obligation on the teacher to teach the pupil and an obligation on the council to pay her. The gaps between the individual contracts when she was not carrying out work for the County Council were 'temporary cessations of work' which were bridged by s 212 of the ERA 1996.

The EAT in *Little v BMI Chiltern Hospital* (UK/EAT/0021/09) held that the fact that the employer could and did send hospital porters home during a shift, without pay for the rest of the shift, when their services were not needed, negated the existence of mutuality of obligation and meant there was only a contract for freelance services, and not, as the porter contended, a succession of specific engagement contracts of employment. The contract itself stated that the porter was an independent contractor who would work on an 'as and when required' basis for an hourly rate. The EAT held that the contract reflected the 'true intentions' of the parties. However, the EAT in *Drake v Ipsos Mori UK Ltd* (UKEAT/0604/11) held that *Little* should not be treated as authority for the proposition that a right to terminate work at will is inconsistent with a contract of employment.

In *Knight v BCCP* (UKEAT/0413/10), the EAT again emphasised the importance of mutuality – without mutual obligations to offer and to accept work, there can be no employment relationship under s 230 of the ERA 1996. Mr Knight was a licensed private hire driver, who was engaged by the respondent company for just over six weeks between 1 September and 14 October 2008. There was no contractual documentation. He was told that he would receive mileage rates for the work that he did, and that he had to provide his car upon the basis that he paid the insurance as well as the running costs including petrol, maintenance bills and other expenses. He was paid by submitting an invoice based on the company's records. He had to pay his own tax and National Insurance contributions and did not have any set working hours. He worked under the company's control to a degree in that it dictated the dress to be worn, how the car was to be presented, how the claimant was to deal with opening doors and procedure at airports and stations. He received wages only for the occasions when he actually worked. The relationship between the claimant and the company terminated when he was asked to complete a detailed security questionnaire in connection with cars provided for government purposes, and he decided he did not want to disclose the detailed information which it required. The issue before the employment tribunal was whether he was entitled to one week's statutory notice pay under s 86 of the ERA 1996, which necessitated his being an employee. The employment tribunal found that Mr Knight was under no obligation to accept work and the company was under no obligation to offer work to him, and as such, he was not an employee. The EAT upheld the tribunal's decision.

See also on mutuality, *Quashie v Stringfellows Restaurants Ltd* [2012] IRLR 536, at **1.3.2.2** below.

Personal service

In *Express and Echo Publications v Tanton* [1999] IRLR 367, the Court of Appeal emphasised that, to be a contract of service, a contract had to contain an obligation on the part of the employee to provide his services personally. Generally, therefore, if a worker is entitled to substitute personal service (ie to ask a replacement to do his work) then that will usually demonstrate that the contract is not a contract of service because the worker lacks the obligation required. However, in *McFarlane v Glasgow City Council* [2001] IRLR 7, the EAT said that a lack of personal service is not necessarily conclusive:

> ... properly regarded, [the decision in] *Tanton* does not oblige the tribunal to conclude that under a contract of service the individual has, always and in every event ... to personally provide his services.

Whether a power to delegate work to a substitute is determinative may depend on whether the right to delegate is fettered and/or the nature of the duties that may be delegated. In *McFarlane*, the claimant could not unilaterally refuse to work; it was only in circumstances where he was unable to attend that a substitute could be provided, and any substitute had to be approved by the employer. In the circumstances he was an employee.

By contrast, in *Real Time Civil Engineering Ltd v Callaghan* (UKEAT/0516/05), the EAT held that the tribunal in this case was wrong to ignore a contractual provision giving an individual an unfettered right to delegate his duties to a substitute simply because the individual had not, in reality, ever done so. The difference in this case was that the individual's right to delegate was unfettered: the agreement contained a term allowing for substitute to be sent without restriction. That term was, held the EAT, inconsistent with a contract of service

In *Autoclenz v Belcher* (above) the Supreme Court confirmed that in determining whether an individual is free to choose whether he will do the work himself or send someone else to do it (in which case he is neither an employee nor a worker), the relative bargaining power of the parties must be taken into account in deciding whether the terms of any written agreement in truth represent what was agreed, and the true agreement will often have to be gleaned from all the circumstances of the case, of which the written agreement is only a part.

Control

In the *Ready Mixed Concrete* case (**1.3.2** above), McKenna J described control as including 'the power of deciding the thing to be done, the way ..., the means ..., the time ... and the place'.

The Court of Appeal, in *Montgomery v Johnson Underwood Ltd* [2001] IRLR 269, confirmed that for a contract of service to exist there had to be control, that control is a separate factor, and no less important than mutuality of obligation when considering whether there is a contract of service. Control requires a general ultimate direct authority over an employee in the performance of his work. Control in itself, however, is not conclusive: an independent contractor can agree to submit himself to the same control as an employee without actually becoming an employee (see, for example, *Ready Mixed Concrete*); and many employees will, by virtue of seniority for example, be subject to very little control.

1.3.2.2   Other matters

An employment tribunal must consider the overall picture. The tribunal should not adopt a 'checklist' approach but consider all aspects, with no single factor being in itself conclusive, and each of which may vary in weight and direction (see eg *Hall v Lorimer* [1994] IRLR 171).

Among matters that may be relevant to consider as to whether the person is an employee are:

(a)   How is the individual paid?

(b)   Who pays tax and National Insurance?

(c)   Who provides the tools and equipment?

(d)   How integral to the business is the individual's role?

(e)   Is the individual paid for sickness and holiday?

(f)   Is the individual subject to the disciplinary and grievance policy?

(g)   Is the individual a member of a company pension scheme?

(h)   Where does the economic risk lie?

(i)   How did the parties view the relationship at the outset

(j)   How was the arrangement terminable?

The Court of Appeal, in *Enfield Technical Services Limited v Payne; Grace v BF Components Limited* [2008] IRLR 500, decided that individuals who characterise themselves as self-employed but who are in fact employees, can still bring unfair dismissal claims, unless they have misrepresented the real nature of the working relationship. In these cases, both claimants had described themselves as self-employed and had not paid tax via PAYE. When the working relationship ended, unfair dismissal claims were brought. The tribunal found, on the facts, that the claimants were employees. The employer argued that it would be contrary to public policy to allow the claim to continue and that the contract had been performed illegally. The Court of Appeal said that a failure to categorise employment status correctly, which deprives the Revenue of tax, does not of itself make a contract illegal, particularly where there is some legal uncertainty about the nature of the relationship. For a contract to be illegal, there must be some false representation about it.

In *Quashie v Stringfellows Restaurants Ltd* [2012] IRLR 536, the EAT said that employment status is not decided by the source or route of payment. The claimant in that case was a lap dancer who was paid entirely from customers' vouchers, which were changed into cash at the end of the night. The employment tribunal decided that she was not an employee, as there was no obligation on the employer to pay her anything. The EAT held that the claimant was an employee and could bring a claim for unfair dismissal. It also held that there was an umbrella contract which covered gaps in the evenings when the claimant did not dance. The case is due to be heard by the Court of Appeal in November 2012.

1.3.3 Workers

A number of statutory employment protections apply not solely to employees but to a wider class of 'worker' (which includes employees). See, for example, s 13 of the ERA 1996 (relating to deductions from wages – see **1.10** below), the National Minimum Wage Regulations 1999 (see **1.8.3.1** below) and the Working Time Regulations 1988 (see **1.11** below).

A worker is defined under s 230(3) of the ERA 1996 to mean:

> an individual who has entered into or works under (or where employment has ceased worked under)
>
> (a)   a contract of employment; or
>
> (b)   any other contract, whether express or implied and (if it is express) whether oral or in writing, whereby the individual undertakes to do or perform personally any work or services for another party to the contract whose status is not by virtue of the contract that of a client or customer of any profession or business undertaking carried on by the individual.

The reference to a contract of employment in para (a) above means that an employee is also a worker. The same definition appears in the National Minimum Wage Regulations 1999 and the Working Time Regulations 1998.

There are thus four requirements that need to be satisfied in limb (b):

(a)   the worker has to be an individual who has entered into or works under a contract;

(b)   with another party for work or services;

(c)   the individual undertakes to do or perform personally the work or services for the other party;

(d)   that other party must not, by virtue of the contract, have the status of a client or customer of any profession or business undertaking carried on by the individual who is to perform the work or services.

As far as the third requirement is concerned, there are a number of authorities dealt with below.

Readers should note again the Supreme Court decision in *Autoclenz* (above) where the Court held that:

> the ET was entitled to hold that the documents did not reflect the true agreement between the parties and that, on the basis of the ET's findings, four essential contractual terms were agreed: (1) that the valeters would perform the services defined in the contract for Autoclenz within a reasonable time and in a good and workmanlike manner; (2) that the valeters would be paid for that work; (3) that the valeters were obliged to carry out the work offered to them and Autoclenz undertook to offer work; and (4) that the valeters must personally do the work and could not provide a substitute to do so. See in particular, per Aikens LJ at para 97. It follows that, applying the principles identified above, the Court of Appeal was correct to hold that those were the true terms of the contract and that the ET was entitled to disregard the terms of the written documents, in so far as they were inconsistent with them.

In *Byrne Brothers (Formwork) Ltd v Baird* [2002] IRLR 96, the EAT held that a tribunal had not erred in holding that various labour-only subcontractors who worked as carpenters in the construction industry were workers within the meaning of the Working Time Regulations, and had therefore correctly concluded that they were entitled to holiday pay: as the applicants undertook to perform work or services for the company personally, they fell within the definition of 'worker' in limb (b) above, notwithstanding that the contract provided that, in certain circumstances, the services could be provided by someone other than the subcontractor with the prior express agreement of the contractor.

The EAT said, usefully:

> Thus the essence of the intended distinction must be between, on the one hand, workers whose degree of dependence is essentially the same as that of employees and, on the other, contractors who have a sufficiently arms-length and independent position to be treated as being able to look after themselves in the relevant respects.
>
> ...
>
> Drawing [the] distinction [between workers and independent contractors] will involve all or most of the same considerations as arise in drawing the distinction between a contract of service and a contract for services – but with the boundary pushed further in the putative worker's favour. It may, for example, be relevant to assess the degree of control exercised by the putative employer, the exclusivity of the engagement and its typical duration, the method of payment, what equipment the putative worker supplies, the level of risk undertaken etc. The basic effect of limb (b) is ... to lower the pass mark, so that cases which failed to reach the mark necessary to qualify for protection as employees might do so as workers (at 101).

The EAT, following *McFarlane* (**1.3.2.1** above), held that a limited power to appoint a substitute was not inconsistent with an obligation to provide services personally and that the purpose of limb (b) is 'to create an intermediate class of protected worker who is on the one hand not an employee, but on the other hand cannot in some narrower sense be regarded as carrying on a business'. In looking at the policy behind limb (b), the EAT said that it was to extend protection to workers who were 'substantively and economically' in the same position as employees.

The EAT emphasised that what was important were the rights and obligations of the parties *under the contract* and not what happened *in practice*, although that 'may shed light' on the contractual position. The EAT thought that the carpenters in *Byrne* were a good example of the kind of workers for whom the intermediate category in limb (b) was designed. The carpenters were clearly not carrying on a business, and Byrne Brothers were not their clients. There was sufficient mutuality of obligation between the parties for it to be said that there was a contract for services within the meaning of limb (b).

In *Premier Groundworks Ltd v Jozsa* (UKEAT/0494/08), the EAT held that an individual who worked under a contract which gave him complete freedom to delegate could not be a worker for the purpose of the Working Time Regulations. The position would be different, according to the EAT, if the right not to perform the obligations depended on some other event, such as whether the party was ill. Here, the freedom was unfettered and therefore the individual could not be a 'worker'. See too *MPG Contracts Ltd v England* (UK/EAT/0488/08), where an option allowing a father-and-son team to appoint a subcontractor (albeit with a provision that the contractor could refuse to accept unsuitable substitutes) meant that the contract was not one to provide services personally, and therefore the claimants were not workers for the purposes of bringing a holiday pay claim.

In *Redrow Homes (Yorkshire) Ltd v Buckborough and Another* (UKEAT/0528/07), the issue was (as it also was in *Redrow Homes (Yorkshire) Ltd v Wright* [2004] IRLR 720) whether workmen (bricklayers) engaged by Redrow to work on its building sites were workers for the purposes of reg 2(1) of the Working Time Regulations, or were self-employed contractors. The standard contract between Redrow and the workmen provided that the men agreed to provide such labour as was necessary to maintain the required rate of progress but were not obliged to perform the labour themselves. The EAT upheld the employment tribunal's finding that the men were workers, and said that its finding that the obligations provision in the contract was a sham did not contain any error of law. The EAT said that an express contractual arrangement could also be a sham where neither party intends the relevant provision(s) in the contract to have effect.

In *Clarkson v Pensher Security Doors Ltd* (UKEAT/0107/07) the EAT held that the purported worker was not a worker but rather that he carried on a business undertaking for a customer. The EAT agreed with the tribunal that the case came very close to the dividing line between the two, and readers should read the decision for further guidance.

In *Yorkshire Window Company Ltd v Parkes* (UKEAT/0484/09) the EAT helpfully drew the following from the authorities:

> We would draw the following principles from the authorities to which we have referred, (a), the question whether or not a contract provides for the performance of personal services is essentially a matter of construction, (b), the court is concerned with construing the contract, rather than with general policy considerations, (c), the fact that the individual chooses personally to supply the services is irrelevant; the issue is whether he is contractually obliged to do so, (d), the right or obligation to employ a substitute will not necessarily mean that there is no obligation on the part of the 'contractor' to perform personal services unless that right to employ a substitute is unfettered, (e), in cases where the 'contractor' is unable as opposed to unwilling, to carry out specified services, and has accepted an obligation to perform those services, but is unable to do so, and where he himself does not bear the costs of employing a substitute, a limited or occasional power of delegation may not be inconsistent with a contract to provide personal services, (f), a worker holds an intermediate position between an employee and someone who carries on his own business undertaking.

The fourth requirement is there, as Mr Recorder Underhill QC (as he then was) noted in *Byrne Brothers (Formwork) Ltd v Baird and Others* [2002] IRLR 96, to:

> create an intermediate class of protected worker, who is on the one hand not an employee but on the other hand cannot in some narrower sense be regarded as carrying on a business. ... it is sometimes said that the effect of the exception is that the regulations do not extend to the 'genuinely self-employed'; but that is not a particularly helpful formulation since it is unclear how 'genuinely' self-employment is to be defined.

It is clear that not all those who might properly be described as self-employed are engaged in a business undertaking. The question whether the 'worker' carries on a business undertaking of which the 'employer' is a client or customer is, of course, closely linked to the issue of whether the 'worker' provides services personally. It must be determined whether the essence of the relationship is that of a worker or somebody who is employed, albeit in a small way, in a business undertaking. In many cases, it might assist, as Langstaff J suggested in *Cotswolds Developments Construction Ltd v Williams* [2006] IRLR 281, para 53, to focus upon 'whether the purported worker actively markets his services as an independent person to the world in general ... or whether he is recruited by the principal to work for that principal as an integral part of the principal's operations'. As Elias J said in *James v Redcats (Brands) Ltd* [2007] ICR 1006, the question is whether the obligation for personal service is the dominant feature of the contractual arrangement or not. If it is, then the contract lies in the employment field; if it is not – if, for example, the dominant feature of the contract is a particular outcome or objective and the obligation to provide personal service is an incidental or secondary consideration – it will lie in the business field and the person concerned will not be a worker.

In *Yorkshire Window Company Ltd v Parkes* (above), the Employment Judge held that the claimant was not an employee because, in particular, he had treated himself as self-employed in relation to VAT and income tax, and prepared accounts on that basis, was entitled to refuse referrals and could elect which leads he wished to pursue. The Judge went on to find, however, that the claimant was a worker because, on the facts, the claimant had to carry out the work personally (there was no unfettered right to provide a substitute) and he was not pursuing a business; the claimant was not conducting a business enterprise of a general character to the benefit of a larger class of beneficiaries. The claimant was required to confine his services to the respondent and did so as the terms of the contract made clear. The EAT upheld the decision.

In *Community Dental Centres Ltd v Sultan-Darmon* (UKEAT/0532/09) the EAT held that a dentist was not a worker (nor an employee) as he did not 'undertake to do or perform personally any work or services' as required by s 230(3) of the ERA 1996 because of the existence of an unfettered right of substitution in his contract. The EAT said that it was not sufficient that the individual might be obliged personally to find a substitute; that analysis was inconsistent with the established authorities.

The Court of Appeal, in *The Hospital Medical Group Ltd v Westwood* [2012] EWCA Civ 1005, had to consider whether a GP who, aside from his job, carried out hair restoration surgery for the respondent's clients on a Saturday morning, was a worker. The claimant brought claims of unlawful deductions, accrued holiday pay and age discrimination. The employment tribunal ruled, applying *Autoclenz v Belcher* (**1.3.2** above), that the claimant was not an employee but that he was a worker within s 230(3)(b) of the ERA 1996. The claimant was 'clearly in business on his own account, and was engaged under a contract for services as a self-employed independent contractor' (para 30). Nevertheless, he was engaged personally to carry out the work himself (as the respondent conceded); he had no right to delegate the work to others; he was engaged by the respondent because of his skills (para 31).

The EAT upheld the decision of the employment tribunal. The EAT said the claimant was not performing work or services for the respondent as a client or customer of any profession or business carried on by him. The Court of Appeal agreed, Maurice Kay LJ commenting that:

> The striking thing about the judgments in *Cotswold* and *Redcats* is that neither propounds a test of universal application. Langstaff J's 'integration' test was considered by him to be demonstrative 'in most cases' and Elias J said that the 'dominant purpose' test 'may help' tribunals 'in some cases' (paragraph 68). In my judgment, both were wise to eschew a more prescriptive approach which would gloss the words of the statute. ... (at [18])
>
> ... HMG was not just another purchaser of Dr Westwood's various medical skills. Separately from his general practice and his work at the Albany Clinic, he contracted specifically and exclusively to carry out hair restoration surgery on behalf HMG. In its marketing material, HMG referred to him as 'one of our surgeons'. Although he was not working for HMG pursuant to a contract of employment, he was clearly an integral part of its undertaking when providing services in respect of hair restoration, even though he was in business on his own account. ... (at [19])

In *Clyde & Co LLP and Another v Bates van Winkelhof* [2012] EWCA Civ 1207, the Court of Appeal held that an equity partner who spent most of her time on secondment in Tanzania was not a worker. The Court of Appeal highlighted that the focus should be on the degree of independence (or dependence) existing between the putative worker and the employer. The Court held that a partnership lacks the relationship of service and control necessary to establish worker status.

BIS has published a 'worker' checklist in connection with national minimum wage claims (search 'national minimum wage worker checklist').

1.3.4   Other relevant qualifying definitions

Although the definitions of 'employee' and 'worker' contained in s 230(1) and (3) of the ERA 1996 are the most common definitions of those terms (see **1.3.2** and **1.3.3**), it is important nonetheless to check what definition is relevant to any particular legislation. Set out below are two areas where wider definitions appear.

1.3.4.1   Public Interest Disclosure Act 1998

So far as a claim under the Public Interest Disclosure Act 1998 (PIDA 1998) is concerned (see **5.5.5**), workers have a right not to be subjected to a detriment on the grounds that they have made a protected disclosure (ERA 1996, s 47B). Employees will be regarded as unfairly dismissed if the principal reason for their dismissal is that they made a protected disclosure (ERA 1996, s 103A). Workers who are dismissed for making a protected disclosure must complain, however, that dismissal is a detriment (ERA 1996, s 47B(2)). Different compensation regimes apply: under s 49(6) of the ERA 1996, workers cannot get more than if they had brought a successful unfair dismissal claim. 'Worker' is given an extended definition beyond the standard definition in s 230(3) of the ERA (see s 43K of the ERA 1996). In particular, the definition is extended to cover agency workers (s 43K(1)(a)), and covers those who would be defined as a worker within s 230(3) if the words 'personally or otherwise' were substituted for 'personally' in s 230(3)(b) (see above) (s 43K(1)(b)). Section 43K(2) contains an extended definition of 'employer'. It provides that with regard to agency and similar workers, 'employer' includes the person who substantially determines the terms on which those workers were engaged. The *Clyde & Co* case referred to at **1.3.3** above was a public interest disclosure case.

Section 43K was considered by the EAT in *Croke v Hydro Aluminium Worcester Ltd* [2007] ICR 1303. The EAT concluded that in construing the definition of 'worker' in s 43K, it was appropriate to adopt a purposive approach. Accordingly, where an individual supplied his services to an employment agency through his own company, and the employment agency, in turn, provided the services of that company to an end-user, it may be that in appropriate circumstances the individual is a 'worker' of the end-user for the purposes of s 43K.

1.3.4.2   Discrimination legislation

By s 83(2) of the Equality Act 2010:

> 'Employment' means ... employment under a contract of employment, a contract of apprenticeship or a contract personally to do work ...

This definition applies to discrimination which is 'because of' any of the protected characteristics (see **Chapter 8**). It is similar, but not identical to the wording that appeared in the old legislation (for example SDA 1975, s 82(1); RRA 1976, s 78; DDA 1995, s 68).

The definition clearly covers employees and workers, and it also extends to individuals who are self-employed, provided that their 'employment' contract obliges them to perform the work personally: in other words, if they are not permitted to sub-contract any part of the work.

The ECJ held in *Allonby v Accrington and Rossendale College* (Case C-256/01) [2004] ICR 1328 that 'the term worker ... cannot be defined by reference to the legislation of the Member States but has a Community meaning. Moreover, it cannot be interpreted restrictively.' It went on to hold that under European law a worker is a person who, for a certain period of time performs services for and under the direction of another person in return for which he receives remuneration, but that the authors of the EC Treaty did not intend the term 'worker', within the meaning of Article 141(1) EC (now Article 157(1) TFEU), to include independent providers of services who are not in a relationship of subordination with the person who receives the services. The question whether such a relationship exists must be answered, said the ECJ, in each particular case having regard to all the factors and circumstances by which the relationship between the parties is characterised.

The UK courts have emphasised that the important question is to ascertain what the dominant objective of the contract was. The Court of Appeal in *Mirror Group Newspapers Ltd v Gunning* [1986] IRLR 27 said the key question was whether the dominant purpose of the contract in that case was the personal execution of any work or labour. It held that the words 'a contract personally to execute any work or labour' (in the extended definition of 'employment' in the SDA 1975, s 82(1)) contemplated a contract the dominant purpose of which is that the party contracting to provide services under it performs personally the work or labour which forms the subject matter of the contract. In *Gunning*, a contract for the distribution of newspapers was not to be considered an 'employment' contract under the discrimination legislation. The dominant purpose of the contract was to secure effective distribution of the paper.

However, according to the Supreme Court in *Jivraj v Hashwani* [2011] UKSC 40, the dominant purpose test is not the key test. The focus must be on the contract and the relationship between the parties. Lord Clarke emphasised the words in the statute 'employment under', and held that:

> [an arbitrator's] role is not one of employment under a contract personally to do work. Although an arbitrator may be providing services for the purposes of VAT and he of course receives fees for his work, and although he renders personal services which he cannot delegate, he does not perform those services or earn his fees for and under the direction of the parties as contemplated in ... *Allonby*. He is rather in the category of an independent provider of services who is not in a relationship of subordination with the parties who receive his services ...

The arbitrator was not therefore a worker within the meaning of the discrimination legislation.

In *X v Mid Sussex CAB* [2011] EWCA Civ 28, the Court of Appeal confirmed that a volunteer worker was not entitled to claim disability discrimination because the legislation does not extend protection to voluntary workers without a contract. The lack of remuneration was held to be the key. A similar interpretation would apply to discrimination on the grounds of race, sex, sexual orientation, religion or belief, and age. The case was heard by the Supreme Court in October 2012.

Note that s 41 of the Equality Act also protects contract workers from being discriminated against by their principals, ie the client who engages them. Such workers may also be separately protected from discrimination by the agency they work for (if it is their employer) (see s 39 and **8.12**). Section 44 and 45 protect partners.

For a recent pre-Equality Act 2010 decision on the meaning of 'contract worker' in discrimination legislation, see *Leeds City Council v Woodhouse* [2010] IRLR 625.

1.3.5 Apprenticeship

In *Thorpe v Dul, Brooksby Melton College and Learning Skills Council* [2003] ICR 1556, the EAT held that a modern apprenticeship is not a contract of employment, and therefore modern apprentices are not automatically protected by unfair dismissal and other statutory rights. However, the EAT also said that there could also be, on the facts in any case, in addition to the apprenticeship, a contract of employment.

1.3.6 Agency workers

Much of the detail in relation to the status of agency workers is beyond the scope of this book, but this is a rapidly developing area of law (see eg *Franks v Reuters and Another* [2003] IRLR 423, CA; *Dacas v Brook Street Bureau (UK) Ltd* [2004] IRLR 358, CA; *Astbury v Gist Ltd* [2007] All ER (D) 480, *Bunce v Skyblue* [2005] IRLR 557, CA and *RNLI v Bushaway* [2005] IRLR 674; *Cable & Wireless* plc v Muscat [2006] IRLR 354, CA). Agency workers may be employees of the agency, or of the end-user or of neither.

In *National Grid Electricity Transmission plc v Wood* [2007] All ER (D) 358 (Oct), the EAT was prepared to uphold a tribunal decision that Mr Wood, who had been supplied to the respondent company by an agency, was employed by the end-user under an implied contract of employment. Case law suggests, however, that tribunals will rarely find implied contracts of service between agency workers and the end-user (the client to whom they are supplied).

In *Dacas* (above), endorsed in *Muscat* (above), the Court of Appeal directed tribunals always to consider the possibility of an implied employment contract between an agency worker and client (or end-user) where there is a triangular relationship between the agency worker, agency and end-user.

The Court of Appeal offered the following guidance to tribunals on when a contract of employment should be implied between the worker and the end-user:

(a)   Where the arrangements between agency, agency worker and end-user are genuine and reflect the actual working relationship – such as where there was no pre-existing employment relationship between the agency, worker and end-user – then it will be a rare case in which the evidence justifies the tribunal implying a contract. Such evidence would need to show that the agency worker is working pursuant to mutual obligations with the end-user, and that these obligations are incompatible with the agency arrangement.

(b)   The mere passage of time does not in itself justify the implication of a contract on the ground of necessity. Something more is required to show that it is necessary to imply a contract.

(c)   It would be more readily open to a tribunal to infer a contract where, as in *Muscat*, the agency arrangement had been superimposed on a pre-existing employment relationship between worker and end-user, although, strictly speaking, the tribunal would be finding that the agency arrangements did not bring the original contract to an end.

The Court of Appeal's view is that whether a contract of employment should be implied between an agency worker and an end-user is a question of fact for the tribunal.

In *Cairns v Visteon Ltd* [2007] IRLR 175, the EAT, while not ruling out the possibility that two employment contracts could exist in parallel between an individual and two employers in respect of the same work, said the concept was problematic, and that there was no good policy reason for extending unfair dismissal protection where an individual already had an express contract of employment with the agency. The EAT went on to say that, for a contract to be implied between the agency worker and the end-user, it is necessary to show that the conduct of the parties is consistent with there being a contract of employment between them. The EAT also held in two other cases (*Heatherwood & Wexham Park Hospitals NHS Trust v Kulubowila* [2007] All ER (CD) 496 and *Astbury v Gist Ltd* [2007] All ER (D) 480) that agency workers were not employees of the end-user.

In *Consistent Group Limited v Kalwak and Others* [2008] IRLR 505, the issue was whether Polish migrant agency workers could be employees of an agency, despite a lack of detailed control over their day-to-day work. In this case, there was a contractual statement that provided that the workers were *not* employees of the agency and that there was no mutuality of obligation between the agency and the workers. The EAT held that the express terms did not reflect the reality and that the arrangements were therefore a sham. The Court of Appeal overruled the EAT, emphasising that it is not possible to imply into a contract a term that conflicts with an express term. If there was nothing to indicate that the relevant terms were included by the parties in order to be deliberately misleading, the finding of 'sham' must be overturned. The case was remitted to the employment tribunal to be reheard.

See also *Protectacoat Firthglow Ltd v Szilagyi* [2009] IRLR 365 and the Court of Appeal decision in *Autoclenz Ltd v Belcher* [2010] IRLR 70 (confirmed by the Supreme Court) at **1.3.2** above.

It was hoped that the Court of Appeal would take the opportunity to consider some of the various and conflicting agency decisions when *James v Greenwich Borough Council* [2008] IRLR 302 came before it on appeal. However, Mummery LJ asserted that 'there is no significant difference between the law stated and applied in the decisions of this court and in those of the EAT. It is apparently thought in some quarters that they are in conflict. I do not think so.'

Ms James had a 'Temporary Worker Agreement' with an employment agency, which found her a position as a housing support worker with Greenwich Council. After several years the Council replaced her with another worker supplied by the agency. In response to her claim for unfair dismissal, the Council disputed her legal status as an employee. She was paid by the agency following receipt by the agency from her of completed weekly timesheets. The tribunal found that the Council's Disciplinary Procedure and Grievance Policy did not apply to Ms James and that she was not entitled to benefit from the Council's sick pay or holiday pay provisions applicable to employees. The decisions of both the tribunal and the EAT were that she was not employed by the Council under a contract of service. The Court of Appeal held that the 'real issue' in agency worker cases is whether a contract should be implied between the worker and the end-user in a tripartite situation of worker, agency and end-user, rather than whether the irreducible minimum of mutual obligation exists. Mutuality is important in deciding whether a contract that has been concluded is a contract of employment or some other kind of contract. The correct approach is for an employment tribunal to decide – as a question of fact – whether, applying common law principles, it is necessary to imply a contractual relationship between the agency worker and the end-user client. In many cases, agency workers will fall outside the scope of protection because neither the workers nor the end-users are in any kind of express contractual relationship with each other and it is not necessary to imply one in order to explain the work undertaken by the worker for the end-user. The Court of Appeal held that the EAT in *James* had not erred in holding that the circumstances did not exist which could justify the inference of an implied contract. The provision of work by the local authority, its payments to the agency, and the performance of the work by Ms James were all explained by their respective express contracts with the agency, so it was not necessary to imply the existence of another contract in order to give business reality to the relationship between the parties. The Court of Appeal expressly approved the guidance given in paras 53–61 of the EAT's decision, and readers advising on this topic should therefore also read the EAT's judgment.

Muschett v HM Prison Service [2010] EWCA Civ 25 is yet another example of the difficulties of establishing a contractual relationship between an agency worker and the end-user. The Court of Appeal emphasised that in tripartite arrangements a contract could only be implied between the agency worker and the end-user where it was necessary to do so to reflect the business reality of the situation. To find necessity, it required evidence from which a tribunal could conclude that the agency relationship no longer adequately reflected how the work was actively being performed. The Court of Appeal in this case said the 'meagre collection of facts' relied upon by the claimant could not justify making a finding that the claimant was an employee.

In *Tilson v Alstom Transport* [2010] EWCA 1038, the Court of Appeal was again reluctant to imply a contractual relationship between the agency worker and the end-user. In this case, the ongoing relationship was conducted on the basis that no contract of employment existed (on two occasions, Alstom asked Mr Tilson to become an employee but on each occasion he declined because he preferred to be an independent contractor); and even though there was evidence of a significant degree of integration of an agency worker into an organisation (Mr

Tilson was supervised by Alstom's managers and had to apply to his line manager to take holiday; he also supervised Alstom staff), the court held that that was not inconsistent with an agency relationship in which there is no contract between worker and end-user. The Court of Appeal also held that the need to apply to a line manager before taking annual leave was not sufficient to justify the implication of a contract. This case reinforces the position that while it is not impossible to find an employment contract between an agency worker and the end-user (see, for an example, *McMeechan v Secretary of State for Employment* [1997] ICR 549), a contract of employment will not be implied where it is not necessary to do so to explain a working relationship. In many such cases, the 'irreducible minimum' requirement for an employment contract – mutuality of obligation and control exercised by the employer – will not be met. It is also likely that deduction of National Insurance and PAYE in such situations will be regarded as a neutral factor (since ss 44–47 of the Income Tax (Earnings and Pensions) Act 2003 necessitate it). The only exception may be where there is evidence that both parties have deliberately entered into a sham arrangement to prevent a relationship of employer and employee from arising (see too *BIS v Studders* (UKEAT/0571/10)).

It should be remembered, of course, that even if the agency worker is not an employee, he may still benefit from some protections, eg the anti-discrimination legislation (see **1.3.4.2**), national minimum wage legislation and working time legislation (see, for example, *Electronic Data Systems Ltd v Hanbury and Brook Street Bureau* (UKEAT/128/00)), as a worker.

1.3.6.1   Agency Workers Regulations 2010

The Agency Workers Regulations 2010 (SI 2010/93), as amended by SI 2011/1941, came into force on 1 October 2011. The Regulations create a right for agency workers to receive the same basic terms and conditions as if they had been directly recruited by the end-user. The detail is beyond the scope of this book. However, a short summary appears below.

The Regulations provide that agency workers (defined as individuals having a contract of employment with the agency or a contract with the agency to perform work and services) will have equal access to facilities (such as canteen, childcare facilities, vacancy lists etc) and information on job vacancies as employees of the end-user from day 1. Otherwise, for the more detailed requirements, such as equal treatment in terms of pay and other basic working conditions (annual leave, rest breaks, rest periods, duration of working time, length of night work – and pregnant agency workers must be allowed to take paid time off for ante-natal appointments), there is a 12-week qualifying period, so short-term agency temps will not qualify for these rights. The 12 weeks do not have to be continuous; there can be breaks between assignments and absences on grounds of, say, sickness or jury service.

The number of hours that the worker has worked during the reference period is calculated differently depending on the type of work done by the worker.

There are four types of work:

(a)   time work;

(b)   salaried hours work;

(c)   output work;

(d)   unmeasured work.

The rules vary according to the type of work done, and readers should consult the Regulations for the detail. For example, lunch breaks will not count as hours worked for time workers but will count for salaried hours workers if they form part of the workers' basic minimum hours under the contract.

In May 2011, the BIS published Guidance on the Agency Workers Regulations 2010. The Guidance seeks to assist in interpreting the Regulations and gives illustrations in relation to issues such as:

- Who is an agency worker?
- What terms and conditions are covered by the requirement of equal treatment?
- Is a comparator needed?
- How to calculate the 12-week qualifying period
- Who will be responsible if the Regulations are breached?

Given that this is a complex and developing area, readers should always ensure that they look at the most up-to-date case law on this topic.

1.3.7 Other categories

In *The New Testament Church of God v Stewart* [2007] IRLR 178, the presumption that all ministers were office holders and not employees was successfully challenged. The Court of Appeal upheld the EAT's decision that a Christian minister was an employee of his church (see too *Ms Preston (formerly Moore) v The President of the Methodist Conference* [2011] EWCA Civ 1581 (currently under appeal to the Supreme Court)).

In *Gladwell v Secretary of State for Trade and Industry* [2007] ICR 264, EAT, the EAT held that the fact that a claimant was a company director with a shareholding of 50% did not preclude him from being an employee. Mr Justice Elias commented, 'a majority shareholder will in practice act as the employer, making decisions on behalf of the company, but that does not prevent him being an employee'.

In *Secretary of State for BERR v Neufeld* [2009] EWCA Civ 280, the Court of Appeal had to determine whether a controlling shareholder of a company could also be an employee. Mr Neufeld claimed to have been an employee (under ERA 1996, s 230) of the company for which he worked. The company was insolvent and he claimed that he was entitled as an employee to a payment from the Secretary of State under s 182 of the ERA 1996 (which provides that employees of insolvent employers can recover certain debts from the National Insurance Fund, including up to eight weeks' arrears of pay, notice pay and a basic award in an unfair dismissal claim). He was a controlling shareholder and a director of the company. The tribunal held that Mr Neufeld was not an employee, but the EAT reversed that finding. The Court of Appeal, after reviewing the authorities, confirmed that the leading case on employees, shareholders and directors was *Secretary of State for Trade and Industry v Bottrill* [1999] ICR 592, and that being a controlling shareholding was one factor which had to be taken into account when deciding, in all the circumstances, whether a person was an employee or not, but that there is no reason in principle why a person who was a shareholder and director of a company could not also be an employee of the company under a contract of employment, even if that person had a controlling interest in, or even total control of, the company.

The Court of Appeal in *Neufeld* approved, in essence, the approach taken by the EAT in *Clark v (1) Clark Construction Initiatives Ltd (2) Utility Consultancy Services Ltd* (UKEAT/0225/07). In that case the EAT concluded that 'what we have to do is to look at the whole picture, which we have done. We should balance out all the factors and make a reasoned conclusion'. The EAT listed three circumstances (although not exhaustive ones) in which it said it might be possible for a tribunal to see through what was on its face a legitimate employment contract:

(a) where the company is itself a sham (ie it is the *alter ego* of the individual) – this would be an 'exceptional' case;

(b) where the contract was entered into for an ulterior purpose, eg to secure a redundancy payment from the Secretary of State;

(c) where the parties do not conduct their relationship in accordance with the contract, either because:

    (i) they never intended to, or

    (ii) the relationship in practice has ceased to reflect the contractual terms.

The EAT then listed a number of other factors which it said would need to be considered when deciding whether to give effect to the contract.

The Court of Appeal held, on the facts, that Mr Neufeld was an employee. The Court summed up the position as follows:

> In a case in which no allegation of sham is raised, or in which the claimant proves that no question of sham arises, the question ... for the court or tribunal will be whether the claimed contract amounts to a true contract of employment. ... [G]iven that the critical question in cases such as those under appeal is as to whether the putative employee was an employee at the time of the company's insolvency, it will or may be necessary to inquire into what has been done under the claimed contract: there will or may therefore need to be the like inquiry as in cases in which an allegation of sham is made. In order for the employee to make good his case, it may well be insufficient merely to place reliance on a written contract made, say, five years earlier. The tribunal will want to know that the claimed contract, perhaps as subsequently varied, was still in place at the time of the insolvency. In a case in which the alleged contract is not in writing, or is only in brief form, it is obvious that it will usually be necessary to inquire into how the parties have conducted themselves under it.

1.4   THE CONTRACT OF EMPLOYMENT

Parties to an employment relationship will often, but not always, put the terms and conditions that govern that relationship into writing. However, there is no legal requirement for the contract of employment to be in writing. It may be written, oral or a mixture of both. In some circumstances the court will imply a contract of employment (see, eg, *Dacas v Brook Street Bureau (UK) Ltd* (**1.3.6**)). Where there is no written contract of employment, the law requires employers to provide what is known as a written statement of terms to their employees. In the absence of any written contract, the written statement should set out some minimum details about the terms governing the employment relationship.

Even where there is a written contract that sets out the express terms which govern the relationship, the courts will in certain situations imply additional terms into that contract (see **1.5**). This section and those following consider the written statement of terms, some of the terms which may be implied into a contract of employment, including the regulation of working time and minimum wage legislation, and the principal terms which should be considered for express inclusion in a written contract, including restrictive covenants. The protection of wages is addressed in **1.10**.

Readers should note the Contracts (Rights of Third Parties) Act 1999. The full operation of the Act is beyond the scope of this book, but in outline, the Act reforms the doctrine of privity of contract but expressly provides that no rights are conferred on a third party to enforce any term of an employment contract against an employee. However, the Act does not prevent third parties from enforcing relevant contractual terms against the employer where, for example, the terms of the contract purport to confer a benefit on a third party, eg a company car. The Act must be considered when drafting employment contracts or compromise agreements (see **6.5**).

Where the employer and the employee have agreed the terms of their contract, those terms cannot be changed without both parties agreeing to the changes. In other words, employers cannot unilaterally change the terms and conditions of the contract. Where an employer does try to impose a unilateral variation on an employee, an employee has four choices (see *Robinson v Tescom Corporation* [2008] IRLR 408):

(a)   to agree to the variation (either expressly, or by continuing to work without protest);

(b)   to resign and complain of unfair constructive dismissal (see **3.4.3**) and wrongful dismissal (see **Chapter 2**);

(c)   to refuse to work under the new terms and force the employer to take such steps as it thinks are appropriate;

(d)   to stand and sue, ie continue to work under protest and seek damages (either for breach of contract – see for example *Rigby v Ferodo* [1987] IRLR 516 – or, if the breach is so serious as to bring the original contract to an end, unfair dismissal).

In *Robinson v Tescom*, the employee agreed to changes 'under protest', but then refused to work under the new terms and was dismissed. The EAT said the decision to dismiss him was fair because, having agreed (albeit under protest) to the changes, he could not then renege on what he had agreed – he was refusing to obey a lawful and reasonable instruction.

Careful regard should be had to the contract to see whether the terms are wide enough to allow for the proposed change. Often a contract will permit variations to certain terms, eg hours of work and place of work. However, employers must also have regard to the implied duty of mutual trust and confidence, even where the contractual terms permit a variation. An employer should, for example, consult with employees before introducing changes.

Note also that terms that purport to give employers the right to change any terms of the contract, eg 'the right to vary this contract from time to time', will be construed narrowly. If the change might produce an unreasonable result, the tribunals must 'seek to avoid such a result' (*Wandsworth LBC v D'Silva* [1998] IRLR 193).

In *Bateman v Asda Stores* (UKEAT/0221/09) the EAT held that conditions in the Asda staff handbook were incorporated in the claimants' contracts of employment, and the wording in the staff handbook was wide enough to permit Asda to change the pay and work structure, with the result that Asda was entitled to impose changes in the claimants' pay and work provisions without the need to obtain their express consent. Note that the employer had consulted and sought agreement, and most employees had agreed to the changes; only one employee (out of 700) alleged financial detriment from the changes.

In *Slade & Others v TNT UK Ltd* (UKEAT/0113/11), the employer sought to change terms of employment by making an offer to 'buy out' certain existing terms, but warned that refusal would result in dismissal with an offer of re-engagement on the proposed new terms. The offer was rejected and the employer dismissed with notice and re-employed on new terms and conditions. The employment tribunal held that the employer did not unfairly dismiss where the terms of offered re-employment did not include the terms of the 'buy out' as part of the new terms (see **Chapter 5**).

Sometimes, when an employer wants to try to change a term of a policy, it will maintain that the term is not contractual and so consent is not needed (see **1.8**).

1.4.1   Types of contract

The two most common types of employment contract are:

(a)   the indefinite contract – this is a 'continuing' contract which is terminable by either the employer or the employee on giving the requisite period of notice; and

(b)   the 'fixed-term' (or 'limited-term') contract – which provides for employment for a fixed (limited), definite period of time (see **1.8.1.2**).

These may be used whether the contract is for full-time or part-time work.

Increasingly, employers are utilising a variety of non-standard contracts, such as zero hour contracts (where the hours to be worked are left (deliberately) undefined, but employees may be required to be available for work at any time or at specified times), in order to achieve flexible working arrangements. These specialist types of contract are beyond the scope of this book.

1.4.2   Written statement of terms

By s 1 of the ERA 1996 (as amended by the EA 2002), the employer must, within no later than two months of employment commencing, give the employee a written statement of terms and conditions relating to the following particulars:

(a)   identity of the parties;

(b)   date employment began;

(c)   date continuous employment began (taking into account any relevant employment with a previous employer);

(d)   scale or rate of remuneration and intervals of pay;

(e)   hours of work;

(f)   any terms relating to:

    (i)   holidays and holiday pay;

    (ii)   sickness and sick pay;

    (iii) pensions and pension schemes;

(g)   length of notice required to determine the contract;

(h)   in the case of non-permanent employment, the period for which it is expected to continue or, if it is for a fixed term, the date it is to end;

(i)   job title or a brief description of work;

(j)   place or places of work;

(k)   particulars of any collective agreements which directly affect the terms and conditions of employment;

(l)   where employees are required to work outside the UK for a period of more than one month, the period of such work, currency in which payment is made, benefits provided and terms relating to the return to the UK;

(m)   details of the disciplinary and dismissal rules and grievance procedures (ERA 1996, s 3) (to avoid the procedures becoming contractual in nature, the s 1 statement should make it clear they are not); these can be set out in the body of the particulars, or reference may be made to another reasonably accessible document;

(n)   whether a contracting out certificate is in force (under the Pension Schemes Act 1993).

If there are no particulars to be entered under any of the heads above, that fact must be stated (ERA 1996, s 2(1)).

Although the statement must be given to the employee, it may refer him to a document that is reasonably accessible and which contains full details of the terms relating to pension schemes and dismissal and disciplinary procedures and grievance procedures (ERA 1996, ss 2(2) and 3(aa)).

Any changes in the terms of employment must be notified by the employer in writing within one month of the change (ERA 1996, s 4).

An example of a statement of terms under s 1 may be found in **Appendix 1**.

1.4.2.1   Exceptions

Excluded classes

No written statement needs to be given to any employee if his employment continues for less than one month.

Written contract

If the contract of employment is in writing and contains all the particulars that need to be referred to under s 1 of the ERA 1996, no separate written statement of terms need be given to the employee (ERA 1996, s 7A). (See **1.8** for written contracts.) Employers may decide not to set out the disciplinary and dismissal rules and grievance procedures in the contract to avoid giving the procedures contractual status (see **Chapter 3**).

1.4.2.2 Disputes about the statement

The written statement of terms given by the employer under s 1 of the ERA 1996 merely states what the contract terms are, it is not the contract itself. The employee may dispute the accuracy of the statement, or, alternatively, the employer may fail to give the employee a written statement. In *Lovett v Wigan Metropolitan Borough Council* [2001] EWCA Civ 12, the Court of Appeal confirmed that a s 1 statement did not form part of the contract of employment. An employee did not agree to any variation of existing terms by signing to 'confirm receipt' of the particulars. If it is intended that the s 1 statement is to have contractual force, it must expressly state so and signing must be stated to confirm agreement to the contractual terms. A mere acknowledgement of receipt will be insufficient to bind an employee.

By s 11 of the ERA 1996, where the employer fails to give the employee a written statement as required, or where a dispute arises as to its accuracy, either party may refer the matter to an employment tribunal. The tribunal's duty is to determine what particulars should have been contained in the written statement. The tribunal does not have power to invent terms or impose terms on the parties which had not been agreed between them (*Eagland v British Telecommunications plc* [1992] IRLR 323, CA). See too *Southern Cross Healthcare v Perkins and Others* [2010] EWCA Civ 1442 where the Court of Appeal said that ss 11 and 12 of the ERA 1996 do not give a tribunal rights to construe the terms of the contract or amend the agreement. Such a power can arise only in the context of a breach of contract claim in the civil courts. The only power the tribunal has is to amend the statutory statement so that it corresponds with any written agreement.

The EA 2002 states that the tribunals must award compensation of two to four (gross) weeks' pay (up to the statutory maximum – £430 as at 1 February 2012) to the employee, where the absence of particulars becomes evident upon a successful tribunal claim being brought under any of the tribunal jurisdictions listed in Sch 5 to EA 2002 (which covers most common tribunal complaints) (EA 2002, s 38). There is no free-standing right to claim compensation. The tribunal must award the minimum of two weeks' pay and may, if it considers it just and equitable in the circumstances, award four weeks' pay (ie a maximum of £1,720 as at 1 February 2012) in respect of the failure. The tribunal does not have to make an award if there are exceptional circumstances that make it unjust to make an award.

1.5 IMPLIED TERMS

In certain situations, even where there is a written statement or a written contract, terms will be implied into the contract. Terms may be implied into a contract of employment either at common law, where there is no express term (see **1.7**), or under statute (see **1.6**). The terms of a collective agreement (an agreement between an employer and a trade union) may be incorporated into a contract of employment by implication. Collective agreements are beyond the scope of this book.

1.6 TERMS IMPLIED BY STATUTE

The Working Time Regulations 1998 (SI 1998/1833) (see **1.11**) provide an example of terms implied by statute, as does the National Minimum Wage Act 1998 (see **1.8.3.1**). The 'equality clause' arising under the Equality Act 2010 (see **8.9.1.1**) is also a term implied by statute.

1.7 TERMS IMPLIED BY COMMON LAW

In addition to terms which are implied by statute, terms may also be implied into a contract by the common law. The principal implied duties are set out below. These may conveniently be divided into employers' duties and employees' duties.

1.7.1 Employers' duties

1.7.1.1 Duty to pay wages and provide work

At common law, the general rule is that an employee has no right to work. Provided that the employer pays the employee, there is no breach of an implied term if the employee is kept idle (*Turner v Sawdon* [1901] 2 KB 653).

There are, however, increasing exceptions to this rule. It has long been established, for example, that workers whose livelihood depends on publicity, for example actors and singers, have the right to work. Similarly, if the employee is paid by commission or is a piece worker, there is an implied duty to provide the employee with work. Furthermore, in *William Hill Organisation Ltd v Tucker* [1998] IRLR 313, the Court of Appeal held that the employee in question had the right to be provided with work during his notice period. The Court of Appeal stated that whether an employee has the right to be provided with work is a 'question of construction of the ... contract in light of its surrounding circumstances'. The Court of Appeal pointed to three factors which, on the facts, supported the right to work:

(a)   The employee was in a specific and unique post, both in substance as well as form. The employee was the only senior dealer – he was the person appointed to conduct a new and specialised business.

(b)   The skills necessary to the proper discharge of such duties as a senior dealer in spread betting required their frequent exercise.

(c)   The terms of the contract itself. The contract provided for the days and hours of work, and specifically imposed on the employee an obligation to work those hours necessary to do the job in a full and professional manner. The court said that if the work was available it was inconsistent with that provision if the employee was bound to draw his pay without doing the work. In addition the contract provided for only a limited power of suspension in narrow circumstances.

Many senior employees will fall within the criteria referred to above, with the result that they will enjoy the right to work (see also **1.8.7.3**). An implied right to work is less likely to be implied into more junior employees' contracts.

In *SG&R Valuation Service v Boudrais* [2008] EWHC 1340, the High Court held that the implied right to work is subject to the qualification that employees have not, as a result of some other breach of contract or duty, made it 'impossible or reasonably impracticable' for the employer to provide work (in this case because the employees concerned had collected confidential information to use with a new employer and had sought to poach staff).

In *Standard Life Healthcare Ltd v Gorman and others* [2009] EWCA Civ 1292, where employees were paid on a commission only basis, the Court of Appeal, whilst holding that they had a right to work, held that where an employee was in breach of his duty of good faith (see **1.7.2.4**), the employer was released from its obligation to provide work.

1.7.1.2 Duty to indemnify employee

The employer is under a duty to indemnify the employee for expenses and liabilities incurred by the employee in the course of his employment (*In re Famatina Development Corporation Ltd* [1914] 2 Ch 271).

1.7.1.3 Duty to take reasonable care of the employee's safety and working conditions

There are implied contractual duties on the employer to provide adequate plant and premises, competent fellow workers and a safe system of work (*Wilsons & Clyde Coal Co Ltd v English* [1938] AC 57). This duty to take reasonable care of an employee's safety and working conditions extends only to the employee's personal safety, not to safeguarding his property.

The employer also has statutory duties in respect of health and safety imposed by the Health and Safety at Work etc Act 1974 (HSWA 1974). Further, the Employers' Liability (Compulsory Insurance) Act 1969 requires the employer to take out employers' liability insurance for the benefit of his employees.

In *Waltons and Morse v Dorrington* [1997] IRLR 488, a term was implied in favour of a non-smoker in a smoking environment, that the employer should provide and monitor, so far as is reasonably practicable, a working environment which is reasonably suitable for the performance of contractual obligations.

1.7.1.4   Duty of mutual trust and confidence

There is a duty of mutual trust and confidence owed by the employer and the employee to each other. As far as the employer is concerned, it was stated in *Woods v WM Car Services (Peterborough) Ltd* [1983] IRLR 413, CA (approved by the House of Lords in *Malik and Another v BCCI SA (in compulsory liquidation)* [1998] AC 20), that employers will not 'without reasonable and proper cause, conduct themselves in a manner calculated or likely to destroy or seriously damage the relationship of mutual confidence and trust between employer and employee'. This is particularly important in the area of constructive dismissal. (See **3.4.3** for further details.)

1.7.1.5   Duty to take reasonable care in giving references

There is an implied term to take reasonable care in compiling or giving a reference and in verifying the information on which it is based. An employer may be liable to the employee or former employee for any economic loss suffered as a result of a negligent misstatement (see *Caparo Industries v Dickman* [1990] 2 AC 605 (re the test to be applied when establishing whether or not a duty of care is owed) and *Spring v Guardian Assurance plc* [1994] IRLR 460 (re references)).

In *Bartholomew v London Borough of Hackney* [1999] IRLR 246, the Court of Appeal held that where an employer decides to give a reference, there is a duty of care to provide a reference that is 'true, accurate and fair' (ie not misleading). By 'fair', the Court of Appeal meant in terms of the overall impression given of the employee, as well as being factually correct in its component parts. In *Kidd v Axa Equity and Law Life Assurance Society plc and Another* [2000] IRLR 301, the High Court rejected an employee's claim that he had a right to a 'full and comprehensive' reference. The court said that the duty owed by a referee is:

> not to give misleading information ... whether as a result of the unfairly selective provision of information, or by the inclusion of facts or opinions in such a manner as to give rise to a false or mistaken inference in the mind of a reasonable recipient.

The EAT held in *TSB Bank plc v Harris* [2000] IRLR 157 that an employee was entitled to resign and claim constructive dismissal on the basis that a reference provided to a prospective employer was in breach of the implied duty of mutual trust and confidence. Ms Harris's employer provided a reference limited to the factual history of Ms Harris's employment. It recorded that there had been 17 complaints against her, 15 more than she knew of, and that four of them had been upheld and eight remained outstanding. The reference said nothing about Ms Harris's character, nor her ability to undertake her job.

The EAT upheld the tribunal's decision that Ms Harris had been unfairly constructively dismissed. The employer should have made Ms Harris aware of the complaints before the reference had been given in order to allow her the opportunity to address the damaging information which was on her file. The reference supplied was unfair and misleading, and not prepared with due skill and care. The approach of the EAT was reinforced by the Court of Appeal in *Cox v Sun Alliance Life Ltd* [2001] IRLR 448. The Court emphasised that the duty of care owed by an employer with regard to the provision of a reference is not only to take reasonable care to provide an accurate reference, but also to take reasonable care to provide a fair one. A reference does not generally 'have to provide a full and comprehensive report on all the material facts concerning the subject'.

In *McKie v Swindon College* [2011] EWHC 469, the High Court held that an employer owed a duty to its former employee to take reasonable care when referring to that former employee in communications with a third party (an email sent by a former employer to a current employer which resulted in the employee's dismissal). This extends the scope of *Spring* to include circumstances beyond that of simply providing a reference. The case is a useful reference for the process that a court will follow in order to determine whether a duty of care is owed.

Employers, especially public authority employers, need to take care that nothing they write when acting as a referee could be taken to amount to an interference with employees' private or family lives, unless one of the exceptions set out in Article 8(2) of the European Convention on Human Rights applies (see **15.4.2**).

The Data Protection Act 1998 (DPA 1998) (see **Chapter 15**) regulates when and how information concerning an employee may be held, obtained and disclosed. An employer who provides a reference will be processing data for the purposes of the DPA 1998. However, the Act excludes the disclosure to employees of references provided for future employment, although employees may be able to obtain the same from the recipient of the reference. It is clear that while there is no common law duty to provide a reference, an employee may be able to see one if it is provided.

1.7.2 Employees' duties

1.7.2.1 Duty to give personal service

The relationship of employer and employee is a personal one, and the employee may not delegate performance of his duties. This can be crucial in determining whether someone is an employee or not (see **1.3** above).

1.7.2.2 Duty to obey reasonable orders

The employee is under a contractual duty not wilfully to disobey a lawful order (*Laws v London Chronicle Ltd* [1959] 2 All ER 285). Neither must the employee act in a manner designed to frustrate the commercial aspect of the contract. A 'work to rule' may amount to a breach of contract if designed to disrupt work (*Secretary of State for Employment v Associated Society of Locomotive Engineers and Firemen (ASLEF) (No 2)* [1972] 2 QB 455).

1.7.2.3 Duty of reasonable care and indemnity

The employee is under a duty to exercise reasonable care and skill in the performance of his duties. An employee will be in breach of this duty if he performs his duties negligently or incompetently. If an employee is in breach of this duty, he is also liable to indemnify the employer for any loss suffered by the employer by reason of the employee's breach (*Lister v Romford Ice and Cold Storage Co Ltd* [1957] AC 555).

1.7.2.4 Duty of fidelity or good faith

The duty of fidelity or good faith is sometimes referred to as the employee's part of the mutual duty of trust and confidence. The duty consists principally of a number of aspects of confidentiality and non-competition, some of which also apply after employment has ceased (see **1.7.2.6–1.7.2.8** and **1.8.6**).

In *Crowson Fabrics Ltd v Rider and Others* [2007] EWHC 2942 (Ch), the High Court held that employees who had copied customer contact details and sales figures during employment, had not acted in breach of their implied duty of confidentiality because the information was not confidential (it was in the public domain). However, they were held to have breached their duty of fidelity and, in the case of the senior employee, the fiduciary duty (see **2.5.3**).

In *Kynixa Ltd v Hynes and Others* [2008] EWHC 1495, the court held that three senior employees had breached their duty of fidelity by deliberately misleading their employer about their intention to work for a competitor, with which they had been in discussions for at least two months prior to departure.

1.7.2.5 Secret profits

An employee must not make a secret profit. If he does so, he can be compelled to account to his employer for the profit made (*Boston Deep Sea Fishing and Ice Co v Ansell* (1888) 39 Ch D 339) (see **2.5.3**).

1.7.2.6 Competition

In the absence of an express prohibition in the contract, taking a job outside working hours is not necessarily a breach of the employee's duty of fidelity, even where that job involves working for a competitor. Much will depend on how damaging that other employment is to the employer's business.

In *Hivac Ltd v Park Royal Scientific Instruments Ltd* [1946] Ch 169, five skilled manual workers who assembled hearing aids worked for their employer's sole competitor on Sundays. The Court of Appeal held that they were in breach of the implied duty of fidelity because it could not be consistent with their contract of employment for them to do in their spare time something which could potentially inflict such harm on their employers. Clearly, the fact that they worked for the only other competitor in the market was of great significance.

For the employee's duty of fidelity to be breached in this situation, the employee must normally occupy a position where he has access to confidential information or trade secrets such that the employer is at risk of such information being passed to a competitor. Therefore, in *Nova Plastics Ltd v Froggatt* [1982] IRLR 146, an odd-job man who worked for a competitor in his spare time was not in breach of contract.

After employment, the ex-employee may compete with his former employer without restriction. Any restrictive covenant which attempts to restrict such competition is subject to the doctrine of restraint of trade (see **1.8.7**).

1.7.2.7 Conflict of interest and duty

During employment, the employee must not allow his duty of fidelity to his employer to conflict with his personal interest. In particular, an employee who is intending to leave his employment and set up in competition may wish to obtain information from his employer or entice away his employer's customers and staff. It is a breach of the duty of fidelity to make lists of existing customers with the intention of using it after the termination of the employment relationship (*Roger Bullivant Ltd v Ellis* [1987] ICR 464) or even deliberately to memorise such a list for such a purpose (*Robb v Green* [1895] 2 QB 315). It is also a breach of the duty to entice away or agree to work personally for existing customers of the employer, or to induce other employees to break their contracts of employment (*Sanders v Parry* [1967] 2 All ER 803). (See also *Kynixa* at 1.7.2.4 above.)

1.7.2.8 Trade secrets and confidential information

During employment, an employee is in breach of his duty of fidelity if he uses or reveals trade secrets or other information which by its nature is confidential, or which has been impressed upon the employee as being confidential (*Faccenda Chicken Ltd v Fowler* [1986] 1 All ER 617). Such other information which by its nature is confidential would include lists of customers (see **1.7.2.7** above). A particular method of doing work, though not a trade secret, could be confidential information if the employee had been told of its confidentiality. However, information of a trivial or mundane character, or information that is available from public sources, cannot be turned into confidential information, even by an express term of the contract.

After employment has ceased, the employee is only prohibited from revealing or using his former employer's trade secrets or highly confidential information equivalent to a trade secret (*Faccenda Chicken Ltd v Fowler* – see **1.8.6**).

1.7.3 Other implied terms

As well as the above general terms, which are seen as a necessary part of contracts of employment, terms may also be implied into contracts where the court is satisfied that the term is necessary to give business efficacy to the contract or that the term is so obvious that the parties must have intended it. It is only appropriate to imply a term where, on a consideration of the express terms of the agreement and the facts and circumstances surrounding it, an implication arises that the parties actually intended the term in question to be part of their original contract.

Terms may also be implied (increasingly rarely) where it is the normal custom and practice to include such a term in contracts of that kind. The custom must be 'reasonable, notorious and certain'. Implication from custom or usage should only normally be on the basis that it does not conflict with an express term.

Lastly, a term may be implied by the courts (albeit rarely) where an intention to include the term (at the time of entering into the contract) is shown by the way the contract has been performed.

1.8   WRITTEN CONTRACTS

Although a contract of employment may be oral, written, or partly oral and partly written, it is advisable in the interests of certainty and to avoid disputes for the contract to be in writing and expressly to set out all the essential terms of the employment. There is no prescribed form for a written contract. An example is set out in **Appendix 1**.

One of the practical difficulties that may occur is deciding what documents form part of the contract and give rise to binding terms. For example, is the disciplinary procedure contractual? This may cause problems if an employer wishes to change a policy. Generally speaking, if it is a term of the contract, it cannot be changed unilaterally, ie without the employee's consent (see **1.4**).

In *Harlow v Artemis International Corporation Ltd* [2008] EWHC 1126, the Court of Appeal said that a redundancy policy, referred to in Mr Harlow's contract but contained in a staff handbook, was an express term of the employee's contract, and he was therefore contractually entitled to an enhanced payment under the policy. The policy spoke of 'entitlement', which set it aside from true policies, said the Court. Just because a document is referred to in a contract, though, does not mean it automatically becomes a contractual term. It will depend on the facts. The EAT held in *Worrall v Wilmott Dixon Partnership* (UKEAT/0521/09) that to incorporate a term of a collective agreement into a contract, the term must be brought to the employees' notice or agreed. It said it was not sufficient for the term simply to be in a readily available document, such as a handbook. The EAT held:

> it cannot be right that a party is bound by a contractual document which he has not received merely because it was a document available to him. The fact that a document was available to the claimant does not show that he had notice of its terms or that he had agreed to them.

On the facts, a term in a collective agreement providing for enhanced redundancy pay was held not to have been incorporated into the claimants' contracts, as there was no evidence of it being brought to the claimants' notice or agreed.

Nevertheless, care needs to be taken if an employer wishes to refer the employee to a policy or procedure but wants to remain free to change that policy or procedure at its disecretion. (See, eg, clause 17 of the sample Service Contract in **Appendix 1**.) A non-exhaustive list of considerations to take into account when determining whether the provisions of a policy were incorporated into a contract of employment was set out in *Albion Automotive Ltd v Walker* [2002] EWCA Civ 946. That case concerned whether employees who had been made redundant were entitled to enhanced redundancy payments because the employers had made such payments on previous occasions. The employees did not have written contracts of employment. Peter Gibson LJ, with whom the other members of the Court of Appeal agreed, endorsed the submission of the employees' counsel (set out at [15]) that when assessing whether a policy originally produced unilaterally by management had acquired contractual status, a number of considerations are relevant, including the following:

(a)   whether the policy was drawn to the attention of employees;

(b)   whether it was followed without exception for a substantial period;

(c)   the number of occasions on which it was followed;

(d)   whether payments were made automatically;

(e)   whether the nature of communication of the policy supported the inference that the employers intended to be contractually bound;

(f)   whether the policy was adopted by agreement;

(g)   whether employees had a reasonable expectation that the enhanced payment would be made;

(h)   whether terms were incorporated in a written agreement;

(i)   whether the terms were consistently applied.

If a policy is not meant to be contractual, the policy or contract should clearly state this. See also *Bateman v Asda Stores* at **1.4** above.

Some of the other *principal* clauses which should be considered for inclusion in a contract and some points to consider when drafting them are outlined below. The desirability of the clauses and their content will vary depending upon whether the employer or employee is being advised.

1.8.1   Duration clause

1.8.1.1   Indefinite contracts

In a contract for an indefinite term, the duration clause should specify the notice period to be given by the employer and the employee to terminate the contract.

In the case of managerial, professional and other senior employees, it may be appropriate to make the notice period fairly long, for example six months to be given by either party. This is mutually beneficial for employer and employee. It means that the employer should not be deprived of the services of a key employee on short notice and it gives the employee a degree of security. It may be worth considering reducing the notice period in the early stages of employment, to allow earlier termination if either the employer finds the employee unsuitable or the employee dislikes the job. For example, only one month's notice might be required to terminate within one year of commencing employment.

For less skilled employees, it may be appropriate to make the notice period shorter, but it must comply with the statutory minimum required by s 86 of the ERA 1996 (see **2.3.3**). In many cases, the contractual notice period would be the statutory minimum.

If there is no express term in the employment contract as to notice, then a term will be implied that the notice be of 'reasonable length'. In *Clark v Fahrenheit 451 (Communications) Ltd* (UKEAT/591/99), the EAT said that determining what is a reasonable length is a mixed question of law and fact and depends on all the circumstances of the case.

1.8.1.2   Fixed (limited)-term contracts

In the case of key, senior employees, the employer may wish to secure the employee's services for a longer period by entering into a fixed-term contract, for example for a period of five years from a specified date. This will bind both the employer and the employee for the fixed period.

If advising the employer on a fixed-term contract, the following matters should also be considered:

(a)   A clause that permits a fixed-term contract to be lawfully ended before expiry is known as a 'break' clause. The 'break' clause may permit the employer, or the employee, or both to have the right to end the contract by giving notice to the other. If a break clause is inserted, it should comply with the statutory minimum notice periods. For example, if the employer is in a strong enough bargaining position, he may wish to insert a clause under which he can terminate the contract at any time by giving the employee three months' notice. This effectively binds the employee for the full fixed term, but allows the employer to bring the contract to an end by giving notice. If there is no express 'break' clause, then the contract cannot be brought to an end by notice. The statutory minimum notice periods are not relevant in that situation.

(c)   Whether or not there is a break clause dealing with notice, it is advisable to insert a 'termination' clause into a fixed-term contract, under which the employer may terminate the contract without notice on the happening of specified events, such as bankruptcy of the employee. This is a more limited form of 'break' clause. In an indefinite contract, such a clause would not be necessary unless the notice period was very long.

(d)   If the employee is a director of the employer company, fixed-term contracts in excess of two years require the approval of the members of the company, otherwise the contract becomes terminable by reasonable notice (Companies Act 2006, ss 188 and 189).

(e)   It is unlawful to treat employees on fixed-term contracts less favourably than permanent employees without objective justification (Fixed-term Employees (Prevention of Less Favourable Treatment) Regulations 2002 (SI 2002/2034)) (see **8.12**).

1.8.1.3 Continuous employment

Section 1 of the ERA 1996 requires the employee to be informed whether any previous employment is continuous with the current employment and the date of commencement of the period of continuous employment (see **1.4.2**). This would normally be dealt with in the duration clause.

1.8.2 Duties and mobility

The duties and mobility clauses are concerned with defining the job which the employee is engaged to perform and the place or places where he can be required to perform it.

1.8.2.1 Job title

The job title or brief description should be stated to comply with s 1 of the ERA 1996. Although s 1 of the Act requires only the job title, the ECJ held in *Helmut Kampelmann and Others v Landschaftsverband Westfalen-Lippe* (Cases C-253/96 to 256/96) [1997] ECR I-6907 that the Proof of Employment Directive requires the employee to be told the nature of his employment, or be given a brief description of his work. The employer may wish to address matters such as job flexibility, or mobility, within a job description.

1.8.2.2 Duties

Defining duties

From the employer's point of view, the employee's duties should be defined widely. The clause should cover all duties that the employer envisages that the employee may be asked to do, and any possible changes in duties. In the case of a senior manager, for example, the contract could require him to carry out 'such duties as the employer may from time to time direct'.

However, even if the duties are widely defined, they will be limited to some extent by the job title. For example, in *Hayden v Cowan* [1982] IRLR 314, the applicant's job title was 'divisional contracts surveyor'. The Court of Appeal held that the employer could not therefore transfer him to any job as a quantity surveyor, despite a term in his contract which stated that he was 'required to undertake, at the direction of the company, any and all duties which reasonably fell within [his] capabilities'.

The duties of junior employees would usually be more narrowly defined. However, the employer must still bear in mind any changes he may wish to make to the employee's duties in the future, so that the changes can be made without the employer being in breach of contract.

How widely duties are defined may be relevant in determining if an employee is redundant (see **4.2.3.2**).

Time devoted to duties

From the employer's point of view, senior employees should be required to devote their whole time and attention to their duties. This does not mean that they have to work 24 hours a day, seven days a week, but it does mean that they are not restricted to specific hours. With junior employees, it is usual to specify the hours to be worked but, if appropriate, the contract should specify that the employee can be compelled to work overtime. Note that the Working Time Regulations 1998 regulate the hours that employees can be required to work (see **1.11**).

Consideration should be given as to whether there should be a term prohibiting the employee from taking part in any other business during employment. In the absence of any express term, an employee is only prohibited from working for a competitor during employment, and only then if he possesses information of a confidential nature (see **1.7.2**). The term prohibiting working for any other business will allow the employer, if appropriate, to obtain an injunction against the employee in the event of breach.

Qualifications

If the employee is required to hold a particular qualification (eg to possess a driving licence), or to pass a test or medical examination, this should be made an express term of the contract. The courts will not imply such a term unless it is necessary to make the contract work (*Stubbes v Trower, Still and Keeling* [1987] IRLR 321).

1.8.2.3 Place of work and mobility

Section 1 of the ERA 1996 requires the place or places of work to be stated (see **1.4.2**). Such a clause, particularly for a senior employee, should be drawn widely so that the employer is entitled to change the employee's place of work if necessary. It might, for example, require an employee to work anywhere within the UK. This can be very important when considering the question of redundancy (see **4.2.2**). If the employee will, or may, be required to work elsewhere, a mobility clause should be included. The mobility clause defines the area within which the employee can be required to work. Even where the contract does contain a mobility clause, the court has held that the employer must not exercise that clause in such a manner as to breach the implied duty of trust and confidence (*United Bank Ltd v Akhtar* [1989] IRLR 507).

Furthermore, it may be argued that a mobility clause is indirectly discriminatory on the grounds of sex, on the basis that it is likely to be more difficult for women than men to comply with the requirement to move, as a greater proportion of women are secondary earners (see **Chapter 10**).

Where there is no express mobility clause, the court is very unlikely to imply one where the written particulars state the place of work as required under ERA 1996, s 1. Even if there is no place of work clause, the court may still refuse to imply a mobility clause where there is no need to do so to give the contract business efficacy (*Aparau v Iceland Frozen Foods plc* [1996] IRLR 119).

The implication of a term is a matter for the court or tribunal, and whether or not a term is implied depends upon the intention of the parties, as collected from the words of the agreement and the surrounding circumstances. An implied term will usually be made in two situations: first, where it is necessary to give business efficacy to the contract, and, secondly, where the term implied represents the obvious, but unexpressed intention of the parties (see **1.7.3**).

Whether the court or tribunal will imply a mobility clause into the contract of employment will therefore depend upon the particular contractual relationship of the parties. If the tribunal is prepared to imply a mobility clause into the contract, as a rule of thumb, it may be possible to expect an employee to be mobile within a reasonable daily travelling distance from his home (see *Jones v Associated Tunnelling Co Ltd* [1981] IRLR 477, where the Court of Appeal held that since the employer was in business as a contractor working at different sites, the parties must have envisaged a degree of mobility). In *O'Brien v Associated Fire Alarms Ltd* [1968] 3 ITR 183, the Court of Appeal would not imply a term requiring an employee to move 120 miles. The Court of Appeal held that the only term that could be implied into the employee's contract was that he should be employed within a reasonable distance of his home. In *Managers (Holborn) Ltd v Hohne* [1977] IRLR 230, the EAT implied a term requiring the employee to work anywhere in Central London, since the employee was a commuter and the whole of central London was accessible to her by public transport.

1.8.2.4 Employee's viewpoint

The above guidelines are expressed from the point of view of the employer. From the employee's viewpoint, it is desirable to have a narrower definition of duties and mobility.

1.8.3 Remuneration, illness and holidays

In order to comply with s 1 of the ERA 1996, terms relating to pay, sickness and sick pay, holidays and holiday pay must be notified to the employee in the contract or s 1 statement.

In *Judge v Crown Leisure Ltd* [2005] IRLR 823, the Court of Appeal held that in order for there to be a legally binding contractual commitment, there must be certainty as to the contractual commitment entered into. Otherwise, a promise amounts to nothing more than a statement of intention. Therefore, on the facts, an employee was not entitled to rely on a promise made at a Christmas party that he would be paid the same as his colleagues 'eventually'.

1.8.3.1 Pay, benefits and commission

The remuneration clause should specify how the employee's remuneration is calculated (eg hourly wage or annual salary) and when payment is due (eg weekly or monthly). The contract should also specify any fringe benefits to which the employee is entitled (eg a company car or medical insurance).

The National Minimum Wage Act 1998 (NMWA 1998) established the legislative framework for the national minimum wage.

The National Minimum Wage Regulations 1999 (SI 1999/584), outlining the detail of the national minimum wage, came into force on 1 April 1999.

The Regulations are secondary legislation authorised under the NMWA 1998. They set out how the national minimum wage (NMW) is to be calculated, the pay reference periods and what employers need to do to comply with the legislation.

The Regulations:

(a)   set the rate of the minimum wage for those aged 21 and over at £6.19 (from 1 October 2012);

(b)   set modified rates for 18–20-year-olds at £4.98 (from October 2011);

(c) provide that workers aged below 18 who have ceased to be of compulsory school age qualify for the national minimum wage. The Regulations set an hourly rate of £3.68 for such workers (from October 2011);

(d) exempt non-employed apprentices under 26 in the first year of their apprenticeship. Persons who are workers on specified Government schemes at pre-apprenticeship level will not be entitled to the NMW, whether they are employed by the employer or not;

(e) set rates for employed apprentices under the age of 19, or 19 or above in their first year of apprenticeship at £2.65 (from 1 October 2012);

(f) set the pay reference period for averaging NMW pay at a maximum of one month;

(g) determine how to calculate hours worked for which the NMW is payable;

(h) require employers to issue a statement of the NMW to workers; and

(i) require employers to keep records.

For salaried workers, rest breaks and lunch breaks may be counted if they are included in the basic minimum hours under the contract. So if someone is employed for 40 hours per week and that includes his lunch break, the employee is entitled to count that time into the number of hours that he works every week.

If an employee is to be remunerated partly by commission, the contract should deal with this. The clause should deal not only with the rate of commission, but also with when it becomes payable.

In the case of *Edmonds v Michael Lawson and Others* [2000] IRLR 391, the Court of Appeal held that a pupil barrister over the age of 26 was not a 'worker' under the NMWA 1998. The Court held that there was no contract of employment because there was no duty on a pupil to do anything asked of him not conducive to his own training and development, as there must be for a contract of apprenticeship to arise.

In *British Nursing Association v Inland Revenue (National Minimum Wage Compliance Team)* [2002] IRLR 480, the Court of Appeal held that nurses who provide a telephone service at night from home were working through the shift even though they could do what they wanted between calls (see too *McCartney v Oversley House Management* (UKEAT/0500/3101)).

With effect from 6 April 2009, with the introduction of the Employment Act 2008, employers have to pay all arrears at the current rate where these are higher than the rate that applied when the underpayment was made. In addition, if an HMRC investigation finds that an employer has underpaid workers, notices of underpayment will require the employer to pay a financial penalty to the Secretary of State within 28 days of service. The penalty is set at 50% of the total underpayment of the NMW. The minimum penalty payable is £100 and the maximum penalty is £5,000. If the employer complies with the notice within 14 days of its service, the financial penalty will be reduced by 50%. The 2008 Act also gives some new powers to help HMRC inspectors carry out their investigations.

For employers who refuse to cooperate with the above civil regime, criminal proceedings are possible. The fine on conviction for each offence is up to £5,000 (level 5) in the magistrates' court, or an unlimited fine in the Crown Court. The Employment Act 2008 also gives HMRC the power to use the search and seize powers in the Police and Criminal Evidence Act 1984 when investigating criminal offences under the NMWA 1998.

1.8.3.2 Deductions

If deductions are to be made from salary or wages, for example, to repay loans from the employer or, in the case of employees who handle money, to recoup any shortages, the contract should give the employer the right to make such deductions. This is to comply with the requirements of the ERA 1996 and is dealt with in more detail at **1.10**.

1.8.3.3 Sick pay

The contract should state whether the employer pays sick pay (other than statutory sick pay). If sick pay is paid, the contract should state the period for which it is payable, how much is payable and whether statutory sick pay is deducted in calculating it. An employee who is off sick for a period of more than three consecutive days is entitled to receive statutory sick pay from his employer.

This clause should also specify that the employer is entitled to require the employee to provide a medical certificate if absent for more than, say, seven days.

With effect from 6 April 2012, the rate of statutory sick pay is £85.85, which is payable for a maximum period of 28 weeks in any three years.

The relationship between holidays and sickness is considered at **1.11.5**.

1.8.3.4 Holidays and holiday pay

The clause should specify how many days paid holiday the employee is entitled to each year and when it can be taken. Note that minimum paid annual leave is now regulated by the Working Time Regulations 1998 (see **1.11**).

1.8.4 Pension

The contract should specify whether or not the employer has an occupational pension scheme which the employee is entitled to join. An employee cannot be compelled to join an occupational pension scheme and is entitled to enter into a personal pension scheme instead.

If the employer has an occupational pension scheme, there will usually be a contracting out certificate in force under the Pension Schemes Act 1993. If there is no contracting out certificate in force, the employee will be entitled to a second State pension under the Second State Pension Scheme (S2P). An employee who is contracted out of S2P pays lower National Insurance contributions.

Employers must, unless exempt (eg employing fewer than five employees, or offering an occupational pension that all staff can join within a year of starting work), give their employees access to a stakeholder pension scheme.

From 1 October 2012, there is a requirement to enrol employees automatically in a pension scheme, and the employer will be obliged to contribute. The new employer duties are being introduced over six years, starting with employers with 120,000 or more employees. Further details may be found at www.pensionsadvisoryservice.org.uk.

1.8.5 Inventions and discoveries

In the case of employees who are likely to make discoveries or inventions, for example senior scientific and technical employees, the employer should ensure that the contract provides that any invention or discovery made in the course of employment belongs to the employer.

Such a clause is subject to the provisions of the Patents Act 1977 and the Copyright, Designs and Patents Act 1988. Details of these Acts are beyond the scope of this book but the basic rule is that inventions made in the course of employment belong to the employer. Other inventions belong to the employee and this cannot be varied by agreement. Even if the invention is made in the course of employment, the employee may be entitled to an award of compensation if the invention is of outstanding benefit to the employer.

1.8.6 Confidentiality

1.8.6.1 During employment

During employment, it is an implied term that an employee shall not reveal any confidential information (*Faccenda Chicken Ltd v Fowler* [1986] 1 All ER 617 – see **1.7.2.8**). Although there is an implied term that the employee shall not reveal any confidential information, it is advisable, in the case of employees who have access to confidential information, to insert an express term making it clear that they may not reveal such information during employment. The clause may also state what information the employer regards as confidential, though mundane information or information already in the public domain cannot be made confidential even by an express clause. The purpose of this clause is to draw the employee's attention to the duty of confidentiality and so to prevent the disclosure of such information.

1.8.6.2   After employment

After employment, only trade secrets and equivalent highly confidential information are protected by the implied term (see *Faccenda Chicken Ltd v Fowler*, **1.8.6.1** above). In *Faccenda Chicken*, the Court of Appeal set out a number of factors to be taken into account to determine whether particular information falls within the category that ought not to be disclosed after the employment has ended (applied recently in *Vestergaard Frandsen Als and Others v Bestnet Europe Ltd and Others* [2009] EWHC 657 (Ch)):

(a)   What was the nature of the employment?

(b)   What was the nature of the information?

(c)   Did the employer tell the employee that he regarded the information as confidential?

(d)   Could the information be easily isolated from the other information which the employee was free to use?

On the facts of *Faccenda Chicken Ltd*, although Mr Fowler's knowledge of customers, sales and prices information was confidential and therefore could not be used or even memorised deliberately during employment, it was not confidential information equivalent to a trade secret, and thus his employer was not entitled to an injunction restraining the former employee from using information which he had generally acquired in his employment. If, however, Mr Fowler had made a copy of the list of customers or deliberately memorised it during his employment, that would amount to a breach of the duty of fidelity and the employer would have been able to restrain him from using that information in a competing business after the employment had ended (see, eg, *Bullivant v Ellis* [1987] ICR 464 and *Robb v Green* above – see **1.7.2.7**)

In *Stephenson Ltd v Mandy* [2000] IRLR 233, the High Court considered whether a distinction could be made between information which had been 'deliberately learned' and that which was 'innocently carried in the head'. The court said such a distinction could not be definitive of what information could be legitimately protected by means of a restrictive covenant. In that case, a list of clients was held to be part of information the employer was entitled to protect, even though some of it was in the employee's head 'innocently'.

In order to prevent an employee taking up a position where he may use such information, a restraint of trade clause (see **1.8.7.1**) should also be included.

While it is well established that an employer cannot enforce restrictive covenants contained in the contract of employment if he is in repudiatory breach (see *General Billposting Company Ltd v Atkinson* [1909] AC 118 and **1.8.7.5**), it seems likely that any express term relating to confidentiality will continue notwithstanding any repudiation of the contract by the employer and that, in the absence of an express provision, the implied duty will, in any event, continue. Nevertheless, the issue is not beyond doubt (*Campbell v Frisbee* [2003] ICR 141).

1.8.7   Restrictive covenants

In order to prevent unfair competition after employment ends, it is advisable for an employer, where it is possible, to insert a restrictive covenant into the employee's contract.

In the absence of an effective restrictive covenant, an ex-employee may compete with the ex-employer, solicit the former customers of the ex-employer and poach its staff.

1.8.7.1   Restraint of trade

A restrictive covenant restraining an ex-employee from working in a competing business or soliciting ex-customers is prima facie void as being in restraint of trade. An employer is not entitled to protect himself against competition as such; he must have an interest to protect.

In order for a restrictive covenant to be enforceable:

(a)   the employer must have a legitimate business interest to protect. Legitimate business interests are:

(i)   trade secrets or other highly confidential information which 'if disclosed to a competitor, would be liable to cause real or significant damage to the owner of the secret which the owner had tried to limit dissemination of' (*Lansing Linde Ltd v Kerr* [1991] 1 All ER 418, CA);

(ii)   trade connections, eg employers' relationships with their customers and clients (goodwill). The employer will have to demonstrate that a breach would result in actual or potential harm to the employer's business (see eg *Jack Allen (Sales and Service) Ltd v Smith* [1999] IRLR 19);

(iii)   the employer's interest in maintaining a stable and trained workforce (see eg *Dawnay, Day & Co Ltd v Braconier d'Alphen & Others* [1997] IRLR 442).

A restrictive covenant can be valid only if imposed on a person who has such information, for example a senior technical employee with knowledge of trade secrets, or a manager or salesperson who has knowledge of trade connections.

In *Thomas v Far plc* [2007] EWCA Civ 118, the Court of Appeal held that an employer was entitled to seek to protect its pricing and financial information by way of a non-compete clause in the contract (see **1.8.7.2**).

(b)   the restraint must also be reasonable in time and area, and it must be no wider than necessary to protect the employer's business interest (ie, the activity prohibited must be no wider than necessary; see **1.8.7.2**).

A restrictive covenant will not be enforced unless its terms are sufficiently clear.

In *Kynixa* (see above at **1.7.2.4**) the High Court upheld terms preventing two employees from competing with their employer ('*in any business competing with the Business*'); from soliciting customers of the employer ('*any person who is, or has been at any time, in the previous 6 months, a customer of the Business*'); and from poaching employees for a period of 12 months ('*solicit or entice away or endeavour to solicit or entice away any consultant, director or employee of the Group engaged in the Business*').

The Court held that the employer:

> had a legitimate interest in seeking to prevent the solicitation of its customers. Equally it had a legitimate interest in seeking to prevent solicitation of [employees]. Given the nature of its business, the competitive nature of the market in which it operated, the fact that the ... [Defendants] were well known to the customers of the Claimant and the fact that with some customers, at least, arrangements for the provision of services by the Claimant between ... it and the customer would remain in place for a fixed period time (measured often in two year periods) but then be reviewed ... a restraint lasting twelve months was entirely reasonable. [The Court] also had regard to the fact that the ... Defendants had a choice about whether or not to enter the shareholder agreement [where the terms were contained] and in each case they chose to do so for (potentially) substantial gain ...

The Court also held that the *anti-competition clause was justified*. The defendants were very senior employees and were privy to confidential information which the claimant was justified in seeking to protect.

1.8.7.2   Contents of the clause

Restrictive covenants can cover competition by the ex-employee after the employment ends, the soliciting of (or dealing with) former customers and clients, and also the poaching of former employees. The basic rules set out above apply to all these areas.

Non-competition

The typical non-competition clause prohibits the employee, for a specified number of months or years after the end of the employment, from carrying on or being associated with the business in which the employer is engaged, within a specified number of miles of the employer's premises at which the employee was employed.

The clause must be no wider than is necessary to protect the employer's business:

(a)   The business activity from which the employee is barred must be no wider than the business in which he was employed. In *Scully UK Ltd v Lee* [1998] IRLR 259, the Court of Appeal refused to grant an injunction enforcing a covenant prohibiting an ex-employee from dealing with companies which were not in direct competition with the former employer. Mr Lee worked as a technical sales engineer for Scully, who were involved in the design and manufacture of systems for use in the oil and gas industry. In January 1997, he resigned from Scully and went to work as a sales manager for a company concerned with the supply of fuel distribution products and gauges. The Court of Appeal struck down a clause which prohibited the ex-employee from having any involvement in any business dealing with the type of equipment provided by Scully, on grounds that it extended to non-competing businesses (ie, businesses not involved in the oil and gas industry) and was therefore wider than necessary to protect their legitimate interests in customer connections and confidential information.

(b)   A time restraint in excess of one year can usually be justified only in exceptional circumstances. One year may be too long in some cases, especially if the employer's trade connections are subject to rapid change.

(c)   The area within which the ex-employee is barred from competing must be reasonable. It must not be wider than the area within which the employer did business.

In *Hollis & Co v Stocks* [2000] IRLR 712, a covenant restraining a solicitor from working (as a solicitor) within a 10-mile radius of a small firm of solicitors in Nottinghamshire for a period of one year was held to be enforceable; and in *Corporate Express Ltd v Day* [2004] EWHC 2943, the court upheld a six-month ban on working for competitors because there was a real risk that the employee would use her knowledge to benefit her new employer.

The Court of Appeal held in *Thomas v Far plc* (see **1.8.7.1**) that a clause in the contract of a managing director of a firm of insurance brokers, which prevented him from competing with the company for 12 months, was enforceable. The employee had argued on appeal that the non-solicitation and confidentiality clauses in the managing director's contract adequately protected the employer and that the non-compete clause was unnecessary. The Court of Appeal held that because of the problems of differentiating between confidential and non-confidential information, and the fact that the solicitation of clients was unlikely to be done by the managing director himself, the non-compete clause was necessary to protect the legitimate business interest. It was accepted, on the facts, that the 12-month non-compete clause did not prevent Mr Thomas from acting as an insurance broker in sectors other than social housing, and since most insurance policies in the social housing sector were for longer than 12 months, the 12-month period was reasonable.

In *Christie Owen & Davies v Walton* [2008] CSOH 37, the Court of Session upheld a non-compete clause that prevented the employee from working for a competitor in the care sector in any capacity, because the employee had been 'materially involved' in the business of the former employer (ie had knowledge of the former employer's client base and potential client base).

Non-solicitation

The non-solicitation clause will prohibit the employee from seeking business from persons who were customers of the employer within a specified period prior to the employee leaving employment. Such a clause is more likely to be upheld if it is restricted to those customers with whom the employee has had personal contact (see, eg, *WRN Ltd v Ayris* [2008] EWHC 1080 (QB) where the term was held to be too wide because it was not restricted to customers with whom the employee had actually dealt). The clause should be no wider than necessary to protect the employer's business. Again, the clause is more likely to be upheld if it is restricted to those persons who were the employer's customers within a comparatively short time prior to the employee leaving. What is reasonable will depend on the nature of the business, eg how often customers come and go.

In *Associated Foreign Exchange Ltd v International Foreign Exchange (UK) Ltd* [2010] EWHC 1178 (Ch) the High Court held that there was insufficient evidence that a non-solicitation restriction of 12 months went no further than was reasonably necessary to protect an employer's legitimate business interests. The contract also contained a six-month non-dealing clause. The High Court refused to grant an injunction to prevent an ex-employee soliciting customers. It said that the non-dealing clause gave the employer adequate protection because the employee in question was not particularly senior and had not played a key part in building up new business for AFEX. Such protection as was sought by the non-solicitation clause would only be appropriate where a business could show that building up a relationship with its potential customers was a long and difficult process involving significant investment in time and money.

Non-poaching

A non-poaching clause will prevent the employee from persuading other employees to go with him to a new employer. Such clauses are probably best restricted to senior employees known to the employee (see, eg, *TSC Europe (UK) Ltd v Massey* [1999] IRLR 22 and, more recently, *UBS Wealth Management (UK) Ltd v Vesta Wealth LLP and Others* [2008] EWHC 1974).

Non-dealing

A non-dealing clause will prevent the employee from dealing with clients even if the clients approach the employee.

In *Beckett Investment Management Group Limited v Hall* [2007] EWCA Civ 613, the Court of Appeal upheld a 12-month non-dealing clause imposed by a holding company, even though on a literal interpretation of the clause the employees were not in breach. Beckett Investment Management Group Ltd (BIMG) was the holding company within a group of companies that provided financial advice. BIMG did not itself provide direct financial advice. This was done by a subsidiary, Beckett Financial Services Ltd (BFS). Hall and Yadev, who were both senior employees employed by BIMG but based at BFS's offices, left to start up their own competing business. Their contracts contained post-termination restrictions preventing them from providing financial advice of a type provided by the Company (defined as BIMG) to certain clients. Hall and Yadev continued to deal with BFS's clients and argued that the non-dealing restriction was unenforceable. The Court of Appeal said that the phrase the business of 'the Company' should be construed as the business undertaken by the subsidiaries. In terms of the length of the restriction, the Court said that 12 months was reasonable having regard to the nature of the financial services business, the seniority of Hall and Yadev, and evidence of an industry standard of 12 months. However, the Court said that a period longer than 12 months would have been unreasonable and unenforceable.

In this case, the clause was trying to protect the business for which the employees were actually working. It is important when drafting such restrictions to ensure that these clauses not only reflect the employee's actual circumstances, but also properly protect the actual business in which they are working.

Enforcement

If the clause is in restraint of trade, either because the employer has no interest to protect or because it is drafted too widely and therefore is unreasonable in time or area, it is void and hence unenforceable.

The 'blue pencil' test

If a clause is drafted too widely and is found to be in restraint of trade, the court may be able to apply the 'blue pencil' test to sever that part of the clause that is too wide and leave the remainder as an enforceable clause. Therefore, if drafting a restrictive covenant, draft for severance so that if one part of a clause is found to be void it can be severed, leaving the remainder valid. The court must be able to sever the offending part by striking a 'blue pencil' through it. The court cannot rewrite the clause (eg by substituting a shorter time-limit). The Court of Appeal in *Scully UK Ltd v Lee* (see above) stated that severance of part of a covenant was permissible only in cases where the obligation to be severed was truly a separate obligation to that to be enforced. If the obligations were in any way interdependent, then severance would not be permitted.

In *Corporate Express Limited v Day* [2004] EWHC 2943, the High Court upheld a restrictive covenant for a senior manager imposing a six-month ban in the post-employment soliciting of clients and the working for 10 named competitors. In *TFS Derivatives Ltd v Morgan* [2005] IRLR 246, the EAT considered a restrictive covenant involving a City equity broker. It concerned the enforceability of a fairly wide-ranging covenant which did not allow the broker for a period of six months following termination of employment to 'undertake, carry on or be employed, engaged or interested in any capacity in either any business which is competitive with *or similar to* a relevant business within the territory, or any business an objective or anticipated result of which is to compete with a relevant business within the territory' (emphasis added). Mrs Justice Cox stated that, if there is ambiguity and two possible constructions, rather than holding that the covenant is an unreasonable restraint of trade, the court should construe it on the basis that the parties are to be deemed to have intended their bargain to be lawful. In this case, rather than holding that the covenant was too wide to be reasonable, she severed the words 'or similar to'.

Drafting a series of cumulative restrictions leaving the court to decide where the line should be drawn (eg restraint for three years, followed by restraint for two years, followed by restraint for one year) is very likely to be void for uncertainty and is not recommended. Particular care needs to be taken where there is a transfer of an undertaking (see **7.4.1.1**).

Mode of enforcement

The employer's remedy when an employee is in breach of an effective restrictive covenant will be an injunction where damages are not an adequate remedy, that is, an injunction to prevent the ex-employee from carrying on a competing business, soliciting customers or poaching staff, whichever is appropriate. The employer may also claim damages if he has suffered pecuniary loss. The employee can be compelled to hand over, for example, copies of lists of customers and details of trade secrets in his possession. See *Roger Bullivant Ltd v Ellis* (at **1.8.6.2** above) and, more recently, *UBS Wealth Management (UK) Ltd v Vestra Wealth LLP* (above), where a business was granted a 'springboard' injunction to prevent a rival business, its founder and four defecting employees from doing business with and attempting to poach clients and other staff. See, most recently, *CEF Holdings Ltd and Another v Mundey and Others* [2012] EWHC 1524, where the High Court determined a number of issues arising out of an employer's attempts to stop its former employees setting up a rival company. The case set out some important principles in relation to without notice injunctions and the obligation of full and frank disclosure. The court also held that a number of restrictive covenants were too wide and invalid or, in some cases, unnecessary.

Effect of wrongful dismissal

If the contract terminates in circumstances where neither party is in breach of contract, or where the employee is rightfully dismissed for his own breach, the restrictive covenant can be enforced by the employer provided it is not void as being in restraint of trade.

However, the House of Lords held in *General Billposting Company Ltd v Atkinson* [1909] AC 118, that an otherwise valid restrictive covenant cannot be enforced if the employee has been wrongfully dismissed by the employer.

Thus, according to *Billposting*, where there is a repudiatory breach of contract by the employer, the employee is released from the obligations under the covenant.

Whilst *Billposting* remains good law, some judges have expressed reservations as to the correctness of the principle (see eg *Rock Refrigeration Ltd v Jones* [1996] IRLR 675). Support for the view that confidentiality covenants can survive wrongful dismissal can be found in *Campbell v Frisbee* [2003] ICR 141.

Note that where the contract expressly provides that payment may be made in lieu of notice, the employer may dismiss the employee without proper notice and still be able to enforce any restrictive covenants (provided they are otherwise reasonable). This is because the employer is not then in breach of contract. This is the principal reason for the inclusion of a pay in lieu of notice provision (see **2.3.3**).

Employee's viewpoint

Ideally, an employee would want to avoid restrictive covenants, or limit them so as not to prejudice his ability to change employment. However, it may be in the employee's interest to agree to a restrictive covenant which is patently too wide and hence unenforceable.

1.8.7.3 'Garden leave' clauses

The term 'garden leave' is used to mean the period of time during which the employee is paid but is required to stay at home rather than attend work. The employer can thus hold the employee to the terms of his contract and prevent him from working for a competitor during the period. The clause will be invoked where either party gives notice of termination but the employer does not want the employee to attend at work during the notice period or to work for a competitor during that period.

A garden leave clause is more likely to be enforceable than a simple restriction precluding the employee joining a competitor for a period post-termination because it ensures that the employee does not suffer financially during the period of garden leave (*Eurobrokers Ltd v Rabey* [1995] IRLR 206). Nevertheless, the clause will not be enforced unless it is a reasonable restraint and the employer can show a legitimate business interest that he is seeking to protect (*Provident Financial Group plc v Hayward* [1989] ICR 160; *Symbian Ltd v Christensen* [2001] IRLR 77).

A long period of garden leave may be unduly onerous for an employee, and it is a matter for the court's discretion as to whether and to what extent the provision should be enforced. The court may, if the restraint during garden leave is drafted too widely, 'whittle it down' to something reasonable.

An employer who wishes to be sure that an employee can be sent home on garden leave should ensure that there is an express clause in the employee's contract sanctioning this course of action. This is because, in some cases (see **1.7.1**), the contract may give the employee the right to be provided with work during the notice period, or such a right may be implied and failure by the employer to observe that right may prevent him from relying on the garden leave clause; indeed, it could amount to a breach of contract by the employer (*William Hill Organisation Ltd v Tucker* [1998] IRLR 313).

In *SG&R Valuation Service v Boudrais* (see **1.7.1.1**), the High Court held that an employer can, however, send an employee on garden leave, in the absence of an express contractual right to do so, where there is evidence of actual wrongdoing by the employee (here helping himself to confidential information as part of a planned move to a competitor).

In *Credit Suisse Asset Management Ltd v Armstrong* [1996] IRLR 450, the court held that there was no relationship between the restrictive covenant and garden leave clause such as to allow the court, in any but an exceptional case, to order a set-off for the period of garden leave against the period covered by the restrictive covenant. Provided that the restrictive covenant was valid, it should be enforced by the court, once the garden leave has come to an end.

Table 1.1 Solicitation, poaching, competition and confidentiality: summary chart

	Solicitation (clients/customers) or Poaching (fellow employees)	Competition	Confidentiality
During contract			
(a) *Implied terms*	Not to solicit customers and/or employees of the employer Not to copy list of customers	Must not compete with employer Cannot 'moonlight' for a competitor if causes harm	Respect any confidential information
(b) *Express terms*	To increase employee's duty and/or clarify implied position	To increase employee's duty – eg devote 'full time' clause – to prevent all moonlighting	To clarify implied position – eg to define what counts as confidential information
After contract			
(a) *Implied terms*	No implied term	No implied term	Only 'highly confidential' information/trade secrets are protected
(b) *Express terms*	Covenant protecting legitimate interest (eg, customer connections/stable workforce). Covenant must be reasonable in terms of (a) the activity prohibited (eg customers with whom employee had personal contact/senior employees known to the employee); and (b) time (eg customers from the last 6 months and for the next 6 months).	Covenant protecting legitimate interest (eg trade secrets) (see *Lansing Linde*). Covenant must be reasonable in terms of (a) the activity prohibited (eg no wider than the business in which employee employed, such as not to work for a competitor); (b) time; and (c) area covered (eg no wider than the area where the employer carries on business).	Covenant protecting legitimate interest (eg trade secrets or other highly confidential information which if disclosed would cause real harm to the employer (*Lansing Linde*)). To clarify the implied position, ie what the employer considers highly confidential information (cannot increase the duty).

1.8.8　Disciplinary and grievance procedures

Details of disciplinary and grievance procedures may be included to comply with s 1 of the ERA 1996 (see **1.4.2**).

1.8.9　Surrender of papers

It is common for the employment contract to require the employee, on the termination of the contract, to surrender all notes and documents that he has in his possession which relate to the employer's business.

1.8.10　Other issues

Consideration should be given to inclusion of other clauses in the contract and policy statements, for example:

(a)　a PILON clause (see **Chapter 2**);

(b)　a whistle-blowing policy (see **5.6.5**);

(c)　computer/telephone usage policies (see **15.5.2**);

(d)　an equal opportunities policy (see **Chapter 8**);

(e)　a health and safety policy;

(f)　a maternity, paternity and parental leave policy (see **Chapter 14**);

(g)　a flexible working policy (see **Chapter 14**).

1.9　HUMAN RIGHTS ACT 1998

From a contractual perspective, the individual rights recognised by the HRA 1998 (see **Chapter 15**) may be given greater weight, especially when they have to be balanced against managerial interests. This could be achieved by two routes. First, the courts may be persuaded to accept that those rights are implicitly incorporated into individual contracts of employment. Secondly, if that is a step too far, it may be argued that they are part and parcel of the development of the implied duty of mutual trust and confidence. Thus, even though the HRA 1998 is not directly enforceable between private individuals, if there is a breach of a Convention right, that may give rise to a claim for breach of contract.

Additionally, as courts and tribunals are obliged to act compatibly with the HRA 1998 (s 6), it has also been argued that the HRA 1998 will impact on the construction of terms of the contract of employment, in particular terms relating to confidentiality and restraint of trade, and the HRA 1998 may well limit the 'scope' of 'managerial prerogative' in the context of giving orders and the obligation of an employee to obey (lawful and reasonable) orders.

Although there is nothing specifically stated in the HRA 1998, it has long been accepted that rights under the European Convention on Human Rights can be waived by contract. The ECtHR's jurisprudence makes it clear, however, that:

(a)　any waiver must be clear and unequivocal;

(b)　simply signing a contract may not amount to a waiver – an employee's attention must be drawn to any specific provision;

(c)　even where there is a waiver in a contract, it is not deemed to be conclusive of the matter; courts will still scrutinise and assess any such waiver.

In *Rommelfanger v Germany* (1989) 62 DR 151, Mr Rommelfanger was a German doctor working in a Catholic hospital. He expressed views on abortion in the press which ran counter to those of the Catholic Church, and was dismissed as a result. In his contract, he had accepted a duty of loyalty to the Catholic Church. It was held that he had accepted a limitation on his freedom of expression but had not thereby deprived himself of the protection of Article 10. Notwithstanding the contractual limitation, the Court maintains a supervisory jurisdiction to look at the substantive issue and weigh up the competing interests of the employer and employee. The Court will give weight to contractual waivers, but there may be situations where the restriction on the right is too extreme, in which case the Court will interfere. As the Catholic Church was an organisation based on certain fundamental convictions and beliefs which it considered essential, it was entitled to its freedom of expression.

In *Ahmad v UK* (1982) 4 EHRR 126, a local authority teacher complained of constructive dismissal after he was refused permission to attend a mosque during working hours. It was accepted by the Court that his right to exercise his freedom of religion (Article 9) could be limited by contractual obligations such as requirements relating to the hours of work, timetabling etc, provided that his employers did not arbitrarily disregard his freedom of religion.

In *Stedman v UK* (1999) 23 EHRR CD 168, the Commission rejected the employee's claim that her employer had breached Article 9 by requiring her to work on Sundays; the employee was not dismissed because of her religious beliefs but because she refused to work her contractual hours (see now, however, s 10 of the Equality Act 2010 – at **8.2.3**).

1.10 PROTECTION OF WAGES

If an employer fails to pay remuneration due under the employment contract, the employee (or worker – see **1.3** above) will often be able to rely on what is commonly referred to as the 'protection of wages' legislation – set out in Pt II of the ERA 1996. This part of the ERA 1996 expressly includes workers as well as employees within its protections (as defined in s 230). The term 'worker' is wider and expressly encompasses an individual who works under a contract of employment (s 230(3)), and will be used below when describing the protection provided. Notice pay is not covered by Pt II and s 14 expressly excludes deductions made in respect of an overpayment of wages or expenses (see **1.10.4** below). The normal remedies for breach of contract are also available in all these situations. Most workers utilise the protection of wages legislation where it is available in addition to or in preference to the normal breach of contract remedies.

Two aspects are considered below: first, the need for authority before the employer is entitled to make deductions from wages; and, secondly, the method of enforcement by employment tribunals.

1.10.1 Deductions from wages

The basic right given to workers by Pt II of the ERA 1996 is stated in s 13, whereby an employer must not make any deduction from wages unless:

(a)   it is authorised by statute (eg Pay As You Earn (PAYE) and National Insurance); or

(b)   it is authorised by the worker's contract; or

(c)   the worker has previously signified in writing his consent to the making of it.

A deduction is defined in s 13(3) as follows:

> Where the total amount of wages paid on any occasion by an employer to a worker employed by him is less than the total amount of wages properly payable by him to the worker on that occasion ... the amount of the deficiency shall be treated ... as a deduction ...

Therefore, if the total amount paid to the worker is less than the total amount properly payable (which will not include pure errors of computation), it will be a deduction.

Non-payment of a sum due may amount to a deduction, provided that the sum relates to a period of employment. Non-payment of wages in lieu of notice after termination of the contract does not therefore fall under the ERA 1996 (*Delaney v Staples* [1991] IRLR 112).

A unilateral reduction in wages may amount to a deduction, as may a non-payment of commission. Note that in *Stringer v HMRC* [2009] UKHL 31, the House of Lords held that non-payment of statutory holiday pay and non-payment in lieu of untaken holiday (under the

Working Time Regulations 1998 – see **1.11**) constitute non-payment of wages. Such claims may be brought under both the Working Time Regulations 1998 (but only in respect of one calendar year) and under the protection of wages provisions as an unauthorised deduction claim (going back six years) (see also **1.10.2** below).

An employer may also make deductions where those deductions are covered by one of the exemptions in s 14 (see **1.10.4**).

If the employer wishes to make any deductions from a worker's wages, for example penalties for substandard work or to recoup 'till shortages' from workers handling money, authority to make the deduction should be specified in the contract.

For workers in retail employment, deductions for cash shortages or stock deficiencies must not, except for the final payment of wages, exceed one-tenth of the employee's gross wages (ERA 1996, s 17).

If the employer wishes to make deductions of a type not provided for in the contract, for example, if the employer makes a loan to be repaid by deductions from wages, the worker must give his written consent to the deduction. (In the example given, this would usually be done in the loan agreement.)

1.10.2   What are 'wages'?

The ERA 1996 prohibits deductions from 'wages', and s 27 of the ERA 1996 defines wages as 'any sums payable to the worker [by his employer] in connection with his employment ... including any fee, bonus, commission, holiday pay or other emolument referable to his employment, whether payable under his contract or otherwise'.

In *Kent Management Services Ltd v Butterfield* [1992] IRLR 394, the EAT held that although the contract described the commissions and bonuses as discretionary and non-contractual, nevertheless both the employer and worker would expect them to be paid unless there were exceptional circumstances. Such payments, which were identifiable sums, were therefore 'wages', whether contractual or not, and the employer could not withhold them even though he was of the opinion that the contract had not been properly performed. If the employer had wanted the right to withhold the payments in certain circumstances then he should have included the necessary authority in the worker's contract.

The EAT held in *Hellewell v AXA Services* (UK/EAT/0084/11) that the contract relieved the employers of any obligation to pay bonuses where, as was the case here, employees had committed gross misconduct. The bonus was not therefore 'properly payable', and thus there was no unlawful deduction (see **1.10.3** below).

In *Coors Brewers v Adcock* [2007] EWCA Civ 19, the Court of Appeal held that claims by employees (who were still employed, so could not bring a tribunal claim for breach of contract) for bonuses under a share scheme, were in reality claims for unliquidated (unspecified) damages and therefore fell outside the scope of an unlawful deduction claim. Wall LJ stated that the unlawful deduction regime applied only to 'a specific sum of money' or an 'identifiable sum'. Where a detailed investigation was required as to the level of the alleged underpayment, the proper route was to bring a breach of contract claim (which in this case would have to be brought in the civil court, as the employees were still employed).

In *Tradition Securities & Futures SA v Alexandre Mouradian* [2009] EWCA Civ 60, the Court of Appeal held that an employee was entitled to bring a claim relating to the amount of his bonus in the employment tribunal under the unlawful deduction from wages provisions because the amount of the bonus was quantifiable according to a precise formula for calculating the bonus.

As stated above, payments in lieu of notice are not wages under ERA 1996, s 27.

1.10.3 'Properly payable'

The Court of Appeal held in *New Century Cleaning Co Ltd v Church* [2000] IRLR 27 that wages will be 'properly payable' only if the worker has a legal (although not necessarily contractual) entitlement to the wages. In *Hellewell v AXA Services* (**1.10 2** above) the EAT confirmed that the claimants were not entitled to a bonus because the contract was clear – no bonus was payable where the employees had committed gross misconduct.

1.10.4 Exceptions

1.10.4.1 Overpayment of wages or expenses

An employer may make deductions to recover overpayments of wages or expenses previously paid by mistake to the worker (ERA 1996, s 14(1)). Any dispute as to the lawfulness of such a deduction must be resolved in the civil courts. Such overpayments are recoverable unless the employer has led the worker to believe the money was his and the worker changes his position (eg spends the money) and the overpayment was not the worker's fault (*Kleinwort Benson Ltd v Lincoln City Council and Other Appeals* [1999] 2 AC 349).

1.10.4.2 Deductions in respect of industrial action

If the worker is not performing any of his duties, the employer may deduct an amount which represents a fair proportion of his salary.

1.10.5 Enforcement

If an employer makes an unauthorised deduction from wages, the worker may present a complaint to an employment tribunal within three months of the payment from which the deduction was made (or within three months of the last in a series of deductions, so allowing a claim to go back more than three months if the underpayments form part of a series). Where the complaint is upheld, the tribunal will order the employer to pay to the worker the amount of the unauthorised deduction (ERA 1996, s 27). Alternatively, an employee could pursue a claim for breach of contract in the civil courts. See also the chart at **5.6.2.5**.

1.11 WORKING TIME REGULATIONS 1998

The Working Time Regulations 1998 (SI 1988/1833) (the Regulations) implement the Working Time Directive (93/104).

The Government has issued guidance on the limits of working time and some of the entitlements provided for in the 1998 Regulations (see http://www.direct.gov.uk). The guidance explains how the Regulations work and how employers may seek to comply with them – what questions they need to consider and what action they should take. The guidance is intended to be just that, and should not be regarded as a complete or authoritative statement of the law.

Note that the Regulations apply to workers as well as employees (see **1.3**). As the definition of worker encompasses that of employee, that term will be used below. What follows is an introduction to the Regulations.

1.11.1 The nature and scope of the Regulations

1.11.1.1 Working time

The Regulations provide that, in relation to a worker, 'working time' means:

(a) any period during which he is working, at his employer's disposal and carrying out his activity or duties;

(b) any period during which he is receiving 'relevant training'; and

(c)   any additional period which is to be treated as working time under a relevant agreement.

The Government's guidance gives some examples:

(i)   On-call time will be working time when a worker is required to be at his place of work – when a worker is away from the workplace when on-call, and accordingly free to pursue his leisure activities, on-call time is *not* working time (see *Sindicato de Medicos de Asistencia Publica (SiMAP) v Conselleria de Sanidad y Consumo de la Generalidad Valenciana* [2000] IRLR 845, ECJ). The ECJ confirmed in *Landeshauptstadt Kiel v Jaeger* [2003] IRLR 804 that the three criteria mentioned in (a) above are cumulative. In the *Jaeger* case the ECJ held that on-call time spent at a hospital was working time, even though the doctor was allowed to sleep when not required, because all three criteria in (a) were met.

In *Hughes v G and L Jones t/a Graylyns Residential Home* (UKEAT/0159/08), the EAT held that working time included the period the care worker was on call between 9pm and 8am, seven days a week, during which time she occupied a flat on site at a reduced rent.

(ii)   A lunch break spent at leisure will not be working time, although a working lunch would be.

(iii) Time spent working abroad will be working time.

(iv)   Time spent travelling to and from a place of work is unlikely to be working time as a worker will probably neither be working nor carrying out his duties, but a worker may well be doing both if he is engaged by travel that is required by the job.

1.11.1.2   Worker

Subject to the exclusions outlined below, the Regulations will apply to individuals over the minimum school leaving age who can be categorised as 'employees' (ie those working under contracts of service or apprenticeship) plus a wider group who undertake to perform personally any work or services (eg freelancers) (see, eg, *Willoughby v County Home Care Ltd* (ET/1100310/99)). Those whose work amounts to carrying out business activity on their own account (with whom there is a relationship of client/customer rather than employer) are excluded; such individuals are likely to be paid on the basis of an invoice rather than receiving wages (see discussion at **1.3**).

The Regulations specifically exclude domestic servants in private households from the provisions of working time and night work. However, they are covered by the provisions on rest periods and annual leave.

The Regulations distinguish between 'adult workers' (workers who have attained the age of 18) and 'young workers' (who are over compulsory school age but below the age of 18). Only adult workers are dealt with below.

1.11.1.3   Excluded activities and sectors of activity

Prior to 1 August 2003, most of the entitlements under the Regulations did not apply to workers in air, road, sea, inland waterway and lake transport; sea fishing and other work at sea; and doctors in training. However, since 1 August 2003, the Regulations now generally apply in full to non-mobile workers within these industries.

Regulation 2 defines a mobile worker as 'any worker employed as a member of travelling or flying personnel by an undertaking which operates transport services for passengers or goods by road or air'. The position with regard to mobile workers in these industries is more complicated, and often mobile workers are protected under sector-specific legislation or are only covered by certain parts of the Regulations.

The armed forces and the police and emergency services are partially exempt from the Regulations.

Young workers in the armed forces, the police and emergency services, the aviation sector and the road transport sector, are covered by the young workers provisions in the Working Time Regulations.

The UK Regulations do now apply to junior doctors.

Detailed consideration of the above provisions is beyond the scope of this book.

1.11.2 Summary of the limits, rights and duties

Almost all of the rights and limits introduced by the Regulations are subject to exceptions and qualifications. The basic provisions with regard to day workers and adults are summarised below. There are also specific provisions relating to night work and young workers which are outside the scope of this book.

1.11.2.1 Limits on working time

Weekly working time

In a 17-week period (which may be extended), no worker is permitted to work more than an average of 48 hours per week.

1.11.2.2 Adult workers' rights

Daily rest period

Eleven consecutive hours' rest in every 24-hour period. See **1.11.4**.

Weekly rest period

An uninterrupted rest period of not less than 24 hours in each seven-day period (in addition to the daily rest period).

Daily rest period

Twenty minutes' rest break, provided that the working day is longer than six hours.

Annual leave

An entitlement to 5.6 weeks' (ie 28 days for a 5-day per week employee) paid annual leave (see **1.11.5**).

1.11.3 Maximum weekly working time

The Regulations set a limit on the amount of working time which may be undertaken by a worker each week. The general rule is that a worker's working time (including overtime) in any reference period shall not exceed an average of 48 hours for each seven days. An employer is under a positive duty to take all reasonable steps, in keeping with the need to protect the health and safety of workers, to ensure that this limit is not exceeded.

1.11.3.1 'Reference period'

For the purposes of the maximum weekly working time-limits, the reference period which applies in the case of a worker is any period of 17 weeks in the course of his employment (unless a relevant agreement (see below) between an employer and a trade union/workforce representative or an individual stipulates which successive periods of 17 weeks amount to such a reference period). This means that, so long as the employee has not worked more than the average in the 17 weeks preceding and including today, then the rules are not breached. In view of this, employers are well advised to put in place early warning systems to check whether an employee is nearing the limit on each rolling period.

The reference period may also be extended to a period not exceeding 52 weeks, by means of a collective or workforce agreement, for objective or technical reasons or reasons concerning the organisation of work. The 17-week reference period is extended to a 26-week period where a worker is engaged in 'special case' activities (eg security or surveillance, hospitals, prisons, broadcasting, tourism, rail transport) where the worker's activities are intermittent.

1.11.3.2 'Average working time'

A worker's 'average working time' is normally calculated by identifying the number of weeks in the reference period (C) and the aggregate number of hours of working time worked by the worker in that period (A) and dividing A by C to produce an average figure. However, where a worker will not have worked certain days during the reference period because of, for example, annual leave, sick leave or maternity leave, A will be increased by the number of hours worked immediately after the reference period during the number of working days on which the worker was absent in the reference period (B).

The Regulations contain the following formula for calculating average working time for each seven days during a reference period:

$$\frac{A + B}{C}$$

In *Barber and Others v RJB Mining (UK) Ltd* [1999] IRLR 308, five pit deputies sought and obtained declarations that they need not work beyond the 48-hour average, irrespective of what their contract required. The High Court ruled that the Regulations imposed a contractual obligation on the employer which was enforceable in the High Court.

1.11.3.3 'Unmeasured' working time

The limit on weekly working time does not apply in relation to a worker where, on account of the specific characteristics of the activity in which he is engaged, the duration of his working time is not measured or predetermined, or can be determined by the worker himself.

Essentially, this applies to workers who have complete control over the hours they work and whose time is not monitored or determined by their employer. The Guidance states that an indicator may be if the worker is able to decide when to do his work and for how long.

The Regulations provide the following examples of situations in which this exception may apply (see reg 20(1)):

(a)   managing executives or other persons with autonomous decision-taking powers;

(b)   family workers (eg family members who work in a shop and live in a flat above it); or

(c)   workers officiating at religious ceremonies in churches and religious communities.

Note, however, that where a 'normal' worker voluntarily works in excess of his contractual hours, those extra hours count towards the 48-hour limit.

1.11.3.4 'Opt out' agreements

A worker may agree in writing with his employer that the 48-hour limit on average working time does not apply to him. Such an agreement may either relate to a specified period or apply indefinitely, but the agreement shall always be terminable by the worker giving not less than seven days' notice to his employer in writing (or such other period of notice not exceeding three months specified in the agreement).

An 'opt out' agreement will be binding only if the employer keeps up-to-date records of workers who have agreed to opt out.

The employer cannot make an employee sign an 'opt out' agreement. A worker will be protected against detrimental treatment if he refuses to sign an 'opt out' agreement. If such a refusal leads to an employee's dismissal, that dismissal will be treated as automatically unfair, irrespective of the length of service of the employee concerned (see, for example, *Brown v Controlled Packaging Services Ltd* (ET/1402252/98)).

1.11.3.5 Sanctions

A failure to observe the weekly working time-limit in respect of a worker will render an employer liable to the sanctions and penalties presently available to the Health & Safety Executive (HSE) and local authorities under health and safety legislation. Under this legislation, the HSE/local authorities can issue improvement and prohibition notices. In extreme cases, criminal proceedings may be commenced, and this may lead to unlimited fines.

As employers have a general duty to protect the health and safety at work of their workers, employers could be in breach of this common law duty of care if the weekly working time-limit is exceeded. This common law duty of care is bolstered by the Regulations which contain a statutory duty on an employer to observe the limits on weekly working time. If the employer fails to observe this statutory duty, a worker may enforce it as a civil claim in the courts.

The Regulations also give workers two further rights if they refuse to work in excess of the maximum weekly working time-limit. First, a worker has the right not to be subjected to any detriment by any act, or any deliberate failure to act, by his employer for (inter alia) refusing to work in excess of an average 48 hours per week. Secondly, an employee shall be regarded as unfairly dismissed (irrespective of length of service) if the principal reason for his dismissal is that he has (inter alia) refused to exceed the weekly limit on his working hours (see **Chapter 5**).

Additionally, as the weekly working units underpin contractual rights, an employee will be entitled to enforce these rights through a contract claim in the civil courts. In the *Barber* case (see **1.11.3.2** above), the High Court indicated that a declaration, rather than an injunction, would normally be the appropriate remedy.

Prosecutions for breach have been few. In 2002, Fourboys newsagent was fined £5,000 because the managers worked, on average, 71.3 hours per week. In 2007, a construction company (CFR Group plc) was fined £750 for breaching reg 4(1) on weekly working time limits.

1.11.4 Rest

The rest entitlements provided by the Regulations differ depending upon whether a person is a worker or a young worker. The rest entitlements provided for young workers are more generous than those provided for workers.

1.11.4.1 Daily rest period

An adult worker is entitled to a rest period of at least 11 consecutive hours in each 24-hour period during which he works for the employer. This entitlement is subject to the following exceptions:

(a)   where working time is unmeasured (see **1.11.3.3**);

(b)   where the worker is engaged in one of the 'special case' activities;

(c)   where a shift worker changes shift and cannot take the daily rest period between the end of one shift and the start of the next one;

(d)   where the worker is engaged in activities involving periods of work split up over the day (eg cleaning staff);

(e)   where the right is modified or excluded by a collective or workforce agreement (see **1.11.6**).

Where any of these exceptions applies (other than the unmeasured working time exception), the employer must allow the worker to take an equivalent period of compensatory rest and, in exceptional cases where this is not possible for objective reasons, the employer must afford the worker such protection as may be appropriate in order to safeguard the worker's health and safety.

1.11.4.2   Weekly rest period

Adult workers are entitled to an uninterrupted rest period of not less than 24 hours in each seven-day period. This right is additional to the daily rest entitlement except where objective, technical or work organisation conditions justify incorporating all or part of the daily entitlement into the weekly rest period. Daily rest and weekly rest should be taken consecutively, ie giving an uninterrupted period of 35 hours.

If the employer so determines, the seven-day reference period can be averaged over a reference period of 14 days. In these circumstances, the employer can choose between:

(a)   two uninterrupted rest periods each of not less than 24 hours in each 14-day period; and

(b)   one uninterrupted rest period of not less than 48 hours in each such 14-day period.

The relevant reference period shall be taken to begin at midnight between Sunday and Monday of each week or (as the case may be) every other week unless a relevant agreement provides to the contrary.

The weekly rest entitlement of adult workers is subject to the same exceptions as are outlined in relation to daily rest (**1.11.4.1** above).

1.11.4.3   Daily rest breaks

Adult workers are entitled to a daily rest break where their daily working time is more than six hours. The details of this rest break (including its duration and the terms on which it is granted) may be set by a collective or workforce agreement. In the absence of such an agreement, the break must be an uninterrupted period of not less than 20 minutes. The worker shall be entitled to spend this break away from his workstation if he has one.

This entitlement is subject to the following exceptions:

(a)   where working time is unmeasured;

(b)   where the worker is engaged in one of the 'special case' activities;

(c)   where the right is modified or excluded by a collective or workforce agreement (see **1.11.6**).

Where (b) or (c) applies, the employer must allow the worker to take an equivalent period of compensatory rest and, in exceptional cases where this is not possible for objective reasons, must afford the worker such protection as may be appropriate in order to safeguard the worker's health and safety. In *Hughes v Corps of Commissioners Management Ltd* [2011] EWCA Civ 1061, the Court of Appeal considered the approach to be taken in assessing the special case exception. Readers should have regard to the case when considering these exceptions.

In *McCartney v Oversley House Management* [2006] IRLR 514, the EAT held that the on-call time of a live-in employee was working time, and could not therefore count as a 'rest period', even if the employee was entitled to 'rest' while on call.

In *Gallacher v Alpha Catering Services* [2005] IRLR 102, the EAT said a 'break' was a period when employees were not at their employer's disposal.

1.11.4.4   Sanctions

A worker may present a complaint to a tribunal that his employer has not allowed him to exercise his right to a daily/weekly rest period or rest break, or has failed to provide an equivalent period of compensatory rest. Such complaints must be brought within three months of the act or omission complained of, unless the tribunal considers that it was not reasonably practicable to bring the complaint within this period. The EAT confirmed in *Miles v Linkage Community Trust Ltd* (UKEAT/0618/07) that time will run from the date of the refusal by the employer.

If the tribunal upholds such a complaint, it must make a declaration to that effect and may also award compensation. The amount of compensation is such as the tribunal considers just and equitable in all the circumstances having regard to the employer's default in refusing to permit the exercise of the worker's entitlement and any loss sustained by the worker as a consequence of that default.

The Regulations also provide that a worker has the right not to be subjected to any detriment by any act, or any deliberate failure to act, by his employer on the ground that the worker has refused (or proposed to refuse) to forgo a rest entitlement, has brought proceedings against the employer to enforce such an entitlement or has alleged that the employer has infringed such a right. If this is the principal reason for an employee's dismissal, the dismissal will be treated as unfair (irrespective of the employee's length of service).

1.11.5 Annual leave (regs 14–15)

At common law in the UK there is no right to holiday or paid holiday. Entitlements to these arise either by reason of an express contractual agreement or by virtue of the 1998 Regulations. The Working Time (Amendment) Regulations 2007 (SI 2007/2079) came into force on 1 October 2007. The 2007 Regulations increased holiday entitlement to 5.6 weeks (28 days for a 5-day per week employee) on 1 April 2009.

A worker's 'leave year' will normally be specified in his contract of employment. If this is not the case, a 'leave year' will start on 1 October 1998 or the date on which an employee commences employment (if later), and each subsequent anniversary of either of these dates.

Regulation 13(9) imposes the following conditions on a worker's entitlement to paid leave:

(a)   the leave may be taken only in the leave year in respect of which it is due;

(b)   a worker's leave entitlement may not be replaced by a payment in lieu (except where the worker's employment is terminated).

The Court of Session held in *MPB Structures Ltd v Munro* [2003] IRLR 350 that payment for annual leave must be made at the time when the leave is taken in order to satisfy the Regulations. Therefore it is not lawful for an employer and worker to choose to 'roll up' holiday pay by agreeing that pay for holidays should form part of the wages paid throughout the year.

The Court of Appeal considered the matter in *Caulfield and Others v Marshalls Clay Products Ltd* [2004] IRLR 564. In this case the employees' holiday pay was incorporated in their hourly rate of pay and was not payable at the time they took their holiday. The employees appealed against a decision that contracts providing for rolled-up holiday pay were not contrary to the Working Time Directive and/or the Working Time Regulations 1998. The Court of Appeal held that the decision in *Munro* that payment for annual leave must be made in association with the taking of the leave was wrong but, that since the matter was not *acte claire*, because of the decision in *Munro*, the issue of the compatibility of rolled-up holiday pay arrangements with the Directive should be referred to the ECJ. The ECJ held (*Robinson-Steele v RD Retail Services Ltd* [2006] IRLR 386) that rolled-up holiday is unlawful as it is contrary to the Working Time Regulations 1998, even if it is clear in the contract of employment what proportion or amount of the rolled-up pay is holiday pay. The ECJ said that holiday pay must be paid in respect of the period when the worker actually takes leave. However, the ECJ does say that payments already made in a clear, transparent way may be offset against a worker's entitlement to payment for holiday taken. BIS advises employers to renegotiate contracts so that statutory holiday pay is paid at the time employees take holiday.

Regulation 13(9)(a) of the 1998 Regulations states that leave can be taken only in the leave year in respect of which it is due. In *Stringer v HMRC* [2009] UKHL 31, the House of Lords held that a claim for non-payment of statutory holiday pay may be brought under both the 1998 Regulations (going back one year) and as a claim under the protection of wages legislation (which allows greater flexibility with regard to the period to which a claim could relate (see **1.10**)). The House of Lords had referred a number of questions to the ECJ relating to holiday pay. The ECJ ([2009] ICR 932) had decided that a worker could carry over untaken holiday due to sickness to the following year, provided there was a contractual provision to this effect. The ECJ also ruled that workers continue to accrue entitlement to paid holiday while on sick leave, and must be entitled to take that holiday at some point, either during sick leave or when they return, or be compensated in lieu if the employee did not return.

In *Zentralbetriebsrat det Landeskrankenhauser Tirols v Land Tirol* (Case C-486/08) the ECJ ruled that a reduction in working hours when moving from a full-time to a part-time job cannot reduce the amount of leave accumulated or the rate at which that leave is paid when it is eventually taken.

Contractual and statutory annual leave will continue to accrue during maternity/adoption leave periods (see **14.3.3.1**).

1.11.5.1   Notice

A worker does not have the right to take leave at any time he chooses. Subject to variation or exclusion by a relevant agreement, a worker is required under reg 15 to give written notice to his employer specifying the dates on which leave is to be taken twice as many days in advance of the earliest day specified in the notice as the number of days to which the notice relates. A similar notice requiring a worker to take leave on particular days may be issued by the employer.

An employer also has the power to issue a notice to a worker requiring him *not* to take leave on particular days. Such a notice must be given to the worker as many days in advance of the earliest day specified in the notice as the number of days to which the notice relates. Again, this right is subject to modification or exclusion by a relevant agreement. (See the decision of the Supreme Court in *Russell v Transocean International* [2011] UKSC 57 on when leave can be taken.)

1.11.5.2   Annual leave and sick pay

In *Pereda v Madrid Mouilidad SA* (Case C-277/08) [2009] IRLR 959 the ECJ said that, under Article 7 of the Directive, workers who are sick during a period of annual leave are entitled to take that leave at a later date, which if it cannot be taken in the current leave year may be taken in a subsequent leave year. This ruling was applied by an employment tribunal in *Shah v First West Yorkshire Ltd* (ET/1809311/09). First West Yorkshire's leave year ran from 1 April to 31 March. Mr Shah had booked four weeks' annual leave from 22 February to 21 March 2009. In January 2009 he broke his ankle and was absent from 15 January to 18 April 2009. He tried to reclaim his annual leave but was told it had been 'lost'. In order to get the Regulations to comply with *Pereda* and the Directive, the tribunal added wording to the end of reg 13(9)(a) as follows:

> save where a worker has been prevented by illness from taking a period of holiday leave and returns from sick leave, covering that period of holiday leave, with insufficient time to take that holiday leave within the relevant leave year; in which case, they must be given the opportunity of taking that holiday leave in the following leave year.

If employees are absent on long-term sick leave, they will be able to accrue holiday, possibly over several years, and could be entitled to a significant lump sum on termination or to take a long period of paid leave on return.

In *NHS Leeds v Larner* [2012] EWCA Civ 1034, the Court of Appeal held that it was not necessary for a sick worker, who was absent for the whole leave year and who did not submit any requests for annual leave during her absence, to have made a formal request for leave in the relevant year to be able to carry it forward (or to have a payment in lieu on termination): holiday which is untaken because an employee is off sick will be carried forward automatically into the next leave year. Mrs Larner, who worked at NHS Leeds, was absent from work for the whole of the 2009–10 holiday year. When Mrs Larner began her period of sick leave, she had not booked any holiday and she did not make any requests to take holiday while she was on sick leave. On 6 April 2010 her employment was ended. She claimed her unpaid holiday pay. NHS Leeds argued that as she had not requested holiday, the entitlement was lost at the end of the pay year. Both the employment tribunal and EAT found that Mrs Larner was entitled to be paid for the annual leave.

The Court of Appeal reviewed the ECJ case law on this area, including *Stringer* (above), *Pereda* (above) and a number of other ECJ decisions, including *Schultz-Hoff v Deutsche Rentenversicherung Bund* [2009] IRLR 214, *Dominguez v Centre Informatique du Centre Ouest Atlantique* (Case C-282/10) and *KHS AG v Shulte* [2012] IRLR 156. The Court of Appeal also allowed the parties to make written submissions in relation to *Neidel v Stadt Frankfurt am Main* (Case C-337/10), another relevant ECJ decision that had been published after the Court of Appeal heard the present case.

The Court of Appeal said that the steady succession of references to the ECJ on holiday pay during long-term sick leave made it 'nervous about offering judicial guidance' that 'may not be of much enduring use or value in practice' and 'could become outdated in quite a short time'. However, the Court did share its 'current understanding of the law' as it applied to this case. In particular, the Court of Appeal emphasised that Article 7 of the the Working Time Directive (rather the 1998 Regulations) had direct effect against NHS Leeds as an emanation of the State.

The Court of Appeal found the following key facts:

(a)   By reason of her sickness throughout her leave year, Mrs Larner was unable to take her paid annual leave entitlement in that year, so she did not lose her entitlement to paid annual leave for that year 2009/10. She was therefore entitled to take paid annual leave at another time when she was not sick and, if necessary, at a time when she could take advantage of the annual leave.

(b)   It would not have been permissible under the Directive for NHS Leeds to pay Mrs Larner compensation in lieu of the leave lost in the 2009/10 leave year. Such a payment could be made only on the termination of the employment relationship.

(c)   The various ECJ rulings do not lay down any requirement to make a request to take paid annual leave or to carry it forward to another leave period. In *Schulte* and *Dominguez*, no prior request was made to take paid annual leave during a period of sick leave or to carry it forward into the following leave year. The request to take paid annual leave referred to in *Pereda* was at a time when the worker was not sick.

The Court of Appeal distinguished the seemingly contradictory EAT ruling in *Fraser v Southwest London St George's Mental Health Trust* [2012] IRLR 100, EAT. In that case, the claimant was a nurse who was off sick and whose right to sick pay expired. Some time later she was certified fit to work and her pay was reinstated. Her pay was later stopped again. The EAT decided that, to be able to claim holiday pay, it was necessary for Ms Fraser to have given formal notice of leave under reg 15 (see **1.11.5.1** above). The Court of Appeal said that the difference in *Fraser* was that there was no evidence that the claimant was unable to take leave when she recovered. She had the opportunity to take leave in the relevant leave year when she recovered but did not. She gave no notice under reg 15 in that period of intention to take annual leave.

The Court of Appeal also considered the position under the notice provisions in reg 15 of the 1998 Regulations. It held that the requirement to give notice would be impractical where the worker is on sick leave and is prevented from taking paid annual leave. It construed reg 15 purposively, so that if the worker had the right under the Directive to take annual leave at another time, it would be fundamentally inconsistent if a private sector worker was required to serve notice to take leave at another time. This therefore extends the application of *Larner* to private employers as well.

The Court of Appeal said that it would not be appropriate for it to use the present case to determine the position in relation to the additional leave to which UK workers are entitled under reg 13A of the 1998 Regulations. The Court concluded that any decision on the additional leave given in the UK would have to wait until a case involving holiday pay during long-term sick leave under the 1998 Regulations. While the case proceeded on the basis of the direct applicability of Article 7 (because the NHS is an emanation of the State), the Court of Appeal suggested that the 1998 Regulations could be construed to give this effect to private sector workers as well.

1.11.5.3   Joiners and leavers

There are special rules relating to joiners and leavers. For joiners, their rights to annual leave are proportionate to the amount of the 'leave year' for which they work. For leavers, workers have a right to be paid in lieu for any untaken leave to which they are entitled.

In *Leisure Leagues UK Ltd v Maconnachie* [2002] IRLR 600, the EAT held that holiday pay should be calculated on the basis of the number of working days in the year (233) and *not* the number of calendar days (365). There is, however, conflicting authority (*Taylor v East Midlands Offender Employment Consortium* [2000] IRLR 760).

The Court of Appeal decided in *Bamsey and Others v Albion Engineering and Manufacturing plc* [2004] IRLR 457 that, when calculating holiday pay, compulsory but non-guaranteed overtime does not need to be taken into account in computing a week's pay.

Regulation 14(4) provides that an employer can recover payment for excess holiday taken by a leaver only if there is express agreement between the employer and employee. That means that if an employer wants to be able to recover compensation from an employee who is leaving and has taken more holiday than that to which he was entitled at the date of termination, this should be provided for in the contract of employment. The EAT confirmed in in *Hill v Chappell* [2003] IRLR 19, that an employer cannot use the ERA 1996 to claw back the money.

1.11.5.4   Sanctions

The sanctions for failing to provide a worker with paid annual leave are very similar to the sanctions which are imposed in respect of a breach of a worker's rest entitlements outlined at **1.11.4.4** above. However, where the complaint is of failure to provide due pay for a period of annual leave or pay in lieu of untaken leave on termination of employment, the tribunal must order payment of the amount due by the employer. (See the chart at **5.7.2.5**.)

1.11.5.5   Law Society practice note

The Law Society has a useful practice note on its website about holiday entitlement, advising on calculating entitlement to paid annual leave, how entitlement is affected by working part time, fixed term or on a temporary contract, and the difference between contractual and statutory entitlement.

1.11.6   Relevant agreements

The Regulations enable workers and employers to enter into agreements to establish the way in which some of the working time rules apply to their own workplaces. Provision is made for the following agreements which, collectively, are referred to as 'relevant agreements':

(a)   workforce agreements, ie agreements with workforce representatives;

(b)   collective agreements with independent recognised trade unions;

(c)   written agreements, ie any other agreement in writing which is legally enforceable between the worker and his employer.

1.11.6.1   Which rights/limits can be modified or excluded?

The main situation in which a written agreement between a worker and his employer can be utilised is to modify or exclude the limits on weekly working time.

Collective or workforce agreements can be used (inter alia) to modify or exclude the following rights:

(a)   length of night work;

(b)   daily and weekly rest periods; and

(c)   rest breaks.

In each case where a collective or workforce agreement is utilised to modify or exclude these rights, the employer must allow the worker wherever possible to take an equivalent period of compensationary rest and, if this is not possible for objective reasons, must afford the worker such protection as may be appropriate in order to safeguard the worker's health and safety.

In *Industry and Commerce Maintenance v Briffa* (UKEAT/021508/07), the EAT held that the basic requirements in reg 15 could be varied or excluded by a contractual term which covered the position and was legally enforceable as a relevant agreement under reg 2.

1.11.6.2   Workforce agreements: the legal requirements

The Regulations lay down detailed provisions with regard to a valid workforce agreement. For example, the agreement has to be in writing, and it cannot last longer than five years.

1.12   CHECKLISTS

1.12.1   Terms and conditions

(1)   Is the individual an employee or a worker? For the definition of 'employee' see s 230(1) of the ERA 1996; for the definition of 'worker' see s 230(3) of the 1996 Act.

(2)   Within two months of starting employment, employers must give their employees a written statement of the main terms of their contract.

(3)   There are certain key terms that *must* be included in a written statement of terms and conditions (see ERA 1996, s 1(3)–(4)).

(4)   Consider whether to include other express terms as well (see **1.4** and **Appendix 1**).

(5)   Check that any restrictive covenants are reasonable in terms of time and area, and are necessary to protect the employer's business interests.

(6)   Check that the National Minimum Wage Regulations and Working Time Regulations are not being broken.

(7)   Check that the employee signs and returns the statement/contract, and that both the employer and the employee have copies.

1.12.2   Summary of basic working time rights, enforcement and exceptions

SUMMARY OF BASIC WORKING TIME RIGHTS

Maximum working week	48 hours/week
Daily break	20 minutes/6 hours
Daily rest	11 hours/24 hours
Weekly rest	24 hours/7 days
Paid annual leave	5.6 weeks/52 weeks

ENFORCEMENT

	Health & Safety etc	Declaration and Compensation	No Detriment	Unfair Dismissal
WORKING WEEK	✓		✓	✓
NIGHT WORK	✓		✓	✓
REST PERIODS		✓	✓	✓
REST BREAKS		✓	✓	✓
ANNUAL LEAVE		✓	✓	✓

EXCEPTIONS

	Written Agreement	Unmeasured Working Time	Special Case Activities	Shift/Split Period Workers	Collective/ Workforce Agreements
WORKING WEEK	✓	✓			
NIGHT WORK		✓	✓		✓
REST PERIODS		✓	✓	✓	✓
REST BREAKS		✓	✓		✓
ANNUAL LEAVE					

1.13 FURTHER READING

Harvey, *Industrial Relations and Employment Law* (Butterworths), Divs A and B.

Lewis, *Employment Law – an adviser's handbook*, 9th edn revised (LAG, 2011).

Selwyn, *Law of Employment*, 17th edn (OUP, 2012).

Blackstone's Employment Law Practice (OUP, 2012).

SUMMARY

This chapter has looked at the various sources of UK employment law (common law, statute, codes of practice and EU law (**1.2** and **1.4**)). It has identified that there are some important differences between employees, workers and those who work for themselves as far as statutory protections are concerned. Certain rights, such as unfair dismissal and the right to a redundancy payment, apply only to employees; others (eg the National Minimum Wage Regulations and the Working Time Regulations) apply to a wider category of worker (**1.3**).

Section 1 of the ERA 1996 provides that employers must give their employees a written statement of the main terms of their contract (**1.4** and **Appendix 1**). A statement of terms and conditions is not a contract, but it does confirm the main express terms of the employment contract. It is not definitive of the entire contract, but it does provide an evidential basis of the most important terms.

Contracts of employment, where both sides agree the terms, may be written or oral, but it is sensible to put them in writing. Even where there is a written contract with express terms, statute and the courts will sometimes imply terms into a contract (**1.4**). The most important implied term is that of mutual trust and confidence. Where this term is broken, it may entitle either side to bring the relationship to an end. If an employer breaches it, it may entitle an employee with the requisite period of continuous employment to resign and claim constructive unfair dismissal (**3.4.3**).

The contract should, as a minimum, deal with all the matters set out in s 1(3) and (4) of the ERA 1996. This includes pay, job description, hours of work, place of work and whether the employee can be made to move, holiday, pension and sickness provisions, the length of notice that needs to be given by either side to terminate the arrangement (s 86 of the ERA 1996 sets out certain minimum notice periods), disciplinary and grievance procedures, and the obligations of confidentiality that an employee owes his employer (**1.4–1.8**, **Appendix 1**). It is also possible to include terms which protect an employer's business after the employee has left. These terms are known as restrictive covenants. They may be expressly included in a contract, so long as they are reasonable in terms of time and area and are necessary to protect the employer's business interests (**1.8.7**).

The protection of wages legislation set out in Pt II of the ERA 1996 protects an employee if an employer fails to pay the proper wages due under the contract, and prevents an employer from making deductions from an employee's wages unless they are authorised (**1.10**).

The Working Time Regulations 1998 set out maximum weekly working hours and provide for certain minimum rights to have breaks and paid annual leave (**1.11**).

CHAPTER 2

TERMINATION OF THE CONTRACT OF EMPLOYMENT – WRONGFUL DISMISSAL

LEARNING OUTCOMES

After reading this chapter you will be able to:

- describe and understand the differences between a claim of wrongful dismissal which is based on a breach of contract and the statutory claim of unfair dismissal, and the remedies that are available for wrongful dismissal

- explain when a wrongful dismissal claim arises

- understand the main ways in which a contract of employment may come to an end and the relevance of notice periods

- understand the significance of constructive dismissal

- understand the relevant principles to apply when calculating an employee's damages following a wrongful dismissal

- understand what remedies are available to an employer if an employee is in repudiatory breach of contract.

2.1 INTRODUCTION

Before considering in detail three of the main potential claims an employee might have on termination of a contract of employment (wrongful dismissal, unfair dismissal and the right to a redundancy payment), it is useful to have a preliminary overview of these claims.

2.1.1 Wrongful dismissal (breach of contract)

This is a common law contractual claim for breach of contract, which may be brought by workers or employees, based solely on the fact that the dismissal by the employer was in breach of contract. The remedy is therefore damages for breach of contract.

For example:

(a)   termination of the contract with no notice or short notice (see **2.3.3**); or

(b)   where the employee/worker establishes he has been constructively dismissed (see **2.3.5**); or

(c)   termination of the contract before the expiry of a limited term where there is no break clause (see **2.3.8**).

A breach of contract claim can be brought in the civil courts or in the employment tribunal. In *London Borough of Enfield v Sivanandan* [2005] EWCA Civ 10, the Court of Appeal held that where a breach of contract claim is struck out (as opposed to being withdrawn – see *Sajid v Chowdhury* [2002] IRLR 113) by an employment tribunal, it is an abuse of process to re-issue it in the civil courts. Even if a claim is withdrawn, it may be an abuse of process to re-issue it if the claim in the employment tribunal covered the same facts and was worth less than £25,000. If a claim is withdrawn but it is intended to pursue the claim in the civil courts, the claimant should tell the employment tribunal that that is the reason the claim is being withdrawn.

There is no limit to the amount of damages recoverable in a court action, although there is a restriction on tribunal awards. This is currently £25,000. Breach of contract claims can be brought in a tribunal where the claim follows termination of the employment together with a claim for unfair dismissal. Claimants need to be aware, though, that if they bring a high-value breach of contract claim in the tribunal, they will not be permitted to seek to recover any excess over £25,000 in the civil courts. The Court of Appeal, in *Fraser v HLMAD* [2006] EWCA Civ 738, said that once the claimant had lodged an ET1 claim form which included a claim for breach of contract for wrongful dismissal, the claims had 'merged' and there was no independent claim left which he could pursue. The Court of Appeal said that claimants wishing to bring high-value breach of contract claims should do so in the civil courts, unless they are willing to limit damages to £25,000.

Limitation periods for bringing claims in the tribunal and courts are also different (see **2.2**).

When considering a breach of contract claim, no account is taken of the reasonableness of an employer's action in terminating the contract. This allows employers to write in contractual provisions entitling them to terminate the contract and dismiss the employee without facing any common law claim for breach of contract (the contractual notice period must not be shorter than the statutory minimum period required by s 86 of the ERA 1996 – see **2.3.3**). So, for example, if an employer dismisses an employee with the correct notice, generally no claim for breach of contract will arise. To redress the balance, in the 1960s, statute began to intervene in the hitherto unfettered rights of the employer. In particular, concepts of fairness and reasonableness were introduced. Two statutory rights given to the employee are the right to claim unfair dismissal and/or the right to claim a redundancy payment on termination.

Note that workers and employees with less than a year's service will also be entitled to bring a claim for unpaid notice if their contract is terminated with insufficient notice (but note that ERA 1996, s 86 – relating to minimum notice periods – applies only to employees).

2.1.2   Unfair dismissal

This is a statutory claim which can be brought only by certain employees who satisfy eligibility criteria. It can be brought only before an employment tribunal.

The success of the claim does not rest on the issue of breach of contract. The tribunal looks instead into whether or not there was a fair reason for dismissal and at the reasonableness of the employer's actions.

A successful applicant may receive a basic award of compensation calculated in accordance with a set formula. In addition, he may receive a compensatory award to compensate for actual financial loss suffered (in a similar way to an award of damages for breach of contract). This compensatory award is subject to a maximum limit, which was £72,300 as at 1 February 2012 (note the limit is subject to revision in February each year – the Secretary of State can, each year, increase or decrease that sum in accordance with the Retail Price Index).

2.1.3 Redundancy payment

This is another statutory claim which is in the nature of a reward for past services; compensation for the loss of a secure job rather than for future financial losses.

The claimant must, again, be eligible and the claim is pursued (where necessary) in the employment tribunal.

The payment is calculated in accordance with a set formula which is the same as the basic award formula for unfair dismissal.

2.1.4 Conclusion

There is overlap, in terms of the remedy afforded to an employee, between the three claims, which is considered after looking in detail at each of them (see **6.8**).

The remainder of this chapter deals with the common law claim of wrongful dismissal in breach of contract.

The statutory claims of unfair dismissal and redundancy payments are dealt with in **Chapters 3–5**.

2.2   WRONGFUL DISMISSAL (DISMISSAL IN BREACH OF CONTRACT)

At common law, an employee (or worker) will have a claim for damages against his employer if the employer has dismissed him in breach of contract. This breach of contract claim is known as the claim for 'wrongful dismissal'. See **2.3** for when termination of the contract amounts to a breach of contract (ie gives rise to a wrongful dismissal claim). If there is no dismissal, there cannot be a claim for wrongful dismissal. Instead, there would be a general breach of contract claim.

This claim may be pursued in the civil courts or in the employment tribunal.

In the courts, the limitation period is six years and there is no upper limit on the level of damages which may be awarded. If the claim is worth less than £5,000 and is pursued in the county court, it will automatically be referred to the small claims track.

If a wrongful dismissal claim is pursued in the employment tribunal, there are certain preconditions:

(a)   the claim must arise or be outstanding on the *termination* of employment. In *Capek v Lincolnshire County Council* [2000] IRLR 590, the Court of Appeal held that tribunals have no jurisdiction to hear claims for breach of contract which are lodged prior to the termination of the employee's contract;

(b)   the employment tribunal will not be able to award more than £25,000 in respect of a contract claim;

(c)   the tribunal cannot hear all claims arising out of an alleged breach – for example claims relating to contractual terms of confidentiality and restrictive covenants are excluded;

(d)   the employer will be able to raise a counterclaim (alleging that the employee has also breached the contract of employment).

(e)   the claim will have to be brought within three months of termination (see **6.3.6**).

2.3   TERMINATION OF CONTRACT

2.3.1   Introduction

At common law, the contract of employment may come to an end in a number of ways. Only if the termination amounts to a breach of contract by the employer will the employee be entitled to claim damages for wrongful dismissal. The main ways in which an employment contract can come to an end are set out below.

2.3.2   Termination by agreement

The parties may at any time agree to bring the contract to an end. Neither party will be in breach of contract and no claim for wrongful dismissal will arise.

2.3.3   Termination by notice

A contract of employment for an indefinite term may be terminated by either party giving the other proper notice. Provided proper notice is given, the contract will terminate with no liability for breach of contract, whatever the reason for the termination. If the contract is ended by the employer with proper notice, there can be no wrongful dismissal claim by the employee because the employer has acted within the terms of the contract.

This rule applies only to contracts for an indefinite term. In the absence of a 'break' clause, limited-term contracts cannot be terminated by notice.

If the contract contains an express term stating the period of notice to be given by either party, then a party giving shorter notice to terminate will be in breach of contract, subject to **2.3.4**. If an expressly agreed period of notice is shorter than the statutory minimum period required by ERA 1996, s 86 (see below), the longer statutory minimum period must be given. The parties should agree the period of notice when the contract is entered into.

In the absence of an express term, it is an implied term of every indefinite contract of employment that it can be terminated by reasonable notice given by either party. What period is reasonable will depend on the facts of each case. The more senior the employee, the longer the period of notice required. The courts have held, for example, that three months was a reasonable period of notice for a salesman and an airline pilot, but only one week was required in the case of a milk carrier. In *Clark v Fahrenheit 451 (Communications) Ltd* (UKEAT/591/99), the EAT held that an employee's seniority and status and the employer's financial position are to be taken into account in determining what is a reasonable period of notice. Clearly, a reasonable amount must not be less than the statutory minimum.

When advising employers on reasonable periods of notice, it must be remembered that for senior, highly-skilled employees, reasonable notice can be quite long. For professional employees such as solicitors, accountants, highly-skilled technical employees, scientists or middle-managers, reasonable notice is likely to be in the region of three to six months. For a very senior employee, such as a managing director, it could be 12 months. For the unskilled and semi-skilled employee, reasonable notice is unlikely to exceed the statutory minimum period required by ERA 1996, s 86. The problem should be avoided by incorporating expressly agreed periods of notice into the employees' contracts.

Where a contract of employment is terminable by notice, s 86 of the ERA 1996 lays down the statutory minimum period of notice which must be given to employees. The statutory minimum period prevails over any shorter contractual period. However, as the parties may agree longer periods, any contractual provisions should be checked as, if these are more beneficial to the employee, they will override the statutory minimum.

The statutory minimum period of notice required to be given by an employer under s 86(1) is:

Period of continuous employment	Notice
1 month to 2 years	1 week
2 years to 12 years	1 week for each year
12 years plus	12 weeks

The only statutory minimum notice required to be given by an employee is one week's notice after one month's continuous employment (s 86(2)).

See **3.5** for the meaning of continuous employment. Either party may waive notice (s 86(3)).

Sometimes the employer will terminate a contract without notice or with short notice but give the employee a payment in lieu of the notice period due ('PILON'). What is the effect of such a payment? There are two possibilities (the second of which is the norm):

(a)   The employee accepts the PILON, although there is no provision in the contract permitting such a payment, and agrees, expressly or impliedly, to waive the requirement for notice. In this case there will either be no breach by the employer, or the breach has been waived by the employee for consideration. In either case, there will be no liability for wrongful dismissal.

(b)   The employer pays the employee in lieu of notice, but there is no provision in the contract permitting such a payment to be made and the employee, while taking the money, does not accept the payment as waiving his right to notice. In this case the employer is in breach of contract and technically the employee could claim wrongful dismissal. However, unless the payment in lieu of notice is significantly less than the damages likely to be awarded (see **2.4.1**), the claim would not be worth pursuing in financial terms.

Note: Where a contract expressly allows the employer to terminate the contract either by notice or by making a payment in lieu of notice, the dismissal does not become wrongful, even if the employer fails to make the payment. The employee's claim in this situation is for a sum due under the contract (a debt owed), *not* for damages for breach of contract (*Abrahams v Performing Rights Society Ltd* [1995] IRLR 486, CA). Because the sum is for the recovery of a debt, the employee is not under a duty to mitigate losses. By contrast an employee who brings a claim for wrongful dismissal is under a duty to mitigate losses (see **2.4**).

In *Cerberus Software Ltd v Rowley* [2001] IRLR 160, the employee's contract provided for termination by either party giving six months' notice. It went on to provide that the employer '*may* make a payment in lieu of notice to the employee'. The Court of Appeal held that in this situation, where the employer gave neither, the case was one of wrongful dismissal and the measure of damages was what the employee would have earned under the contract, subject to the ordinary duty of mitigation. The Court of Appeal distinguished the case from *Abrahams* (above), on the basis that the contract gave the employer the choice whether to pay or not to pay. In *Abrahams* the contractual clause provided that the employee *was* entitled to notice or payment in lieu. Thus, provided a PILON clause is carefully drafted, an employer will still receive the benefit of any mitigation by former employees as the employee's claim will be for wrongful dismissal where the employer gives neither notice nor payment in lieu of notice. However, as the employer has acted in breach of contract, that will render any restrictive covenants in the contract unenforceable (see **1.8.7**).

A PILON paid under the terms of the contract is always regarded as an 'emolument' from that employment and will be chargeable to income tax (*EMI Group Electronics Ltd v Coldicott (Inspector of Taxes)* [1999] IRLR 630, CA). Thus, such payments are not treated as falling within the Income Tax (Earnings and Pensions) Act 2003 exemption relating to termination payments up to £30,000 (see **2.4.1.8**).

Readers should consult the latest information on the HMRC website when giving advice on the tax implications of termination payments (www.hmrc.gov.uk).

2.3.4   Dismissal for employee's breach – 'summary dismissal'

If the employee commits a repudiatory breach of contract, the employer is entitled to treat the contract as discharged, ie to dismiss the employee without notice.

Any repudiatory breach of an express or implied term by the employee will justify the employer dismissing without notice. Non-exhaustive examples would include revealing trade secrets, wilful disobedience of lawful orders, theft from the employer or other gross misconduct and negligence if sufficiently serious. The crucial factor is the seriousness of the breach. It must be repudiatory (or fundamental), ie sufficiently serious to entitle the employer to treat the contract as discharged. For two examples, see (misconduct) *Pepper v Webb* [1969] All ER 216 and (performance) *Alidair v Taylor* [1978] IRLR 82. In *Dunn & Another v AAH Ltd* [2010] EWCA Civ 183, the Court of Appeal held that an employee who had failed to follow instructions to report risk of fraud to HQ over a five-month period had so undermined the duty of trust and confidence by virtue of his wilful neglect of duty that the employer could accept the breach of contract and dismiss without notice.

When dealing with a suspected repudiatory breach, the employer must reserve its position so as not to waive the breach, if it does not intend to take immediate disciplinary action (see *Cook v MSHK Ltd and Ministry of Sound Recordings Ltd* [2009] EWCA Civ 624). Otherwise it will be deemed to have affirmed the contract (and waived the breach).

Dismissal without notice can be justified by discovery of sufficient grounds *after* dismissal has taken place. In *Boston Deep Sea Fishing and Ice Co v Ansell* (1888) 39 Ch D 339, the misconduct of a managing director in taking bribes was discovered only after his dismissal. The tribunal held that the employer could rely on the latter acquired knowledge to justify the decision summarily to dismiss the employee. However, the Court of Appeal held in *Cavenagh v Williams Evans Ltd* [2012] EWCA Civ 697 that the employer could not rely on after-discovered gross misconduct in circumstances where it had already agreed to make a contractual payment in lieu of notice.

If the employer is mistaken about the seriousness of the breach and dismisses without notice in circumstances where he is not entitled to, the employer will have dismissed in breach of contract and be liable for wrongful dismissal (see **2.3.3**). In theory the employee has a choice whether to accept the breach or waive it, but in practice an employee has little choice but to accept the breach because he cannot perform his duties (*Boyo v Lambeth London Borough Council* [1995] IRLR 50).

2.3.5   Resignation and constructive dismissal

Normally, an employee who resigns will have no claim for wrongful dismissal. This is because it is the employee, not the employer, who has terminated the contract. For an example of how difficult it will be for an employee to claim that his unambiguous words of resignation amount to a dismissal, see *Ali v Birmingham City Council* (UKEAT/0313/08). Indeed, if the employee does not give proper notice or terminates a fixed-term contract before its expiry date, it is the employee who will be in breach of contract.

However, if the employer commits a repudiatory breach of an express or implied term of the contract of employment, the employee is entitled to accept the breach, resign and treat the contract as discharged. This is known as a constructive dismissal. The employee must leave within a reasonable time of the breach, otherwise he may be taken to have affirmed the contract and waived the breach. If the employee can establish that he has been constructively dismissed, he will have a claim for wrongful dismissal (dismissal in breach of contract).

Note that the employer's breach must be repudiatory; a minor breach will not entitle the employee to leave and claim that he has been constructively dismissed.

See **3.4.3** for details of constructive dismissal.

2.3.6   Frustration

If the contract of employment is frustrated, it terminates automatically by operation of law. Neither party will be in breach and neither party will have a claim against the other, other than for wages due to the date of frustration. Frustration occurs where, without the fault of either party, some event occurs which prevents performance of the contract. The event must not have been provided for by the contract. The principal events which may frustrate a contract of employment are as follows.

2.3.6.1   The death of either party

The death of the employee clearly frustrates the contract. The death of a sole trader employer will also frustrate the contract. However, if the employees are re-employed by the personal representatives of the deceased, or the business is transferred to another employer who re-employs the employees, continuity of employment will usually be preserved (see **3.5.5**).

2.3.6.2   Illness or injury of the employee

Long-term or permanent illness or injury which prevents the employee from performing his duties *may* frustrate the contract. Factors which will be taken into account in deciding whether or not a contract is frustrated include:

(a)   the nature of the work;

(b)   the length of employment;

(c)   the nature, length and effect of the illness or injury;

(d)   the need for the work to be done and the need for a replacement to do it; and

(e)   whether in all the circumstances a reasonable employer could be expected to wait any longer (*Egg Stores (Stamford Hill) Ltd v Leibovici* [1976] IRLR 376);

(f)   how likely it is that the employee will return to work.

The terms of the contract must also be considered. If the contract makes provision for a period of absence due to ill-health, then the contract would not be frustrated if the employee was likely to return to work within that period.

In practice, especially with contracts terminable by notice, the courts and employment tribunals are extremely reluctant to find that a contract has been frustrated. The effect of holding that a contract is frustrated deprives the employee of any remedy that he might have had if he had been dismissed. Nevertheless, in rare cases the court may find that the contract has been frustrated. In *Collins v Secretary of State for Trade and Industry* (UKEAT/1460/99), the EAT held that a contract had been frustrated by an employee's long-term illness. Of particular relevance, on the facts, was the length of time the employee was off work (three years) and the unlikeliness of any return to work.

2.3.6.3   Imprisonment of the employee

A problem arises when a contract is terminated on the imprisonment of an employee. The employer will allege frustration and termination by operation of law. The employee will argue that he has been dismissed, frustration not being applicable as imprisonment constitutes 'self-induced frustration'. This would give the employee a potential claim for wrongful dismissal, even though in the majority of cases the dismissal would be justified.

The Court of Appeal in *FC Shepherd & Co Ltd v Jerrom* [1987] 1 QB 301 decided the imprisoned employee had no claim. Balcombe LJ found that the frustrating event was the actual imposition of the sentence, not the misconduct by the employee, but Lawton and Mustill LJJ held that the rule against reliance on self-induced frustration only meant that neither party could rely on his own misconduct to establish a defence of frustration. But since the employer was relying on the employee's fault, that requirement was satisfied and thus frustration could succeed.

In *Chakki v United Yeast Co Ltd* [1982] 2 All ER 446, the EAT held that certain elements need to be considered when deciding whether or not a prison sentence has frustrated the contract of employment. It distinguished between a situation where a sentence of imprisonment was a cause of 'instantaneous' frustration of a contract of employment and one where it was merely a 'potentially frustrating event' depending on the time at which frustration occurred, being the time at which the parties became aware of the cause and the likely outcome of the interruption and had to decide on a future course of action. The EAT said:

it seems to us that in some cases a sentence of imprisonment will be similar to an accident or an illness and thus a potentially frustrating event rather than a cause of instantaneous frustration. It has to be recognised, however, that a sentence of imprisonment differs from an accident to an illness in that, unless and until it is varied on appeal, the length of the employee's absence and the affect on the contract of employment is immediately predictable. One has therefore to try to find that moment at which the question of frustration or not has to be determined.

In *Four Seasons Healthcare Ltd v Maughan* [2005] IRLR 324, the EAT held that frustration requires that there should be some outside event or extraneous change of situation, not foreseen or provided for by the parties within the contract. The EAT commented, in a situation where there was a detailed disciplinary procedure in the employment contract which made specific reference to the misconduct which the claimant had been dismissed over (namely physical abuse directed towards residents), 'it seems to us that the presence of such a detailed disciplinary procedure should indeed ... inhibit us from being too ready to find in favour of frustration'. In this case, therefore, the contract was not frustrated until the custodial sentence made its performance impossible. Thus, a very short custodial sentence might not have the effect of frustrating a contract.

2.3.7 Partnerships and companies

The dissolution of a partnership or the winding up of a company may terminate the employees' contracts.

2.3.7.1 Partnerships

Usually, a change of partners where the employer is a partnership will have no effect on the employees' contracts of employment.

However, if the contract is of a personal nature, ie the identity of the partners is material to the contract, then if the relevant partner leaves, the employee's contract will automatically be terminated (*Phillips v Alhambra Palace Co* [1901] 1 KB 59). If the partner leaves voluntarily (eg by retirement), there will be a wrongful dismissal of the employee unless proper notice was given. If the partner dies, the employee's contract will be frustrated. In practice, it is rare for the contract to be of a personal nature, the usual rule being that a change of partners does not affect the employee's contract.

Even if an employee's contract is terminated in such circumstances, there will be no break in the continuity of his employment if he is re-employed by the new partners (see **3.5.5**).

2.3.7.2 Companies

An order for the compulsory winding up of a company and a resolution to wind up an insolvent company will usually terminate the employees' contracts automatically. Dismissal will be wrongful unless proper notice is given. The making of an administration order or the appointment of a receiver by debenture holders would not normally terminate employees' contracts.

2.3.8 Limited-term contracts

At common law, a limited-term contract expires by effluxion of time at the end of the term. For example, a contract for a limited term of three years commencing on 1 February 2010 will come to an end on 31 January 2013 with no liability on either party if it is not renewed.

There is no implied term allowing a party to terminate a limited-term contract before its expiry date. If the employer or employee terminates a limited-term contract, with or without notice, before its expiry date, there will be a breach of contract unless:

(a)   the other party is in repudiatory breach of the contract; or

(b)   there is express power in the contract allowing early termination (a 'break' clause) (see below); or

(c)   the termination is by mutual agreement.

One or both parties (often only the employer) may be able to terminate the contract before the end of the limited term if the contract contains a 'break' clause. A 'break' clause allows a party to bring the contract to an end within the limited term, usually by giving notice. The 'break' clause may, for example, allow the employer to terminate in any circumstances by giving the employee, say, six months' notice, or it may allow termination in specific circumstances only (eg on the employee's bankruptcy or long-term illness) (see **1.8.1.2**).

2.4   EMPLOYEE'S REMEDIES FOR WRONGFUL DISMISSAL

In practice, the employee/worker who is wrongfully dismissed will usually have little choice but to accept the dismissal. It is virtually unheard of for a court to grant an injunction to prevent a dismissal. The employee/worker may then claim damages for wrongful dismissal against the employer.

2.4.1   Damages for wrongful dismissal

2.4.1.1   Introduction

Damages for wrongful dismissal are damages for breach of contract. They are governed by the normal rules of the law of contract:

(a)   the loss claimed must not be too remote, ie it must either arise naturally from the breach or be such as may reasonably be supposed to have been in the contemplation of both parties at the time of contract, as the probable result of the breach (*Hadley v Baxendale* (1854) 9 Exch 341);

(b)   the measure of damages, for loss which is not too remote, is the sum required to put the claimant, so far as money can, in the same position as if the contract had been performed (*Robinson v Harman* (1848) 1 Exch 850).

In *Boyo v Lambeth London Borough Council* [1994] ICR 727, CA, it was held that the correct measure of damages following the employer's repudiatory breach of contract was the amount the employee would be entitled to receive if dismissed in accordance with the terms of the contract.

In the case of wrongful dismissal, damages are usually assessed as follows.

2.4.1.2   Loss of net wages

The starting point in calculating damages in the case of a contract for an indefinite term is the salary or wages that the employee/worker would have earned during the proper notice period. In the case of a fixed-term contract it would be the salary for the remainder of the fixed term. There is an exception in the case of a fixed term where the employer was entitled to terminate under a 'break' clause, in which case it is the salary which would have been earned during the period of notice due under the 'break' clause.

Note that there is a danger in using the term 'ex gratia'. In *Publicis Consultants v O'Farrell* (UKEAT/ 0430/10) Mrs O'Farrell's contract entitled her to three months' notice of termination. The letter of dismissal said she would be paid statutory redundancy pay, holiday pay and a sum which, although equivalent to three months' gross salary, was said to be an ex gratia payment. An issue arose (in her successful unfair dismissal claim) as to whether she was entitled to receive three months' notice pay as damages for her dismissal without notice. The EAT said she was. The starting point in any exercise of the construction of documents must be with the words the parties have used. An 'ex gratia' payment is, on its ordinary construction, a payment made freely and not under obligation. Further, the *contra proferentem* rule meant that, as this was the company's own unilateral document, if it was ambiguous it had to be read with 'the construction least favourable to the author'.

Where an employer fails to follow a contractual disciplinary procedure, the employee is generally only entitled to receive compensation for the wages he would have received during the course of the disciplinary procedure (see *Gunton v London Borough of Richmond* [2000] IRLR 703) plus any contractual notice. This remains the case even if the employee is able to show that the disciplinary process, if followed, would have meant that the employee was not dismissed. This is because, at common law, employers are entitled to dismiss on notice without proper cause. The only recourse for an employee in this situation is to bring an unfair dismissal claim (see **Chapter 5**).

The Court of Appeal held in *Edwards v Chesterfield Royal Hospital NHS Foundation Trust* [2010] IRLR 702 that compensation for reputational damage caused by a flawed disciplinary procedure might be recovered 'at large' as it was not caused by the dismissal but rather by failure to follow an express contractual disciplinary procedure, if that failure led to the misconduct finding and the resultant inability to secure permanent NHS employment. The Court therefore permitted a claim for £4 million loss of earnings to proceed. The Court of Appeal rejected a submission that the principles laid down by the House of Lords in *Johnson v Unisys Ltd* [2001] IRLR 279 (see **2.4.1.5** and **5.6.2.2**) precluded recovery of the lossed claimed. *Unisys* does not apply where there is a breach of an express contractual term – it restricts compensation to the unfair dismissal regime where what is said to cause the loss is the manner of dismissal.

Edwards was appealed to the Supreme Court. A majority of the Supreme Court overruled the Court of Appeal's decision. The majority held that breach of contract claims for an alleged failure to follow an express disciplinary process could not proceed: as the claims for financial loss caused by damage to reputation were inextricably linked to the dismissal process, they fell within the exclusion indentified by the House of Lords in *Johnson v Unisys* and unfair dismissal was the appropriate claim. (There is an excellent and detailed analysis of the case and its significance in IDS Employment Law Brief No 943, February 2012, at p 3 onwards.)

2.4.1.3   Accrued holiday pay

Under the Working Time Regulations 1998, reg 14, the employee/worker will be entitled to payment in lieu of any holiday to which he was entitled but had not yet taken.

In *Leisure Leagues UK Ltd v Maconnachie* [2002] IRLR 600, the EAT gave guidance on calculating holiday pay. The EAT in this case (there is conflicting authority) held that the correct method of calculating holiday pay for a worker with regular hours and an annual salary is to divide the worker's annual salary by the number of working (not calendar) days in a year, multiplied by the number of days' leave the worker has outstanding (see **1.11.5**).

2.4.1.4   Additional loss

In addition to such lost salary or wages, the employee/worker may claim damages for loss of other benefits to which he was entitled under the contract. This would cover lost commission in the case of employees/workers remunerated wholly or partly by commission. It would also cover loss of fringe benefits such as a company car and also loss of pension rights if the employee/worker was entitled to a pension. In *Silvey v Pendragon plc* [2001] IRLR 685, the Court of Appeal held that an employee who was wrongfully dismissed 12 days short of his 55th birthday was entitled to claim damages for loss of significant pension rights that would have accrued when he attained the age of 55.

Loss of pension entitlement may in some cases involve a large sum, and it can be difficult to calculate this loss. There are two forms of pension loss which may be suffered: the loss of the pension position earned to the date of dismissal, and loss of future pension opportunity. Usually the sum lost will be based on the amount of employee's and employer's contributions made to a future pension. Where an employee/worker is close to retirement, the court may look at the cost of purchasing an annuity to produce the pension lost by the employee/worker.

The Government Actuary's Department (GAD), in conjunction with a small committee of tribunal chairmen, has produced guidelines to assist in calculating pension loss. The latest (third) edition of these guidelines was produced in 2003. They may be obtained by searching 'compensation for loss of pension rights'. Readers advising on pension losses must consult the guidelines, although the EAT has said they are not mandatory and tribunals should not adhere to them when to do so would cause an injustice (see *Port of Tilbury (London) Ltd v Birch* [2005] IRLR 92 and *Network Rail Infrastructure v Booth* (EAT/0071/06)). The guidelines draw a distinction between money purchase schemes and final salary schemes, and set out two approaches to calculating future pension losses – a simplified approach and a substantial loss approach. The former is for use where there is either a money purchase scheme or a final salary scheme where there is a relatively short period of continuing pension loss. The substantial loss approach is for use only in cases concerning final salary schemes where there is long-term or whole career loss.

The EAT, in *Sibbit v The Governors of St Cuthbert's Catholic Primary School* (UKEAT/0070/10), set out the correct approach for tribunals to follow when calculating pension loss under the guidelines. The EAT's decision in *Chief Constable of West Midlands Police v Gardner* (UKEAT/0174/11) provides a useful discussion of the various approaches to pension loss calculation.

The Court of Appeal held in *Bentwood Brothers (Manchester) Ltd v Shepherd* [2003] IRLR 364 that an employee should be compensated for 10 years' future loss of pension following an unfair dismissal, even though the award for loss of earnings was for only two and a half years. The Court agreed that whilst Ms Shepherd might well be able to find alternative employment on similar pay, she would not be able to do so with a final salary scheme which she had at Bentwood Brothers.

The employee/worker is only awarded damages for loss of benefits to which he was entitled under the contract. Thus, the established orthodoxy has always been that an employee/worker will not generally be awarded damages for loss of a discretionary contractual payment which he might have expected to receive, such as a Christmas bonus or an annual salary increase (*Lavarack v Woods of Colchester Ltd* [1967] 1 QB 278). However, in *Clark v BET plc and Another* [1997] IRLR 348, the employee successfully argued that, although his contract only entitled him to an annual salary increase 'by such amount as the board shall in its absolute discretion decide', this term amounted to a contractual obligation to increase his salary each year. The court said that contractual provisions relating to salary increases must be interpreted realistically and not on the basis that any discretion would have been exercised to give the employee the least possible benefit. Similar reasoning was applied in respect of a 'discretionary' bonus scheme entitlement under his contract of employment. Similarly in *Clark v Nomura International plc* [2000] IRLR 766, Burton J held that it was a breach of contract for an employer to exercise discretionary powers in a manner that was irrational or perverse. The Court of Appeal held in *Levett v Biotrace International plc* [1999] IRLR 375 that an option to purchase shares did not lapse in circumstances where employment was terminated in breach of contract unless the scheme rules so provided. The Court of Appeal's decision in *Mallone v BPB Industries plc* [2002] IRLR 452 confirms that an employer must not exercise its discretion in an irrational manner (see also *Horkulak v Cantor Fitzgerald International* [2004] IRLR 942).

Damages may also be claimed for the loss of opportunity to earn tips in occupations where tips are usual (eg in the case of waiters and waitresses).

An employee cannot claim damages for breach of contract in respect of a loss of opportunity to bring an unfair dismissal claim (see **Chapter 5**). (See, eg, *The Wise Group v Mitchell* [2005] ICR 896.) The Court of Appeal held in *Harper v Virgin Net Ltd* [2004] IRLR 390 that an employee dismissed in breach of contract with less than one year's service, cannot claim damages for wrongful dismissal on the basis that she lost the chance of recovering unfair dismissal compensation that she would have received if she had been given her *contractual* notice of termination. Brooke LJ stated:

> I do not consider it is open to the courts, through the machinery of an award of damages for wrongful dismissal, to rewrite Parliament's scheme and to place a financial burden on employers which Parliament decided not to impose on them.

Chadwick LJ added that Parliament

> did not – as it easily could have done – postpone the effective date of termination to whichever should be the later of the expiry of the periods of contractual or statutory notice. That must be seen as a deliberate policy choice.

The other reason given for the decision is the need to be consistent with the House of Lords decision in *Johnson v Unisys Ltd* [2001] IRLR 279 (as explained in *Eastwood and Another v Magnox Electric plc* [2004] IRLR 733) (see below and **5.6.2.2**). These cases are authority for the rule that damages for breach of contract cannot include losses arising out of the fact and manner of dismissal.

2.4.1.5 Pecuniary loss only

Damages can usually be claimed for pecuniary loss only, so damages cannot generally be claimed for loss of future prospects or injured feelings (*Bliss v South East Thames Regional Health Authority* [1985] IRLR 308).

In *Malik v BCCI; Mahmud v BCCI* [1997] IRLR 462, HL, it was held that an employee might be entitled to 'stigma' damages, for example where the employer's business was conducted in a wholly dishonest manner which affected the employees' future prospects because of the stigma attaching to their reputations. The Court of Appeal's decision in *Bank of Credit and Commerce International SA (in compulsory liquidation) v Ali and Others (No 3)* [2002] IRLR 460 confirms that loss of employment prospects is almost impossible to prove without strong evidence, preferably from prospective employers.

The House of Lords held in *Johnson v Unisys Ltd* [2001] IRLR 279 that a claimant cannot recover contractual damages for psychiatric illness arising from the dismissal. Their Lordships distinguished the *Malik* case on the basis that that claim arose from a breach of the implied term of trust and confidence *during* the employment relationship; it did not arise on dismissal. Similarly, in *Gogay v Hertfordshire County Council* [2000] IRLR 703, the Court of Appeal held that the employer was in breach of the implied term of trust and confidence when it suspended an employee pending further investigation of a disciplinary charge, because it had no reasonable grounds for suspending her. Mrs Gogay was able to recover damages at common law for psychiatric injury on the facts, because the loss arose from breach of the implied duty of trust and confidence *during* the subsistence of the employment relationship.

The House of Lords in *Eastwood v Magnox; McCabe v Cornwall County Council and Another* [2004] IRLR 733, two cases concerning the overlap between common law claims for damages for breach of trust and confidence, and the statutory unfair dismissal regime, held that a distinction must be drawn between those cases where the employer has breached the term of trust and confidence *prior* to the dismissal – for which an (unlimited) common law claim can be brought – and cases where the *decision* to dismiss amounts to a breach of trust and confidence. These latter cases fall within the statutory unfair dismissal regime, and are therefore subject to the cap on compensation which cannot be circumvented by bringing a breach of contract claim in the civil courts. Lord Nicholls recognised the artificiality of the distinction but said it was nevertheless a distinction that had to be observed. At para 28 of his judgment he said:

> In the ordinary course ... an employer's failure to act fairly in the steps leading to dismissal does not of itself cause the employee financial loss. The loss arises when the employee is dismissed and it arises by reason of his dismissal. Then the resultant claim for loss falls squarely within the *Johnson* exclusion area. ... Exceptionally financial loss may flow directly from the employer's failure to act fairly when taking steps leading to dismissal. Financial loss flowing from suspension is an instance ... [and] cases

... when an employee suffers financial loss from psychiatric or other illness caused by his pre-dismissal unfair treatment.

The existence of such an exclusion area may mean that in some cases a continuing course of conduct, such as a disciplinary process followed by dismissal, may need to be chopped up artificially. Where financial losses flow directly from a pre-dismissal action, that can give rise to a cause of action which arises independently from the dismissal. Lord Nicholls noted two instances where problems will arise: financial losses flowing from suspension without pay and financial losses (as occurred in these two cases) flowing from psychiatric illness caused by pre-dismissal unfair treatment. He said that in such cases 'the employee has a common law cause of action which precedes, and is independent of, his subsequent dismissal'. He went on to note that in some circumstances an employer would be better off dismissing an employee than suspending him.

2.4.1.6 Duty to mitigate

The employee is under a duty to mitigate his loss. Once the employment is terminated, he must take steps to obtain suitable alternative employment. He will be in breach of this duty if he refuses a reasonable offer of re-employment. The employee is not entitled to damages in respect of any loss that has been mitigated or would have been mitigated but for the employee's breach of duty (*Brace v Calder and Others* [1895] 2 QB 253).

The employee is only under a duty to accept reasonable offers of re-employment, not any other job offered. For example, there would be no need to accept an offer involving serious demotion. If the old employer offers to re-engage the employee, the employee would be in breach of his duty to mitigate if he failed to accept, provided that the job offered was reasonable and there was still a relationship of mutual trust and confidence between employer and employee.

2.4.1.7 Benefits reducing loss

If the employer has paid money in lieu of notice to the employee, this will be taken into account in assessing the damages awarded. Certain other benefits received by the employee which reduce his loss will also be set against the damages awarded, for example, jobseeker's allowance and income support. If a pension becomes payable during the period for which damages are claimed, this does not reduce the damages awarded (*Hopkins v Norcross plc* [1994] IRLR 18, CA). The rule on pensions is based on public policy.

Overlap with redundancy payments and awards of compensation for unfair dismissal are dealt with at **6.7**.

2.4.1.8 Tax and National Insurance contributions

The basic rule is that income tax and National Insurance contributions which would have been paid on the wages or salary, if earned, are deducted in assessing damages (*British Transport Commission v Gourley* [1956] AC 185; *Shove v Downs Surgical plc* [1984] IRLR 17). Damages are therefore generally awarded in respect of loss of *net* earnings. This puts the employee in the position as though the contract had been performed.

However, the effect of the Income Tax (Earnings and Pensions) Act 2003 (ITEPA 2003) has to be considered. Guidance on the Act may be found in the HMRC guide CWG2 (2009), *Employer's Further Guide to PAYE and NICs*. It is available on HMRC's website (www.hmrc.gov.uk/guidance/cwg2.pdf.). An employer is exempt from paying tax on termination payments, including damages for wrongful dismissal, which do not exceed £30,000 (ITEPA 2003, s 401). The exemption applies only if the payment is not otherwise subject to tax under any other head; only then can it be taxed as a termination payment. This means considering whether the payment is a contractual payment made in return for services (see for example *Delaney v Staples* [1992] 1 All ER 944 and *SCA Packaging v Revenue and Customs* [2007] EWHC 270 (Ch)). If the payment or benefit is earnings from the employment, tax is due under s 62 of the ITEPA 2003 (and there is no £30,000 exemption). As the employee receives only his net loss of earnings, it is therefore the employer who benefits from the rule. Termination payments exceeding £30,000 are subject to income tax on the excess over £30,000. Therefore, if the damages for wrongful dismissal exceed £30,000, the award of damages will have to be grossed up to compensate the employee for the double tax that the employee will have to pay. Note, however, that pure damages for breach of contract in a tribunal are subject to a £25,000 jurisdictional limit. In reality, damages for breach of contract in a tribunal claim will need to be grossed up only where other awards, such as compensation for unfair dismissal, take the award over £30,000 (see **5.7.2.2**).

For example, in the case of *Shove v Downs Surgical plc* (above), the court assessed the ex-employee's total loss as being £70,300. The court deducted an element for failure to mitigate and accelerated receipt (see **2.4.1.9** below), giving a net loss of £60,729. Damages of £88,447 were therefore payable by the employer to ensure that, after paying tax, the ex-employee was left with £60,729 in his hands, the remainder going to the Revenue.

Note that where the contract of employment contains an express PILON provision, the £30,000 tax and the unlimited National Insurance contributions exemption will not be available in respect of the sum paid by way of compensation or for wrongful dismissal (see *EMI Group Electronics Ltd v Coldicott (Inspector of Taxes)* [1999] IRLR 630 and *Cerberus Software Ltd v Rowley* [2001] IRLR 160). This is because HMRC takes the view that, in such cases, the pay in lieu is due under the contract and is not, therefore, a true severance payment (see **2.3.3**). In practice, this means that awards for unpaid notice pursuant to a PILON clause should always be paid grossed up, because they are taxable as earnings and are not covered by the £30,000 exemption.

Where there is no PILON clause, even if a payment is made, termination without notice is strictly speaking still a breach of contract and the payment does not therefore flow from the contract. Note that the tax position where a contract is terminated without notice and there is a discretion to give a PILON is complex and beyond the scope of the book (see *Richardson v Delaney* [2001] IRLR 663, the Revenue's Tax Bulletin 63, February 2003 and the Revenue's Employment Income Manual 12800 (updated 2010)). (See the chart at **5.6.2.5**.)

2.4.1.9   Accelerated receipt

In the majority of cases, any award of damages for wrongful dismissal will be made after the employee's contract could have been properly terminated by the employer. In this situation, no question of accelerated receipt arises.

However, in the case of a long fixed-term contract, the employee may receive his damages before he would have earned some of the salary that they represent. In this case, a deduction will be made from the damages as the accelerated receipt will allow the employee to invest the money (eg in an annuity) and obtain a return on it (*Bold v Brough, Nicholson & Hall Ltd* [1964] 1 WLR 201). In *Brentwood Brothers (Manchester) Ltd v Shepherd* [2003] IRLR 364, the Court of Appeal questioned whether the 5% discount rate normally applied by tribunals remained appropriate in 2004, given that the discount in personal injury cases was by then 2.5%. The court also held that any deductions should be done on the basis of an appropriate percentage deduction year on year and not one single deduction. The Government is consulting on the personal injury discount rate at the time of writing.

2.4.2   Other remedies

The employee will usually have little choice but to accept dismissal and claim monetary compensation. The courts will not award specific performance of contracts of employment, nor will they usually issue an injunction restraining the employer from terminating the employment in breach of contract. In exceptional circumstances the courts have granted an injunction, the effect of which is to keep the contract alive until proper notice would have expired, but the employer was not required to allow the employee to do work during the period covered by the injunction (*Hill v C A Parsons & Co Ltd* [1972] 1 Ch 305). Occasionally, the courts will grant an interim injunction restraining an employer from dismissing an employee (eg pending an appeal hearing). Such an injunction can be granted only if there is sufficient mutual trust and confidence between employer and employee (*Powell v London Borough of Brent* [1987] IRLR 466). These remedies are exceptional and details are beyond the scope of this book.

2.5 EMPLOYER'S REMEDIES

If the employee is in repudiatory breach of contract, the employer may dismiss him without notice ('summarily') (see **2.3.4**). Other remedies available to the employer include damages, injunction and account of profit.

2.5.1 Damages

Any breach of contract by the employee theoretically entitles the employer to claim damages. In practice, it is a remedy which employers rarely pursue.

(a)   An employee may be in breach of contract by resigning without giving proper notice or leaving before a fixed-term contract has expired. The usual measure of damages in such cases would be the additional cost of providing a substitute to do the work (*National Coal Board v Galley* [1958] 1 WLR 16). The remedy is not usually worth pursuing because the amount involved would usually be too small.

(b)   If an employer suffers loss by reason of the employee's negligence, the employer may be entitled to an indemnity from the employee (see *Lister v Romford Ice and Cold Storage Co Ltd* [1957] AC 555, at **1.7.2.3**). The remedy is rarely pursued, partly because it can lead to bad industrial relations and also because the employer is often insured against the loss. The employee may, anyway, have insufficient funds to meet a substantial award of damages.

(c)   Damages might be an appropriate remedy where the employer has suffered loss by reason of the employee's breach of the duty of good faith, for example where the employee has revealed trade secrets or competed with the employer's business.

2.5.2 Injunction

An injunction may be awarded to an employer to restrain certain actions of an employee where damages would be an inadequate remedy:

(a)   It may be used to restrain or prevent breaches of the duty of fidelity, for example by restraining an employee from using or revealing trade secrets. In *Robb v Green* [1895] 2 QB 315, an employee who had made a list of customers was ordered to deliver up the list and was restrained by injunction from copying it.

(b)   It is the appropriate remedy to enforce a valid restrictive covenant after employment, by restraining the employee from working in contravention of it (see **1.8**).

(c)   Where an employee is required by contract to give a period of notice, the employer might obtain an injunction to prevent him from breaching that term by taking up a new position before expiry of his contractual notice period.

In deciding whether and to what extent to grant an injunction the court will apply the 'balance of convenience' test (*American Cyanamid v Ethicon Ltd* [1975] AC 398). The court will take into account the following factors:

(a)   actual or potential damage to the employer's business (eg loss of important clients who may follow the employee);

(b)   inconvenience (financial and other) to the employee;

(c)   whether the employee has given an adequate undertaking to abide by the contract;

(d)   no more relief should be granted than is absolutely necessary – any injunction need not necessarily be for the full contractual period (*GFI Group Inc v Eaglestone* [1994] IRLR 119).

For a decision which provides a useful analysis of the general principles on injunctions, see *Vestergaard Frandsen Als and Others v Bestnet Europe Ltd and Others* [2009] EWHC 1456 (Ch).

2.5.3   Action for account of profits

Usually in breach of contract claims the measure of damages is the loss suffered by the claimant, and not the profit made by the respondent. Account of profits is, however, assessed on the profits made by the respondent. Until recently, an action for account of profits was available as a remedy only in the special case where there is a breach of the implied duty of good faith, by using the employer's confidential information to make a secret profit (see **1.7.2.5**), or breach of a fiduciary duty (see *Nottingham University v Fishel and Another* [2000] IRLR 471, where the High Court confirmed that the employment relationship is not a fiduciary one but that fiduciary duties may arise from the relationship, *Kynixa Ltd v Hynes and Others* [2008] EWHC 1495, where the High Court held that the company director owed a fiduciary duty and that a second employee was also subject to a fiduciary duty by virtue of her senior status as a clinical services manager, and *Samsung Semiconductor Europe Ltd v Docherty and Another* [2011] CSOH 32, where the Court of Session held that a QA manager who worked with the employer's most important customer was subject to a fiduciary duty). In *Attorney-General v Blake and Jonathan Cape Ltd* [2001] IRLR 36, it was held that exceptionally a respondent may be required, as a remedy for breach of contract, to pay over to the claimant the profits received from the breach, even where the claimant has suffered no financial loss as a result of the breach and the wrongdoer is not in breach of a fiduciary duty. The House of Lords said a useful guide, although not exhaustive, is whether the employer had a legitimate interest in preventing the employee's profit-making activity and, hence, in depriving him of a profit.

2.6   CHECKLIST

(1)   How did contract end – has there been a breach of contract by employer?

(2)   Can employer raise employee's conduct as defence to a wrongful dismissal claim? (Remember after-acquired knowledge can be used.)

(3)   Is contract for a fixed term or terminable on notice?

(4)   What was employee's net pay?

(5)   Are there any factors which will increase/decrease starting point?

(6)   Are damages in excess of £30,000? If so, consider the tax position.

2.7   FURTHER READING

Textbooks dealing with termination at common law include:

Harvey, *Industrial Relations and Employment Law* (Butterworths), Divs A and C.

Duggan, *Wrongful Dismissal: Law, Practice and Precedents*, 2nd edn (Nova Law and Finance, 2011).

Lewis, *Employment Law – an adviser's handbook*, 9th edn revised (LAG, 2011).

Selwyn, *Law of Employment*, 17th edn (OUP, 2012).

Blackstone's Employment Law Practice (OUP, 2012).

SUMMARY

This chapter has looked at the differences between the breach of contract claim known as wrongful dismissal and the statutory claim of unfair dismissal, and at the extent to which they may overlap (**2.1, 2.2**). Provided that a contract is terminated in accordance with any express or implied terms (eg s 86 of the ERA 1996 sets out minimum periods of notice), neither party will be in breach of contract. The chapter has looked at the main ways in which a contract of employment may come to an end and the relevance of notice periods (**2.3**). It has also considered when a summary dismissal claim may be justified (**2.3.4**). It explains the principles to be applied when calculating an employee's damages following a wrongful dismissal (**2.4**) and the remedies available to an employer if an employee is in repudiatory breach of contract (**2.5**). A flowchart summarising wrongful dismissal and breach of contract claims is set out in **Figure 2.1** below.

Figure 2.1 Flowchart: Wrongful Dismissal/Breach of Contract Claims

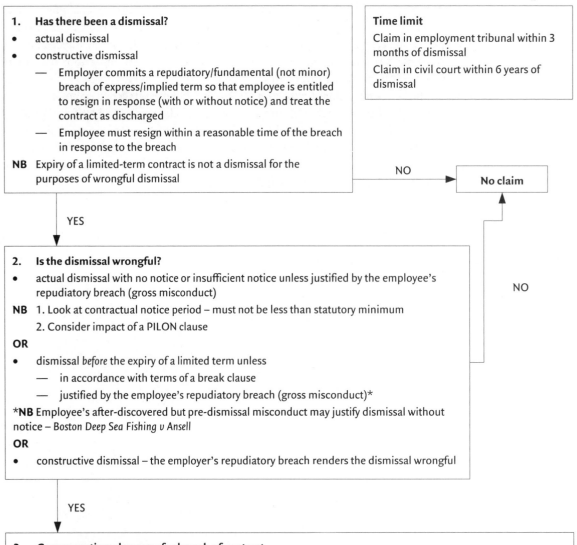

1.   Has there been a dismissal?
- actual dismissal
- constructive dismissal
    — Employer commits a repudiatory/fundamental (not minor) breach of express/implied term so that employee is entitled to resign in response (with or without notice) and treat the contract as discharged
    — Employee must resign within a reasonable time of the breach in response to the breach

NB   Expiry of a limited-term contract is not a dismissal for the purposes of wrongful dismissal

Time limit
Claim in employment tribunal within 3 months of dismissal
Claim in civil court within 6 years of dismissal

NO → **No claim**

YES

2.   Is the dismissal wrongful?
- actual dismissal with no notice or insufficient notice unless justified by the employee's repudiatory breach (gross misconduct)

NB   1. Look at contractual notice period – must not be less than statutory minimum
       2. Consider impact of a PILON clause

OR
- dismissal *before* the expiry of a limited term unless
    — in accordance with terms of a break clause
    — justified by the employee's repudiatory breach (gross misconduct)*

***NB** Employee's after-discovered but pre-dismissal misconduct may justify dismissal without notice – *Boston Deep Sea Fishing v Ansell*

OR
- constructive dismissal – the employer's repudiatory breach renders the dismissal wrongful

NO

YES

3.   Compensation: damages for breach of contract
Normal contractual damages rules (*Hadley v Baxendale*; loss of *net* wages) for proper notice period or until end of limited term (unless break clause)
PLUS any additional *contractual* losses (eg commission, pension, health insurance, car, bonuses, holiday pay, etc)
Reducing factors
payments made (eg payment in lieu)
certain benefits
duty to mitigate
accelerated receipt
Employment tribunal – maximum award £25,000
Civil court – no maximum
NB   Overlapping claims – damages for wrongful dismissal will be set off against any overlapping unfair dismissal compensatory award (usually the 'immediate loss of earning' element) arising from the same dismissal
NB   Compensation may be:
- Increased by up to 25% for an unreasonable failure to follow the Acas Code of Practice
- Decreased by up to 25% for an unreasonable failure to follow the Acas Code of Practice

(Consider too bringing a claim under the Working Time Regulations for unused statutory leave on termination in the absence of a contractual right to payment for unused holiday on termination.)

CHAPTER 3

DISMISSAL – ELIGIBILITY TO PRESENT A STATUTORY CLAIM

LEARNING OUTCOMES

After reading this chapter you will be able to:

- list the eligibility factors that must be satisfied before a person may bring a claim for unfair dismissal and/or a redundancy payment
- explain the difference between an actual and a constructive dismissal
- understand the significance of the non-renewal of a fixed-term contract
- understand the importance of continuity of employment
- calculate continuous employment
- explain when an employment tribunal will not have jurisdiction to hear a claim of unfair dismissal and/or for a redundancy payment.

3.1 INTRODUCTION

In addition to the common law claim for wrongful dismissal (see **Chapter 2**), there are two further claims which may be available to an employee on termination of his employment. These claims arise as a result of statutory rights given to an employee, namely, the right to a redundancy payment and the right not to be unfairly dismissed.

These claims differ from wrongful dismissal in many respects, most notably because not every employee is eligible to present a claim for redundancy or unfair dismissal. In this chapter, we consider the eligibility requirements for both statutory claims.

3.2 ELIGIBILITY FACTORS

In order to claim a redundancy payment or to pursue a complaint of unfair dismissal, a person must:

(a) be an employee;

(b) have been dismissed;

(c) have been continuously employed for the requisite period;

(d)   not be within an excluded class.

In addition, in certain situations, a person may be unable to bring a claim for jurisdictional reasons.

Each of these issues will be considered in more detail below.

3.3 EMPLOYEES ONLY

The claimant must be an employee (ERA 1996, ss 94, 135). An employee is defined as 'an individual who ... works under ... a contract of employment' (ERA 1996, s 230(1)). The self-employed, workers and independent contractors are excluded from entitlement (see **1.3**).

3.4 DISMISSAL

The fact that the contract has terminated does not in itself give rise to a statutory claim.

In order to be entitled to a redundancy payment or to claim unfair dismissal, an employee must show (ie has the burden of proving) that he has been 'dismissed' within the meaning of the legislation. An employee who resigns, leaves by mutual agreement, or whose contract is frustrated has not been dismissed and is not eligible to pursue a statutory claim.

The word 'dismissal' for the purpose of unfair dismissal and redundancy payments is defined by ss 95 and 136 of the ERA 1996, respectively, and differs in one important respect from the common law definition (see (b) below).

Under ERA 1996, dismissal may arise in one of three ways:

(a)   the contract is terminated by the employer; or

(b)   a limited term expires without being renewed; or

(c)   the employee is constructively dismissed.

The following paragraphs consider each of these situations in detail.

3.4.1 The contract is terminated by the employer – actual dismissal

An employee is treated as dismissed if 'the contract under which he is employed ... is terminated by the employer (whether with or without notice)' (ERA 1996, ss 95(1)(a) and 136(1)(a)).

(a)   This includes the most common of the three dismissal situations – where the employer simply gives the employee notice in accordance with the terms of the contract.

(b)   It also covers the situation where the employer terminates the contract without notice, ie he dismisses summarily. In this case, even though the dismissal may have been provoked by the employee's conduct, it is the employer's action in treating the contract as discharged which terminates the contract and thus constitutes dismissal.

> **EXAMPLE**
>
> If an employee is absent without leave and the employer refuses to allow him to return to work, this will operate as a dismissal (*London Transport Executive v Clark* [1981] IRLR 166, CA).

(c)   Occasionally, there is some doubt as to whether there has been a dismissal or a resignation where the words used by the employer are ambiguous.

> **EXAMPLE**
>
> The employer may use the words 'get lost' (or something even less polite) in an argument with the employee. If the employee takes him at his word, can he claim to have been dismissed?

> If the words used by the employer are ambiguous, then the test is to consider how the words would have been understood by the reasonable listener. The test is an objective one and the question of whether or not there has been a dismissal must be considered in light of all the surrounding circumstances (*Southern v Franks Charlesly & Co* [1981] IRLR 278). There is one authority (*Tanner v DT Kean* [1978] IRLR 110) for the proposition that the intention of the speaker is the relevant test, but none of the other cases supports this view.
>
> In *Futty v Brekkes (D & D) Ltd* [1974] IRLR 130, a foreman had a conversation with an employee which ended with the foreman saying 'if you don't like the job, you can f*** off'. The employee left and claimed that he had been dismissed. The tribunal decided that there was no dismissal, but only a 'general exhortation'.
>
> However, note that in appropriate circumstances, speaking to an employee in a disrespectful manner may, through the employer's breach of the implied term of mutual trust and confidence, constitute a constructive dismissal (see **3.4.3**).

(d)   There are cases where the employer will offer the employee a 'choice' – resign or be dismissed. If the employee chooses to resign, as this has been forced upon him by his employer, it will be treated as a dismissal by his employer (see, eg, *Martin v MBS Fastenings (Glynwed) Distribution Ltd* [1983] IRLR 198, CA).

In *Sandhu v Jan de Rijk Transport Ltd* [2007] EWCA Civ 430, an employee was summoned to a meeting and informed that his contract would be ended. He agreed severance terms in the meeting. Both the employment tribunal and the EAT held that he had resigned. The Court of Appeal overturned that finding. The Court said that resignation involves some degree of negotiation, discussion and genuine choice on the part of the employee. In this case, the employee had had no advance knowledge of what was to be discussed in the meeting, no time to take advice and no opportunity for reflection. The Court said he was not negotiating freely and had therefore been dismissed.

3.4.2   A limited term expires without being renewed or is ended early

Unlike the position at common law, the non-renewal of a limited-term contract is treated as a dismissal for the purpose of pursuing the statutory claims.

(a)   An employee is treated as dismissed if 'he is employed under a contract for a limited term and that term expires without being renewed under the same contract' (ERA 1996, ss 95(1)(b) and 136(1)(b)).

(b)   A limited-term contract may contain a 'break' clause under which one party, usually the employer, is entitled to terminate by giving notice before the term expires. If such a contract expires by effluxion of the limited term and the contract is not renewed, the employee is treated as being dismissed under this subsection. If the employer terminates the contract by giving notice under the 'break' clause, the employee is dismissed under s 95(1)(a) or s 136(1)(a) (see **3.4.1**).

3.4.3   The employee is constructively dismissed

Generally, an employee will not be regarded as having been dismissed if he resigns (but see *Southern v Franks Charlesly & Co* [1981] IRLR 278, *Sovereign House Security v Savage* [1989] IRLR 115 and *Greater Glasgow Health Board v Mackay* 1989 SLT 729). However, an employee is treated as dismissed if 'the employee terminates the contract under which he is employed (with or without notice) in circumstances in which he is entitled to terminate it without notice by reason of the employer's conduct' (ERA 1996, ss 95(1)(c) and 136(1)(c)).

(a)   An employee who leaves in such circumstances is said to be constructively dismissed. In order for an employee to treat himself as constructively dismissed within this provision, the employer's conduct must either amount to a significant breach going to the heart of the contract, or show that the employer no longer intends to be bound by one or more of the essential terms of the contract. The employee is then entitled to treat the contract as discharged at common law (*Western Excavating Ltd v Sharp* [1978] QB 761, CA). The test is an objective one; whether the employer intended to breach the contract or not is irrelevant.

(b)   A breach of an express term of the contract by the employer can amount to such a constructive dismissal. Examples would include:

   (i)   *Reduction of pay*

   A unilateral reduction in pay will amount to repudiation of the contract. This would include, for example, reduction in fringe benefits or refusal to pay overtime at overtime rates. In *Cantor Fitzgerald International v Callaghan and Others* [1999] IRLR 234, the Court of Appeal emphasised the importance of pay in any contract of employment; it said there was a crucial distinction between an employer's failure to pay or delay in paying agreed remuneration, perhaps due to a mistake or oversight, which would 'not necessarily' go to the root of the contract, and a deliberate refusal to do so, which the Court said would undermine the whole basis of the contract.

   (ii)   *Job description*

   A fundamental change in the nature of the job will amount to repudiation if there is no term allowing the employer to make such a change. In *Land Securities Trillium Ltd v Thornley* [2005] IRLR 765, EAT, it was held that there was a repudiatory breach when the employer moved the employee from a 'hands on' role to a managerial position, because the contract of employment did not include that flexibility for the employer. In so deciding, the EAT stated that the tribunal should look not only at the claimant's job description, but also at the work she actually did. Although her contract said that the claimant 'would perform to the best of [her] abilities ... any other duties which may reasonably be required of [her]', this, said the EAT, imposed a requirement of reasonableness on any request by the employer.

(c)   A significant breach of an implied term by the employer will entitle the employee to treat himself as constructively dismissed. There is implied into contracts of employment a term that employers will not 'without reasonable and proper cause, conduct themselves in a manner calculated or likely to destroy or seriously damage the relationship of confidence and trust between the employer and employee' (*Woods v WM Car Services (Peterborough) Ltd* [1983] IRLR 413, CA; see also *Malik v BCCI*; *Mahmud v BCCI* [1997] ICR 606, HL and *Baldwin v Brighton and Hove City Council* [2007] ICR 680). This is known as the duty of trust and confidence.

This duty is very wide in its application. Employers have been held to be in breach of this duty by, for example, making unjustified accusations of theft on scant evidence, making unjustified allegations that an employee was incapable of doing his job and falsely telling an employee who wanted a transfer that no vacancies were available. In *Stanley Cole (Wainfleet) Ltd v Sheridan* [2003] IRLR 52, the EAT upheld the tribunal's decision that the unjustified imposition of a final written warning amounted to a repudiatory breach entitling the employee to resign and claim she had been unfairly constructively dismissed; and in *Greenhof v Barnsley Metropolitan BC* [2006] IRLR 98, the EAT held that a serious breach of the employer's duty to make reasonable adjustments (see **Chapter 13**) amounted to a breach of the implied duty of trust and confidence (see also *Shaw v CCL Ltd* (UKEAT/0512/06), where the employer's actions, which amounted to sex discrimination, were held to breach the implied duty (discrimination against an employee will usually amount to a repudiatory breach)). If an employer acts in an unreasonable way there may be a breach of this duty, but the test remains that in *Western Excavating Ltd v Sharp* (see (a) above). The employer's conduct has to amount to a repudiatory breach of contract. In *Brown v Merchant Ferries* [1998] IRLR 682, the Court of Appeal accepted that if the employer's conduct is seriously unreasonable, this may provide evidence that there has been a repudiatory breach of contract but, on the facts, held that the conduct in question fell far short of a repudiatory breach by the employer. Mere unreasonable behaviour is not enough. The Court of Appeal has confirmed that the 'range of reasonable responses' test (see **Chapter 5**) has no relevance to the issue of whether an employee has been constructively dismissed, in *Bournemouth University Higher Education Corporation v Buckland* [2010] EWCA Civ 121 (see below).

In *Morrow v Safeway Stores plc* [2002] IRLR 9, the EAT held that the employment tribunal had erred in holding that although a manager's conduct in giving the applicant a public reprimand amounted to a breach of the implied contractual term of trust and confidence, it was not sufficiently serious to amount to a repudiation entitling the applicant to resign and claim constructive dismissal. The EAT held that where an employer breaches the implied term of trust and confidence, that breach is 'inevitably' fundamental, and thus such a breach goes to the root of the contract and amounts to a repudiatory breach, entitling the employee to resign and claim constructive dismissal. If the employer's conduct is insufficiently serious, there is no breach of the implied term. The EAT remitted the case for re-hearing: was the breach sufficiently serious or not?

Marshall Specialist Vehicles Ltd v Osborne (UKEAT/101/02) is a case concerning when employees can claim constructive dismissal arising out of stress at work. A tribunal had implied a term that employers should take reasonable care to avoid imposing a workload, or acquiescing in an employee's assumption of a workload, that would forseeably cause mental or physical injury. It found that the term had been breached and awarded maximum unfair dismissal damages. The EAT overturned this decision and criticised the tribunal for 'manufacturing' a term which was designed to provide the means to achieve a predetermined result. The EAT stated that there is already a general implied term that employers should take reasonable care for the safety of their employees. To show a breach giving rise to constructive dismissal an employee had to:

(i)   establish that the risk of injury was foreseeable;

(ii)   show that the employer was in breach of its duty;

(iii)   show that the breach was a foreseeable breach.

In *Horkulak v Cantor Fitzgerald International* [2003] IRLR 756, a senior director successfully claimed that the managing director's use of foul and abusive language was in breach of the implied duty of trust and confidence. The High Court held that the frequent use of such language did not 'sanitise its effect' so as to remove its power to offend, and held that the fact that an employee is very highly paid does not entitle an employer to apply a different standard of behaviour in its treatment of the employee.

For some years now there has been a debate about the relevance of the 'range of reasonable responses' test (see **Chapter 5**) when determining whether an employee has been constructively dismissed. For example, the EAT, in *Claridge v Daler Rowney Ltd* [2008] IRLR 672, held that for an employer's mishandling of a grievance to amount to a breach of trust and confidence, it was necessary for the employee to show that the conduct complained of was calculated or likely to destroy or seriously damage the employment relationship, and that the employee will not be able to satisfy that test unless the behaviour is outside the band of reasonable responses. On the facts it was held that a delay of some four and a half months in notifying the employee of the outcome of the grievance was not a fundamental breach; the employer's conduct did not fall outside the band of reasonable responses (see too *Abbey National v Fairbrother* [2007] IRLR 320). In *Savola v Chiltern Herb Farms* [1982] IRLR 166, the Court of Appeal decided that a constructive dismissal (the resignation was in response to a breach of an express term) could be a fair dismissal, ie that in some circumstances an employer who is in breach may still act reasonably. In *Bournemouth University Higher Education Corporation v Buckland* (UKEAT/0492/08) the EAT held that the band of reasonable responses test is not relevant when considering whether an employee has been constructively dismissed. At this stage, held the EAT, the only question for the tribunal is whether the employer had conducted himself in a manner calculated or likely to destroy or seriously damage the employment relationship (although as the EAT stated in *Nationwide Building Society v Niblett* (UKEAT/0524/08), it is perhaps 'difficult to envisage circumstances in which an employer will be in breach of the implied term of trust and confidence unless the employer's conduct has been unreasonable').

The Court of Appeal upheld the *Buckland* decision ([2010] EWCA Civ 121) and held that the only question for the tribunal is whether the employer had conducted himself in a manner calculated or likely to destroy or seriously damage the employment relationship; the range of reasonable responses test should be relevant only when considering whether or not the dismissal (be it actual or constructive) is fair or unfair (see **Chapter 5**). The Court of Appeal also said it was clear as a matter of general contract law that an anticipatory breach of contract could be withdrawn at any time up to the moment of acceptance, but once a repudiatory breach had been committed the defaulting party had 'crossed the Rubicon' and was unable to retreat, ie the breach cannot be cured; the other party could then elect whether or not to accept the breach.

In *RDF Media Group v Clements* [2008] IRLR 207, the High Court gave a very clear explanation of the implied term of trust and confidence (see paras 100–106). Importantly, the High Court held that an employee was not constructively dismissed because he himself was in repudiatory breach of the mutual obligation of trust and confidence. He could not therefore rely on the employer's later breach of the obligation. This applies even where the employer only subsequently finds out about the employee's breach.

The duty not to act in a manner likely to undermine trust and confidence was looked at again by the EAT in *McBride v Falkirk Football Club* (UKEATS/0058/10). The claimant was the Club's under-19s team manager. He resigned after his right to pick his team was arbitrarily removed after an Academy Director was appointed. The tribunal implied into his contract a term that he would relinquish his right to pick his team once an Academy Director was appointed, and on that basis found no breach of contract by the Club, and rejected his claim for constructive dismissal. The EAT, in overturning the employment tribunal's decision and substituting a finding of constructive dismissal, said that the test to be applied in trust and confidence cases was to be judged from an objective standpoint, so that an employer could not rely upon factors in a particular industry – such as 'an autocratic style of management' being 'the norm in football' – as a defence to a breach of the implied term of trust and confidence. The EAT also held that a term ought not to be implied into a contract of employment which contradicted an express term or which was imprecise, unnecessary or not obvious. Useful guidance on when to imply terms in a contact is set out at paras 54 and 55.

In *Assamoi v Spirit Pub Company* (UKEAT/0050/11), the employer upheld an employee's grievance about treatment by his immediate manager and took steps to rectify the situation. The EAT held that this prevented the employee relying on the treatment to show a breach of the implied term of trust and confidence. The actions of the more senior manager had prevented the matter escalating into a state of affairs that would have justified the employee leaving and claiming that he had been constructively dismissed.

(d) A threat to change terms and conditions, and to dismiss an employee if he did not accept the changes, may amount to a constructive dismissal even if the employee resigns before implementation of the changes. The employer's threats could amount to anticipatory breach of contract (*Greenaway Harrison Ltd v Wiles* [1994] IRLR 380). See also *Buckland* (above).

(e) It is not possible to argue that the *manner* of a dismissal is a breach of the implied term of trust and confidence. The House of Lords, in *Johnson v Unisys Ltd* [2001] IRLR 279, was unwilling to develop the common law to imply a contractual term that an employer must carry out a dismissal in good faith, given the existence of the statutory unfair dismissal regimes which specifically cover the process of dismissal. (This decision also had implications for what damages may be recovered in a wrongful dismissal claim – see **2.4.1.5** and **5.6.2.2**.)

(f) It is possible to look to the cumulative effects of the employer's actions. The final act may not in itself amount to a repudiatory breach of contract but could be the 'last straw' entitling the employee to claim constructive dismissal. Where there is a series of incidents, none of which individually amounts to a serious breach but which together amount to a breach of the implied duty of trust and confidence, if the employee continues to work, any implied waiver of the breach will be conditional upon there being no repetition of the breach (*JV Strong & Co Ltd v Hamill* (UKEAT/1179/99)). Where there is a series of incidents, the employee's response has to be measured from the last incident. In *Abbey National plc v Robinson* [2000] All ER (D) 1884, the EAT found that an employee was entitled to claim constructive dismissal when she resigned almost a year after a breach of contract by her employers. There was a series of incidents culminating with the 'last straw' (the withdrawal of a job offer) and her resignation was tendered shortly after that last incident.

Note that, according to the Court of Appeal in *London Borough of Waltham Forest v Omilaju* [2005] IRLR 35, the final straw must contribute something to that breach, although what it adds may be relatively 'insignificant'. If the alleged final straw is an entirely innocuous act (here, a justified refusal to pay) on the part of the employer, this cannot be the last straw.

(g) Founded as it is on the contractual concept of repudiatory breach, the employee must leave within a reasonable period following the breach to avoid being taken as having affirmed the contract and waived the breach. In *Bunning v GT Bunning & Sons Ltd* [2005] EWCA Civ 293, the employer had breached the claimant's contract when it failed to carry out adequate risk assessments when the claimant said she was pregnant. However, the Court of Appeal held that she waived the breach when she accepted an alternative job with the employer.

How long is too long is a question of fact. In *Munchkins Restaurant Ltd and Another v Karmazyn and Others* (UKEAT/0359/09), the waitresses in question put up with the employer's conduct for several years. The tribunal made the point that in its view the waitresses were migrant workers with no certainty of continued employment, save at Munchkins; that there were considerations of convenience for one; that they were constrained by financial and in some cases parental pressure; that they had the fear that they might not obtain other work; that they had the comfort of one manager acting as a cushion until she left; and that they managed, therefore, to find a balance between conduct which was unwelcome and unlawful and the advantages which their job gave them. It was not therefore, according to the EAT, completely beyond the scope of reason to think that women in this particular situation should behave as they did.

Mere delay by itself (unaccompanied by any express or implied affirmation of contract) does not constitute affirmation of the contract, but if it is prolonged it may be evidence of an implied affirmation. In *Mrs A Fereday v South Staffordshire NHS Primary Care Trust* (UKEAT/0513/10), the claimant invoked the grievance procedure, which resulted in a decision adverse to her on 13 February 2009, but she only resigned by a letter dated 24 March 2009. The EAT upheld the employment tribunal's decision that the respondent had repudiated the contract of employment but that the claimant had affirmed the contract by her delay. The EAT held that the employment tribunal was entitled to take the prolonged delay of nearly six weeks between the grievance decision and the claimant's resignation as an implied affirmation, bearing in mind that the claimant was expecting or requiring the respondent (the employer) to perform its part of the contract of employment by paying her sick pay.

Delay is one of many factors to which the tribunal may have regard to when deciding whether the contract has been affirmed. Other relevant factors might be illness, whether a grievance has been raised, whether there are ongoing discussions as to whether or not some accommodation might be reached, etc.

(h)   The employee's acceptance of the breach must be unambiguous and unequivocal (see *Atlantic Air Ltd v Holt* (UKEAT/0602/07), but it need not be communicated to the employer. The employee must resign in response to the employer's repudiatory breach of contract. The employee will not be constructively dismissed if he resigns for some other unconnected reason. The Court of Appeal, in *Weathersfield v Sargeant* [1999] IRLR 94, stated that the fact that an employee left her employment without giving a reason at the time did not preclude her from claiming that she had been constructively dismissed, although such conduct would usually make it more difficult to obtain such a finding. The Court rejected the notion that there could be no acceptance of a repudiation unless the employee told the employer at the time that he was leaving because of the employer's repudiatory conduct.

3.5 CONTINUOUS EMPLOYMENT

In order to be eligible to present a statutory claim, the claimant must have the requisite period of 'continuous employment' prior to the dismissal.

In calculating periods of continuous employment, a month means a calendar month and a year means 12 calendar months. If, for example, an employee commenced employment on 20 April 2012 and worked continuously for his employer from that date, his period of two years' continuous employment is complete on 19 April 2014. (See, eg, *Pacitti Jones v O'Brien* [2005] IRLR 889.)

Continuous employment usually means working for the same employer without a break. Sometimes, employment can be regarded as continuous in spite of short breaks (ERA 1996, s 212(3)(c) (see **3.5.3**)). Sometimes, time spent with a previous employer may be added on (eg where there are 'associated employers', such as teachers within one local education authority who work for different schools).

3.5.1 Periods of employment required

3.5.1.1 Unfair dismissal

From 6 April 2012, for employees who start work on or after that date, to be entitled to present a complaint of unfair dismissal, the dismissed employee must have been continuously employed for a period of not less than two years, starting on the date that employment commenced and ending on the 'effective date of termination' (EDT) (ERA 1996, s 108(1)). For employees who started work before 6 April 2012, one year is required.

It is advisable for employers to review the employment of new employees well before they have been continuously employed for two years. This will enable an employer to dismiss an unsatisfactory employee with proper notice, before he becomes entitled to present a complaint of unfair dismissal. However, note that even if an employee does not have the necessary length of service, he is eligible to present a claim for discrimination if relevant on the facts (see **Chapters 8** and **13**).

Exceptionally, an employee does not need a qualifying period of continuous employment to present an unfair dismissal claim, for example an employee who is dismissed for trade union reasons (**5.5.1**), for having stopped work on health and safety grounds (**5.5.4**), for having asserted a statutory right (**5.5.3**) or because she is pregnant (**Chapter 14**).

3.5.1.2   Redundancy payment

To be entitled to claim a redundancy payment, the dismissed employee must have been employed for a period of not less than two years, starting on the date that employment commenced and ending on the 'relevant date' (ERA 1996, s 155). See further **Chapter 4**.

3.5.2   Calculating continuous employment

3.5.2.1   Unfair dismissal and the effective date of termination

The effective date of termination (EDT) is defined by ss 97 and 145 of the ERA 1996 to mean:

(a)   for an employee whose contract is terminated by notice, whether given by the employer or employee, the date on which that notice expires. In *Palfrey v Transco plc* [2004] IRLR 916, the EAT said that the employee's EDT was his leaving date as agreed with the employer, and not the termination date given in the notice of dismissal (see also *Wedgewood v Ministergate Hull Ltd* (UKEAT/0137/10);

(b)   for an employee whose contract is terminated without notice, the date on which termination takes effect (see *Heaven v Whitbread Group plc* (UKEAT/0084/10)); and

(c)   for an employee with a limited-term contract which expires without renewal, the date on which the term expires.

Usually there should be no problem in applying these rules to ascertain the EDT in the majority of cases. As a rule of thumb, it is the last day on which the employee worked for the employer.

Note that:

(a)   if an employee is dismissed without notice but given wages in lieu, the EDT is still the date the employee was told to go;

(b)   with a constructive dismissal, the EDT is the date of departure, ie the employee's acceptance of the repudiation.

The Court of Appeal held that the EDT is a statutory construct and cannot be fixed by agreement between the parties (*Fitzgerald v University of Kent at Canterbury* [2004] IRLR 300).

The EDT may be important in determining whether an employee has presented a case to a tribunal within the requisite time-limits (see **6.3**). In *Gisda Cyf v Barratt* [2010] UKSC 41, the Supreme Court held that the EDT of an employee dismissed for gross misconduct was the date she opened and read the letter from her employer, informing her of her dismissal.

Extension of EDT in special circumstances

The main purpose of this rule is to ensure that employers do not deprive employees of their statutory rights by wrongfully dismissing them without notice just before they reach the qualifying period to present a claim of unfair dismissal.

In circumstances where the employee is entitled to a statutory minimum period of notice under s 86 of the ERA 1996 (see **2.3.3**), if he is dismissed without notice or with less notice than the statutory minimum, for certain purposes his EDT will be extended by the statutory minimum period of notice to which he was entitled but did not receive (ERA 1996, s 97(2)):

(a)   The EDT is extended only by the statutory minimum period of notice, not by any longer contractual period to which he may have been entitled.

(b)   The EDT is extended only if the employee was entitled to notice. It is not extended if a limited-term contract terminates (except under a 'break' clause), or if an employer is entitled to dismiss the employee without notice.

(c)   A constructively dismissed employee is also entitled to extend the EDT by the statutory minimum period for the purposes of bringing an unfair dismissal claim (see (d) below). The statutory minimum period of notice that would have been due from the employer had the employer terminated, will start to run from the date that the employee gave notice (ERA 1996, s 97(4)).

(d)   The EDT is extended only for some purposes, such as the qualification period to present an unfair dismissal claim, the calculation of awards for such a claim and entitlement to be given a written statement of reasons for dismissal (see **5.2.3**). It does *not* extend the EDT for the purposes of extending the time-limits to present claims.

> **EXAMPLE**
>
> Natalie commenced employment on 3 April 2011. There is no break in her continuity of employment. Her employer wrongfully dismissed her without notice on 30 March 2012. On this date she had been continuously employed for more than one month but less than one year. Under s 86 of the ERA 1996 she was entitled to one week's statutory minimum notice (see **2.3.3**). Her EDT is extended by one week to 6 April 2012 (the seven days' notice starts on 31 March and expires on 6 April), which gives her the necessary one year's continuous employment to present an unfair dismissal claim. (Note: Natalie started work for this employer before 6 April 2012, so she requires only one year's continuous employment to claim unfair dismissal. If she had started on or after 6 April 2012, she would have needed two years.)

3.5.2.2 Redundancy payments and the relevant date

The relevant date is defined by ERA 1996, s 145 in exactly the same way as the EDT is for unfair dismissal (see **3.5.2.1** above).

Extension of the relevant date in special circumstances

Again, the rules are designed to prevent an employer wrongfully dismissing an employee just before he reaches the qualifying period for presenting a redundancy payment claim. Points (a), (b) and (d) at **3.5.2.1** above apply to extension of the relevant date also (s 145(5)).

Point (c) above does not apply. The relevant date will be extended by the statutory minimum period to which the employee is entitled but did not receive, but only where there is an actual dismissal by the employer. The relevant date is *not* extended by the statutory minimum period for the purposes of making a redundancy payment claim where the employee has been constructively dismissed.

> **EXAMPLE**
>
> George commenced employment on 3 April 2011. There is no break in his continuity of employment. He resigns on 30 March 2013, alleging that he has been constructively dismissed. On this date he has been employed for just less than two years. Although, under ERA 1996, s 86, he is entitled to one week's statutory minimum notice, the relevant date will *not* be extended by the statutory minimum period. He is not eligible to claim a redundancy payment.

3.5.3 Continuity of employment

Periods of employment must be continuous. If a period of employment is broken so that it is not continuous with a later period, the employee will commence a new period of employment after the break, starting again at week one. He will not be able to add the old period of employment to the new.

There is a presumption in favour of the employee that employment is continuous (ERA 1996, s 210(5)). This may, however, be rebutted by the employer.

A week counts towards the period of continuous employment if in that week the employee actually works or the employee's relationship with the employer is governed by a contract.

Weeks during which the employee is *not employed* under a contract of employment do not count. However, such weeks *will* count in the following circumstances (ERA 1996, s 212):

(a)   if the employee is absent due to sickness, injury, pregnancy or confinement up to a maximum of 26 weeks;

(b)   if there is a temporary cessation of work (see *Cornwall County Council v Prater* (UKEAT/0055/05)) (the case was appealed to the Court of Appeal on different grounds; there was no appeal on this point ([2006] IRLR 362) and *Ford v Warwickshire CC* [1983] ICR 273, HL (applied in *Hussain v Acorn Independent College Ltd* (UKEAT/0199/10)));

(c)   if the employee is absent in circumstances where, by arrangement or custom, the employee is regarded as continuously in employment (see *Curr v Marks & Spencer plc* [2003] IRLR 74 for a decision of the Court of Appeal on this issue).

It is necessary to rely on these provisions to preserve continuity only where there is no continuing contract of employment. If there is a subsisting contractual relationship, continuity of employment will be preserved, even though the employee does not work due to, for example, sickness or holiday or maternity leave. If an employee is reinstated following an unfair dismissal finding, continuity will be assumed as if there had been no dismissal.

Note that although continuity is a statutory concept, in *London Probation Board v Kirkpatrick* [2005] IRLR 443 the EAT held that it was open to an employer and an employee to arrange (under ERA 1996, s 212(3)(c)) that absence from work could count towards continuity of employment and that reinstatement could qualify as such an arrangement. The EAT said that such arrangements do not have to be agreed before dismissal. As a matter of policy, the EAT said it was preferable for an employer to be able to admit that it had made a mistake and to put it right rather than for an employee to have to bring a claim and require an order for reinstatement via a tribunal or Acas.

3.5.4   Industrial action

Industrial action does not break continuity of employment, but days during which the employee is on strike or locked out by the employer do not count in computing the length of employment (ERA 1996, s 216).

This is achieved by postponing the beginning of the period of continuous employment by the number of days between the last working day before the strike or lockout and the day on which work was resumed.

EXAMPLE

An employee, whose continuous employment commenced on 5 September 2011, goes on strike at lunchtime on Friday 16 November 2012. She resumes work on Tuesday 20 November 2012. Her period of continuous employment will now be treated as beginning on 9 September 2011. It is postponed by the four days (ie 16, 17, 18, 19 November) between the last working day before the strike (15 November 2012) and the day work resumed (20 November 2012). The days 17 and 18 November are 'lost' by the employee, even though they are a Saturday and Sunday and not working days.

3.5.5 Change of employer

The basic rule is that for employment to be continuous, it must be with the same employer. A change of employer will break continuity (ERA 1996, s 218).

Although a change of employer breaks continuity, a change of job with the same employer will not break it.

In the following circumstances, continuity of employment is preserved despite a change of employer:

(a)   there is a transfer of an undertaking within the Transfer of Undertakings (Protection of Employment) Regulations 2006 (see **Chapter 7**);

(b)   on the death of an employer, the employee is employed by the personal representatives of the deceased;

(c)   there is a change of partners who are the employers;

(d)   the new employer is an associated employer of the old employer (ERA 1996, s 218(6)). Employers are associated if one is a company of which the other has control, or if both are companies of which a third person has control (ERA 1996, s 231). Therefore, if an employee is moved between companies within a 'group', his continuity will be preserved.

3.6 EXCLUDED CLASSES

The ERA 1996 excludes certain classes of employee from entitlement to the statutory claims. For example, members of the armed forces, the police service and 'share' mariners are excluded from the right to present a claim of unfair dismissal. Crown employees, 'share' mariners and certain domestic servants employed by close relations are not entitled to redundancy payments. Further details of these exclusions may be found in Harvey, *Industrial Relations and Employment Law* (Butterworths), Division C.

3.7 JURISDICTION

Section 196 of the ERA 1996 provided, inter alia, that the unfair dismissal provisions of the Act did not apply in relation to employment during any period when the employee was working outside Great Britain unless the employee ordinarily worked in Great Britain for the same employer, or his contract was governed by the law of England and Wales (or Scotland). The whole of s 196 was repealed by s 32(3) of the ERA 1999 with effect from 25 October 1999. This repeal left uncertain the extent to which tribunals had jurisdiction to hear unfair dismissal claims under s 94(1) (which states that the right not to be unfairly dismissed applies where the employee 'is employed in Great Britain') where employees worked abroad.

Some issues were resolved by the House of Lords in *Serco Ltd v Lawson* [2006] UKHL 3. Readers should have regard to the decision in cases where the employee is working abroad. Hoffmann LJ, giving the judgment, identified three categories of case:

(a)   where the employee was working in Great Britain at the time of the dismissal (so long as that was not a casual visit) – he said that this was the 'normal' case and s 94(1) would generally apply;

(b)   the peripatetic employee – where the 'commonsense [approach] of treating the base' as the place of employment would apply (see *Todd v British Midland Airways Ltd* [1978] ICR 959); and

(c)   expatriate employees – where there would have to be 'unusual' or 'exceptional' circumstances for an employee to be protected under British employment law.

Two examples were given:

(i)   an employee posted abroad by a British employer for the purposes of a business carried on in Britain,

(ii)   an employee of a British employer operating in a British enclave in a foreign country.

Lord Hoffmann said that there might be other examples of employees who 'have equally strong connections with Great Britain and British employment law' but that he could not think of any.

In *Duncombe and Others v Secretary of State for Children, Schools and Families* [2011] UKSC 36, the Supreme Court held that teachers working abroad in schools in Europe and employed by a UK government department were protected under the expatriate employee category identified in *Serco* above because they were another example of employees who have equally strong connections with Britain – the employees' employment had an overwhelmingly closer connection to Britain than anywhere else. The factors that were important were that the Government employed the employees; their contracts were governed by English law; they were employed in international enclaves and it would be anomalous if a teacher employed by the British Government working in a European school in England were protected but these employees working in a school in another country were not.

Lady Hale, delivering the judgment of the Supreme Court remarked (para 8) that it was a mistake to try to torture the circumstances of one employment to make them fit one of the examples given, for 'they are merely examples of the application of the general principle'. She went on to say:

> In our view, these cases do form another example of an exceptional case where the employment has such an overwhelmingly closer connection with Britain and with British employment law than with any other system of law that it is right to conclude that Parliament must have intended that the employees should enjoy protection from unfair dismissal.

In *Ravat v Halliburton Manufacturing and Services Ltd* [2012] UKSC 1 and *Ministry of Defence v Wallis* [2011] EWCA Civ 231, the courts considered the extent to which, if at all, an employment tribunal can go beyond the three categories of case identified by Lord Hoffmann in *Serco*. In *Wallis*, the Court of Appeal upheld the tribunal's decision that the claimants fell within the expatriate category of employee, making it clear that each case must be decided on its own facts. The fact that the claimants were recruited by the MoD, were eligible for the posts as dependants of serving members of the army posted abroad and were employed on terms governed by English law were all factors which meant that the claimants had 'clear, firm, sound connections with Britain'. In *Ravat*, the Supreme Court, on an appeal from the Scottish Court of Session (which was divided as to the extent to which it was possible to depart from Lord Hoffman's categories), held that a British citizen who lived in England but worked in Libya on what was known as a commuter or rotational basis (he worked 28 days in Libya, then was in England for 28 days), could bring an unfair dismissal claim. He was employed by Halliburton Manufacturing and Services Ltd, a UK subsidiary of Halliburton Inc, a US company. The work he carried out was for the benefit of a German subsidiary of Halliburton Inc. He was paid in sterling and paid UK tax. At the time of his dismissal he was working in Libya. The Supreme Court held that he had sufficiently strong connections with Great Britain to be able to bring a claim of unfair dismissal in England.

In a unanimous judgment, Lord Hope pointed out that Mr Ravat did not fit into any of the three categories identified by Lord Hoffmann in *Serco*. He was not working in Great Britain at the time of his dismissal. He was not a peripatetic employee. He was not working abroad as an expatriate in a political or social British enclave. Nor had he been posted abroad to work for a business conducted in Great Britain, as he was commuting from his home in Preston and the company for whose benefit he was working in Libya was a German company.

Lord Hope referred to the warning given by Lady Hale in *Duncombe* against adopting too restrictive an approach to the problem, and concluded:

> The question in each case is whether section 94(1) applies to the particular case, notwithstanding its foreign elements. Parliament cannot be taken to have intended to confer rights on employees having

no connection with Great Britain at all. The paradigm case for the application of the subsection is, of course, the employee who was working in Great Britain. But there is some scope for a wider interpretation, as the language of section 94(1) does not confine its application to employment in Great Britain ... the starting point needs to be more precisely identified. It is that the employment relationship must have a stronger connection with Great Britain than with the foreign country where the employee works. The general rule is that the place of employment is decisive. But it is not an absolute rule. The open-ended language of section 94(1) leaves room for some exceptions where the connection with Great Britain is sufficiently strong to show that this can be justified. The case of the peripatetic employee who was based in Great Britain is one example. The expatriate employee, all of whose services were performed abroad but who had nevertheless very close connections with Great Britain because of the nature and circumstances of employment, is another. But it does not follow that the connection that must be shown in the case of those who are not truly expatriate, because they were not both working and living overseas, must achieve the high standard that would enable one to say that their case was exceptional. The question whether, on given facts, a case falls within the scope of section 94(1) is a question of law, but it is also a question of degree. The fact that the commuter has his home in Great Britain, with all the consequences that flow from this for the terms and conditions of his employment, makes the burden in his case of showing that there was a sufficient connection less onerous. Mr Cavanagh said that a rigorous standard should be applied, but I would not express the test in those terms. The question of law is whether section 94(1) applies to this particular employment. The question of fact is whether the connection between the circumstances of the employment and Great Britain and with British employment law was sufficiently strong to enable it to be said that it would be appropriate for the employee to have a claim for unfair dismissal in Great Britain.

On the facts, the factors that pointed to a sufficiently close connection with Britain were:

(a)   Mr Ravat's home was in Britain;

(b)   he was paid in sterling;

(c)   he was treated as a commuter under his employer's assignment policy; and

(d)   his contract was stated to be subject to UK law.

The EAT, in *Bleuse v MBT Transport* [2008] IRLR 264, has caused confusion by holding that different rules on jurisdiction apply depending on the statutory basis for the claim. The EAT said that *Serco* applies only where the legislation is primarily a UK concept, but it does not apply where the legislation derives from EU legislation with direct effect (such as the Working Time Regulations). This means that, in these cases, a weaker link with the UK *might* suffice. Bleuse was endorsed by the Court of Appeal in *Duncombe and Others v Secretary of State for Children, Schools and Families* [2010] IRLR 331, which said that the *Serco* test should be modified in its application to UK law where necessary to give effect to directly effective rights derived from EU law – this is likely to have most impact when determining territorial jurisdiction in discrimination cases. However, *Clyde & Co LLP and Another v Bates van Winkelhof* [2012] EWCA Civ 1207 upheld an employment tribunal's decision with regard to jurisdiction and agreed that it was right to apply the *Serco* test of a *sufficiently* strong connection to Great Britain to discrimination claims. Elias LJ did say that, in cases where the employee works *wholly* abroad (on the facts the employee lived and/or worked for part of the time in Great Britain), a comparative approach would be appropriate to decide where the stronger connection is.

3.8 CONTRACTING OUT

Any provision purporting to contract out of the employee's rights under the ERA 1996 is void except in so far as it is permitted by the Act (see eg **6.5**).

3.9 FURTHER READING

Textbooks dealing with eligibility include:

Selwyn, *Law of Employment*, 17th edn (OUP, 2012).

Bowers, *A Practical Approach to Employment Law*, 8th edn (OUP, 2009), chs 13 and 14.

Lewis, *Employment Law – an adviser's handbook*, 9th edn revised (LAG, 2011).

SUMMARY

This chapter has looked at two statutory claims which might be available to an employee on the termination of his employment in addition to the common law claim for wrongful dismissal covered in **Chapter 2** – unfair dismissal and/or for a redundancy payment. It has covered eligibility to present these claims to an employment tribunal. In order to claim a redundancy payment or pursue a complaint of unfair dismissal a person must be an employee (**1.3**), must have been dismissed (actually, constructively or on the expiry of a fixed-term contract) (**3.4**), must have the requisite two years' continuous employment (**3.5**) and must not fall within any of the excluded classes (**3.6**). Additionally, the tribunal must have the necessary jurisdiction to hear the claim (**3.7** and **6.2.1**).

It is therefore sensible always to check the following matters in order to determine if someone is eligible to bring a claim:

(1)   commencement date;

(2)   EDT;

(3)   no break;

(4)   starting date in the event of industrial action;

(5)   two years' service (for employees who started work with their employer before 6 April 2012, one year for unfair dismissal).

REDUNDANCY

LEARNING OUTCOMES

After reading this chapter you will be able to:

- describe the three different definitions of redundancy
- explain how an employee may make a redundancy payment claim
- explain when an employee may lose his entitlement to a redundancy payment
- calculate a redundancy payment.

4.1 INTRODUCTION

An eligible employee, dismissed by reason of redundancy, will be entitled, at a minimum, to a statutory redundancy payment from his employer (ERA 1996, s 163). The contract of employment may provide for more generous payments. *Note:* where an employee is dismissed by reason of redundancy, this may *also* give rise to potential wrongful dismissal and/or unfair dismissal claims (see **Chapters 2** and **5**). The right to claim a redundancy payment is a separate right which will arise irrespective of whether the dismissal is unfair or wrongful.

A redundancy payment is in the nature of a reward for past services, and so an eligible employee is entitled to receive the full payment even when he manages to find another job immediately.

Often the employer accepts that the employee is redundant and will simply calculate the amount of the redundancy payment and make payment without the need for any formal application to an employment tribunal. However, where there is a dispute over the right to receive the payment or over the correct amount, an application will need to be made and the tribunal will determine these matters.

4.1.1 Eligibility

Before advising on the right to a redundancy payment, eligibility must be checked. Employees must have two years' continuous service before they are eligible to claim a redundancy payment (ERA 1996, s 155). There must also, of course, be a dismissal (see **3.4** for the definition of dismissal).

4.1.2 Redundancy

The next point to consider is whether the situation which led to the dismissal fits the statutory definition of redundancy. In other words, is the reason for the dismissal redundancy? If it is not, there will be no right to a redundancy payment. The scope of the definition is considered below at **4.2**.

4.2 DEFINITION OF REDUNDANCY

The definition of redundancy is contained in s 139(1) of the ERA 1996:

> For the purposes of this Act an employee who is dismissed shall be taken to be dismissed by reason of redundancy if the dismissal is wholly or mainly attributable to—
>
> (a)   the fact that his employer has ceased or intends to cease—
>
> > (i)   to carry on the business for the purposes of which the employee was employed by him, or
> >
> > (ii)   to carry on that business in the place where the employee was so employed, or
>
> (b)   the fact that the requirements of that business—
>
> > (i)   for employees to carry out work of a particular kind, or
> >
> > (ii)   for employees to carry out work of a particular kind in the place where the employee was employed by the employer,
>
> have ceased or diminished or are expected to cease or diminish.

Looking at this definition, it may be seen that redundancy occurs in three main situations: job redundancy, place of work redundancy and employee redundancy (our labels). Each of these is now considered in turn.

4.2.1 Cessation of business – 'job redundancy'

Within s 139(1)(a)(i) of the ERA 1996, an employee who is dismissed by reason of the closure of the employer's business will be dismissed by reason of redundancy. This will be the case whether the cessation of business is permanent or temporary.

4.2.2 Cessation or reduction in work at place of employment – 'place of work redundancy'

Here, *the place* where the employee is employed is being relocated (ERA 1996, s 139(1)(a)(ii)). This sounds a simple proposition, but there were, in the past, difficulties in determining whether 'place of work' is where the employee *could be required to work according to the contract of employment* (the 'contractual' test), or alternatively where the employee *actually* works (the 'factual' test). In *Bass Leisure Ltd v Thomas* [1994] IRLR 104, the EAT held that an employee's place of work, for the purposes of redundancy, is a question of 'fact', taking into account where the employee 'actually' worked.

The decision was approved by the Court of Appeal in *High Table Ltd v Horst* [1997] IRLR 513. The applicants were all employed as waitresses by High Table, who provided in-house catering services for city companies. The three applicants had always worked at Hill Samuel, but their contracts did contain a mobility clause. Hill Samuel reduced their requirements and the three applicants were dismissed. The Court held that for the purposes of redundancy, an employee's place of work was not to be decided solely by reference to the contract of employment regardless of where the employee actually worked. The place where the employee was employed for the purposes of s 139(1)(a)(ii) was to be established by a factual inquiry, taking into account the employee's fixed place or changing places of work and any contractual terms which might assist.

The Court said that if an employee had worked in only one location under his contract of employment for the purposes of the employer's business (as was the case, on the facts, in *High Table*), it defied common sense to widen the extent of the place where he was so employed merely because of the existence of the mobility clause. However, if the work of the employee for the employer had involved a change of location, then the contract of employment might be helpful to determine the extent of the place where the employee was employed.

Thus the position is as follows:

(a)   if an employee has worked in only one location, that is his place of work, regardless of any mobility clause in his contract;

(b)   if an employee has worked from several locations, the place of work is still to be established by a factual enquiry, taking into account any contractual terms that might assist in evidencing his place of work, for example a mobility clause.

4.2.2.1   Mobility clauses in the context of a 'place of work' redundancy situation

As noted above, when considering an employee's 'place' of work, the existence of a contractual mobility clause is irrelevant to that particular analysis where the employee worked in one location only.

However, mobility clauses are nevertheless still relevant when considering whether an employee is entitled to a redundancy payment on the facts, even if you have established that there is a redundancy situation within the meaning of s 139. This is because the cause of the dismissal must still be established. To be entitled to a redundancy payment, the employee's dismissal must have been caused by the redundancy situation. Whilst a mobility clause is not always relevant to identifying the place of work (see above), it is still a valid term of the contract. If an employee has a mobility clause in his contract, but refuses to obey a lawful request from his employer to move in accordance with the contractual term, then the dismissal may be due to the employee's misconduct rather than the underlying redundancy situation which has given rise to the need to implement the mobility clause (see *Home Office v Evans* [2008] IRLR 59).

4.2.3   Reduction in requirement for employees to do work of a particular kind – 'employee redundancy'

An employee is dismissed by reason of redundancy within s 139(1)(b) of the ERA 1996 if the reason for his dismissal is that the requirement for employees to do work of a particular kind has ceased or diminished. This will clearly cover the situation where the dismissed employee's own job has disappeared through lack of work, but the section also covers other situations, some of which may not be so obvious.

4.2.3.1   Surplus employees

If the requirement for employees to do the work is reduced, even though the same amount of work is still being done, this will come within the ambit of the section.

> **EXAMPLES**
>
> (a)   Initial overstaffing may mean fellow employees can absorb the work done by the dismissed employee.
>
> (b)   New technology means that some employees are dismissed and replaced by machines.
>
> (c)   A reorganisation of work methods may produce a more efficient system requiring less manpower so some employees are dismissed.
>
> (d)   The work carried out by an employee may be done in fewer hours, so the employer seeks to reduce the employee's hours (not the overall employee headcount). The employee does not agree and is dismissed (see *Packman v Fauchon* (UKEAT/0017/12)).

> (e)   An independent contractor may be taken on to do the same work, for example instead of employing an office cleaner the employer may engage the services of a cleaning company, and the cleaner therefore will be dismissed. Note in this example the effect of the Transfer of Undertakings (Protection of Employment) Regulations 2006 (see **Chapter 7**).

4.2.3.2   Work of a particular kind

What if a change in the nature of a job leads to the dismissal of an employee? Will the dismissal be by reason of redundancy? If the nature of the work has changed fundamentally so that work of a particular kind has ceased or diminished, even though it has been replaced by different work, this will amount to redundancy. For example, in *Murphy v Epsom College* [1984] IRLR 271, as a result of the installation of a new heating system, a plumber was replaced by a heating technician and was held to have been made redundant. The dismissal was for redundancy because the employer no longer needed to carry out work of the particular kind done by him. However, a mere reallocation of duties or introduction of new methods will not amount to redundancy. See, for example, *North Riding Garages Ltd v Butterwick* [1967] 2 QB 56, where no redundancy situation arose when a garage manager was asked to sell cars in addition to his other duties.

The contract test or the function test?

Historically, there have been two conflicting tests used for determining whether work of a particular kind has ceased or diminished: the contract test and the function test. The contract test focused on how the duties of the employee were *defined* in the contract of employment. The function test focused on the duties *actually performed* by the employee. Historically, the contract test prevailed.

According to the contract test, if duties are narrowly defined as the actual job being carried out by the employee, and that job has gone, the employee is redundant. However, if the duties are widely defined in the contract, whilst the job performed by that employee may have gone, there may be other available jobs he could still be required to perform under his contract. In this case his dismissal will not be by reason of redundancy if the alternative job is offered (*Haden Ltd v Cowan* [1982] IRLR 314). According to the function test, if the actual job carried out by the employee has gone, the employee is redundant regardless of whether, under his contract, he could be required to do other work.

However, the EAT held in *Safeway Stores v Burrell* [1997] IRLR 200 that neither the contract nor the function test should be applied. Judge Peter Clark held that the test to establish whether or not a redundancy situation existed under s 139(1)(b) should be a three-stage process:

(1)   Was the employee dismissed? If so,

(2)   Had the requirements of the employer's business for employees to carry out work of a particular kind ceased or diminished, or were they expected to cease or diminish? If so,

(3)   Was the dismissal of the employee caused wholly or mainly by that state of affairs?

In determining at stage (2) whether there was a true redundancy situation, the only question to be asked is whether there was a diminution/cessation in the employer's requirements for *employees* (not the applicant) to carry out work of a particular kind, or an expectation of such a diminution/cessation in the future. The terms of the applicant's contract are irrelevant to that question.

The House of Lords confirmed in *Murray and Another v Foyle Meats Ltd* [1999] IRLR 562 that neither the contract nor the function test is determinative of the matter.

Their Lordships approved the reasoning and conclusion of Judge Peter Clark in the *Safeway* case above (see stages (2) and (3) in *Safeway* above). Lord Irvine held that the definition of redundancy in s 139(1)(b):

> is ... simplicity itself [and] asks two questions of fact. The first is ... whether the requirements of the business for employees to carry out work of a particular kind have diminished. The second ... is whether the dismissal is *attributable*, wholly or mainly to that state of affairs. This is a question of causation. (emphasis added)

Thus, the dismissal of an employee may be attributable to a diminution in the employer's need for employees, irrespective of the terms of the contract or the function which the employee performed. The causal connection between the need for fewer employees to carry out work of a particular kind and the dismissal of the employee is a matter of fact, not law. Clearly at stage (3), contractual terms which allow the employer to move the employee from one job to another (flexibility clauses) may be a relevant fact to take into account. If an employee is asked, for example, to move to another job (under his contractual terms) and refuses, then the dismissal may be due to the employee's misconduct rather than the underlying redundancy situation.

As commentators have pointed out (see Rubenstein [1997] IRLR 197, [1999] IRLR 505), the weakness of the approach in *Safeway* and *Murray* is that no weight is given to the words 'work of a particular kind'. However, the commentator considers that this is also the strength of the House of Lords decision. By directing the focus on causation, a dismissal will now be by reason of redundancy if it is attributable to the business's diminished need for employees to do work of a particular kind. In *Martland and Others v Cooperative Insurance Society and Others* (UKEAT/0220/07 and 0221/07), the EAT held that the words 'work of a particular kind' referred to the generic type of job, not the specific terms and conditions, so where financial advisers were dismissed and immediately offered re-engagement on new terms and conditions, the dismissals were not for redundancy but for some other substantial reason. The job was essentially the same, albeit that time spent selling was to increase by 50% and commission paid was to be reduced.

In *Shawkat v Nottingham City Council NHS Trust (No 2)* [2001] IRLR 555, the Court of Appeal held that the tribunal was entitled to find that dismissal of a thoracic surgeon, following a re-organisation as a result of which he was asked to carry out cardiac surgery in addition to thoracic surgery, was not by reason of redundancy. The requirements for employees to carry out thoracic surgery had not diminished even though a re-organisation changed the work which the employees in the thoracic department, including the applicant, were required to carry out.

It is clear, then, that not all re-organisations will amount to redundancies. The restructuring must, to fall within the statutory definition, entail a reduction in the number of employees required to work of a particular kind. If, for example, the employer dismisses employees and replaces them with less well-paid employees, that will not amount to a redundancy situation.

The EAT also considered the three-stage test in *Hachette Filipacchi UK Ltd v Johnson* (UKEAT/0452/05). The employee had moved to a new position within the company as a project director, 'revitalising' a magazine published by the company. Her old job was filled. Subsequently, the company decided to end production of the magazine in question and the employee was dismissed. The EAT agreed with the employment tribunal that she had been dismissed by reason of redundancy applying the three-stage test: she had been dismissed; the employer's requirements for a project director had ceased; and her dismissal had been caused wholly or mainly by that state of affairs.

4.2.3.3 'Bumping'

'Bumping' occurs where employee A's job disappears. However, employee A is moved to do employee B's job and it is B who is dismissed. In *W Gimber & Sons Ltd v Spurrett* (1967) 2 ITR

308, it was held that the dismissal of B was by reason of redundancy within what is now s 139(1)(b) of the ERA 1996. Work of 'a particular kind', ie A's work, has ceased.

In *Church v West Lancashire NHS Trust* [1998] IRLR 4, the EAT decided it was not bound by *Gimber v Spurrett* and held that dismissal of a 'bumped' employee was not by reason of redundancy. The EAT held that 'work of a particular kind' within ERA 1996, s 139(1)(b) meant work of a particular kind that the *dismissed* employee was employed to do. However, the EAT stated in *Safeway Stores v Burrell* [1997] IRLR 200 that bumping dismissals may be dismissals by reason of redundancy, and the House of Lords confirmed in *Murray and Another v Foyle Meats Ltd* [1999] IRLR 562 that the wording of s 139(1)(b) can include 'bumping' redundancies. Thus, although the House of Lords did not expressly overrule *Church*, it should not be followed in future 'bumping' cases.

4.3 PRESUMPTION OF REDUNDANCY

In many cases there will be no dispute as to whether or not the employee is redundant. However, if the employer will not accept the claim and the employee refers the matter to an employment tribunal, there is a presumption that the dismissal was by reason of redundancy (ERA 1996, s 163(2)). The presumption applies only in the case of a claim for a redundancy payment and may be rebutted by the employer showing that the reason for the dismissal was not redundancy but was for another reason, such as misconduct.

4.4 OFFERS OF RE-EMPLOYMENT

A redundancy payment is intended to compensate the employee for loss of his job with that employer. Therefore, if the employee is re-employed by his employer, or by an associated employer, he does not need compensation and may not be entitled to a redundancy payment.

Section 141 of the ERA 1996 therefore provides that, if the employee is offered a job, he may lose his entitlement to a redundancy payment.

4.4.1 Offers to renew or re-engage

An offer to renew is the offer of the employee's old job back where, for example, the employer secures a new customer and finds that work is beginning to increase again.

An offer of re-engagement involves an offer of a different job with the same or an associated employer.

Even if dismissed by reason of redundancy, an employee will lose his entitlement to a redundancy payment if he unreasonably refuses an offer of suitable alternative employment made in accordance with the provisions of s 141 of the ERA 1996.

4.4.1.1 The offer

By s 141(2)–(4) of the ERA 1996, an employee is not entitled to a redundancy payment if he unreasonably refuses an offer, whether oral or written:

(a)   made by his employer or an associated employer; and
(b)   made before the contract of employment comes to an end;
(c)   to re-employ him in the same or some other suitable employment;
(d)   provided that the renewal or re-engagement is to take effect within four weeks of the end of the original contract.

The employer's offer must comply with all the above requirements, otherwise the employee will be entitled to a redundancy payment, even if he unreasonably refuses it.

4.4.1.2 Acceptance of the offer

If the employee accepts an offer made in accordance with the provisions set out above, the employee is treated as though he had not been dismissed. Thus his continuity of employment is not broken but, as there is deemed to have been no dismissal, there is no entitlement to a redundancy payment. This will be the case whether or not the alternative employment was 'suitable'.

4.4.1.3 Rejection of the offer

If the employee rejects the offer then the question of whether or not he is entitled to a redundancy payment turns on two issues:

(a)   suitability of the alternative offered; and

(b)   the reasonableness of the employee's refusal.

If the alternative offered was unsuitable, the employee will be entitled to a redundancy payment without more analysis. However, if the alternative is suitable, then the second issue must be considered. If the employee has unreasonably refused suitable alternative employment, the right to the redundancy payment is lost.

(a)   The alternative employment has to be suitable for the particular employee and is ultimately a question for the employment tribunal to decide using an objective test. The key factors are pay, nature of duties, status, hours and place. The question is whether the new job is substantially equivalent to the old job. In *Commission for Healthcare Audit and Inspection v Ward* (UKEAT/0579/07), the EAT held that a tribunal is entitled to have regard to the degree of suitability of a job when deciding if a refusal is reasonable. So, if a new job offer is overwhelmingly suitable, it may be easier for the employer to show that a refusal was unreasonable than if suitability is less obvious.

(b)   When looking at the reasonableness of a refusal, a subjective test is used, taking into account personal circumstances, for example domestic circumstances.

Even if a job is deemed suitable, a particular employee may still be reasonable to refuse it. See, for example, *Redman v Devon Primary Care Trust* (UKEAT/0116/2011), where a community nurse was reasonable in refusing a job in a hospital, even though it was a suitable alternative job, because she did not wish to return to hospital nursing. (The case is being appealed to the Court of Appeal. The EAT's decision is, in the authors' view, correct.)

4.4.1.4 Trial period

It may be difficult for the employee to decide whether or not the alternative employment offered is suitable. The employer may also have doubts as to the employee's suitability for the new job. To assist both parties to decide whether the new employment is suitable, s 138 of the ERA 1996 provides that there may be a 'trial period' of four weeks (calendar weeks), beginning with the date on which the employee starts work under the new contract.

In *Optical Express Ltd v Williams* [2007] IRLR 936, the claimant was a manager in charge of a dental clinic. The dental clinic closed and a redundancy situation arose. The claimant was offered an alternative position as manager of an optical store. Whilst she did not consider the post suitable, she accepted a four-week trial period, in accordance with the provisions of s 138 of the ERA 1996. The claimant gave notice to terminate the contract two weeks after the four-week trial period had expired. An employment tribunal upheld her claim for a redundancy payment and stated she had a 'common law' reasonable period in addition to the statutory trial period because this was a constructive dismissal case (her employers were in breach of the implied term of trust and confidence by imposing on her a new contract which was clearly unsuitable). The EAT allowed the appeal and held that where there is an offer and acceptance of a new contract of employment by reference to the four-week trial period in s 138, the claimant could not claim a redundancy payment unless within the trial period she exercised the rights given by s 138 to terminate the contract. It is now clear that where an acceptance of alternative employment is made under the statutory trial period scheme, the employee must give notice of termination within the 4-week statutory trial period in order to receive a redundancy payment.

If either the employer or the employee terminates the contract during the statutory trial period for a reason connected with the change, the original dismissal by reason of redundancy will revive. Whether or not the employee is then entitled to a redundancy payment still turns on whether the alternative employment offered was suitable. However, there will now be evidence available from the trial period.

(a)   There is no 'trial period' if there is no change in the terms of employment, ie if the only change is in the identity of the employer.

(b)   If the new employment involves retraining, the parties may agree, before the employee starts work under the new contract, to extend the trial period. The agreement must specify the date on which the extended period ends.

4.5 CHANGE OF EMPLOYER

4.5.1 Death, etc, of employer

Exceptionally, by s 136(5) of the ERA 1996, where any act by or affecting an employer terminates the contract of employment by operation of law, such termination takes effect as termination by the employer. The effect of this is that if a business closes down by virtue of the death of the employer or dissolution of a partnership then, although at common law the contract may be frustrated, it will be treated as a dismissal for the purposes of redundancy payments. Thus, an eligible employee will, if the business ceases or his job comes to an end, be entitled to a redundancy payment.

This provision may not apply if the employee continues in his job. If he is employed by the personal representatives on the death of an employer, or if there is effectively only a change in partners despite a dissolution of the partnership, the employee will not be dismissed and there will be continuity of employment (see **3.5.5**).

4.5.2 Associated employer

If an employee is re-employed by an associated employer, this will be a re-engagement within **4.4.1**. See **3.5.5** for the definition of associated employer.

4.5.3 Transfer of undertakings

A business closure should be distinguished from a transfer of the business to a new employer. In the latter situation the employees will usually be transferred to the new employer without being dismissed, so the employee will not be entitled to a redundancy payment. This is by virtue of the Transfer of Undertakings (Protection of Employment) Regulations 2006 (see **Chapter 7**).

4.6 COMPUTATION OF THE STATUTORY REDUNDANCY PAYMENT

A redundancy payment is computed by applying a formula based on an age factor, length of service and a 'week's pay' (ERA 1996, s 162). It is not based on loss suffered.

(a)   Working *back* from the date of termination of employment, the employee is entitled to:
   (i)   one-and-a-half weeks' *gross* pay for each complete year of continuous employment in which the employee was 41 or over;
   (ii)   one week's *gross* pay for each earlier year in which the employee was 22 or over (but under 41);
   (iii) half a week's *gross* pay for each earlier year.

(b)   The total number of years to be taken into account is subject to a maximum of 20.

(c)   A 'week's pay' is calculated in accordance with ERA 1996, s 221. In the majority of cases where there is a normal weekly wage, a week's pay would be the *gross* basic pay to which the employee was entitled in the week ending with the dismissal, subject to a statutory maximum of £430 (at February 2012).

EXAMPLE 1

Doris is aged 63 when dismissed in November 2012 by reason of redundancy. Her normal retiring age is 65. She has been continuously employed for 35 years and her gross basic week's pay in her last week was £450.

Her redundancy payment will be:

1½ × 20 (years) × £430 = £12,900.

This is the maximum possible redundancy payment.

The number of years is 20, not 35, as this is the maximum.

The age factor is 1½ as all years that count are aged 41 or over – taking the most 'valuable' year first, ie working back from the date of dismissal.

The 'week's pay' is the maximum of £430, not the £450 actually earned.

EXAMPLE 2

Ron is aged 43 when dismissed by reason of redundancy in November 2012. He has been continuously employed for just over 6 years and his gross basic week's pay in his last week was £580.

His redundancy payment will be:

1½ × 2 years × £430 (= £1,900) (ie for ages 42 and 41)

plus 1 × 4 years × £430 (= £1,720) (ie for ages 40, 39, 38, 37) giving a total of £3,010.

The age factor is 1½ for the 2 complete years worked after the 41st birthday and 1 for the other 4 years.

EXAMPLE 3

Jack is aged 24 when dismissed by reason of redundancy in November 2012. He has been continually employed for 8 years and his gross basic week's pay in his last week was £200.

His redundancy payment will be:

1 × 2 × £200 (= £400) (ie for ages 23 and 22)

½ × 6 × £200 (= £600) (ie for ages 21, 20, 19, 18, 17, 16)

giving a total of £1,000.

The age factor is 1 for 2 complete years worked after the 22nd birthday and ½ for the 6 years between 18 and 21.

Note: The Business Link website (www.businesslink.gov.uk) features an interactive redundancy payment calculator. Select Employment and Skills; Redundancy and Dismissal; Calculate the statutory redundancy pay due to your employee.

4.7 ENFORCEMENT

4.7.1 Employer's liability

The person primarily liable to pay a redundancy payment is the employer. In the majority of cases the employer will simply make the payment without dispute. When the employer makes a statutory redundancy payment, he must give the employee a written statement of how the amount has been calculated (ERA 1996, s 165). The employee can then check its accuracy.

4.7.2 Reference to employment tribunal

If the employer fails to make a payment or there is a dispute about the amount, the employee may refer the matter to an employment tribunal. There is a time limit which must be observed.

By s 164 of the ERA 1996, an employee is not entitled to a redundancy payment unless, within six months of the dismissal:

(a)   a payment is agreed and made; or

(b)   he has given the employer written notice of the claim; or

(c)   a question as to the right to, or amount of, the payment has been referred to an employment tribunal; or

(d)   a complaint of unfair dismissal has been presented to the employment tribunal.

An employment tribunal may, if it considers it just and equitable that the employee should receive a redundancy payment, extend the time-limit to 12 months from dismissal, but employees should regard the six months' time-limit as strict.

It is not necessary to refer the matter to an employment tribunal within six months of dismissal, provided written notice of the claim has been given to the employer within that time.

4.7.3 Employer's insolvency

Where an employee is entitled to a statutory redundancy payment from his employer, but the employer is declared legally insolvent and the redundancy payment remains unpaid, the employee may apply for payment out of the National Insurance Fund to the Redundancy Payment Office (RPO) using Form RP1 (available at www.insolvency.gov.uk). The RPO, if satisfied that the employee is entitled to the payment, will make the payment out of the Fund (ERA 1996, s 166). The RPO then has a statutory right to recover the amount of the payment from the employer. The employee must have claimed the payment from his employer within the relevant time-limit (see **4.7.2**).

4.8 CONSULTATION

4.8.1 Duty to consult representatives

4.8.1.1 The duty to consult under TULR(C)A 1992, s 188

What follows is a very brief introduction to the collective provisions.

Where an employer is proposing to dismiss as redundant 20 or more employees at one establishment within a period of 90 days or less, he should consult the 'appropriate representatives' of any employees who may be affected by the proposed dismissals or measures taken in connection with the dismissals, unless there are special circumstances that mean it is not reasonably practicable to consult (see *GMB and Amicus v Beloit Walmsley Ltd (in administration)* [2004] IRLR 18) (TULR(C)A 1992, s 188, as amended). In *Hardy v Tourism South East* [2005] IRLR 242, the EAT confirmed that the s 188 duty to consult applies even when the employer intends to offer alternative employment to the majority of employees, thereby bringing the number actively dismissed below 20. The employer must also inform the Secretary of State. Failure to do so is a criminal offence.

Redundancy has a different meaning, for the purposes of this consultation exercise, from the s 139 definition set out in **4.2** above. Here, redundancy is defined as a 'dismissal for a reason not related to the individual concerned or for a number of reasons all of which are not so related'. This definition will also, therefore, include a reorganisation where an employer gives notice to end existing terms and offer new terms of employment, and is therefore wider than the s 139 definition.

Consultation must begin in good time. In particular, if 100 or more employees are to be dismissed at one establishment within a 90-day period, the employer must consult at least 90 days before the first dismissal is to take effect; otherwise he must consult at least 30 days before the first dismissal takes effect. Employers should ensure that the consultation period has ended before giving notice of dismissal to those employees who are to be dismissed by reason of redundancy (see *Junk v Kuhnel* [2005] IRLR 310 and *Leicestershire County Council v Unison* [2005] IRLR 920). Even if there are good reasons for shortening the 30-day consultation period, the obligation to consult remains (see *Shanahan Engineering v Unite* (UKEAT/0411/09)).

The obligation to consult includes consulting about ways of avoiding dismissals, reducing the numbers of employees to be dismissed and mitigating the consequences of those dismissals. In *UK Coal Mining Ltd v National Union of Mineworkers (Northumberland Area)* (UKEAT/0397/06), the EAT held that the duty to consult includes consultation over the business reason(s) for a closure. The decision overturned 15 years of established authority. The Court of Appeal referred the matter to the ECJ in *USA v Nolan* [2010] EWCA Civ 1223. The ECJ held (*USA v Nolan* (Case C-583/10)) that it had no jurisdiction to respond to the reference because the Collective Redundancies Directive (98/59/EC) excludes employees of public administrative bodies. In the meantime, employers would be advised to follow *UK Coal Mining*.

Employers who recognise a trade union *must* consult with representatives of that trade union; they cannot choose to consult with elected employee representatives. If there is no recognised trade union, the employer must arrange for employee representatives to be elected and *must* consult with them.

The employer must disclose the reasons for the redundancies, numbers and descriptions of the employees to be made redundant and the method of selection. The consultation must consider the possibility of avoiding or reducing the redundancies and mitigating their effects.

In *GMB and AEEU v Campbells UK Ltd* (ET/26787/96), the tribunal held that it was not enough for an employer who was proposing to close a factory simply to consult on how the ensuing redundancies should be handled. The tribunal stated that consultation must include consultation about ways of avoiding dismissals, and this is so even where what is being proposed is a total shutdown (see also *Middlesborough Borough Council v TGWU and Another* [2002] IRLR 332, EAT). The Court of Appeal stated in *Susie Radin Ltd v GMB and Others* [2004] IRLR 400 that the obligation set out in s 188 placed an 'absolute obligation on the employer to consult, and to consult meaningfully'.

The Government launched a consultation on proposed changes to the rules in June 2012. The closing date for responses was 19 September 2012 (see **4.8.5** below).

4.8.1.2 Protective award

If the employer fails to consult in accordance with the TULR(C)A 1992 provisions, the trade union, elected employee representatives or affected employees may present a complaint to an employment tribunal. If the complaint is well founded, the tribunal must make a declaration to that effect and may make a 'protective award' of wages per employee for such 'protected period' as the tribunal considers just and equitable. A protective award is an award of pay to the employees affected by the failure to consult properly.

The maximum 'protected period' is 90 days. In *TGWU v Morgan Platts Ltd* (UKEAT/0646/02) the EAT ruled that the starting point for tribunals in calculating protective awards should be the maximum period. From there the tribunal should then consider whether there are reasons for reducing the amount. On the facts of the case there were not, as the company had failed to consult at all. Once a protective award is made, relevant employees are entitled to one week's gross pay for each week of the 'protected period'. The award is not capped.

For many years the courts treated protective awards as compensatory in nature (see, for example, *Spillers-French (Holdings) Ltd v USDAW* [1980] ICR 31), but in *Susie Radin Ltd v GMB* [2004] IRLR 400 the Court of Appeal held that the purpose of the protective award was to punish the employer and should act as an effective sanction and deterrent. The Court held that the starting point is the maximum 90 days, which should be reduced only where there are mitigating circumstances.

In *Amicus v GBS Tooling Ltd* [2005] IRLR 683, the EAT agreed that the tribunal was entitled to take into account the fact that the employer had kept employees informed up to the point that the redundancy proposals were formulated. The EAT therefore upheld the tribunal's decision to award 70 days' pay, rather than 90. (See too *Evans v Permacell Finesse* (UKEAT/0350/07).)

In *Lancaster University v UCU* (UKEAT/0278/10), the EAT upheld an award of 60 days' pay where the tribunal had accepted as mitigation the fact that the union had, for a number of years, condoned the employer's practice so far as consultation was concerned.

In *Independent Insurance Co Ltd v Aspinall and Others* (UKEAT/0051/11) there was no recognised union and no employee representative. The employment tribunal upheld a complaint by the individuals who complained, but also extended this to a further 350 employees who had not brought a claim or who had their claims settled or dismissed. The employment tribunal rejected a submission that it only had jurisdiction to make an award in respect of a person who complained. The EAT overturned that decision – which it said would produce an 'absurd result'.

It is a defence to a claim for a protective award for the employer to show that '... there [were] special circumstances which render[ed] it not reasonably practicable for the employer to comply with [the duty to consult]' (TULR(C)A 1992, s 188(7)). In *Clarks of Hove Ltd v The Bakers' Union* [1978] IRLR 366, the Court of Appeal held that 'special circumstances' had to be something out of the ordinary and uncommon, such as a sudden disaster.

4.8.2   Information and Consultation Regulations 2004

Directive 2002/14 gives employees in the covered undertakings a right to be informed about the undertaking's economic situation, informed and consulted about employment prospects, and informed and consulted with a view to reaching agreement about decisions likely to lead to substantial changes in work organisation or contractual relations, including, but not limited to, collective redundancies and transfers (see **Chapter 7**).

The Information and Consultation of Employees Regulations 2004 (SI 2004/3426) (ICE Regulations) apply to undertakings employing 50 or more employees. They require employers to set up information and consultation arrangements to ensure that employees are consulted on a wide range of matters. However, the obligations are triggered only on a valid request from at least 10% of employees.

The detail of the ICE Regulations is beyond the scope of this book, but note that where there is an overlap between the duty under the ICE Regulations and the duty to consult under s 188 (**4.8.1.1** above), the ICE obligations cease to apply once the employer informs the representatives in writing that he will comply with his s 188 duty. BIS has produced a guide for explaining the requirements to inform and consult employees, which is available on its website.

The EAT is empowered to award penalties of up to £75,000 for breaches of the ICE Regulations. In *Amicus v Macmillan Publishers Limited* (UKEAT/0185/07), Macmillan were fined £55,000 for failing to comply with the Regulations. This is the first penalty so awarded. The EAT took into account the following factors in imposing the penalty:

(a)   the fact that the legislation had clearly been ignored;

(b)   Macmillan had committed other breaches of the legislation, including a failure to provide information;

(c)   Macmillan had unacceptably 'dragged its feet' in dealing with the employee request;

(d)   Macmillan had not adequately explained its failure to comply.

The EAT concluded that a penalty of £55,000 was appropriate as it would deter other employers from adopting a similarly 'cavalier' attitude to their obligations, but the breach in this case was not sufficiently grave to warrant the maximum penalty. The EAT in its decision commented that employers must recognise the importance of the rights under the ICE Regulations and that the provisions must be complied with.

See also Chapter 7, at **7.7**, which deals with the (similar but not identical) collective consultation requirements under the 2006 TUPE Regulations.

4.8.3 Duty to notify Secretary of State

Where 20 or more redundancies are proposed there is a duty to notify the Secretary of State of the proposals. Notification is made on form HR1 (available at www.insolvency.gov.uk).

4.8.4 Unfair dismissal

Failure to consult with individual employees about proposed redundancies can render the dismissals unfair (see **5.4.2.3**). Redundant employees in such circumstances may be able to bring claims for a redundancy payment and unfair dismissal.

4.8.5 Proposed changes

The Government has proposed making changes to the rules on collective redundancy consultation. Its proposals include:

(a) issuing a new, non-statutory code of practice on how to conduct consultations;

(b) reducing the minimum consultation period for large-scale redundancies (over 100 employees) from 90 days to 45 or 30 days;

(c) improving guidance for employers and employees on the support available from the Government.

The Government has consulted on these proposed changes; the closing date for responses was 19 September 2012.

4.9 CASE STUDY: REDUNDANCY PAYMENT, UNPAID NOTICE AND HOLIDAY PAY

Facts

(1) R was an independent working men's club. It was not for profit and was registered under the Industrial and Provident Societies Act (IPSA) 1965 with the Financial Services Authority. Its members and employees were governed by the rules of the Club. The premises from which the Club operated were leased to the Club under a full maintenance and repairing lease.

(2) C was employed by R as a bar steward/cleaner. She started work with R in September 1994. She continued to work for R until her dismissal on 28 April 2008. Over that period, she worked approximately 40 hours a week every week, apart from when she took holidays. She was paid £6.00 an hour and took home a net weekly wage of £206 (gross £240).

(3) In or about 28 April 2008, C was informed by a member of R's committee that the Club was in severe financial difficulties and was being wound up. The committee member gave C 48 hours' notice. She was paid one week's notice. She was informed that there was no money to pay her any redundancy payment or any other outstanding monies due to her, such as in respect of untaken but accrued holiday. A subsequent letter received by C indicated that there had been mismanagement at R for several years, and that because of the parlous financial state of R, it had been shut down. Rent has not been paid for several months and various suppliers are owed money. The premises are now being advertised for sale. It does not appear that any steps have been taken with regard to liquidating R. All the committee members have resigned.

(4) Under the provisions of the IPSA 1965, Ch 12, s 57, no individual officer, member or servant is personally liable for any of the debts of the Club. The situation therefore

remains somewhat in limbo as far as the legal status of R is concerned. On the face of it, it appears to be insolvent.

(5)   At the time of the termination of her employment, C, who was aged 57 as at the date of her dismissal, had achieved some 13 years' continuous employment. She was disappointed that none of the committee members had expressed any concerns about her situation and appeared to feel no moral responsibility towards her predicament, notwithstanding that they appeared to have been aware of the Club's difficulties for some time.

Claims

(6)   In her ET1, C brings claims of unpaid notice, breach of contact, unpaid wages and unpaid holiday pay. She also seeks a redundancy payment. She did not complain about unfair dismissal.

Evidence

(7)   C appeared before the Employment Judge (sitting alone) and gave evidence. She produced various items of paperwork, including letters from the Insolvency Service relating to her claim. She also had with her the originals of her pay slips. Although a committee member had submitted a brief ET3/Response Form, which said that R had been wound up, no one appeared for R at the hearing.

Issues

(8)   Although C had a long service record with R, she had not included a claim for unfair dismissal in her ET1. This omission was discussed at a Case Management Discussion (CMD). The notes of this recorded that C said she had not realised she could bring such a claim. By the time the CMD took place, it was over four and half months since the termination of C's contract. The Employment Judge found as a preliminary issue that any claim for unfair dismissal would amount to a new claim, that it was not implicit from the matters set out in the ET1, that it was out of time and that there was nothing to suggest that it was not reasonably practicable for the claim to have been made within the time limit, ignorance of the law per se being no defence.

(9)   On that basis, the Tribunal had to determine the following matters:

(a)   Was C an employee of R?

(b)   Was C entitled to a redundancy payment; and if so, to how much?

(c)   Had C been paid her proper notice?

(d)   Had C been paid the holiday pay due on the termination of her employment?

Findings

(10)   On the basis of the evidence before it, the Employment Judge found as follows:

(a)   C was an employee of R. Although she had no written contract, this was not a difficult issue on the facts. C had worked regularly for R for nearly 14 years. There was no issue that she expected to work each week and expected to be paid for her work. She gave evidence about the hours she worked, from whom she took instructions, that the materials she used, for example, to clean were all provided by R, that she had had her PAYE and National Insurance deducted from her wages, and that she had been paid for her holidays. She produced her wage slips to support this.

(b)   C was entitled to a redundancy payment, as the reason for her dismissal was clearly a reason that fell within the definition in s 139 of the ERA 1996, namely, the closure of the business. C had 13 years' completed service at the date of her dismissal; as she was aged 41 and over for the duration of her employment with R, she was entitled to one and a half week's gross pay for each completed year of continuous service (ERA 1996, ss 162 and 221): 13 x 1.5 x 240 = £4,680. R was ordered to pay to C the sum of £4,680 in respect of a redundancy payment.

(c) R was in breach of C's contract of employment by failing to give her proper notice or to pay her due notice entitlement. Although R paid C one week's notice, under s 86 of the ERA 1996, the statutory minimum period of notice required to be given to an employee with 12 years' plus service is 12 weeks' notice. C is therefore entitled to be paid for 11 weeks' notice at her net weekly wage (£206) per week: 11 x £206 = £2,266. R is ordered to pay damages to C in the sum of £2,266 (net).

(d) C's complaint that R had failed to pay holiday pay due on the termination of the employment was well founded. Regulation 14 of the Working Time Regulations allows an employee to be paid in lieu of any accrued but untaken holiday as at the date of dismissal. As at the date of her dismissal, C had 15 days' holiday accrued and due. C is therefore due payment in respect of 15 days' holiday, calculated on the basis of an eight-hour working day and a net weekly wage of £206 (8 hours x £5.15 (net)) = £41.20 per day rate x 15 = £618 (net). R is ordered to pay to C the sum of £618 (net).

Note: Given that R has been wound up/appears to be insolvent, and that there are no apparent assets, C is unlikely to be able to get any money back from R. In this sort of case, C would be able to make a claim from the National Insurance Fund, by completing Form RP1, in respect of any redundancy pay, unpaid wages (up to a maximum of eight weeks), holiday pay (up to a maximum of six weeks), notice pay (one week after one calendar month's service, rising to one week per year of service up to a maximum of 12 weeks, but new earnings will be taken into account), and any basic award for unfair dismissal. To qualify for a redundancy payment, C will need to show that she has been made redundant, has worked continuously for her employer for two years or more, and that she either made a written claim to her employer for her redundancy payment, or made a complaint to an employment tribunal, within six months of her dismissal. She will be able to attach the Tribunal's decision as evidence of these matters. There is a current limit of £430 a week on the amount C can claim for her weekly pay.

4.10 FURTHER READING

Textbooks covering redundancy include:

Selwyn, *Law of Employment*, 17th edn (OUP, 2012).

See also:

Harvey, *Industrial Relations and Employment Law* (Butterworths), Div E.

Lewis, *Employment Law – an adviser's handbook*, 9th edn revised (LAG, 2011).

Blackstone's Employment Law Practice (OUP, 2012).

SUMMARY

This chapter has set out the mechanisms for making a claim for a redundancy payment. A redundancy payment is in the nature of a reward for past services. Where there is a dispute over the right to receive a redundancy payment or over the amount due, an employment tribunal has jurisdiction to determine the matter (**4.3**). Employees must be eligible to bring a claim. They must have at least two years' continuous service and there must also be a dismissal by reason of redundancy (**3.4**).

The definition of 'redundancy' is contained in s 139(1) of the ERA 1996. Redundancy occurs in three main situations: job redundancy (ie where the business closes down – ERA 1996, s 139(1)(a)(i)); place of work redundancy (ie where there is a cessation or reduction in work *at the place* where the employee works – ERA 1996, s 139(1)(a)(ii)); and employee redundancy (ie there is a reduction in the requirement for employees to do work of a particular kind – ERA 1996, s 139(1)(b)) (**4.2**).

An eligible employee, dismissed by reason of redundancy, will be entitled, at a minimum, to a statutory redundancy payment from his employer (ERA 1996, s 163). The contract of employment may provide for more generous payments.

If the employee is offered a suitable alternative job by his employer, which he unreasonably refuses, he may lose his entitlement to a redundancy payment (ERA 1996, s 141). It is possible to have a trial period of four weeks in order to determine whether the job is suitable (ERA 1996, s 138) (**4.4**). If a business is sold as a going concern, so that employees are not dismissed, they may not be entitled to a redundancy payment (see **Chapter 7** on the transfer of undertakings).

A redundancy payment is calculated by applying a formula based on age, length of service and 'a week's pay' (ERA 1996, s 162) (**4.6**).

Where an employee is dismissed by reason of redundancy, this may also give rise to wrongful (**Chapter 3**) and/or unfair dismissal (**Chapter 5**) claims. The right to claim a redundancy payment is a separate right that will arise irrespective of whether the dismissal is unfair.

Under s 188 of the Trade Unions and Labour Relations (Consolidation) Act 1992 Act obligations are imposed on employers to consult appropriate employee representatives (**4.8**).

In summary, in each case, consider the following.

- Is the employee eligible (**3.4**)?
- Has there been a dismissal (**3.4**)?
- Do the circumstances fit the statutory definition of redundancy (**4.2**)?
- Was the dismissal caused by the redundancy situation?
- Has there been a suitable offer of alternative employment (**4.4**)?
- Is the employee reasonable in refusing this (**4.4**)?

A flowchart showing the redundancy payment system is set out at **Figure 4.1** below.

Figure 4.1 Flowchart: Redundancy Payments

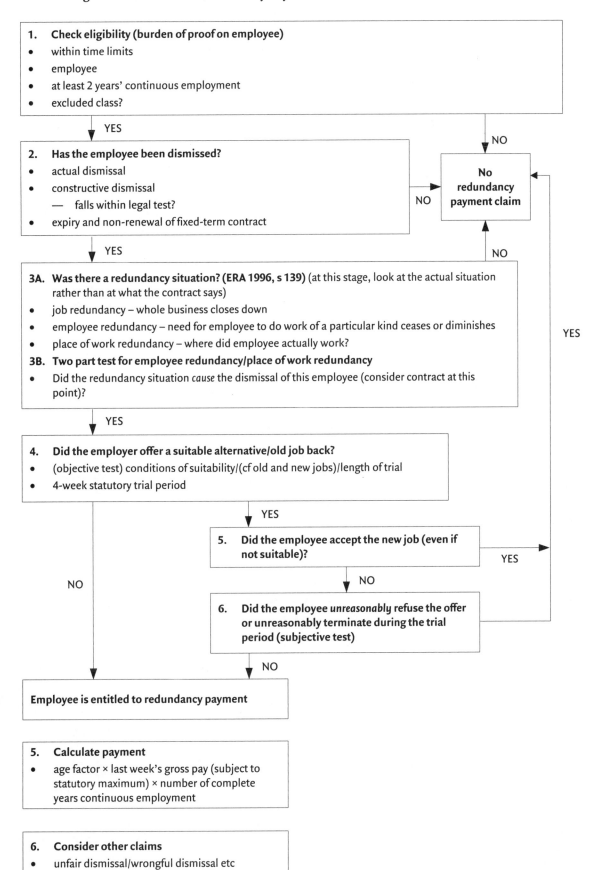

CHAPTER 5

UNFAIR DISMISSAL

LEARNING OUTCOMES

After reading this chapter you will be able to:

- describe the statutory claim of unfair dismissal and how it differs from wrongful dismissal
- list the potentially fair reasons for dismissal set out in ERA 1996, s 98 and understand their ambit
- understand the different procedural steps that should normally be followed before dismissal, depending on the reason for dismissal
- understand the relevance of the Acas Code of Practice on Disciplinary and Grievance Procedures
- understand the significance of BHS v Burchell in a misconduct case
- explain and apply the range of reasonable responses test
- be aware of the relevant maximum for unfair dismissal awards, and understand and be able to apply the relevant principles for calculating damages for unfair dismissal.

5.1 INTRODUCTION

Every eligible employee has the right not to be unfairly dismissed by his employer (ERA 1996, s 94).

At common law, an employer can dismiss any employee whenever he chooses, whether he has any good reason or not. Provided he gives full notice and otherwise complies with the contract, the employee has no remedy. Even where the contract is breached, the award of damages is often relatively small (see **Chapter 2**).

In order to give a measure of protection against dismissal at the whim of the employer, the statutory claim of unfair dismissal introduced the concept of fairness into termination of contracts of employment. The employer must be able to show not only that he had a good reason to dismiss, but also that he acted fairly in, for example, the way in which he handled the dismissal.

5.1.1 Eligible employee

See **Chapter 3** for details of eligibility, but check in particular that the employee has one or two years' continuous employment (ERA 1996, s 108), as relevant. There are exceptions where the dismissal is for a reason relating to, for example, trade union membership, health and safety, or on the grounds of pregnancy. These exceptions are dealt with at **5.5**. In *Moore v The President of the Methodist Conference* (UKEAT/0219/10), the EAT held that ministers can be employees. The decision has been appealed.

5.1.2 Dismissal

The employee must have been dismissed. See **3.4** for the definition of dismissal.

Where an employee intends to rely on s 95(1)(c) of the ERA 1996 – constructive dismissal – rather than on actual dismissal, he should consider using the grievance procedure set out in the Acas Code of Practice on Disciplinary and Grievance Procedures (see **5.4.1** below) before he resigns, or before he submits the ET1. A failure to follow the Code, where it applies, gives tribunals a discretionary power to increase or decrease awards by up to 25%, if they consider that the employer's/employee's failure to comply with the Code was unreasonable.

The Code sets out the process for dealing with grievances, which is as follows:

- Let the employer know the nature of the grievance.
- Hold a meeting with the employee to discuss the grievance.
- Allow the employee to be accompanied at the meeting.
- Decide on appropriate action.
- Allow the employee to take the grievance further if not resolved.
- Overlapping grievance and disciplinary cases: where an employee raises a grievance during a disciplinary process, the disciplinary process may be suspended temporarily in order to deal with the grievance. Where the grievance and disciplinary cases are related, it may be appropriate to deal with both issues concurrently.

To complement the Code, Acas has published guidance. Tribunals cannot adjust awards on account of any failure to follow the guidance, neither are they required to have regard to the guidance.

Where there is an actual dismissal, an employer should also consider the Code (see **5.4.1**). A failure to follow the Code gives tribunals a discretionary power to increase or decrease awards by up to 25% if they consider that the employer's/employee's failure to comply with the Code was unreasonable.

5.1.3 Potentially fair reason for dismissal

The onus is on the employer to show that the dismissal is for one of the five permitted reasons (see **5.2**). If the employer cannot show that the dismissal was for one of these permitted reasons, the dismissal will be unfair.

5.1.4 Fairness

Where the reason for the dismissal falls within one of the five permitted reasons, the tribunal must then go on to decide whether the employer acted reasonably in all the circumstances under ERA 1996, s 98(4) (see **5.3**).

5.1.5 Remedies

Remedies are dealt with at **5.6**.

5.2   REASONS FOR DISMISSAL

The employer must be able to establish that the only or principal reason for the dismissal was a potentially fair reason. The burden of proof is on the employer, but it is not a heavy burden to discharge (see *Kuzel v Roche Products Ltd* [2008] IRLR 530). If he is unable to show that the dismissal was for one of the five permitted reasons, the dismissal will be held to be unfair. This is the case whether there is an actual or a constructive dismissal. Where the employee is basing his claim on a constructive dismissal, the reason for the dismissal given by the employer will be the reason for which the employer allegedly breached the contract.

5.2.1   The five permitted reasons

By s 98(1) and (2) of the ERA 1996, in determining whether a dismissal is fair or unfair, it is for the employer to establish the only or principal reason for the dismissal, and that it is a reason falling within the following:

(a)   relating to the capability or qualifications of the employee to do work of the kind which he was employed to do (s 98(2)(a)); or

(b)   relating to the conduct of the employee (s 98(2)(b)); or

(c)   that the employee was redundant (s 98(2)(c)); or

(d)   that the employee could not continue to work in the position held without contravening some statutory provision (s 98(2)(d)); or

(e)   there was some other substantial reason (SOSR) that could justify the dismissal of an employee holding the position which that employee held (s 98(1)(b)).

The employer should try to ensure that he states the correct reason for dismissal on the ET1 to avoid being at risk of the dismissal being held to be unfair. However, the employment tribunal will seek to discover the real reason for dismissal, and if the employer has made a genuine mistake in how it has labelled the reason, but the factual basis for the dismissal is clear to the employee, the tribunal can ignore an incorrect label. In *Abernethy v Mott, Hay and Anderson* [1974] ICR 323, CA, the employee refused to relocate and was dismissed for redundancy. The tribunal held that the employee was actually fairly dismissed for incapability. The Court of Appeal upheld the fairness of the dismissal, since the facts were clear to the employee at the time of the dismissal and the employer should not be penalised for attaching the wrong legal label.

In *Wilson v Post Office* [2000] IRLR 834, the Court of Appeal confirmed that the characterisation of the reason for a dismissal is a matter of legal analysis, and that since this was not a case in which the employer had tried to change the nature of the case, it was open to the EAT to say that the dismissal was to be characterised as for SOSR when it was originally formulated by the employer in terms of capability. So, where an employer wrongly labels the reason for dismissal, but still seeks to justify the dismissal on factual grounds made clear at the time of dismissal, he will not be bound by the wrong label. (See also *Screene v Seatwave Ltd* (UKEAT/0020/11).)

However, different considerations apply where the employer seeks to change the factual basis of the dismissal. In *Hotson v Wisbech Conservative Club* [1984] ICR 859, the EAT allowed an appeal by Ms Hotson, a club barmaid dismissed for gross inefficiency, because the real reason was suspected dishonesty, which went beyond a mere change of label. The allegation of dishonesty should have been put to the employee at the outset, to allow her to answer it. See too *Screene v Seatwave* (above) (where the EAT said a tribunal was entitled to make its decision on the basis of what it considered to be the real reason for dismissal) and *Perkin v St George's Healthcare NHS Trust* [2005] IRLR 934 (at **5.4.2.5** below).

Thus, provided the factual basis of the employer's argument is adhered to, it should not matter that the wrong reasons are pleaded. However, it would be good practice for an employer to state the reason for dismissal expressly, and, where there is a genuine uncertainty as to which of the reasons apply, state in the alternative. But reasons should not be stated in the alternative unless there is genuine uncertainty, because s 98(1)(a) requires the employer to show the reason or, if more than one, the principal reason.

In *Kuzel v Roche Products Ltd* [2008] IRLR 530, the Court of Appeal confirmed that the burden is on the employer to show the reason for dismissal; but that where the employee asserts there was a different reason, the employee must produce some evidence of that. Where there is such evidence, it will be for the employer to show that the potentially fair reason was, in fact, the principal reason (see also *East Lancs Coachbuilders Ltd v Hilton* (UKEAT/0054/06)). It will then be for the tribunal to consider the evidence and make a finding of fact.

5.2.2 The ambit of the five reasons

This section deals with the ambit or scope of each of the five reasons. If the employer shows the dismissal is for one of these reasons, it has overcome the first hurdle. However, showing the reason does not of itself make the dismissal fair. The employment tribunal still has to decide whether the employer acted reasonably in dismissing the employee for that reason. We shall look at how fairness relates to these reasons in more detail below (see **5.4**).

5.2.2.1 Capability and qualifications

Section 98(2)(a) provides that an employer may fairly dismiss an employee for a reason that 'relates to the capability or qualifications of the employee for performing work of the kind which he was employed by the employer to do'. Capability is defined in s 98(3)(a) as 'capability assessed by reference to skill, aptitude, health or any other physical or mental quality'. There is always the potential for a degree of overlap between conduct and capability.

The incapability or lack of qualification for which the employee is dismissed must relate to the work which the employee was employed to do. Incapability within the provision may be incapability to do the job by virtue of incompetence, or an inherent inability to perform the job. It also extends to the inability of the employee to do his job by reason of illness or injury. Therefore sickness of an employee is a reason which may justify dismissal, even where that illness has been caused by the employer (see **5.4.2.1**).

5.2.2.2 Conduct

The 'conduct' reason may cover misconduct of virtually any nature, but would usually be misconduct within the employment. It would include, for example, disobedience of orders, breach of the duty of fidelity, dishonesty, fighting, sexual harassment, absence without permission, lateness and other breaches of contract or breaches of works rules. To minimise his potential liability for unfair dismissal the employer should have a comprehensive set of disciplinary rules (see **Chapter 1** and the Acas Code of Practice on Disciplinary and Grievance Procedures at **5.4.2.2** below).

Dismissal for misconduct outside employment, such as criminal offences committed elsewhere, will also come within this reason, but for such a dismissal to be fair the outside misconduct must usually have an effect on the employment relationship. For example, if a cashier is charged with a motoring offence, this would have no employment implications. However, a charge of theft clearly could have.

In order for the employer to rely on misconduct to justify a dismissal, the misconduct must have been known to the employer at the time of dismissal. He cannot rely on subsequently discovered misconduct to justify the dismissal (*W Devis & Sons Ltd v Atkins* [1977] AC 931, HL). For example, an employee is dismissed because his employer does not like him. After he leaves, his employer discovers that he has been submitting bogus expense claims. The employer cannot rely on this conduct when giving his reason for the dismissal.

However, note that it is at the point of actual dismissal beyond which after-acquired knowledge cannot be taken into account. The employer is entitled to take into account factors which occur until dismissal, even after notice of termination has been given (*Alboni v Ind Coope Retail Ltd* [1998] IRLR 131, CA), both in determining the reason for the dismissal and whether the employer acted reasonably in the circumstances in treating it as a sufficient reason for dismissal. Note also that after-acquired knowledge may affect the amount of compensation an employee may receive (see **5.6.2**).

5.2.2.3 Redundancy

As we have seen, a dismissal by reason of redundancy may give rise to a claim for a redundancy payment (see **Chapter 4**). However, redundancy is also a potentially fair reason for dismissing an employee. If an employer does not handle a redundancy situation fairly, that can give rise, separately, to an unfair dismissal claim (see **5.4.2.3**). The definition of redundancy has already been dealt with, and the same definition in ERA 1996, s 139 applies here (see **4.2**).

5.2.2.4 Contravention of a statutory provision ('illegality')

Contravention of a statutory provision covers the situation where it becomes illegal by statute either for the employee to work in the position held, or for the employer to employ him in it.

There has long been a common law doctrine of illegality which can defeat claims in contract or tort. The doctrine is rooted in public policy. The underlying principle was identified by Lord Mansfield in *Holman v Johnson* (1775) 1 Cowp 341:

> The objection, that a contract is immoral or illegal as between plaintiff and defendant ... is founded in general principles of policy ... The principle of public policy is this; ex dolo malo non oritur actio. No court will lend its aid to a man who founds his cause of action upon an immoral or an illegal act. If, from the plaintiff's own stating or otherwise, the cause of action appears to arise ex turpi causa, or the transgression of a positive law of this country, there the court says he has no right to be assisted. It is upon that ground the court goes; not for the sake of the defendant, but because they will not lend their aid to such a plaintiff. So if the plaintiff and defendant were to change sides, and the defendant was to bring his action against the plaintiff, the latter would then have the advantage of it; for where both are equally in fault, potior est conditio defendentis.

There are three categories of case where a contract may be tainted with illegality. These were identified by Peter Gibson LJ in *Hall v Woolston Leisure Services Ltd* [2000] IRLR 578 (paras 30–31). The first is where the contract is entered into with the intention of committing an illegal act. The second is where the contract is expressly or impliedly prohibited by statute. The third category is where the contract was lawful when made but has been performed illegally, and the party seeking the assistance of the court knowingly participated in the illegal performance. In the first two types of cases, case law has established that illegality in these situations renders a contract unenforceable from the outset. In the third, illegality may prevent a party from enforcing the contract. In order to fall within the third category, it is traditionally said that there are two requirements:

(a)   knowledge of the illegal performance; and

(b)   participation.

See, for example, *Tomlinson v Dick Evans 'U' Drive Ltd* [1978] IRLR 77 and *Davidson v Pillay* [1979] IRLR 275.

The concept of knowledge requires that the employee must have knowledge of the facts which render the performance illegal. However, it is irrelevant whether the party appreciates that what he is doing is illegal: ignorance of the law is no excuse. In *San Ling Chinese Medicine Centre v Miss Lian Wei Ji* (UKEAT/0370/09) the EAT applied *Hall* and upheld the tribunal's decision that the claimant's contract was not tainted by illegality in circumstances where the claimant's work permit *might* be revoked. There was no illegality unless and until the permit *was* revoked.

In the context of unfair dismissal claims, it is now settled law that if the underlying contract of employment is illegal then it is against public policy to allow the claim to be pursued: *Tomlinson v Dick Evans*, applied in *Davidson v Pillay*, both of which were cited with approval by Peter Gibson LJ in *Hall*. Moreover, the employee cannot count any period during which he was employed under an illegal contract as part of his period of continuous employment for the purpose of obtaining the requisite continuity to pursue a claim: see *Hyland v JH Barker (North West) Ltd* [1985] ICR 861, where continuity was broken by a four-week period during which the employee received a tax-free benefit which both parties knew to be illegal. (See also *Salvesen v Simons* [1994] IRLR 52 and, most recently, *Enfield Technical Services v Payne; Grace v BF Components Ltd* [2008] IRLR 500.)

One of the more common types of dismissal for this reason is the dismissal of the driver of a motor vehicle who is disqualified by a court from driving because of a motoring offence (see, eg, *Appleyard v FM Smith (Hull) Ltd* [1972] IRLR 19). Another common situation that arises is where employers fail to pay an employee's tax and/or National Insurance (see for example *Newland v Simons & Willer (Hairdressers) Ltd* [1981] IRLR 359, *Hewcastle Catering Ltd v Ahmed* [1991] IRLR 473 and *Salvesen v Simons* [1994] IRLR 52).

Another area is the employment of someone who is in the UK illegally, or who does not have permission to work. For all employees employed on or after 29 February 2008, an employer must undertake required checks before an individual commences working. Employers are also required to check at least once every 12 months in relation to employees who have a form of immigration clearance which has an expiry date. An employer is *not* exempt from carrying out checks on employees acquired as a result of a transfer under the Transfer of Undertakings (Protection of Employment) Regulations 2006 (SI 2006/246) (see **1.2.6** and **Chapter 7**).

Employers who are found to have employed someone illegally may be fined up to £10,000 per individual illegal worker. For knowingly employing an illegal worker, the sanctions are up to two years' imprisonment and unlimited fines. (See *Kelly v University of Southampton* (UKEAT/ 0295/07) for a discussion.)

5.2.2.5   Some other substantial reason

Some other substantial reason is not limited by the four reasons above. The employer may show any substantial reason outside the four above as the reason for the dismissal of an employee holding the position held, but the onus of proof is on the employer to show that it is a substantial reason that could justify the dismissal. Provided the reason is not 'whimsical, unworthy or trivial', it will suffice. In *Scott and Co v Richardson* (UKEAT/0074/04), Mr Scott carried out debt recovery services and decided to introduce shift work. Mr Richardson refused to accept the proposed change to his contract of employment on the basis that he should continue to be paid overtime for working in the evening. He was dismissed. The EAT held that what the employer had to demonstrate to the tribunal was that it reasonably believed/ concluded that the reorganisation of working hours had advantages – it was not necessary to go beyond that to see whether it did have those advantages. In this case there was a commercial reason for carrying out the reorganisation, and the EAT said the tribunal was bound to find that the employer had shown that the reason for dismissal was for some other substantial reason.

It is not possible to give a comprehensive list of other reasons which may justify dismissal, but reasons which have been held to be a potentially fair reason for dismissal include refusal to accept a reorganisation affecting working hours (*Muggeridge and Slade v East Anglia Plastics Ltd* [1973] IRLR 163 and *Scott and Co v Richardson* (UKEAT/0074/04)), replacement by a better qualified employee (*Priddle v Dibble* [1978] 1 All ER 1058), end of genuine temporary employment (*Terry v East Sussex County Council* [1977] 1 All ER 567), dismissal because of a clash of personalities between employees (*Gorfin v Distressed Gentlefolk's Aid Association* [1973] IRLR 290; see also *Perkin v St George's Healthcare NHS Trust* [2005] EWCA Civ 1174), marriage of an employee to a competitor, where there was a real risk of a leak of trade secrets (*Foot v Eastern Counties Timber Co Ltd* [1972] IRLR 83), refusal of employees to accept a new restraint of trade clause in their contracts (even if the clause was unreasonable) (*Willow Oak Developments Ltd t/a Windsor Recruitment v Silverwood & Others* [2006] IRLR 607) and loss of trust and confidence in the employee, in exceptional cases (*Ezsias v North Glamorgan NHS Trust* [2011] IRLR 550 and *Governing Body of Tubbenden Primary School v Sylvester* (UKEAT/0527/11)).

5.2.3 Statement of reasons for dismissal

An employee who has been continuously employed for at least two years (or one year if employed by the employer before 6 April 2012) is entitled to request that he be provided by his employer, within 14 days of the request, with a written statement of the reason for his dismissal (ERA 1996, s 92). The statement is admissible in evidence in any proceedings. If a woman is dismissed while pregnant or during her maternity leave period, she is entitled, without prior request, to a written statement (see **14.9.2**).

If the employer unreasonably fails to comply with the request or the particulars given are inadequate or untrue, the employee may present a complaint to an employment tribunal. The time-limit to present the complaint is the same as that for a complaint of unfair dismissal (see **6.3.1**), generally three months from the EDT (see **3.5**). If the complaint is well founded, the tribunal must order the employer to pay the employee two weeks' pay (gross) (ERA 1996, s 93). There is no upper limit on a week's pay for this purpose (ERA 1996, s 227).

5.3 FAIRNESS OF DISMISSAL

For all the permitted reasons, once the employer has shown that the dismissal was for a permitted reason, the tribunal must then decide whether the employer has acted reasonably within s 98(4) of the ERA 1996.

In practice, it is usually relatively easy for the employer to show the reason for the dismissal. Persuading the tribunal that he has acted reasonably on the evidence presented may be more difficult.

By s 98(4) of the ERA 1996, the tribunal must decide whether the dismissal was fair or unfair, having regard to the reason shown by the employer, *and* whether, in the circumstances (including the size and administrative resources of the employer's undertaking), the employer acted reasonably or unreasonably in treating that reason as a sufficient reason for dismissing the employee; *and* that question shall be determined in accordance with equity and the substantial merits of the case.

5.3.1 ERA 1996, s 98(4): general

Each case will turn on its own facts, but there are a number of principles which the tribunal must follow in determining reasonableness.

5.3.1.1 Has the employer acted reasonably?

In *Iceland Frozen Foods Ltd v Jones* [1982] IRLR 439, the EAT summarised the correct approach for the tribunal to adopt in answering the question posed by s 98(4) of the ERA 1996:

(a)   the starting point should always be the words of s 98(4) themselves;

(b)   in applying the section an employment tribunal must consider the reasonableness of the employer's conduct, not simply whether they (the members of the employment tribunal) consider the dismissal to be fair;

(c)   in judging the reasonableness of the employer's conduct an employment tribunal must not substitute its decision as to what is the right course to adopt for that of the employer;

(d)   in many (though not all) cases there is a band of reasonable responses to the employee's conduct within which one employer might reasonably take one view, another quite reasonably take another;

(e)   the function of the employment tribunal, as an industrial jury, is to determine whether in the particular circumstances of each case the decision to dismiss the employee fell within the band of reasonable responses which a reasonable employer might have adopted. If the dismissal falls within the band, the dismissal is fair: if the dismissal falls outside the band, it is unfair.

The question for the tribunal to determine, therefore, is whether the respondent's decision to dismiss the employee fell within the band (or range) of reasonable responses of a reasonable employer. It is sufficient that a reasonable employer would regard the circumstances as a sufficient reason for dismissing – it is not necessary that all reasonable employers would dismiss in those circumstances. However, the tribunal should be careful to not substitute its own view for what the employer should have done, for this would be an error in law which is appealable. Provided that the tribunal does not fall into this error, almost any decision may be justified, because it is for the tribunal to determine what a reasonable employer could or should have done. In *London Ambulance Service NHS Trust v Small* [2009] IRLR 563 the Court of Appeal held that the tribunal substituted its view of the facts for that of the employer. It is useful to quote from the judgment:

41.   The ET ought to have confined its consideration to facts relating to the Trust's handling of Mr Small's dismissal: the genuineness of the Trust's belief and the reasonableness of the grounds of its belief about the conduct of Mr Small at the time of the dismissal. Instead, the ET introduced its own findings of fact about the conduct of Mr Small, including aspects of it that had been disputed at the disciplinary hearing. For example, the ET found that the daughter, who did not give evidence to the ET, had not told Mr Small that her mother was hypertensive and diabetic. Further, on the point whether Mr Small had done a risk assessment before asking the patient to walk, the ET held that there was no evidence that he had failed to carry out a risk assessment, but Mr Suter gave evidence to the ET that the crucial issue before the disciplinary panel was that Mr Small had not carried out a proper patient assessment, before the decision was made.

42.   The ET used its findings of fact to support its conclusion that, at the time of dismissal, the Trust had no reasonable grounds for its belief about Mr Small's conduct and therefore no genuine belief about it. By this process of reasoning the ET found that the dismissal was unfair. In my judgment, this amounted to the ET substituting itself and its findings for the Trust's decision-maker in relation to Mr Small's dismissal.

43.   It is all too easy, even for an experienced ET, to slip into the substitution mindset. In conduct cases the claimant often comes to the ET with more evidence and with an understandable determination to clear his name and to prove to the ET that he is innocent of the charges made against him by his employer. He has lost his job in circumstances that may make it difficult for him to get another job. He may well gain the sympathy of the ET so that it is carried along the acquittal route and away from the real question – whether the employer acted fairly and reasonably in all the circumstances at the time of the dismissal.

For another example of the tribunal wrongly slipping into the substitution mindset, see *Suffolk Mental Health Partnership NHS Trust v Crawford and Another* (UKEAT/0338/10). See *Fuller v The London Borough of Brent* [2011] EWCA Civ 267 for a decision of the Court of Appeal finding that there was no error of law and that a reasonable employment tribunal could find that dismissal was outside the range of reasonable responses.

The approach set out in *Iceland* was re-stated by the Court of Appeal in the joined cases *HSBC (formerly Midland Bank) v Madden; Post Office v Foley* [2000] IRLR 827, CA, and in *London Ambulance Service NHS Trust v Small* [2009] EWCA Civ 220. In *Sarkar v West London Mental Health NHS Trust* [2010] IRLR 508 and *Salford Royal NHS Foundation Trust v Roldan* [2010] IRLR 721, the Court of Appeal appeared to endorse a more interventionist approach by employment tribunals when applying the range of reasonable responses test. In *Roldan*, the Court of Appeal said that the tribunal had been entitled to find that the dismissal was unfair, given the conflict in evidence which meant that the Trust should have investigated the issues in more depth. In *North West London Hospital NHS Trust v Bowater* [2011] EWCA Civ 63, the Court of Appeal upheld an employment tribunal's decision that the decision to dismiss could not possibly be within the band of reasonable responses. The employee had made a lewd comment, but one that 'a large proportion of the population would consider ... to be merely humorous'. The Court said (at [26]):

> It is important that, in cases of this kind, the EAT pays proper respect to the decision of the ET. It is the ET to whom Parliament has entrusted the responsibility of making what are, no doubt sometimes, difficult and borderline decisions in relation to the fairness of dismissal. An appeal to the EAT only lies on a point of law and it goes without saying that the EAT must not, under the guise of a charge of perversity, substitute its own judgment for that of the ET.

In *Graham v The Secretary of State for Work & Pensions (Jobcentre Plus)* [2012] EWCA Civ 903 (a conduct case), the Court said (at [36]) that:

> the ET must then decide on the reasonableness of the response by the employer. In performing the latter exercise, the ET must consider, by the objective standards of the hypothetical reasonable employer, rather than by reference to the ET's own subjective views, whether the employer has acted within a 'band or range of reasonable responses' to the particular misconduct found of the particular employee. If the employer has so acted, then the employer's decision to dismiss will be reasonable. However, this is not the same thing as saying that a decision of an employer to dismiss will only be regarded as unreasonable if it is shown to be perverse. The ET must not simply consider whether they think that the dismissal was fair and thereby substitute their decision as to what was the right course to adopt for that of the employer. The ET must determine whether the decision of the employer to dismiss the employee fell within the band of reasonable responses which 'a reasonable employer might have adopted'. An ET must focus its attention on the fairness of the conduct of the employer at the time of the investigation and dismissal (or any internal appeal process) and not on whether in fact the employee has suffered an injustice.

Note that the 'range of reasonable responses' test applies not just to the substantive reason for the dismissal, but also to the procedural aspects of the employer's actions. In *Sainsbury's Supermarkets Ltd v Hitt* [2003] IRLR 23, the Court of Appeal held that the range of reasonable responses test applied as much to whether a reasonable investigation had been carried out as it does to the reasonableness of the decision to dismiss for the conduct reason. The Court of Appeal confirmed this in *Bournemouth University Higher Education Corporation v Buckland* [2010] EWCA Civ 121.

For a useful discussion of some of the authorities, see *EAGA plc v Tideswell* (UKEAT/0007/11).

5.3.1.2 Matters known to the employer

The employer must generally justify the decision to dismiss on the basis of the information known to him at the time of dismissal (*W Devis & Sons Ltd v Atkins* [1977] AC 931, HL). See also *Alboni v Ind Coope Retail Ltd* [1998] IRLR 131, CA (see **5.2.2.2**). The Court of Appeal held in *Orr v Milton Keynes Council* [2011] EWCA Civ 62 that 'known to the employer' means facts known to the decision maker or facts that he could reasonably acquire through the appropriate disciplinary procedure.

5.3.1.3 Size of the undertaking

The tribunal must take into account the size and administrative resources of the undertaking. An employer with a small workforce might, for example, find it more difficult than a larger firm to find other employees to do the work of an employee who is absent sick for a long period. This might justify a dismissal and replacement of a sick employee in circumstances where a large firm would not be acting reasonably. A small firm is also less likely to have suitable alternative employment for employees who lose their own jobs through redundancy. A small firm may also have less formal disciplinary and consultation procedures than a large one.

5.3.1.4 Does the reason justify dismissal?

The tribunal must decide whether dismissal was within a range of reasonable responses. Would a reasonable employer have demoted or suspended instead?

5.3.1.5 Pressure on the employer

In deciding whether the employer acted reasonably, the tribunal must not take into account any pressure put on the employer, by way of industrial action or the threat of industrial action, to dismiss the employee (ERA 1996, s 107).

5.3.1.6 Breach of contract

The fact that a dismissal is in breach of contract will not of itself render it unfair. The test is whether the employer acted reasonably.

5.3.1.7 Equitable considerations

A long-serving employee deserves more consideration before dismissal. For example, an employee with 20 years' service who is convicted of an offence of dishonesty unrelated to his employment, might be demoted to a position which would not give him an opportunity for breach of trust rather than be dismissed.

5.3.1.8 Consistency

The employer should consider how previous similar situations have been dealt with in the past. Nevertheless, it will be rare that the circumstances of one employee are truly comparable with those of another. In *Hadjioannou v Coral Casinos Ltd* [1981] IRLR 352, the EAT said that inconsistency of treatment would be relevant only in limited circumstances. In *Paul v East Surrey District HA* [1995] IRLR 305, the Court of Appeal held that the employee's dismissal was fair on the ground that there was a clear and rational basis for distinguishing between the cases of the two employees.

5.3.1.9 Human rights

Although the Human Rights Act 1998 (HRA 1998) is only directly effective between victims and public authorities (see **Chapter 15**), for employees pursuing their private sector employers for unfair dismissal, the HRA 1998 may be used to 'shape and determine' the outcome of the claim. In *Pay v Lancashire Probation Service* [2004] IRLR 129, the EAT agreed that the ERA 1996, s 98(4) must be read in a way which is compatible with human rights. However, on the facts, the EAT decided that the activities in which the applicant was involved (performing in fetish clubs and merchandising of products connected with bondage, domination and sado-masochism; photographs were available on the Internet of him involved in these activities) were not private, and that the interference with freedom of expression was justified and accordingly there was no infringement of the applicant's rights under Articles 8 or 10 (freedom of expression) of the European Convention on Human Rights. Mr Pay was a probation officer who worked with sex offenders. The EAT said that the interference with Article 10 was justified on the facts because of the competing interests of the employer to protect its reputation and maintain public confidence. Dismissal was a proportionate response.

In *X v Y* [2004] IRLR 625, the Court of Appeal dealt with the question of whether tribunals must take account of the HRA 1998 (in this case Article 8 of the European Convention) when deciding unfair dismissal claims brought against private sector employers. The majority of the Court of Appeal held that Article 8 was not engaged. Mummery LJ went on to state that there should be no difference in approach, whether the employer is private or public sector. He said the European Convention had an 'oblique' effect rather than a horizontal one, and that the right to respect for private life 'blended' with the law on unfair dismissal, but without creating new private law causes of action against private employers. See **15.4.2**.

It has also been suggested that Article 6 (the right to a fair hearing) might apply to internal disciplinary hearings. In R (G) v The Governors of X School [2011] UKSC 30, the Supreme Court held that Article 6 *may* be engaged in internal disciplinary hearings where the consequences of an internal disciplinary proceeding were sufficiently linked to the determination of an individual's civil rights to practise his chosen profession (in the sense of having a 'substantial influence or effect' on the outcome of a subsequent process which is determinative of civil rights (in this case the outcome of the Independent Safeguarding Authority's process, which could have meant that the claimant's name was added to the register)).

Statutory provisions obliged the school, when it made a serious finding of misconduct, to make a reference to what became the Independent Safeguarding Authority (ISA) (originally the Secretary of State) to consider whether the claimant should be should be placed on the 'children's barred list' and prevented from working with children in the future. Under this statutory framework, the claimant would have a right to legal representation before the ISA; and if dissatisfied with its decision, there was a right of appeal. Applying that test to the facts, the fact that ISA was required by statutory provisions and published guidance to 'exercise its own independent judgment both in relation to finding facts and making an assessment of their gravity and significance', before forming a view as to whether G should be placed on the barred list, was significant in the Supreme Court's view. The Supreme Court considered that the governors' determination that G had been guilty of gross misconduct would *not* have a 'substantial influence or effect' on the ISA's decision-making process. It followed that G's Article 6 rights were not engaged at the internal disciplinary stage, but only at the subsequent ISA hearing (see further **15.4.1**).

Other rights may be of relevance, for example an excessively long period of suspension could amount to inhuman or degrading treatment or punishment under Article 3; or unjustified surveillance of an employee before or as part of an investigation process in a disciplinary matter may be a breach of the right to respect for private life under Article 8 (see **15.4.2**).

5.4 PROCEDURAL UNFAIRNESS

An employer may be justified in dismissing an employee for the substantive reason, but the dismissal may still be unfair if there are procedural defects, for example if employees are unfairly selected for redundancy. These matters are dealt with in **5.4.2** in relation to the different reasons for dismissal.

Under s 10 of the ERA 1999, workers have a statutory right to be accompanied at a disciplinary hearing. This right applies only where the worker 'reasonably requests' the presence of a companion. Where the worker's request is reasonable, the employer must permit the companion to attend (see eg *Roberts v The Regard Partnership* (ET/2104545/09)). Note that while the worker may choose whom he wishes to accompany him, his choice of companion is limited under s 10 to trade union officials or fellow workers. Some organisation will, however, permit a wider choice of companion in their disciplinary procedures.

Note that by virtue of ss 37 and 38 of the ERA 2004 (amending s 10 of the ERA 1999), employers must now allow a companion who accompanies an employee to a disciplinary hearing to address the hearing to put an employee's case, to sum up that case and to respond on the employee's behalf. However, the companion is not entitled to answer questions on the worker's behalf. If the employer fails to tell the employee of his right to be accompanied to a disciplinary hearing, or does not allow a companion to attend, this can be taken into account when considering fairness (see Acas Code of Practice at **5.4.1** below). (Note that these provisions also apply to workers – see **1.3.3**.)

5.4.1 Codes of practice

Any relevant Code (for example, the Acas Code of Practice on Disciplinary and Grievance Procedures, available at www.acas.org.uk) should be considered by the tribunal. If the employer fails to comply with the Code, that will be taken into account by the tribunal when deciding fairness. It may also have an effect on the amount of compensation awarded.

The Acas Code of Practice on Disciplinary and Grievance Procedures is intended to provide basic practical guidance on the key principles that underpin the handling of disciplinary and grievance situations at work. It sets down minimum standards only.

The key points to note are:

- A failure to follow the Code will not in itself make a dismissal automatically unfair, but tribunals can adjust awards by up to 25% for any unreasonable failure to comply with any of its provisions (EA 2008, s 3).
- The Code applies to disciplinary and grievance matters, but the text also refers to performance issues, suggesting that the disciplinary procedure guidance should also be applied to handling capability dismissals.
- The Code does not apply to other dismissals, such as redundancy and the termination of a fixed-term contract. Employers will be required to satisfy a tribunal that the termination procedure is fair according to the general fairness principles set out in the ERA 1996.
- The Code does not require employees to submit a grievance before bringing a tribunal claim, but employees who unreasonably fail to do this may suffer a reduction in any tribunal award of up to 25%.

The Acas Code is not legally binding, but its provisions will be taken into account by employment tribunals where appropriate when deciding whether a dismissal is fair or unfair. In *Lock v Cardiff Railway Co Ltd* [1998] IRLR 358, the EAT emphasised (it was dealing with the old Acas Code) the importance of tribunals examining and taking into account the Acas Code. Not to do so would amount to a misdirection of law.

The Acas Code applies to disciplinary situations, and para 1 states that 'disciplinary situations include misconduct and poor performance'.

The Code sets out the process for disciplinary matters, which is as follows:

- Establish the facts of each case.
- Inform the employee of the problem.
- Hold a meeting with the employee.
- At that meeting, allow the employee to be accompanied.
- Decide on the appropriate action.
- Provide the employee with an opportunity to appeal.

(See **5.4.2.1** and **5.4.2.2** below for further detail.) While an employer may lay down its own procedures, it will need to ensure that these meet the minimum standards of the Acas Code.

Note that the Code does not cover dismissals by reason of redundancy and the non-renewal of fixed-term contracts; but of course, in all cases, employers should follow a fair procedure, as determined by other legislation and case law (see **5.3.2.3** below).

A failure to follow the Code, where it applies, gives tribunals a discretionary power to increase or decrease the unfair dismissal award (and presumably other awards that also arise out of the disciplinary process or dismissal on grounds of misconduct or capability, eg claims of unlawful discrimination, wrongful dismissal, unlawful deduction of wages) by up to 25%, if they consider that the employer's/employee's failure to comply with the Code was unreasonable. It is for the tribunal to decide what uplift (or reduction) would be just and equitable. The full list of claims to which this regime applies is set out in Sch A2 to TULRCA 1992.

To complement the Code, Acas has published guidance. Tribunals cannot adjust awards on account of any failure to follow the guidance, neither are they required to have regard to the guidance. However, it is anticipated that in many cases tribunals will refer to the guidance to assist them in determining whether the employer's handling of misconduct and poor performance matters has complied with general principles of fairness. For that reason, when dealing with disciplinary matters, employers and their advisers should read the relevant section of the guidance and ensure that they comply with it.

5.4.2 Procedural unfairness: particular reasons

The general principles dealt with in **5.3.1** apply to dismissals for any reason. However, where procedural unfairness is concerned, particular reasons may require a particular procedural approach (see below).

The application of an unfair procedure will render a dismissal unfair even though compliance with a fair procedure would have produced the same result of dismissal (*Polkey v AE Dayton Services Ltd* [1987] ICR 301). However, the fact that compliance would have still led to dismissal may be taken into account when considering compensation (a '*Polkey*' deduction) (see **5.6.2.2**).

5.4.2.1 Capability and qualifications

The approach to capability and qualifications should vary depending on whether the incapability is due to incompetence or sickness. The Acas Code covers poor performance/incompetence.

Incompetence

Before dismissing any employee for incompetence, an employer should normally have met with the employee, warned the employee about his standard of work and given him the opportunity to improve. Where appropriate, adequate training should have been given and review periods set down. In some cases, for example where an employee has been moved to a job beyond his capabilities, the employer should consider whether it is possible to move the employee to a job within his capabilities. Acas gives the following example in the guidance:

> A member of staff in accounts makes a number of mistakes on invoices to customers. You bring the mistakes to his attention, make sure he has had the right training and impress on him the need for accuracy but the mistakes continue. You invite the employee to a disciplinary meeting and inform him of his right to be accompanied by a colleague or employee representative. At the meeting the employee does not give a satisfactory explanation for the mistakes so you decide to issue an improvement note setting out: the problem, the improvement required, the timescale for improvement, the support available and a review date. You inform the employee that a failure to improve may lead to a final written warning.

Readers should always have regard to the guidance produced by Acas (see the overview chart reproduced at **5.4.2.2**).

Sickness

The Acas Code does not explicitly cover dismissals by reason of ill-health, but the guidance produced by Acas includes a section dealing with ill-health absences, which employers would be well advised to read.

An employee may be fairly dismissed for long-term sickness. The nature and likely duration of the illness and the length of service of the employee are relevant, as are the needs of the employer. A key employee or an employee in a small firm may need to be replaced by an employer more quickly than a less vital employee or one in a larger firm. Ultimately, the test is whether the employer could reasonably be expected to wait any longer for the employee.

The employer should consult with the employee concerning the nature and likely length of the illness, seek medical advice relating to the condition of the employee and consider whether suitable alternative employment can be offered. Under the Access to Medical Reports Act 1988, the written consent of an employee is required before the employer can obtain a medical report from the employee's specialist or doctor. The medical practitioner must be responsible for the clinical care of the individual. For this reason, reports prepared by occupational doctors are normally exempt. Warnings would not normally be appropriate, but an employee who takes a large number of short breaks for illness could be warned about his attendance record.

The EAT held in *DB Schenker Rail (UK) Ltd v Doolan* (UKEATS/0053/09) that where there is a conflict in medical evidence, the employer need only show that it acted within the range of reasonable responses when preferring the evidence of one expert over another. The decision to dismiss in capability cases is a managerial one for the employer and not a medical one for doctors.

According to the EAT in *Edwards v Governors of Hanson School* [2001] IRLR 733, if an employer has:

> acted maliciously, or wilfully caused an employee incapacitating ill-health, we see no reason why dismissal, however fair the ultimate procedures in themselves, should not lead to a finding of unfair dismissal.

This may mean that a dismissal of an employee on long-term sick absence caused by bullying and mismanagement at work may be unfair.

In *Frewin v Consignia plc* [2003] All ER (D) 314 (Jul), the EAT stated that, when considering the fairness of a dismissal, a tribunal is entitled to take into account the fact that the incapacity was caused by the employer. The EAT said that:

> the weight to be attached to that factor would depend on all the circumstances of the case. In some instances, the existence of causation could render the decision to dismiss unfair; in other cases it might not. Thus the existence of a causative link would not require the conclusion that the decision to dismiss had been unfair or raise any presumption of unfairness. It was merely a factor to be considered and weighed in the balance.

In *McAdie v RBS* [2007] IRLR 895, Mrs McAdie's ill-health was stress-related. The tribunal concluded it had been caused by the way her grievances about various matters had been handled, and by other treatment by her line managers. She was subsequently dismissed on ill-health grounds and brought a claim for unfair dismissal. The employment tribunal held that the dismissal was unfair on the basis that the employer had caused Mrs McAdie's health problems. On appeal, the EAT held that the tribunal had asked itself the wrong question. The question it should have asked was whether it was reasonable for the employer to dismiss Mrs McAdie in the circumstances as they then were, including the fact that its mishandling of the situation had led to her illness. The Court of Appeal upheld the EAT's decision; it stated that the EAT had applied the correct test and had been right to find that Mrs McAdie had not been unfairly dismissed. The fact an employer has caused the incapacity in question cannot preclude him dismissing fairly. However, where the employer is responsible for the incapacity, it may be expected, as the EAT said in this case (approved by the Court of Appeal), to 'go the extra mile in finding alternative employment for such an employee or to put up with a longer period of sickness than would otherwise be reasonable'.

In *First Leeds v Haigh* (UKEAT/0246/07), the EAT held that a capability dismissal will normally be unfair if an employer fails to take reasonable steps to ascertain whether an employee is entitled to an ill-health retirement (see also *Apsden v Webb Poultry & Meat Group (Holdings) Ltd* [1996] IRLR 521).

The impact of the Disability Discrimination Act 1995 should always be considered in relation to an ill-health dismissal. This area is considered further in **Chapter 13.**

5.4.2.2   Conduct

As mentioned previously, the type of misconduct may vary greatly, from incidents of a minor nature (eg bad time-keeping) to gross misconduct (eg theft or divulging trade secrets).

It is important, however, to determine what the real reason for the dismissal is – for example, if the reason for the dismissal is a breakdown in trust and confidence caused by the employee's behaviour, an employer does not need to follow its contractual conduct dismissal procedure (see *Ezsias v North Glamorgan NHS Trust* (UKEAT/0399/09)). In *Ezsias*, the EAT upheld the tribunal's decision that Mr Ezsias had been fairly dismissed for 'some other substantial reason' where Mr Ezsias' behaviour had led to relationships in the department breaking down (see **5.4.2.5**).

The important feature here, when considering the reasonableness of the employer's actions, is how he handled the situation.

The Acas guidance gives the following overview on 'Handling discipline'.

Handling discipline – an overview

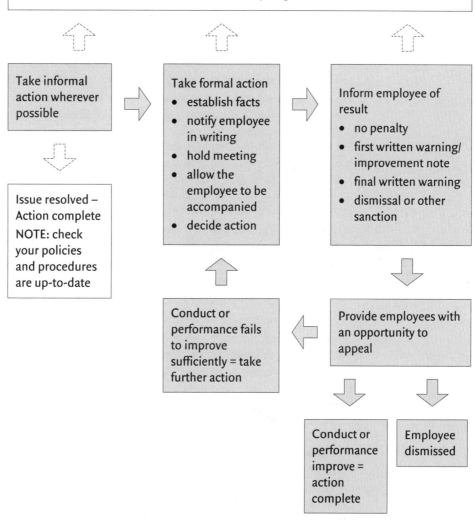

• Always follow the Acas *Code of Practice on disciplinary and grievance procedures*
• It may be helpful to consider mediation at any stage

Take informal action wherever possible

Issue resolved – Action complete
NOTE: check your policies and procedures are up-to-date

Take formal action
• establish facts
• notify employee in writing
• hold meeting
• allow the employee to be accompanied
• decide action

Inform employee of result
• no penalty
• first written warning/ improvement note
• final written warning
• dismissal or other sanction

Conduct or performance fails to improve sufficiently = take further action

Provide employees with an opportunity to appeal

Conduct or performance improve = action complete

Employee dismissed

Source: Acas, Discipline and grievances at work

An extract from the Code follows:

Keys to handling disciplinary issues in the workplace

Establish the facts of each case

5.   It is important to carry out necessary investigations of potential disciplinary matters without unreasonable delay to establish the facts of the case. In some cases this will require the holding of an investigatory meeting with the employee before proceeding to any disciplinary hearing. In

others, the investigatory stage will be the collation of evidence by the employer for use at any disciplinary hearing.

6. In misconduct cases, where practicable, different people should carry out the investigation and disciplinary hearing.

7. If there is an investigatory meeting this should not by itself result in any disciplinary action. Although there is no statutory right for an employee to be accompanied at a formal investigatory meeting, such a right may be allowed under an employer's own procedure.

8. In cases where a period of suspension with pay is considered necessary, this period should be as brief as possible, should be kept under review and it should be made clear that this suspension is not considered a disciplinary action.

Inform the employee of the problem

9. If it is decided that there is a disciplinary case to answer, the employee should be notified of this in writing. This notification should contain sufficient information about the alleged misconduct or poor performance and its possible consequences to enable the employee to prepare to answer the case at a disciplinary meeting. It would normally be appropriate to provide copies of any written evidence, which may include any witness statements, with the notification.

10. The notification should also give details of the time and venue for the disciplinary meeting and advise the employee of their right to be accompanied at the meeting.

Hold a meeting with the employee to discuss the problem

11. The meeting should be held without unreasonable delay whilst allowing the employee reasonable time to prepare their case.

12. Employers and employees (and their companions) should make every effort to attend the meeting. At the meeting the employer should explain the complaint against the employee and go through the evidence that has been gathered. The employee should be allowed to set out their case and answer any allegations that have been made. The employee should also be given a reasonable opportunity to ask questions, present evidence and call relevant witnesses. They should also be given an opportunity to raise points about any information provided by witnesses. Where an employer or employee intends to call relevant witnesses they should give advance notice that they intend to do this.

Allow the employee to be accompanied at the meeting

13. Workers have a statutory right to be accompanied by a companion where the disciplinary meeting could result in:
    •   a formal warning being issued; or
    •   the taking of some other disciplinary action; or
    •   the confirmation of a warning or some other disciplinary action (appeal hearings).

14. The chosen companion may be a fellow worker, a trade union representative, or an official employed by a trade union. A trade union representative who is not an employed official must have been certified by their union as being competent to accompany a worker.

15. To exercise the statutory right to be accompanied workers must make a reasonable request. What is reasonable will depend on the circumstances of each individual case. However, it would not normally be reasonable for workers to insist on being accompanied by a companion whose presence would prejudice the hearing nor would it be reasonable for a worker to ask to be accompanied by a companion from a remote geographical location if someone suitable and willing was available on site.

16. The companion should be allowed to address the hearing to put and sum up the worker's case, respond on behalf of the worker to any views expressed at the meeting and confer with the worker during the hearing. The companion does not, however, have the right to answer questions on the worker's behalf, address the hearing if the worker does not wish it or prevent the employer from explaining their case.

Decide on appropriate action

17. After the meeting decide whether or not disciplinary or any other action is justified and inform the employee accordingly in writing.

18. Where misconduct is confirmed or the employee is found to be performing unsatisfactorily it is usual to give the employee a written warning. A further act of misconduct or failure to improve performance within a set period would normally result in a final written warning.

19.   If an employee's first misconduct or unsatisfactory performance is sufficiently serious, it may be appropriate to move directly to a final written warning. This might occur where the employee's actions have had, or are liable to have, a serious or harmful impact on the organisation.

20.   A first or final written warning should set out the nature of the misconduct or poor performance and the change in behaviour or improvement in performance required (with timescale). The employee should be told how long the warning will remain current. The employee should be informed of the consequences of further misconduct, or failure to improve performance, within the set period following a final warning. For instance that it may result in dismissal or some other contractual penalty such as demotion or loss of seniority.

21.   A decision to dismiss should only be taken by a manager who has the authority to do so. The employee should be informed as soon as possible of the reasons for the dismissal, the date on which the employment contract will end, the appropriate period of notice and their right of appeal.

22.   Some acts, termed gross misconduct, are so serious in themselves or have such serious consequences that they may call for dismissal without notice for a first offence. But a fair disciplinary process should always be followed, before dismissing for gross misconduct.

23.   Disciplinary rules should give examples of acts which the employer regards as acts of gross misconduct. These may vary according to the nature of the organisation and what it does, but might include things such as theft or fraud, physical violence, gross negligence or serious insubordination.

24.   Where an employee is persistently unable or unwilling to attend a disciplinary meeting without good cause the employer should make a decision on the evidence available.

Provide employees with an opportunity to appeal

25.   Where an employee feels that disciplinary action taken against them is wrong or unjust they should appeal against the decision. Appeals should be heard without unreasonable delay and ideally at an agreed time and place. Employees should let employers know the grounds for their appeal in writing.

26.   The appeal should be dealt with impartially and wherever possible, by a manager who has not previously been involved in the case.

27.   Workers have a statutory right to be accompanied at appeal hearings.

28.   Employees should be informed in writing of the results of the appeal hearing as soon as possible.

The Acas guidance gives the following examples:

1.   An employee in a small firm makes a series of mistakes in letters to one of your key customers promising impossible delivery dates. The customer is upset at your firm's failure to meet delivery dates and threatens to take his business elsewhere.

You are the owner of the business and carry out an investigation and invite the employee to a disciplinary meeting. You inform her of her right to be accompanied by a colleague or employee representative.

Example outcome of meeting

At the meeting the employee does not give a satisfactory explanation for the mistakes and admits that her training covered the importance of agreeing realistic delivery dates with her manager. During your investigation, her team leader and section manager told you they had stressed to the employee the importance of agreeing delivery dates with them before informing the customer. In view of the seriousness of the mistakes and the possible impact on the business, you issue the employee with a final written warning. You inform the employee that failure to improve will lead to dismissal and of her right to appeal.

> **Example outcome of meeting in different circumstances**
>
> At the meeting, the employee reveals that her team leader would not let her attend training as the section was too busy. Subsequently the team leader was absent sick and the employee asked the section manager for help with setting delivery dates. The manager said he was too busy and told the employee to 'use her initiative'. Your other investigations support the employee's explanation. You inform the employee that you will not be taking disciplinary action and will make arrangements for her to be properly trained. You decide to carry out a review of general management standards on supervision and training.
>
> 2. A member of your telephone sales team has been to lunch to celebrate success in an exam. He returns from lunch in a very merry mood, is slurring his speech and is evidently not fit to carry out his duties. You decide to send him home and invite him in writing to a disciplinary meeting setting out his alleged behaviour of gross misconduct for which he could be dismissed. Your letter includes information about his right to be accompanied by a colleague or employee representative. At the meeting he admits he had too much to drink, is very apologetic and promises that such a thing will not happen again. He is one of your most valued members of staff and has an exemplary record over his 10 years service with you. You know that being unfit for work because of excessive alcohol is listed in your company rules as gross misconduct. In view of the circumstances and the employee's record, however, you decide not to dismiss him but give him a final written warning. You inform the employee of his right to appeal.

Some principles derived from case law

For serious misconduct, it may be appropriate to skip the imposition of a first written warning and, for gross misconduct, to dismiss without warning (see paras 18–22 of the Code, above). In *Sandwell & West Birmingham Hospitals NHS Trust v Westwood* (UKEAT/0032/09), the EAT held that the question of what amounts to gross misconduct is a mixed question of law and fact: as a matter of law it connotes deliberate wrongdoing or gross negligence. Thus tribunals must consider the character of the conduct and whether it was so serious as to amount to gross misconduct.

It is clear that where a previous warning has expired, it may not be taken into account in a case in which, but for the previous warning, the employer would not have shown a reason for dismissing the employee (*Diosynth Ltd v Thomson* [2006] IRLR 284). However, the Court of Appeal confirmed in *Airbus UK Ltd v Webb* [2008] IRLR 309 that an expired warning may be taken into account where the expired final warning was not the reason, or the principal reason, shown for dismissal, but rather its relevance was to whether the range of reasonable responses to the later misconduct included dismissal for that misconduct. It might also be relevant where an allegation of inconsistent treatment is raised by the employee. The absence of previous misconduct and of a final warning may provide a reason for imposing a lesser penalty on another employee.

If an employee is at risk of dismissal, he must be told of this in advance of the hearing, otherwise the dismissal may be unfair. See, for example, *Boyd v Renfrewshire Council* [2008] CSIH 36. Mr Boyd was summarily dismissed for gross misconduct in 'deliberately and wilfully' taking an unauthorised break and failing to complete his work. The tribunal found that the dismissal was unfair because it had not been alleged until after the disciplinary hearing that Mr Boyd's actions were 'wilful', nor had there previously been any mention of gross misconduct or the possibility of dismissal. The tribunal's decision was upheld by the Court of Session.

The employee should have the right to appeal against any disciplinary action taken. There has been some discussion over the years as to whether an appeal can remedy procedural defects at the initial hearing. Most appeals are not a full rehearing of all the facts and evidence but tend to be reviews of what has gone before. The conventional wisdom was that procedural defects at the initial hearing could only be cured by an appeal which took the form of a full rehearing (which was a matter of substance not label – see, for example, *Whitbread & Co v Mills* [1988] IRLR 501). However, the Court of Appeal in *Taylor v OCS Group Ltd* [2006] EWCA Civ 702 disapproved of that approach, and said that the essential question, when deciding whether a dismissal is fair under ERA 1996, s 98(4), is whether the employer acted reasonably. The Court held that where a first hearing is defective, the appeal can cure the defect if the appeal is comprehensive, and that the distinction drawn in previous case law between reviews and rehearings is not helpful. According to Smith LJ, 'what matters is not whether the internal appeal was technically a rehearing or a review but whether the disciplinary process as a whole was fair'. In *Chaplin v Howard Kennedys Solicitors* (UKEAT/0469/08), the EAT held that a procedural defect was cured at an appeal hearing and thus rendered a dismissal fair.

In most cases of misconduct, notice (or, if the contract so provides, payment in lieu) should still be given in accordance with the contract. However, in the case of gross misconduct, this amounts to a repudiation of the contract by the employee, entitling the employer to terminate without notice or give payment in lieu (see **Chapter 2**).

The exact nature of the employer's disciplinary rules and procedures will depend on the size of the organisation. Larger firms should have a comprehensive set of detailed rules and procedures which should be carefully followed (although a minor deviation will not necessarily lead to a finding of unfair dismissal). A smaller firm may have a much less formal procedure, although it should still ensure that there is a fair investigation and a reasonable sanction.

Suspected misconduct: the approach in *British Home Stores v Burchell* [1978] IRLR 379

What if the employer merely *suspects* misconduct by an employee? He could still be fair in dismissing, provided the tribunal is satisfied that:

(a)   the employer had a genuine belief in guilt (this is really relevant to the reason for the dismissal);

(b)   the employer had reasonable grounds upon which to base the belief; and

(c)   the employer carried out a reasonable investigation.

Note: The burden of proof in relation to (b) and (c) is a neutral one, but (as a result of s 6 of the Employment Act 1980) the onus of proof (with regard to the reason for dismissal) lies on the employer. The first of the three elements of *Burchell* is relevant to reason, *not* reasonableness.

The Court of Appeal held, in *Sainsbury's Supermarkets Ltd v Hitt* [2003] IRLR 23 that the range of reasonable responses test 'applies as much to the question of whether the investigation into the suspected misconduct was reasonable in all the circumstances as it does to ... the decision to dismiss'. In *Gratton v Hutton* (2003) unreported, 1 July, the EAT emphasised that the test is not whether further investigation might reasonably have been carried out but whether the investigation which had been carried out could be regarded by a reasonable employer as adequate. Furthermore, the Court of Appeal held in *Panama v London Borough of Hackney* [2003] IRLR 278 that the employer's failure to obtain evidence to support an allegation of misconduct meant that they had neither reasonable grounds for their belief, nor had they carried out as much investigation into the matter as was reasonable in all the circumstances.

In *Ramsey v Walkers Snack Foods Ltd* [2004] IRLR 754 the EAT confirmed that it is possible to have a fair procedure where witnesses for the employer insist on anonymity because, on the facts, there was a very real fear of reprisals against the witnesses. In *Linfood Cash & Carry Ltd v Thompson* [1989] IRLR 235 the EAT set out guidelines to assist in balancing the need for a fair hearing with protecting witnesses. In outline, the employer should ensure that the information given by the informant is reduced into writing, noting key facts such as date, time and place, clarity of observation, circumstantial evidence, such as the reason for the presence of the informer and why certain small details are memorable, whether the informant has suffered at the hands of the accused or has any other reason to fabricate, whether from personal grudge or any other reason.

Further investigation can then take place, including inquiries into the character and background of the informant or any other information which may tend to add or detract from the value of the information. If the employer is satisfied that the fear is genuine then a decision will need to be made whether or not to continue with the disciplinary process. If it is to continue, it is best if, at each stage of the process, the member of management responsible for the hearing should himself interview the informant and satisfy himself that weight is to be given to the information. The written statement of the informant, if necessary with omissions to avoid identification, should be made available to the employee and his representatives. Full and careful notes should be taken during all stage of the disciplinary process, and if evidence from an investigating officer is to be taken at a hearing, it should, where possible, be prepared in a written form.

The tribunal will want to make clear findings as to the extent of the respondent's investigation into the reasons why the informant is insisting on anonymity, and then carry out a balancing act between the respondent's perceived need to protect the identity of the informant and natural justice that the claimant should know sufficiently the nature of the case against him, applying the band of reasonable responses test.

The EAT confirmed that there is 'no rule of law which renders it incumbent on an employer, when dismissing an employee for misconduct ... [to give] the employee who is liable to be dismissed the opportunity to cross-examine the person making the complaint' (*Santamera v Express Cargo Forwarding t/a IEC Ltd* [2003] IRLR 273).

In *Corus UK Ltd v Mainwaring* (UKEAT/0053/07) the EAT held that there is no obligation to take a witness statement from an employee who 'tips off' an employer about a malingering employee, where the employer subsequently relies on his own evidence (eg, video/medical) before dismissing.

Depending on all the facts, an employer may wish to suspend the employee pending the outcome of an investigation. So long as the employer is not under an obligation to provide the employee with work (see **1.7.1.1**), he will not normally be acting in breach of contract to suspend the employee with pay. Clearly, if there is a contractual clause allowing for suspension with pay, there can then be no argument about breach of the right to be provided with work.

Note, however, that in *Gogay v Hertfordshire County Council* [2000] IRLR 703 (see **2.4.1.5**), the Court of Appeal upheld the High Court's finding that suspension of an employee was in breach of the implied duty of trust and confidence. The woman employee had been suspended (on full pay under a contractual clause) pending the outcome of an investigation. The letter sent to the employee said that 'the issue to be investigated is an allegation of sexual abuse by a young person in our care'. In the event, the investigation concluded that there was no case to answer and that the child had never said anything which might be construed as an allegation of abuse. The Court of Appeal says that it does not inevitably follow that an employee should be suspended merely because there are reasonable grounds for an investigation. There are other options open to an employer, such as transfer. There must be reasonable and proper cause for a suspension.

The Acas guidance makes it clear that suspension with pay may be considered for certain cases such as gross misconduct or where relationships have broken down, or where it is considered that there is a risk to an employer's property or responsibilities to others. However, the guidance emphasises that such suspension should be imposed only after careful consideration and should be reviewed to ensure that it is not unnecessarily protracted.

In *Boys and Girls Welfare Society* [1996] IRLR 129, the EAT said *BHS v Burchell* was inappropriate if there was no conflict on the facts, for example the employee admitted or did not dispute his guilt. Nevertheless, in *Whitbread plc (t/a Whitbread Medway Inns) v Hall* [2001] IRLR 275, the Court of Appeal made it clear that even where misconduct is admitted (so that an employer does not need to prove that it had reasonable grounds for its belief), an employer is still under a duty to follow a fair procedure, such as hearing explanations and considering other penalties besides dismissal (unless the offence is so heinous that a reasonable employer following good industrial practice could conclude that no explanation or mitigation would make any difference to the decision to dismiss). In *John Lewis plc v Coyne* [2001] IRLR 139, an employment tribunal held that a dismissal for making personal telephone calls (which was not denied), in breach of company rules, was unfair because the employer had failed to investigate the seriousness of the offence, including the purpose of the calls, whether there was any element of personal crisis and whether or not the conduct was persistent.

What if an employee is charged with a criminal offence, but denies guilt? This should be grounds for dismissal only where it has employment implications. For example:

(a)   Was the offence committed in the course of employment?

(b)   Was it an offence of dishonesty?

(c)   Was the employee in a position of trust?

(d)   Is the employee to be detained in custody?

The outcome of any subsequent criminal proceedings does not necessarily have any bearing on the issue of reasonableness. For example, in *Da Costa v Optalis* [1976] IRLR 178, the employee in question was dismissed from his job as a bookkeeper for not keeping proper accounts. He was later prosecuted but was acquitted. The employment tribunal held his dismissal to have been fair. The issues involved were different, as was the standard of proof to be applied.

An employer does not have to delay his decision pending the outcome of any criminal proceedings. He may, however, decide to suspend the employee pending the decision of the criminal court. In *A v B* [2003] IRLR 405, the EAT emphasised that 'the investigator ... should focus no less on any potential evidence that may exculpate or at least point to the innocence of the employee as he should on the evidence directed toward proving the charges against him'.

In *Salford Royal NHS Foundation Trust v Roldan* [2010] IRLR 721 the Court of Appeal confirmed that when carrying out an investigation into allegations of gross misconduct, employers should take into account the gravity of the potential consequences on an employee. This may mean a more thorough investigation is required in cases where there are potentially significant consequences for the employee if he loses his job. In *Roldan*, the employee, who was a nurse, lost her work permit and consequently her right to stay in the UK and also became the subject of a criminal investigation by the police.

Social media have increasingly become relevant in unfair dismissal cases (see Acas research paper, *Workplaces and Social Networking – the Implications for Employment Relations* at www.acas.org.uk). Employers often use information posted on Facebook and other social media sites as evidence of employees' wrongdoing. This can give rise to a question whether employers should be entitled to rely on such evidence (have they, for example, breached their employee's privacy in accessing the information – see **Chapter 15**), but there may also be issues about the employee's use of social media sites during working hours. In *Taylor v Somerfield* (ETS/107847/2007) a supermarket warehouse employee was dismissed for posting video footage on YouTube which captured a colleague hitting another colleague with a plastic bag full of plastic bags in one of the employer's warehouses. The footage did not show who the employees were but did reveal the uniforms they were wearing. The footage was taken down after three days and had only eight hits while it was up, three of which were by the supermarket's managers after they discovered the footage was online. The supermarket held a disciplinary process and dismissed the employee for bringing the supermarket into disrepute and breaching health and safety rules. The employment tribunal found there was no evidence to indicate that the supermarket had been brought into disrepute and found the dismissal unfair. (See also *Teggart v TeleTech UK Ltd* (NIIT 00704/11) and *Preece v JD Wetherspoons plc* (ET/2104806/10).) What is important is that employers have a policy on social networking, treat 'electronic behaviour' consistently with 'non-electronic behaviour' and react reasonably to issues around social networking.

Note that where a tribunal finds that the conduct justifying a dismissal was not gross misconduct, so as not to justify summary dismissal (ie without notice), this will not (necessarily) mean that the dismissal is unfair, although it may mean that the dismissal is wrongful if no notice was given.

5.4.2.3   Redundancy

(The Acas Code of Practice on Disciplinary and Grievance Procedures does not apply to redundancy dismissals, but there is an Acas advisory booklet on handling redundancy.)

Where a dismissal is for redundancy, the tribunal must be satisfied that it was reasonable to dismiss *that* employee by reason of redundancy. It is not enough to show that it was reasonable to dismiss *an* employee (*Williams v Compair Maxam Ltd* [1982] IRLR 83).

The essence of a fair redundancy dismissal is (1) fair selection (fair criteria applied fairly), (2) warning and consultation, and (3) alternative employment. In *Polkey v AE Dayton Services Ltd* [1988] ICR 142, HL, it was stated that in the case of redundancy, the employer will not normally act reasonably unless he:

(a)   warns and consults any employees affected or their representatives;

(b)   adopts a fair basis on which to select for redundancy, ie identifies an appropriate pool from which to select, and uses objective criteria and applies those criteria fairly (see *British Aerospace plc v Green* [1995] IRLR 433, CA); and

(c)   takes such steps as may be reasonable to avoid or minimise redundancy by redeployment within his own organisation.

See also *Buchanan v Tilcon Ltd* [1983] IRLR 417, *FDR Ltd v Holloway* [1995] IRLR 400, *John Brown Engineering Ltd v Brown and Others* [1997] IRLR 90 and *King v Eaton* [1996] IRLR 199. Where a trade union is involved, readers should refer to *Williams and Others v Compair Maxam Ltd* (above).

Issues of fairness and reasonableness still need to be judged by reference to the 'range of reasonable responses' test (see *Beddell v West Ferry Printers* [2000] ICR 1263). In *Drake International Systems Ltd v O'Hare* (UKEAT/0384/03), the EAT emphasised that tribunals should not impose their own views as to the reasonableness of the selection criteria or the implementation of the criteria: the correct question was whether the selection was one that a reasonable employer acting reasonably could have made. In *Hendy Banks v Fairbrother* (UKEAT/0691/04) the EAT confirmed that the 'range of reasonable responses' test applied when deciding whether an employer had acted reasonably in selecting a pool for redundancy, ie the group of employees from which those to be made redundant will be selected. The tribunal must first decide whether the pool selected by the employer fell within a 'range of reasonable responses'. In *Wrexham Golf Club Ltd v Ingham* (UKEAT/0190/12) the EAT held that it can be reasonable to focus upon a single employee without developing a pool or even considering developing a pool. In *Leventhal Ltd v North* (UKEAT/0265/04) the EAT upheld a decision that a redundancy dismissal was unfair (on the facts) because the employer had not considered 'bumping' (see also *Fulcrum Pharma (Europe) Ltd v Bonassera and Another* (UKEAT/0198/10) (see **4.2.3.3**). However, in *Halpin v Sandpiper Books Ltd* (UKEAT/0171/11) the EAT held that it was not unreasonable not to 'bump' another employee and that a pool of one was reasonable. (See also *Capita Hartshead Ltd v Byard* (UKEAT/0445/11), where the EAT held that a redundancy dismissal was unfair where the employer used a selection pool of one.) Ultimately, the test is whether the employer has 'genuinely applied its mind' to the composition of the pool and whether the dismissal fell within the range of reasonable responses. The *Capita* case contains a useful summary of the law on redundancy selection.

Having decided upon the pool for selection, the employer must then fairly select for redundancy. There is no one fair method of selection. Last in, first out ('LIFO') is sometimes used as a basis for selection, but following the introduction of the Employment Equality (Age) Regulations 2006 there was concern that LIFO was potentially age discriminatory against younger employees who were presumed to have less service. Both the Acas guide on 'Age in the Workplace' and the Government guide 'Age Positive' counsel against the use of LIFO, although the High Court in *Rolls Royce v Unite the Union* [2008] EWHC 2420 held that including length of service as part of a matrix of selection criteria was not unlawful. LIFO may also be potentially sex discriminatory. However, there are advantages to it, not least that it is completely objective. Where there is a contractual procedure, an employer should follow it.

Some of the selection criteria commonly used include:

(a)   skills or experience;

(b)   standard of work performance or aptitude for work;

(c)   attendance or disciplinary record.

In *De Belin v Eversheds Legal Services Ltd* (ET/1804069/09) the employment tribunal held that a decision to inflate the billing score of a woman on maternity leave was discriminatory on the ground of sex. The decision was upheld by the EAT (UKEAT/0352/10).

Having drawn up fair objective selection criteria, as the Acas booklet on handling redundancies makes clear, 'the selection will still be unfair if those criteria are carelessly or mistakenly applied'.

One of the most difficult questions for tribunals is the extent to which they should examine the marking that has been applied in a selection exercise. It is clear that one of the requirements for fair consultation in a redundancy exercise involves giving an employee sufficient information about and explanation for his scoring so that he understands them and has a meaningful chance to comment on and challenge the scores.

In *Pinewood Repro Limited t/a County Print (County Print) v Page* (UKEAT/0028/10), the employer agreed the selection criteria (attendance, quality, productivity, abilities, skills, experience, disciplinary record and flexibility) with the trade union, ensured that the scoring was carried out by two senior managers and gave the employee a right to appeal his selection for redundancy, but did not explain to Mr Page why he had received lower scores than the two other people in the selection pool. Mr Page was provided with a copy of his scores; he queried why he had been marked down for 'abilities, skills and experience' given his level of qualifications and 27 years' experience. He also queried why he had been marked down for flexibility as he was 'as flexible as the next man'. He was given no explanation as to how the scores had been arrived at, being told only that 'we believe that the scores given by the assessors are responsible and appropriate'. On appeal he was told that the employers were 'satisfied that the scoring was factual and correct'.

A tribunal found that Mr Page had been unfairly dismissed. The EAT upheld its decision and took the opportunity to review the relevant authorities and, whilst cautioning against an impermissible 'microscopic analysis' of scoring by tribunals, indicated that, particularly with subjective criteria, employees should have sufficient information to understand their scores and an opportunity to challenge them.

It is also important that employers make (and keep) written notes of why a particular score was awarded and what it was based on: the EAT in *Page* was critical of the 'complete absence of comments on the scoring sheet'. In *Dabson v David Cover & Sons* (UKEAT/0374/2011), the EAT emphasised, however, that when assessing the fairness of selection for redundancy, the marks awarded in the selection exercise should be investigated only in exceptional circumstances such as bias or obvious mistake.

The employer should always consider whether there are any alternative vacancies before implementing redundancies, and should provide information about the financial prospects of alternative positions (*Fisher v Hoopoe Finance Ltd* (UKEAT/0043/05). The EAT held in *Morgan v The Welsh Rugby Union* (UKEAT/0314/10) that it was fair to apply subjective criteria when deciding whom to appoint to a suitable alternative vacancy where there were multiple applicants. The 'classic' redundancy guidance set out in *Williams v Compair Maxam Ltd* [1982] ICR 156 does not apply where redundant employees are applying for a new and different role. The principles in *Williams* apply to selection for redundancy not selection for a new role, even where redundancies arise in consequence of such a process. The EAT accepted that in new role cases after a reorganisation, the employer's decision must of necessity be forward looking and may involve something more like an interview process than the application of selection criteria. See also *Akzo Coatings plc v Thompson* (UKEAT/117/94) and *Darlington Memorial Hospital NHS Trust v Edwards and Vincent* (UKEAT/678/95).

Note that there are some special cases:

(a)   It is automatically unfair to select an employee for redundancy for a 'trade union' reason (see **5.5.1** for details).

(b)   It is automatically unfair to select an employee for redundancy because she is pregnant. There are also special rules concerning offers of alternative employment to pregnant employees (see **14.9**).

The tribunal will also take into account whether or not the employer has complied with his statutory duties to consult (see **4.8**).

A tribunal's findings of fact may also be relevant as regards compensation. If an employer dismissed an employee without consultation, a tribunal must take account of the possibility of alternative employment arising during the period of consultation (see *King v Royal Bank of Canada Europe* (UKEAT/0333/10)).

5.4.2.4   Illegality

If it becomes illegal for an employee to continue in his employment because to do so would contravene a statutory provision, dismissal will often be fair. However, the employer should consider whether it is possible to redeploy the employee to another job. For example, if a driver has been disqualified from driving, is there any suitable alternative job, such as vehicle maintenance, that he could do without a driving licence? For two cases in this area, see *Kelly v University of Southampton* (UKEAT/0295/07) and *Klusova v London Borough of Hounslow* [2007] EWCA Civ 1127.

In *Connolly v Whitestone* (UKEAT/0445/10) the EAT held that a solicitor who claimed self-employed status with HMRC was not barred from bringing an unfair dismissal claim on the grounds of illegality – the contract would be illegally performed and unenforceable on public policy grounds only if the solicitor knew he was not entitled to claim he was self-employed. (See **1.2.7** above.)

5.4.2.5   Some other substantial reason

The nature of 'some other substantial reason' dismissals are so varied that no specific rules can be laid down. The general principles must be followed and, in particular, the dismissal must be within the reasonable range of responses. For example, in a business reorganisation which involves making changes to certain terms and conditions, the employer must weigh the commercial needs of the business against the detriment suffered by individual employees.

In *Genower v Ealing AHA* [1980] IRLR 297, the applicant was a general administrative assistant in the supplies department of a hospital. In order to solve a problem of corruption, the respondent decided to move certain grades of employees to different posts at different hospitals. The applicant was ordered to become a purchasing officer at another hospital quite outside the terms of his contract. The EAT held that the applicant's resignation amounted to a constructive dismissal but that the dismissal was fair: the respondent had initiated an internal reorganisation with the intention of preventing corruption.

It is clear from the authorities that where it is sought to justify a dismissal as being for some other substantial reason, there must be some kind of pressure on the employer; it is not enough for an employer simply to say that it is convenient or helpful to carry out a business reorganisation or that to do so would reduce employment costs. It is often appropriate to consider the procedural aspects in a similar way to that suggested in *Polkey* (see **5.4.2.3**).

In *Perkin v St George's Healthcare NHS Trust* [2005] EWCA Civ 1174 the Court of Appeal said employers were entitled to dismiss employees for having a difficult personality even if they were technically good at their jobs.

The Court of Appeal held that the three-stage test set out in *BHS v Burchell* [1978] IRLR 379 (see **5.4.2.2** above) applies when dismissing an employee for some other substantial reason (a breakdown in trust and confidence). The tribunal will have to determine whether the employer had reasonable grounds following a reasonable investigation for deciding that trust and confidence has been damaged.

In *Ezsias v North Glamorgan NHS Trust* (UKEAT/0399/09) the EAT upheld the tribunal's decision that Mr Ezsias had been dismissed for 'some other substantial reason' (ie the fact of a breakdown in relationships) rather than for misconduct, and that the dismissal was fair. The tribunal relied upon *Perkin* (see above). The distinction was important because if the tribunal had found that the reason for dismissal was misconduct, the Trust would have had to follow Whitley Council procedures. Those did not apply, however, because Mr Ezsias was found to have been dismissed for 'some other substantial reason' – he was dismissed because of the *fact* that relationships had broken down, not because his behaviour had caused the breakdown.

The EAT did make it clear that, even if the behaviour which had caused the breakdown of working relationships with his colleagues in the department had been the reason for his dismissal, it is possible that the action which the Trust took against Mr Ezsias should have been classified as action taken against him because of his conduct. But it would not *necessarily* follow that it should have been classified in that way. In *Perkin*, the Court of Appeal classified the reason for Mr Perkin's dismissal as coming within the category of 'some other substantial reason', even though it was his manner and management style which had led to the breakdown of relationships. Employers must be clear as to the reason for dismissal because procedure follows the reason.

The EAT also counselled employment tribunals to be on the lookout, in cases of this kind, to see whether an employer is using the rubric of 'some other substantial reason' as a pretext to conceal the real reason for the employee's dismissal.

In *Governing Body of Tubbenden Primary School v Sylvester* (UKEAT/0527/11), a deputy head teacher maintained a friendship, discreetly, with a fellow teacher, who was arrested and suspended for having indecent images of children. Some nine months after it was indicated to her by the School and local education authority that there was nothing wrong in her continuing with this friendship, and with three days' prior warning, she was suspended and disciplinary proceedings were initiated, and ultimately she was dismissed for 'some other substantial reason'. The employment tribunal accepted this but found the dismissal unfair in the circumstances, especially since the employer had not only failed to warn the deputy of the risk to her employment, but also had appeared to condone her conduct in maintaining the friendship.

It was contended that in a case of dismissal for some other substantial reason for loss of confidence, a tribunal was not entitled to have regard to the causes of that loss but should be restricted merely to the fact of it. This was rejected: s 98(4) entitled the tribunal to take a broader view, and the context was analogous to a dismissal for conduct, in which case a warning or its absence was highly relevant to any consideration of fairness.

In *Leach v Office of Communications* [2012] EWCA Civ 959, the Court of Appeal upheld a tribunal's decision that an employee had been fairly dismissed, for 'some other substantial reason' on the basis of a breakdown of trust and confidence, after the police had disclosed to the employer credible but untested allegations that the employee had committed child sex offences. The employer had adopted a sufficiently critical approach to the allegations and had not accepted them at face value. Even though the claimant had denied all of the allegations at a disciplinary hearing, the risk of damage to the employer's reputation was sufficient to justify dismissal. Arguments based on Articles 6 and 8 of the European Convention on Human Rights (which was directly applicable to Ofcom as a public authority employer) were also rejected. The EAT had upheld the tribunal's findings, but Mr Justice Underhill had stated that the EAT did not find the terminology of 'trust and confidence' particularly helpful. He observed 'a growing trend among parties to employment litigation to regard the invocation of "loss of trust and confidence" as an automatic solvent of obligations', which it is not. The Court of Appeal also noted that the duty of trust and confidence was an obligation at the heart of the employment relationship, and was not a convenient label to stick on any situation in which the employer feels let down by an employee or which the employer can use as a valid reason for dismissal whenever a conduct reason is unavailable or inappropriate. Courts are particularly aware that reliance by employers on 'trust and confidence' carries a danger of omitting the procedural safeguards that would apply to a conduct dismissal (see, eg, *Ezsias v North Glamorgan NHS Trust* [2011] IRLR 550, where the EAT pointed out that tribunals must be alert to employers using 'some other substantial reason' as a pretext for dismissal when conduct is the real concern).

In *Windsor Recruitment v Silverwood* (UKEAT/0339/05) the EAT looked at dismissals for refusing to accept a restrictive covenant in terms of some other substantial reason. It said the reasonableness of the covenant was relevant to general fairness, not to the reason.

In *Garside & Laycock v Booth* (UKEAT/0003/11) the EAT held that where a dismissal is for failure to accept a wage cut, the question whether the dismissal is fair for some other substantial reason has to be determined by reference to whether it was reasonable for the employer to dismiss, and not whether it was reasonable for the employee to accept the lesser term offered to him. All employees were asked to take a 5% pay cut. Mr Booth was the only one still refusing. The EAT overturned the tribunal's decision that the dismissal was unfair. The employee's reasonableness in refusing is only one factor to weigh in the balance – the correct focus of the tribunal should be on whether the employer acted reasonably in all the circumstances, not on whether it was reasonable for the employee to resist the attempt to reduce his pay.

In *Slade & Others v TNT UK Ltd* (UKEAT/0113/11), the employer sought to change terms of employment by making an offer to 'buy out' certain existing terms, but warned that refusal would result in dismissal with an offer of re-engagement on the proposed new terms. The offer was rejected and the employer dismissed with notice. Each of those who had been thus dismissed accepted re-engagement on the new terms, but under protest, and reserved their right to claim that their dismissal had been unfair.

The employment tribunal held that the employer did not act unfairly where the terms of offered re-employment did not include the terms of the 'buy out' as part of the new terms. That decision was upheld by the EAT. The tribunal had correctly considered whether the reason for the dismissal was a substantial reason – the burden of proof being on the respondent. If the reason for the dismissals was for a sound business reason, or one which the respondent reasonably believed was a sound business reason, then it would be a substantial reason. It was not necessary for the action to be the only available action to avert a business disaster, but on the other hand a reason must not be trivial. On the facts the tribunal was entitled to find that the reason was a business restructuring, namely a change of remuneration structure with a view to reduction of costs and an increase in efficiency to combat falling revenues and an alarming fall in operating profits. The tribunal found that the respondent had not been successful in all it set out to do in terms of cost reduction, but was satisfied it had an honest and reasonable belief that taking the proposed steps would achieve those aims. Those aims were legitimate and necessary, and constituted a substantial reason satisfying the provisions of s 98(1). That conclusion was not challenged.

The EAT held that the tribunal had correctly considered whether the dismissal was fair having regard to s 98(4) and had legitimately concluded that the employer had acted reasonably. The EAT held that the tribunal applied itself to the correct test and came to a conclusion which was open to it, namely that what the respondent did was within the bands of reasonable responses to the situation in which it found itself: the tribunal rejected the contention that the only reasonable response for the respondent would be to offer re-engagement on terms which included the buy-out sum.

5.5 OTHER SPECIAL CASES

There is a number of other special cases where the normal rules relating to unfair dismissal are varied. In summary, these are:

(a)   pregnancy or maternity-related dismissals (see **Chapter 14**);

(b)   dismissal for trade union reasons (see **5.5.1**);

(c)   selection for redundancy based on either of the above (see **5.4.2.3** and **5.5.1**);

(d)   dismissal following industrial action (see **5.5.2**);

(e)   dismissal for asserting a statutory right (see **5.5.3**);

(f)   health and safety dismissals (see **5.5.4**);

(g)   some dismissals on transfer of a business (see **Chapter 7**);

(h)   dismissals where the worker has made a protected disclosure (see **5.5.5**);

(i)   if the reason for the dismissal relates to a prohibited list (ERA 1996, s 104F(1)) (there is a statutory prohibition on compiling trade union blacklists – see Employment Relation Act 1999 (Blacklists) Regulations 2010 (SI 2010/493).

In the case of pregnancy or maternity-related dismissals, dismissals for trade union reasons (or selection for redundancy on either of these grounds), dismissals for asserting a statutory right, health and safety dismissals, some dismissals for a reason connected with a transfer of a business and dismissals for making a protected disclosure, the dismissal will be 'automatically' unfair. This means that once the tribunal has established that the reason for the dismissal falls under one of these heads, it will not have to go on to consider the reasonableness of the decision under s 98(4).

5.5.1 Dismissals for trade union reasons

The general principle is that an employee is free to join a trade union or not to join as he chooses. Consequently, it is unfair to dismiss any employee either because he is or because he is not a member of a trade union.

By s 152(1) of TULR(C)A 1992:

> ... the dismissal of an employee [is] unfair if the reason for it ... was that the employee—
>
> (a)   was, or proposed to become, a member of an independent trade union, or
>
> (b)   had taken part, or proposed to take part, in the activities of an independent trade union at an appropriate time, or
>
> (c)   was not a member of any trade union, or of a particular trade union ... or [refused] to become or remain a member.

An 'appropriate time' within s 152(1)(b) above is either outside working hours or within them at a time to which the employer has agreed (s 152(2)). 'Activities of an independent trade union' would cover such matters as union meetings. It does not extend to industrial action.

No qualifying period of continuous employment is necessary to bring a claim within this section because employees would be at risk of dismissal for these reasons shortly after commencing employment.

It is automatically unfair to select an employee for redundancy for one of the reasons within s 152 of TULR(C)A 1992 listed above (TULR(C)A 1992, s 153).

Where a complaint is made that the dismissal was on trade union membership grounds, the applicant may also seek interim relief (TULR(C)A 1992, s 161) (ie an injunction to preserve the status quo until a full hearing: in effect reinstatement until final judgment).

5.5.2 Industrial action

Industrial action includes strikes and other industrial action (eg a 'work to rule') by employees and lock-outs by the employer. The right of the employee to present a complaint of unfair dismissal depends whether the industrial action is 'unofficial' or 'other' ('official') industrial action. Basically, industrial action is 'official' if either:

(a)   authorised or endorsed by a trade union; or

(b)   none of those taking part is a member of a trade union.

5.5.2.1 Unofficial industrial action

By s 237 of the TULR(C)A 1992, if at the time of his dismissal the employee was taking part in unofficial industrial action, the employment tribunal has no jurisdiction to hear a complaint of unfair dismissal. This is not to say that the dismissal is fair, but merely that the employee is not eligible to present a claim. This means that in the event of unofficial strikes and other unofficial industrial action, the employer can select employees, such as the ringleaders of the strike, for dismissal without fear of a claim for unfair dismissal.

5.5.2.2 Other industrial action

All employees taking part in official strike action are protected from dismissal during the first 12 weeks of the strike action. There is no qualifying period of employment. Section 238A of the TULR(C)A 1992 provides that a dismissal will be automatically unfair if the reason (or, if more than one, the principal reason for the dismissal) is that the employee took 'protected' industrial action, provided the dismissal occurred within the 12-week period, or if after that period the employee was dismissed when they had ceased to take part in the action, or if the dismissal occurs after the 12-week period, but the employer had not taken proper steps for the purposes of resolving the dispute.

5.5.3 Dismissal for asserting a statutory right

5.5.3.1 ERA 1996, s 104

It is unfair to dismiss an employee (or to select for redundancy) because:

(a)   he has brought proceedings against an employer to enforce a relevant statutory right; or

(b)   he has alleged that the employer has infringed a right of his which is a relevant statutory right.

'Relevant statutory rights' include, for example, claims under s 13 of the ERA 1996 (protection of wages), or a claim to a written statement of terms under ERA 1996, s 1.

No qualifying period of continuous employment is necessary.

Note: there is some scope for an overlap with a public interest disclosure claim (see **5.5.5** below). Section 104 does not cover breaches of contractual obligations (unless it is a wages claim) but the Public Interest Disclosure Act 1998 might cover this. Section 104 does not cover detriments.

5.5.4 Health and safety dismissals

5.5.4.1 ERA 1996, s 100

It is unfair to dismiss an employee who 'stops the job' on health and safety grounds. No period of continuous employment is required.

5.5.5 Public Interest Disclosure Act 1998

5.5.5.1 Introduction

The Public Interest Disclosure Act (PIDA) 1998, often referred to as the 'whistleblower's charter', introduced special rights and protections for workers who disclose wrongdoing by their employers to a third party in specific circumstances. It was introduced after a series of disasters (such as the Zeebrugge ferry, Piper Alpha oil platform and the Clapham rail crash) which highlighted the need for a law to protect workers who 'blew the whistle' in the public interest.

The PIDA 1998 aims to promote better relations between employers and employees over wrongdoing in the workplace, and to end the so-called 'cover-up culture', so that workers are not scared to tell their bosses or others about problems relating to matters such as health and safety or criminal activities for fear of being dismissed or victimised. The Act assumes that whistleblowing is in the public interest. This approach offers some protection to whistleblowers but does little to encourage them. Some commentators have argued that the UK should adopt a similar approach to that in the USA (see the recent Dodd-Frank legislation) which permits a percentage of any fine imposed to be paid to the whistleblower and has encouraged the flow of information to US regulators.

The provisions of the PIDA 1998 apply not just to employees and workers but also to third-party contractors whose work is controlled by an employer. The Act does not create a general right for all whistleblowing. Only certain categories of information will be protected in certain situations. Claims under the PIDA 1998 may be brought in respect of treatment which subjects the claimant to a detriment (ERA 1996, s 47B) and, in respect of employees only, for unfair dismissal (ERA 1996, s 103A). A claim may therefore relate both to treatment during the employment relationship and to the termination of it. This section of the book deals with dismissal claims, whether by an employee or a worker, and is meant only as an introduction to what is a complex topic.

5.5.5.2 Protected disclosure

There are limits on the matters about which an employee may complain. The PIDA 1998 inserts a provision into ERA 1996 (s 43B) which provides that a 'qualifying disclosure' means any disclosure of information which in the reasonable (ie there is an objective element to the test) belief of the worker (ie this is overall a subjective test at the time of disclosure) tends to show wrongdoing of one or more of the following kinds (past, present or future):

(a)   a criminal offence (see *Babula v Waltham Forest College* [2006] EWCA Civ 1154);

(b)   a failure to comply with a legal obligation (see *Parkins v Sodexho Ltd* [2002] IRLR 109 and *Douglas v Birmingham City Council* (UKEAT/0518/02). The Government proposes to amend this provision to ensure that such disclosures are in the public interest to avoid workers using this section to raise concerns about private employment rights (breach of one's own contract) – see the draft Enterprise and Regulatory Reform Bill;

(c)   a miscarriage of justice;

(d)   the health and safety of any individual is endangered;

(e)   the environment is being damaged;

(f)   information relating to any of the above areas is being deliberately concealed.

The Court of Appeal gave guidance in *Babula v Waltham Forest College* [2007] EWCA Civ 1154 as to what is meant by 'reasonable belief'. It held that there may be a qualifying disclosure even if the employee is wrong, so long as the belief was reasonable in the circumstances at the time of the disclosure. Further guidance was provided on this in *Goode v Marks and Spencer plc* (UKEAT/ 442/09). The EAT held in *Cavendish Munro v Geduld* (EAT/0195/09) that, to qualify, the disclosure must disclose information about a situation and not merely make an allegation or assertion (eg saying the words 'have not been cleaned for two weeks' discloses information, whereas saying 'you are not complying with health and safety law' is merely an allegation).

An ancillary activity up to disclosure will not be sufficient. Telling someone something he already knows can be a disclosure (see s 43L).

5.5.5.3   Procedures for disclosure

In order to qualify for protection, there is a tiered disclosure regime:

(a)   a disclosure in good faith to an employer or (where the failure related to a person other than an employer) to that other person (s 43C);

(b)   a disclosure to a legal adviser in the course of obtaining legal advice (s 43D – note this does not need good faith);

(c)   where the employer is appointed under any statute by a Minister of the Crown, a disclosure in good faith to a Minister of the Crown (s 43E);

(d)   a disclosure in good faith to a prescribed person under s 43F. (Details of prescribed bodies and the matters in respect of which they are prescribed are set out in the Public Interest Disclosure (Prescribed Persons) Order 1999 (SI 1999/1549) (as amended). The list includes bodies such as HM Revenue & Customs and the HSE.)

These four methods of disclosure are very specific. In addition, there are two much more general provisions which impose more complex tests:

(a)   A disclosure in good faith, reasonably believing that the information disclosed is substantially true, which is not made for personal gain, where the employee reasonably believes that if he discloses the information to his employer or a prescribed person he will suffer a detriment, or he has previously made a disclosure of substantially the same information to the employer or the prescribed person. In deciding whether it is reasonable for the employee to make the disclosure, the Act lays down a number of circumstances which should be borne in mind, including the identity of the person to whom the disclosure is made, the seriousness of the relevant failure and how the employer responded to the earlier disclosure (s 43G).

(b)   A disclosure of 'exceptionally serious' material such as merits bypassing one of the other procedures.

In *Goode v Marks and Spencer plc* (**5.5.5.2** above), one of the reasons Goode's claim failed was because the tribunal found that his disclosure to the media was different from his internal expressions of concern and did not therefore satisfy the test for the wider disclosure under s 43G(2)(c)(i) which requires a worker to have 'previously made a disclosure of substantially the same information to his employer'.

In *Collins v National Trust* (ET/2507255/05), C was able to avail himself of the 'exceptionally serious circumstances' provisions, such that his disclosure to a local newspaper of a confidential report about dangers on a public beach was protected. (Compare this to the circumstances in *Holbrook v Queen Mary's Sidcup NHS Trust* (ET/1101904/06).)

Employers should have an appropriate disclosure policy in their staff handbooks so as to avoid whistleblowing cases reaching the tribunal. This should ensure they receive early notification of any problems. Since April 2010, claimants bringing a whistleblowing claim against their employer can tick a box on the claim form, requesting that the tribunal forward details of their whistleblowing allegations to the appropriate regulator for investigation.

In *Street v Derbyshire Unemployed Workers Centre* [2004] IRLR 687, the Court of Appeal held that an employee's disclosure was not 'protected' because she had been motivated by a grudge and therefore had not acted in good faith. The Court of Appeal emphasised that a person could 'reasonably believe' in the substantial truth of an allegation, but still not make a disclosure in 'good faith'. It said the phrase did not mean 'honesty'. It said a disclosure would not be made in good faith where the 'dominant or pre-dominant purpose' of making the disclosure was for an ulterior motive and was not for the public interest in the disclosure of wrong-doing. The motive should be 'public spirited' (which is the underlying principle of the whistleblowing legislation). (See also *Smith v Ministry of Defence* (IDS Brief 788/12).) In the Harold Shipman inquiry, Dame Janet Smith, who chaired the inquiry, expressed concerns that the 'good faith' test should be removed from the PIDA 1998. Public Concern as Work believes it should be replaced with a public interest test. The onus is on the employer to show something was not done in good faith.

5.5.5.4   Burden of proof

Employees will be treated as having been automatically unfairly dismissed where the reason or principal reason for the dismissal was that they made a protected disclosure. There is no continuous employment requirement. However, the employee's continuity of employment will still matter.

If the employee has the requisite continuity of employment to bring an 'ordinary' unfair dismissal claim, the burden of proving the reason for the dismissal is on the employer to show that he had a potentially fair reason for the dismissal. There is no burden on the employee to disprove the reason put forward by the employer, but he will have to produce some evidence supporting the positive case that he was dismissed by reason of making a protected disclosure. It will then be for the tribunal to consider the evidence as a whole and make findings of fact on the basis of the direct evidence and/or by reasonable inferences from primary facts established by the evidence (*Kuzel v Roche Products Ltd* [2008] IRLR 530).

Where an employee does not have the requisite continuous employment required for an 'ordinary' unfair dismissal claim, the burden of proof is on the employee to prove that the protected disclosure was the employer's reason or principal reason for the dismissal (see the EAT's reasoning on this in *Kuzel* (UKEAT/0516/06). In a detriment case, the worker must prove that he made the relevant disclosure and prove the detrimental treatment. The employer then has to prove another reason for the treatment. If it does not prove another reason, the tribunal must conclude that it was by reason of the protected disclosure.

5.5.5.5   Standard of proof – causation

In dismissal cases, the standard of proof is different from that in detriment cases (note that where a worker alleges that he was dismissed by reason of making a protected disclosure, he will need to rely on the detriment provisions because only employees are able to allege unfair dismissal). Section 103A of the ERA 1996 requires that the protected disclosure be 'the reason (or, if more than one reason, the principal reason) for the dismissal'. In a case where the claimant has made multiple disclosures, the question is whether the cumulative impact was the principal reason for the dismissal (*El-Megrisi v Azad University (IR) in Oxford* (UKEAT/0448/08)). In detriment cases, the test is whether the protected disclosure *materially influences* the employer's treatment of the whistleblower. That, as the Court of Appeal noted in *NHS Manchester v Fecitt and Others* [2012] IRLR 641, means that there are different tests.

5.5.5.6 Enforcement and remedies

The usual three-month time limit applies for bringing a claim (see **6.3.1**). Where the employee is dismissed, time runs from the date of dismissal. Where the complaint is one of detrimental treatment, this can sometimes be problematic where the act complained of and the detriment occur on different dates – see *Vivian v Bournemouth Borough Council* (UKEAT/0254/10). Where this happens, time runs from the date of the act which has been done on the ground that the worker has made a protected disclosure, not the later date of the detriment suffered as a result. In this case, the act was placing the employee in the redeployment pool, and time ran from that act, not from the consequences of that act. However, it may be found not to have been reasonably practicable to bring the complaint until the detriment occurred, so the claim may be admissible if it is brought within a further reasonable period (see **6.3.1**).

Since April 2010 claimants have been invited to tick a box on the ET1 (see **Chapter 6**) indicating whether their claim includes protected disclosure allegations and, if so, whether the claimant wishes the tribunal to refer the allegation on to the relevant authority.

In whistleblowing case, there is the possibility of 'interim relief' (ERA 1996, s 128). An employee who has been dismissed can ask the tribunal to order the employer to continue to pay his wages through to trial (and any subsequent appeal). An order may be made where the employment judge considers the employee is 'likely to succeed'. 'Likely' means having a 'pretty good chance' of success (see *Taplin v Shippam Ltd* [1978] ICR 1068 and *Raja v Secretary of State for Justice* [2010] All ER (D) 134).

Where an employee has made a protected disclosure and is dismissed for that reason, that is an automatically unfair dismissal (ERA 1996, s 103A). No qualifying period of service will be necessary to bring a claim. There are no limits on the amounts which may be awarded by way of compensatory award, and the tribunal may award reinstatement/re-engagement. It is also unlawful to subject an employee who has made a protected disclosure to any other detriment (ERA 1996, s 47B). That will include dismissal for workers. There is an express provision making it unlawful to contract out of the PIDA 1998. Note that damages will be awarded on different bases, depending on whether the claim is for a detriment (akin to a discrimination claim) or unfair dismissal (unfair dismissal principles will apply). Thus, in detriment cases, compensation can include compensation for injury to feelings.

5.5.5.7 Human Rights Act 1998

Article 10 of the European Convention on Human Rights, as incorporated by the HRA 1998, contains a right to freedom of expression. That includes the right to hold opinions, and to give and receive information and opinions. That right is subject to balancing restrictions such as are necessary in a democratic society. There is considerable overlap between this and the protection offered by the PIDA 1998. However, Article 10 may provide assistance in areas which are not deemed to be 'protected disclosures' under the 1998 Act.

5.6   AWARDS FOR UNFAIR DISMISSAL

The remedies available for an unfairly dismissed employee are either:

(a)   reinstatement or re-engagement; or

(b)   compensation.

Section 112(2) of the ERA 1996 requires an employment tribunal to explain to a successful complainant what awards are available by way of reinstatement and re-engagement, and when they may be made, and to ask the complainant if he wants such an order to be made. The wording is mandatory. A failure to comply with s 112(2) does not render the decision void, but it does make it voidable, depending on whether the failure caused injustice and unfairness (see *Cowley v Manson Timber Ltd* [1995] ICR 367).

5.6.1 Reinstatement and re-engagement

If the employee wants his job back, he may ask for reinstatement or re-engagement. Reinstatement is to his old job as though he had not been dismissed. Re-engagement is in a different job with the same employer, his successor or an associated employer. In the year 2011/12, reinstatement or re-engagement orders were made in only five of all unfair dismissal cases that were successful at tribunal.

5.6.1.1 Availability of the order

In deciding whether to make an order for reinstatement or re-engagement, the tribunal must take into account:

(a) whether the complainant wishes to be reinstated or re-engaged;

(b) whether it is practicable for the employer to comply with the order;

(c) whether it would be just to make the order where the complainant has caused or contributed to his dismissal (ERA 1996, s 116(1)).

The order will not be made unless the employee asks for it. When considering whether to make such an order, the relevant time is the time of the hearing, not the position at the time of dismissal. It is unlikely to be made if the employee substantially contributed to his own dismissal. In practice, few reinstatement or re-engagement orders are made. Those which are made are often found where the employer is a large organisation such that it is practical to order the employee to return. Where, as is often the case, the employment relationship is permanently damaged, an order will not be made. (See, for example, *Central and NW London NHS Trust v Ambimbola* (UKEAT/0542/08), where the EAT held that the existence of mutual trust and confidence was a relevant factor when addressing the issue of practicability of compliance.)

5.6.1.2 Contents of the order

Where the tribunal orders reinstatement in the old job, it will make consequential orders that the employee be paid arrears of pay, maintains seniority and maintains pension rights (ERA 1996, s 114).

Where the tribunal orders re-engagement in a different job, it will make consequential orders relating to the nature of employment, remuneration, arrears of pay, seniority and pension rights (ERA 1996, s 115).

5.6.1.3 Non-compliance with order

If an order for reinstatement or re-engagement is made but not complied with by the employer, the employer cannot be compelled to reinstate or re-engage the employee. The tribunal must then make an award of compensation in favour of the employee instead (ERA 1996, s 117).

This award of compensation will consist of a basic, compensatory and additional award.

The basic award is calculated in the usual way (see **5.6.2.1**).

The compensatory award will be assessed in the same way as usual, but instead of being limited to £72,300 (see **5.6.2.2**), the limit will be the higher of £72,300 (as at February 2012) or the value of the employee's arrears of pay and benefits which should have been paid to him under the original order for reinstatement or re-engagement. The amount of any award already made under s 112(5) shall be deducted from any compensation awarded under s 117.

For example, if the reinstatement order required the employer to pay the employee the sum of £80,000 by way of arrears of pay and the employer fails to comply, the compensatory award will be £80,000 not £72,300.

Lastly, the tribunal must make an additional award unless the employer can satisfy the tribunal that it was not practicable to comply with the reinstatement or re-engagement order. The employer could put forward new evidence to show this. If the tribunal makes an additional award, this will be an amount equivalent to between 26 and 52 weeks' gross pay. A week's pay is subject to a maximum of £430 as at 1 February 2012.

5.6.2　Compensation

If the tribunal considers that the complaint is well founded, but no order for reinstatement or re-engagement is made, it must make an award of compensation. The award will consist of two elements:

(a)　the basic award; and

(b)　the compensatory award (ERA 1996, s 118).

5.6.2.1　Basic award

The basic award is generally calculated in the same way as a redundancy payment, by applying the formula based on age factor, length of service and one week's pay. The same maximum of 20 years' service and £430 (as at 1 February 2012) for one week's pay applies (ERA 1996, s 119). (See **4.6** for details.) A gross weekly figure is used (subject to the maximum cap). The maximum basic award is currently £12,900.

There are, however, a number of differences between the calculations of the basic award and a redundancy payment:

(a)　In certain circumstances, such as where an employee is unfairly dismissed for being a member of a trade union or refusing to be a member of one, or where a health and safety official is dismissed, the basic award is subject to a minimum, which is £5,300 as at February 2012.

(b)　The basic award may be subject to reduction. Section 122(1) and (2) provide that the basic award may be reduced by such sum as is just and equitable having regard to the claimant's unreasonable refusal to accept an offer of reinstatement and/or the claimant's pre-dismissal conduct (even if the conduct did not contribute to the dismissal).

Redundancy payments should also be deducted from the basic award. Note that in *Bowyer v Siemens Communications* (UKEAT/0021/05) the EAT held that a payment made by an employer which purported to be a redundancy payment, but which was not in fact because there was no redundancy situation, could not be set off against the basic award in an unfair dismissal claim. Such a payment could be offset (under ERA 1996, s 122(4)) only where the true reason for the dismissal was redundancy. (In practice, this will have an impact only where the compensatory award exceeds the statutory cap, as usually such sum will be set off against the compensatory award.)

Note, when calculating the basic award, that age, length of continuous service and pay are all artificially defined by statute. This contrasts with the approach to the compensatory award which is almost entirely discretionary. Thus the approach to the calculation of the two awards is necessarily different. The formula for a week's pay is set out in s 229 of the ERA 1996. For continuity of the period of employment, regard needs to be had to s 218 of the ERA 1996.

5.6.2.2　Compensatory award

Unlike the basic award, which is based on a formula, the compensatory award is designed to compensate the employee for the loss that he has suffered.

By s 123(1) of the ERA 1996, the compensatory award consists of 'such amount as the tribunal considers just and equitable in all the circumstances having regard to the loss sustained by the complainant in consequence of the dismissal in so far as that loss is attributable to action taken by the employer'.

In *Tao Herbs and Acupuncture Ltd v Jin* (UKEAT/1477/09), the EAT confirmed that it was not appropriate when assessing compensation under s 123 of the ERA 1996 to take account of the employer's ability to pay (even if it would mean the business went into liquidation): the prime consideration is the loss suffered by the claimant.

In *W Devis & Sons Ltd v Atkins* [1977] AC 931 the dismissal of an abattoir manager was held to be unfair, but because the employer subsequently discovered information suggesting that the employee had been dishonest during his employment, the court held that it was just and equitable to order no compensatory award.

Whether an employee can recover non-economic loss was the subject of discussion in *Johnson v Unisys Ltd* [2001] IRLR 279. The employee received the maximum compensatory award from a tribunal. He then made a claim for breach of contract in the county court, claiming that his dismissal without a fair hearing was in breach of the duty of trust and confidence, and that this breach resulted in his having a mental breakdown. He sought damages for this. His claim was dismissed on two grounds. First, because the implied duty of trust and confidence was said to be inappropriate to the termination of the employment relationship (see **2.4.1.5**) and, secondly, because the employee had already exercised his statutory right to claim unfair dismissal. In the course of his judgment, Lord Hoffmann commented that while 'in the early days' the compensatory award was only there to compensate financial loss, that was:

> too narrow a construction. The emphasis is upon the tribunal awarding such compensation as it thinks just and equitable. So I see no reason why in an appropriate case it should not include compensation for distress, humiliation, damage to reputation in the community or to family life.

However, in *Dunnachie v Kingston Upon Hull* [2004] IRLR 727, the House of Lords unanimously held that damages for non-economic loss are *not* recoverable for unfair dismissal, and that s 123 of the ERA 1996 only allows a tribunal to award financial losses. Thus it is not possible to recover damages for injury to feelings as part of unfair dismissal compensation. This overrides the Court of Appeal's decision (see [2004] IRLR 287).

Dunnachie was heard by the House of Lords at the same time as *Eastwood v Magnox; McCabe v Cornwall County Council and Another* [2004] IRLR 733, two cases concerning the overlap between common law claims for damages for breach of trust and confidence, and the statutory unfair dismissal regime. In these cases the House of Lords confirmed that a common law claim for breach of the implied term of trust and confidence will be allowed for events leading up to the dismissal, but not for the dismissal itself (because that would amount to a circumvention of the statutory cap placed on compensation for unfair dismissal) (see further **2.4.1.5**). So the employee who suffers psychiatric harm arising out of the events leading up to dismissal cannot recover damages for the loss suffered as part of his unfair dismissal claim because such a loss does not flow from the dismissal, but he might be able to bring a personal injury claim and/or a claim for breach of contract in the civil courts for such pre-dismissal loss. Damages for losses arising out of breach of an implied term flowing from the dismissal are only recoverable in an employment tribunal (where the cap on damages applies).

The Supreme Court confirmed that the so-called *Johnson* exclusion area also applies to cases in which the breach relied upon is of an express contractual term (*Edwards v Chesterfield Royal Hospital NHS Foundation Trust* [2011] UKSC 58). Therefore, an employee who is dismissed cannot bring proceedings for breach of contract based on a failure to follow contractual disciplinary procedures because that would, according to the Supreme Court, undermine the statutory unfair dismissal regime (see **Chapter 2**).

In *GAB Robins v Triggs* [2008] IRLR 317 (an unfair constructive dismissal claim), the Court of Appeal held, applying *Johnson* and *Eastwood*, that in assessing the claimant's loss of earnings for unfair dismissal purposes, no regard could be had to losses which flowed from the bullying that led to her taking time off ill and subsequently resigning, and which resulted in reduced earning capacity thereafter. Regard must be had, for the purposes of s 123 of the ERA 1996, only to losses flowing from the dismissal (by which time the claimant was already ill).

The claimant's reduced earning capacity by reason of her illness was not a loss suffered 'in consequence of the the dismissal'. Rather, it was caused by the bullying, and therefore the claimant could recover damages in respect of it only by bringing a separate claim at common law, such as for psychiatric injury.

A tribunal must, in deciding whether to make a compensatory award (see *Saunders v OCS Group* (UKEAT/0051/09)):

(a) identify what loss the employee has suffered at the date of dismissal; and then

(b) decide whether the employer's action (in dismissing the employee) caused the loss.

Heads of loss

Compensation will usually be assessed under the following main heads:

(a) Immediate loss of net earnings to which the employee was entitled, from the date of dismissal to the date of the hearing or until the employee finds a new job, if earlier (provided that job is higher-paid). In *Whelan and Another (t/a Cheers Off Licence) v Richardson* [1998] IRLR 14, the EAT said, when calculating unfair dismissal compensation, that the applicant should be compensated for all losses arising from the date of dismissal until the date on which higher-paid alternative employment is found.

In *Burlo v Langley & Carter* [2006] EWCA Civ 1778, the Court of Appeal dealt with the principles for calculating compensation during an employee's notice period. Ms Burlo worked as a nanny for Mr Langley and Ms Carter. Her employment was subject to a written contract which provided for eight weeks' notice of termination on either side. The contract also provided that, during periods of sickness, the employers would pay 'sickness benefit in accordance with government statutory sick pay legislation'. Following an argument about money, Ms Burlo threatened to resign. Mr Langley said that she would be required to work her notice. Ms Burlo continued at work, but some days later she had a car accident and was provided with a sick note to say that she would be off work for several weeks. In the meantime, her employers engaged another nanny and wrote saying that they would not now require Ms Burlo to work out her notice. Ms Burlo brought a number of claims in the employment tribunal, including claims for wrongful and unfair dismissal. Both these claims succeeded. The tribunal assessed damages for the notice period at £3,440 (eight weeks at her normal weekly wage). They did not explain why they held that the damages should be based on the normal weekly wage rather than on the statutory sick pay to which the employee would have been entitled whilst off sick under her contract of employment. The Court of Appeal held that if Ms Burlo had not been dismissed, she would have received statutory sick pay during her period of absence. Consequently, statutory sick pay was the correct measure of her weekly loss during the notice period. Note, however, that where an employee is entitled only to statutory minimum notice, the employer must pay full pay during the notice period, even where the employee is off work sick (ERA 1996, ss 87 and 88).

In *Paggetti v Cobb* (UKEAT/136/01), the EAT held that when assessing the compensatory (and basic) awards, the tribunal must have regard to the minimum wage.

(b) Future loss of net earnings to which the employee was entitled from the date of hearing until the employee obtains new employment. No award will be made under this head if the employee is permanently re-employed in an equally well remunerated job at the date of hearing. If he loses that new job, the tribunal will have to assess whether the chain of causation has been broken (*Cowen v Rentokil Ltd* (UKEAT/0473/07)). If the employee takes a less well-paid job, he will be compensated for the difference in pay for such period as the tribunal thinks appropriate in the circumstances. If the employee remains unemployed at this date, the tribunal will have to estimate if and when the employee is likely to be re-employed. Compensation for future loss of earnings is not limited to the employee's contractual notice period. The tribunal will take into account local employment conditions, the skills of the employee, his age and general employability. If an employee could and would have worked beyond the age of 65, compensation may be awarded for potential loss of earnings after 65. If evidence shows that the employee would shortly have lost his job anyway, due, for example, to redundancy, compensation will be limited.

(c) Loss of pension rights and net fringe benefits from the date of dismissal to the date at (b) above. The value of lost pension rights is very difficult to calculate, and depends on a number of factors, such as type of scheme, the benefits paid and the benefits receivable on retirement. Employment tribunals may use the guidance produced by GAD (see **2.4.1.4**). In *Port of Tilbury v Birch* [2005] IRLR 92, the EAT said that tribunals should *not* use the guidelines if the parties have their own credible evidence on pension loss. The guidelines are a fallback position only.

(d) Loss of statutory rights. The loss of accrued redundancy rights is compensated for by the basic award, but the tribunal will order a sum for the loss of the right to bring an unfair dismissal claim for one year. Conventionally, this sum is about £350.

The employee may exceptionally also be awarded up to half-a-week's net pay for each week of the statutory minimum period of notice to which he had been entitled at the end of employment. For example, an employee with 20 years' service would have been entitled to the maximum 12-week notice period. He may be awarded ½ × 12 × net weekly pay (ie six weeks) to compensate for the loss of this. This payment will be made only in exceptional circumstances, because it depends on the double contingency that the employee will get a new job and be dismissed from it before building up the same period of notice. More often than not, a tribunal will simply award the £350 above for loss of statutory rights.

(e) Expenses in looking for work; removal expenses incurred in taking up a new job.

(f) A premium for delayed payment may be awarded (the reverse of accelerated receipt – see 'Reducing factors' below) (*Melia v Magna Kansei* (UKEAT/0339/04)).

Compulsory increase of the compensatory award

Section 38 of the EA 2002 states that a tribunal must award compensation to an employee where, upon a successful claim being made under any of the jurisdictions listed in Sch 5 to the EA 2002 (which include unfair dismissal), it becomes apparent that the employer was in breach of his duty to provide full and accurate written particulars (under ERA 1996, s 1). This is not a free-standing claim, it is dependent upon a claim under one of the listed jurisdictions being successful. The tribunal must award the minimum amount of two weeks' pay and may, if it considers it just and equitable, in the circumstances, award a higher amount of four weeks' pay (subject to the maximum of £430 (as at 1 February 2012)). This is on top of any award the tribunal might already have made in respect of the main claim. The tribunal does not have to make any award if there are exceptional circumstances that would make it unjust or inequitable to make an award or increase an award.

Discretionary increase of compensation

Where there has been an unreasonable failure by the employer to comply with the Acas Code, the tribunal has power to increase compensation by up to 25% (TULR(C)A 1992, s 207A). It should be noted that this adjustment option applies to the basic award too.

It remains to be seen what will constitute an unreasonable failure to comply with the Code, and what factors will be relevant to the question of whether it is 'just and equitable' to make an adjustment to an award. In *Lawless v Print Plus* (UKEAT/0333/09), a case decided under the old statutory minimum procedures, the EAT said the factors to be taken into account when considering the size of the uplift include:

(a) whether the procedures were ignored altogether or applied to some extent;

(b) whether the failure to apply the procedures was deliberate or inadvertent;

(c)   whether there are circumstances which might mitigate the blameworthiness of the failure;

(d)   the size and resources of the employer which may aggravate or mitigate the culpability and/or seriousness of the failure.

Note that because s 207A only 'bites' on claims where the relevant Code of Practice applies, and because, as we saw earlier, the only Code of Practice published to date does not apply to dismissals by reason of redundancy or where the dismissal was as a result of the expiry of a fixed-term contract, no adjustment will be made to redundancy payment awards or unfair dismissal awards where the reason for the dismissal was redundancy or expiry of a fixed-term contract. Note also that uplifts can only be applied to employees and not workers (see *Local Government Yorkshire v Shah* (UKEAT/0587/11)).

Maximum award

The compensatory award is subject to a maximum, which is £72,300 for dismissals where the EDT was on or after 1 February 2012 (ERA 1996, s 124). The Enterprise and Regulatory Reform Bill, introduced into Parliament on 23 May 2012, includes powers for the Secretary of State to cap the compensatory award for unfair dismissal at somewhere between one year's national median earnings (around £26,000) and three years' annual average earnings (around £78,000). Alternatively, the Bill includes a power to limit the maximum award to 52 weeks' pay. Consultation closed on 1 November 2012. Note that the maximum does not apply to whistleblowing cases. This maximum is applied *after* any reductions have been made (see below).

Note: The £72,300 maximum applies only to the compensatory element of the award. A claimant could therefore receive £72,300 *plus* a basic award of up to £12,900 (as at 1 February 2012).

Reducing factors

Note that early pension payments should *not* be deducted from the compensatory award (*Smoker v London Fire and Civil Defence Authority* [1991] ICR 449, followed in *Knapton & Others v ECC Card Clothing Ltd* [2006] IRLR 756).

(a)   *Mitigation*

The employee is under a duty to mitigate his loss by taking reasonable steps to obtain alternative employment. Compensation will not be awarded for any loss that should have been mitigated but was not (*Kyndall Spirits v Burns* (EAT/29/02)). The burden of raising and proving an unreasonable failure to mitigate is on the employer. In practice, an employee should keep records of his job applications to show the tribunal that he has tried to mitigate his loss. Where an employee turns down an offer of employment, the ultimate question for the tribunal is whether he acted unreasonably in turning it down. The tribunal must consider all the surrounding circumstances (*Wilding v British Telecommunications plc* [2002] IRLR 524). Failure to mitigate can reduce the compensatory award but not the basic award. Similarly, if the employee has secured an alternative job by the time of the hearing, wages from that new job will be taken into account.

The Court of Appeal in *Burlo* (see 'Heads of loss' above) looked closely at the decision of the National Industrial Relations Court (Sir John Donaldson presiding) in *Norton Tool Co Ltd v Tewson* [1973] 1 WLR 45. It said that *Norton Tool* settled two basic points of law on the calculation of compensation for unfair dismissal in an actual dismissal. First, compensation could not be awarded for injury to feelings. (*Norton Tool* was expressly approved on this point by the House of Lords in *Dunnachie v Kingston upon Hull City Council* (see above).) Secondly, where an employer summarily dismissed an employee in a situation where notice should have been given but was not, an employee was entitled to be awarded compensation for wages in lieu of notice without any deduction for wages which were actually earned, or could have been earned, with an alternative employer during the notice period. In *Babcock FATA Ltd v Addison* [1987] ICR 805, the employer had challenged (unsuccessfully) *Norton Tool* on the wages in lieu of notice point. Although the employer won its appeal on the particular facts in *Babcock*, the Court of Appeal in that case were unanimous in not accepting the contention that *Norton Tool* was wrong in holding that the employee should not have to give credit for the wages that he had received from alternative employment during the period of notice. It was argued in *Burlo* that the House of Lords in *Dunnachie* had impliedly overruled the *Norton Tool* principle that credit need not be given by an employee for other earnings during the notice period. The Court of Appeal said that issue had to be left for another case to determine, but in the meantime a claimant should not have to give credit for monies earned during the notice period. The Court of Appeal in *Stuart Peters v Bell* [2009] EWCA Civ 938 held that this principle does not apply to a constructive dismissal. In a constructive dismissal case, credit has to be given for wages earned during the notice period.

(b)   *Accelerated receipt for future loss of earnings*

See **2.4.1.9** for a discussion of this reducing factor.

(c)   *Ex gratia payments made by the employer to the employee*

(d)   *'Polkey' deductions*

One of the factors that a tribunal has to consider when assessing compensation where there have been procedural failings in the dismissal process, is whether the employee would still have been dismissed if a proper procedure had been followed. If the tribunal concludes that even if a fair procedure had been followed, dismissal would still have occurred, then that can sound in the compensation that is awarded. Such a conclusion can have two main effects:

(i)   on the period of time over which compensation is awarded; and

(ii)   on the actual amount,

in that a percentage reduction (up to 100%) may be made by the tribunal to take account of the tribunal's assessment of the likelihood that dismissal would still have occurred. An employment tribunal's task, when deciding what compensation is just and equitable for future loss of earnings in these circumstances, will almost inevitably involve a consideration of uncertainties. What the tribunal has to do is to 'construct, from evidence not speculation, a framework which is a working hypothesis about what would have happened had the [employer] behaved differently and fairly' (*Gover and Others v Property Care Ltd* [2006] EWCA Civ 286).

In *Polkey v AE Dayton Services Ltd* [1988] ICR 142, the House of Lords ended what was known as the 'no difference' rule, which had allowed procedurally irregular dismissals to be ruled as fair where it could be shown that carrying out a proper procedure would have made no difference to the outcome. Their Lordships said this was not relevant to fairness, but it would sound in the assessment of damages because s 123 of the ERA 1996 refers to 'such amount as the tribunal considers just and equitable in all the circumstances'. Lord Bridge approved the remarks of Browne-Wilkinson J in *Sillifant's Case* [1983] IRLR 91, at 96:

> There is no need for an 'all or nothing' decision; if the industrial tribunal thinks there is a doubt whether or not the employee would have been dismissed, this element can be reflected by reducing the normal amount of compensation by a percentage representing the chance that the employee would still have lost his employment.

In *Lambe v 186K* [2005] ICR 307, the Court of Appeal considered how tribunals should approach the question of compensation in cases where a dismissal might have occurred in any event. Giving the judgment of the Court, Wall LJ (at 323) cited with approval the judgment of Lord Prosser in the Court of Session in *King v Eaton Limited (No 2)* [1998] IRLR 686. The procedure by which an applicant was made redundant in *King* was found to be unfair, and the issue was whether the applicant would have been made redundant had a fair procedure been followed. Lord Prosser stated (at para 19):

> It seems to us that the matter will be one of impression and judgment, so that a tribunal will have to decide whether the unfair departure from what should have happened was of a kind which makes it possible to say, with more or less confidence, that the failure made no difference, or whether the failure was such that one cannot sensibly reconstruct the world as it might have been.

Wall LJ stated that the formulation 'provides tribunals with a straightforward and sensible yardstick with which to approach such cases'. At para 60, Wall LJ adopted that approach and stated:

> [That] approach to the facts of the instant case leads us to the conclusion that on the evidence available to it, the Tribunal was entitled to conclude that in the Appellant's case, whilst both the process of selection for redundancy and the absence of consultation was unfair, it was unlikely that the Appellant would have found alternative employment with the Respondent or any of its associated companies at the conclusion of an extended period of consultation. The Tribunal was entitled to find that what the Appellant wanted was his job back, and that he was not willing to consider the alternative offered by the Respondent, which the Tribunal found was both a promotion and commanded a higher income. In short, this was not a case in which it was impossible for the Tribunal sensibly to reconstruct the world as it never was: the Tribunal was entitled to come to the conclusion that an extended period of consultation should have taken place, but that at the end of it, the Appellant would still have left the Respondent's employment.

Where a fair procedure would have delayed an otherwise inevitable dismissal, compensation will be awarded for the time the procedure would have taken to conduct properly (see, for example, *Slaughter v Breuer* [1990] ICR 730).

In *O'Donoghue v Redcar and Cleveland BC* [2001] IRLR 615, the Court of Appeal upheld the tribunal's finding that the claimant would have been dismissed fairly within a further period of six months because of her antagonistic attitude. Compensation was therefore limited to six months (see also *Gover and Others v Property Care Ltd* [2006] EWCA Civ 286).

In *Software 2000 Ltd v Andrews and Others* [2007] ICR 825, Elias J reviewed and summarised the principles to be extracted from all the authorities on *Polkey*. IDS Employment Law Brief 912 (November 2010) contains a helpful discussion on *Polkey* reductions, including when and how they should be made.

Polkey deductions may be made whether the dismissal is substantively unfair or procedurally unfair, although it will be easier to assess if the failure is procedural (*King v Eaton No 2* [1998] IRLR 686).

(e)   *Discretionary reduction in compensation*

Where there has been an unreasonable failure by the employee to comply with the Acas Code, a reduction of up to 25% is possible. (See the discussion above of the discretionary increase of compensation.)

(f)   *Contributory fault*

If the tribunal finds that the complainant caused or contributed to his dismissal, the compensatory award must be reduced by such proportion as it considers just and equitable (ERA 1996, s 123(6)). If the employee substantially contributed to his own dismissal, this will mean a substantial percentage reduction in the awards, even of 100%, leaving the employee with a finding of unfair dismissal but no compensation. This is usually relevant only in misconduct dismissals. It is unusual in capability dismissals, for example on health grounds, where the employee is not culpable or blameworthy. The tribunal does not necessarily need to reduce basic and compensatory awards by the same percentage, but it often does so in practice. The question for the tribunal is whether, in a misconduct case, the claimant was in fact guilty of the blameworthy or culpable conduct which to any extent caused or contributed to the dismissal. The employer's conduct is irrelevant (*Sandwell & West Birmingham Hospitals NHS*

Trust v Westwood (UKEAT/0032/09), but tribunals must consider mitigating factors before making a reduction.

(g)   *Pre-dismissal misconduct discovered after dismissal*

The tribunal, in deciding what amount is just and equitable, may take into account any misconduct of the employee discovered after dismissal and reduce both the basic and compensatory awards accordingly (ss 122(2) and 123(1)). Post-dismissal conduct is not relevant.

(h)   *Contractual redundancy payments in excess of the basic award.*

(i)   *Payments in lieu – compensatory award only*

If the employee receives a payment in lieu of notice or an ex gratia payment from his employer, this will be taken into account in assessing his compensation (*Babcock FATA Ltd v Addison* [1987] IRLR 173, CA).

Order of compensatory award adjustments

The correct order of adjustments once the net loss is calculated is (see *Ministry of Defence v Wheeler* [1998] IRLR 23, CA, and *Digital Equipment Co Ltd v Clements (No 2)* [1998] IRLR 134, CA):

(a)   deduct payments in lieu/ex gratia payments made by the employer;

(b)   deduct sums earned by the employee from new employment, or make deductions by reason of a failure to mitigate;

(c)   make any *Polkey* deduction;

(d)   make any contributory fault deduction/deduction for misconduct discovered after dismissal (ERA 1996, s 123(6));

(e)   deduct contractual redundancy payment made by the employer which is in excess of basic award;

(f)   add in any award for sums awarded for failure to provide written particulars of employment (EA 2002, ss 31 and 38) (s 31(5));

(g)   reduce the award or increase by up to 25% for a failure to comply with the Acas Code;

(h)   apply statutory cap of £72,300 (as at February 2012) (if appropriate);

(i)   gross up (if appropriate).

5.6.2.3   Interest

Interest may be awarded on compensation for unfair dismissal. However, it begins to run only when the award remains unpaid for 42 days after the decision is sent to the parties.

5.6.2.4   Recoupment of social security benefits

The Employment Protection (Recoupment of Jobseeker's Allowance and Income Support) Regulations 1996 (SI 1996/2349) (as amended and updated by the Welfare Reform Act 2007 and the Social Security (Miscellaneous Amendments) (No 5) Regulations 2010 (SI 2010/2429)) allow the Government to recoup jobseeker's allowance, income support and (from 1 November 2010) income-related employment and support allowance (IRESA) paid to an employee who gets an unfair dismissal award of compensation. These benefits received by the employee are not deducted by the tribunal in computing the compensatory award. (Note: Contributory employment and support allowance is not covered by the recoupment regulations.)

The Employment Tribunals Act 1996 (ETA 1996), ss 16 and 17 operate as follows:

(a)   where the employee has received jobseeker's allowance, income support or IRESA between the EDT and the hearing, the tribunal designates the 'immediate loss of earnings' part of the award as the 'prescribed element' and notifies the Department for Work and Pensions (DfWP);

(b)   the employer withholds the 'prescribed element' from the employee until notified by the DfWP of the amount of jobseeker's allowance, income support and IRESA to be recouped (up to the maximum of the 'prescribed element');

(c)   the amount to be recouped is then paid by the employer to the DfWP and any balance of the 'prescribed element' paid to the employee.

> **EXAMPLE**
>
> Whilst awaiting a hearing, the employee receives income support *totalling* £1,500. The tribunal awards compensation of £10,000.
>
> £2,000 of this represents immediate loss of wages (the 'prescribed element').
>
> The employer pays £8,000 to the employee immediately and tells DfWP that he has retained £2,000.
>
> DfWP tells the employer to account for £1,500.
>
> The employer pays £1,500 to DfWP and £500 to the employee.

Note: the recoupment regulations do not apply to settlements.

5.6.2.5   Taxation

If an award is made for termination of employment that exceeds £30,000, it is subject to taxation (see Income Tax (Earnings and Pensions) Act 2003, Ch 3, Pt 6, s 401(1)). This covers payments for 'being' an employee, including emoluments from the employer and rewards for services past, present and future. Any awards over £30,000 should therefore be grossed up to ensure that the net loss is actually paid to the claimant (see **2.4.1.8**).

A detailed explanation of how taxation impacts in practice on tribunal awards is beyond the scope of this work, but a summary chart is set out in **Table 5.1** below. Tribunals generally make awards that reflect a claimant's losses, but should take into account when doing so any prospective tax liability. From 6 April 2011, employers must deduct PAYE from post-termination payments at the appropriate marginal rate.

> **EXAMPLE**
>
> Suppose a tribunal awards £50,000 as the compensatory element of an award for unfair dismissal. HM Revenue and Customs regards this as taxable as a termination payment. The first £30,000 is tax free (if statutory redundancy has been paid this would count towards the £30,000). The remaining £20,000 is taxed as income. What tax rate is applicable will depend on what the employee has already earned in the tax year. If he has earned only a small amount (so that his total gross earnings in the year do not exceed £37,400) the appropriate tax rate will be 20%. The award will need to be grossed up (which will provide a figure of £24,000 (20,000 × $\frac{120}{100}$)). Then add back in the £30,000. The tribunal will need to award £54,000 to the employee to ensure that the employee is left, after the employer pays tax due, with the true net loss of £50,000.

Table 5.1 Taxation of tribunal awards

Type of Award	Gross/Net	Explanation
Unlawful deduction from wages [ERA 1996, s 24] (see **1.11.1**)	Gross (but see wording in ERA 1996, s 13(3)) NI is also payable	Wages. This is deferred remuneration; it is a contractual payment which is taxable in the hands of the employee. It is not a payment on termination and does not come within the £30K exemption.
Unpaid holiday pay (whether under contract or under WTR) (see **1.12.5**)	Gross NI is also payable	Wages. This is deferred remuneration; it is a contractual payment which is taxable in the hands of the employee. It is not a payment on termination and does not come within the £30K exemption.
Unpaid notice: (a) PILON clause (see **2.4.1.8**)	(a) Gross NI is also payable	(a) This is a contractual payment which is taxable in the hands of the employee. It is not a payment on termination and does not come within the £30K exemption.
(b) No PILON clause	(b) Net (after notional deduction of tax and NI)	(b) This is not a contractual payment but rather is damages for breach of contract. Damages are generally awarded in respect of net loss of earnings as this puts the employee in the same position as if the contract had been performed. An employee is exempt from paying tax on termination payments, including damages for wrongful dismissal, which do not exceed £30K. This sum should be included as part of the £30K exemption as it is a payment on termination under IT(EP)A 2003, Pt 6. Sums in excess of £30K will need to be grossed up.
Damages for wrongful dismissal – generally calculated on basis of a sum equal to the wages payable during the contractual notice period (see **2.4**) (See *British Transport Commission v Gourley* [1955] 3 All ER 796)	Net (after notional deduction of tax and NI)	This is not a contractual payment but rather is damages for breach of contract. An employee is exempt from paying tax on termination payments, including damages for wrongful dismissal, which do not exceed £30K. This sum should therefore be included as part of the £30K exemption as it is a payment on termination. NB: there is a £25K jurisdictional limit on tribunal awards for breach of contract, so in reality this will require grossing up only where other awards, such as compensation for unfair dismissal, take the award over £30K.

Type of Award	Gross/Net	Explanation
Employment Act 2002, s 38 payment (see **5.6.2.2**)	Gross (subject to the weekly pay cap)	This is not wages and therefore is not normally taxable. Not included within the £30K exemption.
UD reinstatement or re-engagement (where arrears of wages etc will have to be paid)	Net	The Court of Appeal in *Wilson v Clayton* [2005] IRLR 108 said this was not earnings but a payment in consequence of dismissal. An employee is exempt from paying tax on termination payments which do not exceed £30,000. This sum should be included as part of the £30,000 exemption.
UD basic award and compensation award (ERA 1996, s 118) (see **5.6.2.1** and **5.6.2.2**)	Net (after notional deduction of tax and NI)	Not taxable *unless in excess of £30K* exemption, when will have to gross up the amount which exceeds £30K. (See *British Transport Commission v Gourley* [1955] 3 All ER 796.)
Compensation award for unlawful discrimination – treated as statutory tort (see **8.13.2.1**)	Net (after notional deduction of tax and NI)	Not taxable unless in excess of £30K exemption, when will have to gross up the amount which exceeds £30K. (See *Walker v Adams* [2001] STC 101.)
Discrimination – injury to feelings and personal injury award (see *Yorkshire Housing v Cuerden* (UKEAT/0397/09)) (see **8.9.2.1**)	Simple figure awarded	If the award relates to conduct before termination then it is not earnings, is not taxable and does not need to be grossed up. If it arises out of the termination of employment then it is taxable.

5.7 CASE STUDY 1: UNFAIR DISMISSAL, REDUNDANCY PAYMENT AND UNPAID WAGES

Facts

(1) R ran a graphic design agency employing a number of designers. C was employed by R as a senior designer. On 1 October 2011, C was given her wage cheque for September. That cheque bounced. By 13 October 2011, the entire workforce, including C, had been sent home on full pay. The workshop was closed. R indicated to its workforce that the company expected a payment and that wages would be honoured. There was considerable uncertainty amongst the members of the workforce as to what was happening, and other than as indicated below, there appears to have been no formal notification to C either of the fact that she was being made redundant, or of when she was being made redundant. C was born on 2 February 1988. She worked for R between June 2009 and October 2011. Her ET1 was dated 28 October 2011. In her ET1, C says that on 28 October 2011 she phoned R to ask what was happening and was told that she was being made redundant. Her basic wage was £30,000 per annum. Her normal working week was 40 hours.

Claims

(2)   C complained in her ET1 of unfair dismissal, and that R had not paid her wages and/or had not paid the notice pay and/or outstanding holiday pay to which she was entitled by her contract.

Evidence

(3)   Oral evidence was heard on oath from C, who produced a bundle of papers relating to her claim, including payslips and her contract of employment. C confirmed that she had not been paid for September or October, and that she had not been given any notice. Her contract confirmed that she was entitled to one month's notice of termination.

Findings

(4)   The decision of the tribunal was that C was unfairly dismissed by R, and that she was entitled to a redundancy payment and wages in breach of contract.

Reasons

(5)   There was some confusion over the effective date of termination for C. One of her colleagues had received a letter confirming that his last date of employment was 20 October 2011, although C had not received such a letter. As C had submitted her ET1 on 30 October 2011, two days after she had been told she was being made redundant, the tribunal concluded that 28 October was the appropriate date from which to assume that the employment relationship with R had ended.

(6)   The tribunal concluded that:

(a)   this was a genuine redundancy situation in accordance with s 139 of the ERA 1996, and that redundancy was the reason for C's dismissal;

(b)   as C had two years' service, she was entitled to a redundancy payment;

(c)   as C had one year's service, she was entitled to complain of unfair dismissal. On the basis of the evidence, the tribunal concluded that her dismissal was unfair. Notwithstanding that there had been some communication with her on 13 October, when she had been sent home on full pay, after that date she was not given any further information about the company's situation and had to find things out for herself. On that basis, there had not been proper, adequate or reasonable warning or consultation. There was clearly no attempt to consider any help or assistance with regard to alternative employment. However, as it was clear that even had there been proper warning, consultation, etc, it was highly likely that C would still have been dismissed, the tribunal made a 100% *Polkey* reduction in respect of the compensatory element of the unfair dismissal award;

(d)   unauthorised deductions had been made from C's wages, in that she had not been paid money properly due and payable in respect of wages, as set out below; further, the tribunal found as fact that R had failed to pay notice pay and holiday pay to which C was entitled.

(e)   in addition, C was owed overtime in respect of hours worked in September.

Remedy

(7)   R was order to pay C:

Unpaid wages awards:

Four weeks' (gross) salary for September	£2,500.00
Four weeks' (gross) salary for October	£2,500.00
September overtime (gross) (45 hours at time and a half) (best estimate)	£3,750.00

Wrongful dismissal award:

Four weeks' salary in lieu of notice (net)   £2,000.00

Holiday pay:

Ten days' unpaid leave (gross)   £1,153.84

TOTAL   £12,403.84

In addition, C was entitled to a redundancy payment/unfair dismissal basic award of 1 x 2 x £400 (max gross week's pay as at date of calculation) = £800. There was no compensatory element to this award in the light of the *Polkey* finding.

GRAND TOTAL   £12,703.84

All the amounts detailed above have been calculated gross unless otherwise stated. Where a sum is stated to be gross, the respondent will account to HMRC directly in respect of tax and National Insurance due thereon as is appropriate.

5.8 CASE STUDY 2: UNFAIR DISMISSAL

Facts

(1) C commenced employment with R (Isle of Sodor Train Company (ISTC)) on 3 December 2004, as a Revenue Protection Assistant based at Sodor Town station. He was summarily dismissed with effect from 3 October 2011, as result of an incident on Sodor Town station on 10 September 2011, when he was accused by a customer of having taken money for two single tickets valued at £5.80, and failing to issue either a receipt or tickets. V (Group Revenue Protection Manager, Isle of Sodor) conducted an investigation into the incident. C was interviewed on 11, 16, 19 and 23 September. He was suspended on basic pay pending the investigation. In addition, W (Senior Revenue Protection Inspector), X (Senior Revenue Protection Inspector), Y (Acting Senior Revenue Protection Inspector) and Z (RO2, Sodor Town) were interviewed.

(2) At the conclusion of the investigatory process, C was invited, by letter dated 23 September 2011, to attend a disciplinary hearing. C was told that he was being charged under para 9 of the ISTC Disciplinary Procedure 'with the following irregularity of gross misconduct', namely, of misappropriating £5.80 of Isle of Sodor Trains' monies. That letter informed C of his right to be accompanied at the disciplinary hearing. C's representative was sent all the relevant paperwork.

(3) A disciplinary hearing was held on 2 and 3 October 2011. H, Group Station Manager, Sodor Town, conducted it. C was accompanied by a trade union representative. Z was called by C to give evidence on his behalf. The hearing was adjourned to enable H and C's trade union representative to view some CCTV footage. At the conclusion of the disciplinary process, H found that:

(a) money was taken from the customers;

(b) the ticket issuing machine was switched off;

(c) no tickets were issued;

(d) the money that was taken was not accounted for and that 'no credible reason has been given for not issuing the tickets', and that 'Therefore I believe that C took the money and did not intend to issue the tickets thereby misappropriating ISTC monies'.

H found that the charge was proved, and he decided that C should be dismissed with immediate effect. H confirmed his decision in writing in a letter dated 3 October. That letter also set out details of the right to appeal against the decision.

(4) C appealed against:

(a) the severity of the punishment; and

(b) the interpretation of the facts by H.

N, Retail Manager, Isle of Sodor, heard the appeal on 10 October 2011. C was again accompanied by his trade union representative. N upheld the decision to dismiss C. N believed that 'it has been proven beyond doubt that C intentionally pocketed the £5.80 by making a conscious decision not to issue the tickets'. His decision was confirmed in writing by letter dated 10 October 2011.

(5) C's contract refers at para 17 to 'Disciplinary and other rules'. At para 2.1, disciplinary procedures are stated to apply to '(f) misconduct or negligence' and '(l) irregularities involving cash'. Procedure Agreement 4 is headed 'Discipline' and an Annex contains the relevant agreed procedure. This allows, inter alia, for witnesses to be called and for the employee to be accompanied. Paragraph 9 states that in cases of 'exceptionally grave misconduct which may warrant summary dismissal' the usual procedure shall not apply. Paragraph 17 of C's contract stated that ISTC may

> at any time ... dismiss without notice, or suspend from duty, and after inquiry, dismiss without notice, or suspend from duty as a disciplinary measure an employee for certain offences including but not limited to ... (c) misconduct or negligence ... (e) cash procedure irregularities (f) a serious or repeated breach of the rules.

Claims

(6) C complained of unfair dismissal. He said in his ET1 Claim Form (box 11) that he believed his dismissal was unfair because 'the company did not properly and thoroughly investigate the matter because they clearly did not take into account all the information I gave them regarding the incident'. C seeks reinstatement. R, in its ET3 Claim Form, maintained that C's dismissal was fair and, in the alternative, that if it were to be found that the dismissal was unfair, that C's own conduct caused or contributed to his dismissal.

Evidence

(7) Disclosure took place in the usual way and paginated bundles were prepared which included extracts from C's personal file, extracts from the ISTC Disciplinary Procedure, other rules and regulations, Procedure Agreement 4, plus papers relating to C's dismissal and a Schedule of Loss from C setting out his claim for compensation.

(8) Although standard directions were made for the exchange of witness statements prior to the hearing, and witness statements were provided by R to C prior to the hearing, C did not provide one. Although R complained about this failure, in the circumstances the tribunal felt that in the light of the pre-litigation correspondence R was well aware of C's case and the grounds of his complaint. As such the tribunal did not believe R had been prejudiced by this failure. On the basis that there was little information in the ET1 about C's case, it was agreed that the tribunal would first of all read the relevant documents and that C would present his evidence first. C, who was not legally represented at the hearing but was assisted by his brother, read out as his evidence-in-chief a letter that he had written to the RMT Regional Organiser dated 21 November 2011, which set out his complaints in some detail. In addition, the tribunal had written statements, on R's side, from P (Group Revenue Protection Manager, Isle of Sodor), who conducted the final part of the investigation, H (Group Station Manager, Sodor Town, who conducted the disciplinary hearing) and N (Retail Manager, Isle of Sodor, who heard C's appeal). Oral evidence was given on oath by all witnesses, except P who affirmed.

(9) At the hearing, all witnesses who gave oral evidence were cross-examined and the tribunal had the opportunity to ask questions of them. C also submitted a written statement from Ms A, whose evidence he wanted the tribunal to take into account, but who was unable to give oral evidence. Although R pointed out that it had not had advance notice of this, having had the opportunity over a short adjournment to consider the contents of the statement, R did not object to the tribunal reading Ms A's statement;

nevertheless, R reminded the tribunal that it had not had the opportunity to cross-examine Ms A.

(10)   There was some discussion during the case about whether the tribunal should see CCTV footage, stills of which had been available at the time of the investigation and the footage of which was viewed as part of the disciplinary hearing. Although both sides agreed that it might be of assistance for the tribunal to see the CCTV in the presence of the parties, unfortunately there was a problem getting the equipment to work and it was not possible to view it during the hearing. After discussion it was agreed that the tribunal would watch the CCTV footage in chambers.

(11)   At the conclusion of the evidence, both sides made oral submissions on liability and remedy. All these matters were taken into consideration by the tribunal before reaching its decision.

The issues to be decided

(12)   The principal issue for the tribunal to determine was whether the dismissal was fair within s 98(4) of the ERA 1996:

  (a)   What was the reason for C's dismissal?

  (b)   Was this a potentially fair reason for dismissal?

  (c)   Was the dismissal substantively fair?

  (d)   Was the dismissal procedurally fair?

  (e)   Depending on the outcome, a remedy might need to be considered.

Submissions

(13)   On behalf of C it was submitted that, on the facts, even if the dismissal was for the potentially fair reason of conduct under s 98(2) of the ERA 1996, R did not act reasonably in treating that as a sufficient reason for dismissal under s 98(4) of the 1996 Act. Procedurally, C said that R did not acknowledge C's denial and did not accept the counter-evidence that was produced. In particular, it was submitted that R's investigation was flawed, and that it did not properly and thoroughly investigate the matter in that:

  (a)   it was neither full nor impartial;

  (b)   evidence was not examined, or was improperly concluded;

  (c)   it was at best based on assumptions and speculation; and

  (d)   it did not take into account all the information C gave to R.

It was submitted that it was unfair to dismiss on suspicion of misconduct without a full examination of the evidence. C said that there was no evidence that he deliberately set out to steal money from the company; there was no evidence that, as per the charge, funds had been misappropriated – no search was made of C and what money was found was in the float bag, which in the event contained more than it should have done because of money added by C. C says that it is not possible to conclude that 'no stone was left unturned in getting to the bottom of the facts'.

(14)   R's representative submitted that the reason for the dismissal was a potentially fair reason, namely, misconduct, and that procedurally R had done all that it should have done. R submitted that it honestly believed that C was guilty of misappropriating £5.80; that there were reasonable grounds for that belief following a reasonable investigation; and that dismissal was within the range of reasonable responses, as C was in a position of trust. In the alternative, it was submitted that if the tribunal found that the dismissal was unfair, then C's conduct caused or contributed to his dismissal and any award should be reduced by 100% to zero.

The law

(15) Where there is a potentially fair reason for dismissal, the tribunal must decide whether the employer acted reasonably or unreasonably in treating that as a sufficient reason for dismissal. The material statutory provisions are set out in s 98(4) of the ERA 1996, which, so far as relevant, read as follows:

> (4)   Where the employer has fulfilled the requirements of subsection (1), the determination of the question whether the dismissal is fair or unfair (having regard to the reason shown by the employer—
>
> > (a)   depends on whether in the circumstances (including the size and administrative resources of the employer's undertaking) the employer acted reasonably or unreasonably in treating it as a sufficient reason for dismissing the employee, and
> >
> > (b)   shall be determined in accordance with equity and the substantial merits of the case.

(16) Tribunals should not, when considering these matters, look at what they would have done but should judge, on the basis of the range of reasonable responses test, what the employers actually did. The appropriate test is whether the dismissal of the applicant lay within the range of conduct that a reasonable employer could have adopted.

(17) The Court of Appeal in the joined cases of *HSBC (formerly Midland Bank) v Madden; Post Office v Foley* [2000] IRLR 827, reiterated that the correct approach for a tribunal to adopt was that set out by the EAT in *Iceland Frozen Foods Ltd v Jones* [1982] IRLR 439, namely, that it was not for a tribunal to substitute its own view as to an employer's conduct and that tribunals should determine in each case whether the decision to dismiss fell within the 'band of reasonable responses' which a reasonable employer might have adopted towards the employee's conduct. That approach was re-emphasised by the Court of Appeal in *Post Office v Burkett* [2003] EWCA Civ 748 and most recently in *London Ambulance Service NHS Trust v Small* [2009] EWCA Civ 220.

(18) Section 98 does not require the dismissing employer to be satisfied, on the balance of probabilities, that the employee whose conduct is in question has actually done what he or she is alleged to have done. The EAT, in *British Home Stores v Burchell* [1978] IRLR 379, held that where an employer *suspects* misconduct, a dismissal can still be fair provided that the employer (i) had a genuine belief in guilt; (ii) had reasonable grounds upon which to base that belief; and (iii) carried out a proper investigation.

(19) The Court of Appeal in *Sainsbury's Supermarkets Ltd v Hitt* [2003] IRLR 23, held that the range of reasonable responses test

> applies as much to the question of whether the investigation into suspected misconduct was reasonable in all the circumstances as it does to other procedural and substantive aspects of the decision to dismiss a person from his employment for a conduct reason. ... The objective standards of the reasonable employer must be applied to all aspects of the question whether an employee was fairly and reasonably dismissed. ... The objective standard ... did not require [the employer] to carry out further investigations of the kind which the tribunal majority considered ought to have been carried out. ... The purpose of the investigation was not to establish whether or not the applicant was guilty of the alleged theft but whether there were reasonable grounds for the employer's belief that there had been misconduct on his part to which a reasonable response was to dismiss him.

(20) The test to be applied in a case of suspected misconduct is not whether further investigation should have been carried out, or whether more could have been done, but whether the investigation that had been carried out could be regarded by a reasonable employer as adequate. Even in the most serious of cases, it is unrealistic and inappropriate to require the standards and safeguards of a criminal trial, but a careful and conscientious investigation of the facts is necessary, and the person carrying out the investigation should focus carefully on the potential evidence, particularly if it points towards innocence, as opposed to concentrating on evidence which goes to

prove the charges being made. In these sorts of cases, the more grave the charges and the potential impact of dismissal, the more rigorous the process that is required.

The tribunal's findings

(21) The unanimous decision of the tribunal was that C was fairly dismissed by reason of conduct. C was a Revenue Inspection Assistant. Trust and integrity are at the heart of such a role. The tribunal believed that in that circumstances, the dismissal of C for the offence charged was within the range of reasonable responses, and that this accordingly was a fair dismissal.

(22) The tribunal found that C's dismissal was for the potentially fair reason of conduct. The dismissal was a result of the employer's belief that C had appropriated money.

(23) The tribunal then considered s 98(4) of the ERA 1996. Since no burden of proof exists on either party to establish the reasonableness or unreasonableness of a dismissal under s 98(4), this is a question for the tribunal to determine 'neutrally'. The tribunal is not able to re-hear the evidence or to re-examine C's case. In particular, it is not for the tribunal to determine whether C is guilty or innocent. This was emphasised most recently by the Court of Appeal in *London Ambulance Service v Small*, where the Court reiterated that a tribunal must review the fairness of the employer's decision to dismiss, not substitute its own view on the facts. The Court of Appeal said the tribunal should have concentrated on the employer's handling of the dismissal rather than making its own findings about Small's conduct.

(24) The tribunal considered the following questions:

(a) *Did R have a genuine belief that C had behaved in the manner alleged?* In the tribunal's judgment, having heard the evidence of H, who conducted the disciplinary interview, and N, who conducted the appeal, and having read and considered the investigatory interviews, R did have a genuine belief that C had behaved in the manner charged. In particular, R believed he had misappropriated the ticket money.

(b) *Did R have reasonable grounds for that belief?* In the tribunal's judgment, R did have reasonable grounds for that belief. The tribunal noted that:

(i) the initial allegation came from a customer;

(ii) there was no dispute that C had taken money from the customer;

(iii) there was no conclusive evidence that C had issued or attempted to issue any tickets: the customer said he had not; the ticket issuing machine 'bleed and print' did not show that any tickets had been issued; the CCTV was inconclusive on this point;

(iv) C had altered his account of what had happened: initially he said that he had issued tickets and had then disposed of them in a plastic rubbish bag – a subsequent search did not produce the tickets; subsequently he said that he must have been confused and had not issued the tickets; later still he said he had not taken any money, or that he must have returned it all to the customer;

(v) C said initially that his ticket issuing machine was switched off because he had 'just' returned from a toilet break – the CCTV showed him at the barrier for an unbroken period of 30 minutes before the incident;

(vi) C failed to do a full cashing-up when asked to do 'an end of shift' and to cash up – he did only a partial cash-up: in particular, he did not remove his float before cashing up; his shift sheet should have shown a surplus of £5.80 but did not.

The tribunal considered that each explanation C gave was examined in full by R. An employer is not obliged to accept a denial, neither is it obliged to accept counter-evidence; what it must do is give it due consideration. The tribunal believes R did this.

C questioned whether there was sufficient evidence of 'intent'. He said that the CCTV appeared to show him trying to issue a ticket. In fact, the tribunal felt that the CCTV was inconclusive on this. H found that 'the money that was taken was not accounted for', that 'no credible reason has been given for not issuing the tickets' and that 'Therefore I believe that C took the money and did not intend to issue the tickets thereby misappropriating ISTC monies'. In answer to a question from C in cross-examination about this, H said he concluded 'intent' because 'no attempt was made to issue a ticket'. In *Post Office v Burkett*, the Court of Appeal said that the crucial question was whether the Post Office's response to the facts before it was reasonable. The question whether there were reasonable grounds for an honest belief had to be answered not by reference to the tribunal's own objective views formed subsequently, but by reference to its assessment of what it was open to a reasonable employer to conclude on the material before it. In the tribunal's judgment, there were sufficient grounds for H to reach the conclusion that he did. C was 'charged' with misappropriating £5.80. Disciplinary hearings are not criminal hearings. The issue for R was, put simply, whether it felt C had made an innocent mistake or not in taking money and not issuing a ticket. It concluded that he had not. In the tribunal's judgment, R was entitled to reach that conclusion on the evidence before it.

(c) *Did R conduct an investigation which was fair and proportionate having regard to the employer's capacity and resources?* This was at the heart of the way C framed his initial complaint – namely, that ISTC did not 'properly and thoroughly investigate the matter because they clearly did not take into account all the information I gave them regarding the incident'. Although there was no attempt made to contact the initial complainant or to elicit a statement from him, in the tribunal's judgment the investigation conducted was fair, full and thorough. There is no obligation as matter of law to turn over every stone. The tribunal concluded that R operated a fair, adequate and reasonable procedure. C was interviewed on a number of occasions. Any matters raised by him in his interviews were followed up and checked. Z was interviewed, all the Revenue Inspection Officers who were involved in the initial process were questioned, and the CCTV was considered. The disciplinary appeal was adjourned to allow C's representative to look at the CCTV footage (as opposed to the stills) and Z gave evidence. In a situation where an employee's livelihood is at stake and the allegation is a serious one, there is a heightened obligation on an employer as to the thoroughness of its investigation. The tribunal had no doubt that this investigation met that standard. In the tribunal's judgment there was a reasonable investigation.

(d) *Other procedural shortcomings.* In addition to the areas identified above, the tribunal looked at whether there were any procedural or other lapses by ISTC. One matter the tribunal considered was the so-called 'Paragraph 9 Summary Procedure'. The Tribunal looked at this against the Acas Code of Practice, which emphasised that workers should be aware of the likely consequences of breaking rules. The tribunal noted that there was no specific list of offences or examples of matters which would amount to serious (or 'exceptionally gross') misconduct, and thus no indication as to precisely when the para 9 procedure would be invoked. Paragraph 9 (which deals with the procedure in cases of 'exceptionally grave misconduct which may warrant summary action') stated that the 'usual' procedure shall not apply. Paragraph 12 contained a list of 'recordable punishments', of which the last was dismissal. Paragraph 17 of C's contract stated that R might

> at any time ... dismiss without notice, or suspend from duty, and after inquiry, dismiss without notice, or suspend from duty as a disciplinary measure an employee for certain

offences including but not limited to ... (c) misconduct or negligence ... (e) cash procedure irregularities (f) a serious or repeated breach of the rules.

Overall, while the tribunal felt that the position could have been spelled out more clearly, in its judgment R's procedure did make clear to C that a possible consequence of misconduct was summary dismissal – the letter summoning C to interview contained a heading that alerted him to this. While the tribunal felt it might be preferable to identify some examples of serious misconduct – as opposed to less serious misconduct – so that the procedure and the possible consequences would be very clearly set out, it did not feel that this was sufficient *per se* to render the dismissal unfair.

The tribunal examined the initial letter informing C that he was to attend a disciplinary hearing, which did not contain any specific mention of the possible consequences of the disciplinary action that was to be taken. It contained a heading, 'Clause 9 Summary Procedure', and it then specified that the charge was considered to amount to gross misconduct. The Clause 9 Summary Procedure states that the usual procedure shall not apply in cases of 'exceptionally grave misconduct, which may warrant summary action'. Again while the tribunal felt it would have been preferable if this letter had set out the possible consequences of the proposed action, bearing in mind that it was not for the tribunal to substitute its own views, it did not feel, either in isolation or taken with the other matters set out here, that this rendered the dismissal procedurally unfair. Both C and his representative appeared to understand the Clause 9 Procedure and its significance.

In general, subject to the above, the tribunal had no criticisms about the way in which the investigatory process or the actual disciplinary hearing were conducted. There was a long, detailed and thorough investigation. The tribunal felt that C was aware of the accusations made against him in advance, and that he was given a proper opportunity to know the case against him and to state his case. It noted that he was entitled to and did call Z at the disciplinary hearing. It also noted that a representative accompanied C to both the disciplinary and the appeal hearings. The tribunal heard no evidence that made it doubt that those conducting the disciplinary hearing and the appeal were anything other than independent, or that they acted in anything but good faith.

(e)   *The substantive decision to dismiss – was it within the range of responses of a reasonable employer in the circumstances?* The Court of Appeal, in *Post Office v Burkett* [2003] EWCA Civ 748, said that the crucial question for a tribunal was whether an employer's response to the facts before it was reasonable. The real question in these cases is whether R acted fairly and reasonably in all the circumstances at the time of the dismissal. If satisfied of R's fair conduct of the dismissal in those respects, the tribunal then has to decide whether the dismissal of C was a reasonable response to the misconduct. In all the circumstances, the tribunal held that decision of H to dismiss C, albeit over a very small sum of money, could not be said to fall outside the range of reasonable responses. The tribunal felt that given that C was in a position of trust in handling money as a Revenue Inspection Assistant, the misconduct that R believed him to have committed amounted to serious dishonesty. Contributory fault arises for decision only if it is established that the dismissal was unfair. As the tribunal had concluded the dismissal was fair, there was no need for it to consider contribution or remedy.

5.9   FURTHER READING

Textbooks include:

Lewis, *Employment Law – an adviser's handbook*, 9th edn revised (LAG, 2011).

Harvey, *Industrial Relations and Employment Law* (Butterworths), Div D1.

Selwyn, *Law of Employment*, 17th edn (OUP, 2012).

Blackstone's Employment Law Practice (OUP, 2012).

SUMMARY

At common law, provided the employer gives the correct notice and otherwise complies with the terms of the contract, he may dismiss any employee he chooses, whether he has a good reason or not (see **Chapter 2**). The statutory claim of unfair dismissal introduced the concept of reasonableness into the termination of contracts of employment. Now every eligible employee (see **Chapter 3**) has a statutory right not to be unfairly dismissed by his employer under s 94 of the ERA 1996.

An employer must be able to establish that the only or principal reason for the dismissal was one of five potentially fair reasons as listed in s 98 of the ERA 1996 (conduct, capability, redundancy, illegality and some other substantial reason) (**5.2**).

Once an employer has shown the existence of one of the five permitted reasons, the tribunal must then decide if the employer acted reasonably, as defined by s 98(4) of the ERA 1996, having regard to the reason shown by the employer, in dismissing the employee (**5.3**).

When deciding whether the dismissal was fair or unfair, in addition to having regard to the reason, the tribunal should also have regard to all the circumstances, including the Acas Code of Practice on Disciplinary and Grievance Procedures (**5.4.1**) and the size and administrative resources of the employer, as well as to equity and the substantial merits of the case. Each case will ultimately turn on its own facts, but tribunals will generally look at both the substantive reason for the dismissal and any appropriate procedure (**5.4**). The test is ultimately one of reasonableness, and tribunals will ask themselves whether the dismissal was within the range of responses of a reasonable employer (see *Iceland Frozen Foods Ltd v Jones* [1982] IRLR 439 (**5.3.1.1**)).

There are a number of special cases where the normal rules relating to unfair dismissal either do not apply or are varied (**5.5**).

The remedies available for unfair dismissal are either reinstatement or re-engagement (together with any consequential awards relating to arrears of pay, etc), or compensation. Awards which exceed £30,000 are subject to income tax and may need to be grossed up to ensure that the net loss is actually paid to the claimant (**5.6**).

In summary, the following questions should be asked:

- Do any of the special rules apply (**5.5**)?
- Is the employee eligible (**Chapter 3**)?
- Has there been a dismissal (**3.4**)?
- Is there a potentially fair reason (**5.2**)?
- Has the employer acted reasonably (**5.3** and **5.4**)?
- Has the employee asked for reinstatement or re-engagement (**5.6.1**)?
- How much will the basic award be (**5.6.2.1**)?
- What are the relevant heads of compensatory award (**5.6.2.2**)?
- Are there any relevant increasing factors?
- Are there any relevant reducing factors?

Figure 5.1 Flowchart: Unfair Dismissal

---

1. **Eligibility** (burden of proof on employee)
- time limits (3 months (less 1 day) from EDT)
- employee
- 2 years' service (for employees employed by current employer on or after 6 April 2012; 1 year for all others)
- not excluded class

↓

2. **Dismissal** (burden of proof on employee)
- expiry and non-renewal of limited-term contract or
- actual dismissal or
- constructive dismissal

NB Definition in *Western Excavating v Sharp*

↓

3. **Reason for dismissal (ERA 1996, s 98(2))** (burden of proof on employer)
- what is the main reason for the dismissal?
- does that reason fall within one of the five potentially fair reasons?

NB If reason is redundancy, consider claim for both unfair dismissal and a redundancy payment

↓

4. **Consider fairness of dismissal (ERA 1996, s 98(4))**
Test – range of reasonable responses (Iceland Frozen Foods)
Question of fact for tribunal
- size and administrative resources of employer
- equity
- sufficiency of the reason given by the employer
- substantial merits
- procedure (depends on reason)
- Acas Code if conduct/capability

↓

5. **Remedies**
- reinstatement (old job back)
- re-engagement (job elsewhere in business)
- compensation
  — basic award: age factor (½/1/1½) x gross weekly pay (max £430 from February 2012) x number of complete years service (max 20 years) (EA 2002, s 38)
  — compensatory award (consider heads of loss/deductions) (max £72,300 from February 2012)
    immediate loss of net earnings etc
    future losses including pension
    mitigation; other deductions (Polkey/contribution)

NB Award (basic and compensatory) can be increased or decreased by up to 25% for unreasonable failure to follow Acas Code

↓

6. **Consider other claims**
- redundancy payment/wrongful dismissal/discrimination

NB Employee cannot be compensated twice for same loss

CHAPTER 6

PRACTICE AND PROCEDURE, SETTLEMENTS AND OVERLAPPING CLAIMS

LEARNING OUTCOMES

After reading this chapter you will be able to:

- describe the relevant employment tribunal procedures for bringing a claim, from submitting a claim form to the giving of a judgment

- understand the different time-limits that apply to tribunal claims

- explain the options that are available other than bringing a tribunal claim

- describe the different ways in which claims may be settled

- understand the significance of overlapping claims

6.1 INTRODUCTION

This chapter deals with the procedure for making a claim to the employment tribunal and, in outline, the hearing of a complaint by the tribunal. It also covers settlement and overlapping claims.

6.2 APPLICATIONS TO THE EMPLOYMENT TRIBUNAL

6.2.1 Jurisdiction

The following claims may all be brought by presenting a complaint to the employment tribunal:

(a) unfair dismissal;

(b) claims of discrimination on the grounds of sex, race, religion or belief, disability, sexual orientation and age from employees and job applicants (Equality Act 2010);

(c) equal pay;

(d) complaints that unlawful deductions from wages have been made under Pt II of the ERA 1996 (these claims may also be brought in the county court);

(e)   redundancy payments;

(f)   complaints in relation to maternity rights, paternity rights, adoption leave rights, parental rights, dependant rights and flexible working rights;

(g)   complaints in relation to failure to provide written reasons;

(h)   complaints of victimisation because an employee has exerted any of his statutory rights;

(i)   certain claims for damages for breach of contract, including (subject to a maximum award of £25,000) wrongful dismissal (contractual claims may also be brought in the county court);

(j)   complaints under the Part-time Workers (Prevention of Less Favourable Treatment) Regulations 2000;

(k)   complaints under some provisions of the Working Time Regulations 1998;

(l)   complaints under the Agency Workers Regulations 2010.

The above list is not exhaustive. In most instances, these claims must be brought by employees, although there are some exceptions (eg, claims under the protection of wages legislation (see **1.10**) and discrimination claims) where claims by workers can be dealt with. For the distinction between a worker and an employee, see s 230 of the ERA 1996 and **1.1.1** and **1.3**.

6.3   TIME-LIMITS IN EMPLOYMENT TRIBUNALS

Time-limits differ depending upon the complaint. The main limits are set out below. A claimant who fails to present a claim in time will generally lose the right to bring the claim, although there are escape clauses. Time-limits go to a tribunal's jurisdiction, so they are not simply matters of procedure that the parties can waive. There are two types of escape clause – that it is 'not reasonably practicable' to present the claim in time, or that it is 'just and equitable' to grant an extension. These are discussed in more detail below.

6.3.1   Unfair dismissal

The time-limits for an unfair dismissal claim are set out in s 111 of the ERA 1996. The complaint must normally be presented to the tribunal within three months starting with the 'effective date of termination' (EDT), or within such further period as the tribunal considers reasonable where it was not reasonably practicable for the complaint to be presented within three months (ERA 1996, s 111). The EDT for this purpose is the basic EDT as defined by s 97 of the ERA 1996 (see **3.5.2**). It is not extended where the employee did not receive the statutory minimum period of notice (see **3.5.2**). The three months start with (ie includes) the EDT (see *Trow v Ind Coope (West Midlands) Ltd* [1967] 2 QB 899 and *Hammond v Haigh Castle & Co Ltd* [1973] ICR 148). This effectively means three months less a day (see *Pacitti Jones v O'Brien* [2005] IRLR 889 (Court of Session)).

In *Gisda Cyf v Barratt* [2010] UKSC 41, the Supreme Court held that in a summary dismissal, the effective date of termination would be the date the employee actually learned of the decision to dismiss. In the case, Barratt dismissed Mrs Syf in a letter, delivered by recorded delivery and signed for by her son, on 30 November 2006. She was expecting the decision letter to arrive, but was away at the time it arrived as her sister was giving birth, and as a result she did not actually open the letter until 4 December. She subsequently presented an unfair dismissal claim on 2 March. If the effective date of termination was the date the letter was sent and received, namely 30 November, then her unfair dismissal claim was out of time. If it was the date she read it, 4 December, then her unfair dismissal claim would have been presented in time. The Supreme Court held that the effective date of termination was 4 December, ie when she actually read the letter. It held that she should not be criticised for wanting the letter to remain at home unopened, instead of asking her son to read to her, as its contents were private. There was nothing to indicate that she had deliberately not opened the letter or gone away to avoid reading it. The Supreme Court stated that, on policy grounds, it was desirable to interpret the time-limit legislation in a way favourable to the employee, and that strict contractual laws concerning termination of contracts should not displace the statutory framework.

In *Wang v University of Keele* (UKEAT/0223/10), the EAT held that, unless a contract specifically provides otherwise, contractual notice, whether oral or written, runs from the day after the notice is given. Dr Wang was given three months' notice of dismissal by a letter e-mailed on the afternoon of 3 November. He read it that afternoon. He presented a claim for unfair dismissal on 2 May. The employment tribunal rejected his claim on the basis that it was a day out of time, saying the notice period ran from 3 November to 2 February. The EAT, having reviewed all the relevant authorities, said that unless there was an express term in the contract, the law does not take account of fractions of a day so notice may not always run from the time of actual knowledge. In cases of oral notice of dismissal given during the working day, notice cannot take effect until the following day.

The complaint should actually be received by the appropriate Regional Office of the Employment Tribunals (ROET) within the appropriate time-limit. For example, s 111 of the ERA 1996 provides that an unfair dismissal claim must be presented (although a tribunal does have the power to extend the period where it was not 'reasonably practicable' to present the complaint within three months – see below) 'before the end of the period of three months beginning with the effective date of termination'. So, if an employee is dismissed on 15 January, his claim form must arrive at ROET before midnight on 14 April. If an employee is dismissed on 30 November, his claim must be presented by 28 February.

The time-limit for presenting a complaint of unfair dismissal should be regarded as strict. Claim forms may be delivered not only by post but also by hand, by fax and by e-mail. Generally speaking, it is up to the party (or his solicitor) to make sure that the claim form is received within the relevant time-limit.

The tribunal's discretionary power to extend the time-limit is subject to a two-part test. First, the tribunal must be satisfied that it was not reasonably practicable for the claim to be presented in time. Secondly, the tribunal must be satisfied that the claim was presented within such further period as the tribunal considers reasonable. In *Palmer v Southend on Sea BC* [1984] ICR 372, the Court of Appeal said that 'reasonably practicable' does not mean reasonably or physically possible but rather something like 'reasonably feasible'. The determination of what is reasonably practicable is a question of fact for the tribunal (see *Miller v Community Links Trust Ltd* (UK EAT/0486/07). The burden of proof is on the claimant.

In *Sealy v Consignia plc* [2002] IRLR 624, the Court of Appeal held that in determining whether it is reasonably practicable for a claim to have been presented in time, a complainant is entitled to rely on the 'ordinary course of post', such that a letter sent by first class post may be assumed to be delivered on the second day after it was posted (excluding weekends and bank holidays), and if it does not so arrive, it may be regarded (for the purposes of an application to extend) as not reasonably practicable for the complaint to be presented in time. The current line of authority stands for three propositions: first, that 'where a claimant does an act within the period prescribed, which in the ordinary event would result in the complaint being made within the specified period, and that is prevented from having its normal and expected result by some unforeseen circumstance', the 'escape clause' is available; secondly, that if the condition is satisfied, it does not matter why the complainant has waited until the last moment; and, thirdly, that the question whether the condition has been satisfied is a question of fact, to be determined by the tribunal on the evidence before it. (See also *Coldridge v HM Prison Service* (UKEAT/0728/04) and *John Lewis Partnership v Charman* (UKEAT/0079/11), where the EAT held it was not reasonably practicable for a claimant to present his unfair dismissal claim in time because he was awaiting the outcome of an internal appeal.)

Where a claim form is sent by e-mail, a claimant is entitled to assume that it will be delivered at the tribunal within an hour (unless there is an indication that it has not been received, such as a bounce-back message). In *Initial Electronic Security Systems Ltd v Avdic* (UKEAT/0281/05), the EAT held the *Consignia* 'escape route' is also available where a claim form is served by e-mail (so long as the claimant sends it at least an hour before midnight on the day time expires). If an e-mail is not received then a tribunal should assume that it was not reasonably practicable for the complaint to be presented in time, and consider whether the claimant acted reasonably promptly in re-submitting the claim form, once he realised it had not been received.

General guideance on e-mail transmission was set out by the EAT in *Initial Electronic Security Systems Ltd v Audic* [2005] ICR 1598. For a contrasting case to *Beasley* (above), see *Powell v Newcastle College Group* (ET/2514148/09).

The remedy of unfair dismissal is sufficiently well known that ignorance of the remedy will not be accepted as an excuse (see *Reed in Partnership Ltd v Fraine* (UKEAT/0520/10), but also *John Lewis Partnership v Charman* (below) and *Walls Meat Co Ltd v Khan* [1979] ICR 52); neither will carelessness by the employee or his adviser. In particular, if the employee's solicitor misses the time-limit, the tribunal will not extend it, subject to wholly exceptional circumstances such as the claimant and the solicitor being misled by the employer as to a material factual matter. This could lead to a negligence claim by the employee against his solicitor.

In *Northamptonshire County Council v Entwhistle* (UKEAT/0540/09) the EAT held that an employment tribunal had erred in finding that it was not reasonably practicable for a claimant to present his unfair dismissal claim in time in circumstances where his solicitor had been negligent; notwithstanding erroneous advice from the employer, the solicitor should have known the limitation period and filed the claim in time. The EAT said that:

> in a case where a claimant has consulted skilled advisers the question of reasonable practicability is to be judged by what he could have done if he had been given 'such [advice] as they should reasonably in all the circumstances have given him'. (para 11)

In *Marks and Spencer plc v William-Ryan* [2005] IRLR 562, the Court of Appeal held that the employment tribunal had been entitled to find that it had not been reasonably practicable for a claimant to present her unfair dismissal claim within three months because she had received misleading information from her employer, who had advised her that she could not present a claim until she had been through the employer's appeal procedure. In *John Lewis Partnership v Charman* (UKEAT/0079/11), the EAT upheld a decision of the employment tribunal that because the claimant was 'young and inexperienced', and prior to his dismissal he knew nothing about employment tribunals or any right to claim for unfair dismissal, it was not reasonably practicable for him to have presented his claim in time. The starting-point, said the EAT, is that if an employee is reasonably ignorant of the relevant time-limits it cannot be said to be reasonably practicable for him to comply with them.

The discovery of new relevant facts can give grounds for an extension of time (see *Machine Tool Industry Research Association v Simpson* [1988] ICR 558 and *Cambridge and Peterborough Foundation NHS Trust v Crouchman* [2009] ICR 1306). Illness of the claimant may also be a relevant factor (see *Chouafi v London United Busways Ltd* [2006] EWCA Civ 689).

Beasley v National Grid (UKEAT/0626/06) is an illustration of how strictly the time-limits are enforced. In that case, the EAT upheld a tribunal decision not to accept an unfair dismissal claim which was presented by e-mail 88 seconds late. The employment tribunal held that it was 'reasonably practicable' to present the claim in time. The claimant knew on 5 May 2006 that the three-month period expired on 6 May 2006, but he misread the e-mail address of place to which the claim form had to be sent and sent it at 23.44 on 6 May 2006 to 'qsi' and not to the correct address, which was 'gsi'. The claim form was returned to the claimant at 23.45 and he sent a test message (rather than the claim form) to the correct address at 23.57 on 6 May 2006. The claimant then sent the claim form to the correct address so that it arrived at 00.01and 28 seconds on 7 May 2006, ie late. The EAT held that the tribunal had considered the reasonable practicability issue properly, taking into account all relevant matters: it had considered whether the claimant knew of the three-month period; the steps taken by him to ensure that the claim was brought in time; and the impediments preventing him from bringing the claim within the prescribed three-month period. The Court of Appeal refused leave to appeal.

Even if a claimant satisfies a tribunal that it was not reasonably practicable to present a claim within the three-month time-limit, the tribunal must still go on to consider whether the claim was presented within such further period as it considers reasonable. The length of any further period will be determined by the facts in any given case. In *Nolan v Balfour Beatty Engineering Services* (UKEAT/0109/11), the EAT said that tribunals must bear in mind the surrounding context, including the primary time-limit and the general principle that litigation should be progressed efficiently and without delay. Tribunals should then go on to consider all the circumstances of a particular case, including what the claimant did; what he or she knew, or reasonably ought to have known, about time-limits; and why it was that the further delay had occurred. The basic rule is that tribunals expect claimants who present a claim late to act to rectify the delay as soon as they become aware of it. In *Marks and Spencer plc v William-Ryan* (above), the Court of Appeal emphasised the importance of considering what a claimant knew and what knowledge she should have had, had she acted reasonably. For two cases where a delay of several months beyond the initial three months was still held to be reasonable, see *Remploy v Brain* (UKEAT/0465/10) and *Locke v Tabfine Ltd t/a Hands Music Centre* (UKEAT/0517/10).

6.3.2 Redundancy payments

An employee will lose his entitlement to a redundancy payment unless, before the end of a period of six months beginning with the 'relevant date', the employee has, where no payment has been made, made a claim in writing to the employer for the payment or presented a claim to the tribunal. The 'relevant date' is defined by s 145 of the ERA 1996 (see **3.5.2**).

6.3.3 Discrimination

Any complaints of discrimination must be brought within three months starting with the date the act or actions to which the complaint relates took place, or such other period as the tribunal considers just and equitable (Equality Act 2010, s 123(1)). (This is considered further at **8.8**.)

This represents a slight change from the pre-Equality Act 2010 position, which provided that a claim was out of time after three months and for a discretion to bring a claim out of time.

6.3.4 Equal pay

There is, in practice, no time-limit for a claim in respect of the ongoing operation of an equality clause whilst still in employment. A claim should be brought within six months of the employee leaving that employment.

6.3.5 Deductions from wages

The time-limit for presenting a claim for unlawful deduction of wages (ERA 1996, s 13) is three months starting with the date of the deduction.

6.3.6 Wrongful dismissal

The time-limit for presenting a claim for wrongful dismissal is three months starting with the EDT, or later if it was not reasonably practicable for the claim to be presented within the time-limit.

6.4 TRIBUNAL RULES

The practice and procedure of employment tribunals is governed by the Employment Tribunals (Constitution and Rules of Procedure) Regulations 2004 (SI 2004/1861). Schedule 1 sets out the Tribunal Rules of Procedure. They have been expressed in plain English wherever possible. The Regulations and Rules apply to the whole of Great Britain. Some of the main provisions of the Rules are discussed below.

Since their inception in 1964, taking a claim to an employment tribunal (or appealing to the EAT) has been free of charge to users. In early 2011, the Government announced its intention, as part of the 'Resolving Workplace Disputes' consultation, to introduce fee-charging into employment tribunals as part of a series of wider reforms 'to support and encourage early resolution of workplace disputes and in order to transfer some of the cost burden from the taxpayer to the users of the system'. On 14 December 2011, the Ministry of Justice published a Consultation Paper entitled 'Charging Fees in Employment Tribunals and the Employment Appeal Tribunal' (CP22/2011). The Ministry of Justice's Response, published on 13 July 2012, was that it intends to introduce a two-stage charging system in the latter half of 2013. The actual amount of the fee will depend on the nature of the claim. 'Level 1' claims (unauthorised deductions from wages and a failure to pay a redundancy payment) will attract a fee of £160 when the claim is issued and a further fee of £230 prior to hearing. 'Level 2' claims, including discrimination, equal pay and unfair dismissal, will attract an issue fee of £250 and a hearing fee of £950. Employers will not be required to pay a fee to file a response. Fees for employers will be possible once a claim has been issued; for example, they will be required to pay to issue a counterclaim in a contract claim or to make a review application. (See **Introductory Note** for more details.)

Regulation 3 states that the 'overriding objective' of the Regulations and Rules is to enable tribunals to deal with cases justly. This includes, so far as practicable:

(a)   ensuring the parties are on an equal footing;

(b)   dealing with the case in ways which are proportionate to the complexity and importance of the issues;

(c)   ensuring that the case is dealt with fairly and expeditiously; and

(d)   saving expense.

The parties have a duty to assist the tribunal in furthering the overriding objective. Tribunals are obliged to apply the overriding objective when interpreting every rule or exercising any power.

Regulation 15 sets out the rules on 'calculating time limits' for any act required under the Rules in Sch 1. (See eg **6.4.2** below.)

The Rules of Procedure themselves are set out in Sch 1 to the Regulations.

The Government has included in Enterprise and Regulatory Reform Bill, which was introduced into Parliament on 23 May 2012, a scheme whereby employment disputes will have to go to Acas for mandatory pre-claim conciliation before they can go to an employment tribunal.

The Government has also decided to introduce fees in employment tribunals and the EAT, and has consulted on the possible arrangements. Two alternative fee structures were proposed. Under the Government's preferred Option 1, the claimant will pay an initial fee to lodge a claim and a second fee to take the claim to a hearing (there will be fees for other steps too). The Government proposes to introduce fees in Summer 2013–14. There will be exemptions (for example where the claimant is in receipt of income support) and recovery by a successful party.

6.4.1   The claim (Rule 1)

The complaint must be made in writing on the prescribed claim form ET1 and must include all 'relevant required information'. (Only the official ETS versions of the forms are acceptable

– they can be downloaded from www.employmenttribunals.gov.uk.) That information is set out in Rule 1(4), which states that the following information must be given:

(a)   each claimant's name;

(b)   each claimant's address;

(c)   each respondent's name;

(d)   each respondent's address;

(e)   details of the claim. In *Grimmer v KLM Cityhopper* [2005] IRLR 596, the EAT held that details of the claim are not the same as 'particulars of claim' – if a claim is felt to be insufficiently particularised, the correct approach is to order further particulars rather than to refuse to admit the claim, so long as the statutory right that it is alleged has been breached is identified. What is important is 'whether it can be discerned from the claim as presented that the claimant is complaining of an alleged breach of an employment right which falls within the jurisdiction of the Employment Tribunal'.

Rule 3(1) states that if a claim is not presented on the prescribed form, or where the claim does not included all the required information, the claim may be rejected. In *Hamling v Coxlease School Ltd* [2007] IRLR 8, a claim was rejected because the ET1 omitted the claimant's address, which was contrary to Rule 1(4)(b). The EAT overturned the decision and held that given that all further communication would be with the claimant's solicitor, whose full contact details had been provided on the form, the claimant's address was neither 'relevant' nor 'material'.

The EAT has also confirmed that the claimant may apply for review of a decision to reject a claim form under Rule 34 if he considers the rejection erroneous – see *Butlins Skyline Ltd and Another v Bemyon* (UKEAT/0042–45/06).

The form should be sent to the appropriate ROET. The complaint must be received at the ROET within the relevant time-limit (see **6.3** above). Generally, as a matter of practice, claims will be held in the 'relevant' tribunal region for the claimant's post code – work or home. However, there is no 'right' for a claimant to have a case heard in a particular region (see *Faleye and Another v UK Mission Enterprise Ltd* (UKEAT/0359/10)). Requests for transfers between regions are purely a matter, subject to any injustice, of discretion for an Employment Judge to determine.

A complaint can be posted, delivered by hand, faxed, sent by e-mail or electronically (see Rule 61). If the time period for presenting the complaint is close to expiry, the complaint should be faxed to the appropriate regional tribunal without delay. It is worth following this up with a telephone call to ensure that it has been received. A careful telephone note, or a copy of the fax transmission sheet, should be kept (see also **6.3.1**).

A copy of the complaint will be sent by the ROET to the employer and to Acas.

6.4.2 Response (Rule 4)

The employer should file a response on prescribed form ET3. Rule 6 states that if a response is not presented on the prescribed form, or where the response does not include all the required information, the response shall be rejected (the respondent can apply for review of that decision under Rule 34 if he considers the rejection erroneous – see *Butlins Skyline Ltd*, at **6.4.1** above).

The form should be submitted within 28 days of the date on which the ET1 was sent by the tribunal to the respondent. Regulation 15(2) states that

> where any act must or may be done within a certain number of days of or from an event, the date of that event shall not be included in the calculation. For example, a respondent is sent a copy of a claim on 1 October. He must present a response to the Employment Tribunal Office … [by] 29 October.

A copy of the response will be sent to all parties.

Rule 4(3) states that the following information must be provided:

(a)   respondent's full name;

(b)   respondent's full address;

(c)   whether or not the respondent wishes to resist the claim in whole or in part; and

(d)   if the respondent wishes to resist, on what grounds.

Rule 4(4) allows the respondent to apply under Rule 11 for an extension of time within which to submit his ET3. Any application for an extension of time must be made within the 28-day limit for responding. Rule 4 states that time will be extended only where the employment judge considers it just and equitable to do so. The application for an extension must be made in accordance with Rule 11.

Where a respondent fails to enter a response within the time-limits (or to apply for an extension under Rule 4(4)) a tribunal may issue a default judgment under Rule 8 (see **6.4.4** below). Rule 9 sets out that a respondent who has not responded will not be entitled to take any part in the proceedings, except, for example, to apply to set aside default judgment.

6.4.3   Applications to amend

Rule 10(2)(q) allows an application to be made to amend a claim or response form. Such applications may give rise to subsidiary considerations about whether claims are made in time. One alternative to seeking to amend an existing claim is to issue a new claim and, if necessary, apply for permission to present it out of time (see **6.3.1** for time-limits and extensions).

The principal authorities with regard to amendments are *Cocking v Sandhurst* [1974] ICR 650, *British Newspaper Printing Corporation (North) Ltd v Kelly* [1989] IRLR 222, *Selkent Bus Co v Moore* [1996] IRLR 661, *Housing Corporation v Bryant* [1999] ICR 123, *Harvey v Port of Tilbury (London) Ltd* [1999] ICR 1030 and *Ali v Office of National Statistics* [2005] IRLR 201. The EAT in *Selkent* stated a number of general principles which it said were applicable to the amendment of tribunal claims:

(4)   Whenever the discretion to grant an amendment is invoked, the tribunal should take into account *all* the circumstances and should balance the injustice and hardship of allowing the amendment against the injustice and hardship of refusing it.

(5)   What are the relevant circumstances? It is impossible and undesirable to attempt to list them exhaustively, but the following are certainly relevant:

(a)   *The nature of the amendment*

Applications to amend are of many different kinds, ranging, on the one hand, from the correction of clerical and typing errors, the additions of factual details to existing allegations and the addition or substitution of other labels for facts already pleaded to, on the other hand, the making of entirely new factual allegations which change the basis of the existing claim. The tribunal have to decide whether the amendment sought is one of the minor matters or is a substantial alteration pleading a new cause of action.

(b)   *The applicability of time limits*

If a new complaint or cause of action is proposed to be added by way of amendment, it is essential for the tribunal to consider whether that complaint is out of time and, if so, whether the time limit should be extended under the applicable statutory provisions ...

(c)   *The timing and manner of the application*

An application should not be refused solely because there has been a delay in making it. There are no time limits laid down in the Rules for the making of amendments. The amendments may be made at any time – before, at, even after the hearing of the case. Delay in making the application is, however, a discretionary factor. It is relevant to consider why the application was not made earlier and why it is now being made: for example, the discovery of new facts or new information appearing from documents disclosed on discovery. Whenever taking any factors into account, the paramount considerations are the relative injustice and hardship involved in refusing or granting an amendment. Questions of delay, as a result of adjournments, and additional costs, particularly if they are unlikely to be recovered by the successful party, are relevant in reaching a decision.

Even in the most extreme case, ie where there is a finding that, as 'a new' claim, that claim would be out of time (allowing for the relevant 'escape clause'), the authorities do not suggest that that would be fatal to an application to amend.

The Court of Appeal in *Office of National Statistics v Ali* [2005] IRLR 201 considered an appeal relating to an application to amend an ET1. The claim form alleged direct racial discrimination. Even though there was an argument about whether it included some aspects of indirect racial discrimination, it did not allege the indirect racial discrimination upon which the employee wished to rely. The details of complaint in the ET1 clearly referred to race as the reason for the treatment of which complaint was made. Mr Ali was originally unrepresented. After counsel was instructed, an application to amend the ET1 was made specifying the basis of a claim for indirect discrimination. The employment tribunal took the view that the ET1 raised the issue of whether there was something about the respondent's recruitment practice which had the effect of excluding black people and concluded that the ET1 included a claim of indirect race discrimination and no amendment was required. The Court of Appeal (Waller LJ) held, at para 39:

> In my view the question whether an originating application contains a claim has to be judged by reference to the whole document. That means that although box 1 may contain a very general description of the complaint and a bare reference in the particulars to an event (as in *Dodd v [British Telecommunications* [1988] IRLR 16]), particularisation may make it clear that a particular claim, for example for indirect discrimination, is not being pursued. That may at first sight seem to favour the less particularised claim as in *Dodd*, but such a general claim cries out for particulars and those are particulars to which the employer is entitled so that he knows the claim he has to meet. An originating application which appears to contain full particulars would be deceptive if an employer cannot rely on what it states. I would for my part think that insofar as *Quarcoopome* [*v Sock Shop Holdings Ltd* [1995] IRLR 353] suggests to the contrary it should not be followed. Therefore I would hold that paragraph 25A seeks to bring into the proceedings a new claim.

For other decisions on amendment see, for example, *Baker v Commissioner of Police of the Metropolis* (UKEAT/0201/09/CEA) and *Enterprise Liverpool Ltd v Jonas and Others* (UKEAT/0112/09). In *New Star v Evershed* [2010] EWCA Civ 870 the Court of Appeal held that adding a public interest disclosure claim to an unfair dismissal claim with similar facts did not require 'wholly different evidence' such that the application to amend should be refused. The claimant sought to add an 'automatic' unfair constructive dismissal claim by asserting that the reason, or principal reason, for his dismissal was that he had made a protected disclosure and that it was a 'whistle-blowing' claim. He had made allegations about being bullied in the context of his unfair dismissal claim, where he argued that they contributed to the intolerable atmosphere causing him to resign. Although the respondent said the allegations were irrelevant to the unfair dismissal claim, they had not been struck out and remained part of the case. The Court of Appeal accepted that this was not a mere 're-labelling' and specific findings would have to be made about the individual components of the public interest disclosure claim; but it upheld the reasoning of the EAT that there was a substantial overlap in the issues.

6.4.4   Late responses and default judgments

Rule 8 allows the tribunal to issue judgment in default in certain circumstances, for example where the respondent fails to serve a response form within 28 days (see **6.4.2**). The judgment can deal with liability, or liability and remedy.

The tribunal may, on application, review the judgment and revoke it under Rule 33. Any application for review must be made within 14 days of the date on which default judgment was sent (Rule 33) (ignoring the day it was sent (reg 15)).

In *Blake Moroak t/a Blake Envelopes v Mr D L Cromie* [2005] IRLR 535, the respondent served its response form 44 minutes late. A letter was sent two days later, which asked for a 44-minute extension. The tribunal rejected the request (stating it had no power to award an extension of time under the new rules because Rule 4(4) states that the request for an extension must be made within the 28 days). The tribunal ordered that the respondent could take no part in the proceedings under Rule 9. However, the tribunal did not actually issue default judgment. (Rule 8 states that it 'may' issue default judgment against a respondent who does not serve a response.) Therefore the respondent was unable to apply for a review of the default judgment under Rule 33. On appeal, the EAT held that the tribunal does have power (under its general powers to review decisions in Rule 34) to review an order declining an extension of time where the interests of justice require, and to direct that the response form be accepted. The EAT also gave guidance as to the factors to take into account when deciding whether to admit a response form late. In particular, it confirmed that the test in *Kwik Save Stores Limited v Swain* [1997] ICR 49 remains the test for extensions of time for a response. In *Kwik Save*, the EAT said:

> it was incumbent on a respondent applying for an extension of time for serving a notice of appearance ... to put before the industrial tribunal all relevant documents and other factual material in order to explain ... both the non-compliance and ... the basis on which it was sought to defend the case on its merits; that an industrial tribunal chairman in exercising the discretion to grant an extension of time to enter a notice of appearance had to take account of all relevant factors, including the explanation or lack of explanation for the delay and the merits of the defence, weighing and balancing them one against the other, and to reach a conclusion which was objectively justified on the grounds of reason and justice; that it was it was important when doing so to balance the possible prejudice to each party ...

6.4.5 Case management

Under the Rules the Employment Judge has wide case management powers. The Employment Judge may, for example, ask the parties to attend or participate in by telephone a case management discussion (Rule 17). This is an interim hearing and may deal with matters of procedure and management of the proceedings. It should be held in private.

The matters listed in Rule 10 are examples of matters which may be ordered by the Employment Judge either at a case management discussion, or through correspondence with the parties or on the Employment Judge's own initiative. For example, the Employment Judge may require:

(a)   a party to provide additional information;

(b)   a party to disclose documents;

(c)   a party to provide written answers to questions;

(d)   attendance of witnesses;

(e)   provision and exchange of witness statements.

The Rules also allow an Employment Judge, for example, to give leave to amend a claim or response form (see **6.4.3**) and to give directions as to expert witnesses.

An example of a pro forma template agenda for a case management hearing is set out in **Appendix 3**.

Employment Judges can suggest to the parties at the case management discussion that the case be referred to judicial mediation. This involves bringing the parties in a case together. The Employment Judge will try to assist the parties to resolve the dispute. The judicial mediation will be heard in private and will be entirely confidential. All jurisdictions (except equal pay) may be referred to the scheme.

The President of the employment tribunals has identified minimum criteria that will be applied in considering whether judicial mediation can be offered. The most significant of these is that the case would be listed in the normal course of events for a minimum of three days. Another important factor in assessing suitability is whether there is an on-going employment relationship (see **6.6** below).

6.4.5.1 Additional information

A request for additional information should first be made directly to the other party before seeking an order from the tribunal. A tribunal may order a party to the proceedings to provide additional information about the grounds upon which he relies and of any facts or contentions relevant thereto, and it may impose a time-limit by which the order is to be complied with.

The purpose of additional information is to remedy any deficiency in the case stated in the claim or response form, in order that the parties will know in advance reasonable details of the nature of the complaints that each side is going to make at the hearing. For example, additional information may be ordered about a vague allegation such as 'the claimant failed to perform her duties satisfactorily'.

6.4.5.2 Disclosure of documents

Again, a request should first be made to the other party before seeking an order. The tribunal has powers similar to those of the county court in ordering disclosure and inspection (CPR 1998, Part 31; see **Civil Litigation**, **Chapter 11**). The CPR provide for disclosure of:

(a) the documents on which a party relies; and

(b) the documents which:

    (i) adversely affect a party's own case,

    (ii) adversely affect another party's case, or

    (iii) support another party's case.

The main purpose of the disclosure and inspection stage of the litigation process is to enable the parties better to evaluate the strength of their opponent's case in advance of the trial. The parties have to reveal to each other the documents which have a bearing on the disputed issues in the case. The process is intended to promote settlements and therefore a saving in costs. It ensures that the parties are not taken by surprise at the trial and that the court has all relevant information in order to do justice between the parties. The Court of Appeal held in *Canadian Imperial Bank of Commerce v Beck* [2009] IRLR 740 that 'the test is whether or not an order for [disclosure] is necessary for fairly disposing of the proceedings ... The fact that some documents may be confidential does not confer immunity on them.'

Privilege

There are some circumstances in which a party will not have to allow the other party to inspect a disclosed document. One of those is where a party relies on the document being protected by legal professional privilege. The rules on privilege are also the same as those that apply in the civil courts. In brief, there are two types of legal professional privilege:

(a) *Advice privilege*

Communications passing between a party and his legal advisers, or between a party's legal advisers, are privileged from inspection, provided they are written by or to the solicitor in his professional capacity and for the sole or dominant purpose of obtaining legal advice or assistance for the client. 'Legal advice' is not confined to telling the client the law; it includes information passed by solicitor to client, or vice versa, so that advice may be sought and given, and it includes advice about what should prudently and sensibly be done in the relevant legal context.

Privilege, however, does not extend without limit to all solicitor/client communications. The range of assistance given by solicitors to their clients has greatly broadened in recent times; for example, many solicitors now provide investment advice to clients.

The scope of legal professional privilege has to be kept within reasonable bounds. See further *Three Rivers District Council and Others v Governor and Company of the Bank of England* [2004] UKHL 48, [2004] 3 WLR 1274.

The privilege extends to communications between a party and his solicitor's employee or agent, and also to communications between a party and a solicitor in his service, for example a solicitor to a government department or in a legal department of a commercial enterprise. The privilege also covers instructions and briefs to counsel, counsel's opinions, and counsel's drafts and notes.

(b)   *Litigation privilege*

(i)   Communications passing between the solicitor and a third party are privileged from production and inspection only if:

(1)   they come into existence after litigation is contemplated or commenced; and

(2)   they are made with a view to the litigation, either for the sole or dominant purpose of obtaining or giving advice in regard to it, or for obtaining evidence to be used in it.

Examples of documents which may come within this head of privilege are a report from an expert obtained by a solicitor with a view to advising his client about existing or contemplated litigation, or witness statements obtained by a solicitor for the purpose of existing or contemplated litigation.

(ii)   Communications between the client and a third party are privileged if the sole or dominant purpose for which they were produced was to obtain legal advice in respect of existing or contemplated litigation, or to conduct, or aid in the conduct, of such litigation. It must be the case that litigation was reasonably in prospect at the time when the document was brought into existence, and that the sole or dominant reason for obtaining the document was to enable solicitors to advise as to whether a claim should be made or resisted, or to have it as evidence.

Where a client is not an individual, this form of privilege is also applied to communications between individuals within that organisation. Thus, a memorandum sent by one partner of a firm to another would be privileged if it was prepared for the dominant purpose of obtaining legal advice in respect of existing or contemplated litigation, or to aid the conduct of such litigation.

In *Scott v Four Seasons (Conservatories) Ltd* (UKEAT/0178/10) the EAT decided that litigation privilege extended to protect advice given by a firm of employment law consultants to the employees and that the claimant did not have the right to inspect such communications. The EAT considered that legal advice given by non-legally qualified staff was not covered by legal advice privilege.

Waiver of privilege

The privilege is the client's and not the solicitor's, and therefore it may be waived by the client but not by the solicitor. Once a copy of a privileged document is served on the other side, the privilege is waived.

Confidentiality

If one party is seeking the disclosure of documents which the other side regards as being of a confidential nature (eg references, assessments, etc), the judge should inspect the documents in order to satisfy himself that disclosure is necessary. The judge will usually order disclosure where the content of the document is relevant and necessary to dispose of the case fairly (see, eg, *Nasse v SRC* [1979] IRLR 465; *Canadian Imperial Bank of Commerce v Beck* [2009] EWCA Civ 619). If appropriate, parts of the documents may be covered up (redacted), for example the name of an employee.

Voluntary disclosure

There is no general duty of disclosure in the absence of an order. However, if voluntary disclosure is made, there is a duty not to be selective by withholding documents and creating a false impression.

Without prejudice communications

In general, without prejudice communications are not disclosable. One exception to that rule is where there is unambiguous impropriety.

The EAT had an opportunity to consider the 'without prejudice' rule in *BNP Paribas v Mezzotero* [2004] IRLR 508. Where settlement discussions between parties are 'without prejudice', communications between the parties are not usually admissible in evidence in tribunal proceedings. In this case, however, the EAT held that for the rule to be effective there must be a genuine dispute between the parties and that, on the facts, there was not, despite the fact that the employee had raised a grievance as to how she was being treated upon her return from maternity leave. The employer called her into a meeting after she raised the grievance and told her it was a 'without prejudice' meeting. The EAT made it clear that the rule applies only where there is already a dispute between the parties, and the communications to which the rule is said to attach must be made for the purpose of a genuine attempt at compromise. More interestingly, the EAT also said that even if there had been a genuine dispute, it was 'unrealistic ... to refer to the parties as expressly agreeing to speak without prejudice, given the unequal relationship of the parties, the vulnerable position of the applicant in such a meeting as this, and the fact that the suggestion was made by the respondent only once the meeting had begun'. The EAT held in essence that the respondent's conduct was an abuse.

In *Brunel University v Vaseghi* [2007] IRLR 592, without prejudice discussions took place in an (unsuccessful) attempt to settle discrimination claims. The discussions were revealed during the course of internal grievance hearings. During the subsequent tribunal hearing, the employees tried to introduce evidence of the without prejudice discussions. The University objected, but the tribunal and EAT allowed the evidence in. The EAT said that failure to allow evidence of what was said during the without prejudice discussions would severely hamper the employees' ability to establish their victimisation claim. The EAT commented that 'in discrimination cases the necessity of getting to the truth of what occurred and if necessary eradicating the evil of discrimination may tip the scales as against the necessity of protecting the "without prejudice" privilege'. The Court of Appeal dismissed the appeal on the basis there had been bilateral waiver. It declined to comment on the suggestion by the EAT below and in *Mezzotero* that there was a particular exception to the without prejudice rule which applied only in discrimination and victimisation cases.

Most recently, in *Woodward v Santander UK plc* (UKEAT/0250/09), the EAT, after considering the leading modern authorities concerning the without prejudice rule and the policy underlying the rule (namely that parties should not be discouraged from settling their disputes by fear that something said in the course of negotiations may be used against them) went on to hold:

58.   Reading the judgment in *Mezzotero* as a whole, we do not think that it establishes any new exception to the without prejudice rule. In paragraph 38 Cox J expressly stated that she would regard the employer's alleged conduct as an exception to the without prejudice rule 'within the abuse principle'....

59.   We doubt whether Cox J intended to say that it was unnecessary, in a discrimination case, to find unambiguous impropriety. We appreciate that paragraph 38 of her reasons, in which she refers to 'the unattractive task of attaching different levels of impropriety to fact sensitive allegations of discrimination', can be read in that way. But Cox J went on to say that she regarded the employer's alleged conduct as 'within the abuse principle'.

60.   We would observe that the policy underlying the 'without prejudice' rule applies with as much force to cases where discrimination has been alleged as it applies to any other form of dispute.

Indeed the policy may be said to apply with particular force in those cases where the parties are seeking to settle a discrimination claim.

61.   Discrimination claims often place heavy emotional and financial burdens on claimants and respondents alike. It is important that parties should be able to settle their differences (whether by negotiation or mediation) in conditions where they can speak freely. A claimant must be free to concede a point for the purposes of settlement without the fear that if negotiations are unsuccessful he or she will be accused for that reason of pursuing the point dishonestly. A respondent must be free to adhere to and explain a position, or to refuse a particular settlement proposal, without the fear that in subsequent litigation this will be taken as evidence of committing or repeating an act of discrimination or victimisation. And it is idle to suppose that parties, when they participate in negotiation or mediation, will always be calm and dispassionate. They should be able, within limits, to argue their case and speak their mind.

62.   What are the limits? To our mind they are best stated in terms of the existing exception for impropriety. This exception, as we have seen, applies only to a case where the Tribunal is satisfied that the impropriety alleged is unambiguous. It applies only in the very clearest of cases. A court or Tribunal is therefore required to make a judgment as to whether the evidence which it is sought to adduce meets this test. Words which are unambiguously discriminatory will of course fall within the exception: see the example given by Cox J at para 37 of *Mezzotero*.

63.   It may at first sight seem unattractive, given the fact sensitive nature of discrimination cases, to exclude any evidence from which an inference of discrimination could be drawn. But it would have a substantial inhibiting effect on the ability of parties to speak freely in conducting negotiations if subsequently one or other could comb through the content of correspondence or discussions (which may have been lengthy or contentious) in order to point to equivocal words or actions in support of (or for that matter in order to defend) an inference of discrimination. Parties should be able to approach negotiations free from any concern that they will be used for evidence-gathering, or scrutinised afterwards for that purpose.

64.   We therefore reject Mr Bacon's submission that there ought to be a wider exception to the without prejudice rule where discrimination is alleged. We do not think such an exception is consistent with the policy behind the rule. We cannot see any workable basis for applying such an exception while preserving the parties' freedom to speak freely in conducting negotiations.

6.4.5.3   'Written answers' to specific questions

The aim of written answers is to identify and narrow the issues; they need not be confined to amplification of the grounds upon which the party relies and are thus wider in scope than additional information. A similar approach is likely to be taken to such requests in the civil courts, so 'fishing' questions, for example, will not be allowed, neither will questions which relate solely to the evidence which a party intends to adduce. They are unlikely to be ordered where other procedural processes would be more appropriate, for example a request for additional information or a request for disclosure.

6.4.5.4   Attendance of witnesses (Rule 10)

The power to issue witness orders is discretionary. The tribunal must be satisfied that the witness's evidence is sufficiently relevant and that it is necessary to issue a witness order to secure his attendance.

6.4.5.5   Provision and exchange of witness statements

Tribunals almost invariably order that the parties' representatives prepare witness statements for the witnesses, and such statements stand as the witnesses' evidence-in-chief. The general rule (since April 2012) is that witness statements should not be read out but should be taken as read. In a case pre-dating the introduction of that rule, the President of the EAT gave guidance on the practice of reading out witness statements in tribunals. In *Mehta v Child Support Agency* (UKEAT/0127/10) he said that very often reading witness statements aloud 'achieves nothing of value' and 'wastes the time of tribunal and the parties', but that sometimes it might be helpful to read out a statement or part of a statement if matters might need clarifying or elucidation, or to help 'settle' an individual before he is cross-examined. He suggested that where both parties were represented, a procedure should be agreed. Where a party is not represented, a tribunal should ensure he understands the implications of what is proposed. Tribunals were cautioned against having a policy of not allowing a claimant to read out his statement – the appropriate procedure should be decided on a case by case basis at the tribunal's discretion. The tribunal will also usually order that statements are exchanged on an agreed date. Further detail may be found in **Civil Litigation, Chapter 12**.

6.4.6 Restricted reporting orders (Rules 49 and 50)

Tribunals, like most courts, should hold most of their proceedings in open court (see European Convention on Human Rights, Article 6 and **6.4.14**). In cases which involve allegations of sexual misconduct, the tribunal may make a restricted reporting order (RRO). The order will prevent publication of the name of the applicant (or respondent, or other persons affected by the allegation) or any other matter that is likely to lead to the identification of the individual in question. The RRO will last until the tribunal's written decision is sent to the parties. Where an allegation of a sexual offence is involved, the central register (see **6.4.12**) may be altered to delete any 'identifying material'. In *X v Stevens* [2002] IRLR 411, the EAT held that even where there is no allegation of a sexual offence, tribunals have the power to make orders analogous to RROs, or to make some provision in respect of confidentiality, so as to protect the identity of an applicant where there has been a finding of fact that the applicant would be deterred from bringing a claim under the SDA 1975 in the absence of such an order.

For two cases reviewing the reporting restriction provisions, see *Tradition Securities and Futures SA and Others v Times Newspapers and Others* (UKEAT/1415/08) and *F v G* (UKEAT/0042/11).

6.4.7 Hearings – general

There are a number of different types of hearing which may be held. Case management discussions were dealt with at **6.4.5** above. The text below deals with pre-hearing reviews hearings. The full hearing is examined at **6.4.8**.

6.4.7.1 Pre-hearing review (Rule 18)

Pre-hearing reviews (PHRs) are interim hearings, which should be held in public (subject to Rule 16 which allows hearings to be in private in certain situations). Rule 18 allows the Employment Judge, at a PHR, amongst other things, to:

(a) determine preliminary issues (eg an issue as to whether the claim was brought in time, or whether the claimant has sufficient continuity of service). The Employment Judge can give judgment at the hearing on preliminary matters, which may result in the proceedings being struck out so that a full hearing is no longer required (see Rule 18(7) below);

(b) issue orders under Rule 10 (general power to manage proceedings), or anything else which can be done at a case management discussion (see **6.4.5** above);

(c) order payment of a deposit under Rule 20 (see **6.4.7.2** below);

(d) consider oral or written representations or evidence.

Rule 18(7) states that a claim or response may be struck out at a PHR, notwithstanding the interim nature of a PHR, if, amongst other things:

(a) the claim or response is scandalous, vexatious or has no reasonable prospects of success;

(b) the manner in which proceedings have been conducted by the claimant or respondent is scandalous, unreasonable or vexatious;

(c) the claimant or respondent has failed to comply with any tribunal orders.

6.4.7.2   Requirement to pay a deposit (Rule 20)

Rule 20 allows for a party to be ordered to pay a deposit of up to £1,000 in order to continue to take part in proceedings, where the Employment Judge considers the claim or response has 'little reasonable prospect of success'. Before so ordering, the Employment Judge must consider the party's ability to pay. The Employment Judge must set out his grounds for making such an order, and give a copy of the document recording his reasons to the parties and explain to the party against whom the order is made that if he 'persists in making those contentions relating to the matter to which the order relates, he may have an award of costs or preparation time made against him and could lose his deposit'. If the party does not pay the deposit within 21 days of receiving the document recording the Employment Judge's reasons for making the order, the claim or response will be struck out.

6.4.7.3   Withdrawal (Rule 25)

Rule 25(1) permits a claimant to withdraw all or part of a claim at any time. Rule 25(4) allows a respondent, where a claim has been withdrawn, to make an application to have the proceedings against him dismissed. If the respondent's application is granted and the proceedings are dismissed, Rule 25(4) says that a claimant cannot commence a further claim against the employer on the same or substantially the same facts (unless the decision to dismiss is successfully reviewed or appealed).

Claimants need to be careful if they start a case in the tribunal and then wish to bring a claim in the civil courts, as a dismissal will prevent them from doing so. Note that Rule 25A states that there will be an automatic dismissal of proceedings where a claim is withdrawn after an Acas settlement. This will also prevent a claimant bringing a fresh claim in a civil court.

6.4.7.4   Role of Acas

A copy of the claim form and response will normally be sent to Acas by the tribunal, because Acas has a statutory duty to endeavour to promote settlement under most employment protection legislation (Employment Tribunals Act 1996 (ETA 1996), s 18, as amended).

6.4.7.5   Preparation for the full hearing

The date, time and place of the hearing will be fixed, and a notice of hearing sent to the parties. Before the date has been fixed, the parties will be asked for dates to avoid. The parties should then ensure that their witnesses will be available.

Before the hearing the parties should prepare a bundle of documents for use at the hearing. The tribunal will often direct who is responsible for preparing the bundle. It should include all correspondence and other documents on which the parties intend to rely, arranged in correct sequence and numbered consecutively. It is desirable, wherever possible, that there should be an agreed bundle. At least six bundles should be available at the hearing, one for each member of the tribunal, one for each side and one for use by the witnesses. Some tribunals ask for the bundle to be lodged in advance of the hearing, others prefer it to be brought to the tribunal on the day of the hearing.

6.4.8   The full hearing

The Employment Tribunals Act 1996 (Tribunal Composition) Order 2012 (SI 2012/988) now allows an Employment Judge to hear unfair dismissal cases sitting alone. Employment Judges were already able to sit alone in certain circumstances, for example in cases brought under Pt II of the ERA 1996 (protection of wages), reg 30 of the Working Time Regulations (holiday pay entitlement) or where the parties consented to this (ETA 1996, s 4(3)). Section 4(5) of the ETA 1996 still provides that, in certain circumstances, an Employment Judge may order a hearing by a full panel, including where there is a likelihood of a dispute arising on the facts. Section 4(5) also provides that the views of any of the parties should be taken into account.

The EAT recently expressed some reservations about judges sitting alone, in *McCafferty v Royal Mail Group* (UKEATS/0002/12). Mr McCafferty was a postman with 19 years' service, who had been dismissed for gross misconduct by reason of alleged dishonesty. The lay members of the tribunal found the dismissal fair. The Employment Judge, in the minority, considered that the dismissal was unfair. On appeal, the decision of the majority that the dismissal was fair was upheld. Lady Smith pointed out that the lay members of the employment tribunal reached their conclusion drawing on their 'valuable common sense'. Lady Smith remarked that this underlines the need to give careful consideration to any views expressed by parties as to whether proceedings should be heard by an Employment Judge and members. The EAT decided in *Sterling Developments v Pagano* (UKEAT/0511/06) that the Employment Judge need not consider s 4(5) before hearing a case alone where neither party made representations.

There is also provision in the ETA 1996 (as amended by s 4 of the Employment Rights (Dispute Resolution) Act 1998) for hearings to be heard by a tribunal judge and one member where the parties consent.

The parties may appear in person, or be represented by a friend, union representative or professional adviser. In England and Wales, public funding is not available for representation at the hearing, although a solicitor may advise prior to the hearing under the Legal Help scheme (subject to the usual restrictions). Note that under the Compensation Act 2006, non-lawyers are prohibited from representing litigants and charging them a fee, unless they are formally registered with and regulated by the Regulated Claims Management Service. Breach of the registration requirements is punishable by up to two years in prison. Free representation does not need to be regulated. A party is not obliged to attend a hearing and a tribunal may hear a case in a party's absence without further inquiry (see *Cooke v Glenrose Fish Co Ltd* [2004] IRLR 866).

The case will usually be opened by the side with the burden of proof for the first point in issue: for example, if it is alleged that the applicant has been constructively dismissed, the applicant will open. If there is no dispute as to dismissal, the respondent will open. Some tribunals will hear an opening speech, others prefer to hear witnesses immediately. There is generally no formal right to make an opening speech. An opening speech should briefly outline the facts (indicating areas of dispute), introduce the evidence and summarise the legal principles involved. In practice, opening speeches are very rare. Witnesses may give evidence under oath or by affirming. Pursuant to Rule 14, the rules of evidence are not strictly applicable. Rule 14(2) provides:

> The tribunal shall, so far as it appears to it appropriate, seek to avoid formality in its proceedings and shall not be bound by any enactment or rule of law relating to the admissibility of evidence in proceedings before the courts of law.

Therefore, for example, the tribunal can hear hearsay evidence. It is a matter for the tribunal to decide the weight to attach to such evidence. Often the witness will have signed a written statement, and this may be used as evidence-in-chief. The tribunal can, and very often will, order the exchange of statements before the hearing (see **6.4.5.5** above). Since April 2012, the general rule is that witnesses should not read out statements (see also **6.4.5.5** above). The tribunal may or may not allow supplementary questions by the witness's representative. This is then followed in the usual way by cross-examination and re-examination. The tribunal may intervene and ask questions of a witness at any time. This frequently happens. Closing speeches may be made by the parties; whoever opened the case will make the final closing speech. The purpose of a closing speech is to review the evidence and to remind the tribunal of the relevant law.

In *Wiggan v Wooler & Co Ltd* (UKEAT/0285/07), the EAT said that it will be rare for a case to be dismissed at half-time on the ground that it has no reasonable prospect of success (see the Court of Appeal decision in *Logan v Commissioner of Customs and Excise* [2004] IRLR 63).

The tribunal will then give its judgment, with reasons (Rules 28–32). The tribunal may give an oral judgment immediately with oral reasons, or may follow an oral judgment with written reasons. If the tribunal gives oral reasons for its decision, the parties may apply, under Rule 30, for written reasons. There is a strict time-limit for doing so. In complex cases, a decision may be reserved to a later date. The decision is formally recorded in a central register held at the Central Office of the Employment Tribunals in Bury St Edmunds. This register is open to the public. Sometimes a tribunal will adjourn at this stage to allow the parties to reach an agreement on quantum. Failing this, evidence will be heard relating to losses, etc (if not already dealt with in examination-in-chief during the hearing). Practice varies as to when the tribunal will hear evidence relating to quantum.

An employment tribunal decision must comply in both form and substance with Rule 30(6). Rule 30(6) provides that written reasons should include

(a)   the issues which the tribunal ... has identified as being relevant to the claim;

(b)   if some identified issues were not determined, what those issues were and why they were not determined;

(c)   findings of fact relevant to the issues which have been determined;

(d)   a concise statement of the applicable law;

(e)   how the relevant findings of fact and applicable law have been applied in order to determine the issues; and

(f)   where the judgment includes an award of compensation or a determination that one party make a payment to the other, a table showing how the amount or sum has been calculated or a description of the manner in which it has been calculated.

A failure to do this will amount to an error of law (see *Balfour Beatty Power Networks Ltd v Wilcox* [2007] IRLR 63). In *Meek v City of Birmingham District Council* [1987] IRLR 250, Bingham LJ (see in particular paras 8 to 12) provided useful guidance on the minimum requirements as to what should be contained in an employment tribunal judgment. Paragraph 8 stated as follows:

> It has on a number of occasions been made plain that the decision of an Industrial Tribunal is not required to be an elaborate formalistic product of refined legal draftsmanship, but it must contain an outline of the story which has given rise to the complaint and a summary of the Tribunal's basic factual conclusions and a statement of the reasons which have led them to reach the conclusion which they do on those basic facts. The parties are entitled to be told why they have won or lost. There should be sufficient account of the facts and of the reasoning to enable the EAT or, on further appeal, this court to see whether any question of law arises; and it is highly desirable that the decision of an Industrial Tribunal should give guidance both to employers and trade unions as to practices which should or should not be adopted.

In other words, tribunals must provide a sufficient outline of the complaint along with a summary of its conclusions and its reasons for reaching those conclusions, so that the parties have enough detail to be able to work out why the decision was made. In *Greenwood v NWF Retail* (UKEAT/0409/09) the EAT re-examined whether a tribunal's written reasons were sufficient. The EAT made it clear that an employment tribunal is required, amongst other things, to decide relevant facts and how those facts should be applied to the law, and that a failure to do so will amount to an error of law. The EAT commented that the 'constituent parts [of a judgment] will need to be more than a formal statement paying lip service to the subparagraphs of the rule'. See also *Mak v Wayward Gallery Ltd* (UKEAT/0589/10).

6.4.9   Costs

Although costs are not often awarded against the losing party in tribunal cases, there are limited powers to make costs orders (ETA 1996, s 13 and Rules 38–48 of the Tribunal Rules). Costs orders can be made only where a party is legally represented at the hearing, and tribunals also have a power to make preparation time orders where a party is not legally represented (see **6.4.9.3**).

The Tribunals Service Annual Report for 2010/11 stated that 132 awards were made in favour of claimants and 355 in favour of respondents. In 2011/12, 116 awards were made in favour of claimants and 1,295 in favour of respondents. The median award was £5, the average £1,292, and there were 38 awards of over £10,000. The largest award, after detailed assessment in the county court, was £36,466.

Three sorts of costs orders may be made:

(a)   costs orders (**6.4.9.1** and **6.4.9.2**);

(b)   preparation time orders (**6.4.9.3**); and

(c)   wasted costs orders (**6.4.9.4**).

There is an excellent detailed IDS Employment Law Brief article on costs orders, preparation time orders and wasted costs orders in employment tribunals in the August 2012 edition (Brief 955, p 13).

6.4.9.1   Costs orders

The general powers to make costs orders are set out in Rule 38. Costs orders can be made only where a party is legally represented. The circumstances in which a tribunal *must* make a costs order are set out in Rule 39: a tribunal *must* make a costs order against a respondent in an unfair dismissal case where reinstatement or re-engagement is in issue and a hearing has to be postponed because of the respondent's failure to adduce evidence about the availability of the suitable employment.

Under Rule 40 a tribunal *may* make a costs order where a PHR or hearing has been adjourned on the application of a party, or:

> where, in the opinion of the tribunal, ... the paying party has in bringing the proceedings, or he or his party's representative has in conducting the proceedings, acted vexatiously, abusively, disruptively or otherwise unreasonably, or the bringing or conducting of the proceedings by the paying party has been misconceived ... a tribunal shall consider making a costs order against a paying party ... [and] having so considered, the tribunal may make a costs order ... if it considers it appropriate to do so.

The definition of 'misconceived' (above) includes 'having no reasonable prospects of success'. In *Daleside Nursing Home v Matthew* (UKEAT/0519/08), the EAT held that the tribunal's decision was perverse where costs were not awarded despite a finding that the claimant had deliberately lied. Note that under Rule 40(2), tribunals may take into account the unreasonable behaviour of a party's representative when awarding costs against that party.

In *Nicolson v Highlandwear Ltd* [2010] IRLR 859, the EAT allowed an appeal against a tribunal's refusal to award costs against an employee, where the tribunal found it was open to an employee to pursue an unfair dismissal claim purely in order to obtain a 'simple finding' of unfair dismissal 'without the objective of obtaining money'. The EAT pointed out that the ET1 form specified only three remedies and, unlike a discrimination claim, there was no provision for a declaration as a remedy. Commentators have pointed out that an employee may bring a claim to clear his name. It is also, arguably, inconsistent with *Telephone Information Services Ltd v Wilkinson* [1991] IRLR 148, where the EAT held that an employer's offer to pay the maximum unfair dismissal compensation did not render it frivolous or vexatious for the employee to continue the claim when unfairness was not admitted.

A legal representative is defined as a person who has a general qualification within the meaning of s 71 of the Courts and Legal Services Act 1990 (Rule 38(5)).

The tribunal may also make a costs (or preparation) order under Rule 47, essentially where a party has paid a Rule 20 deposit and lost the case. The deposit will be used in full or part settlement of the costs award (see **6.4.7.2**).

The power to award costs is exercised relatively infrequently in practice, but regard should be had to the case law in this area as costs awards are becoming more common.

6.4.9.2   Amount of costs (Rule 41)

Costs include fees, disbursements or expenses incurred by or on behalf of a party in relation to the proceedings (Rule 38(3)). They can include the costs of an in-house employed lawyer (see Rule 38(5)).

The costs ordered will either be a specified sum not exceeding £20,000, an agreed sum or a sum assessed by the civil courts (Rule 41). Rule 41(2) states that a tribunal may have regard to the paying party's ability to pay when considering (i) whether to make a costs order, or (ii) how much it should be, but there is no absolute duty to take this into account (see *Jilley v Birmingham & Solihull Mental Health Trust* (UKEAT/0584/06)). There currently is conflicting authority on when a tribunal must enquire about a party's ability to pay (see *Doyle v West London Hospitals NHS Trust* (UKEAT/0271/11) and *D'Silva v NATFHE* (UKEAT/0126/09)). In *Walker v Heathrow Refuelling Services Co Ltd* (UKEAT/0366/04), the EAT looked at, in the context of EAT costs (where the same Rule applies), what was relevant when taking into account the ability of a claimant to pay costs. The EAT said, in making an order that the claimant pay £1,250 towards the respondent's costs, that the following two factors were relevant:

(a)   that the claimant had recovered a sum of money as part of the proceedings (in this case an award of £2,520); and

(b)   that any legal fees the claimant was ordered to pay were likely to be met by the union that was funding his claim.

The Court of Appeal offered some advice to tribunals when deciding whether to make costs orders in late withdrawal cases, in *McPherson v BNP Paribas* [2004] IRLR 558. Mr McPherson had withdrawn his tribunal claim about two weeks before the hearing, citing ill health. There were doubts about the extent of his ill health. He had also failed to comply with a number of tribunal orders. The tribunal and the EAT held that the late withdrawal, when taken against the background of his non-compliance with tribunal orders, amounted to unreasonable conduct. He was ordered to pay all of BNP Paribas's costs. The Court of Appeal agreed that Mr McPherson had acted unreasonably, but allowed his appeal to the extent that it varied the amount of costs he should have to pay. It held (Mummery LJ) that:

> it would be legally erroneous if, acting on a misconceived analogy with the CPR, tribunals took the line that it was unreasonable conduct for employment tribunal claimants to withdraw claims and that they should accordingly be made liable to pay all the costs of the proceedings. It would be unfortunate if claimants were deterred from dropping claims by the prospect of an order for costs on withdrawal, which might well not be made against them if they fought on to a full hearing and failed. ... withdrawal could lead to a saving of costs. Also, ... notice of withdrawal might in some cases be the dawn of sanity and the tribunal should not adopt a practice on costs, which would deter applicants from making sensible litigation decisions. On the other side, ... tribunals should not follow a practice on costs, which might encourage speculative claims, by allowing applicants to start cases and to pursue them down to the last week or two before the hearing in the hope of receiving an offer to settle, and then, failing an offer, dropping the case without any risk of a costs sanction. The solution lies in the proper construction and sensible application of rule [40]. The crucial question is whether, in all the circumstances of the case, the claimant withdrawing the claim has conducted the proceedings unreasonably. It is not whether the withdrawal of the claim is in itself unreasonable.

6.4.9.3   Preparation time orders

Tribunals have the power to make 'preparation time orders' (Rules 42–46), where parties are not legally represented (see Rule 38(4)), in respect of carrying out preparatory work relating to the hearing. The grounds for making such orders are the same as for a costs order (see Rules 39 and 40). The Rules allow a rate of £32 per hour (from 6 April 2012) (up to a maximum of £20,000), in the same circumstances in which costs orders may be made. This may include time spent by the party (or its employees). Note that Rule 42(3) does not allow for preparation time to be awarded for time spent at any hearing, although it might cover time outside the tribunal rooms between hearings (*Andrews v Eden College and Others* (UKEAT/0438/10)). Rule 45 deals with the assessment of preparation time orders.

Note: it is not possible to make both a costs order and a preparation time order in the same proceedings against the same party (Rule 46), although it is possible to make an order that either a costs order or a preparation time be made, leaving it to final determination to decide which order it will be (Rule 46(2); see *Ramsay v Bowercross Construction Ltd* (UKEAT/0534/07)).

6.4.9.4 Wasted costs orders

Rule 48 permits tribunals to make a 'wasted costs' order against a party's representative (except not-for-profit representatives) as a result of 'any improper, unreasonable or negligent act or omission' by the representative. In *Mitchells Solicitors v Funkwerk Information Technologies* (UKEAT/0541/07), the EAT said that the threshold for a wasted costs order was high. The representative must not only have acted improperly, unreasonably or negligently, but must also have lent assistance to proceedings which amount to an abuse of process. Rule 48 is based on the wasted costs provision set out in s 51(7) of the Senior Courts Act 1981 for civil courts. The Court of Appeal's guidance on s 51(7), as set out in *Ridehalgh v Horsefield* [1994] 3 WLR 462, is therefore relevant and should be consulted.

In *Ratcliffe Duce & Grammer v Binns* (UKEAT/0100/08), the EAT confirmed that a wasted costs order cannot be made against a solicitor simply because the employment tribunal thinks that the client's pursuance of his claim is unreasonable and that the solicitor should have known that it was. (See also *Godfrey Morgan Solicitors Ltd v Cobalt Systems Ltd* [2012] ICR 305.)

6.4.9.5 Proposals for reform

The former President of the EAT, Mr Justice Underhill, recently conducted a review of employment tribunal practice and procedure, and proposed a new set of tribunal rules that are now the subject of a formal consultation. No major substantive changes to the current costs regime are envisaged: a tribunal would continue to have the same powers as now to make costs orders, preparation time orders and wasted costs orders, although Underhill J has recommended that s 13 of the ETA 1996 be amended to allow a party who has been represented by a non-lawyer to recover that person's charges or expenses as part of a costs award. Currently, any costs award above £20,000 has to be referred to the county court for detailed assessment; it has been recommended that that cap should be removed so that Employment Judges will also be able to conduct such assessments.

6.4.10 Review of tribunal decisions

A party may, within 14 days, ask for decisions and judgments of the tribunal to be reviewed in defined circumstances (Rule 34). See *Sodexho v Gibbons* (UKEAT/0318/05) for a decision about tribunals' powers of review.

6.4.11 Appeals to the EAT

An appeal may be made from a decision of the employment tribunal, on a point of law only, to the EAT. As with employment tribunals, the EAT must guard against substituting its own subjective response to an employer's conduct (see *Brent v Fuller* [2011] ICR 806). The EAT must pay proper regard to the decision of the employment tribunal, 'to whom Parliament has entrusted the responsibility of making what are, no doubt sometimes, difficult and borderline decisions' (see *Bowater v North West London Hospitals NHS Trust* [2010] IRLR 331).

Determining what is the difference between a question of law and findings of fact and inference is crucial, but difficult: an error of law can be found if a tribunal fails to make a finding of fact where there is uncontroverted evidence, or has made a finding contrary to all the evidence. But there is no error of law where some evidence points one way and some evidence points another way (see *Yeboah v Crofton* [2002] IRLR 634).

Any appeal must be made within 42 days after written reasons are sent out by the tribunal. The EAT's time-limit is enforced strictly (see, eg, the Court of Appeal's decision in *Greg O'Cathail v Transport for London* [2012] EWCA Civ 1004). The Employment Appeal Tribunal (Amendment) Rules 2004 (SI 2004/2526) came into force on 1 October 2004. A new Practice Direction dealing with EAT procedure came into force on 26 May 2008. The 2004 Rules introduce the overriding objective for the first time into the EAT procedural rules. They also set out instructions as to the documents to be submitted when lodging an appeal, improve the procedures for weeding out unmeritorious appeals, and also bring costs rules in the EAT into line with the new costs rules for employment tribunals.

The Government announced a consultation on legal aid reforms on 15 November 2010. The Government proposes to remove all Legal Help and Representation on employment matters for appeals to the EAT. The Government announced in December 2011 that no changes would now take place before April 2013.

6.4.12 The public tribunal register

The public tribunal register will no longer record applications and will contain only judgments and written reasons. Claims which are settled will no longer be matters of public knowledge.

6.4.13 Enforcement

Employment tribunals are not responsible for enforcement of an award. This must be done in the civil courts as if it were a county court judgment.

Section 27(1)–(4) of the Tribunals, Courts and Enforcement Act 2007, which came into force on 1 April 2009, removes the previous requirement to register unpaid tribunal awards before they can be treated as enforceable. Claimants may go directly to the county court (or High Court) for enforcement. Form N322B, which is available on the court services website (http://www.hmcourts-service.gov.uk), needs to be completed to allow enforcement of a decision or an Acas settlement (Form COT3).

Employers or individuals who fail to pay employment tribunal or EAT awards in England and Wales, will now be added to the *Register of Judgments, Orders and Fines* once enforcement proceedings are brought against them (Register of Judgments, Orders and Fines (Amendment) Regulations 2009 (SI 2009/474)).

6.4.14 Contingency fee agreements

Because employment tribunal cases are considered non-contentious by The Law Society, such cases can be run by solicitors on a contingency fee basis. Readers should have regard to the Damages-Based Agreements Regulations 2010 and The Law Society Guidance published in May 2010.

6.4.15 Human Rights Act 1998

Under Article 6 of the European Convention on Human Rights, everyone is entitled, 'in the determination of his civil rights and obligations', to 'a fair and public hearing within a reasonable time by an independent and impartial tribunal established by law'. Any party to an employment-related dispute, whether it takes place in the courts or before a tribunal, is therefore entitled to a fair trial. Case law from Strasbourg has, however, suggested that employment disputes may not come within the definition of 'civil rights and obligations' because they are essentially concerned with private rights. Nonetheless, under the HRA 1998, courts and tribunals are obliged to act compatibly with the HRA 1998 (s 6), and therefore, when determining an employment dispute between private parties, will still have to apply Convention rights.

Inherent in the concept of a fair trial is equality of arms between the parties. This may render the lack of legal representation in employment tribunal proceedings open to challenge, although because such proceedings are set up to be conducted in a practical and straightforward manner, without undue formality, such a challenge may not succeed. The ECtHR has held that the unavailability of legal assistance in respect of complex issues is a breach of the principles of a fair trial. The Scottish Executive made a decision to make public funding available in some circumstances to individuals pursuing employment cases in Scotland amid fears that a failure to do so is in contravention of Article 6. Public funding is available where the claimant can show that his claim is arguable and too complex for him to litigate without assistance. The Lord Chancellor stated on 5 July 2001 that he was 'confident' that the public funding in England and Wales is fully compliant with the European Convention on Human Rights.

Readers should refer to **Chapter 15** for cases involving the HRA 1998.

6.4.16 Proposed reform of Tribunal Rules

In November 2011, the Government commissioned the former President of the EAT, Mr Justice Underhill, to lead a working group to conduct a fundamental review of the rules of procedure governing employment tribunal proceedings. The terms of reference were:

(a) Cases to be managed in a way that is proportionate to the nature of the issues involved, with the importance of saving expense considered throughout.

(b) Proceedings to be handled quickly and efficiently, with an emphasis on helping proceedings to resolve themselves otherwise than through judicial determination at hearings and dealing robustly and, so far as appropriate, consistently with cases where they appear to have little or no reasonable prospect of success, with a view to fairness for all parties and the tribunal and its resources.

(c) Rules to be both simple and simply expressed, in particular given the significant proportion of unrepresented parties using employment tribunals.

(d) Proceedings to have as much certainty as the nature of particular cases allows, and that in particular that:

(i)   like cases are treated alike (with as much use made of standardised orders and directions as possible, building on the good work already developed around Case Management Discussion agendas);

(ii) rules are exercised, and orders are made, in a manner that is consistent, so far as appropriate, across Great Britain (backed, where necessary and appropriate, by relevant and published practice directions).

At the end of June 2012, Mr Justice Underhill wrote to the Government attaching a draft set of new Rules that the working group recommended should be made in place of the current Rules. The new Rules are less than half the length of the old ones. Mr Justice Underhill says that this has been achieved 'not only by more succinct wording but also by leaving out many rules that simply prescribe administrative practice and by leaving some general case-management discretions unglossed'.

Provision has been made for the employment tribunal Presidents to issue guidance on matters of practice. Provision is also included for stronger case management, including:

(a) an initial sift stage at which every case will be reviewed by an Employment Judge on the papers after the claim form and response have been received; and

(b) removing the present distinction between case management discussions and pre-hearing reviews and combining them together as a 'preliminary hearing' which can decide matters of case management and substantive preliminary issues (Rules 39–42).

Express provision has been made in the draft Rules to encourage the parties to settle where possible, and to take advantage of the various forms of ADR available (including the services of Acas and judicial mediation) (Rules 2 and 39(e)). The regime in the current Rules governing the setting aside of default judgments has been replaced with a simpler and more flexible regime (Rules 17–21).

Provision has been included for a specific rule allowing tribunals to set timetables for oral evidence and submissions, and to enforce them by guillotines where necessary (Rule 50), in an effort to prevent disproportionately lengthy questioning and submissions.

A new rule has been included governing when anonymity and restricted reporting orders may be made, providing for a more flexible regime which allows tribunals to take appropriate steps to balance the important principles of open justice and freedom of expression on the one hand and of privacy and effective justice on the other. The rule apparently goes beyond the explicit rule-making powers conferred by ss 11 and 12 of the ETA 1996, but the working group believes that the Ministry of Justice has the necessary powers to implement it.

Consultation on the new Rules closed on 23 November 2012. The Government proposes that the new Rules will come into force in 2013.

6.5 SETTLEMENTS

Many complaints are settled without a hearing. In 2011/12, for example, 50% of all cases were withdrawn or settled before a full hearing. Thirty-three per cent were settled through Acas and 27% were withdrawn (ET and EAT statistics 2011/12). The usual terms of settlement involve the employee agreeing not to start or proceed with a claim in consideration of the employer making a monetary payment and sometimes agreeing to provide a reference. Employers should be careful when providing a reference in these circumstances. A negligent reference which causes loss may be actionable by the recipient (*Hedley Byrne & Co Ltd v Heller & Partners Ltd* [1964] AC 465) or by the employee (*Spring v Guardian Assurance plc and Others* [1994] 3 All ER 129) (see **1.7.1.5**). Even in cases where the employer has a reasonable chance of success, it may be worth settling to avoid the cost of a tribunal hearing. This is a commercial decision to be taken by the employer. The effect of the recoupment regulations is also avoided (see **5.7.2.4**).

Broadly, by s 203 of the ERA 1996, any provision in an agreement is void in so far as it purports to exclude or limit the operation of any of the provisions of the Act, or to preclude a person from bringing any proceedings under the Act before an employment tribunal, unless:

(a) a conciliation officer has taken action under s 18 of the ETA 1996. Conciliation officers are designated by Acas. Where a complaint is presented to a tribunal, it is the duty of the Secretary of the Tribunals to send copies of all documents to an appropriate conciliation officer. The officer's duties are to promote a settlement and ensure that both parties understand its effect. He does not have a duty to ensure that the settlement is fair (*Moore v Duport Furniture Products Ltd* [1980] IRLR 158, CA). He must be involved in promoting the settlement. He will not merely 'rubber-stamp' an agreement already reached between the parties.

Note that personal injury claims cannot be settled through Acas, but if both parties agree, waivers in respect of existing claims can be included in the agreement.

It is common practice to exclude all possible claims by the employee in return for the settlement. However, care should be taken in drafting. In *Bank of Credit and Commerce International SA (in liquidation) v Ali and Others (No 1)* [2001] 2 WLR 735, the House of Lords held that a COT3 agreement containing a general release under which the employee accepted an additional payment on being dismissed for redundancy which was expressed as being 'in full and final settlement of all or any claims whether under statute, common law or in equity of whatsoever nature that exists or may exist' did not preclude a claim for 'stigma' damages which the parties could not have contemplated at the time the agreement was signed because the decision in *Malik* was not handed down until some eight years later. The House of Lords held that clear language leaving no scope for doubt is needed for an employee to be held to have intended to surrender rights and claims of which they were unaware and could not have been aware. Similarly, in *Royal National Othopaedic Hospital Trust v Howard* [2002] IRLR 849, the EAT held that an agreement settling a complaint of sex discrimination which was stated to be 'in full and final settlement ... of all claims which the applicant may have against the respondent' did not preclude her from bringing a victimisation claim later. The EAT held that, if such a result is intended, the language must be absolutely clear and leave no room for doubt that the agreement relates to future claims; or

(b) a written agreement (a 'compromise agreement') is entered into. In order for a compromise agreement to be binding it must comply with the following conditions:

(i) it must be in writing, identify the adviser, relate to the particular complaint and state that the relevant statutory conditions are satisfied,

(ii) the employee or worker must have received advice from a relevant independent adviser as to the terms and effect of the proposed agreement and, in particular, its effect on his ability to pursue his rights before an employment tribunal, and

(iii) there must be in force, when the adviser gives the advice, a contract of insurance, or an indemnity provided for members of a profession or professional body, covering the risk of a claim by the employee or worker in respect of loss arising in consequence of the advice.

A person is a relevant independent adviser:

(a) if he is a qualified lawyer;

(b) if he is an officer, official, employee or member of an independent trade union who has been certified in writing by the trade union as competent to give advice and as authorised to do so on behalf of the trade union;

(c) if he works at an advice centre (whether as an employee or a volunteer) and has been certified in writing by the centre as competent to give advice and as authorised to do so on behalf of the centre; or

(d) if he is a person of a description specified in an order made by the Secretary of State, eg a Fellow of the Institute of Legal Executives employed by a solicitors' practice.

However, a person is not a relevant independent adviser:

(a) if he is employed by or is acting in the matter for the other party or a person who is connected with the other party;

(b) in the case of a person within (b) or (c) above, if the trade union or advice centre is the other party or a person who is connected with the other party;

(c) in the case of a person within (c) above, if the complainant makes a payment for the advice received from him; or

(d) in the case of a person within (d) above, if any condition specified in the order in relation to the giving of advice by persons of that description is not satisfied.

A qualified lawyer is a barrister or solicitor who holds a practising certificate.

The conditions are applied strictly, such that if any one of the conditions is not satisfied the agreement is not binding.

Note: The compromise agreement must relate to the particular complaint; a compromise agreement which seeks to exclude all possible claims will fall foul of ERA 1996, s 203, which contains restrictions on contracting out of statutory rights. In *Sutherland v Network Appliance Ltd* [2001] IRLR 12, the applicant's employment with the respondent was settled on agreed terms by way of a compromise agreement. The terms stated that the settlement was in 'full and final settlement of any claims you may have against the company'. The EAT confirmed that the agreement was void in respect of statutory claims but held that the agreement was enforceable to the extent that it contained a compromise of contractual claims. Thus a compromise agreement must only seek to settle those statutory claims which have already been raised (either by presentation to the tribunal or raised by the employer prior to the issue of proceedings). The Court of Appeal gave guidance on compromise agreements in *Hinton v University of East London* [2005] IRLR 522. Smith LJ stated that it is not adequate for compromise agreements to use 'a rolled up expression such as "all statutory rights"'. Instead the particular proceedings must be identified, 'either by a generic description such as "unfair dismissal" or by reference to the section of the statute giving rise to the claim'. She agreed with Mummery LJ's statement that 'it is good practice for the particulars of the nature of the allegations and of the statute under which they are made or the common law basis of the alleged claim to be inserted in the ... agreement in the form of a brief factual and legal description'. Readers should pay careful attention to this case when drafting compromise agreements.

Where an agreement is concluded either through a conciliation officer or as a compromise agreement, any proceedings will normally be adjourned generally. If the employer complies with the agreement, the employee is barred from continuing with his complaint. If the employer does not comply with the agreement, the employee can either return to the tribunal to continue with the complaint, or sue for breach of contract in the county court or High Court or the tribunal itself.

In *Collidge v Freeport plc* [2008] EWCA Civ 485, the Court of Appeal held that an employer was entitled to withhold payment under a compromise agreement where the employee was in breach of a warranty he had given in the agreement, whereby the employee stated that he knew of no circumstances which would amount to a repudiatory breach of contract.

Where a settlement does not bind an employee, any sums paid under it will be taken into account by the tribunal in making any award. However, as a result of s 124(5) of the ERA 1996, the maximum compensatory award (£72,300 as at February 2012) must be applied only after all deductions have been made.

Similar rules on settlement apply to claims under the SDA 1975, s 77(4)(aa), the RRA 1976, s 72(4)(aa), the TULR(C)A 1992, s 288(2A), and the DDA 1995, s 9(2)(b).

Whatever method of settlement is used, the employee's adviser should ensure that any personal injury claims or claims arising out of employment pension benefits are expressly excluded from the settlement.

The Enterprise and Regulatory Reform Bill, introduced into Parliament on 23 May 2012, provides for compromise agreements to be renamed 'settlement agreements'. Consultation closed on 23 November 2012.

6.5.1   Recording the settlement

Once a claim has been presented, this needs to be withdrawn by the claimant in one of two ways:

(a)   the terms of the settlement may be recorded and registered with the employment tribunal on Form COT3. This is the usual method used where a settlement is reached after a conciliation officer has taken action;

(b)   alternatively, the claimant may merely decide to withdraw his claim to the tribunal, for example in compliance with a compromise agreement. Form COT4 can be used for this purpose, or a letter to the tribunal will suffice.

An amendment has been inserted into the Enterprise and Regulatory Reform Bill, introduced into Parliament on 23 May 2012, to include a new provision in the ERA 1996 to make it easier for employers to make settlement offers to employees without this being admissible in subsequent unfair dismissal proceedings. An employer would be able to make an offer to 'pay off' an employee before any performance management or disciplinary proceedings had started, and before any dispute had arisen between them. Such offers would still be admissible in evidence in discrimination claims and any claims of automatically unfair dismissal, and they would also be admissible if anything 'improper' is said or done. Consultation closed on 23 November 2012.

6.6 ALTERNATIVES TO TRIBUNAL PROCEEDINGS

Acas was given power to run a statutory arbitration scheme, as an alternative to the employment tribunal for unfair dismissal cases, by the Employment Rights (Dispute Resolution) Act 1998. The ACAS Arbitration Scheme (England and Wales) Order 2001 (SI 2001/1185) is intended to be 'confidential, informal, relatively fast and cost-efficient'. Procedures are 'non-legalistic' and flexible. Awards are final, with very limited opportunity to appeal. The scheme applies only to unfair dismissal complaints or claims under the flexible working law (see **14.19**). Full details of the scheme, including a guide to the scheme, may be found on the Acas website (www.acas.org.uk). To use the scheme, both the employer and the employee must agree to enter into voluntary arbitration. An Acas officer will listen to the arguments of both sides and decide whether compensation should be awarded and, if so, how much.

The arbitrator cannot deal with 'jurisdictional matters' (eg whether the worker was an employee; whether the complaint was presented in time; or whether the employee has sufficient continuity of service). A dispute is referred to arbitration by the parties entering into an arbitration agreement. A waiver form under which the parties agree to arbitration and waive the right to return to the employment tribunal must accompany the agreement. If the employee withdraws from the scheme his claim is dismissed. The employer cannot unilaterally withdraw from the scheme.

Once the parties have agreed to arbitration the procedure in outline is as follows.

At least 14 days before the arbitration hearing each party must send to the Acas Arbitration Section:

(a)   a written statement of case;
(b)   supporting documents;
(c)   a list of witnesses.

In deciding whether the dismissal was fair or unfair, the arbitrator must have regard to general principles of fairness and good conduct rather than legal rules. He must still apply EU law and the HRA 1998. Witnesses cannot be cross-examined by the parties; it is for the arbitrator to establish facts.

The arbitrator's decision must identify the reason for dismissal, the main considerations taken into account in reaching the decision, state the decision, the remedy awarded and the date it was made. Awards are binding and there is generally no right of appeal.

As indicated above (see **6.4.5**), Employment Judges can suggest to the parties at the case management discussion that the case be referred to judicial mediation. Judicial mediation is voluntary and provides parties to an employment tribunal claim with a confidential, alternative settlement option that tries to avoid the need for a full merits hearing. It operates in addition to, and not as a substitute for, the role of Acas or privately negotiated settlements. The judicial mediation takes place in private. A trained Employment Judge acts as an impartial mediator to try to help the parties to resolve their dispute. This judge will not hear the case if the mediation fails.

The principal criteria which identify cases as being suitable for judicial mediation are:

(a)   a full hearing has been fixed for the substantive issues of at least three days in length;

(b)   the case will usually involve at least one element of discrimination although some other complex cases are included;

(c)   the claims are generally single claims, but occasionally judicial mediation can incorporate small multiples (ie two or three claimants);

(d)   there must be no proceedings in other jurisdictions; and

(e)   there must be no insolvency involved.

If a settlement is achieved, the terms are agreed in writing. The parties may finalise the settlement terms by entering into a compromise agreement or by using a COT3 Form if Acas is involved. The Law Society has now published a Practice Note to support judicial mediation. This is available at www.lawsociety.org.uk/productsandservices/practicenotes/judicialmediation.page.

Acas also offers a pre-claim conciliation scheme. The details are available on the Acas website (see above).

6.7 OVERLAPPING CLAIMS AND AWARDS

A dismissed employee may have more than one potential claim against his employer. For example, a dismissal that is both unfair and without proper notice or within a fixed term may give rise to both an unfair dismissal claim and a wrongful dismissal claim. If an employee is unfairly selected for redundancy, he will be entitled to a redundancy payment and be able to present an unfair dismissal claim. All three claims of wrongful dismissal, redundancy payment and unfair dismissal would be available to the employee unfairly dismissed without proper notice by reason of redundancy.

6.7.1 Wrongful and unfair dismissal

The wrongful dismissal claim is a breach of contract action which may be brought as a court action or pursued in an employment tribunal. The unfair dismissal claim is pursued only in an employment tribunal. Both may be pursued. In the case of a less well-paid employee who is entitled to only a short period of notice, the unfair dismissal claim is usually more advantageous, as compensation for future loss may extend beyond the employee's notice period.

If both claims are brought, and both succeed, the basic principle is that compensation will not be awarded for the same loss twice. The tribunal will deduct the breach of contract damages awarded from the compensatory award for unfair dismissal.

6.7.2 Redundancy payment and unfair dismissal

The redundancy payment will be set against the unfair dismissal award. Usually it will simply offset the basic award, but if it exceeds the basic award (eg because the basic award has been reduced by contributory fault) the remainder will reduce the compensatory award. The excess redundancy payment should be deducted *after* the other deductions (eg for contributory fault) have been made (see **5.6.2.2**).

6.7.3 Redundancy payment and wrongful dismissal

Since a redundancy payment is a reward for past services, and a wrongful dismissal payment is an award for future loss, a redundancy payment is not taken into account in awarding damages for wrongful dismissal.

6.7.4 A discriminatory dismissal

If a person is dismissed for reasons relating to sex or race or disability, this is not automatically unfair but, in practice, will often be found to be unfair.

A claim for unfair dismissal may be pursued alongside a discrimination claim. Discrimination awards are not subject to any maximum figure and may include an award in respect of injured feelings. In addition, no eligibility conditions need be satisfied. As against this, the award for unfair dismissal includes a basic award in addition to compensation. Alternatively, re-engagement or reinstatement may be ordered. If both claims are pursued, s 126 of the ERA 1996 provides that compensation cannot be awarded again in respect of any loss or other matter which has already been taken into account in dealing with the other claim. (See **Chapters 8–13** for further details of discrimination claims.)

6.7.5 Compensation

The general rule of the compensation regime is that the employee cannot be compensated twice for the same *financial* loss.

---

1. **Compensation in respect of time spent at work**
- unfair dismissal basic award
- redundancy payment
- no other regimes

NB Employee will not be paid both

---

2. **Compensation in respect of actual losses**
- unfair dismissal compensatory loss to date of employment tribunal hearing
- wrongful dismissal damages (eg notice)
- discrimination pecuniary loss claims to date of employment tribunal hearing

NB Employee can recover these only once

---

3. **Compensation in respect of future losses**
- unfair dismissal compensatory loss from date of employment tribunal hearing
- discrimination future pecuniary loss claims from date of hearing

NB Employee can recover these only once

See further the diagram set out below.

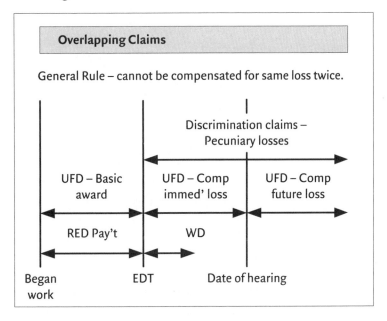

6.8 CASE STUDY: UNFAIR DISMISSAL

(1)   Chronology and facts

(2)   Particulars of response

(3)   Tribunal orders

(4)   Witness statement

(5)   Judgment

IN THE GUILDSHIRE EMPLOYMENT TRIBUNAL   CASE NUMBER: 1234/2010

BETWEEN

MRS JANE MINNERY   Claimant

- and -

GUILDSHIRE PRIMARY CARE TRUST ('PCT')   Respondent

CHRONOLOGY of
EVENTS

NUMBER	EVENT	DATE
1	Claimant commences employment with the Respondent	08/09/2006
2	Claimant's daughter made allegations of child abuse – Claimant's children taken into care	26/01/2010
3	Claimant's children voluntarily accommodated per Section 20 of The Children's Act 1989	29/01/2010
4	Claimant contacts acting senior nurse manager to notify Respondent of need to take emergency annual leave – no mention of superseding allegations	29/01/2010
5	A one-week sick note is received by the Respondent from the Claimant	05/02/2010
6	A further ten-day sick note received by the Respondent from the Claimant	09/02/2010
7	Case Conference meeting – children placed on the Child Protection Register for emotional and physical abuse & Respondent notified	09/02/2010 14/02/2010
8	Claimant informed of her suspension by the Respondent	15/02/2010
9	Children returned to the family home	22/02/2010
10	Guildshire Police state that no criminal prosecution will be taken against the Claimant but that a notation will be made on the Criminal Records Bureau register.	01/03/2010
11	Dr Francis meets with Claimant to assess the Claimant's fitness/competence to work	30/04/2010
12	Dr Francis' investigations recommend Claimant is dismissed	21/05/2010
13	Disciplinary panel meeting chaired by the PCT's Group Manager for Children's Services	02/07/2010
14	Written confirmation of outcome of Disciplinary hearing	10/07/2010
15	Claimant notifies the Respondent of her wish to appeal against the disciplinary panel's decision to dismiss her	17/07/2010
16	Appeal panel hearing chaired by the PCT's Director of Children Services	07/09/2010
17	Written confirmation of outcome of Appeal hearing	10/09/2010

NUMBER	EVENT	DATE
18	Proceedings commenced in Tribunal. The Claimant alleges unfair dismissal on the grounds that: • Insufficient evidence presented to the hearing to justify dismissal • Decision based primarily on suspicion rather than evidence of wrongdoing • PCT's decision based on the CRB notation but those who presented the PCT's case could not say how long it would remain on file • The allegation of abuse was retracted • It was not true that the claimant did not have an insight on how personal life would impact on job – the claimant outlined that she would use reflection, support of colleagues and supervision, along with policies and procedures to deal with similar child protection issues. • No formal warnings given • Previous good service not taken into account	05/10/2010
19	Tribunal Hearing: The Tribunal had an agreed bundle of documents The Tribunal had Witness Statements from the Claimant on her own behalf; and from Dr M Francis, Consultant Paediatrician for the PCT; the PCT's Group Manager of Children's Services who chaired the disciplinary hearing; and the PCT's Director of Children Services who chaired the appeal hearing.	17–19/12/ 2010

Tribunal's findings of fact

1. The Claimant began her employment with the Respondent in September 2005, starting as a student health visitor. She qualified in August 2006. The Claimant's line manger told Dr Francis, the Trust's consultant paediatrician, that she had always found the Claimant to be hardworking, reliable and flexible. She assessed the Claimant as being a good colleague.

2. The Claimant has two daughters who live with her.

3. On 12 January 2010 the Claimant spoke to her line manager about allegations that had been made against her by her daughter which involved allegations of physical abuse, being hit with a belt by her mother.

4. Social services wrote to the Respondent on 14 February 2010, reporting that both the Claimant's daughters had been removed from the family home on 26 January due to allegations of physical harm made by one daughter. The children had been placed on the Child Protection Register under categories of 'physical harm and emotional abuse' on 9 February.

5. The Respondent suspended the Claimant on 15 February. The decision to suspend was made because of the serious nature of the allegations. The Claimant remained on full pay and was told that the suspension was a neutral act, not disciplinary.

6. Dr Francis was asked by the Respondent to investigate. By the time he met with the Claimant her children had returned home, and the Claimant had signed a written agreement saying she would not cause emotional harm to her daughters and that she would work in partnership with the authorities.

7. Dr Francis interviewed the Claimant's line manager, the council's social worker and the Claimant.

8. The social worker told Dr Francis that she was concerned about the Claimant's perception of child abuse and physical chastisement. The Claimant was, she said, still attributing her actions to her upbringing and culture.

9. Dr Francis noted that no criminal charges were brought against the Claimant but that the investigation carried out by the police would appear as a notation on the Criminal Records Bureau record.

10. Dr Francis interviewed the Claimant on 30 April 2010. He asked her about her practice as a health visitor. He then asked her about the recent events and for her assessment of how the incident would affect her work. The Claimant said that she did not think that it would affect her work, and that children were the priority in the service and that she would not impose her own values on her work. The Claimant told Dr Francis that her daughter had retracted her allegations, but there was no evidence of this. The Claimant appeared to think, Dr Francis notes, that if this was the case then there was no issue for the Respondent to take up with her.

11. Dr Francis recommended dismissal for the following reasons:

    (i)   The Claimant's refusal fully to accept responsibility for the offence that had occurred, instead attempting to justify her action because of her culture, knowing full well, through her child protection and health visitor training, that this was not acceptable. Instead the Claimant continued to focus on issues relating to her being misconstrued and misrepresented in the child protection investigation.

    (ii) The Claimant's unwillingness to acknowledge that the events which occurred in her private life would impact on her work and practice as a health visitor.

    (ii) His concern that the Claimant's experiences would affect her attitude and her ability to work jointly with agencies involved in child protection investigations, and in particular with social services.

    (iv) His concern that because of the issues raised in the investigation, the Claimant's duty to assess risks and make appropriate referrals to social services where there were child protection concerns might be affected, as this was dependent not just on her knowledge but also on her attitude. The concern was that it would be difficult for any manager to have confidence that the Claimant was making the correct decisions and taking appropriate actions, especially in child protection cases, given the independent way that health visitors work.

12. Dr Francis was also concerned about whether the Claimant could maintain her credibility among her colleagues and other professionals if they became aware of events that had occurred, and that the Respondent would be taking a risk if it continued to employ her as a health visitor. Should there be any other child protection issues in connection with the Trust's clients, where her judgment was called into question because of this background, the Respondent could be seen to be at fault.

13. Dr Francis also produced a document entitled: 'Management case relating to Jane Minnery'. The risks were listed as follows:

    1. 'The welfare, safety and health of children must always be paramount. This is an overriding responsibility of Guildshire PCT.

    2. As a health visitor [the Claimant] will present a risk to the children and families she will be working with because her current knowledge and attitude could impair her judgment and her ability to manage cases appropriately.

    3. The organisation will be at risk if it continues to employ a health visitor who has been the executor of child abuse, and whose CRB check will contain a notification of this abuse.'

14. The Claimant was told in a letter dated 4 June 2010 that there would be a disciplinary hearing on 26 June 2010 to consider her dismissal due to the Claimant's conduct, and in light of the need to protect children and of the risk to the children and the PCT.

15. The Claimant was told that the hearing could result in the termination of her employment, and that she was entitled to be accompanied to the hearing by a trade union representative or friend or colleague. The disciplinary hearing took place on 2 July 2010, not 26 June, at the Claimant's request as she wanted to go on holiday to recover from the trauma of recent events.

16. At the hearing Dr Francis presented the Respondent's case, summarising its concerns as that the Claimant had not seen the problem that he was trying to highlight to her when he had questioned her. He said that she was unable to make the connection between what she had experienced personally and how it could possibly affect her ability to do her job. He did not believe she was capable of being credible to other professionals, and he thought that it could be a problem employing someone carrying a CRB notation. For this reason she should be dismissed, he said. The Respondent made it clear to the Claimant that it was not concerned with the details surrounding her children being taken into care. The Respondent was only concerned with its duty to protect clients from potential harm and with how what had happened had affected the Claimant's ability to carry out her job. The Respondent had to investigate that risk.

17. The Claimant's representative asked the Claimant a series of questions to enable her to give answers which would deal with the Respondent's apparent concerns. The Claimant confirmed that she would follow the Respondent's policies and procedures should she have to deal with a child at risk. She did not explain how that would work in practice. The Claimant confirmed that she did not feel compromised as a health visitor since the incident.

18. The Respondent wrote the Claimant a letter of dismissal dated 10 July 2010. The reasons given for the decision to dismiss were:

    • It has been deemed not suitable for you to continue in your role as a health visitor due to 'some other substantial reason'. That is, given the PCT's overriding responsibility to protect its clients, the potential risk of employing a frontline health visitor with a CRB notation for physical and mental abuse of children outweighs the arguments to continue to employ you in that capacity.

    • For the same reason it has been deemed not suitable for the PCT to offer you alternative employment within adult services as a 'Registered General Nurse'. The Claimant was offered an administrative post.

19. The Claimant was told that her employment would be terminated with three months' notice, and she was told of her right to appeal within 21 days. Otherwise the dismissal would take effect from date of the hearing, 2 July 2010.

20. The Claimant did appeal on 17 July 2010. The appeal hearing was heard on 7 September. The central theme in the appeal was that as no evidence of wrongdoing had ever been presented against her, she should not have been dismissed. The Claimant relied heavily upon the absence of any formal finding of guilt against her as a result of the investigation carried out by the police and social services. She also stated that allegations by family members had subsequently been retracted, which should have made a difference to the outcome of the disciplinary hearing.

21 The CRB notation was discussed at the appeal hearing. The Respondent confirmed that it had relied on the police and social services investigation, which had concluded that there was insufficient evidence for a criminal prosecution but that there was enough for a CRB notation, which reflected the seriousness of the allegations.

22. The appeal panel decided as follows:

    • The panel had serious concerns about the impact of Jane Minnery working with vulnerable children and her lack of insight.

- The appeal hearing considered whether she was suitable for a clinical alternative and decided (like the disciplinary panel) that the risks were too great.

- The panel had confidence in the professional advice that personal behaviour impacts on professional behaviour, and confirmed that as a health visitor advising on child protection, there would be a risk.

- The panel did not have confidence in the level of the Claimant's acceptable behaviour in parenting.

23. It had been noted during the hearing that the Claimant would not be supervised unless she reported a case to her team leader. As a band 7 employee she would be expected to assist with supervising junior staff and to have an in-depth knowledge of child protection matters, and to take a lead role in resolving those issues within families.

24. The appeal panel confirmed the disciplinary panel's decision on 10 September 2010. The panel had reviewed the earlier decision to ensure it was fair and reasonable, taking into account the facts and circumstances.

25. It had been apparent to the appeal panel that the Claimant lacked insight into how her private behaviour could impact on her professional ability to make objective decisions about vulnerable children. The advice the panel had received was that the Claimant's conduct towards her children could not be separated from the risks presented by her continuing to work as a health visitor. The Respondent has to be responsible for children in the borough, and the children's needs remain paramount.

26. The appeal panel therefore agreed with the panel that the risks in continuing to employ the Claimant as a health visitor were too high.

IN THE GUILDSHIRE EMPLOYMENT TRIBUNAL   CASE NUMBER: 1234/2010

BETWEEN

MRS JANE MINNERY   Claimant

- and -

GUILDSHIRE PRIMARY CARE TRUST   Respondent

PARTICULARS OF RESPONSE

1. The Respondent is a Primary Care Trust commissioning and providing health services to members of the general public in the Guildshire area.

2. It is admitted that the Claimant was employed as a Health Visitor by the Respondent from September 2006 to July 2010. It is admitted that the Claimant was dismissed. It is not admitted that the dismissal was unfair.

3. Unless admitted in these Particulars of Response the Respondent denies all of the Claimant's allegations.

4. The Respondent has an overriding duty and responsibility to protect members of the public, especially children, who use the services it commissions or provides. That duty includes ensuring that any employee who comes into contact with children presents no risk of harm. Section 11 of the Children Act 2004 places a statutory duty on NHS bodies, amongst others, to make arrangements to safeguard and promote the welfare of children. Statutory guidance was first issued in 2005 and revised guidance was published in April 2007. The NHS bodies that are covered by this statutory duty include Strategic Health Authorities, NHS Trusts, NHS Foundation Trusts and Primary Care Trusts.

5. As part of its overriding duty to protect the welfare of children the Respondent has to ensure that staff coming into contact with children present no risk in themselves to the children who are referred to services operated or commissioned by the Respondent. It is averred that this overriding duty is such that the Respondent must also consider any potential risk to service users and act accordingly.

6. As stated above the Claimant was employed by the Respondent as a Health Visitor. In that role she regularly came into contact with vulnerable children. In February 2010 it was brought to the Respondent's attention that a Child Protection Section 47 investigation had been undertaken by Social Services together with a police investigation in respect of the Claimant's two children. Both children were put on the Child Protection Register and placed in foster care.

7. Although the police subsequently confirmed that no further action would be taken against the Claimant, they made a notation with the Criminal Records Bureau ('CRB'). The Claimant's two children were returned to her care in due course.

8. Because of the Respondent's overriding duty subject to the Children Act 2004 and also the Children Act 1989 ('The welfare, safety and health of children must always be paramount'), the Respondent considered it imperative to initiate an investigation into the Claimant's conduct and professional suitability to be in contact with children. The investigation was undertaken by Dr Francis, Consultant Paediatrician. The Claimant was invited by letter dated 4 June 2010 to a disciplinary hearing.

9. The disciplinary hearing took place on 2 July 2010 and the Claimant was notified of the outcome by letter dated 10 July 2010. The panel concluded that the Claimant was unable to continue in her role as a Health Visitor due to its overriding duty to protect clients, and the potential risk of continuing to employ a health visitor with a CRB notation for physical and emotional abuse outweighed arguments to continue to employ her in that role. Equally the Respondent did not consider it suitable to continue to employ the Claimant as a Registered General Nurse within the Adult Service, and as such the

Claimant's contract as a health visitor with the Respondent would terminate three months from 2 July. The Respondent offered to re-deploy the Claimant into an administrative post.

10. The Claimant appealed the decision of the disciplinary panel by letter dated 17 July 2010. An appeal hearing took place on 7 September 2010. The appeal panel upheld the decision of the disciplinary panel and the Claimant was notified of that decision by letter dated 10 September 2010.

11. The Human Resources Manager subsequently had a telephone conversation with the Claimant and discussed vacant posts within the Respondent. The posts included a clerical officer post and a post as a personal assistant. It was left for the Claimant to express an interest in either post but the Claimant failed to do so. The Claimant would certainly have been appointed to the clerical officer position if she had confirmed she wanted that post.

12. In all the circumstances the Respondent maintains that the dismissal was fair. The Respondent denies that the Claimant was unfairly dismissed as alleged and denies that the Claimant is entitled to the relief sought or at all.

Advocate & Co
Solicitor for the Respondent
19 October 2010

IN THE GUILDSHIRE EMPLOYMENT TRIBUNAL   CASE NUMBER: 1234/2010

BETWEEN

MRS JANE MINNERY   Claimant

- and -

GUILDSHIRE PRIMARY CARE TRUST   Respondent

NOTICE OF ORDERS

Notice under Rule 10(8) Employment Tribunals Rules of Procedure 2004 of Orders made by a Judge under Rule 10

TO ALL PARTIES

Employment Judge Hazel has made the following Orders on his own initiative. Under Rule 12(2) any party affected by the Order may apply to have it varied or revoked. Such an application must be made in writing to this office before the date ordered for compliance and must include reasons for the application. A party who is legally represented is required by Rule 11(4) to provide to all other parties in writing the information set out in that Rule.

ORDERS

1. **DISCLOSURE OF DOCUMENTS:**
    On or before **29th November 2010** each party shall send to the other a list of the documents in their possession or control relevant to the claims and to the grounds of resistance. Additionally, the Claimant shall send to the Respondent a 'schedule of loss', ie a written statement of what is claimed, including a breakdown of the sums concerned showing how they are calculated; and the Claimant's list of documents should include any documents relevant to the schedule of loss.

2. **INSPECTION OF DOCUMENTS:**
    If either party requests a copy of any document on the other party's list, that other party shall provide a clear photocopy within 14 days of the request. Alternatively, that other party shall allow the requesting party on reasonable notice and at a reasonable time to inspect the original documents on the list and to make photocopies of them. That inspection shall take place where the documents are normally situated, but the parties may agree that inspection shall take place at some other convenient location. The provision of copies in compliance with this order shall entitle the supplying party to reimbursement of reasonable copying expenses, but not to delay or withhold provision of the copies pending such reimbursement.

3. **BUNDLE OF DOCUMENTS:**
    For the Hearing, the parties shall agree a bundle of documents limited to those which are relevant to the determination by the Tribunal of the issues in the case. Because it appears likely that the Respondent has most of the original documents, the Respondent shall create the bundle unless the parties specifically agree otherwise. On or before **20th December 2010** the Claimant shall notify the Respondent of the relevant documents to be included on behalf of the Claimant. On or before **27th December 2010** the Respondent shall provide to the Claimant a clear, indexed, paginated copy of the bundle, assembled in chronological order (save in respect of formal policies or procedures, which may be placed together) and containing all the relevant documents which any party wishes to be included. The Respondent shall also bring 4 copies to the Hearing (3 for the Tribunal and one for any witness).

4. **WITNESS STATEMENTS:**
    Not later than **7 days** before the hearing the parties shall exchange written witness statements (including one from a party who intends to give evidence). The witness statement should set out all of the evidence of the relevant facts which that witness intends to put before the Tribunal. If it is intended to refer to any document, the witness statement should refer to page/s in the agreed bundle. A failure to comply with this order may result in a witness not being permitted to give evidence because it has not been disclosed in a witness statement; or in an adjournment of the hearing and an appropriate order for costs caused by such adjournment. Each party shall bring 4 copies of any such witness statement to the hearing. The Claimant's statement should contain evidence relevant to the schedule of loss.

5. **HEARING TIME:**
    The case will be listed for a **3 days** hearing on the Chairman's estimate of the time required for it. That estimate is intended to include the time needed for considering the oral and written evidence; each party's closing statements; the consideration and delivery of the judgment of the Tribunal; and consideration and judgment on remedy, if arising. The Tribunal will require the case to be completed within the time allocated to it and the parties must now consider the question, whether that time is adequate. If you consider that the hearing may require a time longer than that which has been set aside for it, you must write to the Tribunal as soon as possible, giving your own estimate of the time required, with reasons, and with an indication of the extent of the witnesses and documents which constitute the evidence in the case.

CONSEQUENCES OF NON-COMPLIANCE

FAILURE TO COMPLY with any:

(a) Orders made under the Rules and set out in this Notice may result in a Chairman or Tribunal making an Order in respect of costs of preparation time against the party failing to comply and/or, subject to notice under Rule 19, making an Order to strike out the whole or part of the claim or response, including an Order that the Respondent shall be debarred from responding to the claim altogether; and/or

(b) Order for inspection or disclosure may result upon summary conviction in a fine of up to £1,000 being imposed upon the party in default under Section 7(4) of the Employment Tribunals Act 1996.

IN THE GUILDSHIRE EMPLOYMENT TRIBUNAL   CASE NUMBER: 1234/2010

BETWEEN

MRS JANE MINNERY   Claimant

- and -

GUILDSHIRE PRIMARY CARE TRUST   Respondent

WITNESS STATEMENT OF
DR MIKE FRANCIS

I, Dr Mike Francis MAKE OATH AND SAY as follows:

1.   I am employed as a Consultant Paediatrician by Guildshire Primary Care Trust. The statements made within this witness statement are based upon facts within my own knowledge, save where I have indicated the source of my information or belief. Where matters are not directly within my knowledge, I believe them to be true.

2.   I was appointed as the Designated Doctor for Child Protection for Guildshire in 1997 and continue to hold that post. I have worked in the speciality of paediatrics for 23 years, and I have had a significant experience managing cases where child abuse is suspected. In the last 13 years as Consultant Paediatrician and Designated Doctor for Child Protection, I have led the service strategically in the field of safeguarding children. I provide advice and supervision to clinicians, social workers and other professionals, and also to senior management within the health organisations locally.

3.   I make this statement in support of the Respondent in respect of the claim that has been commenced by the Claimant in the Employment Tribunal alleging unfair dismissal.

4.   I was asked by the Head of Children's Services for the Respondent to undertake an investigation surrounding allegations of physical abuse that had been made about the Claimant by her children. I wrote to the Claimant on 23 March 2010 informing her of my role and explaining that as part of my investigation I would be obtaining information about the allegations from Guildshire County Council Social Services and the section 47 investigation that had been completed. (A section 47 investigation requires the Local Authority to make enquiries when a child is suspected to be suffering, or likely to suffer, significant harm, in order to enable the Local Authority to decide whether it should take any action to safeguard and promote the welfare of the child.) I told the Claimant that as part of the investigation I would need to interview the relevant people concerned, which included herself, and I would write to her in due course to arrange a date for that interview. I told her she would be able to be accompanied by a trade union representative, work colleague or friend at the interview. I gave her my contact details so that she could contact me if she had any queries. (p52 Hearing Bundle)

5.   I arranged to meet the Claimant on 19 April, but she cancelled that appointment two days beforehand (p55) and we eventually met on 30 April 2010. The Claimant was accompanied at the meeting by her representative from the Royal College of Nursing, and notes were taken by my personal assistant.

6.   At the start of the meeting I again confirmed that I had been asked to conduct an investigation by the Respondent and explained the reasons for the investigation, ie that it had been alleged that the Claimant had physically abused her children. I told her that I would prepare a report following our meeting which would be sent to her prior to being finalised, and at that point she would be asked to sign a copy of the final version.

7.   The Claimant told me that after qualifying as a health visitor in 2007 she was offered a substantive post as a health visitor with the Respondent. She said that her caseload was heavy, but she received support from the senior health visitors with whom she worked and also her manager and supervisor.

8.   I explored with the Claimant the allegations and what had happened afterwards. She told me that she understood that the allegations had to be investigated but said that she felt what she had told the social worker had been misconstrued. One of the allegations that had been made was that she had hit her children with a belt. The Claimant told me that she had been asked by the social worker if she had ever hit her children with a belt but she said that the children were only ever smacked on their bottoms with the hand. She did concede that in the culture she came from, using a belt as a means of punishment was acceptable, but she said that through her health visitor training she had realised that was not the way forward. She was concerned that the report prepared by social services incorrectly conveyed what had been discussed and what she had said at the child protection conference when she and her partner had been interviewed by the Senior Practitioner, Child Protection Investigation Team, although she did accept that she had been given an opportunity to check the report and correct any inaccuracies. I took it that she had objected to the report, but she confirmed that the comments she had been concerned about were still in the report, so I presume that the social worker felt that the report was an accurate reflection of what had been discussed.

9.   The Claimant also told me that she did not consider that the allegations about abuse, and the fact that her children had been taken into care, would affect her work as a health visitor. She told me that the children with whom she came into contact through her work were her priority, and she assessed each case on the evidence and merits, and not according to her personal beliefs or cultural background. The notes of my meeting with the Claimant are at page 68.

10.   Also as part on my investigation I interviewed the Claimant's immediate line manager (p66); the social worker who conducted the investigation into the abuse allegations (p71); and I also reviewed the Child Protection Conference report (p80) prepared by the social worker; and liaised with Guildshire Police (p86).

11.   When I interviewed the social worker on 19 April 2010, she confirmed that she had not had any contact with the Claimant's family prior to the allegations, although one of her colleagues had been involved previously. She explained that the Claimant had acknowledged hitting her children with her hand and had in the past hit the elder daughter with a belt, but there had been no physical signs of abuse on either of the children, although the elder daughter had told her school that she was afraid to go home as she might be beaten. This had been mentioned to teachers at the school on a number of occasions but it was the first time that social services had been involved, and the referral by the school was prompted by the elder daughter alleging, on 26 January, that the Claimant had grabbed her around the neck and shaken her several times. Whilst the social worker confirmed that the elder daughter had subsequently stated that the smacking by hand and belt at home had stopped, she did not say that it had never happened; and the social worker felt that the daughter was intelligent and articulate, and had been reliable and consistent in the accounts that she had given.

12.   The social worker told me that the Claimant had said that she (the Claimant) had been treated in the same manner at home when she was a child, ie hit with a belt, and that such chastisement was culturally acceptable. She said that the Claimant told her that following her health visitor training, she realised that type of behaviour was wrong, although the social worker suspected that it was possible that the abuse had continued after that point in time. Although the Claimant, when she was interviewed during the child protection conference on 8 February 2010, confirmed that she had smacked both children in the past and had used a belt on the hands of the elder child, and appeared to have taken responsibility for her actions, that acknowledgement and acceptance for that type of punishment was subsequently retracted by the Claimant. However, when the Claimant's children were interviewed on 26 April, the social worker was told that the smacking by belt and hand had stopped, which would suggest to me that at some point in time in the past the Claimant had used a belt to punish her children.

13.   As a result of the initial Child Protection Conference, it was recommended that the Claimant and her partner should attend meetings and parenting courses, to which they agreed. The fact that the Claimant had two jobs also probably contributed to the stress that the Claimant was under, and would not have helped with the Claimant's attempts to cope with her children at home. I was told that the next review was due on 26 April (p87), but at the time of our meeting the children remained on the Child Protection Register, although there were no active concerns about their welfare at that time. I explained to the council's social worker that my concerns were around the Claimant's ability to care for her children without using physical violence or emotional pressure. I also had some concerns about the advice that she would give to clients, and whether she could properly decide when a referral was necessary if there were child protection concerns.

14.   I met the claimant's line manager on 2 May 2010. She confirmed that she first met the Claimant when the Claimant was training to be a health visitor, and she became her line manager in August 2008. She told me that although she did not monitor the Claimant's work each day, when the Claimant was sick her cases were allocated to other health visitors who did not discover any issues with the management of her cases. She found the Claimant to be hard-working and reliable.

15.   Her line manager confirmed that health visitors worked independently and effectively managed themselves, but they could contact their line managers if there were problems, specifically with child protection issues. I asked her to explain how the Claimant could be monitored or supervised if she came back into practice. She was unable to explain how such monitoring would take place as it was not something that had happened before. I explained that I had concerns about the Claimant's attitude towards Social Services which could perhaps affect her willingness to report appropriate child protection issues.

16.   In addition to interviewing the above-named witnesses, I also carefully studied the initial Child Protection Conference report (p80), which was appendix 7 of my report. The report confirmed that following the allegations made on 26 January 2010, the Claimant's two daughters were made subjects of a Police Protection Order and placed in local authority care. On 29 January the Claimant and her partner agreed to the children remaining in foster care, and then proposed that the children should be placed with family members rather than remaining in foster care, which happened on 6 February. The report noted that both the Claimant and her partner had admitted physically chastising their children, which included smacking the children's bottoms with their hands and hitting the elder child on the hand with a belt, but later commented that it was not illegal to chastise children reasonably.

17.   The report noted that both the Claimant and her partner agreed to sign a parental agreement, by which they agreed not to use any form of physical chastisement at any time against their children in the family home. In addition, the Claimant and her partner accepted that disciplining their children by the use of physical chastisement was not acceptable and could not continue.

18.   The report also noted that although the Claimant and her partner had admitted using a belt to chastise their elder daughter, that admission was retracted to some extent later by the Claimant, as it was reported that, according to her, there had been a misunderstanding in relation to the use of the belt and she had not used it for two years to punish her elder daughter.

19.   The report recommended that the children should be placed on the Child Protection Register under the category of Physical Abuse, and whilst it was proposed that the children should be returned to the family home on a gradual basis, they should be closely monitored by professionals to ensure their safety, and the Claimant and her partner were to attend a parenting course, amongst other requirements.

20. I also contacted Guildshire Police to determine if any formal charges had been made against the Claimant and her partner, and I was informed that they had not been cautioned and there was insufficient evidence to proceed with a criminal prosecution. I was told, however, that the incident would show up on a CRB check, but whether or not the information was released would depend upon the nature of the job for which the Claimant applied (p54). I was also subsequently informed by the social worker that the children had been removed from the Child Protection Register as they were no longer considered to be at risk of harm, and the Claimant and her partner had agreed to cooperate with the Child Protection Plan, and the children were classified as Children in Need (p87).

21. In the light of the evidence that I had gathered, the witnesses I had interviewed, including the Claimant, and the report from the Initial Child Protection Conference, I had to decide whether or not I considered the Claimant presented a risk to clients, and children in particular, if she was allowed to resume her job as a health visitor. I felt that the Claimant was not able to accept responsibility for her actions in relation to her children, and continued to deny that she had done anything wrong when I interviewed her. The Claimant was of the view that as her children had been returned to her then that was evidence that there had not been any abuse and that nothing wrong had occurred. I could not see any degree of reflection about the events that had happened, which is what I would have expected, and especially from somebody working as a health visitor.

22. Although the Claimant's children had been returned to her, this did not mean that there was no risk, or no continuing risk, or that there had not been any abuse. I must explain that child protection issues are based on the balance of probabilities. Initially the balance of probabilities in this case was that the children had either been significantly harmed, or were at risk of significant harm. Subsequently, when the children's names were removed from the register, it was felt that the risks were not as high as previously because of the work that had gone into the case.

23. Upon concluding my investigation I had to consider whether or not I could recommend that the Claimant should be allowed to return to her job as a health visitor, albeit with supervision, or if I should recommend that she could not work with vulnerable clients, particularly children. I felt that the Claimant would need extensive supervision, and I came to the conclusion that as health visitors by the nature of the job work on their own a lot, it would have been difficult to be entirely confident that the Claimant did not pose a risk to children, either through failing to identify a risk or by condoning practices that she might have considered to be acceptable. I came to the conclusion that this was too high a risk to accept. The Children Act 2004 (p162) places a statutory obligation to promote and safeguard the welfare of children. Not only did I believe that to have allowed the Claimant to return to her position as a health visitor would have put that duty in jeopardy, but fundamentally I believe that my duty, and that of the Respondent, is to try to address the imbalances that exist when children are involved. The overriding duty of the Respondent, and its employees, is to protect and safeguard the welfare of children generally, and especially those considered to be at risk. It was my professional opinion that to return the Claimant to her role as a health visitor would have meant that the Respondent would not have been fulfilling its obligations and duty to protect the welfare of children, and as such I had to recommend that the Claimant should be dismissed from her position as a health visitor.

24. I prepared a Management Statement of Case (p90) for the hearing, and on the basis of the risks I had assessed as to allowing the Claimant to continue to work as a health visitor, I recommended that she should be dismissed from that post. I presented the Management Case at the hearing on 2 July 2010. I had no further involvement with the matter after that date save for my involvement as a witness for the Respondent in respect of the claim brought by the Claimant in the Employment Tribunal.

I confirm that the contents of this my witness statement are true.

Signed:

Date:

Judgment of the Employment Tribunal

The unanimous decision of the Tribunal is that the Claimant's dismissal was for some other substantial reason and was fair and reasonable in the circumstances.

REASONS

1. The Claimant brought a claim of unfair dismissal against the Respondent. The Respondent resisted her complaint.

EVIDENCE

2. The Tribunal had before it an agreed bundle of documents. The Tribunal had witness statements from the Claimant on her own behalf; and from Dr Francis, Consultant Paediatrician, Mr Y, Group Manager Children's Services and Z, Director of Adult and Children Services; all on behalf of the Respondent.

ISSUES

3. The tribunal had to determine the following issues:
   (a) the reason for the Claimant's dismissal
   (b) whether the reason fell within one of the permitted reasons under s 98(2) ERA 1996, and if so;
   (c) whether the Respondent had conducted a reasonable investigation on which to base its beliefs with regard to the Claimant;
   (d) whether it was reasonable in all the circumstances for the Respondent to treat it as a sufficient reason for dismissing the Claimant.

FINDINGS OF FACT [see the facts at pp 196–199 above]

LAW

4. The tribunal needs to consider the reason for the Claimant's dismissal and whether that reason is one that is proved by the employer; as the burden is on the employer to show the reason for the dismissal and that it is a reason falling under sub-section (2) of section 98 ERA 1996 or some other substantial reason of a kind such as to justify the dismissal of an employee holding the position which the employee did.

5. It is the Respondent's case that they dismissed for SOSR.

6. In order to prove that the dismissal has been for SOSR, the Respondent would need to prove that it is a substantial reason and thus not frivolous or trivial.

7. If the tribunal decides that the reason for dismissal is proven by the employer and that it is one of the reasons set out in section 98(2) ERA 1996, then the tribunal needs to decide if it was fair and reasonable in all the circumstances. The tribunal has to decide whether taking into account all the relevant circumstances, including the size and administrative resources of the employer's undertaking and the substantial merits of the case, the employer has acted reasonably treating that reason as a sufficient reason for dismissing the employee. In determining this, the tribunal has to be mindful not to substitute its views for that of the employer.

8. The tribunal is also aware of the Police Act and the Home Office Circular 5/2005 entitled 'Criminal Records Bureau: Local checks by police forces for the purpose of enhanced disclosure'.

APPLYING THE LAW TO THE FACTS:

Was the dismissal unfair?

9. In our judgment Dr Francis' investigation was thorough and fair. In conducting his investigation Dr Francis interviewed the Claimant after interviewing most of the

witnesses. The brief that he was given by the Respondent was properly focused in that he was not concerned with the details of what occurred between the Claimant's daughter and herself so much as with the Claimant's reaction to what had happened and her perspective on it, given the nature of her duties as a health visitor. After Dr Francis saw the Claimant he met her line manager who was supportive of the Claimant and stated that in her opinion the Claimant had been hard-working, reliable as a colleague and flexible whenever cover was required in managing their caseload.

10.   The line manager confirmed that health visitors work independently, self-supervising on the whole, and that they would be monitored only if there were issues of concern.

11.   When Dr Francis met the Claimant he asked her wide-ranging questions which allowed her the opportunity to give her version of the incident, and also to discuss broadly how the incident might affect her practice and influence her thinking or how she would work to ensure it did not do.

12.   In our view Dr Francis was correct not to reinvestigate the child's allegations. As the Claimant's employer the Respondent's only interest in the situation would be how what has occurred in the Claimant's private life affects her ability to do her job. In order to do so, it was able to rely on the findings and judgment of the police and social services after their investigation into the child's allegations.

13.   The social services and the police had decided that the children needed to be placed on the Register, even for a short period of time. Also, that although the children were returned to the family eventually, work needed to be done with both parents around parenting issues thrown up by the incident, and this occurred over a number of weeks from the date of the incident.

14.   Lastly, the Respondent was aware from information provided by the police that there would be a notation on any Criminal Records Bureau disclosure that was obtained in respect of the Claimant in relation to working with children or vulnerable adults.

15.   From those circumstances it was quite right for the Respondent to accept the fact that the Claimant had behaved in such a way toward her daughter that it warranted a CRB notation, even if there had been no conviction at the magistrates' court.

16.   The disciplinary hearing was a hearing in which the Respondent balanced the risks involved in continuing to employ the Claimant (who it was aware, and which was noted in the minutes, had a good record prior to this incident and who would now have a CRB notation if a search were made); and the risks posed to the children in need within its catchment area, being the need to protect the safety of children, the risk to children and the risk to the PCT. The Respondent is entitled to weigh up those risks.

17.   It was noted that if the Claimant was a new applicant for a job as a health visitor, with a CRB notation for physical and emotional abuse of her own children she would not have been employed. The difference is that the Claimant is an existing employee with a previous unblemished record. As she was a longstanding employee, it was the Respondent's duty to treat the Claimant fairly and reasonably, and to consider in the light of her previous employment with the Respondent whether or not that outweighed the risks.

18.   In our judgment the Respondent was also entitled to take into consideration some of the inconsistencies in the evidence which was given by the Claimant to the Respondent in interviews and at the hearing. The Claimant stated that she used to condone chastisement with a belt, but that she stopped doing so when she undertook health visitor training and learnt this was not a suitable way to discipline her children. However, the Claimant became a qualified health visitor three years before the incident but she stated that she stopped using the belt against her children only two years prior to the incident. That would mean she continued to use the belt even after she completed her training, and therefore challenges her earlier statement.

19. The Claimant also stated during the course of the internal proceedings that she no longer believed that physical chastisement of children was appropriate. However, in her answer to Dr Francis at the investigatory interview, she stated that she would not impose her own values on her work and that each case was to be judged on its own merit and not on her beliefs. This would tend to suggest that she continues to believe that that method of discipline is still appropriate but that she is endeavouring to keep those beliefs to herself. There is a significant difference between the two positions.

20. In presenting her case to the Respondent at the disciplinary and appeal hearing and at the tribunal Hearing, the Claimant appeared to be suggesting that the fact that there was no evidence of abuse, that there had been no conviction at the magistrates' court, and that the children were returned to her and removed from the at risk register, meant that the Respondent should not have considered that anything significant had occurred but should instead consider that everything had, in effect, 'gone back to normal'. This would suggest to the Respondent that the Claimant did not appreciate that the fact that this had occurred at all would give the Respondent cause for concern.

21. The Respondent is therefore, in the tribunal's judgment, correct in its judgment that it could not have any confidence that the Claimant's personal opinions had in fact changed with regard to the correct methods for disciplining children. Instead it appears that the Claimant was going to keep her personal feelings to herself, which is different and less reliable.

22. The Respondent's real concern was that if the Claimant did not consider that whatever was happening with a particular child was wrong or was inappropriate, she was unlikely even to be aware that she had condoned it, and would not have flagged it up for advice from anyone.

23. When questioned about how she saw issues in her personal life affecting her work, the Claimant's answer was that there were policies and procedures that dealt with those issues. This answer demonstrated that she was not aware of a potential conflict between her apparent beliefs and the duties of the job.

24. The Respondent weighed up its duty towards the Claimant and the risks involved in continuing to employ her. The risks outweighed any duty towards her as a longstanding employee with no previous disciplinary record and a good work record, and this is why the decision was made to dismiss her.

25. It is therefore our judgment that the decision to dismiss was for some other substantial reason and that it was reasonable in all the circumstances that it should be considered as an appropriate reason for dismissing the Claimant.

26. The Respondent not only took into account the CRB notation but also took into consideration the Claimant's attitude to the existence of the notation, the investigation by social services and the police, and the effect of the whole incident on her practice. The claimant showed that she had failed to analyse the situation in a way which showed she appreciated the risks that faced the Respondent.

27. The Respondent was not weighing up the risk that the Claimant might abuse children; this was not the issue. The issue was that she might observe something in her work that should give her cause for concern and cause her to report the family to the authorities, but that she would not do so because she would not consider what she had observed as wrong or worrying. There were concerns that if she harboured personal views that physical chastisement of children with a belt or a hand was actually acceptable in her 'culture' or otherwise, she would not take up the issue with the family or her employers, as appropriate, and as required by the Respondent in satisfaction of its duties to protect children in its care.

28. The Claimant's job required her to work independently. The Respondent therefore had to be reassured that she would be able to perform her duties professionally and without any personal issues clouding matters. And even though the Claimant states that she

would not allow them to do so, the possibility that she might still hold those beliefs reasonably gave the Respondent cause for concern.

29. The Respondent is an independent organisation and is entitled to come to its own decision based on the facts. The Respondent's decision to dismiss that Claimant for some other substantial reason was fair and reasonable in the circumstances, and although it was unfortunate, considering the Claimant's unblemished work record up until that date, it was not unfair.

Signed

....

Employment Judge

Judgement sent to the Parties on

....

and entered on the Register

....

For Secretary of the Tribunals

6.9   FURTHER READING

Lewis, *Employment Law: an adviser's handbook*, 9th edn revised (LAG, 2011).

Cunningham and Reed, *Employment Tribunal Claims – Tactics and Precedents*, 3rd edn revised (LAG, 2010).

Blackstone's Employment Law Practice (OUP, 2012).

Barnett, Palka and Hay, *Costs in Employment Tribunals* (Jordans, 2010)

SUMMARY

A wide range of different statutory claims may be brought by presenting a complaint to an employment tribunal (**6.2**). In most instances these claims must be brought by employees, but some claims by workers may also be dealt with (**1.3** and **6.2**). There are a number of different time-limits within which claims to tribunals must be submitted, depending upon the nature of the complaint. Care needs to be taken with these rules as the time-limits are relatively short (in most cases three months) and enforced strictly (**6.3**). For example, an unfair dismissal claim must normally be presented within three months starting with the effective date of termination (EDT – see **3.5.2**), or within such further period as the tribunal considers reasonable where it was not reasonably practicable for the complaint to be presented within three months (ERA 1996, s 111). The EDT for these purposes is the basic EDT defined by ERA 1996, s 97.

The practice and procedure of employment tribunals is governed by Rules set out in s 1 of the Employment Tribunals (Constitution and Rules of Procedure) Regulations 2004. These cover such matters as the form and substance of the claim form (ET1) and the response (ET3), case management, ancillary applications for information or documents, pre-hearing reviews and costs (**6.4**).

Many employment tribunal claims are settled without a hearing. Settlements, to be binding, may be negotiated either through an Acas conciliation officer or via a compromise agreement (**6.5**).

There are options other than bringing tribunal proceedings, including using ADR, the Acas statutory scheme and judicial mediation (**6.6**).

A dismissed employee may have more than one potential claim against an employer, eg unfair dismissal, wrongful dismissal and a redundancy payment claim. However, as a general rule an employee cannot be compensated twice for the same financial loss (**6.7**).

The following practical steps should be taken when bringing a claim:

- Consider whether to bring the claim in the tribunal or in a civil court (see **Chapter 1**).
- Check that the tribunal has jurisdiction. There is a list of all the tribunal jurisdictions at www.employmenttribunals.gov.uk/FormsGuidance/jurisdictionList.htm.
- Check time-limits. For example, for unfair dismissal, a claim must be received by the tribunal within three months starting with the EDT (or within such further period as the tribunal considers reasonable in all the circumstances: ERA 1996, s 111). In discrimination cases or complaints relating to non-payment of wages or holiday pay, the three-month period begins when the matter complained about happened. This may mean that time can start running in some cases before termination of employment. There are special rules for equal pay and redundancy payment claims.
- Submit the claim on the approved ET1 form and ensure all required information is provided.

- If the claim is posted (it is also possible to send it using a downloadable pdf via the employment tribunals website), the postcode for the place where the employee normally worked should be used to identify the correct tribunal office address to use. If the employee has never worked for the respondent, identify the correct tribunal office postal address by using the postcode for the place where the matter being complained about happened. There is a list on the employment tribunal website which indicates the correct tribunal office: www.employmenttribunals.gov. uk/Documents/HearingCentres/Postcodelist_1stApril2010.pdf.

- Once the tribunal office has received and accepted the claim, it will give it a case number. If the claim is accepted, the tribunal office will send a letter to confirm this, together with a booklet about what the next steps are. At the same time, the tribunal office will send the respondent a copy of the claim form together with a form [ET3] for its response. In most cases, the tribunal office will also send a copy of the claim to Acas. The forms and guidance notes are available on the employment tribunal website.

- If the claim is not accepted, the tribunal office will return the form with a letter explaining the reason why the claim has not been accepted and what action needs to be taken. In these cases it will be very important to ensure that the form is resubmitted within the time limits.

- The response form and guidance notes are available on the employment tribunal website. If a response is not on the approved form, is not received within the specified time limit, or does not contain: (i) the employer's full name and address; (ii) whether the employer wants to defend all or part of the claim; and (iii) the grounds on which the claim is being defended, it will not be accepted.

- If the response is not accepted, it will be returned by the tribunal office. In these cases it will be very important to ensure that the form is resubmitted within the time-limits.

- If the response is accepted, a copy will be sent to the claimant. In most cases, a copy will also be sent to Acas.

- If no proper response is received within 28 days, the tribunal may consider issuing a default judgment. A default judgment allows an Employment Judge to give a decision about the claim without the employer being present.

- A respondent should consider whether it wishes to make a counterclaim. Any such counterclaim must be made within six weeks of receiving the copy of the claim from the tribunal office. If a counterclaim is being made, the tribunal office can be asked to send the appropriate form.

- It is possible to apply to the tribunal to ask it to review a default judgment. Any such application must be made in writing within 14 days of the date the default judgment was sent by the tribunal office. (An Employment Judge may extend the time limit for reviewing a default judgment but only if it thinks it is just and equitable to do so.) Any such application must say why the default judgment should be changed or withdrawn. When the employer is applying for a review of a default judgment, the application must include: (i) the respondent's response to the claim; (ii) an application to extend the time limit for presenting the response; and (iii) an explanation of why a response containing the necessary information or an application to extend the time limit for response was not provided within the time limit for responding. The tribunal has the power to refuse to review the default judgment, confirm it, change it or withdraw it.

- Once the claim and response have been received and accepted, the parties need to consider whether there are any issues they want to be dealt with or any orders which should be made before the claim should proceed further. The tribunal may give directions or orders on a variety of matters (see **6.4.5**), including further information, documents and witnesses. If a party decides that it needs more information or documents from the other party, it should first ask for these to be provided voluntarily by writing to the other party, giving a reasonable time limit for responding. If matters do not get resolved voluntarily, a party should write to the tribunal and ask the tribunal to issue an order.

- The main hearing will determine whether the claim succeeds or fails (ie on liability) and, if it succeeds, what remedy is appropriate. A full hearing will normally be conducted by a full tribunal which includes an Employment Judge and two non-legal members.

- A pre-hearing review (see **6.4.7.1**) can be held to determine jurisdictional issues, for example: (i) whether the claim or response should be struck out; (ii) questions of entitlement to bring or defend a claim; (iii) if either side's case appears weak, whether a deposit needs to be paid and, if so, how much, before that side can go ahead. This type of hearing is normally held in public before an Employment Judge sitting alone, but may also be held over the phone.

- In a straightforward case, the tribunal will issue, of its own motion, a short set of directions to help the parties prepare for the substantive hearing. In a more complex case, the tribunal may hold a case management discussion to deal with any outstanding matters. It may be held over the phone or in person. It is normally held in private. A case management discussion will normally seek to: (i) clarify the issues in the case; (ii) decide what orders should be made about matters such as documents and witnesses; and (iii) decide the time and length of the full hearing. The time and length of the full hearing will be given automatically in the standard directions.

- The length of time allocated to a case includes time for: (i) the substantive hearing on liability; (ii) any issues or evidence on remedy; and (iii) the tribunal to deliberate and deliver a judgment. Hearing dates are postponed only where there is a good reason and/or it is in the interests of justice to postpone a hearing.

- All or part of a claim (or responses) may be withdrawn at any time before or during the hearing, by telling the tribunal and the other parties in writing. Withdrawals should be done as soon as possible.

- If a case settles before the hearing, the parties should let the tribunal office know as soon as possible.

- Prior to the hearing it will be necessary for the parties to prepare and agree between them a bundle of documents for use at the hearing (see **6.4.7.5**). This is usually done by the respondent. It will also be necessary for the parties to have prepared witness statements for their witnesses and to have provided copies of these in advance in accordance with any case management directions to the other party. Signed copies must be brought to the tribunal.

- See **6.4.8** for the conduct of the main hearing, **6.4.9** for the rules on costs, and **6.4.10** and **6.4.11** for reviews and appeals.

TRANSFER OF UNDERTAKINGS

LEARNING OUTCOMES

After reading this chapter you will be able to:

- explain when the Transfer of Undertakings (Protection of Employment) Regulations 2006 apply
- identify what constitutes a 'relevant transfer'
- list and understand the *Spijkers* factors
- understand the effect of a 'relevant transfer' and who is covered by it
- describe the implications of dismissals connected to a transfer
- explain the impact of a transfer on an employer's ability to vary the terms of a contract of employment
- be aware of the requirements to inform and consult under the Regulations.

7.1 INTRODUCTION

In this chapter, we consider the protection afforded to employees by the Transfer of Undertakings (Protection of Employment) Regulations 2006 (SI 2006/246) ('the 2006 Regulations').

The BIS Guide, *Employment Rights on the Transfer of an Undertaking*, July 2009 (www.berr.gov.uk/files/file20761.pdf), summarises the effect of the Regulations as follows:

> Broadly speaking, the effect of the Regulations is to preserve the continuity of employment and terms and conditions of any employees who are transferred to a new employer when a relevant transfer takes place. This means that employees employed by the previous employer (the 'transferor') when the transfer takes effect automatically become employees of the new employer (the 'transferee') on the same terms and conditions (except for certain occupational pensions rights). It is as if their contracts of employment had originally been made with the transferee employer. However, the Regulations provide some limited opportunity for the transferee or transferor to vary, with the agreement of the employees concerned, the terms and conditions of employment contracts for a range of stipulated reasons connected with the transfer. ... The Regulations can apply regardless of the size of the transferred business: so the Regulations equally apply to the transfer of a large business with thousands of employees or of a very small one (such as a shop, pub or garage). The Regulations also apply equally to public or private sector undertakings and whether or not the business operates for gain, such as a charity.'

The 2006 Regulations were introduced to comply with various EC Directives concerning the transfers of undertakings. The main Directives are:

(a)   the Acquired Rights Directive (77/187/EC);

(b)   the Acquired Rights Directive (98/50/EC);

(c)   the Acquired Rights Amendment Directive (2001/23/EC).

At common law in the UK, the transfer of an undertaking by one employer to another automatically terminates the employee's contract of employment, ie there is a dismissal. In this situation the reason for the dismissal will generally be redundancy (as the employer's requirement for employees to do work of a particular kind has ceased or diminished). Should the undertaking's new owner require the employee's services, he will offer a new contract of employment, and can do so on whatever terms he likes. Depending on the timing of the dismissal, the employee may still retain continuity in this situation (see ERA 1996, s 218(2) and *Clark & Tokely Ltd (t/a Spellbrook Ltd) v Oakes* [1998] 4 All ER 353). The 2006 Regulations altered the legal position by providing that where there is a 'relevant transfer', there will not be any automatic termination of the contract of employment. There will not be a dismissal simply because there is a transfer. In that situation, the employee will transfer with the undertaking and will be employed by the new owner under his original contract. If there are any dismissals, whether actual or constructive, and whether before or after the transfer, if those dismissals are connected with the transfer, they will be automatically unfair unless, effectively, there is a genuine redundancy situation (see **7.5** below).

7.2   WHEN DO THE 2006 REGULATIONS APPLY?

7.2.1   Applicability

The 2006 Regulations contain a number of exclusions and limitations. The most important ones are as follows:

(a)   There must be a transfer from one person to another; consequently, there must be a change in the employer, not merely in the ownership. The 2006 Regulations do not, therefore, apply to share sale transfers or where a purchaser buys a majority shareholding in a company, thereby gaining control. This is because there is no change in the identity of the employer. (See *Brookes and Others v Borough Care Services and CLS Care Services Ltd* [1998] IRLR 636, EAT, for confirmation of this principle.) A transfer which is caught by the Regulations can occur alongside or after a share sale (see, for example, *Millam v The Print Factory (London) 1991 Ltd* [2007] IRLR 526).

The ECJ in *Allen and Others v Amalgamated Construction* (Case C-234/98) [2000] IRLR 119 ruled that the 1981 Regulations were capable of applying to transfers between two companies belonging to the same group, or where one subsidiary subcontracts work to another, provided the transfer involves the transfer of an 'economic entity' (see **7.2.2**). By way of guidance, the Regulations have been found to apply to mergers, sale of part of a going concern, changes of franchisee, sale of a sole trader's business or partnership. The Regulations do not apply to transfers by share takeover, or to transfers of assets only. For example, on insolvency the receiver may break up the business and sell off its assets to various buyers, the plant to one buyer and the premises to another.

Only a transfer of an undertaking or a service provision change (see **7.2.2**) will be covered by the 2006 Regulations.

(b)   The EAT, in *Holis Metal Industries v GMB* [2008] IRLR 187, confirmed that the Regulations can apply where the ownership of a company is transferred to a company operating outside the EU.

(c)   There are special provisions regarding insolvency (regs 8 and 9) which are beyond the scope of this book, but where there are bankruptcy or insolvency proceedings (but not administration proceedings – see *OTG Ltd v Barke and Others* (UKEAT/0320/09)), contracts of employment will not be transferred automatically.

(d)   Regulation 4 (automatic transfer of contract of employment together with all rights and liabilities (see **7.3.1** and **7.4**)) does not apply to rights under or in connection with an occupational pension scheme (reg 10). For this purpose, any provisions of an occupational scheme which do not relate to benefits for old age, invalidity or survivors are treated as not being part of the pension scheme, with the result that these benefits will be transferred. Some pension protection is now afforded to employees transferred by virtue of the Pensions Act 2004 (see **7.4.1.3**).

(e)   Regulation 4 (above) also does not transfer any liability of any person to be prosecuted for, convicted of and sentenced for any criminal offence. So, for example, if the transferor is liable to be prosecuted for breach of the HSWA 1974, that liability cannot pass to the transferee on the transfer of a business (reg 4(6)).

(f)   Regulation 7 (dismissals connected to the transfer are automatically unfair unless economic, etc reason) applies only to employees who satisfy the usual qualifying conditions for unfair dismissal protection (see **Chapter 3**); for example, two years' continuous employment (see **7.5**).

7.2.2   A relevant transfer – reg 3

The 2006 Regulations apply only to what are known as 'relevant transfers', which may occur in a wide range of situations. There are two broad categories of relevant transfers: business transfers (reg 3(1)(a)); and service provision changes (reg 3(1)(b)). Some transfers will comprise both a business transfer and a service provision change. The two definitions are not mutually exclusive – as long as one definition is satisfied, it does not matter if the other one is not.

We shall look at both types of relevant transfer in more detail below.

Regulation 3 also endeavours to clear up some areas where there had previously been uncertainty. It makes clear that the 2006 Regulations:

(a)   apply to public and private undertakings engaged in economic activities, whether or not they are operating for gain;

(b)   can apply to a transfer or service provision change howsoever effected, notwithstanding:

   (i)   that the transfer of an undertaking, business or part of an undertaking or business situated in the UK pre-transfer is governed or effected by the law of a country or territory outside the United Kingdom, or that the service provision change is governed or effected by the law of a country or territory outside Great Britain;

   (ii)   that the employment of persons employed in the undertaking, business or part transferred, or, in the case of a service provision change, persons employed in the organised grouping of employees, is governed by any such law.

As far as a business transfer is concerned (see **7.2.2.1** below), the 2006 Regulations apply so long as the undertaking itself (comprising, amongst other things, premises, assets, fixtures and fittings, and goodwill as well as employees) is situated in the UK; and so far as a service provision change is concerned, provided there is an organised grouping of employees situated in the UK immediately before the service provision change (therefore if an employee is part of team but works abroad, that should not prevent the Regulations from applying; but if the whole team worked abroad, that would fall outside the definition);

(c)   apply to a transfer of an undertaking, business or part of an undertaking or business (which may also be a service provision change) where persons employed in the undertaking, business or part transferred ordinarily work outside the UK, provided, of course, that the undertaking itself is situated in the UK immediately before the transfer;

(d)   do not apply to an administrative reorganisation of public administrative authorities or the transfer of administrative functions between public administrative authorities (Note: many such transfers are in fact covered by similar protection under other statutes, eg the Local Government Act 2003 applies in relation to the reorganisation of service provision within local government. See the Cabinet Office Statement of Practice, 'Staff Transfers in the Public Service', available at: www.civilservice.gov.uk/publications/staff_transfers/publications_and_forms/pdf/stafftransfers.pdf for more details.)

Regulation 3 also provides that:

(e)   a relevant transfer may be effected by a series of two or more transactions;

(f)   a relevant transfer may take place whether or not any property is transferred to the transferee by the transferor.

7.2.2.1   Business transfers

Under reg 3(1)(a), a business transfer is 'a transfer of an undertaking, business or part of an undertaking or business situated immediately before the transfer in the United Kingdom to another person where there is a transfer of an economic entity which retains its identity'. Regulation 3(2) defines 'economic entity' as 'an organised grouping of resources which has the objective of pursuing an economic activity, whether or not that activity is central or ancillary'. The expression 'organised grouping of resources' is derived from *Suzen v Zehnacker Gebaudereinigung GmbH Krankenhausservice* [1997] IRLR 255.

At the heart of this definition is the principle that to qualify as a business transfer, the identity of the employer must change. This is why the Regulations do not apply to transfers by share takeover because, when a company's shares are sold to new shareholders, there is no transfer of a business or undertaking – the same company continues to be the employer.

The key ECJ case outlining the general tests to be applied in determining whether there is a business transfer is *Spijkers v Gebroeders Benedik Abattoir CV* [1986] ECR 1119, ECJ. In *Spijkers*, the transferor owned and ran a slaughterhouse. The business came to an end, whereupon the premises, certain goods and all employees bar Mr Spijkers were transferred to the transferee. It was held that the fact that there was a break in time between the old business ceasing and the new one starting, and the lack of a transfer of goodwill, did not prevent the application of the Acquired Rights Directive. The Court said:

> It appears from the general structure of Directive 77/187 and the wording of Article 1(1) that the Directive aims to ensure the continuity of existing employment relationships in the framework of an economic entity irrespective of a change of owner. It follows that the decisive criterion for establishing the existence of a transfer within the meaning of the Directive is whether the entity in question retains its identity.

> Consequently, it cannot be said that there is a transfer of an enterprise business or part of a business on the sole ground that its assets have been sold. On the contrary, in a case like the present, it is necessary to determine whether what has been sold is an economic entity which is still in existence, and this will be apparent from the fact that its operation is actually being continued or has been taken over by the new employer, with the same economic or similar activities.

> To decide whether these conditions are fulfilled it is necessary to take account of all the factual circumstances of the transaction in question, including the type of undertaking or business in question, the transfer or otherwise of tangible assets such as buildings and stocks, the value of intangible assets at the date of transfer, whether the majority of the staff [in terms of numbers or skills] are being taken over by the new employer, the transfer or otherwise of the circle of customers and the degree of similarity between activities before and after the transfer and the duration of any interruption in those activities. It should be made clear, however, that each of these factors is only a part of the overall assessment which is required and therefore they cannot be examined independently of each other.

So, from *Spijkers* and later ECJ decisions, we may state that the decisive criterion for establishing the existence of a transfer within the meaning of the Directive is whether the entity in question retains its identity after the transfer. The key question is whether there is a transfer of an economic entity that retains its identity.

In *Holis Metal Industries Ltd v GMB* (see **7.2.1**), the EAT held that the 2006 Regulations might apply to a transfer from the UK to a non-UK country; the test is the same – is there an economic entity and has it transferred?

Is there an economic entity?

Regulation 3(2) defines 'economic entity' as 'an organised grouping of resources which has the objective of pursuing an economic activity, whether or not that activity is central or ancillary'. The reference to 'economic' appears to suggest that the 'undertaking' being transferred does need to have some sort of cost centre.

The BIS Guide says that:

> the economic entity test ... means the Regulations apply where there is an identifiable set of resources (which includes employees) ... and that set of resources retains its identity after the transfer.

The definition applies to the transfer not just of an undertaking but also of part of an undertaking. An illustration is *Fairhurst Ward Abbotts Limited v Botes Building Limited* [2004] IRLR 304, where an operation was split into two geographical units when it was re-tendered, and it was held that there were transfers to each of the two successful new contractors.

Even though it pre-dates the 2006 Regulations, the domestic authority that gives the best general guidance on whether there has been a business transfer is *Cheesman v R Brewer Contracts* [2001] IRLR 144 (approved by the Court of Appeal in *Balfour Beatty Power Networks Ltd v Wilcox* [2007] IRLR 63).

In *Cheesman*, when looking at the question whether there was an undertaking, the EAT said that:

(a)   there needs to be found an economic entity, which is stable and discrete and whose activity is not limited to performing one specific works contract, an organised grouping of wage earners and assets enabling the exercise of an economic activity;

(b)   the entity must be sufficiently structured and autonomous but will not necessarily have significant assets;

(c)   in certain sectors the entity can essentially be based on manpower;

(d)   the identity of the entity emerges from factors such as its workforce, management staff, the way work is organised and operating methods.

In *Fairhurst Ward Abbotts Ltd* (above), the Court of Appeal confirmed that there is no requirement that the part of an undertaking transferred is itself a separate economic entity in the hands of the transferor; it is enough if part of a larger stable economic entity is identified for the first time as a separate economic entity on the occasion of the transfer separating a part from the whole.

This is therefore essentially a factual exercise. Once it has been determined that an entity exists, it is then necessary to ask 'Has that entity transferred?'

Has that entity transferred?

The *Spijkers* factors (see above) are particularly pertinent here. The decisive criterion established by *Spijkers* is whether 'the entity in question retains its identity'. This may be ascertained by looking at whether its operations are continued or resumed after the transfer. *Spijkers* laid down seven factors that tribunals should consider:

(a)   the type of undertaking or business;

(b)   the transfer or otherwise of tangible assets such as building, equipment and stocks;

(c)   the value of intangible assets at the date of transfer (eg goodwill);

(d)   whether the majority of the staff (in terms of numbers or skills) are being taken over by the new employer;

(e)   the transfer or otherwise of the circle of customers;

(f)   the degree of similarity between activities before and after the transfer;

(g)   the duration of any interruption in those activities.

The ECJ in *Spijkers* emphasised that all factors must be taken into account and that 'they cannot be examined independently of each other'.

The EAT confirmed in *Cheesman* (above) that where an economic entity can function without assets, the lack of assets transferred does not preclude a transfer; and where no staff are transferred, the reasons why may be relevant. (In *ECM (Vehicle Delivery Service) Ltd v Cox and Others* [1999] IRLR 559, the Court of Appeal held that the tribunal was entitled to have regard to the reasons why the employees were not taken on by the transferee – namely because it wished to avoid the (old Regulations) applying.) The EAT overturned the decision of the tribunal that there was no transfer where the workforce of the transferor was not taken on. A tribunal should ask itself which, if any, of these factors are present. If the answer is all of (or in some cases several of) the above factors, it is generally going to be safe to assume that there has been a transfer of a stable economic entity.

The BIS Guidance suggests that 'resources' in reg 3(2) includes not only tangible and intangible assets but also employees. It is unclear how the reg 3(2) definition will work where only part of a large business is transferred, as it may be difficult to ascertain (particularly if resources are shared by different parts of the business) whether resources transferred were part of an 'organised grouping' capable of satisfying the reg 3 requirement. The Guidance states that in this situation the resources in question do not need to be used exclusively by the part of the business being transferred for the 2006 Regulations to apply.

For useful case law on the implications of the transferee not taking on former employees, see *RCO Support Services Ltd and Another v Unison and Others* [2002] ICR 751 and *Astle and Others v Cheshire County Council and Another* [2005] IRLR 12.

In *Camden Primary Care Trust and University College London v Skittrall and Others* (UKEAT/0078/05) (a contracting out case), UCL's degree level course in podiatry was taken over by the University of East London (UEL). The parties agreed that the Transfer Regulations applied. Six staff objected to the transfer and a tribunal was asked to make a preliminary determination as to whether there had been a relevant transfer. The tribunal said there had not, primarily because the economic entity had not retained its identity after the transfer as the course offered by UEL was a new, distinct course. The EAT said the tribunal had defined the economic entity too narrowly. If the economic entity was the UCL degree course in podiatry, there could never be a transfer unless UCL had successfully re-tendered for the contract tendered by Camden PCT. The differences that the tribunal found between the two courses were changes to the mode of delivery and location rather than changes to the actual *activity*. The EAT said that the course had retained its identity.

In *Jouini v Princess Personal Service GmbH (PPS)* [2007] IRLR 1005 a group of workers comprising administrative staff and temporary staff who were transferred to a temporary work agency were held to fall within the scope of the Directive. Dr John McMullen, Professor of Labour Law at Leeds University, has described the case as 'an excellent example of how the jurisprudence of the ECJ is built up in an incremental way from which the Court applies accrued principles to new situations'.

In *Klarenberg v Ferrotron Technologies GmbH* [2009] IRLR 301, the ECJ held that where a business was integrated into the transferee business to the extent that employees were integrated into different units, undertaking duties relating to the existing business, there was still a relevant transfer. There was no need for a transferee to retain the same organisational structure, as long as some functional link was maintained so that the transferee continued the same or a similar economic activity. A change in organisational structure did not prevent the Directive applying.

In *Wood v London Colney Parish Council* (UKEAT/0528/09), the EAT held that a temporary cessation in running a bar (caused by the loss of the premises licence) meant that the economic entity was suspended, but there was still a relevant transfer when the new owner later obtained his own licence.

7.2.2.2 Service provision changes

Background

As noted earlier, the most typical situation where the 2006 Regulations apply is the sale of a business as a going concern. Regulation 3(1)(b) was introduced in order to reduce uncertainty about whether changes in service provision contracting would be captured by the Regulations or not.

Since the early 1980s, one of the developing trends within the public and private sector has been to externalise service functions, such as cleaning, catering, maintenance and IT systems, support and development. In this way, a particular organisation can concentrate its efforts on the core business, leaving ancillary services to those better equipped and qualified to provide them. Further, it allows businesses to deal more effectively with fluctuating demand for support services. Such externalisation has often involved contracting out, a process where the ancillary function which the organisation no longer wishes to manage is awarded, by contract, to another organisation. Contracting out is one of the most common 'atypical' transfer situations.

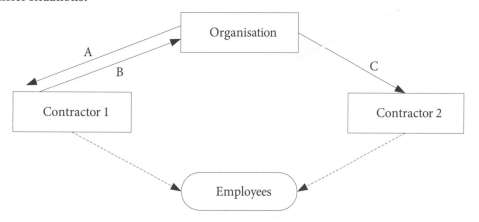

'First generation' contracting out occurs where the organisation awards a contract for some ancillary function to contractor 1 (arrow A). 'Second (third, fourth, etc) generation' contracting out occurs where an organisation ends a contract with one contractor (arrow B), and awards it to another (arrow C). Here, there is no contract between contractor 1 and contractor 2. The 1981 Regulations were, eventually, held to be capable of applying to all these scenarios.

When determining whether a business had retained its identity before and after the transfer, the courts focused on the nature of the activity rather than on the nature of the business. For example, on the contracting out of a canteen, the courts focused on whether a canteen existed after the transfer, rather than on whether the canteen (ie substantially the same business as before) existed after the transfer. In this way, it was not easy to see circumstances in which contracting out would fall outside the scope of the Acquired Rights Directive, and hence the

Regulations, because where an organisation contracts out services, by definition, those activities will be continued or resumed by the (new) contractor.

In *Suzen v Zehnacker Gebaudereinigung GmbH Krankenhausservice* [1997] IRLR 255, the ECJ held that the Directive did not apply to the dismissal of a cleaner. Mrs Suzen was employed by Zehnacker as a cleaner at secondary church-run school, whose premises Zehnacker had contracted to clean. Mrs Suzen was dismissed along with seven other cleaners at the school when Zehnacker lost the contract. She claimed that the dismissal was automatically unfair, relying upon the Acquired Rights Directive.

The ECJ determined that the Directive did not apply to a change of contractor if there was no accompanying transfer from one undertaking to another of significant tangible or intangible assets, or taking over by the new employer of a major part of the workforce, in terms of their numbers and/or skills, assigned by the transferor to the performance of the contract:

> The decisive criterion for establishing the existence of a transfer within the meaning of the Directive is whether the entity in question retains its identity, as indicated inter alia by the fact that its operation is actually continued or resumed ...

> For the Directive to be applicable, however, the transfer must relate to a stable economic entity whose activity is not limited to performing one specific works contract. The term entity thus refers to an organised grouping of persons and assets facilitating the exercise of an economic activity which pursues a specified objective ... the fact that the service provided by the old and new awardees of a contract is similar does not therefore support the conclusion that an economic entity has been transferred. An entity cannot be reduced to the activity entrusted to it ... the mere loss of a service contract to a competitor cannot therefore by itself indicate the existence of a transfer within the meaning of the Directive.

The ECJ felt able to come to this conclusion on the same authority as it had done in *Spijkers* (see **7.2.2.1**), namely, whether the entity in question retains its identity. This is because the factors to be taken into account in determining whether the entity in question retains its identity are varied and may be applied by the courts at their discretion. In *Suzen*, the decisive criterion applied was whether there was an accompanying transfer from one undertaking to another of significant tangible or intangible assets or taking over by the new employer of a major part of the workforce (in terms of numbers or skills), ie *Suzen* sets a minimum precondition in these situations.

The 2006 Regulations aim to clear up most, if not all, of the previous uncertainties by including an express provision that the 2006 Regulations will apply to a 'service provision change'.

Service provision changes

Regulation 3(1)(b) states that a service provision change may exist in any one of three possible situations, provided that certain specified conditions are satisfied. The three situations are:

(a) *activities cease to be carried out by a person ('a client') on his own behalf and are carried out instead by another person on the client's behalf ('a contractor')* – contracting out (ie client to contractor) (reg 3(1)(b)(i));

(b) *activities cease to be carried out by a contractor on a client's behalf (whether or not those activities had previously been carried out by the client on his own behalf) and are carried out instead by another person ('a subsequent contractor') on the client's behalf* – second generation contracting (ie contractor to contractor) (reg 3(1)(b)(ii)); or

(c) *activities cease to be carried out by a contractor or a subsequent contractor on a client's behalf (whether or not those activities had previously been carried out by the client on his own behalf) and are carried out instead by the client on his own behalf* – contracting back in-house (ie contractor to client) (reg 3(1)(b)(iii)).

The preconditions which must be satisfied (reg 3(3)) are that:

(a)   immediately before the service provision change:

   (i)   there is an organised grouping of employees situated in Great Britain which has as its principal purpose the carrying out of the activities concerned on behalf of the client,

   (ii)   the client intends that the activities will, following the service provision change, be carried out by the transferee other than in connection with a single specific event or task of short-term duration; and

(b)   the activities concerned do not consist wholly or mainly of the supply of goods for the client's use. If there is a mixture, the service element will need to be predominant. (See *Pannu and Others v Geo W King (in liquidation) and Others* (UKEAT/0021/11) for a case in which the EAT upheld a decision that this exclusion applied.)

The wording of reg 3(3)(a) does not therefore cover transactions where there is no identifiable group of employees dedicated to meeting one client's needs.

Analysis

A service provision change will occur when a client who engages a contractor to do work on its behalf is either:

(a)   reassigning such a contract; or

(b)   bringing the work 'in-house'.

Note that reg 2 provides that 'contractor' includes sub-contractors.

It will *not* be a service provision change if:

(a)   the contract is wholly or mainly for the supply of goods for the client's use (eg client engages a contractor to supply sandwiches and drinks to its canteen every day to sell on to staff) (see *Pannu* (above)); or

(b)   the activities are carried out in connection with a single specific event or a task of short-term duration. This suggests that where something is a 'one-off' job it will not be covered by the 2006 Regulations. There is a lack of clarity in the drafting of this exception. This wording may be read in one of two ways: either the exclusion applies to an activity (an 'event' or 'task') that is a one-off job *and* is of short duration, or it applies where the service activity in question is either a single specific event *or* a task of short-term duration.

The BIS Guidance supports the former interpretation, giving as an example two hypothetical contracts covering security for the Olympic Games. The first contract concerns the provision of security advice to the event organisers and covers a period of several years running up to the event. The second contract concerns hiring staff to protect athletes during the Games themselves. Both contracts are one-off in the sense that they relate to a specific event. The first contract runs for a significantly longer period than the second and would be covered by the Regulations, but the second would not. Ultimately, this will be a question for a domestic court to decide.

This issue was considered by the EAT in *Liddell's Coaches v Cook* (UKEATS/0025/12), with the EAT disagreeing with the BIS Guidance: the phrase, it said, must be considered disjunctively. A single specific event did not need to be of short-term duration.

Note: These are exceptions to reg 3(1)(b). Regulation 3(1)(a) may still apply in such situations, facts permitting.

Under reg 3(3)(a)(i), for there to be a service provision change, there does not have to be an 'economic entity' before the alleged transfer, so long as there is an organised grouping of employees and the other tests above are met. The term 'organised grouping of employees' is probably best summarised by the word 'team' (but note it is also stated that a single-employee can satisfy the test – reg 2(1)). The EAT held in *Argyll Coastal Services Ltd v Mr I Stirling and Others*

(UKEATS/0012/11) that the phrase 'organised grouping of employees' 'connotes a number of employees ... organised for the purpose of carrying out activites ... who work as a team'. Further, it does not matter whether the new contractor takes on any of the old contractor's employees; the transferee cannot now seek to argue that the 2006 Regulations do not apply because he did not take on any employees. So long as the same activities are carried out for the client before and after the transfer, there is a transfer.

See also *Eddie Stobart Ltd v Moreman* [2012] IRLR 356, where the EAT gave helpful guidance on the concept of an 'organised grouping of employees':

> The paradigm of an 'organised grouping' is indeed the case where employees are organised as 'the [Client A] team', though no doubt the definition could in principle be satisfied in cases where the identification is less specific .

Where the grouping comes about by virtue of 'coincidences of working patterns', that is unlikely to be enough – there needs to be an element of planning and deliberate organisation.

The BIS Guidance offers the following anlaysis:

> This is intended to confine the Regulations' coverage to cases where the old service provider (ie the transferor) has in place a team of employees to carry out the service activities, and that team is essentially dedicated to carrying out the activities that are to transfer (though they do not need to work exclusively on those activities). It would therefore exclude cases where there was no identifiable grouping of employees. This is because it would be unclear which employees should transfer in the event of a change of contractor, if there was no such grouping. So, if a contractor was engaged by a client to provide, say, a courier service, but the collections and deliveries were carried out each day by various different couriers on an ad hoc basis, rather than by an identifiable team of employees, there would be no 'service provision change' and the Regulations would not apply.

In one of the first cases to consider the new law, the tribunal held in *Hunt v Storm Communications Ltd and Others* (ET/2702546/06) that there was a service provision change when the client terminated its contract with Storm and awarded a new contract to a different agency. The claimant was employed by Storm as an account manager who spent about 70% of her time working on one client's account. The tribunal held that there was a 'service provision change'; the claimant was an 'organised grouping of employees' whose principal purpose was to provide services to the client, and the same activity was carried on when the new agency took over the account previously managed by Storm.

In *Kimberley Group Housing Ltd v Hambley* [2008] IRLR 682, the EAT gave some guidance on applying the provisions. First, the tribunal should identify the activities which the current supplier has ceased to carry out. On the facts, the tribunal found that the activities were of providing suitable accommodation and related supported services to asylum seekers in the towns concerned. The EAT did not interfere with this decision but it did comment that 'care may need to be taken ... in deciding what constitutes the relevant activities'. Secondly, it should ask whether an organised grouping of employees had as its *principal* purpose the carrying out of those particular activities. The tribunal found that there was and the EAT agreed. The EAT stated that the word 'principal' qualifies the purpose and that '[a] distinction is to be drawn between a principal purpose and one which is merely ancillary'. Lastly, the tribunal should ascertain whether the new contractor(s) are engaged in the same activities as the old contractor. In this case they were, given the finding that the relevant activities were of providing suitable accommodation and related supported services to asylum seekers in the towns concerned.

In *Clearsprings Management Ltd v Ankers and others* (UKEAT/0054/08), the EAT confirmed that while under the 2006 Regulations one transferor could transfer the provision of a service to more than one transferee, there may be some circumstances in which, if the relevant activities are sufficiently split up and fragmented between a number of new contractors of the service, there is no service provision change. On the facts, the EAT agreed with the tribunal that, because the allocation of asylum seekers showed no obvious pattern of re-allocation to the three incoming contractors, the activity carried on by Clearsprings, the outgoing contractor, was so fragmented that no relevant transfer took place within the meaning of reg 3 of the 2006 Regulations.

In *Metropolitan Resources Ltd v Churchill Dulwich Ltd* [2009] IRLR 700, the EAT held that the question for tribunals is simply whether, on the facts, one of the three situations set out in reg 3(1)(b) exists and whether the conditions set out in reg 3(3) are satisfied, and that a commonsense and pragmatic approach is required. The tribunal should ask itself whether the activities carried on by the alleged transferee are fundamentally or essentially the same as those carried out by the alleged transferor. The answer to that question will be one of fact and degree, to be assessed by the tribunal on the evidence in the individual case before it. The pre-2006 case law is irrelevant for this purpose.

For an example of a case where it was held that a change of contractor did not fall within the 'service provision' definition because of a difference in activity before and after the change of contractor, see *OCS Group UK Ltd v Jones* (UKEAT/0038/09). The EAT refused to overturn the tribunal's decision that a canteen service which provided hot meals prepared by chefs was very different from a counter selling pre-prepared sandwiches and that therefore the 2006 Regulations did not apply.

In *Enterprise Management Services Ltd v Connect-Up Ltd and Others* (UKEAT/0462/10), the EAT set out a statement of the law:

> (2) The expression 'activities' is not defined in the Regulations. Thus the first task for the Employment Tribunal is to identify the relevant activities carried out by the original contractor: see *Kimberley*, para 28; *Metropolitan*, paras 29–30. That was the issue on appeal in *OCS*, where the Appellant's challenge to the activities identified by the Employment Tribunal failed.
>
> (3) The next (critical) question for present purposes will be whether the activities carried on by the subsequent contractor after the relevant date ... are fundamentally or essentially the same as those carried on by the original contractor. Minor differences may properly be disregarded. This is essentially a question of fact and degree for the Employment Tribunal (*Metropolitan*, para 30).
>
> (4) Cases may arise (eg [*Clearsprings*]) where the division of services after the relevant date, known as fragmentation, amongst a number of different contractors means that the case falls outside the service provision change regime, as explained in *Kimberley* (para 35).
>
> (5) Even where the activities remain essentially the same before and after the putative transfer date as performed by the original and subsequent contractors, [a service provision charge] will only take place if the following conditions are satisfied:
>
>> (i) there is an organised grouping of employees in Great Britain which has as its principal purpose the carrying out of the activities concerned on behalf of the client;
>>
>> (ii) the client intends that the transferee post-service provision change will not carry out the activities in connection with a single event of short-term duration;
>>
>> (iii) the activities are not wholly or mainly the supply of goods rather than services for the client's use. ...
>
> (6) Finally, by reg 4(1) the Employment Tribunal must decide whether each Claimant was assigned to the organised grouping of employees.

In *Nottinghamshire Healthcare NHS Trust v Hamshaw and Others* (UKEAT/0037/11), the EAT held that there was no TUPE transfer in circumstances where a Healthcare NHS Trust which ran a care home shut the home and re-housed the residents into homes of their own. The residents' care was transferred to two new independent providers.

According to the EAT, there was neither a transfer of an economic entity retaining its identity under reg 3(1)(a) nor a service provision change under reg 3(1)(b). Under the new arrangements, former residents were to live in their own flats. The care provided was different. The economic entity had lost its identity. Nor was there a service provider change because the activity carried on by the new provider was not 'fundamentally or essentially' the same as the service provided before the change.

By analogy with *ECM v Cox* (above at **7.2.2.1**) it is possible that tribunals will be sceptical about deliberate fragmentation, which they may regard as a TUPE avoidance measure, but no such cases have emerged yet.

The statement of law set out in *Enterprise Management Services Ltd* (above) was endorsed in *Johnson Controls Ltd v Campbell and Another* (UKEAT/0042/12). The EAT added that the identification of 'activity' is critical in many cases and that tribunals must be careful to ensure that they do not take too narrow a view of that term. The EAT said that:

> if for instance the activity performed by a given employee is after a service provision change to be performed by two or three employees in the transferee or, in a 3(1)(b)(iii) situation, by the client itself, then it may well be that the approach of the Tribunal should recognise that the same activity may well be carried on, though it is performed now by three people rather than by the one person who earlier performed it.

In *McCarrick v Hunter* [2012] EWCA Civ 1399, the Court of Appeal upheld the EAT's decision that there cannot be a service provision change in circumstances in which the client changes as well as the service provider.

7.2.2.3 Cross-border transfers of undertakings

There has long been uncertainty about whether the Directive/Regulations apply in relation to the transfer of a UK-based business even if the purchaser is outside the European Union. This was looked at by the EC Commission, which reported on 18 June 2007. It did not reach a definitive conclusion! In *Holis Metal Industries Ltd v GMB & Newell Ltd* [2008] IRLR 187, the EAT said the UK Regulations could apply transnationally.

7.2.2.4 Time of transfer

Practically speaking, a transfer of an undertaking may extend over a period of time rather than being an event staged to take place for the purposes of the Acquired Rights Directive and the 2006 Regulations at any one particular moment in time. However, the legal requirement for certainty, so as to be able to identify, at the least, the date when a transfer took place, may conflict with practical realities. Sometimes the point of transfer is expressly pinpointed in sale documentation or otherwise agreed by the parties, but if it is not, tribunals have to identify as best they can when the actual transfer took place. The date of transfer may be important.

The ECJ considered the 'time' of transfer in *Celtec v Astley* (Case C-478/03) [2005] IRLR 647, where it had to decide whether a relevant transfer could be a gradual process occurring over a period of several years. The ECJ ruled that the use of the word 'date' (singular) in the Acquired Rights Directive, combined with the need for legal certainty, meant that the claimants in that case had to be able to point to a specific date on which they said the transfer occurred. A transfer *cannot* occur over a period of time (see paras 32–36). The ECJ went on to find:

> 29. ... the reference to 'date of a transfer' in [the Acquired Rights Directive] is designed to identify the workers who may rely on the protection established by that provision. That protection therefore covers workers assigned to the unit affected by the transfer whose contract of employment or employment relationship is in force on the 'date of a transfer' and not those who have ceased to be employed by the transferor on that date (see Case 19/83 *Wendelboe and Others* [1985] ECR 457, paragraphs 13 and 15) or those who were engaged by the transferee after that date (see *Ny Mølle Kro*, cited above, paragraphs 24 to 26).

> 30. Both the choice of the word 'date' and reasons of legal certainty indicate that, in the mind of the Community legislature, the workers entitled to benefit from the protection established by [the] Directive must be identified at a particular point in the transfer process and not in relation to the length of time over which that process extends.

> 36. In those circumstances, the term 'date of a transfer' in [the Directive] must be understood as referring to the date on which responsibility as employer for carrying on the business of the unit in question moves from the transferor to the transferee.

In support of that interpretation, the Court observed, first, that the Acquired Rights Directive gives the Member States the option of providing that, after the date of transfer, the transferor is to be liable, alongside the transferee, for the obligations arising from a contract of employment or employment relationship. Such a rule implies that in any event those obligations are transferred to the transferee on the date of the transfer (*Rotsart de Hertaing v Benoidt SA and IGC Housing Service SA* (Case C-305/94) [1997] IRLR 127, para 23).

Lastly, the Court considered that to allow the transferor or transferee the possibility of choosing the date from which the contract of employment or employment relationship is transferred would amount to allowing employers to derogate, at least temporarily, from the provisions of the Directive, whereas those provisions are mandatory, and it is thus not possible to derogate from them in a manner unfavourable to employees (*Rotsart de Hertaing*, paras 17 and 25).

Having established that the Directive refers to a transfer taking place on a particular date, the ECJ went on to consider the issue of how that date was to be identified. The ECJ referred to Article 1(1) of the Acquired Rights Directive, which refers to the change in the legal or natural person responsible for carrying on the business and who continues or resumes the operation. The ECJ concluded that what was significant was to identify 'the date on which responsibility as employer for carrying on the business of the unit in question moves from the transferor to the transferee'.

Following the ECJ's ruling that a relevant transfer cannot take place over a period of time but only on a specific date, the House of Lords gave its opinion on the actual facts in *Celtec*. The House of Lords had to decide whether the date of the transfer was the date the employees were originally seconded. Their Lordships found that there was a deemed transfer of the claimants' contracts to the Training and Enterprise Council at the date of the original secondment, even though for three years the claimants thought they were civil service employees. This was when responsibility for carrying on the business had passed to the transferee.

In all cases, in determining when a relevant transfer takes place it will be essential to consider when responsibility for carrying on the business had transferred. In practice, if the transfer is a sale of a business and there is a gap between exchange of contracts and completion, it will be the date of completion which is the date of transfer for the purposes of reg 4.

7.3 EFFECT OF A RELEVANT TRANSFER

Once it has been established that a relevant transfer has occurred, it is necessary to consider what effect that has on the employment relationship.

7.3.1 Automatic transfer of contracts of employment

Regulation 4(1) of the 2006 Regulations provides:

> Except where objection is made under paragraph (7), a relevant transfer shall not operate so as to terminate the contract of employment of any person employed by the transferor and assigned to the organised grouping of resources or employees that is subject to the relevant transfer, which would otherwise be terminated by the transfer, but any such contract shall have effect after the transfer as if originally made between the person so employed and the transferee.

In other words, an employee's contract of employment does not end by reason of the transfer; instead the contract will be transferred from the old employer to the new on the existing terms and conditions, and with the employee's existing continuity of service (see *Jackson v Computershare Investment Services plc* [2008] IRLR 70). (Employees do, however, have the right to object to the transfer of their contracts (see **7.3.2.3**).) Note that the reference to employees is likely to include workers too (see reg 2(1)).

In *G4S Justice Services (UK) Ltd v Anstey* [2006] IRLR 588, the EAT held that employees who had been dismissed for gross misconduct but who had an internal appeal pending at the date of a relevant transfer had their employment preserved only for the purpose of the appeal. If the appeal failed, the dismissal stood and the employees would not have been employed immediately before the transfer. If the appeal succeeded and the dismissal was set aside then it 'vanished', and the employees would be treated as if they were employed immediately before the transfer, so they continued in employment with the transferee.

Regulation 4(2) states that on the completion of a relevant transfer:

(a)   all the transferor's rights, powers, duties and liabilities under or in connection with any such contract shall be transferred by virtue of this regulation to the transferee; and

(b)   any act or omission before the transfer is completed, of or in relation to the transferor in respect of that contract or a person assigned to that organised grouping of resources or employees, shall be deemed to have been an act or omission of or in relation to the transferee.

The employees, in other words, have the same rights against the transferee as they had against the transferor and their continuity of employment is not affected by the transfer.

Regulation 8 sets out the position in respect of insolvent businesses. The detail is beyond the scope of this book.

7.3.2   Who is covered by reg 4(1)?

Regulation 4(3) states that any reference:

to a person employed by the transferor and assigned to the organised grouping of … employees that is subject to a relevant transfer, is a reference to a person so employed immediately before the transfer, or who would have been so employed if he had not been dismissed in the circumstances described in regulation 7(1) …

Regulation 4(3) clearly applies to all employees employed by the transferor immediately before the transfer. In *Secretary of State for Employment v Spence* [1986] IRLR 248, CA, the Court of Appeal said that the phrase 'immediately before' means at the precise moment of transfer.

However, reg 4(3) of the 2006 Regulations also applies to employees who would have been so employed had they not been unfairly dismissed in the circumstances described in reg 7(1) (see **7.5**). This statutory provision encapsulates the House of Lords' judgment in *Secretary of State for Employment v Litster* [1989] IRLR 161. In that case the employees were dismissed one hour before the transfer. The House of Lords made it clear that a transferee may still be liable for any claims arising out of a pre-transfer dismissal, and reg 4(3) preserves that rule. This means that a transferee cannot circumvent the 2006 Regulations by insisting that the transferor dismiss some or all of the workforce prior to completion.

Thus a relevant transfer will:

(a)   transfer the contracts of anyone who is employed by the transferor immediately before the relevant transfer and who is assigned to the relevant group of employees that is the subject of the transfer. Their contracts of employment will transfer to the transferee and they will be employed by the transferee under the terms and conditions of those contracts;

(b)   pass liability for any pre-transfer dismissals falling within the circumstances described in reg 7(1) to the transferee. In other words, the transferee will be liable for any claims arising out of pre-transfer dismissals (actual or constructive (see reg 4(11)), or 'deemed' (see reg 4(9)) – see **7.3.2.1**) if those dismissals were by reason of the transfer, or for a reason connected with the transfer where no economic, technical or organisational (ETO) reason exists, and those dismissals will be automatically unfair (see **7.5**).

Although the dismissal is effective (see **7.6**) and the employee is therefore not employed by the transferee, all rights, duties, and liabilities relating to his previous employment will transfer in addition to the claim of unfair dismissal, including, for example, any wrongful dismissal claim or any claim for discrimination.

7.3.2.1   Meaning of dismissal

Dismissal includes actual and constructive dismissal (see reg 4(11) at **7.3.2.3**). However, the term also includes, for the purpose of the 2006 Regulations, 'deemed' dismissal. This is because reg 4(9) provides that:

> ... where a relevant transfer involves or would involve a substantial change in working conditions to the material detriment of a person whose contract of employment is or would be transferred under paragraph (1) [of reg 4], such an employee may treat the contract of employment as having been terminated, and the employee shall be treated for any purpose as having been dismissed by the employer.

The wording in reg 4(9) is wider than the meaning of constructive dismissal, where the employee must prove that he resigned as a result of a repudiatory breach of contract (see **Chapter 3**). The regulation will apply even when there is no breach of contract.

The BIS Guidance suggests that a major relocation of the workplace which makes it difficult or much more expensive for an employee to travel, or the withdrawal of a right to a tenured post, is likely to fall within this definition.

The EAT considered the meaning of reg 4(9) in *Tapere v South London and Maudsley NHS Trust* (UKEAT/0410/08). The EAT pointed out that there are two components to reg 4(9):

(a)   a 'substantial change in working conditions';

(b)   'to the material detriment of a person whose contract of employment is ... transferred'.

The EAT held that the term 'working conditions' should be interpreted widely following the decision of the ECJ in *Merckx and Neuhuys v Ford Motors Belgium SA* [1996] IRLR 467. In that case, salesmen were transferred to a new dealership at a different workplace without any guarantee as to client base or sales figures, so that there was potential for an adverse impact on commission. These components were regarded by the ECJ as 'working conditions'. The phrase therefore applies, according to the EAT, to contractual terms and conditions as well as physical conditions. On the facts, therefore, a change of workplace was a change to 'working conditions'. The question of whether it is a change of substance is, according to the EAT, a question of fact, and the employment tribunal will need to consider the nature, as well as the degree, of the change in order to decide whether it is substantial. The character of the change is likely to be the most important aspect of determining whether the change is substantial. In *Merckx*, the ECJ regarded the change as substantial because it was a change in remuneration. The EAT gave another example: a change in the method of salary payment. Moving from cash payment to bank, or from weekly to monthly payment would be a change of substance, even if the amount of remuneration was not altered. Therefore a change of workplace, on the facts, is also a change of substance.

On the phrase 'material detriment', the EAT held that 'material' simply means not trivial or fanciful, and that what has to be considered is the impact of the proposed change from the employee's point of view. On the facts of *Tapere* the change of location meant potential disruption to child-care arrangements and a longer journey, or an altered journey involving travelling on the M25, which the appellant did not find attractive. The tribunal should ask whether the employee regarded those factors as detrimental and, if so, whether that was a reasonable position for the employee to adopt. On the facts the claimant was therefore deemed to have been dismissed under reg 4(9).

In *Abellio London Ltd (Formerly Travel London Ltd) v Musse and Others* [2012] IRLR 360 (EAT), the EAT held that a move from north to south of the river in London (six miles) was substantial and that an increase in the working day of one to two hours was a material detriment, and that it was irrelevant that the contract contained a mobility clause. There was therefore a reg 4(9) dismissal, notwithstanding that there was no breach of contract.

Note that an employee who resigns in reliance on reg 4(9) cannot make a claim for notice pay. The employee should give notice and work it out (reg 4(10)).

7.3.2.2   Employees whose contracts would 'otherwise have been terminated by the transfer'

Those employees whose contracts would not be terminated by the transfer do not come within reg 4. This may, for example, apply to an employee who is retained by the transferor and redeployed in some other part of his operation within the terms of the employee's contract or with his consent. Such redeployment should take place before the transfer.

Where part of a business is transferred, employees will not be affected by reg 4 if they did not work in the part transferred. Even employees who perform duties in relation to the part transferred (eg administrative duties) will not be covered unless they are assigned to the part transferred, ie the organised grouping.

The question of whether an employee is assigned to the relevant grouping is a question of fact. The 2006 Regulations do not provide much by way of assistance as to what is meant by 'assigned'. Regulation 2(1) provides that it means 'assigned other than on a temporary basis'. For the time being, therefore, existing domestic and European case law will still be relevant. See, for example, *Securiplan v Bademosi* (UKEAT/1128/02) and *Gale v Northern General Hospital* [1994] IRLR 292. In general the case law confirms that where the employee was assigned is a matter of overall impression for the tribunal. This may often be decided as a mathematical question of how the employee spent most of his time, but sometimes a different approach may be called for.

The BIS Guidance suggests that in determining whether an assignment is temporary, factors such as 'the length of time the employee has been there and whether a date has been set by the transferor for his return or re-assignment to another part of the business or undertaking' should be taken into account.

Regard should also be had to the test laid down in *Botzen v Rotterdamsche Droogdok Maatschappij BV* (Case 186/83) [1986] 2 CMLR 50, ECJ. The ECJ said, in summary, that the test is whether there is a transfer of the part of the undertaking to which the employees 'were assigned and which formed the organisational framework within which their employment relationship took effect'.

Useful guidance on the *Botzen* test was given by the EAT in *Duncan Webb Offset (Maidstone) Ltd v Cooper and Others* [1995] IRLR 633. Factors which should be taken into account include how much time was spent on different parts of the business, how much value has been given to each part, what the contract said about the employee's duties, and how the cost of the employee was shared between the various parts of the business.

Further guidance may be found in the Court of Appeal decision in *CPL Distribution Ltd v Todd* [2003] IRLR 23. In *Argyll Coastal Services Ltd* (see **7.2.2.2** above), the EAT confirmed that involvement in carrying out the activity will not necessarily mean that the employee was assigned to the organised group, eg where the employee was covering for a colleague.

In *Carsway Cleansing Consultants Ltd v Richards & Cooper Cleaning Services* (UKEAT/629/97), the EAT held that an employer could not 'off-load' an unwanted employee by deliberately moving him to a part of the undertaking that the employer knew was about to be transferred. The EAT held that such an act was fraudulent and, accordingly, void. The employee was not 'employed in the part of the undertaking' being transferred.

In *Kimberley Group Housing v Hambley* (above at **7.2.2.2**) the EAT held that there may be a transfer to more than one transferee under the Regulations. On the facts there were two overlapping contracts post-transfer, providing for activities done pre-transfer by one provider. By analogy with *Duncan Webb* above, the EAT found that the transferor's employees transferred to the transferee taking over the majority of the services, in this case Kimberley which took over 79% of the activities performed in one area and 97% in the other area of the country.

7.3.2.3   The employee's right of objection

In the UK, employees can object to the transfer of their employment contract. If they do this, their employment is treated as terminated by operation of law and there is no dismissal.

Regulation 4(7) states:

> Paragraphs (1) and (2) shall not operate to transfer the contract of employment and the rights, powers, duties and liabilities under or in connection with it of an employee who informs the transferor or the transferee that he objects to becoming employed by the transferee.

Under reg 4(8):

> Subject to paragraphs (9) and (11), where an employee so objects, the relevant transfer shall operate so as to terminate his contract of employment with the transferor but he shall not be treated, for any purpose, as having been dismissed by the transferor.

And under reg 4(11):

> Paragraphs (1), (7), (8) and (9) are without prejudice to any right of an employee arising apart from these Regulations to terminate his contract of employment without notice in acceptance of a repudiatory breach of contract by his employer.

The transfer of the contract of employment and rights, powers, duties and liabilities under and in connection with it, will not occur if the employee informs the transferor or the transferee that he objects to becoming employed by the transferee. In that event, the transfer will terminate the employee's contract of employment with the transferor, but he will not be treated for any purpose as having been dismissed by the transferor, ie he will be regarded as having resigned (reg 4(7) and (8)) unless the reason for the objection is that the transfer will involve a significant and detrimental change in working conditions (reg 4(9)), or the employee is alleging constructive dismissal (reg 4(11)) (see **7.3.2.1** above), in which case liability will transfer. Therefore, if an employee exercises this right, he will lose all his rights against both the transferor and the transferee, unless he has been caused to resign by a change in working conditions or a breach of contract by his employer. Interestingly, the Court of Appeal has held that as the effect of the objection was that the contract of employment did not transfer to the transferee, neither did liability for any claims flowing from the constructive dismissal, which therefore remained with the transferor (see *Tapere v South London and Maudsley NHS Trust* (UKEAT/0410/08)). In a case of this type, reg 4(3)/*Litster* does not apply (*University of Oxford v Humphreys* [2000] IRLR 183, CA).

There is nothing to prevent an employee in this situation being re-engaged by the transferee on new terms, although his continuity would be broken.

The right of employees to object to a transfer of their employment on a business transfer was also considered in *Senior Heat Treatment Limited v Bell* [1997] IRLR 614. In this case, the employer decided to move its Heat Treatment Department to a vacant factory and new employer six miles away. The employees were given the following options:

(a)   transfer to the new factory and new employer;

(b)   opt out of the transfer and receive a payment equivalent to statutory redundancy pay, pay in lieu of notice and a further ex gratia sum.

The employees were given a form on which to state their preference. Having ticked the box objecting to the transfer, they received payments in accordance with the severance package. However, they had *already* signed employment contracts with the new employer and then turned up for work for the new employer the following Monday. When they were dismissed 10 months later, they claimed unfair dismissal and/or redundancy payments in the employment tribunal.

When the case reached the EAT, it was found that on the peculiar facts of this case the former employees were entitled to count their employment before the transfer towards their continuity of service, and as a result they had two years' service and could bring claims in the employment tribunal. The reasoning was that the employees had already signed contracts with the new employer before they completed the forms provided by their old employer. As a result, the EAT found they had not objected to the transfer even though they had said they wished to 'opt out' of it.

Opting out was also considered by the EAT in *Capita Health Solutions v BBC and McLean* (UKEAT/0034/07). The BBC transferred its occupational health unit to an outside contractor. Mrs McLean 'objected' and 'resigned' on the day before the transfer, stating that she would work 'a period of secondment' with the contractor while she served out her notice. The employment tribunal said that on the facts, Mrs McLean had not objected and her contract still transferred. The EAT agreed. Regulation 4 states that an objection will stop a transfer occurring and end the contract. There is no provision for working out notice. If Mrs McLean had objected successfully, she could not have continued as the BBC's employee.

It is now clear that neither the general application of the automatic transfer principle nor the existence of the employee's right to object is subject to a precondition that employees have knowledge of both the fact of a transfer and the identity of the transferee (*Secretary of State for Trade and Industry v Cook and Others* [1997] ICR 288, EAT).

Note that according to the High Court, employees may object after a transfer where they do not know the identity of the transferee pre-transfer, so long as they do so promptly (see *New ISG Ltd v Vernon* [2008] IRLR 115). In this case the High Court, interpreting the 2006 Regulations purposively, made it clear that where the identity of the buyer is not known until the sale is completed, the right to object would be meaningless if it could be exercised only pre-sale.

7.4   WHAT THE TRANSFEREE ACQUIRES

The transferee inherits those employees employed by the transferor on their existing terms and conditions, assuming that they do not object (reg 4(2)).

Equally, the transferred employee has no right to insist that he be given the benefit of any superior terms and conditions enjoyed by the transferee's existing staff. In addition, the transferee inherits the legal responsibilities for any employees dismissed by reason of the transfer or for a reason connected with the transfer, where no ETO reason exists (see **7.5.2** below).

7.4.1   Rights transferring – employees employed immediately before the transfer

The transferee inherits all the employees employed immediately before the transfer, together with all the contracts of employment of the transferred employees. The transferee cannot pick and choose which employees to take on. The only exceptions to this are where:

(a)   employees are 'temporarily' assigned to the 'organised grouping' (see **7.3.2.1**);

(b)   the employee has objected (see **7.3.2.2**).

The transferee also inherits all the accrued rights and liabilities connected with the contract of the transferred employee (except for criminal liabilities (reg 4(6)) and some benefits under an occupational pension scheme (see **7.4.1.3**)).

If, for example, the transferor was in arrears with wages at the time of the transfer, the employee can sue the transferee as if the original liability had been the transferee's. The transferor is relieved of his former obligations without any need for the employee's consent.

All liability for tortious claims, for example personal injury claims, will also pass to the transferee (*Bernardone v Pall Mall Services Group and Others* [2000] IRLR 487, CA). Note that where an entitlement is inextricably linked to the identity of the transferor (eg profit-sharing schemes), the employee's post-transfer entitlement, according to the EAT in *MITIE Managed Services Ltd v French* [2002] IRLR 512, is to participate 'in a scheme of substantial equivalence'.

Equally, the transferee may sue an employee for a breach of contract committed against the transferor prior to transfer.

The transferee will also inherit all the statutory rights and liabilities which are connected with the individual contract of employment, for example unfair dismissal, redundancy and discrimination.

Regulations 11 and 12 contain provisions requiring the transferor to notify the transferee in writing of 'liability' information about an employee who is 'assigned to the organised grouping of employees or resources that is the subject of a relevant transfer'. This includes providing details of the identity and age of the employee, the particulars of employment (ERA 1996, s 1), and information relating to disciplinary and grievance procedures involving the employee. If a transferor fails to provide this information in whole or part, the transferee may complain to an employment tribunal, which may award compensation of not less than £500 per employee (see **7.7**).

The transferred employee's period of continuous employment will date from the beginning of his period of employment with the transferor, and the statutory particulars of terms and conditions of employment, which every employer is obliged to issue, must take account of any continuity enjoyed by virtue of the Regulations.

7.4.1.1 Restrictive covenants

In the case of restrictive covenants, these will normally be expressed in terms of protecting customers of the transferor. In essence, following the transfer of an undertaking a restrictive covenant should be read as being enforceable by the transferee, but only in respect of customers of the transferor who fall within the protection. (Great care needs to be taken if restrictive covenants are re-drafted post-transfer. See *Credit Suisse First Boston (Europe) Ltd v Padiachy and Others* [1998] IRLR 504 and *Credit Suisse First Boston (Europe) Ltd v Lister* [1998] IRLR 700.)

7.4.1.2 Collective agreements

Under the 2006 Regulations, any collective agreements made with a union by the transferor are deemed to have been made by the transferee (reg 5). Further, the transferee is deemed to recognise the trade union to the same extent as did the transferor (reg 6). In effect, the transferee steps into the shoes of the transferor. Neither the 2006 Regulations nor the general law prevent the employer from seeking to derecognise the union entirely, or from amending the basis of the recognition. This lack of an effective remedy undermines the protection given to trade unions on a relevant transfer. Note that the ERA 1999 contains detailed statutory procedures for the recognition and de-recognition of trade unions for collective bargaining. The procedures are beyond the scope of this book.

Individually, however, there may be 'hangovers' from previous union recognition. Of course, all terms of the individuals' contracts including those pursuant to the collective agreements will be deemed to have been made between the transferee and the employee. It follows that, notwithstanding derecognition of the union by the transferee, the right to have pay determined by collective bargaining can persist.

This was considered in *Whent and Others v T Cartledge Ltd* [1997] IRLR 153. This case concerned employees of a local authority who worked within the street lighting department. Their contracts of employment stated that their pay under the main terms and conditions would be in accordance with the NJC (National Joint Council for Local Authorities' Administrative, Professional, Technical and Clerical Services) agreement. The NJC agreement is essentially a collective agreement negotiated between national representatives of local authorities and recognised trade unions.

The local authority then contracted out its street lighting functions to a private sector contractor (ie the new employer), expressly terminating the collective bargaining machinery and any recognition rights. The contractor reassured the employees that their existing terms and conditions remained in force.

Some months later, the annual pay review came along. The employees argued that they were entitled to a pay increase as agreed under the NJC collective bargaining process. They claimed that it did not matter that they were no longer local authority employees. The contractor argued that it was nonsense for it to be bound by the results of pay negotiations in which it had played no role.

The EAT held that the relevant part of the NJC agreement had been incorporated into the individual contracts. The incorporated terms included not only the rate of pay and general terms which existed at the time of the transfer, but also the terms providing for the collective bargaining mechanism itself. It would therefore be the NJC and not the contractor which would set the level of pay. The collective bargaining mechanism itself transferred with the transfer. The fact that the employer had derecognised the union was irrelevant.

In *Alemo-Herron and Others v Parkwood Leisure Ltd* [2010] EWCA Civ 24, the Court of Appeal considered the impact of the ECJ's decision in *Werhof v Freeway Traffic Systems GmbH & Co KG* [2006] IRLR 400 on the decision in *Whent* and held that *Whent* was effectively overruled by the ECJ's judgment that the collective agreement did not transfer to the transferee. The case has been appealed to the Supreme Court.

7.4.1.3 Pensions

Regulation 10 provides that regs 4 and 5 do not apply to occupational pension schemes (although a contractual provision that an employer would pay a certain percentage of salary into a personal pension fund would transfer). However, separate regulations have been issued under the Pensions Act 2004, which provide that when a relevant transfer occurs and employees had the benefit of an occupational pension scheme (with employer contributions) before transfer, the transferee *must* provide membership of an equivalent scheme. The detail is beyond the scope of the book; see Transfer of Employment (Pension Protection) Regulations 2005 (SI 2005/649) and www.dwp.gov.uk.

7.4.1.4 'Liability for failure to consult'

Regulation 15(9) makes the transferor and the transferee jointly and severally liable in respect of compensation payable as a result of a failure to consult (see **7.7**).

7.4.2 Rights and liabilities which are not assigned under the 2006 Regulations

The 2006 Regulations do not have the effect of assigning:

(a)   criminal liabilities (reg 4(6)); or

(b)   liability (in a health and safety context) under a continuation order.

7.5 DISMISSAL OF AN EMPLOYEE BECAUSE OF/CONNECTED TO A RELEVANT TRANSFER

If an employee is dismissed (whether actually (see **3.4.1**), or constructively (see **3.4.3**) or within the meaning of reg 4(9) (see **7.3.2.1**) and whether before or after the transfer), if the sole or principal reason for the dismissal is either (i) the transfer, or (ii) a transfer-connected reason that is *not* an economic, technical or organisational (ETO) reason entailing changes in the workforce then, by reg 7 of the 2006 Regulations, the dismissal is automatically unfair (ie there is no need to consider whether the dismissal is reasonable in accordance with ERA 1996, s 98(4) (reg 7(1)).

If the sole or principal reason for the dismissal is a reason connected with the transfer that is an ETO reason entailing changes in the workforce (of either the transferor or the transferee) before or after a relevant transfer, there is no automatically unfair dismissal, and (without prejudice to the application of s 98(4) of the ERA 1996) the dismissal shall, for the purposes of ss 98(1) and 135 of the 1996 Act, be regarded as having been for redundancy where s 98(2)(c) of that Act applies (see **5.2.1**), or otherwise for a substantial reason of a kind such as to justify the dismissal of an employee holding the position which that employee held (reg 7(2)and (3)).

Regulation 7(4) states that reg 7 applies irrespective of whether the employee in question is assigned to the organised grouping of resources or employees that is, or will be, transferred. This means that the protection of reg 7 is available to all employees. It is important, therefore, that transferees are aware that their existing employees, as well as the transferring employees, are protected against transfer-related dismissal.

If dismissals are not because of or connected to the transfer, normal unfair dismissal rules apply and liability will lie with the employer who dismissed.

To bring a claim of unfair dismissal arising out of a transfer-related dismissal, an employee still needs to have a minimum of one or two years' continuous employment (dependent on when the employment commenced).

7.5.1 When is a dismissal by reason of the transfer itself?

It will be a question of fact for the tribunal to determine whether a dismissal is by reason of the transfer itself, or for a reason connected with the transfer (see **7.5.2**). The BIS Guidance gives the following example in connection with changing terms and conditions, but it is useful by way of analogy:

Q.   What is the difference between an action that is by reason of the transfer itself and that which is for a reason which 'is connected with' the transfer?

A.   Where an employer changes terms and conditions simply because of the transfer and there are no extenuating circumstances linked to the reason for that decision, then such a change is prompted by reason of the transfer itself. However, where the reason for the change is prompted by a knock-on effect of the transfer – say, the need to re-qualify staff to use the different machinery used by the transferee – then the reason is 'connected to the transfer'.

In the authors' opinion, a dismissal following collusion between a transferor and a transferee with regard to dismissals (ie the transferee was involved in some way in the decision to dismiss) might be regarded as a dismissal by reason of the transfer itself, but as yet there is no authority supporting this proposition. In *Wheeler v Patel* [1987] IRLR 211 (a case decided under the old law), Mrs Wheeler was employed by the vendor of a shop in his business which he proposed to sell. Before the shop was transferred to a prospective purchaser, Mrs Wheeler was dismissed, in order to achieve agreement for sale. The EAT held (under the old law) that this dismissal was for a reason connected with the transfer, but it may be seen under the new law as a dismissal by reason of the transfer itself.

7.5.2 When is a dismissal for a reason connected with the transfer?

It is a question of fact whether or not a dismissal is for a reason connected with the transfer. Although dismissals which occur shortly before or after the transfer are likely to be found to be connected with it, if not by reason of it, an employee may have difficulty convincing the tribunal that a dismissal which took place weeks or even months before the transfer was by reason of the transfer or for a reason connected with the transfer. An employee dismissed prior to the transfer will come under reg 7 if he can prove that, at the time the dismissal took place, a transferee had been found and that the dismissal was connected to the transfer under negotiation. Clearly, where there is collusion between the transferor and transferee (see *Wheeler* at **7.5.1** above), this will, at the very least, be a transfer-connected reason.

Less clear is whether it is sufficient for the employee to show that his dismissal was in connection with transfers generally. There was a conflict of EAT decisions under the 1981 Regulations on this point.

In *Ibex Trading Company Ltd v Walton and Others* [1994] IRLR 564, the EAT held that the actual transferee had to be identified. Dismissal in respect of transfers generally was not sufficient. The employees were held to be dismissed by reason of 'a' transfer, rather than 'the' transfer.

However, in *Harrison Bowden Ltd v Bowden* [1994] ICR 186, and subsequently in *Morris v John Grose Group Ltd* [1998] IRLR 499 and *CAB Automotive Ltd v Blake and Others* (UKEAT/0298/07), the EAT held that the words 'the transfer' did not necessarily have to refer to the particular transfer that had actually occurred. That this is the correct approach was confirmed by the Court of Appeal in *Spaceright Europe Ltd v Baillavoine and Another* [2011] EWCA Civ 1565, although the case is under appeal to the Supreme Court. In the authors' view, the approach confirmed by the Court of Appeal is correct.

This approach accords with the ECJ's analysis. The ECJ has stated that the proper approach to the issue of whether dismissals were made in connection with a transfer was to look *back* in time and consider what had happened. On the basis of this method of analysis, the fact that no transferee can be identified at the moment of dismissal does not prevent employees' rights from being protected by the Acquired Rights Directive. In the *Spaceright* case, the claimant was the managing director of a business which was up for sale. Although no buyer had been identified, a view had been taken that an incumbent managing director was too expensive for a purchaser. The claimant was dismissed, ostensibly on the grounds of redundancy, but the business was always going to need a managing director, and there was always going to be an ongoing business. The EAT agreed that the dismissal was connected with the transfer which was contemplated.

So, for example, if employees are dismissed because customers become aware of the transferor's plans to contract out part of a business and, in view of the uncertainty, they decide to take their business elsewhere, this is likely to be seen as a reason connected with the transfer.

In *Dynamex Friction Ltd and Another v Amicus and Others* [2008] IRLR 515, when the company got into difficulties, joint administrators were appointed. The administrators decided to dismiss the workforce on the basis that the company had no money to pay them. The Court of Appeal upheld the tribunal decision that the sole reason for the dismissals was economic, as there was no money to pay the workforce, and so was not transfer-related. It was the administrator's decision to dismiss, and just because there was collusion between the director of the insolvent company and the transferee did not make the dismissals transfer-related in circumstances where the administrator was not involved in the collusion.

7.5.3 Establishing an ETO reason which entails a change in the workforce if the dismissal was connected to the transfer

If there is a dismissal for a reason (which is not an ETO reason) connected with the transfer, the transferee (ie the new employer) will be liable for all claims by the dismissed employee (reg 4(3)). If the dismissal was for an ETO reason which entails a change in the workforce, then liability for a pre-transfer dismissal will lie with the transferor (ie the old employer). Liability for a post-transfer dismissal will always lie with the transferee.

If there is an ETO reason, the dismissal will be either for redundancy, or for 'a substantial reason' under s 98(1) and s 135 of the ERA 1996. Even where the employer can show such a reason, the employment tribunal must still be satisfied that the employer has acted reasonably within s 98(4) of the ERA 1996.

The employer must show an ETO reason entailing a change in the workforce, otherwise the dismissal will be automatically unfair.

Note that the wording of reg 7 mirrors the wording of reg 4(4) (see **7.6** below) There is no statutory definition of an ETO reason. According to the BIS Guidance, it is likely to include:

(a)   a reason relating to the profitability or market performance of the transferee's business (ie an economic reason);

(b)   a reason relating to the nature of the equipment or production processes which the transferee operates (ie a technical reason); or

(c)   a reason relating to the management or organisational structure of the transferee's business (ie an organisational reason). (See (a) below.)

Likewise there is no statutory definition of the phrase 'entailing changes in the workforce'. The BIS Guidance points out that previous interpretations of the phrase by the courts under the 1981 Regulations (see below) restricted it to changes in the numbers employed, or to changes in the functions performed by employees. A functional change could involve a new requirement on an employee who held a managerial position to enter into a non-managerial role, or to move from a secretarial to a sales position. Two cases in particular have provided authoritative guidance on what the phrase means (see (b) below):

(a)   To be an ETO reason within reg 7, an 'economic' reason must relate to the future conduct of the business as such, and does not include dismissing employees simply to obtain an enhanced price or to achieve an agreement for sale (*Wheeler v Patel*, **7.5.1** above; *Spaceright*, **7.5.2** above).

The Court of Session confirmed in *Hynd v Armstrong* [2007] IRLR 338 that a transferor employer cannot rely on the transferee's reason for dismissal in order to establish an 'economic, technical or organisational reason' so as to provide a potential defence under the Regulations. In this case a pre-transfer dismissal of a solicitor by the transferor because the transferee did not require him was held to be automatically unfair. The Court of Session held that it is 'reasonably clear' that the Transfer Directive would not 'permit dismissal in such circumstances'. A transferor can only rely on a reason of its own.

Sarah Lamont of Bevan Brittan summarises the practical effects of the case:

- Where an employee is dismissed by the transferor prior to the transfer, the reason for the dismissal must relate to the transferor's future conduct of its business in order to be an ETO reason

- That will never be the case where, as here, the transferor has no intention of continuing the business after the transfer

- Often this situation arises where the transferor carries out dismissals at the request of the transferee, who does not want to take on the employees concerned, usually because it will leave him overstaffed and he does not want to carry out a redundancy exercise after the transfer

- Where there are pre-transfer dismissals in connection with the transfer and there is no ETO reason, liability for unfair dismissal will pass to the transferee under TUPE

- Although this is a case decided under TUPE 1981, it would apply equally to TUPE 2006, which replaced and amended the old version of the Regulations

- As a Court of Session case, this decision is not strictly binding on tribunals in England and Wales or the EAT sitting in England, but it is likely to be followed by them in practice.

(b)   The ETO reason must entail a 'change in the workforce'. For a change in the workforce there has to be a change in the composition of the workforce, or possibly a substantial change in job descriptions (*Berriman v Delabole Slate Ltd* [1985] IRLR 305, CA). Changes in the identity of the individuals who make up the workforce do not constitute changes in the workforce itself so long as the overall numbers and functions remain the same.

In *London University v Sackur* (UKEAT/0286/06), an employer, following a transfer and wanting to harmonise terms and conditions after a period of consultation lasting two years, dismissed staff and offered to re-engage them on new terms. The EAT upheld a tribunal's finding of fact that a transfer of an undertaking was the sole reason for the dismissal of the employees, even though the dismissals occurred two years after the transfer. They then looked at whether harmonisation of terms was an ETO reason. Referring to *Berriman*, they said that that case established that for an ETO reason to entail changes in the workforce, it must involve changes in the 'strength' or 'establishment' of the workforce. That means changes in the overall numbers or functions of employees. Effectively, therefore, an ETO reason entailing a change in the workforce will have to be a genuine redundancy situation. A mere change in the terms and conditions enjoyed by the workforce will not suffice, neither will the mere substitution of one employee for another. Consequently, a transferee who provokes an actual or a constructive dismissal by attempting to change the terms and conditions of the transferred employees to harmonise with those of his existing workforce would be unable to rely on the defence. The EAT in *Meter U Ltd v Hardy and Others* [2012] IRLR 367 followed the guidance in *Berriman*, as did the EAT in *The Manchester College v Hazel and Another* (see below).

For a case in which the tribunal's finding that the change to the claimants' bonus scheme was done for an ETO reason entailing a change in the work force, see *Nationwide Building Society v Benn & Others* (UKEAT/0273/09). In that case the principal reason for the change in a bonus scheme was connected to the claimants' job functions since it was driven by the product range and funds available to the respondent at that time.

In *Spaceright* (**7.5.2** above), the Court of Appeal held that there was no ETO reason entailing a change in the workforce. The reason did not relate to the conduct of the business as a going concern; the business was always going to need a managing director. It did not involve a diminution in the number of employees in the transferred business: the claimant was replaced. The reason was related to the sale of the business, not to the conduct of the business.

In *The Manchester College v Hazel and Another* (UKEAT/0642/11 and 0136/12), the EAT upheld a tribunal's decision that harmonisation of terms and conditions six months after a transfer did not effect changes in the workforce, and that as dismissals were connected to the transfer they were automatically unfair. Shortly after a transfer of the provision of offender learning services from the Prison Service to the College, which resulted in the transfer of 1,500 employees, the College realised that large cost savings were needed. As part of a raft of proposals, it asked two employees to take pay reductions (of 18% and 13.2%). They refused and were dismissed. The EAT held that simple harmonisation of terms was not an ETO reason (although it did confirm that there can be an ETO reason even where there is not a change to numbers and functions). The appropriate remedy, on the facts, was reinstatement on the new terms and conditions but at the old salaries, which would be frozen until other employees caught up.

The employer will need to make sure that a dismissal for redundancy is fair within other employment legislation, eg that selection for redundancy is fair and not based simply on the fact that the person is a transferred employee. Dismissed employees may also be entitled to a redundancy payment if they have been employed for two years or more. Employers must further ensure that the required period for consultation with employees' representatives is allowed (see **7.7** below). As it will sometimes be unclear whether the 2006 Regulations apply, and therefore whether the previous or the new employer is responsible for making redundancy payments (because if the 2006 Regulations do not apply then liability for the dismissals will not pass to the transferee but will remain with the transferor), employees are best advised to make any claims against both employers at an employment tribunal.

In certain circumstances reg 9 allows for variations to be agreed to where a transferor is subject to 'relevant insolvency proceedings' (as defined). The detail of this is beyond the scope of this book.

7.5.4 Summary

In summary, therefore:

(a) Where the sole or principal reason for a dismissal is either the transfer itself or a reason connected with the transfer that is not an ETO reason, the dismissal will be automatically unfair under reg 7(1). Irrespective of whether the dismissal occurred before or after the transfer, the claim will be against the transferee.

(b) Where the sole or principal reason for a dismissal is not the transfer itself but is a reason connected with the transfer that is an ETO reason, under reg 7(2) and (3) the dismissal will be potentially fair on the basis of either redundancy (in which case a redundancy payment may also be appropriate) or some other substantial reason, subject to the normal unfair dismissal tests. In this situation, while the transferee will remain liable for any post-transfer dismissals, the transferor will be liable for pre-transfer dismissals.

(c) Where the sole or principal reason for a dismissal is unconnected with the transfer, the usual unfair dismissal principles will apply.

(d) An employee who has been dismissed, or who has resigned in circumstances in which he considers he was entitled to resign because of the consequences or anticipated consequences of the transfer, needs to have the requisite continuous employment, although the qualifying period does not apply where an employee claims that he was dismissed for asserting his statutory rights under the 2006 Regulations (reg 19) (see **5.5.3**).

(e) Any complaints must be brought within three months of the date when employment ended.

(f) Because it may be unclear whether claims should be made against the previous employer or the new employer, employees should consider whether to claim against both employers.

7.6 POST-TRANSFER VARIATIONS TO TERMS AND CONDITIONS

One of the aims of the 2006 Regulations was to clarify what the position was post-transfer, where variations were made to contracts. The Regulations ensure that employees retain the same terms and conditions post-transfer as they enjoyed pre-transfer, and that they are not penalised when they are transferred by being given inferior terms and conditions. This is achieved by two routes. First, the 2006 Regulations state (reg 4(1)) that the contract of employment of any transferred employee 'shall have effect after the transfer as if originally made between the person so employed and the transferee'. This ensures that the pre-existing terms and conditions are transferred across on the first day of the employee's employment with the transferee. Secondly, by way of reinforcement, the Regulations also impose limitations on the ability of the transferee and employee to agree variations to those terms and conditions. In particular, reg 4(4) states:

> Subject to regulation 9, in respect of a contract of employment that is, or will be, transferred by paragraph (1), any purported variation of the contract shall be void if the sole or principal reason for the variation is—
>
> (a) the transfer itself; or
>
> (b) a reason connected with the transfer that is not an economic, technical or organisational reason entailing changes in the workforce.

Thus both the transferor and the transferee are prevented from varying contracts where the sole or principal reason is the transfer itself, or a reason connected with a transfer which is not 'an economic, technical or organisational reason entailing changes in the workforce'. Note that the wording of reg 4(4) mirrors the wording of reg 7. See **7.5.3** above for discussion of the meaning of the phrases 'economic, technical or organisational reason' and 'entailing changes in the workforce'. If contracts are varied for these reasons then those variations are rendered void by the Regulations. As far as the distinction between a reason relating to 'the transfer itself' and 'a reason connected with the transfer', the BIS Guidance suggests that where an employer changes terms and conditions simply because of the transfer and there are no extenuating circumstances linked to the reason for that decision, such a change is prompted by reason of the transfer itself. However, where the reason for the change is prompted by a knock-on effect of the transfer – say, the need to re-qualify staff to use the different machinery used by the transferee – then the reason is 'connected with the transfer'.

Regulation 4(5) states:

> Paragraph (4) shall not prevent the employer and his employee, whose contract of employment is, or will be, transferred by paragraph (1), from agreeing a variation of that contract if the sole or principal reason for the variation is—
>
> (a)   a reason connected with the transfer that is an economic, technical or organisational reason entailing changes in the workforce; or
>
> (b)   a reason unconnected with the transfer.

Thus the 2006 Regulations permit a transferee or a transferor to agree to vary an employment contract with an employee where the sole or principal reason is either unconnected with the transfer, or is a reason connected with the transfer but which falls within the definition of an 'economic, technical or organisational reason entailing changes in the workforce'. Note that an employer cannot unilaterally change or impose new terms and conditions without the agreement of the employee (see *Regent Security Services v Power* [2008] IRLR 226). The BIS Guidance suggests that a reason unconnected with a transfer could include the sudden loss of an expected order by a manufacturing company, or a general upturn in demand for a particular service or a change in a key exchange rate.

Where a change occurs after the transfer, it will be a question of fact whether the change was for a reason connected with the transfer. One relevant factor will be the length of time between the date of the transfer and the change, but the gap is only one factor. In *Taylor v Connex South Eastern Ltd* (UKEAT/1243/99), the EAT held that there was still a connection between the transfer and an attempt to force changes in terms and conditions two years after the relevant transfer, because the subject matter of the insistence by the respondents on the contractual change was an important term which had been transferred across on the occasion of the transfer.

In *Norris and Others v Brown & Root Ealing Technical Services Ltd* (UKEAT/386/00), the EAT upheld the finding of the tribunal that the reason for the dismissals (for refusing to accept new terms and conditions), which took place two years and four months after the transfer, was to do with needing to save money as a result of under-funding and was not connected to the transfer.

It is unlikely that an attempt by a transferee to change the terms and conditions of a transferring employee in order to harmonise them with those of the existing workers would be covered by this wording. Any wish to harmonise terms and conditions is really a reason directly connected with the transfer, and it is difficult to see how it could fall within the wording of reg 4(5). There is no hard-and-fast rule as to how long after a transfer it would 'safe' for the transferee to vary contracts because of the passage of time. The BIS Guidance points out that while there is likely to come a time when the link with the transfer can be treated as no longer effective, this must be assessed in the light of all the circumstances of the individual case and will vary from case to case.

In *Regent Security Services v Power* (above), the Court of Appeal held that favourable transfer-related variations (where no ETO existed) are valid, notwithstanding the statutory language.

In summary, therefore, the Regulations draw a distinction between four situations:

(a)   cases where the sole or principal reason for a purported contractual variation is the transfer itself;

(b)   cases where the sole or principal reason is a reason connected with the transfer that is not an ETO reason entailing changes in the workforce; and

(c)   cases where the reason is connected with the transfer but is for an ETO reason, or is entirely unconnected with the transfer; and

(d)   cases where the changes are entirely to the benefit of the employee.

In the first two situations any purported variation will be void, but this will not prevent a valid variation being agreed in the last two situations.

Note that reg 9 allows for variations to be agreed in certain circumstances, where a transferor is subject to 'relevant insolvency proceedings' (as defined). The detail of this is beyond the scope of this book.

7.6.1   Practical advice

Where acting for a transferee, it is imperative to carry out full due diligence of all transferring employees' terms and conditions, since the transferee will inherit on those terms and conditions, and may not be able to vary the terms and conditions even with the employees' consent (see also **7.7.1**).

Where acting for the transferee, an indemnity should be gained from the transferor in the event of there being any difference between the terms and conditions detailed in the due diligence process by the transferor, and the actual terms and conditions on which employees transfer across.

A transferee who wishes to be sure that old terms and conditions do not apply, and/or to harmonise terms and conditions with the existing workforce, may dismiss those employees post-transfer or get the transferor to dismiss pre-transfer, with a view to re-engaging them on new terms. Such dismissals will be effective, but will give rise to the risk of unfair dismissal claims. Such dismissals will be 'automatically' unfair, unless there is an ETO reason. In *Berriman* (**7.5.3** above), the Court of Appeal held that an ETO reason entailing changes in the workplace involves more than a mere change in terms and conditions. If transferees wish to have contractually binding and harmonious terms, they will have to bear in mind the potential costs of any consequential unfair dismissal claims. Alternatively, they will have to try to ensure that changes are not connected with the transfer.

7.7   THE PROVISION OF INFORMATION AND CONSULTATION UNDER THE 2006 REGULATIONS

Regulations 11–16 of the 2006 Regulations impose duties upon both the transferor and the transferee to provide information to each other, and to provide information to and consult the representatives of employees who may be affected by the transfer.

7.7.1   The provision of employee liability information

Article 3(2) of the Acquired Rights Directive gives Member States the option to introduce provisions 'to ensure that the transferor notifies the transferee of all the rights and obligations which will be transferred to the transferee ... so far as those rights and obligations are or ought to have been known to the transferor at the time of the transfer'. As a result, from 6 April 2006, under the 2006 Regulations, transferors became obliged, for the first time, to give transferees written information about 'any person employed by [the transferor] who is assigned to the organised grouping of resources or employees that is the subject of a relevant transfer' and all the associated rights and obligations towards them (reg 11), ie 'employee liability information'. This information includes, for example, the identity and age of the employees who will transfer, information contained in the employees' written particulars of employment under s 1 of the ERA 1996, any disciplinary and grievances procedures within the last two years, details of any claims that the transferor reasonably believes might be brought and information about any collective agreements. This is aimed at helping the transferee to prepare for the arrival of the transferred employees, and ensuring that it is fully aware of all its inherited obligations.

The obligation includes a duty to provide employee liability information relating to any person who would have been employed by the transferor and assigned to the organised grouping of resources or employees that is the subject of a relevant transfer immediately before the transfer if he had not been dismissed in the circumstances described in reg 7(1) (see **7.5**), including, where the transfer is effected by a series of two or more transactions, a person so employed and assigned, or who would have been so employed and assigned, immediately before any of those transactions (reg 11(4)).

The information, which need not be provided all in one go, should be given in writing or in any other form that is accessible to the transferee (eg as computer data files). The information may also be provided via a third party. For example, where a client is re-assigning a contract from an existing contractor to a new contractor, that client organisation may act as the third party in passing the information to the new contractor. The information must be provided not less than 14 days before the transfer or, if special circumstances make this not reasonably practicable, as soon as reasonably practicable thereafter (reg 11(6) and (7)). There is no provision entitling the transferor and the transferee to agree to contract out of the duty to supply the employee liability information.

If the transferor does not provide this information, within three months after the transfer the transferee may complain to an employment tribunal that the transferor has failed to comply with any provision of reg 11. The tribunal may make a declaration and award such compensation, as it considers just and equitable. Compensation starts at a minimum of £500 for each employee in respect of whom the information was not provided or was defective (reg 12).

7.7.2   The duty to inform and consult

Regulation 13 of the 2006 Regulations imposes duties upon both the transferor and the transferee to provide information to, and to consult, the representatives of employees who may be affected by the transfer.

An employer must inform and consult appropriate representatives, who may be:

(a)   elected employee representatives;

(b)   representatives of an independent trade union recognised by an employer. (Where there is a recognised trade union, the employer must consult with representatives of that trade union rather than with employee representatives.)

Regulation 14 lays down detailed requirements for the election of employee representatives. See the BIS Guidance for more information on how this works. Representatives and candidates for election have certain rights and protections to enable them to carry out their function properly. The dismissal of an elected representative will be automatically unfair if the reason, or the main reason, related to the employee's status or activities as a representative. An elected representative also has the right not to suffer any detriment short of dismissal on the grounds of his status or activities. Candidates for election enjoy the same protection.

The obligation to consult and provide information applies in relation to:

> any employees of the transferor or the transferee (whether or not assigned to the organised grouping of resources or employees that is the subject of a relevant transfer) who may be affected by the transfer or may be affected by measures taken in connection with it; and references to the employer shall be construed accordingly.

Categories of 'affected employees' might include not only the individuals who are to be transferred, but also their colleagues in the transferor who will not transfer but whose jobs might still be affected by the transfer, and their new colleagues in employment with the transferee whose jobs might also be affected by the transfer.

7.7.2.1 The duty to inform

The obligation to provide information arises whenever a relevant transfer is planned. The information must be provided 'long enough before a relevant transfer to enable the employer to consult with the employees' representatives' (reg 13(2)). There is no firm guidance on time limits. In particular, it is clear that they are not the same as redundancy time limits, ie 90 or 30 days. In practice, consultation under the Regulations often lasts for relatively short periods. The information to be given to the representatives is to be delivered to them personally or by post, or (in the case of union representatives) sent by post to the union's head office.

The employer of affected employees must inform all the appropriate representatives of the following:

(a) the fact that a relevant transfer is to take place;

(b) when it is to take place (approximately);

(c) the reasons for it;

(d) the legal, economic and social implications of the transfer for the affected employees;

(e) the measures which he envisages taking (eg if a re-organisation will result) in relation to those employees (and if no measures are envisaged, that fact);

(f) if the employer is the transferor, the measures, in connection with the transfer, which he envisages the transferee will take in relation to any affected employees who will become employees of the transferee after the transfer (and if no measures are envisaged, that fact). The transferee must give the transferor the necessary information so that the previous employer is able to meet this requirement.

7.7.2.2 The duty to consult

If action is envisaged which will affect the employees, the employer must consult the representatives of the employees affected about that action. The consultation must be undertaken with a view to seeking agreement of the employee representatives to the intended measures (reg 13(6)). In practice, this means that the management must consider representations made and reply to the same; and if they choose to reject them, they should state the reasons for this. There is clearly an obligation to negotiate in good faith. The employer must consider any representations made by the appropriate representatives and reply to those representations; and if he rejects any of those representations, he must state his reasons (reg 13(7)). The employer must permit the appropriate representatives access to any affected employees, and must provide them with such accommodation and other facilities as may be appropriate (reg 13(8)).

It is a defence for the employer to show that there were special circumstances which rendered it not reasonably practicable to perform the duty in question, provided that he took whatever steps to perform that duty as were reasonably practicable in the circumstances. The tenor of the case law is that this defence is to be construed extremely narrowly. The circumstances must be out of the ordinary and relate to the particular situation and not merely to general circumstances which may create pressure or problems for the employer.

Confidentiality will not in itself be enough to invoke the defence. A mere desire to preserve confidentiality, rather than it being a prerequisite for the purchase to go ahead, will not be adequate.

With regard to a financial crisis in a redundancy situation, the tribunal will look to the practicability of consultation in light of the suddenness of the situation and the extent of prior knowledge.

There is no case law on the point which often arises in the context of listed companies, ie whether the defence is available where the disclosure of information would amount to a disclosure of price-sensitive information. In the authors' view, this argument is unlikely to persuade most employment tribunals. The tribunal would no doubt counter-suggest that appropriate representatives could have been asked to agree to confidentiality obligations and that the Listing Rules allow a company to disclose information about impending developments/negotiations to employee or trade union representatives.

7.7.2.3   Failure to comply

The relative inadequacy of the remedy for a failure to inform and consult means that many companies will probably opt to put other business concerns, such as confidentiality, ahead of their obligations under the 2006 Regulations.

Any of the affected employees, or their appropriate representatives, may bring a complaint (no later than three months after the date of the transfer) to an employment tribunal (reg 15). They can choose against whom they bring their complaint. Where either the transferor or the transferee is the sole defendant, he may seek to join the other employer to the case. The 2006 Regulations resolve one previous area of uncertainty, as to whether the transferor or the transferee was liable for any award made by a tribunal for a failure to comply: both the transferee and the transferor are now jointly and severally liable in respect of any compensation payable (reg 15(9)).

If a complaint is upheld, the tribunal must make a declaration and has a discretion to order the employer to pay appropriate compensation to such descriptions of affected employees as may be specified in the award. 'Appropriate compensation' in reg 15 means such sum not exceeding 13 weeks' pay for the employee in question as the tribunal considers just and equitable having regard to:

(a)   the seriousness of the failure of the employer to comply with his duty;

(b)   any loss sustained by the transferee attributable to the matters complained of; and

(c)   the terms of any contract between transferor and transferee under which the transferor may be liable to pay a sum to the transferee in respect of failure to provide such information (reg 16(3)).

The last provision is to prevent any element of double recovery. It is for a tribunal to decide when it would be 'just and equitable' to award less than the maximum, although the Government has commented that if a failure was 'minimal or trivial', the minimum award need not apply. Note that whether a week's pay for this purpose is subject to the statutory maximum (currently £450) imposed by s 227 of the ERA 1996 was the subject of an appeal in *Zaman v Kozee Sleep Products Ltd* (EAT/0312/10). The EAT said that even though reg 16 did cross-refer to s 227 of the ERA 1996, there was no intention to apply the cap. If there had been such intention, it would have been necessary either to amend s 227 to include a specific reference or include an express provision in the 2006 Regulations. The Court of Appeal confirmed in *Sweetin v Coral Racing* [2006] IRLR 252 (following *Susie Radin Ltd v GMB* [2004] IRLR 400 – see **4.8.1.2**) that where there is a complete failure to engage in the consultation process, a tribunal should start at the 13-week maximum and work down as appropriate (see eg *Cable Realisations Ltd v GMB Northern* [2010] IRLR 42 and *Todd v Care Concern* (UKEAT/0057/2010)).

Compensation for a failure to inform and consult cannot be set off against other obligations, for example damages for breach of contract or for a 'protective award' under the collective redundancy obligations.

In *Royal Mail Group v CWU* [2009] EWCA Civ 1045, Royal Mail was planning to transfer a number of post office branches to WH Smith. It believed, however, that no employees would transfer as a result because they were offering voluntary redundancy and/or redeploying staff using an express contractual right. Because Royal Mail believed no staff would transfer, it believed there was no need to inform and consult the union about the transfer. The CWU complained to an employment tribunal, which found that Royal Mail had failed to comply with the obligation to inform and consult. The EAT and the Court of Appeal disagreed and overturned the tribunal's decision. They accepted that where an employer genuinely believes that no transfer will take place, it will not be in breach of its obligations to inform and consult.

7.7.3 Other duties to consult and inform

In addition to the obligations under regs 11–16 of the 2006 Regulations, the Information and Consultation of Employees Regulations 2004 (SI 2004/3426) (implementing the EC Directive on information and consultation) apply to undertakings employing 50 or more employees. The Regulations provide for a comprehensive scheme of consultation and the provision of information to employees (see **4.8.2**).

Again, where there is an overlap, the 2004 Regulations cease to apply once the employer has notified the representatives that he will be complying with his duties under the 2006 Regulations.

7.8 FURTHER READING

BIS Guide, *Employment Rights on the Transfer of an Undertaking*.

Selwyn, *Law of Employment*, 17th edn (OUP, 2012).

Blackstone's Employment Law Practice (OUP, 2012).

Harvey, *Industrial Relations and Employment Law* (Butterworths), Div F.

SUMMARY

At common law in the UK, the transfer of a business undertaking by one employer to another would automatically terminate the employee's contract of employment, ie there is a dismissal. The Transfer of Undertakings (Protection of Employment) Regulations 2006 alter the legal position by providing that where there is a 'relevant transfer', there will not be any automatic termination of the contract of employment simply by reason of the transfer. Where there is a 'relevant transfer' the employee will transfer to the new owner and will be employed by him on the same terms as under his original contract. If there are any dismissals, whether actual, constructive or deemed, and whether they are before or after the transfer of the business, if those dismissals are connected with the transfer, they will be automatically unfair unless, effectively, there is a genuine redundancy situation (an economic, technical or organisational (ETO) reason for the dismissal; **7.1**).

For the 2006 Regulations to apply, there must be a transfer from one person to another; consequently, there must be a change in the employer, not merely in the ownership. The 2006 Regulations do not therefore apply to transfers by share takeover or to transfers of assets only, or to a situation where a purchaser buys a majority shareholding in a company, thereby gaining control. This is because there is no change in the identity of the employer – in all these situations it will remain the same company. The 2006 Regulations do apply to mergers, sales of part of a going concern, changes of franchisee, sale of a sole trader's business or partnership and to transfers between two companies belonging to the same group, or where one subsidiary subcontracts work to another, provided the transfer involves the transfer of an 'economic entity' (see *Allen and Others v Amalgamated Construction* (Case C-234/98) [2000] IRLR 119) (**7.2**).

Regulation 3 of the 2006 Regulations expressly covers 'service provision changes' such as contracting-out exercises (eg catering, cleaning, security) where services are outsourced, insourced or assigned to a new contractor. However, the Regulations will not apply to service provision changes that take place 'in connection with a single specific event or task of short term duration'.

Regulation 4(3) of the 2006 Regulations operates so as to transfer the contracts of any individuals who are:

(a)   employed by the transferor immediately prior to the transfer (or would have been had they not been dismissed for a reason connected with the transfer – in this latter situation the dismissal will be effective but liability for any claims the dismissed employee may have may fall upon the transferee); and

(b)   assigned to the relevant grouping of employees that is transferred.

The Regulations state that there will be no transfer of employees who are only 'temporarily assigned' to a particular undertaking (**7.3** and **7.4**).

Regulations 4(4) and 7(1) clarify when the 'economic technical or organisational' (ETO) defence applies, and the ability to change terms and conditions on a transfer.

The 2006 Regulations permit variations of contract, which may be agreed between transferees and transferred employees, and which either are done for a reason unconnected with the transfer or done for a reason connected with the transfer that is an ETO reason entailing changes in the workforce. 'Entailing changes in the workforce' is not defined in the 2006 Regulations, but it has been interpreted by tribunals under predecessor Regulations as meaning changes in the 'numbers' employed.

Regulation 4(7) and (8) allow an employee to object to a transfer, but specify that where this right is exercised, the employee shall be treated as having resigned (**7.5** and **7.6**).

Regulations 8 and 9 cover what happens where there is a rescue of failing businesses.

Regulations 11 and 12 create an obligation for the current employer to provide employee information to the transferee, so that the transferee is made fully aware of the employees' rights, obligations and liabilities upon transfer (**7.7**).

Flowcharts showing the steps to be taken to determine whether a dismissal before a relevant transfer or a dismissal on or after a relevant transfer is fair, are set out in **Figures 7.1** and **7.2** respectively below.

Figure 7.1 Dismissals before a relevant transfer

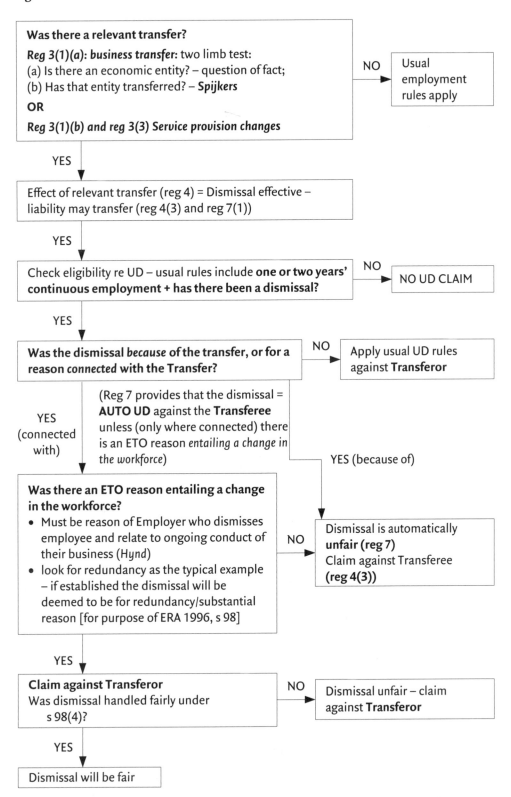

NB – ALSO check for redundancy payment claims and/or WD claims. Claim will be against the same party as the claim for UD.

Figure 7.2 Dismissals on or after a relevant transfer

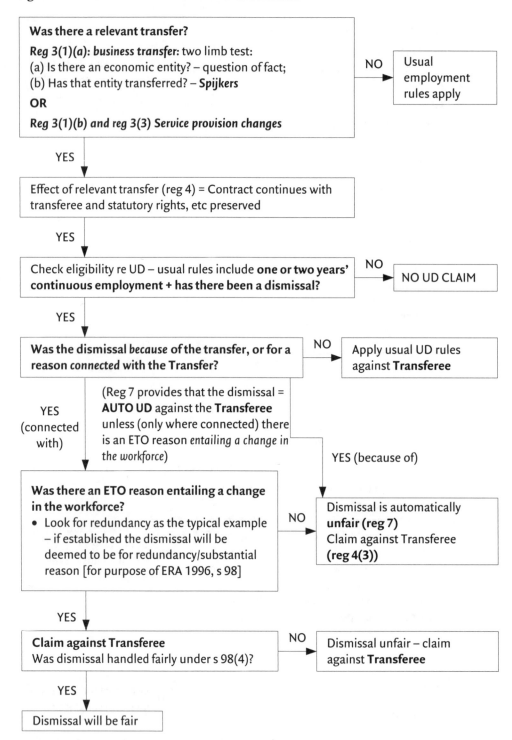

NB – ALSO check for redundancy payment claims and/or WD claims. Claim will be against the Transferee.

DISCRIMINATION AND EQUAL PAY

LEARNING OUTCOMES

After reading this chapter you will be able to:

- understand the underlying principles of discrimination law and when and to whom it applies in an employment context
- list the grounds ('protected characteristics') in the Equality Act 2010 upon which discrimination is deemed unlawful
- describe and explain each of the protected characteristics
- list the four types of prohibited conduct
- understand the significance of occupational requirements and the reasonable steps defence
- describe the remedies available where a complaint of discrimination is made out.

8.1 INTRODUCTION

The first anti-discrimination legislation was passed in 1965. In February 2005, the Government set up the Discrimination Law Review to address long-term concerns about perceived inconsistencies in the then existing discrimination law framework. The Review was tasked with considering the fundamental principles of discrimination legislation and its underlying concepts, and the opportunities for creating a clearer and more streamlined framework of equality legislation. In June 2007, the Department for Communities and Local Government published a Consultation Paper, *A Framework for Fairness: Proposals for a Single Equality Bill for Great Britain*. This was followed in June and July 2008 by two Command Papers published by the Government Equalities Office: *Framework for a Fairer Future – the Equality Bill* (Cm 7431); and *The Equality Bill – Government Response to the Consultation* (Cm 7454).

A single Equality Bill, intended to harmonise and consolidate in one place most existing anti-discrimination and equality legislation (such as the SDA 1975, the RRA 1976 and the DDA 1995), was published on 27 April 2009. The Bill contained 205 clauses and 28 Schedules. The Government also published in April 2009, *Equality Bill: Assessing the impact of a multiple discrimination provision* (a summary of responses was published in October 2009). In June 2009, the Government published *Equality Bill: Making it work – Policy proposals for specific duties*, and in January 2010 *Equality Bill: Making it work – Ending age discrimination in services and public functions*.

The Equality Act 2010 received Royal Assent on 8 April 2010. The Act replaces most of the previous discrimination legislation and, as well as codifying the different strands of the old statute-based law on discrimination (eg, direct discrimination still occurs when 'someone is treated less favourably than another person because of a protected characteristic'), also makes a number of changes to the existing law (eg, employees may now complain about harassment even if it is not directed at them, if they can demonstrate that it creates an offensive environment for them). Additionally, it extends some aspects of the old law (eg, associative discrimination – direct discrimination against someone because he or she associates with another person who possesses a protected characteristic). Under the old law, discrimination by association applied only to race, religion and belief, and sexual orientation. It has now been extended to cover age, disability, gender reassignment and sex. There are also some entirely new concepts (eg, the concept of discrimination arising from disability, which occurs if a disabled person is treated unfavourably because of something arising in consequence of his or her disability). Most of the employment provisions came into force on 1 October 2010. Some consequential amendments to the Act were introduced by the Equality Act 2010 (Consequential Amendments, Saving and Supplementary Provisions) Order 2010 (SI 2010/ 2279) – see, eg, **8.4.3** below). There are no transitional provisions in the Act. Section 137 prevents complaints brought and determined under the pre-Equality Act 2010 legislation being re-litigated under the 2010 Act.

A number of provisions have not yet been implemented, and in March 2011 the Government announced that it would not be implementing the 'dual' discrimination provisions.

Acas has published a useful table setting out the main changes. This is reproduced opposite.

The Equality and Human Rights Commission (EHRC) has created a series of non-statutory guidance documents to help explain the Act and provide practical examples on how the law has changed. Its website has detailed guidance (running to hundreds of pages) for employers, workers, service providers, service users, education providers and public sector bodies. The Guidance for Employers appears under the following headings:

1. What equality law means for you as an employer: when you recruit someone to work for you
2. What equality law means for you as an employer: working hours, flexible working and time off
3. What equality law means for you as an employer: pay and benefits
4. What equality law means for you as an employer: training, development, promotion and transfer
5. What equality law means for you as an employer: managing workers
6. What equality law means for you as an employer: dismissal, redundancy, retirement and after a worker has left
7. Good equality practice for employers: equality policies, equality training and monitoring

Similar guidance notes are available for workers (except for No 7). All the guidance notes may be accessed at www.equalityhumanrights.com/advice-and-guidance/guidance-equality-act-2010/equality-act-2010-guidance/.

Equality Act 2010
What's new & what's changed: at a glance

Key

Description	Colour
Characteristic covered in existing legislation – **no changes**	(black)
Characteristic covered in existing legislation – but some **changes**	Changes
Characteristic not covered in existing legislation – **now covered**	New
Characteristic not covered in existing legislation – still **not covered**	(white)

Definitions

Direct discrimination — Someone is treated less favourably than another person because of a protected characteristic (PC)

Associative discrimination — Direct discrimination against someone because they associate with another person who possesses a PC

Discrimination by perception — Direct discrimination against someone because the others think they possess a particular PC

Indirect discrimination — Can occur when you have a rule or policy that applies to everyone but disadvantages a particular PC

Harassment — Employees can now complain of behaviour they find offensive even if it is not directed at them

Harassment by a third party — Employers are potentially liable for harassment of their staff by people they don't employ

Victimisation — Someone is treated badly because they have made/supported a complaint or grievance under the Act

	Age	Disability	Gender Reassignment	Race	Religion or Belief	Sex	Sexual Orientation	Marriage & Civil Partnership	Pregnancy & Maternity
Direct discrimination	New	New	New						
Associative discrimination	New	New	New						
Discrimination by perception		New	New			New	New		
Indirect discrimination		New	New	Changes	Changes				
Harassment	Changes	Changes	Changes	New	New		Changes		
Harassment by a third party	New	New	New	New	New	Changes	New		
Victimisation	Changes	Changes	Changes	Changes	Changes	Changes	Changes	Changes	Changes

In line with its statutory powers (Equality Act 2006, s 14(1)), the EHRC has also published codes of practice on employment and equal pay (covering sex, race). The purpose of these codes is to explain the new statutory provisions of the Equality Act 2010. They draw on precedent and case law. The codes came into force on 6 April 2011. Courts and tribunals must take into account any part of the code that appears to them relevant to any questions arising in proceedings. They may be found at www.equalityhumanrights.com/advice-and-guidance/information-for-advisors/codes-of-practice/.

The Acas website (www.acas.org.uk) also contains a wealth of guidance on the new law.

This chapter and the following chapters on discrimination set out the new law. All the chapters on discrimination refer by way of illustration and example to the pre- and post-Equality Act 2010 case law. Although the Government believes, in many places, that there have been no changes, care is still needed where pre-Equality Act 2010 case law is relied upon.

8.1.1 Background

The general common law rule is that an employer is free to offer employment to whomsoever he chooses (*Allen v Flood and Taylor* [1898] AC 1). This common law freedom has been restricted by statute. The employer may be in breach of statutory requirements if he discriminates against a person on the grounds of:

(a)   sex or marital status;

(b)   gender reassignment;

(c)   race;

(d)   religion or belief;

(e)   sexual orientation;

(f)   trade union membership;

(g)   part-time work;

(h)   age;

(i)   disability;

(j)   fixed (limited)-term work;

(k)   pregnancy and maternity.

In all areas of discrimination law it is important to appreciate the influence of EU law. In the area of sex discrimination, the Equal Treatment Directive (76/207) provided that there should be no discrimination on grounds of sex, either directly or indirectly, nor by reference to marital or family status, in access to employment, training, working conditions, promotion or dismissal. The UK first implemented the Directive by way of the SDA 1975, which made it unlawful to discriminate against women, men, married persons or persons who intend to undergo, or have undergone, a gender reassignment. The Equal Treatment (Amendment) Directive (2002/73) amended the Equal Treatment Directive, most importantly by adding definitions of 'sexual harassment' and 'harassment'. The UK initially implemented the changes required by the Directive in October 2005, by way of the Employment Equality (Sex Discrimination) Regulations 2005 (SI 2005/2467).

Influenced by international law and EU law (the Race Discrimination Directive (2000/43)), the RRA 1976 prohibited discrimination on the grounds of colour, race, nationality or ethnic or national origins.

Article 157 TFEU (ex 141 EC) established the principle that men and women should receive equal pay for equal work. This was implemented into UK law by way of the Equal Pay Act (EPA) 1970 (as amended).

The Framework Directive for Equal Treatment in Employment and Occupation (2000/78) required Member States to implement legislation prohibiting discrimination on grounds of sexual orientation and religion. The UK enacted law to comply with its EU obligations by way of the Employment Equality (Religion or Belief) Regulations 2003 (SI 2003/1660) ('the Religion or Belief Regulations'), the Employment Equality (Sexual Orientation) Regulations 2003 (SI 2003/1661) ('the Sexual Orientation Regulations') and the Disability Discrimination Act 1995 (Amendment) Regulations 2003 (SI 2003/1673), which amended the DDA 1995. The Sexual Orientation Regulations were amended in 2005 to take account of the Civil Partnership Act 2004. A revised Code of Practice on Racial Equality in Employment came into effect in April 2006. The Employment Equality (Age) Regulations 2006 (SI 2006/1031) ('the Age Regulations') were the last plank of the UK's implementation of the Equal Treatment Framework Directive.

The Equality Act 2006 received Royal Assent on 16 February 2006. It provided for the establishment of the EHRC, which came into being in October 2007. The EHRC took on the work of the former equality Commissions (the EOC, the DRC and the CRE), and additionally assumed responsibility for promoting equality and combating unlawful discrimination in three new strands, namely sexual orientation, religion or belief, and age. The EHRC also has responsibility for the promotion of human rights.

Much of the UK legislation referred to above has now been consolidated into the Equality Act 2010. All references in **Chapters 8** to **13** to 'the Act' are to the Equality Act 2010.

In May 2012, the Government announced various proposed changes to the Equality Act 2010 aimed at reducing 'red tape' in equality law. It consulted on repealing provisions in the Act that make employers liable for harassment by third parties. That consultation closed on 7 August 2012. There is also a consultation concerning employment tribunals' power to make wider recommendations on an employer's policies and procedures on discrimination, and the use of the statutory questionnaire procedure in discrimination cases. The view of the consultation was that the power of employment tribunals to make wider recommendations was unlikely to serve a practical purpose, or to be an appropriate or effective legal remedy for employment tribunals. The procedure for obtaining information was intended to increase pre-hearing settlements and reduce tribunal loads, but it has apparently not had this effect. The consultation sought views on proposals to repeal these two measures. That consultation also closed on 7 August 2012. The Government published its response to the consultation on 10 October 2012 and has announced that it intends to abolish the statutory questionnaire procedure, remove tribunals' power to make recommendations and repeal the provisions on third party harassment. The Government is also intent on pressing ahead with changes to the remit of the EHRC (see www.homeoffice.gov.uk for further information).

8.1.2   Who is protected?

The Act protects, amongst others, employees (s 39), job applicants (s 39), contract workers (s 41), office holders (s 50) and trade union members (s 57). It also protects employees after their employment has ended (s 108). Section 83(2) of the Act defines 'Employment' as '(a) employment under a contract of employment, a contract of apprenticeship or a contract personally to do work'. This definition is wider than the definition of 'employee' in s 230(1) of the ERA 1996 (see **1.3.2** and **1.3.4.2** above).

Sections 39 and 40 make it unlawful for an employer to discriminate against, or to harass or to victimise employees and people seeking work. It applies where the employer is making arrangements to fill a job, and in respect of anything done in the course of a person's employment (see **8.4** below). Section 40 also makes the employer liable for harassment of its employees by third parties, such as customers or clients, over whom the employer does not have direct control. Section 41 makes it unlawful for a person (referred to as a 'principal') who makes work available to contract workers to discriminate against, harass or victimise them (see *Leeds City Council v Woodhouse* [2010] IRLR 625).

Section 108 makes it unlawful to discriminate against or harass someone after a relationship covered by the Act has ended (see **8.4** below).

There is a general interpretation section in s 212, and an index to defined expressions in s 214 and Sch 28.

8.1.3 Territorial jurisdiction

Unlike previous discrimination legislation, the Act does not deal with territorial scope. Most of the old legislation applied to employment 'at an establishment in Great Britain', and provided protection to those who work 'wholly or partly' in Great Britain as well as to those who work wholly outside Great Britain but fulfil specific criteria. It is therefore left to employment tribunals to determine whether the Act applies.

According to the Explanatory Notes, the decision to remove territorial scope from the Act follows the precedent of the ERA 1996 (s 196, which determined whether it applied to employees who ordinarily work outside Great Britain, was repealed by the Employment Relations Act 1999.) This means that when determining whether they have jurisdiction to hear a claim brought under the Act, tribunals will have to follow the test laid down by the House of Lords in *Serco Ltd v Lawson* (see **3.7**).

The Court of Appeal in *British Airways Plc v Mak and Others* [2011] EWCA Civ 184 held that an employment tribunal had jurisdiction to hear age and race discrimination cases brought against British Airways by Chinese national, Hong Kong-based former cabin crew employees who had been compulsorily retired at 45, when other cabin crew who were working out of London and other bases were not forced to retire at that age. The claimants spent as little as 5% of their time working in Great Britain, but that time involved carrying out integral flight cycle duties, plus essential training. Although the case was decided under the Age Regulations and the Race Relations Act, the Court of Appeal's analysis of the factual background in *Mak*, which led to it finding that the employees worked 'partly in Great Britain' remains highly relevant to any determination of jurisdictional issues under the Act.

In *Clyde & Co LLP and Another v Bates van Winkelhof* [2012] EWCA Civ 1207, the Court of Appeal upheld an employment tribunal's decision with regard to jurisdiction and agreed that it was right to apply the *Serco v Lawson* test to discrimination and/or whistleblowing claims (see **3.7**). In this case, Mrs Bates van Winkelhof spent the majority of her time working abroad, and on that basis the Court confirmed that the test to be applied is whether an individual has a sufficiently strong connection with Great Britain. In cases where the individual works wholly abroad, a comparative exercise will be appropriate (ie connections with Great Britain will need to outweigh connections with the other jurisdiction).

8.1.4 Interpretation

Section 137 provides that any final finding in a claim brought under the previous discrimination legislation is to be treated as conclusive in proceedings under the Act. A finding is considered final when an appeal against it is dismissed, withdrawn or abandoned, or where the time-limit for appealing against it has expired. This is intended to prevent matters from being relitigated under the Act.

8.1.5 Scope of this and following chapters on discrimination

This chapter deals with the matters which are common to all the protected characteristics. It, together with **Chapters 9, 10** and **11,** deals with discrimination on the grounds of sex, race, religion or belief, marriage and civil partnership, pregnancy and maternity, and sexual orientation. This chapter also looks briefly at equal pay, discrimination against part-time workers and discrimination on grounds of trade union membership or activities.

Chapter 12 deals with age discrimination and **Chapter 13** covers discrimination on the ground of disability, because these follow slightly different regimes from the other protected characteristics.

8.2 PROTECTED CHARACTERISTICS

Section 4 of the Equality Act 2010 sets out certain 'protected' characteristics. These are the grounds upon which discrimination is deemed unlawful.

The characteristics relevant to this chapter and **Chapters 9–11** are:

- gender reassignment (s 7)
- marriage and civil partnership (s 8)
- race (s 9)
- religion or belief (s 10)
- sex (s 11)
- sexual orientation (s 12)
- pregnancy and maternity (s 18).

The characteristic relevant to **Chapter 12** is age (s 5) and to **Chapter 13** is disability (s 6 and Sch 1). The definitions in relation to the protected characteristics of age and disability are dealt with separately in **Chapters 12** and **13**. Pregnancy and maternity, which are dealt with separately in s 18, are dealt with under direct discrimination (see **9.4**).

The EHRC Code contains a wealth of information, and tribunals are obliged to take it into account when it appears relevant. Readers should refer to the Code for further guidance.

8.2.1 Sex

Sex is defined in s 11 of the Act:

> In relation to the protected characteristic of sex—
>
> (a) a reference to a person who has a particular protected characteristic is a reference to a man or to a woman;
>
> (b) a reference to persons who share a protected characteristic is a reference to persons of the same sex.

8.2.2 Race

'Race' is defined in s 9 of the Act:

> (1) Race includes—
>
>   (a) colour;
>
>   (b) nationality;
>
>   (c) ethnic or national origins.
>
> (2) In relation to the protected characteristic of race—
>
>   (a) a reference to a person who has a particular protected characteristic is a reference to a person of a particular racial group;
>
>   (b) a reference to persons who share a protected characteristic is a reference to persons of the same racial group.
>
> (3) A racial group is a group of persons defined by reference to race; and a reference to a person's racial group is a reference to a racial group into which the person falls.
>
> (4) The fact that a racial group comprises two or more distinct racial groups does not prevent it from constituting a particular racial group.
>
> (5) A Minister of the Crown may by order—
>
>   (a) amend this section so as to provide for caste to be an aspect of race;
>
>   (b) amend this Act so as to provide for an exception to a provision of this Act to apply, or not to apply, to caste or to apply, or not to apply, to caste in specified circumstances.

...

The Explanatory Notes give the following examples:

- Colour includes being black or white.
- Nationality includes being a British, Australian or Swiss citizen.
- Ethnic or national origins include being from a Roma background or of Chinese heritage.
- A racial group could be 'black Britons' which would encompass those people who are both black and who are British citizens.

The courts have often had to consider the meaning of 'ethnic origins'. In *Mandla and Another v Dowell Lee and Another* [1983] 2 AC 548, HL, Lord Fraser identified two essential characteristics of an ethnic group:

(a)   a long shared history; and

(b)   a cultural tradition of its own.

On that basis, for example, Sikhs are a distinct ethnic group for these purposes.

In addition to these essential characteristics, his Lordship identified others which, although not essential, could be expected to be displayed, such as a common language, or a common geographical origin. The principles in *Mandla* have been applied in a number of cases, so, for example, gypsies have been held to constitute an ethnic group, but not Rastafarians.

In *BBC Scotland v Souster* [2001] IRLR 150, the Court of Session confirmed that the Scots and English are separate racial groups, defined by reference to their national origins (although not by reference to their ethnic origins).

In *Dizedziak v Future Electronics Ltd* (UKEAT/0270/11), the EAT upheld a decision that the claimant had been subjected to direct discrimination on grounds of her nationality when she was instructed by her line manager not to speak in 'her own language' at work (the claimant was a Polish national).

8.2.3   Religion or belief

Religion or belief is defined in s 10 of the Act:

(1)   Religion means any religion and a reference to religion includes a reference to a lack of religion.

(2)   Belief means any religious or philosophical belief and a reference to belief includes a reference to a lack of belief.

(3)   In relation to the protected characteristic of religion or belief—

(a)   a reference to a person who has a particular protected characteristic is a reference to a person of a particular religion or belief;

(b)   a reference to persons who share a protected characteristic is a reference to persons who are of the same religion or belief.

The Explanatory Notes give the following examples:

- The Baha'i faith, Buddhism, Christianity, Hinduism, Islam, Jainism, Judaism, Rastafarianism, Sikhism and Zoroastrianism are all religions for the purposes of this provision.
- Beliefs such as humanism and atheism would be beliefs for the purposes of this provision but adherence to a particular football team would not be.

Note: Jews may also a constitute a racial group under the definition in s 9 (see **8.2.2**).

The Explanatory Notes state that the criteria for determining what is a 'philosophical belief' are that it must:

(a)   be genuinely held;

(b)   be a belief and not an opinion or a viewpoint based on the present state of information available;

(c)   be a belief as to a weighty and substantial aspect of human life and behaviour;

(d)   attain a certain level of cogency, seriousness, cohesion and importance; and

(e)   be worthy of respect in a democratic society, compatible with human dignity and not conflict with the fundamental rights of others.

So, for example, any cult involved in illegal activities would not satisfy these criteria. (For a detailed discussion of what is meant by cogency, etc, see, for example, *R (Williamson) v Secretary of State for Education* [2005] 2 AC 246 and *Campbell and Cosans v UK* (1982) 4 EHRR 293.)

In *Devine v Home Office* (ET/2302061/04), a claimant sought to argue that his sympathy for underprivileged asylum seekers was a demonstration of the Christian virtue of charity and should be protected from religious discrimination. A tribunal rejected the claim on the grounds, inter alia, that it was too vague and the claimant had at no point put himself forward as a Christian.

In *Hussain v Bhullar Bros* (ET/1806638/04), a tribunal held that attendance at home following the bereavement of a close family member was a religion-based practice or belief. The tribunal applied a generous meaning to 'religion' and 'religious belief ', and held that if a person genuinely believes that his faith requires a particular course of action then it is sufficient to make it part of his belief. It said that attempting to differentiate between cultural manifestation, traditions and religious observance would lead to 'unnecessary complications and endless debate'.

In *McClintock v Department of Constitutional Affairs* [2008] IRLR 29, the EAT said that to constitute a belief, there must be a religious or philosophical viewpoint in which one actually believes; it is not enough to have an opinion based on some real or perceived logic, or based on information or lack of information.

It is not clear whether and to what extent this definition will cover political beliefs: communism and other political beliefs may be protected as a philosophy. In early cases decided under the previous Religion or Belief Regulations 2003, tribunals rejected arguments that political beliefs were protected (see eg *Williams v South Central Limited* (ET/2306989/03), *Baggs v Fudge* (ET/1400114/04) and *Finnon v Asda Stores Limited* (ET/2402142/05)).

In *McConkey v The Simon Community* [2009] UKHL 24, the House of Lords had to consider whether the refusal to employ someone because he had in the past approved of the use of violence to achieve political ends, was unlawful under the Northern Ireland fair employment legislation, which covers religious belief *and* political opinion. The respondent was a charity providing services to homeless people in Northern Ireland. It refused to employ the claimant after a check showed that he had a conviction for violent crime, received while he was a member of a proscribed paramilitary organisation. The claimant said that this was discrimination on the grounds of his Republican political beliefs. The House of Lords drew a distinction between a belief/opinion and action in support of that belief/opinion, and said that it may be lawful to refuse to employ someone on the ground of that person's conduct – which would be applied equally to someone who had Loyalist views, if that person had a criminal record. Their Lordships added that the use of violence for political ends was not a political opinion. While the wording of the Equality Act 2010 is different (it refers to religious or philosophical belief), the approach and interpretation adopted in this case are likely to be similar.

Recent judgments suggest a willingness to adopt a fairly broad approach to what beliefs are covered. In *Nicholson v Grainger plc* [2010] IRLR 4, the EAT adopted a more expansive approach when it upheld a tribunal decision that an employee's belief that action was needed urgently to address climate change, could amount to a philosophical belief as it was cogent, serious, coherent and worthy of respect in a democratic society. The EAT rejected the argument that political or science-based beliefs could not fall with the meaning of 'philosophical belief'. See also *McFarlane v Relate Avon Ltd* [2010] IRLR 872 (where the Court of Appeal sought to draw a (fine) distinction between the holding of a belief system and its communication or manifestation in the workplace) and the tribunal cases of *Kelly v Unison* (ET/2203854/08) (where the question was whether a person who was a Marxist/Trotskyite could argue that he was dismissed because of his political beliefs), *Hashman v Milton Park (Dorset) Ltd* (ET/3105555/09) (a gardner's belief in the sanctity of life, extending to a fervent anti-fox hunting belief, was a protected philosophical belief), *Lisk v Shield Guardian Ltd* (ET/3300873/11) (a belief that individuals should wear poppies was too narrow to constitute a protected belief) and *Mr D Maistry v The BBC* (ET/1313142/10) (a journalist's belief in the 'higher purpose' of public service broadcasting was a philosophical belief).

In November 2012, the ECtHR upheld a complaint by Arthur Redfearn, a bus driver in Bradford (serving a largely Asian population) who was dismissed when he stood as a BNP candidate, that he had been discriminated against on the grounds of political opinion or affiliation, which put the UK in breach of Article 11 of the ECHR (freedom of association) (*Redfearn v UK* [2012] ECHR 1878).

This was a case heard in the UK courts before the Religion or Belief Regulations 2003 were implemented. The Court of Appeal (see *Redfearn v Serco Ltd t/a West Yorkshire Transport Service* [2006] IRLR 623) rejected Mr Redfearn's claim that he had been discriminated against on racial grounds. (He did not have sufficient service to bring an unfair dismissal claim.) Mummery LJ concluded, 'properly analysed' Mr Redfearn's complaint is of discrimination on political grounds, which falls outside the anti-discrimination laws: Mr Redfearn was not dismissed simply because he was white – so he was not discriminated against, and Serco would have dismissed any driver of any race who stood for a similarly racially-segregated political party – so he did not suffer indirect discrimination either. The Religion or Belief Regulations 2003 (which have now been replaced by the Equality Act 2010) did contain protection for 'philosophical beliefs', but early decisions rejected arguments that this phrase included 'political beliefs'; and BNP members have not managed to persuade tribunals that their membership amounts to a philosophical belief (see eg *Wingfield v North Cumbria Trust*).

The ECtHR has previously distinguished between political opinions that are legal but extreme (eg the National Front) and those that are illegal (eg supporting terrorism). In this case, the ECtHR was split 4:3 in Mr Redfearn's favour. It did not find that Mr Redfearn was either unfairly dismissed or discriminated against; it held that there was not a proper opportunity for him to argue his case. While s 10 of the Equality Act 2010 (replacing the Religion or Belief Regulations 2003) does not expressly include political beliefs, the Equality Directive 2007/78/EC contains no such qualification; it is arguable that Serco, which was treated as a private employer, is an emanation of the state, such that the Equality Directive was directly enforceable against it. At the time the case was argued before the Court of Appeal, the BNP was characterised as a party that confined its membership to white people. Since then, following proceedings brought against the BNP by the EHRC, this is no longer strictly true, which may make it harder to dismiss BNP members from sensitive posts. The Government's response to the case is awaited, in particular whether it will extend s 10 of the Equality Act 2010 to cover political beliefs.

There are two particularly tricky issues when looking at religion or belief discrimination. One concerns the extent to which law protects the manifestation of beliefs as opposed to the holding of them, particularly at work (see *McFarlane v Relate* (above) and **10.2.3** below). The other is the apparent conflict with the protection of sexual orientation (see *Ladele v London Borough of Islington* (**9.2.5.1**) and *McFarlane v Relate* – note that both claimants in these cases have taken their cases to the ECtHR under Articles 9 and 14 of the ECHR).

8.2.4 Sexual orientation

Sexual orientation is defined in s 12 of the Act:

> (1)   Sexual orientation means a person's sexual orientation towards—
>
> (a)   persons of the same sex,

> (b) persons of the opposite sex, or
>
> (c) persons of either sex.
>
> (2) In relation to the protected characteristic of sexual orientation—
>
> > (a) a reference to a person who has a particular protected characteristic is a reference to a person who is of a particular sexual orientation;
> >
> > (b) a reference to persons who share a protected characteristic is a reference to persons who are of the same sexual orientation.

The Explanatory Notes give examples:

- A man who experiences sexual attraction towards both men and women is 'bisexual' in terms of sexual orientation even if he has only had relationships with women.
- A man and a woman who are both attracted only to people of the opposite sex from them share a sexual orientation.
- A man who is attracted only to other men is a gay man. A woman who is attracted only to other women is a lesbian. So a gay man and a lesbian share a sexual orientation.

8.2.5 Gender reassignment

Gender reassignment is defined in s 7 of the Act:

> (1) A person has the protected characteristic of gender reassignment if the person is proposing to undergo, is undergoing or has undergone a process (or part of a process) for the purpose of reassigning the person's sex by changing physiological or other attributes of sex.
>
> (2) A reference to a transsexual person is a reference to a person who has the protected characteristic of gender reassignment.
>
> (3) In relation to the protected characteristic of gender reassignment—
>
> > (a) a reference to a person who has a particular protected characteristic is a reference to a transsexual person;
> >
> > (b) a reference to persons who share a protected characteristic is a reference to transsexual persons.

The Explanatory Notes give examples:

- A person who was born physically male decides to spend the rest of his life living as a woman. He declares his intention to his manager at work, who makes appropriate arrangements, and she then starts life at work and home as a woman. After discussion with her doctor and a Gender Identity Clinic, she starts hormone treatment and after several years she goes through gender reassignment surgery. She would have the protected characteristic of gender reassignment for the purposes of the Act.
- A person who was born physically female decides to spend the rest of her life as a man. He starts and continues to live as a man. He decides not to seek medical advice as he successfully 'passes' as a man without the need for any medical intervention. He would have the protected characteristic of gender reassignment for the purposes of the Act.

Note that the requirement under the Sex Discrimination Act of being under medical supervision has been removed. This is because gender reassignment is recognised as a personal process rather than a medical one.

8.2.6 Marriage and civil partnership

Marriage and civil partnership is defined in s 8 of the Act:

> (1) A person has the protected characteristic of marriage and civil partnership if the person is married or is a civil partner.
>
> (2) In relation to the protected characteristic of marriage and civil partnership—
>
> > (a) a reference to a person who has a particular protected characteristic is a reference to a person who is married or is a civil partner;
> >
> > (b) a reference to persons who share a protected characteristic is a reference to persons who are married or are civil partners.

The Explanatory Notes give examples:

- A person who is engaged to be married is not married and therefore does not have this protected characteristic.
- A divorcee or a person whose civil partnership has been dissolved is not married or in a civil partnership and therefore does not have this protected characteristic.

Marriage and civil partnership does not include those who are single and cohabiting.

8.2.7 Pregnancy and maternity leave

See **9. 4** below.

8.3 PROHIBITED CONDUCT

The Act outlaws:

(a)   direct discrimination (s 13) (see **Chapter 9**);

(b)   indirect discrimination (s 19) (see **Chapter 10**);

(c)   harassment (s 26) (see **Chapter 11**);

(d)   victimisation (s 27) (see **Chapter 11**);

(e)   instructing, causing, inducing and helping discrimination;

in relation to each of the protected characteristics. There are some differences with regard to age and disability. These characteristics are therefore dealt with separately in **Chapters 12** and **13**.

The Act also outlaws discrimination where a person is absent from work because of gender reassignment (s 16) (see **9.3**) and discrimination where a woman is absent from work as a result of pregnancy or illness caused by the pregnancy (s 18) (see **9.4**).

The prohibited conduct gives rise to a cause of action only if it falls within an area that the Act makes unlawful. The relevant part of the Act for employment purposes is Part 5 'Work'. Section 120 provides that an employment tribunal has jurisdiction to determine complaints relating to a breach of Part 5 provisions (see **8.4** for the relevant unlawful acts).

The EHRC non-statutory guidance on 'What equality law means for you as an employer: when you recruit someone to work for you' gives the following examples of the various types of discrimination:

> You must not treat a person **worse** than someone else just because of a protected characteristic (this is called **direct discrimination**).
>
> For example:

> - An employer does not interview a job applicant because of the applicant's ethnic background.
> - An employer says in a job advert 'this job is unsuitable for disabled people'.

> You must not do something to someone in a way that has a worse impact on them and other people who share a particular protected characteristic than on people who do not have that characteristic. Unless you can show that what you have done, or intend to do, is **objectively justified**, this will be **indirect discrimination**. 'Doing something' can include making a decision, or applying a rule or way of doing things.
>
> For example:

> A job involves travelling to lots of different places to see clients. An employer says that, to get the job, the successful applicant has to be able to drive. This may stop some disabled people applying if they cannot drive. But there may be other perfectly good ways of getting from one appointment to another, which disabled people who cannot themselves drive could use. So the employer needs to show that a requirement to be able to drive is objectively justified, or they may be discriminating unlawfully against people who cannot drive because of their disability.

You must not treat a disabled person **unfavourably** because of something connected to their disability where you cannot show that what you are doing is **objectively justified**. This only applies if you know or could reasonably have been expected to know that the person is a disabled person. This is called **discrimination arising from disability**

For example:

> An employer tells a visually impaired person who uses an assistance dog that they are unsuitable for a job because the employer is nervous of dogs and would not allow it in the office. Unless the employer can objectively justify what they have done, this is likely to be discrimination arising from disability. The refusal to consider the visually impaired person for the job is unfavourable treatment which is because of something connected to their disability (their use of an assistance dog). It may also be a failure to make a reasonable adjustment.

You must not treat a person worse than someone else because they are **associated with** a person who has a protected characteristic.

For example:

> An employer does not give someone the job, even though they are the best-qualified person, just because the applicant tells the employer they have a disabled partner. This is probably direct discrimination because of disability by association. Direct discrimination cannot be justified, whatever the employer's motive.

You must not treat a person worse because you incorrectly think they have a protected characteristic (**perception**).

For example:

> An employer does not give an applicant the job, even though they are the best-qualified person, because they incorrectly think the applicant is gay. This is still direct discrimination because of sexual orientation.

You must not treat a person badly or **victimise** them because they have complained about discrimination or helped someone else complain or have done anything to uphold their own or someone else's equality law rights.

For example:

> An employer does not shortlist a person for interview, even though they are well-qualified for the job, because last year they said they thought the employer had discriminated against them in not shortlisting them for another job.

You must not **harass** a person.

For example:

> An employer makes someone feel humiliated by telling jokes about their religion or belief during the interview. This may amount to harassment.

In addition, to make sure that disabled people have the same access, as far as is reasonable, to everything that is involved in getting and doing a job as a non-disabled person, you must make **reasonable adjustments**.

Before looking in detail at each of these types of discrimination, we shall first consider what constitutes an unlawful act of discrimination. Discrimination is not in itself outlawed: it must be accompanied by an unlawful act.

8.4   UNLAWFUL ACTS OF DISCRIMINATION – IN THE EMPLOYMENT FIELD

Unlawful discrimination in the employment field against job applicants and employees/ workers is prohibited by ss 39 and 40 of the Act. These sections make it unlawful for an employer directly or indirectly to discriminate against, victimise or harass employees and people seeking work. They apply where the employer is making arrangements to fill a job, and in respect of anything done in the course of a person's employment.

Other sections create causes of action for contract workers (s 41), police officers (ss 42–43), partnerships (ss 44–46), barristers and advocates (ss 47–48), office holders (ss 49–52, Sch 6) and trade union members (s 57). Section 108 prohibits discrimination and harassment against former employees and other groups referred to in this section. For a recent pre-Equality Act 2010 decision on the meaning of 'contract worker' in discrimination legislation, see *Leeds City Council v Woodhouse* [2010] IRLR 625, where the Court of Appeal rejected a submission that it is necessary for the alleged contract worker to show that the respondent had control or influence over the work that he did.

8.4.1 Recruitment

Under s 39(1) of the Act:

> An employer (A) must not discriminate against a person (B)—
>
> (a)   in the arrangements A makes for deciding to whom to offer employment;
>
> (b)   as to the terms on which A offers B employment;
>
> (c)   by not offering B employment.

Section 39(3) contains an identical provision with regard to victimisation, and s 40(1) protects job seekers from harassment.

Readers should note that under the Immigration, Asylum and Nationality Act 2006, an employer is expected to ensure that any migrant workers whom it employs are eligible to work in the UK. Section 15 of the 2006 Act provides that an employer who employs a person subject to immigration control who does not have the right to take employment, shall be guilty of a civil offence and liable to payment of a civil financial penalty (see **1.4**). The 2006 Act allows employers to avoid the penalty if they have carried out specific checks on documents. Checking the documents of prospective employees provides an employer with what is known as a 'statutory excuse'. For workers with a time-limit on how long they can stay in the UK, employers must repeat the document checks at least once a year to retain the 'statutory excuse'. The 2006 Act also (s 21) makes it a criminal offence knowingly to employ someone who has no permission to work in the UK. (For a case where the EAT considered the immigration rules, see *Kelly v University of Southampton* (UKEAT/0295/07).)

Since 29 February 2008, tough new penalties have been in force for anyone caught employing illegal migrants. However, an employer also needs to take care that, when implementing or exercising measures to prevent illegal working, he also avoids unlawful discrimination. While taking proper steps to ascertain that an employee does have a right to work, careful consideration must be given to when to ask questions of applicants to avoid discriminating on the grounds of race (see, eg, *Osborne Clarke Services v Purohit* [2009] IRLR 341).

An updated Code of Practice for all employers on the avoidance of unlawful race discrimination in recruitment practice while seeking to prevent illegal working came into effect in February 2008. The Code states that 'information about eligibility to work in the UK ... should preferably be verified in the final stages of the selection process, to make sure that the appointment is based on merit alone and is not influenced by other factors'. The current version of the Code is available on the Home Office UK Border Agency website at <http://www.ukba.homeoffice.gov.uk/sitecontent/documents/employersandsponsors/preventingillegalworking/currentguidanceandcodes/antidiscriminationcode2008.pdf>.

Also available on the website is the Home Office UK Border Agency 'Comprehensive Guidance' for employers on preventing illegal working: <http://www.ukba.homeoffice.gov.uk/sitecontent/documents/employersandsponsors/preventingillegalworking/currentguidanceandcodes/comprehensiveguidancefeb08.pdf> and <http://www.ukba.homeoffice.gov.uk/sitecontent/documents/employersandsponsors/preventingillegalworking/currentguidanceandcodes/whatemployersneedtoknow.pdf>.

Specific guidance is also available for employers on the status of asylum seekers, refugees and those with Humanitarian Protection at

<http://www.ukba.homeoffice.gov.uk/sitecontent/documents/employersandsponsors/
preventingillegalworking/currentguidanceandcodes/guide-for-employers-asylum.pdf>.

The best way for employers to ensure that they do not discriminate is to treat all job applicants
the same way at each stage of the recruitment process. In other words, to carry out document
checks on all prospective employees and not make assumptions about a person's right to work
based on that person's background, appearance or accent. A step-by-step guide to employing
migrants and conducting the appropriate right to work checks is available on the Business
Link website at <www.businesslink.gov.uk/emw>.

The various EU equality directives permit positive action. Section 159 of the 2010 Act allows
(but does not require) an employer to take a protected characteristic into account when
deciding whom to recruit, where persons who share a protected characteristic suffer a
disadvantage connected to the characteristic, or participation in an activity by persons who
share a protected characteristic is disproportionately low. This can be done only where
candidates are equally qualified. This does not allow employers automatically to prefer such
candidates. Each case must be considered on its merits, and any action must be a
proportionate means of addressing such disadvantage or under-representation.

8.4.2 Promotion and dismissal

Under s 39(2) of the Act:

> An employer (A) must not discriminate against an employee of A's (B)—
>
> (a)   as to B's terms of employment;
>
> (b)   in the way A affords B access, or by not affording B access, to opportunities for promotion,
> transfer or training or for receiving any other benefit, facility or service;
>
> (c)   by dismissing B;
>
> (d)   by subjecting B to any other detriment.

Dismissal, for the purposes of the Act, includes constructive dismissal (s 39(7)). Detriment
does not include harassment (s 212).

Section 39(4) contains an identical provision with regard to victimisation, and s 40(1)
protects employees from harassment.

8.4.3 Post-employment discrimination

Section 108 prohibits discrimination after the employment relationship has ended. Where an
employment relationship has come to an end, it is unlawful for the employer to discriminate
against the former employee or by harassing the former employee where the discrimination
arises out of and is closely connected to that former relationship.

The Explanatory Notes give examples, one of which is:

> A[n] ... employer refuses to give a reference to an ... ex-employee because of his or her religion or
> belief. This would be direct discrimination.

However, if the post-employment treatment which is being challenged constitutes
victimisation, it must be dealt with under the victimisation provisions and not under s 108
(see **11.7.2**).

8.4.4 Advertisements

Under the old discrimination legislation, there were specific provisions about discriminatory
advertisements (for example in s 29 of the RRA 1976 and s 38 of the SDA 1975; there was
never a specific prohibition in the now repealed Age Regulations). These were all repealed by
the Act, along with the specific sections of the Equality Act 2006 which dealt with advertising.
There is no specific provision in the Act regarding discriminatory advertisements, so
publishers are no longer required to prove they relied reasonably on an assurance from the
creator of an advertisement. Instead, s 13 of the Act, which prohibits direct discrimination, is

intended to embrace discriminatory advertisements. The Explanatory Notes gives this as an example of direct discrimination:

> If an employer advertising a vacancy makes it clear in the advert that Roma need not apply, this would amount to direct race discrimination against a Roma who might reasonably have considered applying for the job but was deterred from doing so because of the advertisement.

The EHRC has enforcement powers which cover both direct and indirect discrimination, and may bring prosecutions against employers.

8.5 OCCUPATIONAL REQUIREMENTS

Schedule 9, Pt 1, para 1 to the Equality Act 2010 provides that:

(1)   A person (A) does not contravene a provision [in relation to recruitment, training or dismissal] by applying a requirement to have a particular protected characteristic, if A shows that, having regard to the nature or context of the work—

    (a)   it is an occupational requirement,

    (b)   the application of the requirement is a proportionate means of achieving a legitimate aim, and

    (c)   the person to whom A applies the requirement does not meet it (or A has reasonable grounds for not being satisfied that the person meets it).

The Act therefore provides a general exception to what would otherwise be unlawful direct discrimination in relation to work.

The exception in para 1 applies where being of a particular sex, race, religion or belief, sexual orientation – or not being a transsexual person, married or a civil partner – is a requirement for the work, and the person to whom it is applied does not meet it (or, except in the case of sex, does not meet it to the reasonable satisfaction of the person who applied it). The requirement must be crucial to the post and not merely one of several important factors. It also must not be a sham or pretext. In addition, applying the requirement must be a proportionate way of achieving a legitimate aim, ie it must be the least restrictive way of achieving the aim.

Examples of para 1 occupational requirements given in the Explanatory Notes to the Act include:

- The need for authenticity or realism might require someone of a particular race, or sex for acting roles (for example, a black man to play the part of Othello) or modelling jobs.
- Considerations of privacy or decency might require a public changing room or lavatory attendant to be of the same sex as those using the facilities
- Unemployed Muslim women might not take advantage of the services of an outreach worker to help them find employment if they were provided by a man.

Schedule 9, Pt 1, para 2 to the Act provides for exceptions in relation to religious requirements relating to sex, transsexuals, married persons and civil partners, and sexual orientation:

(1)   A person (A) does not contravene a provision by applying [in relation to recruitment, training or dismissal] a requirement to which subparagraph (4) applies if A shows that—

    (a)   the employment is for the purposes of an organised religion,

    (b)   the application of the requirement engages the compliance or non-conflict principle, and

    (c)   the person to whom A applies the requirement does not meet it (or A has reasonable grounds for not being satisfied that the person meets it).

    ...

(5)   The application of a requirement engages the compliance principle if the application is a proportionate means of complying with the doctrines of the religion.

(6)   The application of a requirement engages the non-conflict principle if, because of the nature or context of the employment, the requirement is applied so as to avoid conflicting with the strongly held religious convictions of a significant number of the religion's followers.

The exception in para 2 allows the employer to apply a requirement to be of a particular sex or not to be a transsexual person, or to make a requirement related to the employee's marriage or civil partnership status or sexual orientation, but only if:

(a) appointing a person who meets the requirement in question is a proportionate way of complying with the doctrines of the religion; or

(b) because of the nature or context of the employment, employing a person who meets the requirement is a proportionate way of avoiding conflict with a significant number of the religion's followers' strongly held religious convictions.

Examples of para 2 occupational requirements given in the Explanatory Notes to the Act include:

- a requirement that a Catholic priest be a man and unmarried.
- unlikely to permit a requirement that a church youth worker who primarily organises sporting activities is celibate if he is gay, but it may apply if the youth worker mainly teaches Bible classes.
- would not apply to a requirement that a church accountant be celibate if he is gay.

In *Sheridan v Prospects for People with Learning Disabilities* (ET/2901366/06), a tribunal held that a Christian charity providing support services for people with learning disabilities could not rely on the (as it was then) 'genuine occupational requirement' exemption to operate a blanket 'Christians only' policy as the work was primarily secular in nature: it could not be said that being of a particular religion was essential for performing the functions of the post.

8.6 VICARIOUS LIABILITY

Under s 109 of the Act, an employer is vicariously liable for acts of discrimination by his employees during the course of their employment. This is so whether or not the acts were done with the employer's knowledge or approval. However, it is a defence for the employer to show that he took such steps as were reasonable to prevent an employee doing the act complained of.

8.6.1 Course of employment

In *Jones v Tower Boot Co Ltd* [1997] IRLR 168, CA, Mr Jones was subjected to acts of racial harassment by other employees, including having his arm burnt with a hot screwdriver; having metal bolts thrown at his head; having his legs whipped with a piece of welt; and being called 'chimp', 'monkey' and 'baboon'. The EAT held that the acts complained of could not by any stretch of the imagination be regarded as an improper mode of performing authorised tasks, and found for the employers. This decision initially caused much concern because no one is employed to harass another employee. However, the Court of Appeal reversed the decision because the EAT had erred in applying the old common law test of an employer's vicarious liability. The words 'in the course of employment' should be interpreted in the sense in which they are employed in everyday speech and not restrictively by reference to the old principles laid down for establishing an employer's vicarious liability for the torts committed by an employee. Otherwise, the more heinous the act of discrimination, the less likely it would be that the employer would be liable. Note, too, that the House of Lords re-assessed the test used to establish the vicarious liability of employers at common law for the tortious acts of employees. The decision in *Lister and Others v Hesley Hall Ltd* [2001] IRLR 472 brings the statutory and common law approaches to vicarious liability more in line. (For an interesting, more recent decision on the scope of vicarious liability – but not specifically in a discrimination context – see *Maga v Birmingham Roman Catholic Archdiocese Trustees* [2010] All ER (D) 141.)

In *Chief Constable of the Lincolnshire Police v Stubbs and Others* [1999] IRLR 81, a police officer was found to be acting 'in the course of employment' when he subjected the applicant to inappropriate sexual behaviour, even though the incidents occurred at social gatherings either immediately after work or at an organised leaving party. They were not chance meetings. The officer's employer was, on the facts, held to be vicariously liable for his actions under s 41 of the SDA 1975.

In *Sidhu v Aerospace Composite Technology Ltd* [2000] IRLR 602, the Court of Appeal upheld the tribunal's decision that a racial assault upon the applicant by a colleague during a family day out organised by the employer had not taken place 'in the course of employment', since the outing was in a public place, the employees had attended during their own time, and the majority of those attending were family and friends of the employees as opposed to employees.

8.6.2 'Reasonable steps' defence

Section 109(4) sets out the 'reasonably practicable' defence:

> In proceedings against A's employer (B) in respect of anything alleged to have been done by A in the course of A's employment it is a defence for B to show that B took all reasonable steps to prevent A—
>
> (a)   from doing that thing, or
>
> (b)   from doing anything of that description.

This defence is often unsuccessful. The employer must take preventative action. A written equal opportunities policy is unlikely to succeed unless it is implemented actively.

The European Recommendation and Code of Practice on the Dignity of Women and Men at Work (92/131/EEC) makes specific recommendations to employers on how to combat sexual harassment. Tribunals will look at whether employers have complied with these recommendations in deciding whether the employer is liable. The Code recommends that:

(a)   employers should issue a policy statement which expressly states that all employees have the right to be treated with dignity, that sexual harassment at work will not be permitted or condoned and that employees have the right to complain about it should it occur;

(b)   the policy should then be communicated to all employees so that they are aware that they have a right to complain and to whom they should complain. In this way, employees are made aware of the likely consequences of engaging in sexual harassment;

(c)   managers and supervisors have a particular duty to ensure that sexual harassment does not occur in the area for which they are responsible; they should explain the policy to their staff, and be responsive and supportive in confidentiality to anyone who complains;

(d)   managers and supervisors should be given training on their responsibilities in relation to sexual harassment and to ensure that they are aware of the factors which contribute to a working environment free from sexual harassment.

The Code also makes some recommendations as to the procedures which employers should follow when dealing with allegations of sexual harassment:

(a)   both formal and informal methods of resolving the problems created by harassment should be available;

(b)   employers should designate someone to provide advice and assistance to employees who are subjected to sexual harassment;

(c)   a formal procedure should specify to whom complaints should be brought, and also set out an alternative if complaining to that person would be inappropriate for the employee in question;

(d)   internal investigations of complaints should be seen to be independent, objective and handled with due respect for the rights of both the complainant and the alleged harasser. Those carrying out the investigation should not be connected with the allegations;

(e)   violations of the employer's policy on sexual harassment should be treated as a disciplinary offence.

Useful guidance was also provided by the (former) CRE and EOC. For example, the CRE's 2005 Code stated that:

> The aim of an equal opportunity policy is to make sure that:
>
> (a)   No job applicant or worker receives less favourable treatment than another, on racial grounds;
>
> (b)   No job applicant or worker is placed at a disadvantage by requirements, provisions, criteria ... unless ... a necessary and appropriate means of achieving a legitimate aim; and shown to be justifiable on other than racial grounds;
>
> (c)   People from underrepresented racial groups are given training and encouragement to achieve equal opportunity within the organisation.

The sample policy on equal opportunities in employment published by the (former) CRE is extracted below:

> _____ [organisation's name] is committed to building an organisation that makes full use of the talents, skills, experience, and different cultural perspectives available in a multi-ethnic society, and where people feel they are respected and valued, and can achieve their potential regardless of race, colour, nationality, national or ethnic origins.
>
> _____ will follow the recommendations of the CRE's statutory Code of Practice on Racial Equality in Employment in all its employment policies, procedures and practices.
>
> The aims of this policy are to ensure that:
>
> •   no one receives less favourable treatment, on grounds of race, colour, nationality, or ethnic or national origins, or is disadvantaged by any conditions, requirements, provisions, criteria, procedures or practices that cannot be justified on non-racial grounds, or victimised for taking action against racial discrimination or harassment, or instructed or put under pressure to discriminate against, or harass, someone on racial grounds;
>
> •   the organisation is free of unwanted conduct that violates the dignity of workers or creates an intimidating, hostile, degrading, offensive or humiliating environment;
>
> •   opportunities for employment, training and promotion are equally open to candidates from all racial groups; and
>
> •   selection for employment, promotion, transfer and training, and access to benefits, facilities and services, will be fair and equitable, and based solely on merit.
>
> This policy applies to all aspects of employment, from recruitment to dismissal and former workers' rights.
>
> We will take the following steps to put the policy into practice and make sure it is achieving its ends.
>
> •   The policy will be a priority for the organisation.
>
> •   ___ (named senior manager and job title) will be responsible for the day-to-day operation of the policy.
>
> •   The policy will be communicated to all workers and job applicants, and will be placed on the organisation's intranet and website.
>
> •   Workers and their representatives and trade unions will be consulted regularly about the policy, and about related action plans and strategies.
>
> •   All workers will be trained on the policy; on their rights and responsibilities under the policy, and on how the policy will affect the way they carry out their duties. No one will be in any doubt about what constitutes acceptable and unacceptable conduct in the organisation.
>
> •   Managers and workers in key decision-making areas will be trained on the discriminatory effects that provisions, practices, requirements, conditions, and criteria can have on some racial groups, and the importance of being able to justify decisions to apply them.
>
> •   Complaints about racial discrimination or harassment in the course of employment will be regarded seriously, and may result in disciplinary sanctions, and even dismissal. The complaints procedure will be published in a form that is easily accessible.

- Opportunities for employment, promotion, transfer and training will be advertised widely, internally and externally, and all applicants will be welcomed, irrespective of race, colour, nationality or ethnic or national origins.
- All workers will be encouraged to develop their skills and qualifications, and to take advantage of promotion and development opportunities in the organisation.
- Selection criteria will be entirely related to the job or training opportunity.
- Information on the ethnic and racial backgrounds of workers and applicants for employment, promotion and training will be collected and analysed, to monitor each stage of the recruitment process. The information will be held in strictest confidence and will only be used to promote equality of opportunity and prevent unlawful racial discrimination.
- If the data show that people from a particular racial group are under-represented in particular areas of work, lawful positive action training and encouragement will be considered for workers and others from that group, to improve their chances of applying successfully for vacancies in these areas.
- Grievances, disciplinary action, performance assessment, and terminations of employment, for whatever reason, will also be monitored by racial group.
- Requirements, conditions, provisions, criteria and practices will be reviewed regularly, in the light of the monitoring results, and revised, if they are found to, or might, discriminate unlawfully on racial grounds.
- All contracts between ____ and contractors to supply goods, materials or services will include a clause prohibiting unlawful racial discrimination or harassment by contractors and their staff, and by any sub-contractors and their staff. The clause will also encourage contractors and potential contractors to provide equality of opportunity in their employment practices.
- An equal opportunities action plan will be drawn up, with racial equality targets and timetables, to show what steps the organisation plans to take to achieve equality of opportunity.
- The effectiveness of the policy and the plan will be monitored regularly. A report on progress will be produced each year, and published via the intranet, the website, the staff newsletter, notice boards, and the annual report.
- Customers and clients will be made aware of the policy, and of their right to fair and equal treatment, irrespective of race, colour, nationality or ethnic or national origins.

This policy has been endorsed by ____ [an appropriate senior person] and has the full support of the management/board.

The policy was approved on ____ [insert date], following consultation with senior managers, workers, workers' representatives and trade unions.

Overall responsibility for the effectiveness of this policy lies with ___ [an appropriate senior person].

All staff are responsible for familiarising themselves with this policy. Managers must also make sure their workers know about, and follow, the policy.

For further information, please contact [insert name and details].

In *Caspersz v Ministry of Defence* (UKEAT/0599/05), the EAT held that the tribunal was correct to take the two-stage approach referred to in *Canniffe v East Riding of Yorkshire Council* [2000] IRLR 555, which is that a tribunal should:

(a) identify whether a respondent took any steps at all to prevent the employee from doing the act or acts complained of; and

(b) having identified what steps, if any, the employer took, consider whether there were any further acts that the employer could have taken which were reasonably practicable.

The EHRC's Code of Practice suggests that reasonable steps will include training and implementation of an equality policy. An extract appears below:

18.5 It is essential that a written equality policy is backed by a clear programme of action for implementation and continual review. It is a process which consists of four key stages: planning, implementing, monitoring and reviewing the equality policy.

...

18.7 A written equality policy should set out the employer's general approach to equality and diversity issues in the workplace. The policy should make clear that the employer intends to develop and apply procedures which do not discriminate because of any of the protected characteristics, and which provide equality of opportunity for all job applicants and workers.

Planning the content of equality policies

18.8 Most policies will include the following:

- a statement of the employer's commitment to equal opportunity for all job applicants and workers;
- what is and is not acceptable behaviour at work (also referring to conduct near the workplace and at work-related social functions where relevant);
- the rights and responsibilities of everyone to whom the policy applies, and procedures for dealing with any concerns and complaints;
- how the policy may apply to the employer's other policies and procedures;
- how the employer will deal with any breaches of policy;
- who is responsible for the policy; and
- how the policy will be implemented and details of monitoring and review procedures.

18.9 It will help an employer avoid discrimination if the equality policy covers all aspects of employment including recruitment, terms and conditions of work, training and development, promotion, performance, grievance, discipline and treatment of workers when their contract ends. ...

Planning an equality policy – protected characteristics

18.10 It is recommended that adopting one equality policy covering all protected characteristics is the most practical approach. Where separate policies are developed, such as a separate race equality or sex equality policy, they should be consistent with each other and with an overall commitment to promoting equality of opportunity in employment.

Implementing an equality policy

18.11 An equality policy should be more than a statement of good intentions; there should also be plans for its implementation. The policy should be in writing and drawn up in consultation with workers and any recognised trade unions or other workplace representatives, including any equality representatives within the workforce.

...

Promotion and communication of an equality policy

18.13 Employers should promote and publicise their equality policy as widely as possible and there are a number of ways in which this can be done. Promoting the policy is part of the process of effective implementation and will help an employer demonstrate that they have taken all reasonable steps to prevent discrimination.

18.14 Employers may use a number of methods of communication to promote their policy, including:

- email bulletins
- intranet and/or website
- induction packs
- team meetings
- office notice boards
- circulars, newsletters
- cascade systems
- training
- handbooks
- annual reports.

18.15 These methods of communication may not be appropriate in all cases.... Employers must also consider whether reasonable adjustments need to be made for disabled people so that they are able to access the information.

18.16 Promoting and communicating an equality policy should not be a one-off event. It is recommended that employers provide periodic reminders and updates to workers and others such as contractors and suppliers. Employers should also periodically review their advertising, recruitment and application materials and processes ...

Implementing an equality policy – training

18.18 Employers should ensure that all workers and agents understand the equality policy, how it affects them and the plans for putting it into practice. The best way to achieve this is by providing regular training.

18.19 Some workers may need more specific training, depending on what they do within the organisation. For example, line managers and senior management should receive detailed training on how to manage equality and diversity issues in the workplace.

18.20 The training should be designed in consultation with workers, their workplace representatives and managers and by incorporating feedback from any previous training into future courses.

18.21 Employers should make sure in-house trainers are themselves trained before running courses for other workers. External trainers also need to be fully informed about the employer's policies, including their equality policy ...

Monitoring and reviewing an equality policy

18.23 Equality monitoring enables an employer to find out whether their equality policy is working ...

8.6.3 Personal liability of employees

By virtue of s 110 of the Act, the employee for whose act the employer is liable (or would be so but for establishment of a defence that he took all reasonably practicable steps) is deemed to have aided that unlawful act. This means that the complainant may claim against both the employer and the employee who carried out the act of discrimination. It is not now necessary (as it was under the previous legislation) to show that the employee or agent knew that the act was unlawful. Section 111 covers instructing, causing or inducing contraventions of the Act, codifying the situation in *Weathersfield Ltd v Sargent* [1999] IRLR 94. It permits the intended victim to bring proceedings even if the instruction has not been carried out. Both the EHRC and B and/or C (if they are subjected to a detriment as a result of A's conduct, even where the instruction is not carried out) may bring enforcement proceedings in relation to any breach.

Note that if the employer is not vicariously liable for the acts of the employee because the acts did not take place during the course of employment, there can be no claim against the employee who carried out the discriminatory act. However, if the acts were committed during the course of employment then, even if the employer establishes the reasonably practicable defence, the employee may still be personally liable (*Yeboah v Crofton* [2002] IRLR 634). The Explanatory Notes give this example:

> A factory worker racially harasses her colleague. The factory owner would be liable for the worker's actions, but is able to show that he took all reasonable steps to stop the harassment. The colleague can still bring a claim against the factory worker in an employment tribunal.

The EAT held, in *Barlow v Stone* (UKEAT/0049/12), that an employment tribunal had jurisdiction to consider a claim of victimisation brought by an employee against a fellow employee even though no claim had been brought against their mutual employer. It will be interesting to see if the decision survives challenge.

8.7 RETIREMENT

The age at which the State retirement pension becomes payable is permitted to be discriminatory (EC Directive 79/7, Article 7). It is currently 65 for a man and between 60 and 65 for a woman. The State pension age for a woman will increase gradually from 2010, so that by 2020 it will be 66. If a woman was born before 5 April 1950, she can get her State pension from age 60; if she was born after 6 April 1955, she can get her State pension at 65; if she was born between April 1950 and April 1955, the date at which she can get her State pension will vary between 60 and 65, depending on her actual date of birth. The White Paper, *Security in Retirement*, proposed increasing the State pension age by one year in every decade, to reach 68 in 2046, but the Government announced in October 2010 that it will bring this forward so that the State pension age will be 66 by 2020. There will therefore be a gradual increase in the State pension age for men and women from 65 to 66 starting in 2018.

8.8 ENFORCEMENT AND REMEDIES

Enforcement proceedings may be brought either by an individual, or by the EHRC. The EHRC has power to investigate discriminatory practices and may serve a non-discrimination notice. Additionally, the EHRC can give assistance to an individual pursuing a claim.

The EHRC issued a Code of Practice which came into force on 6 April 2011. Whilst breach of the Code does not give rise to any legal liability, tribunals must take it into account if relevant.

The employment tribunal derives its jurisdiction from s 113 and ss 120–135 of the Act. An employment tribunal has jurisdiction, inter alia, to determine a complaint relating to a contravention of Part 5 (work) (ss 39–83), s 108 (prohibited conduct where work relationships have ended). Note that members of the armed forces must have first utilised the armed forces procedure before they can complain to an employment tribunal under Part 5 (s 121).

8.8.1 Enforcement by an individual

8.8.1.1 Time-limits

A complaint should be made to an employment tribunal within three months of the act complained of or such other period as the tribunal thinks just and equitable (s 123). In *London Borough of Southwark v Afolabi* [2003] IRLR 220, the Court of Appeal held that a tribunal is not required to go through the matters listed in s 33(3) of the Limitation Act 1980 as a checklist in considering whether it is just and equitable to extend time, provided no significant factor has been left out of account by the tribunal in exercising its discretion. The Court of Appeal confirmed in *Apelogun-Gabriels v London Borough of Lambeth* [2002] IRLR 116 that there is no general principle that it will be just and equitable to extend the three-month time-limit where the delay was caused by the applicant seeking to deal with the matter internally. In *Robertson v Bexley Community Centre* [2003] IRLR 434, the Court of Appeal emphasised that the exercise of discretion should be the exception rather than the rule. In *Carter v London Underground* (UKEAT/0292/08), the claimant's severe depression was a factor that was considered relevant.

Where there is a continuing act of discrimination, the three months do not start to run until the discrimination ceases. Where the discrimination consists of a failure to do something, the time-limit starts to run when the person decides not to do the thing in question. The concept of 'continuing acts' of discrimination has generated much case law over the years and is a matter that requires very careful consideration. Note that the Act states (s 212(2) and (3)) that a reference (however expressed) to an act includes a reference to an omission; and a reference (however expressed) to an omission includes a reference to:

(a)   a deliberate omission to do something;

(b)   a refusal to do it;

(c)   a failure to do it.

Continuing acts are distinguishable from one-off acts which have continuing consequences; time will run from the date of the one-off act complained of. Readers should consider the Court of Appeal decision on the question of continuing acts for further guidance (see *Hendricks v Commissioner of Police for the Metropolis* [2003] IRLR 96). See also *Aziz v FDA* [2010] EWCA Civ 304 for a more recent Court of Appeal decision.

8.8.1.2 Questionnaire procedure (s 138)

In October 2010 the Government published the Equality Act 2010 – Discrimination and Other Prohibited Conduct – Questions and Answers Forms, together with guidance to assist in completion of both forms. The forms and guidance may be found on the GEO's website.

The complainant can deliver a standard form of questionnaire to the respondent, to enable the complainant to decide whether to institute proceedings and, if so, how to present his case. The questionnaire can be served before the complaint is issued within three months of the act complained of, or within 28 days after presentation of the complaint. (Later service is possible, but only with leave of the tribunal.)

Although the respondent is not obliged to reply to the questionnaire, he will be well advised to do so: failure to reply, or the giving of evasive replies, can enable the tribunal to draw an inference that discrimination has occurred. The respondent has a period of eight weeks in which to reply. In D'Silva v NATFHE (UKEAT/0384/07), the EAT held that an employer's failure fully to answer a questionnnaire does not automatically raise a presumption of discrimination. The real significance is whether the failure can support an inference that the employer committed the discriminatory act: there will be situations in which a failure to deal with a questionnaire, however reprehensible, has no bearing at all on the employer's defence. See too Deer v Walford and Another (UKEAT/0283/10). (Note that tribunals may also draw inferences from evasive, incorrect or no replies in documents that are not the statutory questionnaire – see Dattani v Chief Constable of West Mercia Police [2005] IRLR 327.)

The Government has announced that the questionnaire procedure is to be abolished, although the date the change will be brought in is not yet known (see the draft Enterprise and Regulatory Reform Bill). The Government takes the view that the questionnaire process did not assist in pre-hearing settlements or in reducing claims, but in fact created a significant burden for employers.

8.8.2 Remedies

Under the previous discrimination legislation, tribunals' powers to award the same remedies were to be exercised where the tribunal considered it just and equitable to do so. Section 124 does not contain the words 'just and equitable', but because the words referred to the choice of remedy and not the amount of compensation to be awarded, the authors do not consider that the change of wording is significant.

8.8.2.1 Declaration, orders and recommendations

Under s 124 of the Act, if the complaint is well founded:

(2)   The tribunal may—
   (a)   make a declaration as to the rights of the complainant and the respondent in relation to the matters to which the proceedings relate;
   (b)   order the respondent to pay compensation to the complainant;
   (c)   make an appropriate recommendation.

(3)   An appropriate recommendation is a recommendation that within a specified period the respondent takes specified steps for the purpose of obviating or reducing the adverse effect of any matter to which the proceedings relate—
   (a)   on the complainant;
   (b)   on any other person.

Failure to comply with a recommendation in so far as it relates to the complainant, without reasonable excuse, can lead to an increase in the compensation ordered (s 124(7)).

The power to make a recommendation does not include a power to recommend that the employee should be promoted to the next suitable vacancy (British Gas v Sharma [1991] IRLR 101). However, in a change to the old law, recommendations no longer have to be aimed only at reducing the negative impact on the individual claimant(s) of the respondent's actions which gave rise to the successful claim, but may be aimed at reducing that impact on the wider workforce.

Examples given in the Explanatory Notes include the following:

A tribunal could recommend that the respondent:
   –   introduces an equal opportunities policy;
   –   ensures its harassment policy is more effectively implemented

-      sets up a review panel to deal with equal opportunities and harassment/grievance procedures;
-      re-trains staff; or
-      makes public the selection criteria used for transfer or promotion of staff.

In *Lycée Français Charles de Gaulle v Delambre* (UKEAT/0563/10), the EAT upheld the tribunal's recommendations that the respondent circulate the judgment to the Governing Board and management team, that the respondent review existing equal opportunities policies, and that it undertake a programme of formal equality and diversity training.

The Government has announced that it intends to repeal the power to make recommendations, although no provision has been included in any current legislation.

A declaration is an important statement of the decision. Most tribunals' findings result in a compensation order. The tribunal has power to order the respondent to pay compensation of an amount corresponding to the damages that could be ordered in a county court. There is no upper limit to the amount that may be ordered. Unlike compensation for unfair dismissal, compensation for discrimination is awarded on tortious principles. This means that the tribunal must, as far as it can, put the claimant in the position he would have been in 'but for' the discriminatory act. An employee has a duty to mitigate his losses. Although the Act no longer specifically refers to an award being made if the tribunal considers it just and equitable to do so, there is no reason to believe this will change the way in which tribunals make such awards.

There had been some uncertainty as to whether a compensatory award for discrimination may be reduced to take account of contributory fault. In *Way v Crouch* [2005] IRLR 603, the EAT concluded that compensation in discrimination cases may be subject to a deduction for contributory conduct on the part of the claimant (although the EAT found no grounds for any such deduction on the facts of the case). The EAT held that since an award of compensation in a discrimination case is of an amount corresponding to any damages that could have been ordered by a county court, it followed that any such award must be subject to the Law Reform (Contributory Negligence) Act 1945, which allows for reduction in compensation where the claimant's *conduct itself amounts to negligence or breach of a legal duty and contributed to the damage suffered.* This appears to be a much higher test than that applied in unfair dismissal cases. The EAT did not elaborate, however, on the kind of situations which would be likely to give a tribunal grounds for holding that a victim of discrimination has contributed to the loss or injury he has suffered.

8.8.2.2 Assessment of compensation

In deciding the appropriate level of compensation, the following matters will be taken into account:

(a)   Pecuniary loss arising directly from an act of discrimination, including past loss to the date of the hearing and future losses (to put the claimant in the position he would have been if the discrimination had not occurred). As far as the duty to mitigate is concerned, see *ICTS (UK) Ltd v Tchoula* [2000] IRLR 643, where undertaking a period of retraining was not treated as a failure to mitigate.

(b)   Injury to feelings. Whilst an award for injury to feelings is not made automatically, in the majority of cases it will be almost inevitable. Awards for injury to feelings are compensatory: they should not be about punishment; they should be just to both parties. Awards need to be sufficient to command public respect for the policy underlying anti-discrimination legislation. Case law suggests that it is appropriate for awards to bear some broad similarity to the range of awards in personal injury cases. In *HM Prison Service and Others v Johnson* [1997] IRLR 162, the EAT found no grounds for interfering with a tribunal's award of £21,000 compensation for injury to feelings and £7,500 for aggravated damages to an employee who had suffered racial discrimination over a period exceeding 18 months.

In *Vento v Chief Constable of West Yorkshire Police* [2003] IRLR 102, the Court of Appeal handed down guidance on awards for injury to feelings. The Court said that the top band of awards should normally be between £15,000 and £25,000, and apply only to the most serious cases. The middle band of £5,000–£15,000 should be used for serious cases not meriting the top award, and awards of £500–£5,000 should be made for less serious cases (eg, an isolated incident). Awards of less than £500 should be avoided. The EAT set out new guideline figures in *Da'Bell v NSPCC* (UKEAT/0227/09) to take account of inflation:

(i)   The lower band – the upper limit for this band has risen from £5,000 to £6,000.

(ii)   The middle band – the upper limit has risen from £15,000 to £18,000.

(iii) The upper band – the upper limit has risen from £25,000 to £30,000.

The EAT decision in *St Andrews School v Blundell* (UKEAT/0330/09) reviews some post-*Vento* authorities.

(c)   Aggravated damages where the respondent has behaved in a high-handed, malicious, insulting or oppressive manner. Aggravated damages, which are an aspect of the injury to feelings award, are compensatory in nature, not punitive (see *Commissioner of Police for the Metropolis v Shaw* (UKEAT/0125/11). The power to award aggravated damages is not statutory; it derives from other, non-statutory torts.

In *Shaw*, the EAT considered the three categories of circumstances identified in the Law Commission Report on Aggravated, Exemplary and Restitutionary Damages (1997) (Law Comm No 247) which may attract an award of aggravated damages. The first concerned the *manner* in which the wrong was committed. The distress caused by an act of discrimination may be made worse by its being done in an 'high-handed, malicious, insulting or oppressive' way (May LJ used this expression in *Alexander v Home Office* [1988] ICR 685). The EAT warned that this should not be treated as an exhaustive definition of the kind of behaviour which may justify an award of aggravated damages, pointing out that, as the Law Commission Report made clear, an award may be made in the case of any exceptional or contumelious conduct which has the effect of seriously increasing the claimant's distress. The second circumstance identified in the Report was the respondent's motive. The EAT said that conduct which is spiteful or vindictive, or based on prejudice or animosity, is more likely to cause distress. The third circumstance was the respondent's conduct after the tort which related to it. This might include, depending on the circumstances, a failure to apologise.

The EAT commented on the difficulty of distinguishing between the injury caused by the discriminatory act itself and the injury attributable to the aggravating elements: tribunals had to be aware of the risks of compensating claimants under both heads for the same loss. The ultimate question is whether the overall award is proportionate to the totality of the suffering caused. The EAT cautioned on the dangers of focusing too much on the conduct – which could lead down the dangerous route of equating damages with punishment. While the EAT expressed doubt as to the desirability of awarding aggravated damages as a separate head of compensation, as there was no 'bright line' by which to distinguish what part of the injury to the claimant's feelings resulted from the core act and what resulted from an exceptional feature, it felt the practice had been approved too many times to suggest that it was wrong, but suggested a better way of dealing with it might be to include it as a subheading of injury to feelings, ie 'injury to feelings in the sum of £x, incorporating aggravated damages in the sum of £y'. This might reduce the risk of a tribunal unwittingly introducing a punitive element into the calculation.

In *Zaiwalla & Co and Another v Walia* [2002] IRLR 697, the EAT held that employment tribunals can, exceptionally, award aggravated damages by reference to the conduct of the respondent in defending a claim. The Court of Appeal upheld an award of aggravated damages in *BT v Reid* [2004] IRLR 327. The Court said that on the facts the tribunal was entitled to take into account the fact that the transgressor was not punished and was indeed promoted before the charges against him were determined. The Court emphasised it was not 'laying down any principle that an employer cannot promote [in the circumstances, but it may, depending on the facts,] demonstrate the high-handedness of an employer'. The employee must have some awareness of the improper conduct or motive (*Ministry of Defence v Meredith* [1995] IRLR 52). Conduct in the course of litigation may be taken into account (*City of Bradford Metropolitan Council v Arora* [1991] IRLR 165, CA). In *Tameside Hospital NHS Foundation Trust v Mylott* (UKEAT/0352/09 and UKEAT/0399/10), the EAT quashed a tribunal award of aggravated damages where the tribunal found that a manager had acted in a brusque and insensitive manner towards the employee, and that in giving evidence she was dismissive and evasive: none of these was sufficient to support the making of an award of aggravated damages.

(d)   Exemplary damages may be awarded in discrimination cases but are rare. Exemplary damages punish the wrongdoer and should be awarded only for 'arbitrary and outrageous use of executive power' (see, eg, *Kuddus v Chief Constable of Leicestershire Constabulary* [2001] UKHL 29).

   In *Husain v Chief Constable of Kent* (ET, 6 April 2006), the employment tribunal awarded exemplary damages of £5,000 due to the seriousness of the discrimination. The police force had suggested that Mr Husain had falsified his qualifications and professional experience, and had circulated a report to this effect to other forces. Subsequently, Mr Husain was arrested and detained when he applied for a new job. The tribunal held that the suggestion that he was falsifying his qualifications was the result of racial stereotyping.

   In *Ministry of Defence v Fletcher* (UKEAT/0044/09), the EAT looked at the relationship between aggravated and exemplary damages, and upheld the aggravated damages award but overturned the exemplary damages award, finding no 'conscious and contumelious' wrongdoing.

(e)   Compensation for personal injury (psychiatric or physical injury) caused by the discrimination – see *Sheriff v Klyne Tugs (Lowestoft) Ltd* [1999] IRLR 481, CA. In *HM Prison Service v Salmon* [2001] IRLR 425, a female prison officer was awarded £21,000 for injury to feelings and £11,250 for personal injury in respect of psychiatric damage caused by sexual harassment. On appeal, the EAT recognised that there was a risk of double recovery, but that in principle injury to feelings and psychiatric injury are distinct, although in practice not always easy to separate.

   In *Essa v Laing Ltd* [2004] IRLR 313, the Court of Appeal held that compensation for unlawful discrimination is not limited to cases of reasonably foreseeable harm. A claimant simply has to show that the discrimination caused the harm. (See also *Taylor v XLN Telecom* (EAT/0383/09) for confirmation that a claimant is entitled to recover for injury (to feelings or personal injury) attributable to the act complained of (eg a racially motivated dismissal) and does not have to prove that the injury resulted from actual knowledge of the discrimination.)

(f)   In a case of indirect discrimination where the respondent proves that there was no intention to treat the claimant unfavourably, a tribunal cannot award damages to a claimant unless it has first considered making either a declaration or a recommendation (s 124(4) and (5)). The EAT held, in *JH Walker Ltd v Hussain and Others* [1996] IRLR 11, that a person will have intended an act if he intended the consequences of his act, ie he knew when he did the act that those consequences would follow and he wanted those consequences to follow. So, in this case, the company knew that the Islamic festival of Eid was important to Muslim employees, that only they were affected by prohibiting holidays from May to July, and that they were required to work on that day. Such discrimination was not, therefore, unintentional.

(g)   Pregnancy dismissals – loss of career prospects or congenial employment does not form a separate head of damage and should be catered for in the award for injury to feelings ((b) above). Estimated child-care costs should be set off against future loss of earnings.

(h)   Accelerated receipt – a discount should normally be applied (see **2.4.1.9**).

(i)   Section 207A of the TULR(C)A 1992 gives the tribunals discretion to increase or reduce awards by up to 25% where the employer or employee unreasonably fails to comply with the 2009 Acas Code.

(j)   Taxation – see the chart at **5.6.2.5**.

(k)   Interest – tribunals must consider whether to award interest. Any award must be calculated in accordance with the Employment Tribunal (Interest on Awards in Discrimination Cases) Regulations 1996 (SI 1996/2803). Interest on past pecuniary losses will generally be awarded from the midpoint date between the act of discrimination and the date of the tribunal hearing. Interest on injury to feelings runs from the date on which the unlawful act took place to the date of leaving. The rate from July 2009 is 0.3%. Note that there is no upper limit on the amount of compensation which may be awarded.

8.8.2.3   Joint and several liability

Employees who are held to have knowingly aided the employer are treated as if they themselves did the unlawful act(s), and tribunals have power to make a separate award against each respondent (see *Gilbank v Miles* [2006] IRLR 538). In practice, tribunals often make substantial awards against an employer and a small award against any individual who has been found to have committed any actual acts of discrimination. Tribunals may also treat the parties as joint tortfeasors and make one award against all respondents jointly and severally.

In *Way and Another v Crouch* [2005] IRLR 603, the EAT held that it is proper to make both the employer and any individual who has been found to have committed any actual acts of discrimination liable on a joint and several basis. In practice this allows the employee to sue the individual harasser for the full amount of any compensation if the employer turns out to be insolvent. The EAT emphasised that when making joint and several awards, tribunals must apportion the respective shares, so that if a claimant chooses to enforce against only one respondent, that respondent can still seek a suitable contribution. Any apportionment should be on the basis of respective culpability (and not on the financial strengths of the parties).

In *Munchkins Restaurant Ltd and Another v Karmazyn and Others* (UKEAT/0359/09), the EAT said (casting doubt on *Way v Crouch*) that the appropriate principle where there is an award of joint and several liability is that any one of the respondents is liable for the full extent of the damages to the claimant. Although, as between respondents, a respondent may have a right to seek contribution from a co-respondent, depending upon the relative contribution and responsibility of each of the respondents to the wrong which has been done, that should not affect the position of a claimant, who is entitled, if the award is joint and several, to receive the full extent of his award from any of the respondents as he chooses. The EAT held:

> as a matter of general approach, where there is more than one respondent to a claim ... a Tribunal will have to decide whether or not it is to make a joint and several award. In some cases the reason for it doing so will be obvious and need very little elaboration.

In *London Borough of Hackney v Sivanandan and Others* (UKEAT/0075/10) the employment tribunal found complaints of victimisation were valid and determined that the respondents were jointly and severally liable to pay the claimant £421,415. The tribunal declined to apportion liability as between the respondents. The EAT dismissed the council's appeal against the tribunal's decision that the award be joint and several, and held that (not following the dicta in *Way v Crouch* (above) that the Civil Liability (Contribution) Act 1978 provides a basis for the apportionment of the liability of 'concurrent' discriminators) where an employer and employee are jointly liable for the loss caused, each is liable for the entire award of compensation and there is no basis for the apportionment of damages. In *Brennan and Others v Sunderland District Council and Others* (UKEAT/0286/11), the EAT approved *Sivanandan* and said that the employment tribunal has no jurisdiction to determine claims for contribution under the Civil Liability (Contribution) Act 1978.

8.8.3 Removal of contractual term

Section 142 provides that a contractual term 'is unenforceable against a person in so far as it constitutes, promotes or provides for treatment of that or another person that is of a description prohibited by this Act'. The provisions also provide that a county court may, on the application of an interested party, make an order removing or modifying a term which is unenforceable against that party (s 143).

In *Mead-Hill v The British Council* [1995] IRLR 478, an employee sought to rely on these provisions in relation to a mobility clause. It was held that the insertion of the clause could amount to indirect discrimination against women, who form a higher proportion of secondary earners and, as such, are less likely to be able to relocate. However, it was open to the employers to show justification irrespective of sex.

8.9 EQUAL PAY AND THE EQUALITY CLAUSE

8.9.1 Introduction

What follows is merely a very brief introduction to this complex area of the law, the detail of which is beyond the scope of the book. The law was previously contained in the EPA 1970 as amended (principally by the SDA 1975); it is now contained in Pt 5 (work), Ch 3 (equality of terms) of the Equality Act 2010, which is designed to ensure that men and women within the same employment receive equal pay (and other contractual terms) for equal work. Equal pay for men and women for equal work is a requirement of EU law under Article 157 TFEU (ex 141 EC). The law works by implying an 'equality clause' into a contract. Lord Nicholls, in *Glasgow City Council and Others v Marshall and Others* [2000] 1 WLR 333, set out what was regarded as the proper approach (under the old law as set out in s 1 of the EPA 1970) to equal pay claims.

It is important to consider whether the claim is one that should be brought under the equal pay provisions, or one that should be brought under the discrimination provisions (above):

- If the less favourable treatment relates to the payment of money which is regulated by a contract of employment, only the equal pay provisions can apply.
- If the employee is treated less favourably than an employee of the other sex who is doing the same or broadly similar work, or whose work has been given an equal value under a job evaluation, and the less favourable treatment relates to some matter which is regulated by the contract of employment of either of them, only the equal pay provisions can apply. However, if the less favourable treatment relates to a matter which is not included in the contract, only the sex discrimination provisions can apply.
- If the less favourable treatment relates to a matter (other than the payment of money) in a contract, and the comparison is with workers who are not doing the same or broadly similar work, or work which has been given an equal value under a job evaluation, only the sex discrimination provisions can apply.
- Lastly, if the complaint relates to a matter which is regulated by an employee's contract of employment, but is based on an allegation that an employee of the other sex would be treated more favourably in similar circumstances (ie it does not relate to the actual treatment of an existing employee of the other sex but rather requires a hypothetical comparator), only the sex discrimination provisions can apply.

The distinctions are crucial in practice because there are different time-limits.

In *Birmingham City Council v Abdulla and Others* [2012] UKSC 47, the Supreme Court decided that equal pay claims, which would have been out of time in an employment tribunal, could be brought in the High Court.

8.9.1.1   The equality clause

Section 64(1) states that ss 66 to 70 apply where:

    (a)   a person (A) is employed on work that is equal to the work that a comparator of the opposite sex (B) does;

    ...

By s 66:

    (1)   If the terms of A's work do not (by whatever means) include a sex equality clause, they are to be treated as including one.

    (2)   A sex equality clause is a provision that has the following effect—

        (a)   if a term of A's is less favourable to A than a corresponding term of B's is to B, A's term is modified so as not to be less favourable;

        (b)   if A does not have a term which corresponds to a term of B's that benefits B, A's terms are modified so as to include such a term.

This has the effect of implying an equality clause into the contract of employment of a woman (or man), so that she (or he) is entitled to be treated no less favourably than a man (or woman) in the same employment.

Section 65 deals with what is meant by equal work:

    (1)   For the purposes of this Chapter, A's work is equal to that of B if it is—

        (a)   like B's work,

        (b)   rated as equivalent to B's work, or

        (c)   of equal value to B's work.

    (2)   A's work is like B's work if—

        (a) A's work and B's work are the same or broadly similar, and

        (b)   such differences as there are between their work are not of practical importance in relation to the terms of their work.

It will be necessary for a claimant in an equal pay case to be able to point to an actual (not hypothetical) comparator (however, note that no comparator is needed if it can be shown that the reason for not paying a woman the same as a man is because she is pregnant – see *Alabaster v Woolwich plc and DWP* [2005] IRLR 576). In *Walton Centre for Neurology v Bewley* (UKEAT/0564/07), the EAT held that a woman's successor in the job cannot be used as a comparator for the purposes of an equal pay claim. The comparator must be employed contemporaneously or be a predecessor. If there is no actual comparator available, the woman must bring a claim of direct sex discrimination claim against the employer. The example given in the Explanatory Notes is as follows:

> An employer tells a female employee 'I would pay you more if you were a man' ... In the absence of any male comparator the woman cannot bring a claim for breach of an equality clause but she can bring a claim of direct sex discrimination ... against the employer.

8.9.1.2   Defences

It is a defence to an equal pay claim to show that the difference in pay is due to a material factor which is relevant and significant, and which does not directly or indirectly discriminate against the worker because of her sex (s 69) . If there is evidence that the factor which explains the difference in terms is not directly discriminatory but would have an adverse impact on people of her sex (that is, without more, it would be indirectly discriminatory), the employer must show that it is a proportionate means of meeting a legitimate aim or the sex equality clause will apply. For these purposes, the long-term objective of reducing pay inequality will always count as a legitimate aim.

The EAT provided a useful step-by-step summary of the defence in *Bury Metropolitan Borough Council v Hamilton and Others; Council of the City of Sunderland v Brennan and Others* (UKEAT/0413–5/09):

(1) It is necessary first to identify the explanation for the differential complained of. (In the language of the statute, this is the 'factor' to which the differential is 'due'; but the terminology of 'explanation' used by Lord Nicholls in *Marshall* [*Glasgow City Council v Marshall* [2000] ICR 196] is generally less clumsy.) The burden of proof is on the employer.

(2) It is then necessary to consider whether that explanation is 'tainted with sex'. What that not altogether happy metaphor means is that the explanation relied on must not itself involve sex discrimination, whether direct or indirect (see per Lord Browne-Wilkinson in *Wallace* [*Strathclyde Regional Council v Wallace* [1998] ICR 205], at pp 211H–212A and per Lord Nicholls in *Marshall*, at pp 202H–203A).

(3) In considering whether the explanation involves direct or indirect discrimination, the ordinary principles of the law of discrimination apply. That means that:

(a) if the differential is the result of direct discrimination (in the sense established in *Nagarajan v London Regional Transport* [1999] ICR 877) the defence under section 1(3) will fail;

(b) if the differential involves indirect discrimination of either the 'PCP' or 'Enderby' type – as to this distinction, see para 16 below – the defence will fail unless the employer proves that the differential is objectively justified, applying the classic proportionality test;

(c) if the employer's explanation involves neither direct nor indirect discrimination the defence will succeed, even if the factor relied on cannot be objectively justified – this is most vividly illustrated by the 'mistake' cases such as *Yorkshire Blood Transfusion Service v Plaskitt* [1994] ICR 74 and *Tyldesley v TML Plastics* [1996] ICR 356, approved in *Wallace*.

(4) In conducting the exercise under (3), the ordinary principles governing the burden of proof in discrimination claims will apply. Thus if the claimant shows a prima facie case of discrimination (in the sense explained in *Madarassy v Nomura International plc* [2007] ICR 867), the burden shifts to the employer to prove the absence of discrimination.

In *Allen and Another v GMB* [2008] IRLR 690, the Court of Appeal upheld a tribunal decision that the GMB Union indirectly discriminated against union members by recommending acceptance of a 'single status' pay deal which grossly underestimated the compensation to be paid to female equal pay claimants. Although the objective of securing a fair single status pay deal was legitimate, the means used by the union were not proportionate. Permission to appeal to the House of Lords was refused.

In *Clark v Metropolitan Police Authority* (Mayor and City of London Court, Case No OMY00263, 26 May 2011), a part-time female inspector successfully challenged the Metropolitan Police's pay scheme. While, on its face, the terms were equal, and both full- and part-timers were paid for the hours they were due to work (for full-timers 40 hours and for part-timers according to their rotas), any hours worked over this were not paid. The effect was that if part-time and full-time inspectors worked the same number of hours but that number was greater than the part-timers' rota hours, the full-timers would be paid more. That pay differential was tainted by sex, as 96% of part-timers were women and 86% of full-timers were men. The Metropolitan Police Authority argued that the scheme had been agreed through collective bargaining, but the court said that was not sufficient to justify the inequality.

The equality clause does not apply to any provision affording women special treatment in connection with pregnancy or childbirth

8.9.1.3 Enforcement

In the event of a breach of the equality clause, the remedy is to present a complaint to an employment tribunal within six months of the end of the employment contract, or in some circumstances to bring a breach of contract claim in the civil courts within six years (*Birmingham City Council v Abdulla and Others* [2012] UKSC 47). The tribunal, if the complaint is well founded, may award arrears of remuneration and damages going back for up to six years for breach of the equality clause.

Note that unlike in sex discrimination claims, damages for non-pecuniary loss (such as injury to feelings and aggravated damages) cannot be recovered in equal pay claims (because such claims are based on contract and are not based on a statutory tort as in a discrimination claim) – see *City of Newcastle upon Tyne v Allan* [2005] IRLR 504.

8.10   PART-TIME WORKERS

The Part-time Workers (Prevention of Less Favourable Treatment) Regulations 2000 (SI 2000/ 1551) implement the European Part-time Work Directive (97/81/EC). Clause 4(1) of the Directive provides that:

> In respect of employment conditions, part-time workers shall not be treated in a less favourable manner than comparable full-time workers solely because they work part time unless different treatment is justified on objective grounds.

What follows is an overview. In addition to the 2000 Regulations, the Government has published Best Practice Guidance (see www.bis.gov.uk).

The 2000 Regulations make it unlawful for employers to treat part-time workers less favourably than full-time workers (unless different treatment can be objectively justified) in their terms and conditions, in areas such as:

(a)   hourly rates of pay;

(b)   overtime rates;

(c)   access to occupational pension schemes;

(d)   training;

(e)   (pro rata) holiday entitlement;

(f)   (pro rata) maternity/paternal leave;

(g)   (pro rata) sick pay.

Part-time workers should also be treated no less favourably when being selected for redundancy, unless the different treatment can be justified objectively.

The 2000 Regulations apply to 'workers', not just 'employees'. A part-time worker who is treated less favourably than a full-time worker is now able to bring a claim regardless of whether he or she is a man or a woman. Before the 2000 Regulations came into force, because part-time work is overwhelmingly done by women, claims of indirect sex discrimination were possible, but only by women part-time workers. Nevertheless, at present, if advising women, it would seem wise to run claims under both the Equality Act 2010 and the 2000 Regulations. Readers should consult the Regulations for detailed guidance.

The first case on what is required to make a part-time worker comparable with a full-time worker was decided by the House of Lords on 1 March 2006 (*Matthews v Kent and Medway Towns Fire Authority* [2006] IRLR 367). Retained firefighters (ie, part-time firefighters) claimed parity of employment terms with full-time, regular firefighters. They sought to belong to the pension scheme, and to be paid the same rate for additional duties and sick pay. The Court of Appeal ([2004] IRLR 697) held that retained firefighters are not engaged in the same or broadly similar work as regular firemen having regard to their level of qualification, skills and experience. The House of Lords said that the tribunal (which, along with the EAT, had found that the new workers were engaged on different contracts and that the Part-time Workers Regulations did not apply) had taken the wrong approach to the question of whether the workers did the same or broadly similar work. Their Lordships said that the question to ask is whether the main duties and responsibilities of the two jobs were the same or similar. This will involve looking at the work done by both groups, and taking into account similarities and differences. If the answer to the above question is 'Yes', the next stage is to look at the differences and decide whether they are so important as to prevent the work being regarded as the same or broadly similar. Their Lordships commented that just because the full-timers carried out some extra tasks, this would not prevent the jobs being the same or broadly similar. The case was sent back to the tribunal for reconsideration.

In *Carl v University of Sheffield* (UKEAT/0261/08), a part-time teacher of shorthand complained that she had been treated less favourably than a full-time sociology lecturer, who was better qualified and taught at a higher level. She also argued that she could use a hypothetical comparator. The EAT said that a hypothetical comparator was not permissible in respect of a claim of less favourable treatment in a part-time work context. A claimant must be able to point to a real comparator. The claimant also failed in her claim based on an actual comparator, as the difference in skills and qualifications meant (unlike in *Matthews v Kent and Medway Towns Fire Authority*) that she had not identified an actual full-time comparator.

In *McMenemy v Capita Business Services Ltd* [2007] IRLR 400, the Court of Session held that it was not discriminatory to fail to give a part-time worker a Bank Holiday Monday off in lieu, where his normal working days were Wednesday to Friday. The reason he did not receive a Bank Holiday Monday off in lieu was not because he worked part time, but because he did not work on Mondays. A full-time worker who worked, say, Tuesday to Saturday would have been treated in the same way as the claimant. It is important to note that the business in which the worker worked, operated seven days a week. The outcome would probably be different for a business operating Monday–Friday.

The BIS Guidance *Part-time workers. The law and best practice – a detailed guide for employers and part-timers* (URN No 02/1710), states that 'allowing full-timers the day off, but not part-timers, is clearly less favourable treatment and unlawful under the regulations unless there is objective justification'. It suggests that to comply with the law, an employer must treat part-time workers as favourably as it treats full-time workers:

> In some circumstances, it may be enough simply to give workers a paid day off if their day of work happens to coincide with the public holiday, without giving time off in lieu to those who would not ordinarily work on that day. This may produce a fair result, for example where a shift system means that full-time and part-time workers are equally likely to be scheduled to work on a public holiday. However, where workers work fixed days each week, such a practice could put part-timers at a disadvantage. For example, because most bank and public holidays fall on a Monday, those who do not work Mondays will be entitled to proportionately fewer days off. In many workplaces, these workers will predominantly be part-timers. In such cases, it may be necessary to remove the disadvantage suffered by those staff who do not receive particular days off as a result of their particular working pattern, for example by giving all workers a pro rata entitlement of days off in lieu according to the number of hours they work. Whatever approach they choose to adopt, employers should bear in mind that it is unlawful to treat part-timers less favourably than comparable full-timers unless there is objective justification for doing so.

Although the language used is the language of discrimination, there is no provision to make any award for injury to feelings. No adjustment to compensation for failure to comply with the 2009 Acas Code is possible, because a claim under the Regulations is not one of the listed Sch 2 jurisdictions.

The ECJ has recently ruled (see *Istituto nazionale della previdenza social (INPS) v Bruno* [2010] IRLR 890) on how the Part-time Work Directive applies to occupational pension rights. This case suggests that the protection goes beyond mere access to such schemes. In *O'Brien v Ministry of Justice* (Case C-393/10) the ECJ held that if fee-paid, part-time judges are workers, the national law that excludes fee-paid judges from the pension scheme is discriminatory, unless it can be objectively justified. The case was heard by the Supreme Court on 4 July 2012.

8.11   FIXED-TERM EMPLOYEES

The Fixed-term Employees (Prevention of Less Favourable Treatment) Regulations 2002 (SI 2002/2034) work on a similar basis to the Part-time Workers Regulations 2000 (see **8.10**). However, there is one important distinction. The Fixed-term Employee Regulations apply only to employees, not to the wider category of workers. Unfortunately, there is no definition of 'employee' in the Regulations, and it is not clear whether the narrower ERA 1996, s 230 definition (see **1.3.2**) or the wider discrimination definition (see **1.3.4.2**) will apply. It may be fruitful in this regard to look at the definition set out in the applicable EC Directive (Council Directive 99/70/EC, Framework Agreement on Fixed-term Work).

The detail of the legislation is beyond the scope of this book but, briefly, the 2002 Regulations cover the following:

(a)   A right for a fixed-term employee not to be treated less favourably than a comparable permanent employee on the grounds that he is a fixed-term employee, unless objectively justified. Objective justification is deemed to be made out where the fixed-term employee's contractual rights are, as a whole, at least as favourable as the permanent employee's. Otherwise, the employer will have to show that there is an objective reason for treating the fixed-term employee less favourably. The BIS Guidance gives an example an employee on a three-month fixed-term contract, who is not provided with a company car because the cost of doing so is so high, and the employee's travel needs can be met in another way.

(b)   An obligation on employers to advertise permanent vacancies in such a way as is reasonably likely to come to the fixed-term employee's attention.

(c)   A right to receive a written statement of reasons for treatment, if the employee believes less favourable treatment has occurred.

(d)   Provision that any dismissal for seeking to enforce these rights is automatically unfair.

(e)   Provision that a fixed-term contract will be converted to a permanent contract upon the next renewal/extension if the employee has been employed on a fixed-term contract for over four years (unless the employer can demonstrate an objective justification for continued fixed-term employment). The BIS Guidance gives as an example professional sports people, where it is traditional practice for employees to work on fixed-term contracts.

For some case law on the 2002 Regulations, see *Bleuse v MBT Transport Ltd* [2008] IRLR 264, *Duncombe and Others v Secretary of State for Children, Schools and Children* [2011] UKSC 14 and *The Manchester College v Mr M Cocliff* (UKEAT/0035/10).

8.12   TRADE UNION MEMBERSHIP OR ACTIVITIES

Section 137 of the Trade Union and Labour Relations (Consolidation) Act 1992 (TULR(C)A 1992) abolishes the pre-entry closed shop (ie the refusal to employ a person who is not a member of a trade union). It also prohibits an employer from refusing to employ someone because he is a member of a trade union or takes part in trade union activities.

8.12.1   Refusal of employment

It is unlawful to refuse to employ a person on the grounds that he is, or is not, a member of a trade union. It is also unlawful to refuse to employ a person if he does not agree to become, or remain or cease to be a member of a trade union (TULR(C)A 1992, s 137(1)).

8.12.2   Remedies

The complainant may apply for interim relief (see **5.5.1**). If a person has been refused employment on the grounds that he is, or is not, a member of a trade union, he may present a complaint to an employment tribunal within three months of the act complained of.

The tribunal may make an order for compensation, or a recommendation that the effect of the act be obviated or reduced. This could involve, for example, a recommendation that the complainant be offered employment. If a recommendation is not complied with, the compensation award can be increased. The maximum compensation currently awardable is £72,300 (at February 2012).

8.13   DISCRIMINATION UNDER THE HUMAN RIGHTS ACT 1998

The European Convention on Human Rights was incorporated into domestic law by the Human Rights Act (HRA) 1998. This means that individuals are able to enforce Convention rights in the UK's domestic courts and tribunals (see **Chapter 15**).

Article 14 of the European Convention on Human Rights ('the Convention') contains a wide prohibition against discrimination. It states that the enjoyment of rights and freedoms set forth in the Convention shall be secured:

> without discrimination on any ground such as sex, race, colour, language, religion, political or other opinion, national or social origin, association with a national minority, property, birth or other status.

However, Article 14 does not create any 'freestanding' right to freedom from discrimination, and is thus limited to the right to enjoy the other Convention rights without discrimination. There is a proposal for a new Protocol to the Convention which would create a freestanding substantive right to freedom from discrimination. For such a right to become part of the HRA 1998 would require fresh UK legislation.

There have been a number of cases before the European Court of Human Rights (ECtHR) looking at violations of Article 14 by States in connection with education policies relating to the children of Roma parents (see, eg, *DH and Others v The Czech Republic* (App No 57325/00) and *Sampanis v Greece* (App No 32526/05), which contain useful statements on indirect discrimination and the shifting burden of proof).

Article 9 of the Convention contains a right to freedom of thought and religion. It will cover, for example, religious groups who are not currently covered under the definition of 'race' under the Equality Act 2010 (eg Muslims; Rastafarians). If employers discriminate on grounds of belief or religion, that will be unlawful. In previous cases before the ECtHR, the Court has been restrictive of these rights and has given only limited protection. See the case of *Ahmad v UK*, referred to at **1.9**, where the ECtHR accepted that the right could be limited by contractual provisions.

Even though discrimination on grounds of sexual orientation has, until very recently, not been covered by UK or EU law, sexual orientation has been recognised as part of an individual's private life under Article 8 of the Convention. If there is a dismissal on such grounds, Article 8 can be used to give strength to an argument that there is an unfair dismissal. If there is an act by a public authority, Article 8 will give rise to a direct cause of action. Article 8, in conjunction with Article 14, was significant in *EB v France* (App No 43546/02), where the ECtHR found breaches of the Convention when a lesbian's application to adopt a child was refused.

Particularly gross forms of harassment and discrimination may amount to inhuman or degrading treatment under Article 3 of the Convention.

8.14   FURTHER READING

Barnard, *The Substantive Law of the EU: The Four Freedoms*, 3rd edn (OUP, 2010).

Barnard, *EU Employment Law*, 4th edn (OUP, 2012).

Wadham, Ruebain, Robinson and Uppal, *Blackstone's Guide to the Equality Act 2010*, 2nd edn (OUP, 2012).

Harvey, *Industrial Relations and Employment Law* (Butterworths), Vol 2, Divs K and L.

Lewis, *Multiple Discrimination – A Guide to Law and Evidence* (Central London Law Centre, November 2010).

The Government Equalities Office (GEO) website:
www.equalities.gov.uk/equality_act_2010.

The Advisory, Conciliation and Arbitration Service (Acas) Guidance at:
www.acas.org.uk.

See also the Acas advisory booklet, *Tackling discrimination and promoting equality – good practice guide for employers*, available from the Acas website at www.acas.org.uk/publications.

SUMMARY

The general common law rule is that an employer is free to offer employment to whomsoever he chooses (*Allen v Flood and Taylor* [1898] AC 1). This common law freedom has been restricted by statute. The EC Equal Treatment Directive (76/207) provides that there should be no discrimination on grounds of sex, either directly or indirectly, nor by reference to marital or family status, in access to employment, training, working conditions, promotion or dismissal. In the UK, under the provisions of the Equality Act 2010, an employer may be in breach of statutory requirements if he discriminates against a person on a large number of protected characteristics including:

(a)   sex, maternity, pregnancy or marital status;

(b)   gender reassignment;

(c)   colour, race, nationality or ethnic or national origins;

(d)   religion or belief;

(e)   sexual orientation;

(f)   age;

(g)   disability (**8.1**).

The Equality and Human Rights Commission (EHRC) has responsibility for promoting equality and combating unlawful discrimination on grounds of sex, race, disability, sexual orientation, religion or belief, and age. It also has responsibility for the promotion of human rights.

This chapter has looked at the matters which are common to all the protected characteristics. Provisions in the Equality Act 2010 relating to age and disability discrimination are in some ways different from the other protected characteristics, and so age discrimination (**Chapter 12**) and disability discrimination (**Chapter 13**) are dealt with separately.

Four main types of discrimination in the employment field are outlawed by UK legislation on these grounds. These are:

(a)   direct discrimination (ie being subject to less favourable treatment than others because of sex, race, religion or belief, sexual orientation, age, etc) (see **Chapter 9**);

(b)   indirect discrimination (ie the application of a provision, criterion or practice which disadvantages people of a particular sex, race, religion or belief, sexual orientation, age, etc) (see **Chapter 10**);

(c)   harassment (unwanted conduct that violates a person's dignity, or creates an intimidating, hostile, degrading, humiliating or offensive environment for him or her having regard to all the circumstances, including the perception of the victim) (see **Chapter 11**); and

(d)   victimisation (because the victim has been subject to a detriment because he has done a protected act) (see **Chapter 11**).

In most cases, indirect discrimination may be justified 'objectively' where the discrimination is a 'proportionate means of achieving a legitimate aim' (**Chapter 10**).

Discrimination is outlawed (Equality Act 2010, ss 39 and 40) in the employment field against job applicants (ie recruitment) and employees and former employees. It is unlawful for a person, to discriminate against a person employed by him (**8.4**):

(a)   in the way he affords him or her access to opportunities for promotion, transfer or training, or to any other benefits, facilities or services; or

(b)   by dismissing him or her, or subjecting him or her to any other detriment.

An employer may have a defence under the occupational requirements provisions of the Equality Act 2010 (**8.5**) and under the 'reasonable steps' defence (**8.6.2**), if he can show that he took such steps as were reasonably practicable to prevent an employee doing the act complained of. Employers may be vicariously liable for the acts of their employees during the course of employment (**8.6**).

Remedies and enforcement are dealt with at **8.8**. Tribunals may, on making a finding of discrimination, as they consider just and equitable, make:

(a)   an order declaring the rights of the complainant;

(b)   an order requiring the respondent to pay the complainant compensation; and/or

(c)   a recommendation that the respondent take, within a specified period, practicable action to obviate or reduce the adverse effect of any act of discrimination.

The general principle as far as compensation is concerned is that, as far as possible, complainants should be placed in the same position as they would have been but for the unlawful act (see *Ministry of Defence v Wheeler* [1998] IRLR 23). In addition to awarding compensation for foreseeable damage arising directly from the unlawful act, a tribunal has jurisdiction to award compensation for personal injury, including both physical and psychiatric injury, and for injury to feelings (**8.8.2.2**).

DIRECT DISCRIMINATION

LEARNING OUTCOMES

After reading this chapter you will be able to:

- understand the definition of direct discrimination
- explain what is meant by 'less favourable treatment'
- describe how direct discrimination protects women who are pregnant or on maternity leave
- explain what is meant by the shifting burden of proof
- list the potential remedies that are available where a complaint of discrimination is made out.

9.1 INTRODUCTION

This chapter considers direct discrimination in respect of the following protected characteristics listed in s 4 of the Equality Act 2010 ('the Act') (see **8.2.1**):

- gender reassignment (s 7)
- marriage and civil partnership (s 8)
- race (s 9)
- religion or belief (s 10)
- sex (s 11)
- sexual orientation (s 12)
- pregnancy and maternity (s 18).

This chapter refers, by way of illustration and example, to the pre- and post-Equality Act 2010 case law.

9.2 DIRECT DISCRIMINATION

9.2.1 Definition

Direct discrimination occurs where the reason for a person being treated less favourably than another is a protected characteristic listed in s 4 of the Act (see **9.1**). This definition is broad enough to cover cases where the less favourable treatment is because of the victim's association with someone who has that characteristic (eg is disabled – see **Chapter 13**), or because the victim is wrongly thought to have it (eg a particular religious belief) (see **9.2.4**).

Note that men cannot claim privileges for women connected with pregnancy or childbirth. Direct discrimination cannot be justified (save in age discrimination cases).

The definition of 'direct discrimination' is set out in s 13 of the Act:

(1)   A person (A) discriminates against another (B) if, because of a protected characteristic, A treats B less favourably than A treats or would treat others.

...

(4)   If the protected characteristic is marriage and civil partnership, this section applies to a contravention of Part 5 (work) only if the treatment is because it is B who is married or a civil partner.

(5)   If the protected characteristic is race, less favourable treatment includes segregating B from others.

(6)   If the protected characteristic is sex—

(a)   less favourable treatment of a woman includes less favourable treatment of her because she is breast-feeding;

(b)   in a case where B is a man, no account is to be taken of special treatment afforded to a woman in connection with pregnancy or childbirth.

(7)   Subsection (6)(a) does not apply for the purposes of Part 5 (work).

(8)   This section is subject to section ... 18(7) [see **9.4**].

The Explanatory Notes give examples:

- If an employer recruits a man rather than a woman because she assumes that women do not have the strength to do the job, this would be direct sex discrimination.

- If a Muslim shopkeeper refuses to serve a Muslim woman because she is married to a Christian, this would be direct religious or belief-related discrimination on the basis of her association with her husband.

- If an employer rejects a job application form from a white man who he wrongly thinks is black, because the applicant has an African-sounding name, this would constitute direct race discrimination based on the employer's mistaken perception.

- If an employer advertising a vacancy makes it clear in the advert that Roma need not apply, this would amount to direct race discrimination against a Roma who might reasonably have considered applying for the job but was deterred from doing so because of the advertisement.

In *Islington Borough Council v Ladele* [2010] IRLR 111, the EAT explained direct discrimination as follows (para 32):

The concept of direct discrimination is fundamentally a simple one. A claimant suffers some form of detriment (using that term very broadly) and the reason for that detrimental treatment is the prohibited ground. There is implicit in that analysis the fact that someone in a similar position to whom that ground did not apply (the comparator) would not have suffered the detriment. By establishing that the reason for the detrimental treatment is the prohibited reason, the claimant necessarily establishes at one and the same time that he or she is less favourably treated than the comparator who did not share the prohibited characteristic.

Only direct discrimination because of age may be justified (Article 6 of the Framework Directive and Equality Act 2010, s 13(2); see *Seldon v Clarkson Wright and Jakes* [2012] UKSC 16, **Chapter 12**.)

9.2.2 Dual discrimination

Section 14 of the Act is aimed at what is known as 'intersectional' multiple discrimination. This was an area that was not properly covered under the previously existing law (see, eg, *Bahl v Law Society* [2004] IRLR 799), but see more recently *O'Reilly v BBC* (ET/2200423/2011), which suggests that where a claimant brings a dual discrimination case and the tribunal finds that part of the reason for less favourable treatment is one of the protected characteristics, the claimant will succeed. Intersectional multiple discrimination occurs when the discrimination involves more than one protected characteristic and it is the unique combination of characteristics that results in discrimination, in such a way that they are inseparable. This often occurs as a result of stereotyped attitudes or prejudice relating to particular combinations of the protected characteristics, eg refusing to give a job to an older woman, but being willing to employ an older man.

Section 14 provides for the discrimination prohibited by the Act to include direct discrimination because of a combination of two protected characteristics ('dual discrimination'), eg disability and gender, or disability and race. The Government considers it too complicated and burdensome to allow claims on three or more different discrimination grounds. Not all protected characteristics are covered by the dual discrimination provisions – marriage and civil partnership, and pregnancy and maternity are excluded. The Government said that it had heard no evidence of any problems arising in practice from a combination of these characteristics and others. Further, as pregnancy and maternity claims do not involve a comparator (see below at **9.4**), it would be difficult to combine them with a claim based on a protected characteristic which does entail such a requirement.

The Explanatory Notes give the following examples:

- A black woman has been passed over for promotion to work on reception because her employer thinks black women do not perform well in customer service roles. Because the employer can point to a white woman of equivalent qualifications and experience who has been appointed to the role in question, as well as a black man of equivalent qualifications and experience in a similar role, the woman may need to be able to compare her treatment because of race and sex combined to demonstrate that she has been subjected to less favourable treatment because of her employer's prejudice against black women.

- A bus driver does not allow a Muslim man onto her bus, claiming that he could be a 'terrorist'. While it might not be possible for the man to demonstrate less favourable treatment because of either protected characteristic if considered separately, a dual discrimination claim will succeed if the reason for his treatment was the specific combination of sex and religion or belief, which resulted in him being stereotyped as a potential terrorist.

It is not clear under s 14(1) whether a comparator can share one but not both of the characteristics, or whether he or she must share neither of them. It may not be easy to find an exact comparator. The approach of the House of Lords in *Shamoon v Chief Constable of the Royal Ulster Constabulary* [2003] IRLR 285 is worth reading on how to approach this difficult area.

In a 2009 discussion document, the Government Equality Office estimated that 7.5% of discrimination cases would include claims of dual discrimination, and that there would be a 10% increase in discrimination cases once s 14 is in force.

Section 14 applies only to direct discrimination; there is no equivalent provision for dual discrimination in indirect discrimination (but see *Ministry of Defence v DeBique* (UKEAT/0048/09 and 0049/09) – **10.2.5**)

Section 14 was not brought into force when the majority of the Equality Act 2010 became effective in October 2010. On 23 March 2011, the Chancellor of the Exchequer, George Osborne, suggested that £350 million worth of specific regulations would go – including the Equality Act's costly dual discrimination rules. Further, the Government's Equality Office has removed dual discrimination from its list of provisions that are still being considered. Notwithstanding this, the approach in *O'Reilly* may mean that such claims will still be able to be pursued.

The London Law Centre has published a very helpful Multiple Discrimination Guide, available at www.londonlawcentre.org.uk (Publications).

9.2.3 Association and perception

Associative and perceptive discrimination were covered under some but not all of the old discrimination legislation. For example, while the Employment Equality (Age) Regulations

2006 (SI 2006/1031) defined direct age discrimination as occurring where A treats B less favourably than others 'on grounds of B's age', the RRA 1976 referred to 'on racial grounds'. This wider wording meant that discrimination was not just with regard to the race of the person concerned – it could be with regard to the race of someone else.

The wording of the definition of 'direct discrimination' in the Act is wide enough to now cover both associative and perceptive discrimination: the reference in s 13 (see **9.2.1**) is to treatment 'because of [protected characteristic]' as opposed to 'on grounds of' A's protected characteristic. This broader wording removes the need to consider whether the complainant's protected characteristic was the reason for the treatment complained of. It means that so-called 'associative discrimination' is covered. If A treats B less favourably because B cares for an elderly relative, A may be held to have discriminated against B *because of age*, even though B's age is not the reason for the treatment.

The Explanatory Notes state that direct discrimination occurs where the reason for a person being treated less favourably than another is a protected characteristic listed in s 4, and that the definition (save in the case of marriage and civil partnership) is broad enough to cover cases where the less favourable treatment is because of the victim's association with someone who has that characteristic (eg, is black) (association), or because the victim is wrongly thought to have it (eg, a particular religious belief) (perception).

In *Showboat Entertainment Centre v Owens* [1984] IRLR 7, a white employee was dismissed for failing to obey an order not to admit young black men into an amusement arcade; this was held to be a discriminatory dismissal. He was discriminated against on the grounds of someone else's race. In *Showboat*, Browne-Wilkinson P said (at para 11):

> Therefore the only question is whether Mr Owens was treated less favourably 'on racial grounds'. Certainly the main thrust of the legislation is to give protection to those discriminated against on the grounds of their own racial characteristics. But the words 'on racial grounds' are perfectly capable in their ordinary sense of covering any reason for an action based on race, whether it be the race of the person affected by the action or of others.

The decision in *Showboat* was subsequently approved by the Court of Appeal in *Weathersfield Ltd v Sargent* [1999] IRLR 94, which was another case in which an employee had resigned and was found to have been constructively dismissed, after having been given an unlawful instruction to discriminate on racial grounds against blacks and Asians. The crucial test under the old case law was whether the protected characteristic had a significant influence on the outcome which it was claimed was discriminatory.

For other recent, albeit pre-Equality Act cases, illustrating the likely approach in this area, see *Saini v All Saints Haque Centre* [2009] IRLR 74, *English v Thomas Sanderson Blinds Ltd* [2009] IRLR 206 and *Lisboa v Real Pubs Ltd* (EAT/0224/10).

Note that a different approach applies where the reason for the treatment is marriage or civil partnership, in which case only less favourable treatment because of the victim's status amounts to discrimination. It must be the victim, rather than anybody else, who is married or a civil partner, and a perception that the victim is married or a civil partner is not sufficient.

It is not clear how perception discrimination will work for disability (see **13.3.9**).

9.2.4 Reason for the less favourable treatment

Section 13 of the Act uses the words 'because of' where the previous legislation used the words 'on grounds of'. As explained above (**9.2.3**), the Explanatory Notes state that this difference in wording does not change the legal meaning of the definition but rather is designed to make it more accessible to the ordinary user of the Act. In *Amnesty International v Ahmed* [2009] IRLR 884, Mr Justice Underhill stated that:

> there can be no objection to the use of the phrase 'because of' if used as a synonym for the phrase 'on grounds of' as long as the phrase is not used to import a 'causation' (or a 'but for') test.

It remains to be seen whether the courts and tribunals continue to follow the case law applying the old statutory test of 'on grounds of' (see the example at **9.2.5.1**).

Note: It is not necessary for the prohibited characteristic to be the only or even the main reason for the treatment; it is sufficient that it had a significant influence on the outcome (*Nagarajan v London Regional Transport* [1999] IRLR 572, HL).

9.2.5 What is less favourable treatment?

Less favourable treatment is a wide concept: it covers any 'disadvantage' (see, eg, *Jeremiah v Ministry of Defence* [1979] IRLR 436). It does not require any tangible loss (see *Chief Constable of West Yorkshire Police v Khan* [2001] IRLR 830). A mere deprivation of choice will be sufficient to found a claim of less favourable treatment (see, eg, *Gill v El Vino Co Ltd* [1983] QB 425 and *R v Birmingham City Council, ex p Equal Opportunities Commission* [1989] IRLR 173).

Although there was some suggestion in recent but pre-Equality Act 2010 case law that the test may be a subjective one (see *Chief Constable of West Yorkshire v Khan*), the wording in s 13 appears to suggest that the test is objective: the question is whether the complainant would have been treated:

(a)   differently; and

(b)   more favourably,

had it not been because of sex, race, religion or belief, sexual orientation, gender reassignment or marital/civil partnership status. The reason for the less favourable treatment must be because of sex, race, etc. The tribunal must ask what the 'conscious or subconscious reason for treating the claimant less favourably was' (*Nagarajan v London Regional Transport* [1999] IRLR 572, HL).

What amounts to less favourable treatment is for the tribunal to decide, but the hurdle is generally not a difficult one to satisfy. In considering the meaning to be given to 'less favourable', the courts have generally adopted the same test as that applied to determine whether a 'detriment' has occurred. In *Chief Constable of West Yorkshire Police v Khan* (above), the employer refused to give the claimant a reference, and he claimed that this was racially discriminatory. The employer argued that the claimant was better off without a reference, because any such reference would have been unfavourable and that there was, therefore, no less favourable treatment. The House of Lords held it was enough that the claimant 'could reasonably say that he would have preferred not to have been treated differently in this way'.

9.2.5.1 Comparison by reference to circumstances

Analysis

The Explanatory Notes explain that s 23 provides that like must be compared with like in cases of direct discrimination. The treatment of the claimant must be compared with that of an actual or a hypothetical person – the comparator – who does not share the same protected characteristic as the claimant (or, in the case of dual discrimination, either of the protected characteristics in the combination) but who is (or is assumed to be) in not materially different circumstances from the claimant.

The use of the words 'would treat' in s 13(1) (see **9.2.1**) allows for a hypothetical rather than an actual comparator. The relevant circumstances of the complainant and the comparative group should be the same or not materially different. In *Chief Constable of West Yorkshire v Vento* [2001] IRLR 124, the EAT made an important point about comparing like with like and the use of hypothetical comparators where there is no actual comparator. In such cases, where the tribunal has to construct the probable treatment of a hypothetical comparator, it is legitimate to see how unidentical but not wholly dissimilar instances had been dealt with in the past. This would not infringe the principle of comparing like with like. For example, a woman might say that cases of alleged misconduct are investigated swiftly and in detail by the employer, whereas there was a slow and half-hearted investigation into her claim of sexual harassment. Thus, in the *Vento* case, the EAT held that the tribunal had not erred in constructing an inference from the hypothetical case of how the employers had treated four actual, unidentified but not wholly dissimilar comparators. The Court of Appeal approved *Vento* in *Balamoody v United Kingdom Central Council for Nursing, Midwifery and Health Visiting* [2002] IRLR 288, and ruled that the question of the correct comparator is a question of law.

The House of Lords emphasised the importance of the hypothetical comparator in *Shamoon v Chief Constable of the Royal Ulster Constabulary* [2003] IRLR 285. Their Lordships stated that 'in most cases a suitable actual comparator will not be available and a hypothetical comparator will have to constitute the statutory comparator'. As Michael Rubenstein notes in 'Highlights IRLR May 2003', 'the way others are treated whose circumstances are insufficiently similar to be actual comparators then becomes evidence of how a hypothetical comparator would be treated'. In *Shamoon*, the House of Lords also indicated that instead of relying on like with like comparators, a claimant may rely on the 'evidential significance' of non-exact comparators in support of an inference of direct discrimination, even though their evidential value will become weaker the greater the difference in circumstances.

Lord Nicholls said (at para 11) that:

> employment tribunals may sometimes be able to avoid arid and confusing disputes about the identification of the appropriate comparator by concentrating primarily on why the claimant was treated as she was. Was it on the proscribed ground which is the foundation of the application?

This approach has been adopted in a number of subsequent cases (see eg *Amnesty International v Ahmed* [2009] IRLR 884, *Ladele v The London Borough of Islington* (see 'Cases' below), *Aylott v Stockton-on-Tees Borough Council* [2010] IRLR 994 (at para 37: 'there is no obligation on the ET to construct a hypothetical comparator in every case'), *Martin v Devonshires Solicitors* [2011] ICR 352 and *JP Morgan Europe Ltd v Chweidan* [2011] EWCA Civ 648). Most recently, in *Cordell v Foreign and Commonwealth Office* [2012] ICR 280, Underhill J, while acknowledging that where there was an actual comparator the 'less favourable treatment' question might be the easiest route, described the 'reason why' question as 'in truth fundamental ... but where there is [no actual comparator] it will usually be better to focus on the reason why question than to get bogged down in the often arid and confusing task of "constructing a hypothetical comparator"'.

Cases

In *Hussain v Bhullar Bros* (see 8.2.3), although the tribunal held that attendance at home following the bereavement of a close family member was a religion-based practice or belief, the claim failed on the basis that the claimant, who was a Muslim, could not prove that the employer would have treated non-Muslims in the same situation any differently.

In *Khan v Direct Line Insurance plc* (ET/1400026/06), the issue arose of a suitable comparator for a Muslim employee who alleged direct discrimination on grounds of (the pre-Equality Act 2010 test – see 9.2.4) his religion or belief, where his employer offered alcohol as an incentive. The employment tribunal held that he had not been discriminated against, because a non-Muslim tee-totaller would have been in the same position.

In *Eweida v BA* (ET/2702689/06), the employment tribunal held that it was not necessary to give a Christian employee privilege over other employees when allocating shifts, to accommodate her desire to attend church services on Sundays. The tribunal held that to do so would amount to a form of preferential treatment on grounds of religion.

In *Martin v Parkham Foods* (ET/1800241/06), the tribunal held that 'the Respondent did not deal with the Claimant's grievances as forcefully as it might have done had they related not to homophobia but to other issues'. The comparator would be someone raising a grievance on other grounds. The employer would have treated that grievance more forcefully. The employer should have taken further steps, eg training and meetings, and referred to homophobia in the warning notices.

In *Chondol v Liverpool City Council* (UKEAT/0298/08), the EAT said that debating the correct characterisation of the comparator was 'less helpful than focusing on the fundamental question of the reason why the claimant was treated in the manner complained of', and referred to the tribunal's finding that 'it was not on the ground of his religion that he received this treatment, rather on the ground that he was improperly foisting it on service users'.

In *Azmi v Kirklees Metropolitan Borough Council* [2007] IRLR 484, the EAT upheld a tribunal's decision that the suspension of a teaching assistant for refusing an instruction not to wear a veil when assisting a male teacher in front of pupils, was not directly discriminatory on the grounds of religion or belief. Mrs Azmi had not been treated less favourably than a comparator (a person who wore a face covering) would have been in similar circumstances.

In *Glasgow City Council v Mr D McNab* [2007] IRLR 476, the EAT upheld a tribunal's decision that an atheist teacher employed by a local authority-maintained Catholic school had suffered direct discrimination when he was refused an interview for the post of Acting Principal Teacher of Pastoral Care. The post was not on the list of positions for which the Roman Catholic Church required a teacher to be Catholic, and therefore the Council should not have presumed that the Church would not have approved the appointment. There was no occupational requirement. A local authority has no religious ethos and cannot take advantage of the occupational requirements even in respect of employment in a religious school.

In *Ladele v The London Borough of Islington* [2010] IRLR 211, Ms Ladele was the registrar at Islington Council. She said that same-sex civil partnerships conflicted with her strict Christian beliefs, and refused to conduct same-sex civil partnership ceremonies. She was disciplined by the Council as a result. The EAT said that Ms Ladele was disciplined because she was refusing to carry out her duties, not because of her religious beliefs. Elias J said:

> The proper hypothetical or statutory comparator here is another registrar who refused to conduct civil partnership work because of antipathy to the concept of same sex relationships but which antipathy was not connected [to] or based upon his or her religious belief.

The Court of Appeal agreed with that view and therefore held that there was no basis upon which the employment tribunal could have made a finding of direct discrimination.

In *Dansie v The Commissioner of Police for the Metropolis* (UKEAT 0234/09), D, a police recruit, was forced to cut his shoulder length hair or face disciplinary action. It was common ground the a female police recruit would not have been required to cut her hair. D claimed he had been unlawfully discriminated against on the ground of his sex. The EAT, in upholding the tribunal's decision, said that requiring a conventional standard of appearance is not in itself discriminatory, provided that, looking at the code as a whole, neither sex is treated less favourably as a result of its enforcement.

In *McFarlane v Relate Avon Ltd* [2010] ICR 50, EAT, the claimant entered into a contract of employment with the employer as a paid counsellor in August 2003. Upon doing so he signed up expressly to the employers' equal opportunities policy. The claimant is a Christian. In the course of his employment he experienced no difficulties of conscience in counselling same-sex couples where no sexual issues arose. At length, however, he sought to be exempted from any obligation to work with same-sex couples in cases where issues of psycho-sexual therapy ('PST') were involved. The EAT held that the tribunal was correct in its finding that there was no direct discrimination:

> [W]e concluded, firstly, that it was necessary for an actual or hypothetical comparator to be identified and, secondly, that an appropriate comparator would be another counsellor who, for reasons unrelated to Christianity, was believed by the respondent to be unwilling to provide PST counselling to same sex couples and therefore unwilling to abide by the respondent's Equal Opportunities and Ethical Practice

Policies. The question, therefore, is whether the respondent would have treated [such] a comparator differently, and in our view it would not.

In other words, while religious belief was the claimant's motivation for his actions, the employer had dismissed him because he refused to comply with its equal opportunities policy.

Both *Ladele* and *McFarlane* were heard by the ECtHR in September 2012.

In *Dziedziak v Future Electronics Ltd* (UKEAT/0270/11) the EAT upheld the tribunal's conclusion that the claimant, who is Polish, was subjected to direct discrimination on grounds of nationality when told by her line manager that she should not speak to colleagues 'in her own language', as those words demonstrated an 'instrinsic link' with her nationality.

9.2.5.2 Motive

The motive or intentions behind the action are irrelevant and there is no defence once direct discrimination has been proved (see *Birmingham City Council v EOC* [1989] AC 1155). For example:

(a)   If the only woman remaining on a work experience scheme is withdrawn 'for her own good', this will be direct discrimination.

(b)   If the temporary appointment of a black person as a refuse collector is withdrawn due to fear of industrial action by the other workers, this will amount to direct discrimination even though the employer's intention was not to discriminate but to avoid disrupting the service.

In *Amnesty International v Ahmed* (UKEAT/0447/08), Amnesty declined to appoint a northern Sudanese woman to the position of researcher because it was concerned that her ethnic origin might compromise her impartiality and her safety. The tribunal upheld the claim of direct discrimination, as 'but for' her Sudanese origins she would have been appointed. The EAT upheld the tribunal's finding and approach. It made clear that the explanation for the discrimination was irrelevant and that this was a clear case where the employer's decision was overtly made on basis of the claimant's race (see *James v Eastleigh BC* [1990] 2 AC 751). Underhill J referred to the 'reason why' question as the discriminator's 'motivation' and to the explanation for the discrimination as his 'motive'. He explained (at paras 33–34):

> In some cases the ground, or the reason, for the treatment complained of is inherent in the act itself. If an owner of premises puts up a sign saying 'no blacks admitted' race is, necessarily, the ground on which (or the reason why) the black person is excluded. *James v Eastleigh* is a case of this kind ... In cases of this kind what was going on inside the head of the putative discriminator – whether described as his intention, motive, his reason or his purpose – will be irrelevant. The 'ground' of his action being inherent in the act itself, no further inquiry is needed. It follows that, as the majority in *James v Eastleigh* decided, a respondent who has treated a claimant les favourably on the ground of his or her sex or race cannot escape liability because he had a benign motive.

> But that is not the only kind of case. In other cases – of which *Nagarajan* is an example – the act complained of is not itself discriminatory but is rendered so by a discriminatory motivation, ie by the 'mental processes' (whether conscious or unconscious) which led the putative discriminator to do the act ... Even in such a case, however, it is important to bear in mind that the subject of the inquiry is the ground of, or reason for, the putative discriminator's actions, not his motive; just as in the kind of case considered in *James v Eastleigh*, a benign motive is irrelevant.

What is important, therefore, is to discover what caused someone to act as he did, as opposed to a consideration of that person's motive, intention, reason or purposes; or to put it another way, in order to establish if direct discrimination has occurred, it is necessary to identify only 'the factual criteria that determined the decision made by the discriminator', as opposed to the motive for the discrimination. The 'but for' test is simply one way of identifying the factual criterion that have been applied; another way is to ask what the facts were that the discriminator considered to be determinative when making the relevant decision. Note, however, that the 'but for' approach may not be appropriate in victimisation cases (see *Martin v Devonshires Solicitors* (**9.2.5.1** above) and **Chapter 11**).

9.2.6 Irrelevance of alleged discriminator's characteristics

Section 24 of the Act provides that it is no defence to a claim of direct discrimination that the alleged discriminator shares the protected characteristic with the victim. The discriminator will still be liable for any unlawful discrimination.

The Explanatory Notes provide an example:

> An employer cannot argue that because he is a gay man he is not liable for unlawful discrimination for rejecting a job application from another gay man because of the applicant's sexual orientation.

9.2.7 Stereotypical assumptions

Stereotypical assumptions may amount to direct discrimination. For example:

(a)   Assuming that a woman with young children will be an unreliable employee is direct discrimination.

(b)   Assuming that the husband is the breadwinner and that his wife will resign and follow him, in the event of the husband being relocated, without asking the wife what her intentions are, also amounts to direct discrimination.

The courts have held, however, that it is not discriminatory to take into account natural differences between the sexes, for example to tell men that their hair must be worn above the collar, whereas, although women are allowed long hair, they are also subject to a rule prohibiting 'unconventional hair styles'.

9.3   GENDER REASSIGNMENT AND ABSENCE FROM WORK

Section 16 of the Act provides that it is also discrimination against transsexual people if they are treated less favourably for being absent from work because they propose to undergo, are undergoing or have undergone gender reassignment than they would be if they were absent because they were ill or injured. Transsexual people are also discriminated against in relation to absences relating to their gender reassignment if they are treated less favourably than they would be for absence for reasons other than sickness or injury and it is unreasonable to treat them less favourably.

The Explanatory Notes give an example:

> A female to male transsexual person takes time off work to receive hormone treatment as part of his gender reassignment. His employer cannot discriminate against him because of his absence from work for this purpose.

9.4   PREGNANCY AND MATERNITY DISCRIMINATION

Section 18 of the Act defines what it means to discriminate because of a woman's pregnancy or maternity, as distinct from her sex, in specified situations within work. It protects a woman from discrimination because of her current or a previous pregnancy. It also protects her from maternity discrimination, which includes treating her unfavourably because she is breast-feeding, for 26 weeks after giving birth, and provides that pregnancy or maternity discrimination as defined cannot be treated as sex discrimination. Maternity is defined in s 213 of the Act. There is no definition of pregnancy.

Section 18 provides as follows:

> (1)   This section has effect for the purposes of the application of Part 5 (work) to the protected characteristic of pregnancy and maternity.

(2)   A person (A) discriminates against a woman if, in the protected period in relation to a pregnancy of hers, A treats her unfavourably—

    (a)   because of the pregnancy, or

    (b)   because of illness suffered by her as a result of it.

(3)   A person (A) discriminates against a woman if A treats her unfavourably because she is on compulsory maternity leave.

(4)   A person (A) discriminates against a woman if A treats her unfavourably because she is exercising or seeking to exercise, or has exercised or sought to exercise, the right to ordinary or additional maternity leave.

(5)   For the purposes of subsection (2), if the treatment of a woman is in implementation of a decision taken in the protected period, the treatment is to be regarded as occurring in that period (even if the implementation is not until after the end of that period).

(6)   The protected period, in relation to a woman's pregnancy, begins when the pregnancy begins, and ends—

    (a)   if she has the right to ordinary and additional maternity leave, at the end of the additional maternity leave period or (if earlier) when she returns to work after the pregnancy;

    (b)   if she does not have that right, at the end of the period of 2 weeks beginning with the end of the pregnancy.

(7)   Section 13, so far as relating to sex discrimination, does not apply to treatment of a woman in so far as—

    (a)   it is in the protected period in relation to her and is for a reason mentioned in paragraph (a) or (b) of subsection (2), or

    (b)   it is for a reason mentioned in subsection (3) or (4).

In *Webb v EMO Air Cargo (UK) Ltd* [1993] IRLR 27, the House of Lords held that to dismiss a woman because she was pregnant, or to refuse to employ her because she was or might become pregnant, was unlawful direct discrimination. In *Brown v Rentokil Ltd* [1998] IRLR 445, the ECJ held that dismissal during pregnancy for absences due to incapacity for work 'must ... be regarded as essentially based on the fact of pregnancy'. The ECJ decided that since pregnancy can affect only women, action taken on the grounds of a pregnancy-related illness constitutes direct discrimination on the grounds of sex.

Section 18 of the Act codifies the *Webb* decision above and sets out the meaning of discrimination because of a woman's pregnancy or pregnancy-related illness, or because she takes or tries to take maternity leave. Under s 18, a person discriminates against a woman in relation to her pregnancy or maternity leave if, during the protected period of her pregnancy and maternity leave, he treats her less favourably because of her pregnancy (or an illness resulting from it) or maternity leave. The period during which protection from these types of discrimination exists is the period of pregnancy and any statutory maternity leave to which the woman is entitled. Section 13 (see **9.2.1**) does not apply during these periods. There is no need for a comparator during the protected period. Where a woman is treated unfavourably because of pregnancy or a pregnancy-related illness, and the decision to treat her in that way was taken during the protected period but not implemented until after the end of that period, the treatment is regarded as occurring during the protected period (s 18(5)).

The Explanatory Notes give examples:

- An employer must not demote or dismiss an employee, or deny her training or promotion opportunities, because she is pregnant or on maternity leave.
- An employer must not take into account an employee's period of absence due to pregnancy-related illness when making a decision about her employment.

Section 18(7) means that a claim in respect of pregnancy and maternity discrimination during the protected period cannot be brought as direct sex discrimination under s 13. A claim for direct discrimination outside that protected period would fall under s 13. It is not clear if this means a comparator is needed, or whether it was intended that pregnancy should not be covered outside the protected period, but the authors think that the former is correct, bearing in mind EU law.

In *Sahota v The Home Office* (UKEAT/0342/09), the EAT considered the extent to which discrimination on the ground that an employee was receiving IVF treatment was to be regarded as discrimination on the ground of her pregnancy. It was common ground that after implantation, the claimant was to be regarded as being pregnant. The EAT, considering a decision of the ECJ in *Mayr v Backerei und Konditorei Gerhard Flockner OHG* [2008] IRLR 387, held that the pregnancy principle applied to adverse treatment during the interval between follicular puncture and an imminent or immediate implantation attempt, but said it did not go any wider.

In *Nixon v Ross Coates Solicitors* (UKEAT/0108/10) the EAT held that gossip about the paternity of a baby that a female employee was expecting (following her behaviour at an office party) amounted to sex discrimination, pregnancy discrimination and harassment.

In *Eversheds v De Belin* (UKEAT/0352/10), the EAT held that the obligation to protect employees who are pregnant or on maternity leave is limited to treatment that is 'reasonably necessary [meaning proportionate] to compensate them for the disadvantages occasioned by their condition'. In this case, the claimant had been scored lower in a redundancy exercise than a colleague who was on maternity leave solely because the colleague was given a maximum notional score for one of the criteria. The EAT upheld the tribunal's finding of sex discrimination and unfair dismissal: the maternity benefit applied was disproportionate because there were less discriminatory alternative measures that could be adopted, such as measuring performance at a time when both candidates were still at work. Thus, the claimant who had been disadvantaged by this was entitled to claim sex discrimination. However, applying the approach in *Polkey* (see **5.6.2.2**), as there was cogent evidence that the claimant would have been made redundant in any event some nine months later, the claim was remitted to a different tribunal to consider whether the claim for loss of earnings should be capped or discounted on that basis.

9.5 BURDEN OF PROOF

9.5.1 The shifting burden of proof

The legislation provides that where a complainant can establish facts from which the tribunal could decide that there has been a contravention of a provision of the Act, the tribunal *must* make a finding of unlawful discrimination *unless* the employer shows it did not contravene the provision (s 136). The Explanatory Notes explain that the burden of proving a case starts with the claimant. Once the claimant has established sufficient facts which, in the absence of any other explanation, point to a breach, then the burden shifts on to the respondent to show that it did not breach the Act. This means that the complainant does have to establish some facts from which a tribunal could decide that there has been discrimination.

The EAT had the chance to consider the burden of proof in *Barton v Investec Henderson Crosthwaite Securities Ltd* [2003] IRLR 332 (a sex discrimination case decided under the old law but which will apply to the 2010 Act). Ansell J gave guidance on the new burden of proof in practice in direct discrimination claims. That guidance was amended by the Court of Appeal in *Igen Ltd and Others v Wong* [2005] IRLR 258 and approved again in *Madarassy v Nomura International plc* [2007] EWCA Civ 33. Although these cases involved sex or race discrimination, the Court of Appeal in *Igen* made it clear that they apply to all the discrimination strands. The revised guidance is as follows:

1. [It] was for the claimant who complained of sex discrimination to prove on the balance of probabilities facts from which the tribunal could conclude, in the absence of an adequate explanation, that the respondent had committed an act of discrimination against the claimant which was unlawful ...

2.   If the claimant did not prove such facts he or she would fail.

3.   It was important to bear in mind in deciding whether the claimant had proved such facts that it was unusual to find direct evidence of sex discrimination. Few employers would be prepared to admit such discrimination, even to themselves. In some cases the discrimination would not be an intention but merely based on the assumption that 'he or she would not have fitted in'.

4.   In deciding whether the claimant had proved such facts, it was important to remember that the outcome at this stage of the analysis by the tribunal would therefore usually depend on what inferences it was proper to draw from the primary facts found by the tribunal.

5.   It was important to note the word 'could' in s [136]. At this stage the tribunal did not have to reach a definitive determination that such facts would lead it to the conclusion that there was an act of unlawful discrimination. At this stage a tribunal was looking at the primary facts before it to see what inferences of secondary fact could be drawn from them.

6.   In considering what inferences or conclusions could be drawn from the primary facts, the tribunal must assume that there was no adequate explanation for those facts.

7.   Those inferences could include, in appropriate cases, any inferences that it was just and equitable to draw in accordance with s [138] ... from an evasive or equivocal reply to a questionnaire or any other questions that fell within s [138] ...

8.   Likewise, the tribunal must decide whether any provision of the relevant code of practice was relevant and if so take it into account in determining such facts ... This meant that inferences might also be drawn from any failure to comply with any relevant code of practice.

9.   Where the claimant had proved facts from which conclusions could be drawn that the respondent had treated the claimant less favourably on the ground of sex, then the burden of proof moved to the respondent.

10.   It was then for the respondent to prove that he had not committed, or as the case might be, was not to be treated as having committed, that act.

11.   To discharge that burden it was necessary for the respondent to prove, on the balance of probabilities, that the treatment was in no sense whatsoever on the grounds of sex, since 'no discrimination whatsoever' was compatible with the burden of proof Directive (Council Directive 97/80/EC).

12.   That required a tribunal to assess not merely whether the respondent had proved an explanation for the facts from which such inferences could be drawn, but further that it was adequate to discharge the burden of proof on the balance of probabilities that sex was not a ground for the treatment in question.

13.   Since the facts necessary to prove an explanation would normally be in the possession of the respondent, a tribunal would normally expect cogent evidence to discharge that burden of proof. In particular, the tribunal would need to examine carefully explanations for failure to deal with the questionnaire procedure and/or code of practice.

To summarise, the claimant must prove, on the balance of probabilities, facts from which a tribunal could conclude, in the absence of an adequate explanation, that the respondent has discriminated against the claimant. The claimant must produce some evidence of discrimination before the burden will pass to the respondent. If the claimant does this then the respondent must prove that it did not commit the act. This is known as the shifting burden of proof – once the claimant has established a prima facie case (which will require the tribunal to hear evidence from the claimant and the respondent to see what proper inferences may be drawn (see *Madarassy v Nomura International* above and below)), the burden of proof shifts to the respondent to disprove the allegations, which will require consideration of the subjective reasons that caused the employer to act as he did. The respondent will have to show a non-discriminatory reason for the difference in treatment.

On the facts of *Barton v Investec*, the EAT found that Mrs Barton had produced sufficient evidence of sex discrimination to shift the burden of proof to the respondent, but that the tribunal had not considered what the employer's explanation was. The EAT found that, in hearing her claim for equal pay, the tribunal erred in that it failed to take into account Investec's reluctance to answer Mrs Barton's questionnaire and provide her with the information she requested concerning pay and bonuses.

The Court of Appeal in *Madarassy v Nomura* (above) took a further look at the burden of proof in discrimination cases. Essentially, it upheld the approach of the Court of Appeal in *Igen* and said that 'the correct legal position' was made plain in paras 28 and 29 of the judgment. The material parts of those paragraphs stated as follows:

28.   ... It is for the complainant to prove the facts from which ... the employment tribunal could conclude, in the absence of an adequate explanation, that the respondent committed an unlawful act of discrimination. It does not say that the facts to be proved are those from which the employment tribunal could conclude that the [respondent] 'could have committed' such act.

29.   The relevant act is, in a race discrimination case ... , that (a) in circumstances relevant for the purposes of any provision of the ... Act ...(b) the alleged discriminator treats another person less favourably and (c) does so on racial grounds. All those facts are facts which the complainant, in our judgment, needs to prove on the balance of probabilities ...

The Court emphasised that the Court of Appeal in *Igen* expressly rejected the argument that it was sufficient for the complainant simply to prove facts from which the tribunal could conclude that the respondent 'could have' committed an unlawful act of discrimination. It held that the bare facts of a difference in status and a difference in treatment indicate only a possibility of discrimination:

They are not, without more, sufficient material from which a tribunal 'could conclude' that, on the balance of probabilities, the respondent had committed an unlawful act of discrimination.

Evidence supporting a prima facie case might include breaches of the Codes of Practice (the tribunal must consider the reason for the failure – see *Tera (UK) Ltd v Mr A Goubatchev* (UKEAT/0490/08)), or an evasive reply to a questionnaire (see **8.8.1.2**). Evidence against a prima facie case might be, for example, evidence of how the respondent treats (or mistreats) others (and not just the complainant). In *Laing v Manchester City Council* [2006] IRLR 748, the claimant's case failed at the first stage because the respondent gave evidence that the claimant was treated in the same way as all subordinate employees.

Usefully, the Court of Appeal in *Madarassy* made it clear (at paras 56 and 70) that although s 136 involves a two-stage test, the tribunal does not hear evidence in two stages; rather, it will hear all the evidence in a case before applying the two-stage analysis. Readers should study the case before advising in discrimination cases. In *Gay v Sophos plc* (UKEAT/0452/10) the EAT confirmed that the tribunal is not obliged to follow the two-stage approach: if it finds that the employer was motivated by non-discriminatory considerations, the burden of proof has been discharged.

The burden of proof was considered most recently by the Supreme Court in *Hewage v Grampian Health Board* [2012] UKSC 37. The Supreme Court declined to give any further guidance beyond Igen and Madarassy. Lord Hope, giving the unanimous judgment, reiterated that a complainant must prove facts from which the tribunal could conclude, in the absence of an adequate explanation, that the respondent had committed an act of unlawful discrimination, 'so the prima facie care must be proved, and it is for the claimant to discharge that burden'. Lord Hope repeated (at para 32) what Underhill J had pointed out in *Martin v Devonshires Solicitors* [2011] ICR 352 (at para 39), to the effect that:

it is important not to make too much of the role of the burden of proof provisions. They will require careful attention when there is room for doubt as to the facts necessary to establish discrimination. But they have nothing to offer where the tribunal is in a position to make positive findings on the evidence one way or the other.

9.5.2   Case law – drawing inferences

9.5.2.1   Cases decided prior to *Barton v Investec*

In *Strathclyde Regional Council v Zafar* [1998] IRLR 36, the House of Lords held that mere unreasonable treatment by the employer 'casts no light whatsoever' on the question whether he has treated the employee 'unfavourably' (see also *Martins v Marks and Spencer plc* [1998] IRLR 326). In *Law Society and Others v Bahl* [2003] IRLR 640, the EAT agreed that mere unreasonableness is not enough. Elias J commented that:

> all unlawful discriminatory treatment is unreasonable, but not all unreasonable treatment is discriminatory, and it is not shown to be so merely because the victim is either a woman or of a minority race or colour ... Simply to say that the conduct was unreasonable tells nothing about the grounds for acting in that way ... The significance of the fact that the treatment is unreasonable is that a tribunal will more readily in practice reject the explanation given for it than it would if the treatment were reasonable.

A tribunal must also take into consideration all potentially relevant non-discriminatory factors that might realistically explain the conduct of the alleged discriminator.

These cases are still useful and relevant.

9.5.2.2   Cases decided after Barton v Investec

In *University of Huddersfield v Wolff* [2004] IRLR 534, the EAT overturned the tribunal's decision that, since there was less favourable treatment and a difference in sex, the burden shifted to the employer to provide an explanation. The EAT stated that 'the burden moves where the applicant has proved facts from which inferences could be drawn that the respondents have treated the applicant less favourably on the grounds of sex'. It is clear that more than simply being of a different sex/race is required to shift the burden of proof.

In *Igen Ltd and Others v Wong* (see **9.5.1** above), the Court of Appeal stated: 'The finding of unexplained unreasonable conduct enabled the Tribunal to draw the inferences satisfying the requirements of the first stage.' So it seems that unreasonable behaviour by an employer, combined with a relevant difference (sex, race, etc) may lead to a finding that the claimant has satisfied the initial evidential burden. However, Gibson LJ warned tribunals against:

> too readily infer[ring] unlawful discrimination on a prohibited ground merely from unreasonable conduct where there is no evidence of other discriminatory behaviour on such ground, [although on the facts] the tribunal was not wrong in law to draw that inference.

In *Moonsar v Fiveways Express* [2005] IRLR 9, the EAT held, applying the Barton guidelines (**9.5.1** above), that downloading pornography in an office or other place where it could be seen by a woman gave rise to a prima facie case of less favourable treatment (by affecting the woman's dignity and creating an intimating atmosphere) which shifted the burden of proof onto the employer to establish a non-discriminatory reason, such as the woman was party to what was going on. The employment tribunal had found that the conduct of the male employees did not amount to sex discrimination by way of sexual harassment because the claimant had not complained of the behaviour at the time and the images had not been shown to her. The EAT said that the fact that the claimant did *not* complain at the time did not afford a defence where the behaviour was so obvious and there was evidence that she found the behaviour unacceptable. Having established that there was a case to answer, the burden then shifted to the employer to show that the conduct was not discriminatory.

In *DKW Ltd v Adebayo* [2005] IRLR 514, a race case, the EAT gave guidance on the level of evidence that is required to establish a prima facie case so that the burden of proof passes to the employer. The claim in *Adebayo* followed the summary dismissal of an employee of black African origin, employed as a senior trader, for breach of trading guidelines. The claim for race discrimination was based on the fact that other traders who had breached the guidelines in the same way had not been disciplined. The EAT confirmed that the tribunal was correct to accept that the applicant had established a prima facie case not only because other, white traders had not been disciplined for the same offence, but also because there had apparently been a number of procedural failings in the way the employers dealt with the case. The employers had failed to put forward an adequate explanation, and the fact that they had a genuine belief in the applicant's misconduct was not sufficient. The case establishes that all that an applicant needs to do is to show some primary facts from which inferences could be drawn. The EAT emphasised that it is not sufficient at the first stage for an applicant to show simply that a comparator of a different race was promoted to a post for which the applicant had also applied – he would need to show that a comparator of a different race was promoted to the post *and* that he was at least as well qualified.

In *Mohmed v West Coast Trains Ltd* (UKEAT/0682/05), the EAT upheld the tribunal's finding that the applicant had failed to prove facts from which a tribunal could conclude, in the absence of a non-discriminatory explanation from the employer, that the employer had discriminated against him. The EAT said that it was open to the tribunal to conclude that no inference of less favourable treatment could be drawn in circumstances where it was agreed that the employee could maintain his beard at one fist's length, in accordance with his religion, provided it was tidy. No prima facie case of unlawful discrimination had been made out.

The Scottish Court of Session in *Bvunzai v Glasgow City Council* [2005] CSIH 85 upheld a tribunal's decision that it would be legitimate to draw an adverse inference that an interview panel's assessment of the claimant at interview was influenced by racial factors. That inference was based on the manner in which the claimant and another applicant for the job were scored, and the fact that the respondent was unable credibly to explain how it had scored the job applicants. Moreover, the respondent had also departed from its Code of Conduct and could not credibly explain why.

In *Komeng v Sandwell Metropolitan Borough Council* (UKEAT/0592/10) the EAT said that tribunals should take care before accepting an employer's explanation that the treatment was meted out by reason of poor administration. In the circumstances, the tribunal must consider carefully why the claimant was treated the way he was.

9.6 CASE STUDY: DIRECT RACE DISCRIMINATION CLAIM – BURDEN OF PROOF

Facts

(1)　C was employed as a cleaning supervisor by Veryclean Bus Services Ltd (R) at its main London depot, from 25 April 2011 until her dismissal on 30 September 2011. R's business is that of providing bus-cleaning services. R has over 500 members of staff across 15 sites. R issued an equal opportunities policy in 2006. R's workforce consists of people from a variety of racial and national origins. C worked 40 hours per week, from 6pm until 2.30am on each weekday night. Her job involved management responsibilities, supervising in total 30 night and day workers at the depot. C's main job role was to ensure the proper and adequate cleaning of buses that were bought to the depot as part of a weekly maintenance and service check. At the end of the maintenance and service work, R needed to clean the buses, prior to their being sent back into service. It was C's responsibility to oversee that cleaning operation. With effect from 1 June 2011, C's line manager changed. There was no evidence that, prior to X becoming C's line manager, there had been any concerns about the way in which C carried out her job. X became dissatisfied (based partly on comments that he said he received from London Underground about the state of some of the buses, and based partly on his own observations) about the standard of the cleaning and spoke about this to C informally on two occasions, on 20 July and 11 August. C maintained she had given X legitimate explanations for what he had observed. X noted on the second of these occasions that C's perception was that he was picking on her.

(2)　In addition to the two incidents on 20 July and 11 August, there were a number of other criticisms recorded by X about C on 19/08, 22/08, 28/08, 4/09 and 20/10. The final incident (20/10) related to an occasion on which X recorded that when he arrived at the site, he was told by a cleaner that C had gone home, that she had not told him, that he had tried to phone her and that she had said that she was sick. C did not deny that she was at home sick on this date.

(3) Following that incident, X hand-delivered to C's home a letter of termination giving C one week's notice. The letter set out no reasons for the termination. Notwithstanding that R had a disciplinary procedure which was stated to apply to all staff after the completion of their probationary period, there had been no investigation, and no disciplinary process or procedure was followed. Subsequently, in response to a suggestion by C's representative that the dismissal was discriminatory, X wrote

> As you are aware, C's employment with Veryclean Bus Services was less than 12 months, therefore we are under no legal obligation to supply you with the reasons for her dismissal. However, in the interest of fairness, openness and to dispel any suggestion that there may have been discrimination of any description, I am prepared to do so on this occasion. During her employment with us the following issues in regard to her performance conduct were raised but failed to be adequately addressed:
>
> • Failure to perform the necessary quality control measures that were fundamental to her role. For example, the completion and standard of the rota cleaning.
>
> • Failure to take reasonable action to ensure that the staff reported to her while performing their duties adequately and conducting themselves properly.
>
> • Failure to advise her area manager of absence from site.
>
> • Complaints from clients regarding the standard of cleaning.
>
> Should C wish to exercise her right of appeal we are willing to extend the deadline for this request to 10 October 2011 as per your request.

(4) C's representative responded, stating that his client believed that she had been dismissed on the grounds of her race and that, in particular, she believed that there was an informal policy of replacing black workers with white Portuguese workers.

(5) On 11 October 2011, C submitted a race questionnaire to R; and on 26 October, she submitted an appeal against the termination of her employment. She made no mention of or nor complained about discrimination in that appeal. That appeal stated:

> I was not given any warning and carried out my duties to the best of my knowledge. We have to clean rota buses before they are inspected and before the engineers get to repair them and repair could last up to two days sometimes even longer and the buses are sent back during the day with oil/grease etc.

No appeal took place. R subsequently submitted additional information in response to the questionnaire.

(6) After C was dismissed, her job was offered to M, a black African, who was a supervisor at an another of R's bus depots, who turned it down. Subsequently, a Portuguese worker, N, took over C's position.

Claims

(7) C's complaint is that her dismissal amounted to direct discrimination under s 13 of the Equality Act 2010 on racial grounds. She is of black African origin. The alleged less favourable treatment is her dismissal and the manner of her dismissal. As C had less than one year's service with R, she was unable to bring an unfair dismissal claim arising out of her dismissal.

(8) R says it has not discriminated against C. It says the dismissal was not because of C's race.

Evidence

(9) Disclosure took place in the usual way and paginated bundles were prepared which included extracts from C's personal file, extracts from the staff handbook on *Disciplinary Procedures, Grievances and Appeals*, papers relating to the C's dismissal and a Schedule of Loss from C setting out her claim for compensation.

(10) Statistically, the evidence proved in response to the RRA questionnaire showed that there were 11 black African leavers out of a total of 30 leavers between April 2011 and February 2012. This was one-third of the total. If the class was widened out to include all black (as opposed to white) leavers then the total was 19 out of 30, which would be two-thirds of the total leavers. In terms of information relating to X, he supervised a total of nine sites. As regards the other site supervisors or managers, out of nine, one was Portuguese, two were South American, one was Asian and one was Eastern European. The remainder were black Africans.

(11) Witness statements were exchanged prior to the hearing. At the hearing all witnesses who gave oral evidence were cross-examined and the tribunal had the opportunity to ask questions of them.

(12) At the conclusion of the evidence, both sides made oral submissions on liability and remedy.

(13) All these matters were taken into consideration by the tribunal before reaching its decision.

The issues to be decided

(14) The tribunal will have to determine:
   (a) Has C been treated less favourably than a real or hypothetical comparator?
   (b) If so, is the comparator from a different racial group from C?
   (c) If so, has C proved facts from which the tribunal could conclude that the difference in treatment was because of race?
   (d) If so, has R proved that it did not treat C less favourably in any sense whatsoever because of race?

(15) Depending on the outcome of the matters, the tribunal will have to determine what amount of compensation, if any, should be awarded.

Submissions

(16) R submitted that the tribunal needed to take note that there was a very diverse ethnic pattern within R's workforce, which was also affected by influxes of different nationalities. It submitted that C was not doing her job. It accepted that if this was an unfair dismissal case, the dismissal would be unfair, but said that that was not relevant to this claim. R submitted that there was an informal practice with regard to employees with less than one year's service, but there was nothing in writing about that. R referred the tribunal to *Igen Ltd v Wong* [2005] IRLR 258, where the Court of Appeal set out a number of guidelines with regard to the burden of proof. R submitted that, in the first instance, the burden did not shift from C to R. In the alternative, it submitted that if the burden did shift, R had discharged its obligations in terms of showing that C's dismissal was not connected in any way whatsoever to her race. R said that the fact that it did not comply with its own disciplinary procedures could not shift the burden of proof on its own; even if there was unreasonableness, there needed to be something else to shift the burden. The evidence was that the post was initially offered to M, who was a black African like C. Alternatively, if the burden shifted then there was an adequate explanation, which was that provided by M.

(17) C submitted that the appropriate comparator was a white Portuguese person. In that context, it was submitted that N, who eventually took over the post, might well be a suitable actual comparator, but in any event, C said that a hypothetical white Portuguese comparator would suffice. She said that the tribunal needed to look at the imbalance between black non-Portuguese and white Portuguese/others. C's case was that X had a policy of dismissing black workers and replacing them with Portuguese workers, and that she had been a victim of this policy. C's evidence was that there had been mainly black Africans in the workplace before X started work. After X arrived, 22 out of 39 staff

were white, of whom 16 were white European. C says she complained about race discrimination to X in August 2011. There was a suspicion that the notes of these meetings had not been recorded contemporaneously as X had claimed. R had not applied its own procedure. There was no reason for the dismissal. As far as *Igen v Wong* is concerned, C had been dismissed, no – and no fair – procedure had been followed, and C had been displaced by a Portuguese worker; these matters were, she said, sufficient to shift the burden of proof.

(18)   As far as statistics were concerned, C relied upon the statistics which indicated that out of 10 white leavers, 6 had been dismissed and 4 had resigned (one of whom returned); and that there had been 17 black leavers, of whom only 2 had resigned. Proportionately, she said, it was significant that there had been a large number of black leavers over a relatively short period of time. C submitted that the burden of proof shifted to R, who needed to provide an explanation. She said that R had failed to show that in no way whatsoever was race the reason for C's dismissal.

Tribunal findings

(19)   The unanimous judgment of the tribunal was that C's complaint of racial discrimination was not made out and it was dismissed.

(20)   *Comparator.* C's chosen comparator was a white Portuguese person who would not have been dismissed in the way and in the circumstances that C was, and/or who was promoted when C was dismissed.

(21)   *Has C proved facts from which the Tribunal could conclude that the treatment was because of her race?* The tribunal found as follows:

21.1   C had been treated unreasonably, in that no proper process had been followed with regard to any investigation or disciplinary hearing in connection with allegations about her conduct or capability; R had failed in that regard to follow its own procedures; however, the tribunal accepted the evidence advanced by both R's witnesses, which the tribunal regarded as being supported by the documents, that R had in practice disregarded a fair procedure when it dismissed *anyone* who had less than a year's service. The tribunal noted in particular that the dismissal letter sent to C was in virtually identical terms to (i) that sent by X's predecessor, Y, who was white British [against whom no complaint was or had been made] and (ii) that sent by X to B, described as white European; and (iii) was not dissimilar in terms to that sent by X to D, described as white European. As indicated by the EAT in *Laing* and approved by the Court of Appeal in *Madarassy*, having regard to all the evidence, the treatment or mistreatment (of others by the alleged discriminator) can be a highly material fact. On balance, the tribunal did not believe that the unreasonable treatment meted out to C was aimed only at her or at individuals of her race; it believed that all employees with less than one year's service were treated in this dismissive and unfair way by R. The tribunal was not convinced on the evidence before it that M and/or the hypothetical comparator would have been treated differently from C in similar circumstances relating to dissatisfaction with the way they carried out their jobs. On that basis, the tribunal did not find that this amounted to a proven fact from which it could conclude that C's less favourable treatment was because of race.

21.2   R was inconsistent in the reason it gave for C's dismissal – it had originally given no reason for the dismissal; subsequently it had said it was for 'operational' reasons; later, the letter of explanation set out reasons relating to C's capability. The tribunal accepted that R knew staff with less than a year's service did not have to be given a reason for dismissal. On balance, the tribunal did not believe that this alleged inconsistency amounted to a proven fact from which it could conclude that C's less favourable treatment was because of race.

21.3 A white Portuguese person eventually got C's job. Having heard the sworn testimony of M, who was a black African, the tribunal was satisfied that he had been offered the job by R. The tribunal did not find that the eventual appointment of a white Portuguese man amounted to a proven fact from which it could conclude that C's less favourable treatment was because of race. Neither did it give rise to any inference that C's treatment was because of race.

21.4 *Statistical evidence*. As far as statistics were concerned, there had been mainly black Africans in the workplace before X arrived. After he arrived, 22 out of 39 staff were white, of whom 16 were white European. Out of a total of 29 leavers between April 2011 and February 2012, there were 10 (British and European) white leavers, (6 of whom were dismissed and 4 of whom had resigned (one of whom returned)); in contrast there had been 19 (African, British and European) black leavers, of whom only 2 had resigned. Proportionately, C relied on these figures to support her allegation that X was dismissing black Africans and replacing them with white Europeans. There was no specific information available as to who, in terms of race, had replaced those who had been dismissed over this period, although by extrapolation from the information to answers in the Questionnaire, it would appear that out of a total of 69 staff recruited, 23 were black Africans, of whom 11 left [just under 50%] and 22 were white Europeans, of whom 6 left [just under 25%]. There is clearly, on any analysis, a very high turnover of staff – of 69 recruited, 30 had left and 39 had remained. The statistics relating to black leavers did on their face appear to be significant – there was a higher proportion of black leavers over that period, and particularly black leavers who were dismissed (17/29 compared to 6/29). R relied upon the fact that, out of the sites managed by X and/ or over which he had responsibility for recruitment, almost half of the managers who were in a position directly comparable to that of C were black African. There was only one Portuguese manager. Further, if the leaving figures were narrowed down from the broad groupings replied upon by C [all blacks against all whites], so as to focus on the treatment of black Africans against white Europeans, the apparent disparity between dismissals decreased quite significantly – 11 black Africans compared to 6 white Europeans. The statistics indicated that 6 out of 10 white people were dismissed rather than resigned, and that 17 out of 19 black people were dismissed rather than resigned. There was a slight weighting in favour of black people over white people in the tribunal's judgment, when looked at in the round; while the statistical evidence provided some support for C's thesis, it was not particularly determinative and was not, in isolation, sufficient to amount to a fact from which it could conclude that this dismissal was because of race. It was not enough to shift the burden onto R to give an explanation.

(22) On balance, therefore, it was the tribunal's judgment that C had not succeeded in discharging the initial burden of proof to show facts from which the tribunal could conclude that her dismissal because of race, and she accordingly did not get to stage two, such as to require an explanation from R.

(23) The tribunal added that in case it was wrong with regard to its assessment of the evidence at stage one, it would in any event have found that R had proved that it did not treat C any less favourably in any sense whatsoever because of race. In particular, the tribunal found R had proved to its satisfaction two matters, which it regarded as compelling, namely, that:

23.1 prior to the appointment of N, the job had been offered to M, who had turned it down;

23.2 R treated everyone with less then one year's service in the same unreasonable way.

(24) On that basis, it was the unanimous decision of the tribunal that C's claim for race discrimination failed.

SUMMARY

This chapter has looked at direct discrimination in respect of the following protected characteristics listed in s 4 of the Equality Act 2010:

(a)   sex, maternity, pregnancy or marital status;

(b)   gender reassignment;

(c)   colour, race, nationality or ethnic or national origins;

(d)   religion or belief;

(e)   sexual orientation (**9.1**).

(Age and disability are dealt with in separate chapters.)

One of the four main types of discrimination in the employment field outlawed by UK legislation is direct discrimination. Direct discrimination occurs when the reason for a person being treated less favourably than another is because of one of the protected characteristics (sex, race, religion or belief, sexual orientation, age, etc). The definition of direct discrimination is set out in s 13 of the Equality Act 2010 (**9.2**).

Less favourable treatment is a wide concept, which covers any 'disadvantage' – it does not require any tangible loss (**9.2.5**). Motive or intention is irrelevant and there is no defence once direct discrimination has been proved (save for age discrimination). There are special rules relating to pregnancy and maternity (**9.4**).

The burden of proving discrimination is a shifting one. The burden starts with the claimant. Once the claimant has established sufficient facts which, in the absence of any other explanation, point to a breach, the burden shifts to the employer. Section 136 provides that where a complainant can establish facts from which a tribunal could decide that there has been a contravention of a provision of the Equality Act 2010, the tribunal *must* find unlawful discrimination, *unless* the employer shows that it did not contravene the provision (**9.5**).

Remedies and enforcement are dealt with at **8.8**. Tribunals may, on making a finding of discrimination, as they consider just and equitable, make:

(a)   an order declaring the rights of the complainant;

(b)   an order requiring the respondent to pay the complainant compensation; and/or

(c)   a recommendation that the respondent take, within a specified period, practicable action to obviate or reduce the adverse effect of any act of discrimination.

The general principle as far as compensation is concerned is that, as far as possible, complainants should be placed in the same position as they would have been but for the unlawful act (see *Ministry of Defence v Wheeler* [1998] IRLR 23). In addition to awarding compensation for foreseeable damage arising directly from the unlawful act, a tribunal has jurisdiction to award compensation for personal injury, including both physical and psychiatric injury, and for injury to feelings (8.8.2.2).

A flowchart summarising direct discrimination is set out at **Figure 9.1** below.

Figure 9.1 Flowchart – Direct Discrimination

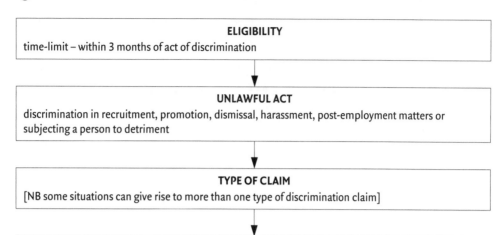

ELIGIBILITY
time-limit – within 3 months of act of discrimination

UNLAWFUL ACT
discrimination in recruitment, promotion, dismissal, harassment, post-employment matters or subjecting a person to detriment

TYPE OF CLAIM
[NB some situations can give rise to more than one type of discrimination claim]

DIRECT DISCRIMINATION
- Has C been treated differently and less favourably because of a protected characteristic?
- Need actual or hypothetical comparator (*Shamoon*)
- *Barton v Investec/Igen v Wong*
  - initial evidential burden on C to prove facts from which ET could conclude that reason for less favourable treatment is because of sex, etc
  - legal burden passes to R to show cogent reason for less favourable treatment; it was in no way whatsoever to do with C's sex, etc
  - if R's explanation is inadequate, ET must find that R committed an act of unlawful discrimination
- Exception. Is there an occupational requirement (OR) exception?

NO DEFENCE

VICARIOUS LIABILITY
R will be vicariously liable for acts of employees committed in the course of employment (*Jones v Tower Boot Co/Chief Constable of Lincolnshire Police v Stubbs*) unless R took all reasonably practicable steps to stop/avoid the discrimination (statutory defence – s 109(4))

REMEDIES
- declaration of employee's rights
- recommendation that employer take action to alleviate or reduce the effect of the discrimination
- order for compensation (no maximum)
  - pecuniary losses
  - aggravated damages if employer has behaved in a high-handed, malicious, insulting or aggressive manner
  - injury to feelings (*Vento/Da'Bell*)
  - psychiatric or physical injury
  - possibility of exemplary damages
  - increase/decrease for any unreasonable failure to comply with the Acas Code of Practice

INDIRECT DISCRIMINATION

LEARNING OUTCOMES

After reading this chapter you will be able to:

- understand the definition of indirect discrimination
- explain what is meant by the shifting burden of proof
- describe how the justification defence works
- list the potential remedies that are available where a complaint of indirect discrimination is made out.

10.1 INTRODUCTION

This chapter considers indirect discrimination in respect of the following protected characteristics listed in s 4 of the Equality Act 2010 (see **8.2.1**):

- gender reassignment (s 7)
- marriage and civil partnership (s 8)
- race (s 9)
- religion or belief (s 10)
- sex (s 11)
- sexual orientation (s 12)
- pregnancy and maternity (s 18).

This chapter refers, by way of illustration and example, to the pre- and post-Equality Act 2010 case law.

10.2 INDIRECT DISCRIMINATION

10.2.1 Definition

Indirect discrimination occurs when there is equal treatment of all groups but the effect of the provision, criterion or practice imposed by an employer has a disproportionate adverse impact on one group, unless the requirement can be justified. The definition of indirect discrimination is set out in s 19 of the Act:

(1) A person (A) discriminates against another (B) if A applies to B a provision, criterion or practice which is discriminatory in relation to a relevant protected characteristic of B's.

(2) For the purposes of subsection (1), a provision, criterion or practice is discriminatory in relation to a relevant protected characteristic of B's if—

(a) A applies, or would apply, it to persons with whom B does not share the characteristic,

(b)   it puts, or would put, persons with whom B shares the characteristic at a particular disadvantage when compared with persons with whom B does not share it,

(c)   it puts, or would put, B at that disadvantage, and

(d)   A cannot show it to be a proportionate means of achieving a legitimate aim.

Baroness Hale said in *Secretary of State for Trade and Industry v Rutherford and Another* [2006] IRLR 551, HL, that some points stand out:

(a)   the concept is normally applied to a rule or requirement which *selects* people for a particular advantage or disadvantage;

(b)   the rule is applied to a group of people who *want* something. The disparate impact complained of is that they cannot have what they want because of the rule, whereas others can.

The Explanatory Notes provide examples:

•   A woman is forced to leave her job because her employer operates a practice that staff must work in a shift pattern which she is unable to comply with because she needs to look after her children at particular times of day, and no allowances are made because of those needs. This would put women (who are shown to be more likely to be responsible for childcare) at a disadvantage, and the employer will have indirectly discriminated against the woman unless the practice can be justified.

•   An observant Jewish engineer who is seeking an advanced diploma decides (even though he is sufficiently qualified to do so) not to apply to a specialist training company because it invariably undertakes the selection exercises for the relevant course on Saturdays. The company will have indirectly discriminated against the engineer unless the practice can be justified.

Other examples based on the old law include the following:

(a)   A Sikh boy who was refused entrance to public school unless he cut his hair and stopped wearing a turban was indirectly discriminated against (*Mandla (Sewa Singh) and Another v Dowell Lee and Another* [1983] 2 AC 548; see now the approach in *R (on the application of Watkins-Singh) v Aberdare Girls' High School and Another* [2008] EWHC 1865 and *G v Headteacher and Governors of St Gregory's Catholic Science College* [2011] EWHC 1452, discussed at **10.2.3** below).

(b)   To impose a requirement that a job applicant must weigh at least 12 stone would be discriminatory against women unless the minimum weight was a genuine requirement of the job.

(c)   The imposition of an age requirement of 17½ to 28 for promotion to executive officer was held to be indirect 'discriminatory', as more women than men would be out of the labour market between those ages having children. It could also discriminate against immigrant applicants, who may obtain qualifications at a later age than those educated in the UK.

(d)   The requirement that an employee should work full time as opposed to part time may indirectly discriminate against women (*Home Office v Holmes* [1984] 3 All ER 549).

(e)   In order to increase efficiency a company decided that no holidays could be taken during the May to July peak period. When Eid fell in June 1992, the company refused to make any exceptions to its policy, even though its Muslim employees offered to work extra hours to compensate. The rule was indirectly discriminatory (*JH Walker Ltd v Hussain and Others* [1996] IRLR 11).

(f)   A requirement to be available for duty 24 hours a day, seven days a week, taken together with a restriction on bringing relatives abroad to facilitate childcare, was indirectly discriminatory on grounds of sex and race (*Ministry of Defence v De Bique* (UKEAT/0048/09)).

10.2.2 Meaning of provision, criterion or practice

This will cover informal and formal working practices, and will therefore allow for examination of, for example, recruitment and promotion policies and working practices that do not operate as absolute requirements for the job in question (see, eg, *BA plc v Starmer* [2005] IRLR 862).

10.2.3 Impact of provision – disadvantage

Once a provision, etc has been established, the complainant must show that the provision, etc is to the detriment of his or her group. Before any assessment of the impact of the provision, etc can be made, the appropriate pool for comparison must be identified. There has been some doubt as to whether the identification of the appropriate pool for comparison is a question of fact or law for the tribunal. If it is a question of fact, that means that a tribunal's decision cannot easily be appealed.

However, in *Allonby v Accrington and Rossendale College and Others* [2001] IRLR 364, Sedley LJ characterised the identification of the pool as a 'matter ... of logic', such that once the provision, etc has been identified, 'there is likely to be only one pool which serves to test its effect'. If the wrong pool is used, this will probably now be an error of law.

In *Jones v University of Manchester* [1993] IRLR 218 (a claim under the SDA 1975), the University had advertised a post requiring a graduate aged between 27 and 35. Mrs Jones argued that this indirectly discriminated against women. She was aged 46. The pool for comparison, Mrs Jones argued, should be graduates who had obtained their degrees as mature students. The tribunal agreed and upheld her complaint, as statistics showed that the proportion of women graduates obtaining their degrees as mature students (aged over 25) who could comply with the requirement was considerably smaller than the proportion of male graduates who had obtained their degrees as mature students. However, the EAT held that the wrong pool for comparison had been chosen, and the Court of Appeal upheld this view. The Court held that the appropriate pool for comparison was all men and women with the required qualifications for the job, not including the requirement complained of (ie, all graduates with relevant experience, ignoring age, and not just those who had graduated as mature students).

It will often be the case in recruitment situations that the appropriate pool for comparison is all those who are qualified for the post in question, including all those who would be so qualified were it not for the alleged discriminatory requirement. In other cases, where the complainant alleges that a practice of the employer is discriminatory, the pool might be the workforce to whom that requirement applies (see, eg, *London Underground Ltd v Edwards* [1998] IRLR 364, where the pool was all London Underground train drivers).

Once a pool for comparison has been established, the tribunal must consider whether the provision, etc would put persons of the group in question at a particular disadvantage when compared to persons of the other group. Thus, for example, in a indirect sex discrimination claim, the tribunal must compare the proportion of women within the pool who suffer a disadvantage with the proportion of men. Under the old law it was necessary to show that the proportion of one sex or one race *who could comply* with the requirement was considerably smaller than that of the comparative group. The use of the word 'would' suggests that statistical evidence will not always be required to prove this. The tribunal will be able to consider the likely impact of the proposed provision, etc. Michael Rubenstein comments in the *Equal Opportunities Review* (No 118) that 'it will be sufficient if it can be shown, perhaps via economic or sociological evidence, that the practice would be likely to have an adverse impact on the group to which the [complainant] belongs'.

In *London Underground Ltd v Edwards* (above) (a sex discrimination case), London Underground imposed a requirement to work flexible hours. All 2,023 men could comply (100%) and 20 out of the 21 women could comply (95.2%). The Court of Appeal held that the requirement was

indirectly discriminatory. The Court of Appeal accepted that a percentage difference of no more than 5% would often lead a tribunal to the conclusion that the 'considerably smaller' requirement had not been made out. However, by taking into account wider national statistics (10 lone mothers for each father), the Court of Appeal was able to uphold the tribunal's findings of indirect discrimination. A similar approach was taken by the EAT in *Chief Constable of Avon Constabulary v Chew* [2001] All ER (D) 101 (Sep), (UKEAT/503/00).

In *Hacking and Paterson and Another v Wilson* (UKEAT/0054/09), the EAT commented that society has changed, and men now take on more childcare responsibilities. Whether the statistics bear that out is, in the authors' view, doubtful.

In *Cross and Others v BA plc* [2005] IRLR 423, the EAT upheld the tribunal's decision that the provision, providing for a compulsory retirement age of 55 for cabin crew and pilots, was to the detriment of a considerably larger proportion of women than men. The statistics presented to the tribunal showed that 90.28% of men were disadvantaged compared to 98.55% of women; and that 9.72% of men could comply with the provision, etc, compared to 1.45% of women. The employer argued on appeal that the tribunal should have ignored the smaller advantaged group and instead concentrated on the disadvantaged group statistics; it would, according to the employer, have been bound to find that there was no clear case of adverse impact. The EAT held that the tribunal was entitled to look at all the figures; and that in cases of less obvious adverse impact it should use more than one form of comparison.

In 1998, a challenge was launched to the UK's cut-off age of 65 for unfair dismissal claims and redundancy compensation (*Secretary of State for Trade and Industry v Rutherford and Another* [2006] IRLR 551, HL). In the absence of any age equality legislation at that time, the claim was brought based on indirect sex discrimination. Mr Rutherford had been made redundant in 1998 at the age of 67 by his employer, Harvest Town Circle Ltd. He claimed that the cut-off age of 65 indirectly discriminated against men, because more men than women continued to work past 65. Harvest subsequently went into liquidation and the defence of the claim was taken over by the Secretary of State. A tribunal held that the cut-off provisions did amount to indirect sex discrimination against men. It found, after a detailed statistical analysis, that in the pool of employees affected by the cut off, the proportion of men who were disadvantaged (ie all those over 65) was greater than the proportion of disadvantaged women. The EAT ([2001] IRLR 599 and [2003] IRLR 858) and the Court of Appeal ([2004] IRLR 892) disagreed with the way the tribunal had analysed the statistics. The case went to the House of Lords, which gave its decision on 3 May 2006. Unhelpfully, while there was a unanimous conclusion that there was no unlawful discrimination, each of their Lordships adopted a slightly different approach. However, the analysis in the House of Lords judgment of the principles of and the approach to the indirect discrimination claims is important, and should be considered fully by anyone wishing to bring or defend an indirect discrimination claim. The point to note here is that the House of Lords focused on the *advantaged* group in this case.

However, the Court of Appeal, in *Grundy v BA plc* [2007] EWCA Civ 1020, held that the employment tribunal did not err when it focused on the *disadvantaged* group, where the women disadvantaged outnumbered men 14:1, rather than on the make-up of the advantaged group, which contained 99% of all employees in the relevant pool, when deciding whether the practice disadvantaged considerably more women. The Court said that there is no rule that the focus should be on the advantaged or disadvantaged group. It depends on the facts. The pool, said the Court of Appeal:

> must be one which suitably tests the particular discrimination complained of; [there is no universal formula for locating the correct pool]. It needs to include, but not be limited to, those affected by the term of which complaint is made, which can be expected to include both people who can and people who cannot comply with it.

In *Somerset CC and Another v Pike* [2009] EWCA Civ 808, the Court of Appeal held that rules in the Teachers' Pension Scheme that prevented retired teachers who returned to part-time work from joining the scheme (those who returned full-time were allowed to rejoin) could be indirectly discriminatory. Mrs Pike took early retirement from teaching on grounds of ill-health in 1993. She returned to part-time work in 1994, but under the rules of the Scheme she was prevented from rejoining the Scheme. It was argued that this amounted to indirect sex discrimination because it disadvantaged a substantially higher proportion of women than men, as women are statistically more likely to work on a part-time basis. An employment tribunal decided that the correct pool of comparison was the whole of the teaching profession, which resulted in only a slightly adverse disparate impact of the rule on women of 0.3%. On that basis the tribunal found no detriment. The EAT held that the pool should consist only of teachers wishing to return to work, and excluding those who were not included in the post-retirement rules. On this basis, the disparity in relation to women assessed over a 13-year period was more significant – 15% more women than men were in non-pensionable employment and, comparing the proportion of advantaged women over the same period, 38% more men than women were advantaged. The Court of Appeal, applying the House of Lords decision in *Rutherford* (above), agreed. By adopting the entire teaching profession as the pool of comparison, the employment tribunal had brought into the equation people who had no interest in the advantage or disadvantage in question. The case was remitted to the employment tribunal to consider whether or not the rule could be justified.

In *Eweida v British Airways* [2009] IRLR 78, the EAT said that a dress code that prevented an employee from wearing a visible cross was not unlawful indirect discrimination. British Airways' policy did not permit personal items of jewellery to be visible over a uniform unless they were mandatory religious items which could not be concealed. When E insisted on wearing her cross visibly, having been warned not to do so, she was sent home. She was offered an alternative job for which a uniform was not required, but she refused it. She said that the policy was indirectly discriminatory. The EAT said that the policy did not put Christians as a group at a *particular disadvantage*, as there was no evidence that other Christians felt disadvantaged, and this decision was upheld by the Court of Appeal ([2010] EWCA Civ 80). Permission to appeal to the Supreme Court was refused.

In *G v Headteacher and Governors of St Gregory's Catholic Science College* [2011] EWHC 1452, the High Court had to consider whether a school's uniform and hair policy, which prohibited boys from wearing their hair in cornrows, was unlawful discrimination on sex and/or racial grounds. G, who was 11 and of African-Caribbean ethnicity, was due to start his secondary education at St Gregory's Catholic Science College, a strict but high-performing inner-London school. Since birth, G had not cut his hair and, in accordance with family tradition, kept his hair in cornrows. African-Caribbean girls were permitted to wear their hair in cornrows as the School recognised that this helped keep long hair neat and under control. The school's written uniform policy did not explicitly prohibit cornrows for boys, but the cornrow ban was outlined at an introductory meeting at the school in September 2009, which G missed. G was unwilling to comply with the school's policy and was therefore unable to take up his place at the school. He subsequently brought judicial review proceedings alleging that the school's policy amounted to indirect race discrimination and sex discrimination. (He has also launched a claim for damages in the county court alleging sex and race discrimination.)

The school had a strong Catholic ethos. One of its principal aims behind the ban on cornrows was to keep gang culture out of the school, to avoid ethnic tensions and violence. The school considered that distinctive haircuts could be 'badges of ethnic or gang identity in an aggressive or unwelcome sense and can help foster disunity rather than unity'. It therefore adopted a zero tolerance approach to all male hairstyles.

To prove indirect race discrimination, G had to show that the school's policy placed a racial group at a particular disadvantage and also that he, as an individual, suffered that disadvantage. The case is a good example of the difficulties of proving group discrimination where not all those who share a protected characteristic are equally affected by the policy.

Compare *Mandla* (see **10.2.1(a)**), where all Sikh men are required to wear their hair long and would be disadvantaged by a prohibition on wearing turbans, with *Eweida* (above) where the Court found that the employee's belief in the requirement to wear a visible cross was a personal one. The courts have been clear that 'the whole purpose of indirect discrimination is to deal with the problem of group discrimination' (per Elias J in *Eweida*), but there is no agreement as to how large or small a group must be to be protected. The Court of Appeal in *Eweida* expressed concern that a wide interpretation of 'group' risks placing 'an impossible burden on employers to anticipate and provide for what may be parochial or even factitious beliefs in society at large'.

In G's case, the judge concluded that the 'group disadvantage test' was satisfied as there was evidence that there were groups of African-Caribbean ethnicity who, for reasons based on their culture and ethnicity, regard the cutting of their hair to be wrong, so that it is necessary for them to keep their hair in cornrows. Collins J said:

> It may be that those who regard it as an obligation rather than a preference are in the minority, but on the material before me, I am satisfied that there is a group who could be particularly disadvantaged by a refusal to permit them to wear their hair in cornrows.

The judge also concluded that the school's refusal to allow G to attend school, and the trauma he suffered in being turned away on his first day, amounted to a sufficient individual disadvantage. The judge rejected the school's defence of justification, namely that its policy was a 'proportionate means of achieving a legitimate aim'. Collins J concluded that although the aim of the policy was legitimate, the school's argument that introducing exceptions would undermine the whole uniform policy was not a valid one. He concluded that a blanket policy without exceptions could not be justified.

The judge rejected G's sex discrimination claim. Applying *Smith v Safeway* [1996] ICR 868, he concluded a dress code will not be discriminatory where it enforces a common standard of conventionality for both men and women. On the facts, the school's rationale for permitting African-Caribbean girls to wear their hair in cornrows (keeping long hair neat and under control) was not evidence of sex discrimination.

10.2.4 Complainant's disadvantage

The complainant must suffer a disadvantage. Hypothetical cases cannot be brought. The House of Lords confirmed in *Shamoon v Chief Constable of the Royal Ulster Constabulary* [2003] IRLR 285 that, in order to qualify as a disadvantage, the disadvantage must arise in the employment field. But once this requirement is satisfied, as the House of Lords confirmed in *Shamoon*, the only other limitation that can be read into the words is:

> Is the treatment of such a kind that a reasonable worker would or might take the view that in all the circumstances it was to his detriment? An unjustified sense of grievance cannot amount to 'detriment' … [b]ut … it is not necessary to demonstrate some physical or economic consequence.

An obvious example of disadvantage in the employment context is not getting promoted or being dismissed.

In *Keane v Investigo and Others* (UKEAT/0389/09), the EAT dismissed the claimant's claims of age discrimination because she had applied for jobs only in order to claim compensation, and on that basis had not suffered a detriment (ie she had no interest in the job vacancies).

10.2.5 Dual discrimination

There is no equivalent to s 14 of the Act for indirect dual discrimination (see **9.2.3**). However, in *Ministry of Defence v DeBique* (UKEAT/0048/09), the EAT held that the claimant, a female soldier from St Vincent with childcare commitments, had been the victim of sex and race discrimination by reason of two 'provisions, criteria or practices' (PCPs): one requiring that she be available for deployment on a 24/7 basis ('the 24/7 PCP'), which disadvantaged her as a female single parent; the second prohibiting her from inviting a member of her extended family not of British origin to stay with her in Services Family Accommodation (and thereby assist with childcare) ('the immigration PCP'), which disadvantaged her as a foreign national. On this basis, the EAT upheld the employment tribunal's conclusion that indirect discrimination claims under the RRA 1976 and the SDA 1975 were made out when the combined effect of the two PCPs were considered. The EAT commented that 'discrimination is often a multi-faceted experience' and should not be artificially compartmentalised. When the two PCPs were considered together, their discriminatory effect could not be justified.

10.2.6 Employer's defence

The employer must show that the provision, etc is 'a proportionate means of achieving a legitimate aim' (s 19(2)(d) of the Act). The Directive uses slightly different language: 'objectively justified by a legitimate aim and the means of achieving that aim are appropriate and necessary'. The (old) CRE commented as follows:

> It is our belief that the 'proportionality test' is a more limited test than that provided for by the Directive ie that the means used are 'appropriate and necessary'.

In *Allonby v Accrington and Rossendale College and Others* [2001] IRLR 364, the Court of Appeal made it clear that:

> once an employment tribunal has concluded that [the provision, etc] has a disparate impact on a protected group it must carry out a critical evaluation of whether the reasons demonstrate a real need to take the action in question. This should include consideration of whether there was another way to achieve the aim in question.

Courts and tribunals must carry out a balancing exercise between the degree of discrimination caused and the object or aim to be achieved, taking into account the surrounding circumstances (*Cobb v Employment Secretary* [1989] IRLR 464). However, the means used to achieve a legitimate aim might be proportionate but there could still be an alternative way to achieve the aim.

The Supreme Court held, in *Homer v Chief Constable of West Yorkshire Police* [2012] UKSC 15, that to be proportionate, a measure must be an appropriate and necessary means of meeting the aim.

So, for example, a rule prohibiting beards in a chocolate factory may be considered a proportionate response and justifiable in the interests of hygiene, but rather than not employing bearded persons, the employer should look at other means of achieving the objective, such as the covering up of beards. The 'appropriate and necessary' test requires consideration of whether there are less discriminatory alternative measures to achieve the aim; the proportionality test requires the same consideration.

In *Hardys & Hansons v Lax* [2005] EWCA Civ 846, (a case under the SDA 1975), the Court of Appeal held that the 'range of reasonable responses' test (see **5.3.1.1**) does not apply when tribunals have to decide whether an otherwise discriminatory practice is objectively justified. (See too *Board of Governors of St Matthias Church of England School v Crizzle* [1993] ICR 401, *Azmi v Kirklees Metropolitan Borough Council* [2007] IRLR 484 and *Allen v GMB* [2008] IRLR 691.) The Court in *Hardys* said that the principle of proportionality required the tribunal to take into account the reasonable needs of the business. But it had to make its own judgment, upon a fair and detailed analysis of the working practices and business considerations involved, as to whether the proposal was reasonably necessary. The reasonableness qualification did *not* permit the margin of discretion or range of reasonable responses for which the respondent contended. The Court also added that, where an employer is relying on the economic needs of the business, it would be expected to adduce sufficient evidence of that business need to enable the tribunal to 'set out at least a basic economic analysis of the business and its needs'.

Examples under the old and new definitions of 'indirect discrimination' include the following:

(a)   In *Panesar v Nestlé Co* [1980] ICR 144, a factory rule prohibiting beards and long hair had a disproportionate impact on Sikhs, but it was held to be objectively justified on the grounds of hygiene.

(b)   In *London Underground Ltd v Edwards* (a sex discrimination case) (**10.2.3** above), the EAT held that the tribunal was entitled to find that the employers had not justified the requirement to work flexible hours. There was good evidence that the employer could have made arrangements which would not have been damaging to its business plans but which would have accommodated the reasonable needs of its employees.

(c)   There is some conflicting case law on whether cost alone may be relied upon to justify an otherwise discriminatory policy. In *Cross and Others v BA plc* (**10.2.3** above), a case decided under the equivalent of the new law, the EAT held that the employment tribunal had been entitled to take the cost to the employer of changing the offending provision into account when deciding whether the employer could justify the provision. The EAT added that costs could not be the sole justification, but they were nevertheless a relevant factor. (See also *BA plc v Starmer* [2005] IRLR 862, where the employer failed in its attempt to justify a refusal to halve the hours of a full-time female airline pilot with childcare responsibilities.) In *Woodcock v Cumbria Primary Care NHS Trust* [2012] EWCA Civ 330, the Court of Appeal held that a dismissal carried out in such a way as to avoid additional costs to the Trust of the employee attaining the age of 50 years before the end of his notice period, and thus being entitled to enhanced redundancy payments, was justified because the decision to terminate his employment by reason of redundancy was genuine and legitimate, and it was a part of that aim to ensure that the Trust also saved money through the timing of the notice given (the 'costs plus' approach).

(d)   In *Williams Drabble v Pathway Care Solutions Ltd and Another* (ET/2601718/04), the employment tribunal held that the employer had indirectly discriminated against a Christian employee when it imposed a requirement to work on Sundays. The employer had imposed a provision, criterion or practice on all staff, but it put practising Christians at a disadvantage and the employer was not able, on the facts, to show that the requirement to work on Sundays was a proportionate means of achieving a legitimate aim.

(e)   In *Azmi v Kirklees Metropolitan Borough Council* [2007] IRLR 484, the tribunal's finding was that refusing to permit a Muslim woman teacher to wear a full veil did not amount to indirect religious discrimination because the treatment was justified – the need to communicate effectively was a legitimate aim and was proportionate – the woman could wear a veil at all other times when not working directly with the children.

(f)   In *London Borough of Islington v Ladele* [2010] IRLR 211 (see **9.2.6.1** above), the Court of Appeal accepted that Islington's policy of requiring all registrars to officiate at civil partnerships did indirectly discriminate on grounds of religion (it 'put a person such as Ms Ladele, who believed that civil partnerships were contrary to the will of God, "at a disadvantage when compared with other persons", namely those who did not have that belief'), but the Court went on to say that the aim of providing the service on a non-discriminatory basis was a proportionate means of achieving a legitimate aim.

The Court, in considering the question of justification, agreed with the EAT which had said:

> Once it is accepted that that the aim of providing the service on a non-discriminatory basis was legitimate – and in truth it was bound to be – then ... it must follow that [Islington] were entitled to require all registrars to perform the full range of services.

(g)   In *Mayuuf v Governing Body of Bishop Challenor Catholic Collegiate School and Another* (ET/3202398/2004) (see <www.practicallaw.com/3-369-5996>), the claimant's beliefs required attendance at a mosque every Friday. The school required him to teach at that time (in 2003/04), and he brought a claim of indirect discrimination. The tribunal held that the school's actions were objectively justified, balancing the discriminatory effect on Mr Mayuuf against:

(i)   declining standards in maths and the new arrangements in place;

(ii)   the fact that all the Year 11 maths classes had to take place at the same time, so that pupils could be moved up or down between sets according to ability;

(iii)   the fact that it was impossible to rewrite the timetable to free the relevant period; and

(iv)   the fact that providing a supply teacher would have affected the continuity of education and have been too costly.

(h)   In *Joseph Estorninho v Zoran Jokic t/a Zorans Delicatessen* (ET/2301487/06), the claimant was held to have been indirectly discriminated against when he was told that he would be required to work on Sundays. As a practising Catholic he attended church on a Sunday, and he was thereby placed at a 'particular disadvantage' compared with non-Catholics. Moreover, the employer had not considered other ways of arranging Sunday working, and thus had not adopted proportionate means.

(i)   In *Cherfi v G4S Security Services Ltd* (UKEAT/0379/10), the EAT upheld the tribunal's decision that a requirment that security guards be on site during the whole of their shift was a proportionate means of achieving a legitimate aim, in circumstances where the claimant had access to an on-site prayer facility and had been offered different shifts.

10.3 BURDEN OF PROOF

The burden of proving objective justification is on the employer ('which he cannot show to be a proportionate means of achieving a legitimate aim'). The employer needs to produce cogent evidence that the justification defence is made out (see *British Airways v Starmer* [2005] IRLR 862 and *Osborne Clarke Services v Purohit* [2009] IRLR 341). However, the claimant has to show some evidence of disparate impact before the burden of proof is placed on the employer. The Court of Appeal held in *Bailey and Others v The Home Office* [2005] IRLR 369 that the tribunal had been entitled to conclude that there was a prima facie case of discrimination where the advantaged group was predominantly male but the disadvantaged group was mixed, containing both men and women. Waller LJ made clear the claimant's burden:

> ... thus, where a difference in pay is established, and statistics seem to indicate a possibility of a disproportionate impact on women when looking at both the advantaged and disadvantaged groups as a whole, those statistics must provide sufficient evidence to get those carrying the burden over the hurdle of placing the onus on the employer ...

The Court of Appeal's judgment was given before a new definition of 'indirect discrimination' was brought into effect in October 2005 by the Employment Equality (Sex Discrimination) Regulations 2005. The definition in the Equality Act 2010 is identical. Commentators, at the time the new definition became law, queried *when* the burden of proof shifts in an indirect discrimination case. Taking the new definition into account, Claire Hockney of the EOC suggested that the burden of proof would transfer to the employer where the claimant could show:

(a)   the existence of a provision, criterion, practice, etc; and

(b)   facts that 'indicate a possibility' that a particular group has been disadvantaged without the need to provide supporting statistics.

She said that:

> arguably, the intention of the legislation is that all the claimant is required to do is produce some evidence (even their own oral evidence) from which a tribunal could infer disparate impact. Once they do this the burden shifts to the respondent to show otherwise by cogent evidence.

A respondent could, at this stage, for example, put in evidence showing others are also at a disadvantage. This analysis still appears relevant today.

10.4 REMEDIES

See **8.8**. In a case of indirect discrimination, where the tribunal is satisfied there was no intent to discriminate, the tribunal must not award compensation without first considering whether to make a declaration or recommendation (s 124(4) and (5)).

SUMMARY

This chapter has looked at indirect discrimination in respect of the following protected characteristics listed in s 4 of the Equality Act 2010:

(a)   sex, maternity, pregnancy or marital status;

(b)   gender reassignment;

(c)   colour, race, nationality or ethnic or national origins;

(d)   religion or belief;

(e)   sexual orientation (**8.1**).

(Age and disability are dealt with in separate chapters.)

One of the four main types of discrimination in the employment field outlawed by UK legislation is indirect discrimination. Indirect discrimination occurs when there is equal treatment of all groups but the effect of a provision, criterion or practice imposed by an employer has a disproportionate adverse impact on one group, unless the requirement can be justified. The definition of indirect discrimination is set out in s 19 of the Equality Act 2010 (**10.2**).

Once a provision, etc has been established, the complaint must show that it is to the detriment of his group, ie it would put persons of the group at a particular disadvantage. The complainant must also suffer a disadvantage, so hypothetical cases cannot be brought (**10.2.3** and **10.2.4**). An employer has a defence to an indirect discrimination claim if he can show that the provision, etc is a 'proportionate means of achieving a legitimate aim' (**10.2.6**).

The burden of proving discrimination is a shifting one. The burden starts with the claimant. Once he has established sufficient facts which, in the absence of any other explanation, point to a breach, then the burden shifts to the employer. Section 136 provides that where a complainant can establish facts from which a tribunal could decide that there has been a contravention of a provision of the Equality Act 2010, the tribunal *must* find unlawful discrimination *unless* the employer shows it did not contravene the provision (**10.3** and **9.5**).

Remedies and enforcement are dealt with at **8.8**. Tribunals may, on making a finding of discrimination, as they consider just and equitable, make:

(a)   an order declaring the rights of the complainant;

(b)   an order requiring the respondent to pay to the complainant compensation; and/or

(c)   a recommendation that the respondent take, within a specified period, practicable action to obviate or reduce the adverse effect of any act of discrimination.

The general principle as far as compensation is concerned is that, as far as possible, complainants should be placed in the same position as they would have been but for the unlawful act (see *Ministry of Defence v Wheeler* [1998] IRLR 23). In addition to awarding compensation for foreseeable damage arising directly from the unlawful act, a tribunal has jurisdiction to award compensation for personal injury, including both physical and psychiatric injury, and for injury to feelings (**8.8.2.2**).

A flowchart summarising indirect discrimination is set out at **Figure 10.1** below.

Figure 10.1 Flowchart – Indirect Discrimination

ELIGIBILITY
time limit – within 3 months of act of discrimination

UNLAWFUL ACT
discrimination in recruitment, promotion, dismissal, harassment, post-employment matters or subjecting a person to detriment

TYPE OF CLAIM
[NB some situations can give rise to more than one type of discrimination claim]

INDIRECT DISCRIMINATION
- Has R applied a provision, criterion or practice that applies equally to all?
- Does that provision put persons of one group at a particular disadvantage compared to others?
  – Particular disadvantage?
  – Pool of comparison required?
- Has C suffered a disadvantage?

POTENTIAL DEFENCE: JUSTIFICATION
Can R show provision is a proportionate means of achieving a legitimate aim?

VICARIOUS LIABILITY
R will be vicariously liable for acts of employees committed in the course of employment (*Jones v Tower Boot Co/Chief Constable of Lincolnshire Police v Stubbs*) unless R took all reasonably practicable steps to stop/avoid the discrimination (statutory defence – s 109(4))

REMEDIES
- declaration of employee's rights
- recommendation that employer take action to alleviate or reduce the effect of the discrimination
- order for compensation (no maximum)
  – pecuniary losses
  – aggravated damages if employer has behaved in a high-handed, malicious, insulting or aggressive manner
  – injury to feelings (*Vento/Da'Bell*)
  – psychiatric or physical injury
  – possibility of exemplary damages
  – increase/decrease for any unreasonable failure to comply with the Acas Code of Practice

HARASSMENT AND VICTIMISATION

LEARNING OUTCOMES

After reading this chapter you will be able to:

- explain what is meant by harassment and what the different types of harassment are
- explain when employers are liable for the acts of third parties
- explain what is meant by victimisation
- list the potential remedies that are available where a complaint of harassment or victimisation is made out.

11.1 INTRODUCTION

This chapter considers harassment and victimisation in respect of the following protected characteristics listed in s 4 of the Equality Act 2010 (see **8.2.1**):

- gender reassignment (s 7)
- race (s 9)
- religion or belief (s 10)
- sex (s 11)
- sexual orientation (s 12).

Section 26 (harassment) does not include marriage and civil partnership, or pregnancy and maternity: this is because pregnancy and maternity are covered by harassment related to sex, and as there is no evidence that people have been harassed due to marriage and civil partnership, it was not considered necessary to include these characteristics. These grounds are not covered by European law. One view is that harassment relating to those matters may be brought under s 13 as direct discrimination; another view is that as s 26 does not specifically disapply those protected characteristics, they are still included.

This chapter refers, by way of illustration and example, to the pre- and post-Equality Act 2010 case law.

11.2 BURDEN OF PROOF

The reversed burden of proof applies in both harassment and victimisation cases (s 136). Thus, where a prima facie case of harassment or victimisation is made out by a claimant, the tribunal will be required to find for the claimant unless the defendant can prove that his or her conduct was not unlawful (see **9.5** and **10.3**).

11.3 HARASSMENT

11.3.1 Definition

The definition of harassment is set out in s 26 of the Act.:

(1)   A person (A) harasses another (B) if—

    (a)   A engages in unwanted conduct related to a relevant protected characteristic, and

    (b)   the conduct has the purpose or effect of—

        (i)   violating B's dignity, or

        (ii)   creating an intimidating, hostile, degrading, humiliating or offensive environment for B.

(2)   A also harasses B if—

    (a)   A engages in unwanted conduct of a sexual nature, and

    (b)   the conduct has the purpose or effect referred to in subsection (1)(b).

(3)   A also harasses B if—

    (a)   A or another person engages in unwanted conduct of a sexual nature or that is related to gender reassignment or sex,

    (b)   the conduct has the purpose or effect referred to in subsection (1)(b), and

    (c)   because of B's rejection of or submission to the conduct, A treats B less favourably than A would treat B if B had not rejected or submitted to the conduct.

(4)   In deciding whether conduct has the effect referred to in subsection (1)(b), each of the following must be taken into account—

    (a)   the perception of B;

    (b)   the other circumstances of the case;

    (c)   whether it is reasonable for the conduct to have that effect.

...

As with direct discrimination, s 26 prohibits harassment based on association and perception; to bring a claim, a victim of harassment does not have to possess the 'protected characteristic' himself: '... A engages in unwanted conduct *related to* a relevant protected characteristic' (s 26(1)(a)) (emphasis added).

Note that under the law, where the complaint is about harassment, the complainant cannot also claim direct discrimination, because 'detriment' does not include subjecting a person to harassment: see the definition of 'detriment' in s 212(1) of the Act: '"detriment" does not, subject to subsection (5), include conduct which amounts to harassment'.

There are three different types of harassment:

(a)   'Characteristic-related harassment' applies to all the protected characteristics listed in **11.1** above. It involves unwanted conduct which is related to a relevant characteristic and has the purpose or effect of creating an intimidating, hostile, degrading, humiliating or offensive environment for the complainant, or violating the complainant's dignity.

(b)   Sexual harassment is unwanted conduct of a sexual nature, where this has the purpose or effect of creating an intimidating, hostile, degrading, humiliating or offensive environment for the complainant, or violating the complainant's dignity.

(c)   The third type of harassment is treating someone less favourably because that person has either submitted to or rejected sexual harassment, or harassment related to sex or gender reassignment which had the purpose or effect of creating an intimidating, hostile, degrading, humiliating or offensive environment for the complainant, or violating the complainant's dignity.

Each will be dealt with in more detail below.

11.3.2 Characteristic-related harassment

European Union law defines harassment (Equal Treatment Directive (Recast) 2006/54) as:

> where unwanted conduct related to the [sex, etc] of a person occurs with the purpose or effect of violating the dignity of a person, and of creating an intimidating, hostile, degrading, humiliating or offensive environment.

To be unlawful under the old law, harassment had to be 'on the ground' of sex, etc. In *Equal Opportunities Commission v Secretary of State for Trade and Industry* [2007] IRLR 327, the EOC successfully challenged the UK legislation (in so far as it dealt with harassment in sex cases) in judicial review proceedings. The EOC submitted that the use of the words 'on the ground of' in SDA 1975, s 4A imported causation into the Act, requiring an investigation of the reason for the conduct complained of, whereas the Directive, by referring to conduct 'related to' the sex, etc of a person, defined harassment by association with sex, etc. The High Court held that:

> the use of the words 'on the ground of her sex' impermissibly imports causation – the reason why issue – into the concept of harassment. There can be conduct which is related to sex, but not of a sexual nature, which has the effect of creating an offensive working environment for a woman ... That would not fall within [the law] on a straightforward reading, as it would not be conduct on the ground of the woman's sex.

The law was amended in 2008 where the characteristic was sex, which meant that there were different definitions depending on the characteristic in question.

The Equality Act 2010 follows through that change in respect of all the protected characteristics in **11.1**: harassment no longer needs to be 'on the grounds' of but rather 'related to' a protected characteristic. The view is therefore that causation is no longer relevant, and that no comparator is needed. This means that an employer can no longer rely on the *Brumfitt* type defence by arguing that its conduct was not discriminatory because it treated everyone alike (in *Brumfitt v MOD* [2005] IRLR 4 (a case decided under the old test), the complainant lost her case because the obscene language used by the alleged harasser was directed at both men and women).

The Explanatory Memorandum to the 2008 amendments gave an example which is still useful: where male colleagues dislike a female colleague and decide to put the office equipment on a high shelf to make it hard for her to reach it, the old definition would not help as the men are acting out of dislike rather than because their colleague is a woman, ie not on the 'ground of her sex'; under the new definition such conduct might be actionable because it is 'related to sex', ie woman are on average shorter than men.

It is not necessary to have the protected characteristic in order to be covered by the protection. In *English v Thomas Sanderson Blinds Ltd* [2008] IRLR 342, Mr English complained about homosexual banter directed at him. He was not a homosexual and his colleagues knew this. He found the banter degrading and offensive. The Court of Appeal concluded that he had been harassed within the definition: although the banter was not based on a perception or assumption that he was homosexual, it was enough that Mr English was taunted as if he were gay. The banter created a degrading and hostile working environment, on the grounds of sexual orientation.

The new law also covers a person who is a witness to harassment. The Explanatory Notes provide an example:

> • A white worker who sees a black colleague being subjected to racially abusive language could have a case of harassment if the language also causes an offensive environment for her.

11.3.3 Sexual harassment

Sexual harassment encompasses any conduct of a sexual nature which has the purpose or effect of violating a person's dignity or of creating an intimidating, hostile, degrading, humiliating or offensive environment. Conduct of a sexual nature is not defined in the Act. The example given by the Equality and Human Rights Commission (EHRC) is unwelcome sexual advances – touching, standing too close, the displaying of offensive pictures.

The Explanatory Notes provide an example:

- An employer who displayed any material of a sexual nature, such as a topless calendar, may be harassing her employees where this makes the workplace an offensive place to work for any employee, female or male.

11.3.4 Less favourable treatment

An employer may also be liable where there is less favourable treatment of a person by reason of that person's submission to or rejection of sex- or gender reassignment-related harassment or sexual harassment which had the purpose or effect of violating that person's dignity or of creating an intimidating, hostile, degrading, humiliating or offensive environment.

The Explanatory Notes provide an example:

- A shopkeeper propositions one of his shop assistants. She rejects his advances and then is turned down for promotion which she believes she would have got if she had accepted her boss's advances. The shop assistant would have a claim of harassment.

11.3.5 'Purpose or effect ...'

All three types of harassment require that the conduct has the purpose or effect of (s 26(1) – see **11.3.1**):

(i)   violating B's dignity, or

(ii)   creating an intimidating, hostile, degrading, humiliating or offensive environment for B.

If the conduct was intended to have the effect of violating dignity or creating a hostile, etc environment, it amounts to harassment whatever the actual effect. If there is no such intent then the conduct may be treated as having the effect of violating dignity or creating a hostile, etc environment only if 'it should reasonably be considered as having that effect'; as part of that assessment, the victim's perspective is a relevant circumstance to take into account (s 26(4)). It is therefore for the tribunal to decide, based on the evidence, whether the effect of the conduct was to create a hostile, etc working environment.

In *Richmond Pharmacology v Dhaliwal* [2009] IRLR 336, the EAT noted that the fact that, at least in some cases, there will be substantial overlaps between the questions that arise in relation to each element (eg, the question whether the conduct complained of was 'unwanted' will overlap with the question of whether it creates an adverse environment for the employee) and between the two defined proscribed consequences (many or most acts which are found to create an adverse environment for an employee will also violate her dignity). The EAT went on to state that:

> ... an employer may be held liable on the basis that the effect of his conduct has been to produce the proscribed consequences even if that was not his purpose; and, conversely, that he may be liable if he acted for the purposes of producing the proscribed consequences but did not in fact do so (or in any event has not been shown to have done so). In most cases the primary focus will be on the effect of the unwanted conduct rather than on the employer's purpose ...
>
> A respondent should not be held liable merely because his conduct has had the effect of producing a proscribed consequence: it should be reasonable that that consequence has occurred. That ... creates an objective standard. The proscribed consequences are, of their nature, concerned with the feelings of the putative victim: that is, the victim must have felt, or perceived, her dignity to have been violated or an adverse environment to have been created. That can, if you like, be described as introducing a 'subjective' element; but overall the criterion is objective because what the tribunal is required to consider is whether, if the claimant has experienced those feelings or perceptions, it was reasonable for her to do so. Thus if, for example, the tribunal believes that the claimant was unreasonably prone to take offence, then, even if she did genuinely feel her dignity to have been violated, there will have been

no harassment within the meaning of the section. Whether it was reasonable for a claimant to have felt her dignity to have been violated is quintessentially a matter for the factual assessment of the tribunal. It will be important for it to have regard to all the relevant circumstances, including the context of the conduct in question. One question that may be material is whether it should reasonably have been apparent whether the conduct was, or was not, intended to cause offence (or, more precisely, to produce the proscribed consequences): the same remark may have a very different weight if it was evidently innocently intended than if it was evidently intended to hurt.

In *Weeks v Newham College of Further Education* (UKEAT/0630/11), the EAT held that the word 'environment' is a 'state of affairs', which may be created by one incident if the effects are of longer duration.

An extract from the former Gender Equality Unit's guidance is set out below. We have amended it to take account of the new Act. Although it is no longer published, the authors believe it is still useful.

What the law says ...

... [T]he [law] has made it explicit that harassment [related to] the complainant's sex, and sexual harassment are unlawful. Harassment is now a distinct form of discrimination ...

Test for harassment – subjective or objective? To what extent is the test for harassment based on the complainant's personal perception?

Case law has established the way tribunals consider whether harassment has taken place. It has recognised that it is of particular importance to take account of the reasons why a person is claiming they have been harassed, and in the majority of circumstances, the complainant's view will be the key factor. However, the complainant's perception will not be the only factor, and the tribunal needs to consider all the facts in the case before deciding whether unlawful harassment has in fact taken place. It is important for an objective consideration of a claimant's subjective perception to take place if a just decision is to be reached.

An illustration of the kind of conduct that a tribunal may consider it unreasonable for a claimant to view as sexual harassment might be a situation where a man brushes against a female colleague as they both leave the office to go to a meeting. The woman complains that he deliberately rushed through the door at the same time as she did so that he would come into physical contact with her.

In such a case, a tribunal looking at all the facts may well consider it unreasonable to view this conduct as harassment. Conversely, if the tribunal finds on the facts that there was a pattern of similar incidents in which the man has ended up in physical contact with the woman, the tribunal may consider that unlawful harassment had taken place. The key issue however is that conduct can be harassment if it has the purpose or effect of creating an intimidating etc environment, so unintentional conduct can be harassment too.

Ultimately though, it will be for a tribunal or court to rule on the facts of each case (not on the basis of how they would view the conduct) as to whether conduct should reasonably be considered as having the effect of harassing the complainant. In doing so, they will weigh up all the circumstances and will take particular account of the complainant's perception of the conduct and its effect on her.

...

- Harassment can be an action which takes place simply because someone is a woman, or a man – such as purposely putting crucial equipment on a high shelf which can only be reached by tall people (mainly men). **Note:** this is unwanted conduct related to a person's sex that **is not** 'of a sexual nature'.

- Sexual harassment is an additional and different prohibition covering situations where the unwanted conduct is sexual in nature – such as a person making unwelcome sexually explicit comments or giving unwelcome verbal sexual abuse. **Note:** this is unwanted conduct which is not necessarily related to a person's sex but **is** 'of a sexual nature'.

- It is prohibited to make a decision which is unfavourable to someone because they have rejected or submitted to harassment as defined above – for instance refusing someone a job because they would not submit to particular unwanted conduct, or refusing someone promotion because they did submit to it.

...

Harassment and sexual harassment are unlawful if they have the purpose or effect of violating the complainant's dignity or creating an intimidating, hostile, degrading, humiliating or offensive environment. This can include unintentional behaviour.

Sexual harassment

There are many different situations that could be construed as sexual harassment. Individual men and women will have differing opinions of what they regard as such behaviour (for instance, when horseplay becomes harassment, or when photographs are offensive) and decisions will have to reached in the circumstances of the individual case. But either a serious 'one-off' occurrence or an accumulation of less serious occurrences can be harassment under the [Act].

The [Act] does not specify the detail of what constitutes 'conduct of a sexual nature'. We expect that the courts will determine this widely taking account of the facts of an individual case. However, such conduct would not be restricted to language or actions with connotations relating to genitalia, sexual acts, etc.

The best way of ensuring that employers and individuals know their responsibilities and rights in this complex area is through practical guidance to help interpret the legislation. ...

Harassment [for a reason related to] the complainant's sex

- A sole woman in a team always gets asked to take notes and make tea/coffees because it's considered 'women's work'.

- A female HR manager was subjected to humiliating and embarrassing remarks [which were not sexual in nature] by her line manager. In one incident the line manager depicted the claimant as 'an airhead'. The tribunal found this to be insensitive and to have gender undertones – it being a term more frequently applied to a woman than a man.

- A male claimant working in an environment which was predominantly staffed by women complains about the climate and culture created by the abuse and treatment of him by his female colleagues, eg belittling comments about men.

- Derogatory comments relating to the person's gender, eg 'don't worry your pretty little head about it', 'she's is not thinking straight today – it must be the time of the month', 'you're looking a bit fat – do you have a bun in the oven?' ...

- A pregnant worker subjected to derogatory comments implying she will no longer be up to the job as a result of her pregnancy. [**Note: this could also be sexual harassment, depending on the context**].

Sexual harassment

- ...

- A woman is offended by a calendar of nude women that one of her male co-workers has hung on the office wall. Again, a Tribunal is likely to find that this is sexual harassment.

    ...

- On three occasions, male colleagues working in the same room as the claimant download pornographic images onto a computer screen. Viewed objectively, the behaviour complained of clearly has potential to cause affront to a female employee working in close proximity to the men and is thus to be regarded as degrading or offensive to her as a woman. The fact that the claimant does not complain to her employer is irrelevant, given the obviously detrimental effect that the behaviour has in undermining her dignity at work.

- A female model (X) is subjected to repeated unwanted sexual advances from another female model (Y) who is employed by the same company and is responsible for engaging models for photographic shoots for advertising purposes. X claims that during a shoot, Y came to her hotel room and attempted to kiss her. X rebuffed her advances. Y also sent the model suggestive text messages and invited her to visit a sex shop. [**Note: this example illustrates that because sexual harassment is 'unwanted conduct of a sexual nature', it does not have to be male/female but can be carried out by someone of the same sex**]

- A city worker (of either gender) required to go to team outings to strip-clubs despite making it clear that s/he was not happy to do so.

11.4 EMPLOYERS' LIABILITY FOR THE ACTS OF THIRD PARTIES

Employers could, until 2003, be liable for the acts of a person who was not an employee. In *Burton and Another v De Vere Hotels* [1996] IRLR 596, the applicants were employed as casual waitresses at one of the respondent's hotels, working at a dinner organised by the City of Derby Round Table. The stand-up comedian Bernard Manning had been booked as the guest speaker. The two women were working in the banqueting hall where Mr Manning was speaking. He used words such as 'wog', 'nigger' and 'sambo', and said that 'darkies were good at giving blow jobs'. The applicants brought claims under the RRA 1976. The tribunal held that the respondent was not liable because it was not the respondent which subjected the applicants to the racial harassment. The EAT held the respondent liable. The EAT said that an employer subjects an employee to racial harassment if he causes or permits racial harassment to occur in circumstances which he can control, whether it happens or not, and where an application of good employment practice would prevent or reduce the harassment. In the present case, it would have been good employment practice for the manager to warn his assistants to keep a look out for Mr Manning, and to withdraw the waitresses if things became unpleasant.

However, in *Macdonald v Advocate General for Scotland; Pearce v Governing Body of Mayfield Secondary School* [2003] IRLR 512, the House of Lords disapproved of the decision in *Burton*. Their Lordships stated that whilst an employer's failure to prevent third parties committing acts of sexual/racial harassment might amount to discrimination by the employer, it would do so only if the employer failed to take such steps *because* of the employee's sex/race.

In *EOC v Secretary of State for Trade and Industry* (**11.3.2** above), the High Court agreed with the EOC that the law needed to be re-cast so as to facilitate claims that an employer subjected an employee to harassment by knowingly failing to protect that employee from repetitive harassment by a third party, such as a supplier or customer. The High Court said that:

> [s]o long as [the law] is framed in terms of unwanted conduct engaged in on the ground of a woman's sex by the employer, it is difficult to see how an employer could be held liable for the knowing failure to take steps to prevent harassment by others, since such knowing failure would have to amount to unwanted conduct by the employer on the ground of her sex.

Section 40 of the 2010 Act now states:

(1)   An employer (A) must not, in relation to employment by A, harass a person (B)—

        ...

(2)   The circumstances in which A is to be treated as harassing B under subsection (1) include those where—

        (a)   a third party harasses B in the course of B's employment, and

        (b)   A failed to take such steps as would have been reasonably practicable to prevent the third party from doing so.

(3)   Subsection (2) does not apply unless A knows that B has been harassed in the course of B's employment on at least two other occasions by a third party; and it does not matter whether the third party is the same or a different person on each occasion.

(4)   A third party is a person other than—

        (a)   A, or

        (b)   an employee of A's.

The Explanatory Notes give an example:

- A shop assistant with a strong Nigerian accent tells her manager that she is upset and humiliated by a customer who regularly uses the shop and each time makes derogatory remarks about Africans in her hearing. If her manager does nothing to try to stop it happening again, he would be liable for racial harassment.

Employers are therefore currently liable for repetitive harassment by third parties such as clients or customers, unless they have taken reasonable steps to prevent such harassment. This liability is triggered where the employer is aware that the employee has been harassed on at least two occasions by a third party (which need not be the same third party). So, a one-off incident will not be sufficient.

As Michael Rubenstein pointed out in the May 2008 edition of *Equal Opportunities Review*, there are a number of potential problems with the wording. It appears that it will not cover a situation where the employer knows there is a problem with a client or customer and others have complained before but only once. It does not appear to cover the situation where the employer knows the third party is a harasser from other employees but places a different employee in a vulnerable position. There is nothing in the new provisions that make it clear how close or how far apart the two other occasions have to be.

There is no guidance as to what 'reasonably practicable' steps an employer might take to avoid liability. It might be useful to have regard to the guidance at **8.6.2** above.

It is clear that for an employer to be liable under s 40 there will need to be a finding both that there were reasonably practicable steps for an employer to take to prevent the harassment *and* that the employer failed to take those steps.

Following a Government consultation in May 2012, proposals in the current Enterprise and Regulatory Reform Bill will remove the third party harassment provision from the Equality Act 2010. There was considerable opposition to the repeal of this provision in the consultation (71% to 20% agreeing with repeal), but the Government said that no evidence was provided in support of retaining the provision and employees have other potential avenues of redress.

11.5 PROTECTION FROM HARASSMENT ACT 1997

The Protection from Harassment Act 1997 allows for victims of harassment to claim damages and/or injunctive relief in the civil courts and to prosecute in the criminal courts. To bring a claim under the 1997 Act, it is not necessary to show that the harassment was done on any particular prohibited ground or basis. Harassment is not defined in the Act, but it includes 'alarming [a]person or causing a person distress'. The Act prohibits a course of conduct (defined as at least two occasions of harassment) that amounts to harassment, or which a person knows, or ought to know, amounts to harassment. There is no statutory defence available to an employer under the Act, which enables victims of harassment in the workplace to pursue claims against their employer through the civil courts (through the principle of vicarious liability) and/or through the employment tribunal (see *Majrowski v Guy's and St Thomas's NHS Trust* [2005] IRLR 340, CA (upheld by the House of Lords [2006] UKHL 34) and *Banks v Ablex Ltd* [2005] IRLR 357 for two decisions in this area).

Claims under the 1997 Act have a number of advantages over other more traditional 'employment' routes such as discrimination or unfair dismissal. The provisions will apply to workers as well as to employees. Unlike an unfair dismissal claim, compensation for injury to feelings can be recovered as well as loss of earnings. Claims under the 1997 Act can be brought in the courts, so there is no three-month limitation on bringing the claim. However, the realisation that the Act might give rise to claims for damages for what might be viewed as relatively trivial acts of harassment, led the Court of Appeal to re-examine what amounted to harassment under the Act. In *Conn v Sunderland City Council* [2007] EWCA Civ 1492, the trial judge found that two incidents involving verbal threats amounted to harassment under the Act and awarded a small sum by way of damages. The Court of Appeal made it clear that 'bad-mannered' behaviour should not give rise to criminal penalties or a civil claim for damages. It held that for the Protection from Harassment Act to be engaged, harassment had to amount to conduct that is, viewed objectively, likely to cause distress to the victim and is unacceptable and oppressive, and probably criminal. There must be two or more incidents which are each sufficiently serious.

However, see now *Veakins v Kier Islington Ltd* [2009] EWCA Civ 1288, where the Court of Appeal provided guidance on the sort of conduct that would be needed before an employee could successfully bring a claim under the Protection from Harassment Act 1997. In the leading judgment given by Maurice Kay LJ, the Court emphasised that:

> since *Majrowski*, courts have been enjoined to consider whether the conduct complained of is 'oppressive and unacceptable' as opposed to merely unattractive, unreasonable or regrettable. The primary focus is on whether the conduct is 'oppressive and unacceptable' albeit that the court must keep in mind that it must be of an order which 'would sustain criminal liability'.

One of the perceived limitations on a claim under the Protection from Harassment Act was the requirement for harassment to arise out of a course of conduct, ie conduct occurring on at least two occasions. However, the provisions implemented by the Act now import a similar requirement into claims of third party harassment.

11.6 CASE STUDY: HARASSMENT

Facts

(1)   R1 is the operator of an adventure park. R2 is an employee of R1. He is the operations manager of R1, and was the line manager of C, who was a member of his operations team. C had been in post for nine months. On a previous occasion, another member of the operations team, 'F', complained informally to 'S' (the managing director of R1) about R2's conduct towards her, following which she then submitted a formal grievance in writing. C says she had a number of informal conversations with R2, making him aware that she was uncomfortable with his engaging her in conversations of an explicit sexual nature and/or making sexual innuendos. R2 says that staff accepted a level of ribald language and that swearing was common amongst all staff.

(2)   Following one particular incident when R2 made further remarks that C regarded as lewd, C sent R1 a letter giving one month's notice of her intention to resign. In this letter she said she had recently 'found working conditions intolerable due to your apparent disregard for the welfare of staff and your resultant failure to appropriately address or bring about a satisfactory conclusion regarding my concerns about R2 and the sexist and abusive behaviour others females and I have repeatedly endured'. She enclosed a copy of a diary she had been keeping, which she said contained examples of R2's behaviour. R1 did not take her complaint seriously and did nothing about it. C subsequently left.

(3)   C issued a claim form to the employment tribunal.

Claims

(4)   C complained of harassment under s 26(1) and (2) and of direct discrimination because of sex under s 13.

(5)   C claimed against R1 and R2.

(6)   She indicated on the claim form that she only wanted compensation.

(7)   R1 and R2 did not admit that the alleged incidents of discrimination relied upon by C took place, and denied that any incidents that did take place were acts of discrimination.

Evidence

(8)   Disclosure took place in the usual way, and paginated bundles were prepared which included extracts from C's personal file, extracts from the staff handbook on *Grievances and Appeals*, papers relating to previous complaints and a Schedule of Loss from C setting out her claim for compensation.

(9) Witness statements were exchanged prior to the hearing.

(10) At the hearing all witnesses who gave oral evidence were cross-examined and the tribunal had the opportunity to ask questions of them. On C's behalf, oral evidence at the hearing was given by C and F. C also submitted witness statements from a number of former employees who did not appear to give evidence. As their evidence could not be tested by cross-examination, the tribunal gave their testimony less weight evidentially. For R1 and R2, oral evidence was given by R2, S, T, and W (a junior manager).

(11) At the conclusion of the evidence, both sides made oral submissions on liability and remedy.

(12) All these matters were taken into consideration by the tribunal before reaching its decision.

The issues to be decided

(13) C complained of both characteristic (sex)-related harassment and sexual harassment and direct sex discrimination. Where R1's conduct was directed at other female staff, it was characteristic-related harassment. R1 does not admit that the alleged incidents took place, and denies that any incidents that did take place were acts of harassment. The tribunal will need to determine:

    13.1 whether R2 subjected C to harassment either by way of conduct of a sexual nature directed at her, or by way of conduct directed at other female staff;

    13.2 whether R1 was responsible for any such harassment.

    13.3 The direct discrimination claims related to the way R1 responded to C's complaints about R2 and to the act of C's resignation.

(14) Depending on the outcome of the matters, the tribunal will have to determine what amount of compensation, if any, should be awarded.

Tribunal findings

(15) The unanimous decision of the tribunal is that:

    15.1 R1 and R2 unlawfully discriminated against C;

    15.2 R1 and R2 are to pay C £5,419.77 by way of compensation.

Reasons

Harassment claim

(16) The tribunal took account of s 136 of the Equality Act 2010 on the burden of proof. It noted that in *Igen v Wong* [2005] IRLR 258 (a race discrimination case determined under pre-Equality Act 2010 legislation), subject to one amendment, the Court of Appeal upheld the guidance given by the EAT in a sex discrimination case, *Barton v Investec Securities Ltd* [2003] ICR 1205, in particular, to summarise that guidance, that it is for the claimant who complains of sex discrimination to prove on the balance of probabilities facts from which the tribunal could conclude, in the absence of an adequate explanation, that the employer has committed an unlawful act of discrimination against the claimant. Where the claimant proves facts from which inferences could be drawn that the employer has treated the applicant less favourably on the grounds of sex, then the burden of proof moves to the employer. It is then for the employer to prove that he did not commit, or, as the case may be, is not to be treated as having committed, that act. To discharge that burden it is necessary for the employer to prove, on the balance of probabilities, that the treatment was 'in no sense whatsoever on the grounds of sex', since 'no discrimination whatsoever' is compatible with the Burden of Proof Directive 97/80. That requires a tribunal to assess not merely whether the employer has proved an explanation for the facts from which such inferences can be drawn, but further that it is adequate to discharge the burden of proof on the balance of probabilities that sex was

not a ground for the treatment in question. The tribunal also noted the decision of the Court of Appeal in *Madarassy v Nomura International plc* [2007] EWCA Civ 33, which emphasised that the court in *Igen* expressly rejected the argument that it was sufficient for the complainant simply to prove facts from which the tribunal could conclude that the respondent 'could have committed an unlawful act of discrimination'. It held that the bare facts of a difference in status and a difference in treatment only indicate a possibility of discrimination. 'They are not, without more, sufficient material from which a tribunal "could conclude" that, on the balance of probabilities, the respondent had committed an unlawful act of discrimination'.

(17) The tribunal also considered the definition of harassment set out in s 26(1) and (2) of the Equality Act 2010. It noted that both types of harassment required that the conduct complained of had the purpose or effect of violating C's dignity or creating an intimidating, hostile, degrading or humiliating or offensive environment for C. It noted the case of *Reid and Bull Information Systems Ltd v Stedman* [1999] IRLR 299 (a pre-Equality Act 2010 case but one which it considered remained relevant on overall approach). It noted that in *Wileman v Minilec Engineering Ltd* [1988] IRLR 144, the EAT acknowledged that a person may be happy to accept the remarks of A or B in a sexual context and be wholly upset by similar remarks made by C; and that in *Driskel v Peninsula Business Services Ltd* [2000] IRLR 151, the EAT had held that a tribunal should not lose sight of the significance of the sex of both the complainant and the alleged discriminator. Sexual badinage with a heterosexual male by another man could not be completely equated with like badinage by him with a woman.

Tribunal's findings

Workplace culture

(18) The tribunal found from the evidence of a number of witnesses that general ribald banter and mickey-taking was common in the workplace, and that there was a lot of sexual banter and swearing. It was not a 'cloistered' environment. There was also girly gossip about sex. R2 struggled with the 'overly emotional' reaction of some of the young women to his remarks, which left him bewildered. The tribunal noted that C was open in discussion about her relationship with her boyfriend. Overall it found C was uncomfortable with R2's conversations and behaviour, and R2 knew this but persisted with his conduct. This was backed up by the diary that C kept. The tribunal held that even in an environment where it was accepted that bad language was commonplace, the continued use of this sort of language when objection has been taken to it, particularly when it is used by a more senior manager to his junior staff, was not acceptable conduct. The tribunal found therefore that harassment was made out under s 26(2) but not under s 26(1). The tribunal did not believe that any of R2's language or behaviour was directed specifically at C because of her sex.

(19) It held S did not do enough to set standards for his staff about this. Neither did he really take it seriously. It found there was a stark contrast between the way he treated C and the way he responded to a previous complaint about another member of staff. The tribunal found that the different treatment was not, however, because of C's sex; it stemmed from the fact that S was not willing to tolerate any criticism of R2 because he considered him a valuable asset. The tribunal was not satisfied that this treatment fell within the definition of direct discrimination.

(20) On balance, the tribunal found that the comments made by R2 did amount to sexual harassment – his intention was irrelevant. It also found that given that C's resignation was caused principally by R2's remarks and S's failure to take her concerns seriously, those actions amounted to less favourable treatment because of her sex. An employer is vicariously liable for the acts of employees carried out within the course of their employment. R2 carried out these acts of harassment during the course of his

employment. R1 had not sought to avail itself of the 'reasonably practicable steps' defence in s 109 of the Equality Act 2010. On that basis, the tribunal found R1 was liable for the acts of R2 and the omissions of S.

Remedies

(21)   Section 124 of the Equality Act 2010 sets out the remedies available on a finding of discrimination. The general principle as far as compensation is concerned is that, as far as possible, complainants should be placed in the same position as they would have been but for the unlawful act (see *Ministry of Defence v Wheeler* [1998] IRLR 23). Another way of looking at it is to ask what loss has been caused by the discrimination in question. It is important to remember that the loss must be caused by the discrimination and, secondly, that the loss must not be too remote a consequence of the discrimination. In *Skyrail Oceanic Ltd v Coleman* [1981] ICR 864 (a pre-Equality Act 2010 sex discrimination claim), Lawton LJ explained this by saying that, 'Compensation is to be awarded for foreseeable damage arising directly from an unlawful act of discrimination'. Compensation for unlawful discrimination falls under two heads: financial loss, and non-financial loss. Financial loss covers matters such as loss of earnings, both past and future; while non-financial loss covers matters such as injury to feelings. In addition to awarding compensation for foreseeable damage arising directly from the unlawful act, an employment tribunal has jurisdiction to award compensation by way of damages for injury to feeling and personal injury, including both physical and psychiatric injury, caused by the unlawful discrimination. Where compensation is assessed under the discrimination regime, the Employment Protection (Recoupment of Jobseeker's Allowance and Income Support) Regulations 1996 do not apply.

(22)   Principles relating to compensatory awards for injury to feelings for unlawful discrimination are set out in *Armitage and HM Prison Service v Johnson* [1997] IRLR 162, *Vento v Chief Constable of West Yorkshire Police* [2003] IRLR 102 and *Da'Bell v NSPCC* (UKEAT/0227/09). *Da'Bell* set out new guideline figures which the tribunal inserted into the *Vento* guidance. In *Vento*, the Court of Appeal observed that there were three broad bands of compensation for injury to feelings, as distinct from compensation for psychiatric or similar personal injury: (1) The top band should normally be between £18,000 and £30,000. Sums in this range should be awarded in the most serious cases, such as where there has been a lengthy campaign of discriminatory harassment on the ground of sex or race. Only in the most exceptional case should an award of compensation for injury to feelings exceed £30,000. (2) The middle band of between £6,000 and £18,000 should be used for serious cases which do not merit an award in the highest band. (3) Awards of between £500 and £6,000 are appropriate for less serious cases, such as where the act of discrimination is an isolated one or a one-off occurrence. Defining injury to feelings is more a broadbrush exercise of estimation than of calculation, comparison with precedents or cold logic.

(23)   Since the Court of Appeal's ruling in *Sheriff v Klyne Tugs (Lowestoft) Ltd* [1999] ICR 1170 (a race discrimination case), tribunals have jurisdiction to award compensation for personal injury arising out of unlawful sex, race or disability discrimination. This includes compensation for psychiatric illness. In *HM Prison Service v Salmon* [2001] IRLR 425, the EAT considered the possibility of overlap and double recovery where a tribunal awards separate sums for psychiatric damage and injury to feelings. The EAT accepted that injury to feelings can cover a wide range of injury, from minor upset to serious and prolonged feelings of humiliation and depression, and that in practice psychiatric damage may be compensated under this heading. It also accepted that there was a risk of double recovery where separate awards were made, and stated that tribunals should be aware of the risk.

(24)   In *Snowball v Gardner Merchant Ltd* [1987] IRLR 397, the EAT said that evidence as to the complainant's attitude to matters of sexual behaviour was relevant and admissible for

the purpose of determining the degree of injury to feelings that the complainant suffered as a result of sexual harassment. Compensation for sexual harassment must relate to the degree of detriment, and evidence as to whether she had talked freely to fellow employees about her attitude to sexual matters was relevant for determining whether the claimant was unlikely to be very upset by a degree of familiarity with a sexual connotation, so as to challenge the alleged detriment suffered and any hurt feelings

Tribunal's findings

(25)   C had less than one year's continuous service. A sensible average weekly figure for her wages was £173.41. This was agreed by the parties. C did not have a job to go to when she resigned. She obtained some part-time work over the Christmas period. She later went full-time. That work is on-going. She set out in her Schedule of Loss the details of these earnings. In her current job she was getting paid more than she had earned with R1 (approx £202.00 per week). C said she was depressed as a result of her treatment. She referred to her GP's notes, indicating that she was struggling with money problems and had headaches, and continued to suffer anxiety and headaches. However, she was now working a 40-hour week without any sickness problems.

(26)   The tribunal can make separate awards against R1 or R2. It is common in such cases to make a larger award against the employer and a smaller award against the individual harasser. The tribunal can also make one award and make both parties jointly and severally liable for that award. When making joint and several awards, tribunals must apportion the respective shares, so that if a claimant chooses to enforce only against one respondent, that respondent can still seek a suitable contribution from the other respondent. Any such apportionment should be on the basis of respectively culpability. The tribunal in this case made only one award. While R2 was the perpetrator, S's attitude was primarily responsible for what happened in allowing R2 to continue with his objectionable conduct. The tribunal concluded that S (and therefore R1) was substantially culpable for what happened. The tribunal apportioned blame on the basis of 20% to R2 and 80% to R1.

(27)   *Compensatory element.* By the date of the hearing, taking account of C's actual earnings over the period against what she would have earned, her actual losses were £1,419.77. There were no future losses continuing to accrue.

(28)   In terms of an award for *injury to feelings*, the tribunal felt that this case fell towards the top of the lower *Vento* band, in that it had not found there was any deliberate or ongoing campaign against C, but this was not just one isolated incident; a number of lewd remarks were made, which occurred as a result of a careless disregard for C's sensitivities once they had been made known. Judging from the medical evidence, there were no lasting effects suffered by C. In the circumstances, the tribunal made an award, inclusive of interest of £5,000 for injury to feelings.

(29)   Accordingly, the tribunal found that the respondents were to pay C a total sum of £6,419.77. The Recoupment Regulations do not apply to this award.

11.7   VICTIMISATION

The victimisation provisions aim to give protection to workers who bring complaints of discrimination or other proceedings aimed at enforcing compliance with equal treatment principles.

11.7.1   Definition

The definition of victimisation is set out in s 27 of the Act:

(1)   A person (A) victimises another person (B) if A subjects B to a detriment because—

(a)   B does a protected act, or

(b)   A believes that B has done, or may do, a protected act.

(2)   Each of the following is a protected act—

(a)   bringing proceedings under this Act;

(b)   giving evidence or information in connection with proceedings under this Act;

(c)   doing any other thing for the purposes of or in connection with this Act;

(d)   making an allegation (whether or not express) that A or another person has contravened this Act.

(3)   Giving false evidence or information, or making a false allegation, is not a protected act if the evidence or information is given, or the allegation is made, in bad faith.

...

The Explanatory Notes make it clear that the Act changes the old law, in that there is no longer a requirement for the tribunal to construct an appropriate comparator. However, a comparison of the claimant's treatment with that of an appropriate comparator will often be an effective way of establishing the reason for the treatment.

The Explanatory Notes give examples:

- A woman makes a complaint of sex discrimination against her employer. As a result, she is denied promotion. The denial of promotion would amount to victimisation.

- A gay man sues a publican for persistently treating him less well than heterosexual customers. Because of this, the publican bars him from the pub altogether. This would be victimisation.

- An employer threatens to dismiss a staff member because he thinks she intends to support a colleague's sexual harassment claim. This threat could amount to victimisation.

- A man with a grudge against his employer knowingly gives false evidence in a colleague's discrimination claim against the employer. He is subsequently dismissed for supporting the claim. His dismissal would not amount to victimisation because of his untrue and malicious evidence.

Some of the case law based on the pre-Equality Act 2010 law is still relevant. In *Chief Constable of West Yorkshire Police v Khan* [2001] 1 WLR 1947, the House of Lords confirmed that the less favourable treatment must be by reason of the protected act (ie motivated by it). In this case, the reason the employer refused to provide a reference was to preserve his position in pending litigation and not the fact that the worker had commenced proceedings.

According to the Court of Appeal in *Nagarajan v London Regional Transport* [1998] IRLR 73, there must be *conscious motivation* by the discriminator to treat the employee less favourably because of the protected act. The case was appealed to the House of Lords. Their Lordships (Lord Browne-Wilkinson dissenting) held that the Court of Appeal had erred in holding that the alleged victimiser must have been consciously motivated by the race relations legislation. The question that must be asked, according to their Lordships, is 'did the defendant treat the employee less favourably because of his knowledge of a protected act?'. If the answer to that question is yes, the case will fall within the law, even if the victimiser did not consciously realise that he or she was prejudiced by the defendant having done the protected act (*Nagarajan v London Regional Transport* [1999] IRLR 572).

The EAT held in *Pasab Ltd t/a Jhoots Pharmacy and Another v Woods* (UKEAT/0454/11) that the protected act must be the reason (conscious or subconscious) for the treatment. In this case, the reason for treatment was 'genuinely separable' from the protected act. The Court of Appeal heard the appeal on 24 October 2012.

In *St Helens Metropolitan Borough Council v Derbyshire* [2004] IRLR 851, [2005] EWCA Civ 977, [2007] IRLR 540, the EAT upheld a tribunal finding that female catering staff who had brought equal pay claims had also been victimised. The employer wrote to all catering employees (not just the women who brought the claims) and said that if the claims were successful the cost of a school meal would rise so as to 'make provision of the service wholly unviable', which might lead to large numbers of redundancies. The employer also wrote to the women concerned and said, amongst other things, 'I am greatly concerned about the likely outcome of this matter ... [I would urge you to consider] the original offer of settlement'. The EAT held that this constituted victimisation and stated that a direct threat of dismissal or other sanction made to the individual claimant is not a necessary element for establishing less favourable treatment.

This decision was upheld on appeal by the House of Lords, which held that while an employer may seek to dissuade an employee from bringing a claim, it must seek to avoid putting unreasonable pressure on the employee. In this case, the House of Lords held that the letter was not reasonable and therefore amounted to victimisation.

11.7.2 Protection of former employees

Section 108 protects against post-employment discrimination and harassment, but s 108(7) states expressly that 'conduct is not a contravention of this section in so far as it also amounts to victimisation of B by A' (see **8.4.3**). The Explanatory Notes state 'if the treatment which is being challenged constitutes victimisation, it will be dealt with under the victimisation provisions and not under this section'. Section 39(4) deals expressly with victimisation against current employees, but makes no reference to former employees. Claimants will have to point to the House of Lords' decision in *Rhys-Harper v Relaxion Group plc* [2003] IRLR 484 to argue that s 39(4) should be interpreted as protecting former employees (see **8.4.2**). In that case, the House of Lords held that the (then) victimisation provisions could apply to post-termination treatment because former employees can claim to have suffered a 'detriment'. (See too *Bullimore v Pothecary Witham Weld Solicitors and Another* (UKEAT/0189/10).)

The EAT heard an appeal in September 2012 as to whether the Equality Act 2010 covers post-employment victimisation (*Jessemey v Rowstock Ltd and Another*). Judgment is awaited.

SUMMARY

This chapter has looked at harassment and victimisation in respect of the following protected characteristics listed in s 4 of the Equality Act 2010:

(a) sex;

(b) gender reassignment;

(c) colour, race, nationality or ethnic or national origins;

(d) religion or belief;

(e) sexual orientation (**8.1**).

(Age and disability are dealt with in separate chapters.) Harassment does not include marriage and civil partnership, or pregnancy and maternity (**11.1**).

Two of the four main types of discrimination in the employment field outlawed by UK legislation are harassment and victimisation.

Harassment is unwanted conduct that violates a person's dignity, or which creates an intimidating, hostile, degrading, humiliating or offensive environment for that person having regard to all the circumstances including the perception of the victim. The definition of 'harassment' is set out in s 26 of the Equality Act 2010 (**11.3**).

There are three different types of harassment (**11.3**):

(a) 'characteristic-related harassment', which involves unwanted conduct which is related to a relevant characteristic and has the purpose or effect of creating an intimidating, hostile, degrading, humiliating or offensive environment for the complainant, or violating the complainant's dignity;

(b) sexual harassment, which is unwanted conduct of a sexual nature, where this has the purpose or effect of creating an intimidating, hostile, degrading, humiliating or offensive environment for the complainant, or violating the complainant's dignity;

(c) treating someone less favourably because that person has either submitted to or rejected sexual harassment, or harassment related to sex or gender reassignment which had the purpose or effect of creating an intimidating, hostile, degrading, humiliating or offensive environment for the complainant, or violating the complainant's dignity.

Employers will be liable for repetitive harassment by third parties such as clients or customers, unless they have taken reasonable steps to prevent such harassment. A one-off incident will not be sufficient (**11.4**).

The victimisation provisions aim to give protection to workers who bring complaints of discrimination or other proceedings aimed at enforcing compliance with equal treatment principles. Victimisation occurs when a person has been subject to a detriment because he has done a 'protected act'. This may include bringing a tribunal claim or giving evidence in connection with such a claim. The definition of 'victimisation' is set out in s 27 of the Equality Act 2010.

The same shifting burden of proof applies in both harassment and victimisation cases (**11.2** and **9.5**). Section 108 protects against post-employment discrimination and harassment. This does not apply to victimisation (**11.7.2**).

Remedies and enforcement are dealt with at **8.8** above. A flowchart summarising harassment and victimisation is set out at **Figure 11.1** below.

Figure 11.1 Flowchart – Harassment and Victimisation

ELIGIBILITY
time limit – within 3 months of act of discrimination

UNLAWFUL ACT
discrimination in recruitment, promotion, dismissal, harassment, post-employment matters or subjecting a person to detriment

TYPE OF CLAIM

[NB some situations can give rise to more than one type of discrimination claim]

HARASSMENT	**VICTIMISATION**
<ul><li>character-related harassment – unwanted conduct related to a protected characteristic; or</li><li>sexual harassment – unwanted conduct of a sexual nature; or</li><li>less favourable treatment – where C has rejected unwanted conduct of a sexual nature or conduct related to sex of gender reassignment;</li><li>which has the purpose or effect of violating C's dignity or creating an intimidating, hostile, degrading, humiliating or offensive environment for C;</li><li>if unintended, having regard to all the circumstances, including C's perception, should conduct be reasonably considered as having that effect?</li></ul>	<ul><li>has C been subject to a detriment because C has done a protected act (eg brought/ intends to bring proceedings or has given/intends to give evidence or information in connection with such proceedings)?</li><li>No comparator needed</li></ul>

NO DEFENCE

VICARIOUS LIABILITY

R will be vicariously liable for acts of employees committed in the course of employment (*Jones v Tower Boot Co/Chief Constable of Lincolnshire Police v Stubbs*) unless R took all reasonably practicable steps to stop/avoid the discrimination (statutory defence – s 109(4))

REMEDIES

- declaration of employee's rights
- recommendation that employer take action to alleviate or reduce the effect of the discrimination
- order for compensation (no maximum)
  - pecuniary losses
  - aggravated damages if employer has behaved in a high-handed, malicious, insulting or aggressive manner
  - injury to feelings (*Vento/Da'Bell*)
  - psychiatric or physical injury
  - possibility of exemplary damages
  - increase/decrease for any unreasonable failure to comply with the Acas Code of Practice

AGE DISCRIMINATION

LEARNING OUTCOMES

After reading this chapter you will be able to:

- understand the underlying principles of age discrimination law, and when and to whom it applies in an employment context
- list the four types of prohibited conduct
- describe how the justification defence works in a direct age discrimination claim
- describe how the justification defence works in an indirect age discrimination claim
- explain how a compulsory retirement age may operate
- describe the remedies available where a complaint of age discrimination is made out.

12.1 INTRODUCTION

This chapter considers age discrimination. The Framework Directive for Equal Treatment in Employment and Occupation (2000/78) required Member States to implement legislation prohibiting discrimination on grounds of age by 2 December 2006. The UK enacted law to comply with its Community obligations by way of the Employment Equality (Age) Regulations 2006 (SI 2006/1031) ('the Age Regulations'), which were the last plank of the UK's implementation of the Equal Treatment Framework Directive. These have now been consolidated and harmonised in the Equality Act 2010. The EHRC has responsibility for the promotion of equality and combating discrimination on the grounds of age (see **8.1**).

The protection against discrimination because of age applies to all employers, private and public sector, and employment agencies, vocational training providers, trade unions, professional organisations, employer organisations, and trustees and managers of occupational pension schemes. It applies to employees, job applicants, ex-employees, contract workers, office holders and partners. The protection applies to a broad definition of workers and employees (see **1.3**). As with sex, race, disability, religious belief and sexual orientation discrimination, 'employment' is defined as 'employment under a contract of service or of apprenticeship or a contract personally to execute any work or labour' (s 83). This is a wider definition than that of 'employee' in the ERA 1996, and means that certain categories of individuals who are not covered by other statutory rights (eg job applicants, office holders, police officers and the self-employed) are covered by the Equality Act 2010.

Much of the terminology used is familiar discrimination terminology: under the Act direct age discrimination is prohibited (ie persons being subject to less favourable treatment than others because of their age) as well as indirect age discrimination (ie the application of a provision, criterion or practice which disadvantages people of a particular age), although (unlike other forms of discrimination) direct age discrimination can be justified 'objectively' where the discrimination is a 'proportionate means of achieving legitimate aim'. Both harassment (being unwanted conduct that violates a person's dignity, or creates an intimidating, hostile, degrading, humiliating or offensive environment for that person having regard to all the circumstances, including the perception of the victim) and victimisation (because the victim has brought proceedings under the Act, or has given evidence or information in connection with proceedings under the Act) are also prohibited.

12.2 THE PROTECTED CHARACTERISTIC

Section 4 of the Equality Act 2010 sets out certain 'protected' characteristics (see **8.2**). These are the grounds upon which discrimination is deemed unlawful. Age is listed as a protected characteristic in s 5:

(1)   In relation to the protected characteristic of age—

   (a)   a reference to a person who has a particular protected characteristic is a reference to a person of a particular age group;

   (b)   a reference to persons who share a protected characteristic is a reference to persons of the same age group.

(2)   A reference to an age group is a reference to a group of persons defined by reference to age, whether by reference to a particular age or to a range of ages.

This section establishes that where the Act refers to the protected characteristic of age, it means a person belonging to a particular age group. An age group includes people of the same age and people of a particular range of ages. Where people fall in the same age group, they share the protected characteristic of age.

The Explanatory Notes give the following examples:

- An age group would include 'over fifties' or twenty-one year olds.
- A person aged twenty-one does not share the same characteristic of age with 'people in their forties'. However, a person aged twenty-one and people in their forties can share the characteristic of being in the 'under fifty' age range.

Section 14 provides for the discrimination prohibited by the Act to include direct discrimination because of a combination of two protected characteristics ('dual discrimination'), eg age and gender, or disability and race (see **9.2.3**). The Government considers it too complicated and burdensome to allow claims on three or more different discrimination grounds.

12.3 PROHIBITED CONDUCT

As referred to at **12.1** above, there are four main types of age discrimination outlawed in the employment field by the Equality Act 2010 so far as the protected characteristic of age is concerned:

(a)   direct discrimination (s 13), eg refusing employment on the ground of a person's being too young or too old;

(b)   indirect discrimination (s 19), eg refusing employment on the ground of a person's having too few or too many years' service;

(c)   harassment (s 26);

(d)   victimisation (s 27).

These will be dealt with in more detail below.

12.4   UNLAWFUL ACTS OF DISCRIMINATION

As with sex and race, etc, discrimination in the employment field against job applicants, employees and former employees is prohibited by ss 39 and 40 of the Act. These sections make it unlawful for an employer to discriminate against, victimise or harass employees and people seeking work. The prohibition applies where the employer is making arrangements to fill a job, and in respect of anything done in the course of a person's employment. The provisions apply to recruitment, terms and conditions, promotions, transfers, dismissals and training. See **8.4** for more details.

In *Keane v Investigo and Others* (UKEAT/0389/09), K a 51-year-old accountant with a number of years' experience, applied for a large number of positions that were advertised as being for a recently-qualified accountant with limited experience. She was not interviewed for these posts and brought tribunal proceedings against 11 agencies, a number of whom settled. There were five left by the time of the tribunal hearing. At the hearing it was argued that K had no genuine interest in the jobs and had brought the claims to make a broader point about age discrimination. The tribunal found that there was no direct or indirect discrimination as K did not want the jobs. The EAT upheld that decision, finding that there was no 'less favourable treatment' or 'disadvantage' caused to K:

> [W]e do not see how an applicant who is not considered for a job in which he or she is not in any event interested can in any ordinary sense of the word be said to have suffered a detriment – or to be more precise, to have been (comparatively) unfavorably 'treated' or put at a 'disadvantage'.

12.5   OCCUPATIONAL REQUIREMENTS

See **8.5** for a more detailed discussion of occupational requirements.

12.6   DIRECT DISCRIMINATION

12.6.1   Definition

Direct discrimination occurs where the reason for a person being treated less favourably than another is a protected characteristic listed in s 4 of the Act (see **9.2.1**).

The definition of 'direct discrimination' in connection with a person's age is the same as for sex, race, etc, and is set out in s 13 of the Act:

> (1)   A person (A) discriminates against another (B) if, because of a protected characteristic, A treats B less favourably than A treats or would treat others.
>
> (2)   If the protected characteristic is age, A does not discriminate against B if A can show A's treatment of B to be a proportionate means of achieving a legitimate aim.

The Explanatory Notes give the following by way of example:

> If the manager of a nightclub is disciplined for refusing to carry out an instruction to exclude older customers from the club, this would be direct age discrimination against the manager unless the instruction could be justified.

Acas gives the following example of direct discrimination in its booklet *Age and the Workplace*:

> Whilst being interviewed, a job applicant says that she took her professional qualification 30 years ago. Although she has all the skills and competences required of the job holder, the organisation decides not to offer her the job because of her age.

Note that, unlike the other types of protected characteristics, direct age discrimination can be justified (see **12.6.2**): for age, different treatment that is justified as a proportionate means of meeting a legitimate aim is not direct discrimination.

The definition is wide enough to cover discrimination by association, ie cases where the less favourable treatment is because of the victim's association with someone who has the protected characteristic. It is also (see **9.2.4**) wide enough to include discrimination on the ground of a person's apparent age; it will not be a defence for the employer to say that the person in question appeared to be older or younger than he or she in fact was. This would apply where, for example, someone is refused employment because he looks too old or too young.

It is therefore unlawful to decide not to employ someone on the ground of age, to dismiss him, to refuse to provide him with training, to deny him promotion, to give him adverse terms and conditions, or to retire him without an objective justification.

In *Swann v GHL Insurance Services UK Ltd* (ET/2306281/07), an employment tribunal decided (by a majority) that a flexible benefits package containing a medical insurance option, where the premium was calculated according to age, did not amount to unlawful age discrimination, because all the employees were given the same flexible benefits package and the calculation of the package was not age-related. (See also *Live Nation (Venues) UK Ltd v Hussain* (UKEAT/ 0234/ 08), where the EAT overturned the tribunal's funding of direct age discrimination.)

12.6.2 Justification

One important distinction between direct age discrimination and most other forms of direct discrimination under UK law, is that direct age discrimination can be justified objectively. Although the provisions of the Act do not use the term 'justification', it is clear that direct discrimination on the ground of age will be lawful if the treatment in question is shown to be a proportionate means of achieving a legitimate aim. This is likely to involve a balancing exercise between the discriminatory impact of the treatment in question and the legitimate aim of the employer. It will be for employment tribunals to decide how they will approach the issue of justification, but the test is not an easy one, and it will undoubtedly be necessary to provide evidence of the decision-making process that was undertaken.

As far as proportionality is concerned, this will involve an employer showing that what it is doing is necessary to achieve the legitimate aim and is the least onerous way of doing so. It will be open to employers to demonstrate that any aim they are pursing is legitimate. Examples of treatment that a court or tribunal may find to be a proportionate way of achieving a legitimate aim could include setting age requirements in order to ensure the protection of, or to promote the vocational integration of, people in a particular age group, or the fixing of a minimum age to qualify for certain advantages linked to employment in order to recruit or retain older people. Acas gives the following advice in *Age and the Workplace*:

- if your aim is to encourage loyalty then you ought to have evidence that the provision or criterion you introduce is actually doing so;
- the discriminatory effect should be significantly outweighed by the importance and benefits of the legitimate aim;
- you should have no reasonable alternative to the action you are taking. If the legitimate aim can be achieved by less or non discriminatory means then these must take precedence.

Legitimate aims are likely to include economic factors such as business needs and efficiency, health and safety, particular training requirements, facilitation of employment planning and the need for a reasonable period of employment before retirement. Cost alone cannot be a legitimate aim. A legitimate aim must be proportionate and must correspond with a real need of the employer – economic efficiency may be a real aim, but saving money because discrimination is cheaper than non-discrimination is not legitimate. The legitimate aim cannot be related to age discrimination itself. The July 2005 Consultation Paper on the implementation of the predecessor provisions to the Equality Act 2010 (as set out in the Age Regulations 2006) gave as an example a retailer of trendy fashion items who wants to recruit young shop assistants in order to target young shoppers. Trying to attract a young target group will not be a legitimate aim because this has an age-discriminatory aspect to it. It may, however, be legitimate for a business to recruit staff with the right image to assist sales to a target market.

Bloxham v Freshfields Bruckhaus Deringer (ET/2205086/06) was the first significant claim to be brought before a tribunal under the direct discrimination provisions of the Age Regulations 2006. The tribunal found that Mr Bloxham (who, when he retired at 54, had a 20% reduction applied to his pension following a change to the scheme rules) had been discriminated against on the grounds of age, but that Freshfields justified this because they needed to make changes to their pension scheme to avoid disadvantaging younger partners. The legitimate aim here was the promotion of 'intergenerational fairness'. Freshfields were not relying on cost as their defence – costs reasons alone cannot justify discrimination (*Cross v British Airways* [2006] IRLR 804).

In *Swann v GHL Insurance Services UK Ltd* (see **12.6.1**), an employment tribunal held that a flexible benefits package which contained a medical insurance option, where the premium was calculated on age, even if it was less favourable treatment (and the majority found it was not) was justified because:

(a)   there was a legitimate aim (improving the effectiveness of recruitment and retention of staff); and

(b)   the introduction of the benefits package, based on professional advice, was a proportionate means of achieving that aim.

In *MacCulloch v ICI plc* (UKEAT/0119/08), the EAT gave some useful general guidance on the correct approach to the justification defence (see, in particular, para 10 of the decision). See too *Loxley v BAE Systems Land Systems (Munitions and Ordinance) Ltd* (UKEAT/0156/08), where the EAT remitted a decision back to the employment tribunal because it had failed to deal appropriately with justification, and in particular with the issue of proportionality.

There have been cases under the Age Regulations 2006 dealing with objective justification in connection with policies of compulsory retirement at 65. However, such policies needed to be justified objectively. In *Hampton v Lord Chancellor and the Ministry of Justice* [2008] IRLR 258 and *Seldon v Clarkson Wright and Jakes* (ET/1100275/07), the tribunals accepted that compulsory retirement of workers at 65 was direct age discrimination. In *Hampton*, it was argued that it was necessary in order to maintain a reasonable flow of recorders (who were office holders and not employees) and a reasonable flow of candidates for full-time judicial posts. The tribunal accepted that these were legitimate aims, but held that the policy was not a proportionate means of achieving those aims – there were a number of other ways to ensure them. Further, the Ministry of Justice failed to produce any evidence to show that compulsory retirement at 70 would affect this aim. The Government has now changed the compulsory retirement age for part-time judges to 70.

In *Seldon*, a partner in a law firm was compulsorily retired at age 65. The tribunal found that the policy was objectively justified – there were legitimate aims (including allowing others to enter the partnership and giving realistic opportunities to plan for vacancies) and compulsory retirement at 65 was a proportionate means of achieving these aims within a partnership. The EAT ([2009] IRLR 267) agreed that the firm could rely on matters such as succession planning and the opportunity for junior lawyers to be promoted as legitimate aims. The Court of Appeal upheld the tribunal's decision that the rule was a proportionate means of achieving the legitimate aims of workforce planning and providing associates with a chance of promotion. The Court of Appeal ([2010] IRLR 865) held that the fact that a retirement age of 66 would have been less discriminatory to some did not mean that a retirement age of 65 was unlawful. There was no evidence that choosing a different retirement age would have made a difference to the recruitment or retention of staff. The Court of Appeal said that the aims pursued by employers must at least be consistent with the social or labour policy of the UK which satisfied the implementation of the Age Regulations 2006, but did not gave any further details as to what that would mean in practice. The Supreme Court held ([2012] UKSC 16) that it is possible to justify a compulsory retirement age but ruled that direct age discrimination can only be justified by reference to an aim which is of 'a public nature interest' and is consistent with social policy aims. The case was remitted to the employment tribunal to make a decision on the facts.

The Court of Appeal held, in *Woodcock v Cumbria PCT* [2012] EWCA Civ 330, that cost alone cannot justify discrimination, but that where there is another factor (here there was a redundancy situation too) the discrimination can be justified on a 'costs plus' basis.

12.7 INDIRECT DISCRIMINATION

Indirect discrimination occurs when there is equal treatment of all groups but the effect of the provision, criterion or practice imposed by an employer has a disproportionate adverse impact on one group, unless the requirement can be justified.

The definition of 'indirect discrimination' in connection with a person's age is the same as for sex, race, etc, and is set out in s 19 of the Act:

(1)   A person (A) discriminates against another (B) if A applies to B a provision, criterion or practice which is discriminatory in relation to a relevant protected characteristic of B's.

(2)   For the purposes of subsection (1), a provision, criterion or practice is discriminatory in relation to a relevant protected characteristic of B's if—

(a)   A applies, or would apply, it to persons with whom B does not share the characteristic,

(b)   it puts, or would put, persons with whom B shares the characteristic at a particular disadvantage when compared with persons with whom B does not share it,

(c)   it puts, or would put, B at that disadvantage, and

(d)   A cannot show it to be a proportionate means of achieving a legitimate aim.

For example, in *Kraft Foods v Hastie* (UKEAT/0024/10), Kraft had an 'exceptionally generous' contractual redundancy scheme. Because of the high levels of payment under the scheme, it capped redundancy payments at the sum that a redundant employee would have earned if he had remained in employment until normal retirement age. Mr Hastie, who was 62, had his redundancy payment capped at £76,560. This was what he would have earned if he had remained employed until 65. If no cap existed, he would have received about £90,000. He complained that the cap amounted to indirect discrimination on grounds of age, as it would only 'bite' against older workers. The EAT held that the cap was justified. The company's aim of preventing employees receiving a 'windfall' met a legitimate aim, namely giving appropriate payments to employees to compensate them for future loss of earnings. They said the cap was a proportionate means of achieving that aim.

See **Chapter 10** for more a more detailed analysis of the underlying principles of indirect discrimination.

12.7.1 Age groups

Bringing a claim for indirect age discrimination will involve comparing the claimant's 'age group' with another group. Section 5(2) states that 'age group' means 'a group of persons defined by reference to age, whether by reference to a particular age or a range of ages'. There is no further definition of age groups in the Act. This was the same wording as used by the Age Regulations 2006. However, it is still unclear whether 'age group' will be interpreted widely or narrowly. Acas suggests that companies could undertake age monitoring using age bands 16–21, 22–30, 31–40, 41–50, 51–60, 60–65 and 65+. Whatever age group an employee chooses, it will still be open to an employer to challenge the group on the basis that it is not appropriate.

In *Chief Constable of West Yorkshire Police v Homer* [2009] IRLR 262, the EAT overturned a tribunal finding of indirect age discrimination where an employer introduced a requirement that, to be graded at the top grade and to receive the higher salary linked to that grade, an employee had to have a law degree. The tribunal had concluded that there was discrimination directed against those without a law degree who were within the 60–65 age bracket. The tribunal considered the issue of justification but concluded that, although the employers were seeking to achieve a legitimate objective, namely the recruitment and retention of staff of an appropriate quality, nonetheless the imposition of this criterion was not a proportionate means of achieving it. The EAT held that there was no discrimination. It held that such a requirement did not put a 61-year-old employee at a particular disadvantage on the grounds of his age, even though he could not have obtained a degree (studying part-time) before he retired. He was treated in precisely the same way as everyone else. The requirement for a law degree was not something required only of those over a certain age. Neither was it in principle more difficult for an older person to obtain the qualification than it was for a younger person. Any disadvantage could properly be described as the consequence of age, but it was not the consequence of age discrimination (para 39). However, had the claimant been able to establish the requisite age group disadvantage, the EAT would have upheld the finding that any age discrimination was not justified, as the requirement was not a proportionate means of achieving the recruitment and retention of appropriately qualified staff. The Court of Appeal agreed with the EAT ([2010] All ER (D) 189) that the employee's problem was not his age per se, but rather that he would retire before he could get the necessary qualification. The Supreme Court ([2012] UKSC 15) disagreed with the Court of Appeal and held that the employer did indirectly discriminate on grounds of age, subject to justification. Therefore, a requirement which works to the comparative disadvantage of a person approaching compulsory retirement age is discriminatory on grounds of age.

In *Rainbow v Milton Keynes Council* (ET/1200104/2007), an advert looking for teachers 'in the first five years of their career' was held to be indirectly discriminatory. Employees in the claimant's age group (over 60) were likely to have more than five years' teaching experience and would therefore be disadvantaged.

12.7.2 Justification

There are limited circumstances in which it is lawful to treat people differently because of their age. The same test of justification is used for indirect age discrimination as for direct age discrimination (see **12.6.2** above) although, post *Seldon*, it will, it seems, be harder to justify direct age discrimination because the test is narrower. There must be a social policy aim. In other words, an employer must show a legitimate aim and that the policy is a proportionate means of achieving that aim. The wording of the original EU Directive (Article 6.1(c)) gives as one example setting age requirements to ensure the protection or promotion of people in a particular age group, and as another the fixing of a maximum age for recruitment or promotion, based either on the training requirements of the post in question or on the need for a reasonable period in employment before retirement. The Acas booklet suggests that 'economic factors such as business needs and efficiency' could constitute a legitimate aim for the purposes of justification (see **10.2.6**).

For example, the setting of a maximum upper age for a course (eg 25 years old), which is designed to encourage 'new blood' into a particular profession or vocation, will be unlawful unless it can be shown to be a proportionate means of achieving a legitimate aim. In an example such as this, detailed information about the needs of the particular profession would have to be provided as part of that justification. There would need to be an explanation why 'new blood' has to be 'young blood', and consideration of whether the message the employers are sending out (ie that people over the age of 25 do not have a positive contribution to make to the profession) is the right one.

In *Rolls Royce Plc v Unite* [2009] IRLR 576, an issue arose as to whether a collectively agreed redundancy selection matrix which included an award of points for length of service was indirect age discrimination. The Court of Appeal said that rewarding long service was a reasonable and legitimate policy. It held that, viewed objectively, including a length of service criterion amongst a substantial number of other criteria was proportionate. The legitimate aim was to reward loyalty, and to achieve a stable workforce in the context of a fair process of redundancy selection. (For cases looking at contractual redundancy schemes based on age, see *MacCulloch v ICI plc* [2008] IRLR 846 and *Loxley v BAE Systems (Munitions and Ordnance) Ltd* [2008] IRLR 853.)

An occupational requirement may also provide a defence (see **8.5** above). For example, hiring actors is likely to be covered by an occupational requirement, as the age of the character portrayed is likely to be a relevant consideration. For more detailed discussion of some of the common features of indirect discrimination, such as the meaning of 'provision, criterion or practice', 'disadvantage' and the application of the justification defence, see **10.2** above.

In *HM Land Registry v Benson* (UKEAT/0197/11), the EAT said that an employer's decision not to select employees aged 50–54 for voluntary redundancy/early retirement because they were too expensive was justified indirect age discrimination. The selection of cheapness as a criteria, which allowed the releasing of as many employees as possible within budget, was a proportionate means of achieving this legitimate aim. The EAT, while considering that whether this was a 'costs plus' case was debatable, did not need to challenge the tribunal's finding of fact on that (see **10.2.6** above).

12.8 HARASSMENT AND VICTIMISATION

As with the other areas covered by discrimination legislation, harassment is a specific separate ground of complaint. The definitions used in connection with a person's age are identical to those used for sex, race, etc, ie harassment includes behaviour that is intimidating, hostile, degrading, humiliating or offensive.

The IDS Brief, *Focus on Age Discrimination* (805, May 2006), gave some useful practical examples of the protection against harassment provisions:

- an employee whose father works in the same office is subjected to jokes about the father's age. Even though the victim's own age is not the subject of the jokes, this behaviour may still qualify as harassment on the ground of age
- an older employee is not asked to after-work drinks and events as his younger colleagues believe he would not fit in with their social culture. As this is likely to make the older worker feel excluded, it could come within the definition of offensive conduct
- an older employee is subjected to jokes about baldness, wrinkles, etc. Any offensive behaviour based on physical traits that become apparent as one gets older could be argued to be on the ground of age.

In *Lambert v BAT (Investments) Ltd* (ET/3100897/08), the tribunal held that an e-mail entitled 'The perks of being over 50' amounted to 'unwanted conduct which had the effect of violating [the claimant's] dignity'.

The victimisation provisions aim to ensure that individuals are not discouraged from bringing complaints of age discrimination. The protected acts include bringing proceedings under the Act; giving evidence in connection with a case; and alleging that someone has done something which would be unlawful under the Act. Victimisation cannot be justified.

See **Chapter 11** for a more detailed analysis of the underlying principles of victimisation and harassment.

12.9 EXCEPTIONS

Many service-related benefits (see Sch 9, para 10) and the minimum pay rates applicable to younger workers under the minimum wage legislation (Sch 9, para 11) are exempt from the provisions of the Act. Schedule 9, Pt 2 also makes special provision for exemption of or modification to the normal rules in the case of retirement and enhanced redundancy payments (para 13). While certain age-related criteria have been removed (the upper and lower age limits for redundancy payments), the two-year qualifying service period, the length of service used to calculate the payment, and the age-based multipliers for unfair dismissal and redundancy payment awards all remain.

There are a number of other grounds set out in Sch 9, Pt 2 on which otherwise discriminatory acts are lawful: see, eg, para 14 (life assurance) and para 15 (childcare provision for children of a particular age group). The full details of these are beyond the scope of this book.

12.10 VICARIOUS LIABILITY

Section 109 provides that employers are vicariously liable for any acts of their workers, done in the course of their employment, that are unlawful under the Act. Likewise, it extends to the acts of agents. This is so whether or not the acts were done with the employer's knowledge or approval. However, it is a defence for the employer to show that he took such steps as were reasonably practicable to prevent an employee doing the act complained of. See **8.6** for a more detailed discussion of vicarious liability.

12.11 BURDEN OF PROOF

The burden of proof for age discrimination is the same as in all the other main areas of discrimination, as set out in s 136(2) of the Act, namely:

> If there are facts from which the court could decide, in the absence of any other explanation, that a person (A) contravened the provision concerned, the court must hold that the contravention occurred.

In other words, once a complainant has established facts from which a tribunal could conclude there has been discrimination, the tribunal will have to make a finding of discrimination, unless the employer proves he did not commit the act of discrimination (see **9.5**).

In *McCoy v McGregor & Sons Ltd, Dixon and Aitken* (IT/00237/07), the tribunal held that a job advert requiring 'youthful enthusiasm', taken in the context of other evidence, gave rise to a prima facie case of direct discrimination and therefore shifted the burden to the employer.

12.12 PRACTICAL CONSIDERATIONS

12.12.1 Advertising and recruitment

Care should be taken with the language used in job advertisements. Words such as 'mature', 'senior', 'energetic' and 'junior' could all be problematic. Advertisements should focus on the job requirement and the tasks, and not on the person. Consider why and, if so, what experience is needed. Care also needs to be taken about where job advertisements are placed. Recruitment criteria need to be looked at to see if they could have a discriminatory impact. Avoid focusing on a particular age group to satisfy customer prejudice or targets. Using an agency to recruit staff does not avoid the risk of age discrimination.

12.12.2 Application forms and interviews

The Acas booklet recommended banishing questions about age and date of birth from application forms, and suggests that this information could be collected through a separate diversity monitoring form. Application forms should also avoid requesting information from which a job applicant's age can be inferred, unless such information is necessary (eg the dates when an applicant attended school). Employers should consider why they need this information so that, if necessary, they can avail themselves of the justification defence. Interviewers should have had age diversity training. Make sure that each candidate is asked the same questions in the same order. Focus on the job requirement, the tasks involved and the competencies needed for the job.

12.12.3   Contracts

Employment contracts, policies and procedures, and terms and conditions all need to be checked to ensure that they comply with the Act. If any policies or practices are potentially discriminatory, consideration will need to be given as to whether they can be justified. The Act requires that if changes are to be made to the contracts of more than 20 employees, there must be collective consultation with either unions or employee representatives. Similar consultation obligations apply as are to be found in large-scale redundancy situations.

12.12.4   Pensions and insurance benefits

The provisions of the Act relating to pensions are set out in s 61. While the Act makes it unlawful for trustees and managers of occupational pension schemes to discriminate against members or prospective members on the ground of age, there are lots of exemptions (which are beyond the scope of this book) (see for example s 197 and Schs 7 and 9). BIS published 'Guidance on the Age Regulations and their impact on pension schemes' in December 2006, which is still a useful reference.

The Act, like the Age Regulations, outlaws age discrimination in respect of employment-related insured benefits (private medical, motor insurance, etc). The cost to employers of providing insured benefits in relation to older staff, particularly those over 65, can be very high. Insurance companies are free to impose age limits or higher premiums on insurance policies, as insurance providers are not covered by the age discrimination legislation. There is concern amongst both employer and employee organisations that the absence of any exemptions for insurance benefits may cause employers to level down or remove insured benefits for all staff.

The Government has not ruled out introducing an exemption for insured benefits, but to date no action has been taken.

12.12.5   Dismissal and retirement

12.12.5.1   The position under the Age Regulations 2006 – a default retirement age

One of the key features of the Age Regulations 2006 was the introduction of a default retirement age of 65, and the prohibition of a compulsory retirement age below 65 unless it could be objectively justified. This meant that dismissing an employee by reason of retirement was a potentially discriminatory act unless the employee was at or over the age of 65 and a set procedure was followed. Retirement below the age of 65 would amount to age discrimination unless the retirement could be justified as a proportionate means of achieving a legitimate aim.

Section 98(2) of the ERA 1996 was amended also to include the employee's retirement as a further potentially fair reason (s 98(2)(ba)), and the upper age limit of 65 for bringing claims for unfair dismissal and redundancy rights was removed, giving older workers the same rights to claim unfair dismissal or receive a redundancy payment as younger workers, unless there is a genuine retirement.

12.12.5.2   The Heyday challenge

Heyday (an organisation which helps people prepare for and make the most of retirement), supported by Age Concern, challenged regs 3 and 30 of the Age Regulations 2006 on the basis that they contravened Article 6(1) of the EU Equal Treatment Framework Directive (2000/78/EC). The High Court referred the issue to the ECJ (*Age Concern v Secretary of State for Business, Enterprise and Regulatory Reform* (CO/5485/2006)). The ECJ, in a different case (*Felix Palacios de la Villa v Cortefiel Services* (Case C-411/05) [2007] IRLR 989 – see **3.7**), decided that a compulsory retirement age of 65 in Spain did not breach the Directive on the basis that it met a legitimate aim in seeking to promote employment opportunity and could be objectively justified.

In September 2008, the Advocate-General handed down his opinion in the *Age Concern* case. He recommended to the court that it is legitimate to allow a general justification defence and that reg 30 (permitting employers to dismiss employees aged 65 or over if the reason is retirement) is not incompatible with the Equal Treatment Framework Directive, provided the regulation is objectively justified within the context of national law. The decision of the full court followed this opinion. The ECJ ruled that the UK's compulsory retirement age of 65 was not in breach of the Framework Directive, provided there was a legitimate aim related to employment and social policy. Following the ECJ's judgment, the case returned to the High Court to decide whether regs 3 and 30 of the Age Regulations 2006 properly implemented the Directive. The High Court ([2009] EWHC 2336) held that the UK's default retirement age of 65 and reg 3 allowing objective justification of direct discrimination, were both lawful.

Notwithstanding the ECJ's decision, the Government decided to conduct a consultation exercise on the default retirement age. The consultation ended on 1 February 2010. The Government abolished the default retirement age on 1 October 2011.

12.12.5.3   The new provisions

If an employer wishes to retire an employee after 6 April 2011, the employer will have to ensure that a fair procedure is followed under the ordinary unfair dismissal rules. Retirement is no longer a potentially fair reason for dismissal, so employers will need to show that the dismissal was for one of the potentially fair reasons for dismissal set out in s 98 of the ERA 1996 (capability, conduct, illegality, redundancy or some other substantial reason). This will mean that if an employer feels that an employee is under-performing then the employer should deal with the employee in the same manner as any other under-performing employee, ie by following a fair capability process that focuses on the employee's performance and not on his age. There has been concern that older employees will be particularly sensitive to this, and employers will have to ensure that any such disciplinary/capability procedures are handled sensitively and fairly.

Employers may still be able to operate a compulsory retirement age provided that they can justify it objectively. They must show that the discrimination is a proportionate means of achieving a legitimate aim. In its consultation on the default retirement age (see **12.12.5.2**), the Government set out guidance on the proportionate means of achieving a legitimate aim. 'Proportionate' means that what the employer is doing is actually achieving its aim; the discriminatory effect should be significantly outweighed by the importance and benefits of the legitimate aim; and the employer should have no reasonable alternative to the action it is taking. If the legitimate aim can be achieved by other or less discriminatory means, the employer must then opt for that route. 'Legitimate' means taking into account economic factors such as the needs and the efficiency of running of a business; the health, welfare and safety of the individual (including protection of young people or older workers); and the particular training for that job.

The Government pointed out in its consultation that a legitimate aim must correspond with a legitimate need of the employer. The aim of saving money by removing older workers who might be paid more than younger workers is not by itself a legitimate aim. Employers will not be able to rely on generalised assumptions as evidence of justification; they will have to provide valid evidence if their retirement ages are challenged (see *Hampton* and *Seldon* at **12.6.2** above). In *Martin v Professional Game Match Officials Ltd (PGMOL)* [2010] ET/2802438/09, an employment tribunal held that a retirement age of 48 for football referees was direct age discrimination and could not be justified as a proportionate means of achieving a legitimate aim. The tribunal held that a compulsory retirement policy could be a proportionate means of achieving a legitimate aim only if it could be shown that there was no less discriminatory way of achieving that aim. It was not satisfied that this was the case here. In addition, the PGMOL had not produced evidence to demonstrate why it had selected 48 as the retirement age. Other countries had adopted other ages. The ECJ appears to have adopted a less rigid approach in

Petersen v Berufungsausschuss für Zähn für den Bezirk Westfalen-Lippe [2010] All ER (D) 233, where a German law setting a maximum age limit of 68 for dentists to be accredited to work in the German national health service was found to be lawful and an appropriate and necessary means of giving younger generations the opportunity of working.

In *Rosenbladt v Oellerking Gebäudereinigungsgesellschaft mbH* (Case C-45/09) [2011] IRLR 51, the ECJ held that a compulsory retirement age of 65 in a contract of employment, while prima facie discriminatory on the grounds of age, could be justified on the basis of a legitimate aim of seeking to promote access to employment by means of 'better distribution of work between the generations' (see too *Prigge v Deutsche Lufthansa AG* (Case C-447/09), ECJ).

In *Fuchs and Another v Land Hessen* (Joined Cases C-159/10 and C-160/10) the ECJ was asked to decide a number of questions arising out of a German law which stipulated that permanent civil servants must retire at 65 years. The two claimants – both prosecutors in the German legal system – were subject to a retirement age of 65 years, with the option to request an extension to 68 years (if this proved to be in the interest of their employer). Both claimants requested to work beyond retirement. Their requests were rejected, and as a result they brought age discrimination claims. The German national court doubted whether this provison complied with the Equal Treatment Directive and thought it might really be budgetary savings which were the rationale for the retirement decision. On the facts, the ECJ held that the law was justified.

The ECJ accepted that it is a legitimate aim for an employer to impose a compulsory retirement age to achieve 'the aim of establishing a balanced age structure amongst their workforce in order to enable staff planning and encourage the recruitment and promotion of young people, improve personnel management and avoid performance disputes with older workers'. This suggests therefore that where an employer has a required retirement age in place in order to avoid disputes over older workers' fitness to work, this is a justifiable aim, along with (para 50) an aim of encouraging a younger workforce. The ECJ also seems to adopt a test of whether it is 'reasonable' to adopt a retirement age (paras 60 and 83), rather than whether it is proportionate to do so.

The Court also suggested that Member States could rely on budgetary constraints when justifying retirement age if considered alongside other factors (such as social, political or demographic issues), but that budget alone should not be considered a legitimate aim, but did not specifically deal with whether cost alone can justify discrimination (see *Cross v British Airways* and *Woodcock v Cumbria PCT* at **10.2.6** above). At present, it appears that there is a consistent line of authority from the ECJ adopting a less stringent approach to the issue of justifying compulsory retirement ages than in the UK courts.

12.12.5.4   Practical issues arising from the abolition of the statutory retirement regime

As indicated above, it is still possible for employers to have a compulsory contractual retirement age, providing they can objectively justify it. Otherwise, an employer will need a reason for dismissing an older employee. Where, for example, an employee's skills are in decline owing to age, an employer will have to deal with this under the heading of capability – age alone will not free an employer from having to show that a dismissal was reasonable.

In essence, commentators have advised that there are now broadly two options for employers – to have and operate a contractual retirement age and be willing and able to justify it (s 13(2) of the Act) if an employee complains of direct discrimination; or to treat retirement on a case by case basis using ordinary capability and disciplinary procedures; but otherwise to leave it up to employees to decide when they want to retire. Clauses in contacts specifying that the contract may come to an end automatically when the employee reaches his 65th birthday may need to reviewed.

With regard to the first option, as indicated above, there is a consistent body of decisions from the ECJ adopting a liberal stance towards justifying compulsory retirement ages. The EHRC's Code of Practice on Employment – which is admissible as evidence – should be referred to. In *Seldon* (above) the tribunal accepted that the following aims were potentially legitimate aims:

- retention reasons – giving senior solicitors the opportunity of partnership so that they do not leave;
- facilitating partnership and workforce planning so as to provide promotion opportunities (and see the Acas booklet, *Working within the DRA*, and *Rosenblatt* (above)); and
- limiting the need to expel partners by way of performance management.

Additional reasons which might be considered include:

- health and safety – for example where a role relies on physical fitness or good eyesight;
- cost (see the problems highlighted in *Cross* and *Woodcock* at **10.2.6** above);
- declining performance.

In addition to be a legitimate aim, the retirement age will have to be a proportionate response. The EHRC Code of Practice states (para 4.31) that:

> EU law views treatment as proportionate if it is an appropriate and necessary means of achieving a legitimate aim. … it is sufficient that less discriminatory measures could not achieve the same aim. A balance must be struck between the discriminatory effect of the practice and A's reasons for applying it, taking into account all the relevant facts.'

Even where an employer can show that a compulsory retirement age is justified, it will still be necessary where an individual is to be dismissed to show that the dismissal was for a potential fair reason. The most likely category of the five potentially fair reasons for dismissal that could be used here would appear to be some other substantial reason. Where there is no contractual date, an employer will have to rely on one of the other potentially fair reasons, from which capability seems to be the one most employers will probably rely on. For a detailed analysis of capability dismissals, see **5.2.2.1** and **5.4.2.1** above. It should be noted that in addition to capabilities and qualifications, the definition of capability includes skills, aptitude and health as well as 'any other physical or mental quality'.

12.12.6 Redundancy

Note that enhanced redundancy schemes may be unlawful if they pay out based on differential age grounds (likely to be direct discrimination unless exempted under Sch 9 or objectively justified) or on length of service (indirect discrimination unless exempted under Sch 9 or objectively justified). Paragraph 13 of Sch 9 to the Equality Act 2010 allows for enhanced redundancy schemes that essentially mirror the statutory redundancy payment scheme, although employers can derogate from the statutory cap on a week's wage and/or the multiple used.

(For cases under the pre-Equality Act 2010 law looking at contractual redundancy schemes based on age, see *MacCulloch v ICI plc* [2008] IRLR 846, *Loxley v BAE Systems (Munitions and Ordnance) Ltd* [2008] IRLR 853 and *Kraft Foods v Hastie* (above at **12.7**).

12.13 ENFORCEMENT AND REMEDIES

Chapter 3 of the Act contains the enforcement and remedies regime. Readers are referred to **8.8** for a more detailed discussion of enforcement and remedies. In essence, the same regime applies as applies to the other grounds of discrimination. Section 124 permits the making of a declaration of rights, an order to pay compensation and a recommendation that the employer take, within a specified period, specific steps for the purpose of obviating or reducing the adverse effect on the complainant or any other person of any matter to which the complaint relates.

In *Thomas v Eight Members Club and Killip* (ET/2202603/07), a claimant was awarded £1,500 for injury to feelings (the lowest band in the *Vento* range – see **8.8.2.2**) where her employer was found to have discriminated against her because she was thought too young to do the job. (She had insufficient service to bring an unfair dismissal claim and immediately found another job, so her compensation was limited to an injury to feelings award.) Provision is also made for the use of questionnaires (see s 138). See **8.8.1.2** for a more detailed discussion of the usefulness of questionnaires.

12.14 FURTHER READING

Although these works focus on the provisions of the Age Regulations 2006, they are nonetheless still worth looking at:

Kapoor (ed), *Age Discrimination: A Guide to the New Law* (The Law Society, October 2006).

Sprack, *Guide to the Age Discrimination Regulations 2006* (Tottel, 2006).

O'Dempsey, Jolly and Harrop, *Age Discrimination Handbook* (LAG, 2006).

The three-part IDS Employment Law Brief (October/November 2008, 863–65) provided a detailed focus on employment tribunal decisions on the Age Regulations 2006.

The three-part IDS Employment Law Brief, *Focus on Age Discrimination* (May/June 2006, 805) also provided a detailed analysis of the Age Regulations 2006. Part 2 used some useful examples born of the experience in Ireland following the passing of the Employment Equality Act 1998.

Age and the Workplace: Putting the Employment Equality (Age) Regulations 2006 into Practice, published by Acas, provides guidance for employers and providers of vocational training. At the back of the employer leaflet is an Appendix containing flowcharts in relation to retirement dismissals, and template letters in relation to the 'duty to consider' process. A parallel information leaflet – *Age and the Workplace* – is available for employees. Both are available online from the Acas website at <www.acas.org.uk>.

The 'Age Positive' website (<www.agepositive.gov.uk>) also contains useful guidance and advice for employers on good practice. See too the website of the Equality Challenge Unit at <www.ecu.ac.uk/guidance/age/faqs.htm>.

See also Bowers, *A Practical Approach to Employment Law*, 8th edn (OUP, 2009), ch 10.

SUMMARY

Age is a protected characteristic under s 4 of the Equality Act 2010 (**12.2**). The provisions of the 2010 Act apply to employees, job applicants, ex-employees, contract workers, office holders and partners. They outlaw age discrimination in terms of recruitment, promotion and training, transfers and dismissals (**12.4**); ban all retirement ages below 65 (except where objectively justified); and remove the current upper age limits for unfair dismissal and redundancy (**12.12.5**).

Four main types of age discrimination in the employment field are outlawed by UK legislation. These are:

(a)   direct discrimination (ie being subject to less favourable treatment than others because of age) (**12.6**);

(b)   indirect discrimination (ie the application of a provision, criterion or practice which disadvantages people of a particular age) (**12.7**);

(c)   harassment (unwanted conduct that violates a person's dignity, or creates an intimidating, hostile, degrading, humiliating or offensive environment for him having regard to all the circumstances including the perception of the victim) (**12.8**); and

(d)   victimisation (because the victim has been subject to a detriment because he has done a protected act) (**12.8**).

Much of the terminology used is familiar 'discrimination' terminology. Unlike other forms of discrimination, both direct and indirect age discrimination may be justified 'objectively' where the discrimination is a 'proportionate means of achieving legitimate aim' (**12.6.2** and **12.7.2**). Harassment and victimisation cannot be justified.

The Equality Act 2010 also removes the age limits for statutory sick pay, statutory maternity pay, statutory adoption pay and statutory paternity pay. The Employment Equality (Age) Regulations 2006, Sch 6 further introduced a right for employees to request to be permitted to work beyond retirement age, and a duty on employers to consider that request, and a requirement for employers to give at least six months' notice to employees about their intended retirement date so that individuals might plan better for retirement and be confident that 'retirement' is not being used as a cover for unfair dismissal. The Regulations also made changes to the existing unfair dismissal regime. In particular, 'retirement' is now a potentially fair reason for dismissal. The Equality Act 2010 does not affect the age at which people may claim their State pensions.

Remedies and enforcement are dealt with at **8.8** above.

Disability Discrimination

LEARNING OUTCOMES

After reading this chapter you will be able to:

- understand the underlying principles of disability discrimination and how it differs from other areas of discrimination
- explain the four cumulative elements that make up the meaning of 'disability'
- list the six types of prohibited conduct and explain how they differ from each other
- describe the remedies available where a complaint of disability discrimination is made out.

13.1 INTRODUCTION

This chapter considers disability discrimination. Traditionally, disability discrimination has been treated differently from discrimination because of sex, race, religion or belief, etc. The pre-Equality Act 2010 legislation, the Disability Discrimination Act 1995 (DDA 1995) (as amended by the Disability Discrimination Act 1995 (Amendment) Regulations 2003 and the Disability Discrimination Act 2005) was different from other discrimination legislation in a number of ways. In relation to sex, race, religion or belief, etc, the emphasis is on treating all people the same. In disability discrimination, the opposite is often the case – a person's individual circumstances have to be considered, and such consideration is crucial to avoid discrimination. Many of the differences that existed between the DDA 1995 and the rest of the UK anti-discrimination legislation have been maintained in the Equality Act 2010, eg the concept of 'reasonable adjustments' (see **13.5.2** below), whereby employers need to treat disabled people differently in order to achieve substantive equality.

The relevant parts of the 2010 Act in so far as they relate to disability discrimination were implemented in October 2010.

The Equality and Human Rights Commission (EHRC) has responsibility for the promotion of equality and for combating discrimination on the grounds of disability. The EHRC published a Code of Practice on Employment, which came into force on 6 April 2011.

The protection against discrimination because of disability applies to all employers, private and public sector, and employment agencies, vocational training providers, trade unions, professional organisations, employer organisations, and trustees and managers of occupational pension schemes. It applies to employees, job claimants, ex-employees, contract workers, office holders and partners. The protection applies to a broad definition of workers and employees (see **1.3**). As with sex, race, age, etc, 'employment' is defined as 'employment under a contract of employment, a contract of apprenticeship or a contract personally to do work' (s 83). This is a wider definition than that of 'employee' as contained in the ERA 1996, and means that certain categories of individuals who are not covered by other statutory rights (eg job claimants, office holders, police officers and the self-employed) are covered by the Equality Act 2010.

Much of the terminology used is familiar discrimination terminology; under the Act direct disability discrimination is prohibited (ie being subjected to less favourable treatment than others because of disability) as is indirect disability discrimination (ie the application of a provision, criterion or practice which disadvantages the disabled person). Both harassment (being unwanted conduct that violates a person's dignity, or creates an intimidating, hostile, degrading, humiliating or offensive environment for him having regard to all the circumstances, including the perception of the victim) and victimisation (because the victim has brought proceedings under the Act, or has given evidence or information in connection with proceedings under the Act) are also unlawful. However, some of the terminology is new and relevant to disability discrimination only (eg the duty to make reasonable adjustments; discrimination arising from a disability).

13.2 THE PROTECTED CHARACTERISTIC

Section 4 of the Act sets out certain 'protected' characteristics (see **8.2**). These are the grounds upon which discrimination is deemed unlawful. Disability is listed as one of the protected characteristics in s 4.

13.3 THE MEANING OF 'DISABILITY' AND 'DISABLED PERSON'

13.3.1 Introduction

Crucial to the operation of the disability discrimination regime in the Act are the definitions of 'disability' and 'disabled person' in s 6. This section establishes who is to be considered as having the protected characteristic of disability and is a disabled person for the purposes of the Act.

Section 6 provides as follows:

> (1)   A person (P) has a disability if—
>
>> (a)   P has a physical or mental impairment, and
>>
>> (b)   the impairment has a substantial and long-term adverse effect on P's ability to carry out normal day-to-day activities.
>
> (2)   A reference to a disabled person is a reference to a person who has a disability.
>
> (3)   In relation to the protected characteristic of disability—
>
>> (a)   a reference to a person who has a particular protected characteristic is a reference to a person who has a particular disability;
>>
>> (b)   a reference to persons who share a protected characteristic is a reference to persons who have the same disability.
>
> (4)   This Act (except Part 12 and section 190) applies in relation to a person who has had a disability as it applies in relation to a person who has the disability;
>
> accordingly (except in that Part and that section)—
>
>> (a)   a reference (however expressed) to a person who has a disability includes a reference to a person who has had the disability, and
>>
>> (b)   a reference (however expressed) to a person who does not have a disability includes a reference to a person who has not had the disability.

A person has a disability, therefore, if he has:

- a physical or mental impairment, which has
- a substantial and
- long-term adverse effect on his ability to carry out
- normal day-to-day activities. (s 6(1))

A 'disabled person' means a person who has a disability (s 6(2)). In essence, s 6 requires a tribunal to look at four different (cumulative) conditions.

Section 6 replaces similar provisions in the DDA 1995. The stated intention was that the 2010 Act would make it easier for a person to show that he is disabled. It introduces one major change from the DDA 1995, by removing a previous requirement to consider a specific list of eight capacities (such as mobility or speech, hearing or eyesight) which were said to constitute 'normal day-to-day activities', when considering whether or not a person was disabled (see **13.3.3** below). This change is intended to make it easier for some people to demonstrate that they meet the definition of a 'disabled person'.

A number of other sources also provide assistance, including Sch 1 to the Act; the Equality Act 2010 (Disability) Regulations 2010 (SI 2010/2128); and the draft 'Guidance on matters to be taken into account in determining questions relating to the definition of disability' ('the draft Guidance') which came into force on 1 May 2011. The Guidance is published by the Office for Disability Issues (ODI) which is a cross-government organisation that works with government departments, disabled people and a wide range of external groups: see www.officefordisability.gov.uk. The Guidance does not impose any legal obligations in itself, nor is it an authoritative statement of the law. However, para 12 of Sch 1 to the Act requires that an adjudicating body which is determining for any purpose of the Act whether a person is a disabled person must take into account any aspect of the Guidance which appears to it to be relevant.

We look at each of the various elements of the definition of 'disability' in more detail below.

13.3.2   The impairment condition

The claimant must have a physical or mental impairment. There is no definition in the Act of either physical or mental impairment. The Guidance states that the term should be given its ordinary meaning. Examples given include sensory impairments, organ specific diseases such as asthma, progressive diseases such as MS, and mental health conditions such as depression, OCD and eating disorders. The Guidance states that if the condition amounts to an impairment, it is not necessary to consider how the impairment was caused, and confirms the pre-Equality Act 2010 case law reported at **13.3.2.1** below in this respect.

The Equality Act 2010 (Disability) Regulations 2010, which came into force on 1 October 2010, provide that an addiction to alcohol, nicotine or any other substance will not be an impairment for the purposes of the Equality Act 2010. In addition, a tendency to set fires, a tendency to steal, a tendency to physical or sexual abuse of other persons, exhibitionism (a compulsive desire to expose one's genital organs publicly), voyeurism (obtaining sexual pleasure from the observation of people undressing and having intercourse) and seasonal allergic rhinitis (hay fever) (although it may be taken into account for the purposes of the Act where it aggravates the effect of any other condition) are not recognised as impairments.

The 2010 Regulations also confirm that people who are certified blind, severely sight impaired, sight impaired or partially sighted by a consultant ophthalmologist are deemed disabled, and will automatically qualify for protection under the Act.

13.3.2.1 Pre-Equality Act 2010 case law

In *Dunham v Ashford Windows* [2005] IRLR 608, the EAT held that general learning disabilities could amount to a mental impairment; and in *Paterson v The Commissioner of Police of the Metropolis* (UKEAT/0635/06), that the claimant's dyslexia had an adverse effect on his normal day-to-day activities (being written assessments of work).

The Guidance emphasises that it is not how an impairment is caused that is important, but rather the effect it has. In *Power v Panasonic UK Ltd* [2003] IRLR 151, the EAT said that where depression was caused by alcohol addiction, the fact that the *cause* of the impairment was an addiction did not mean it was not covered.

In *J v DLA Piper UK LLP* (UKEAT/0263/09) the claimant's job offer was withdrawn soon after she revealed a history of depression. She tried (unsuccessfully) to convince the tribunal that she was in fact disabled and so entitled to protection under the pre-Equality Act 2010 legislation (DDA 1995). She maintained that her disability consisted of clinical depression, being a 'mental impairment which has a substantial and long-term adverse effect on [her] ability to carry out normal day-to-day activities'. She asserted that the condition had an adverse effect on her ability to concentrate. The tribunal decided that J did not suffer from a sufficiently well-defined impairment. J appealed and submitted that the existence of an impairment will, in most cases, be evident from the existence of an adverse effect on a claimant's ability to carry out day-to-day activities, and so the tribunal should examine that issue first. The EAT accepted that there will be cases where identifying the nature of the impairment in question involves difficult medical questions and that, in most such cases, it will be easier and legitimate for the tribunal to 'park' that issue and first consider adverse effect: it will not always be essential to identify a specific 'impairment' (within the words of s 1 of the DDA 1995) if the existence of one can be established from evidence of an adverse effect on the claimant's abilities.

Thus it may be easier to address the second and third conditions at **13.3.3** and **13.3.4** below first, ie whether there is a substantial effect on ability to carry out day-to-day activities. In the event that the tribunal decides that those conditions are made out, an impairment may be inferred. So if, for example, the claimant's symptoms have a substantial effect on normal day-to-day activities caused by symptoms characteristic of depression, the tribunal is likely to conclude that the impairment condition is also made out: that the claimant is suffering from clinical depression. In this case the medical evidence was ambiguous. The EAT stated that it remains good practice for the tribunal to state its conclusions on the issues of impairment and effect separately, as recommended in *Goodwin v Patent Office* (see **13.3.3.1**), but, in reaching those conclusions, the tribunal need not proceed by rigid consecutive stages. Specifically, where there may be a dispute about the existence of an impairment, it will make sense to make findings on the question of substantial adverse effect and then consider impairment in the light of those findings.

13.3.3 The adverse effect on normal day-to-day activities condition

The tribunal must ascertain whether the identified impairment adversely affects the claimant's ability to carry out normal day-to-day activities. These are not defined in the Act. The Guidance states that the term 'normal day-to-day activities' are things that people do on a regular or daily basis such as shopping, reading, getting dressed, etc. The Guidance confirms that the term is not intended to include activities which are normal only for a particular person or group of people. In any individual case, the activities carried out may be highly specialised, for example the playing of a particular game, taking part in a particular hobby, playing a musical instrument, playing sport or performing a highly-skilled task. Impairments which affect only such an activity and have no effect on 'normal day-to-day activities' are not covered. Nevertheless, the EAT held in *Cruickshank v VAW Motorcast Ltd* [2002] IRLR 24 that if, while at work, a claimant's symptoms have a significant and long-term effect on his ability to perform day-to-day tasks, such symptoms should not be ignored simply because the work itself is specialised, so long as the effect of the disability can be measured in terms of the claimant's ability to carry out day-to-day tasks. The Guidance confirms this.

The Guidance says as follows:

> It is not possible to provide an exhaustive list of day-to-day activities, although guidance on this matter is given here and illustrative examples of when it would, and would not, be reasonable to regard an impairment as having a substantial adverse effect on the ability to carry out normal day-to-day activities are shown in the Appendix. In general, day-to-day activities are things people do on a regular or daily basis, and examples include shopping, reading and writing, having a conversation or using the telephone, watching television, getting washed and dressed, preparing and eating food, carrying out household tasks, walking and travelling by various forms of transport, and taking part in social activities.

> The term 'normal day-to-day activities' is not intended to include activities which are normal only for a particular person, or a small group of people. In deciding whether an activity is a normal day-to- day activity, account should be taken of how far it is normal for a large number of people, and carried out by people on a daily or frequent and fairly regular basis. In this context, 'normal' should be given its ordinary, everyday meaning.

> A normal day-to-day activity is not necessarily one that is carried out by a majority of people. For example, it is possible that some activities might be carried out only, or more predominantly, by people of a particular gender, such as applying make-up or using hair curling equipment, and cannot therefore be said to be normal for most people. They would nevertheless be considered to be normal day-to-day activities.

The Guidance gives these examples:

> A woman plays the piano to a high standard, and often takes part in public performances. She has developed carpal tunnel syndrome in her wrists, an impairment that adversely affects manual dexterity. She can continue to play the piano, but not to such a high standard, and she has to take frequent breaks to rest her arms. This would not of itself be an adverse effect on a normal day-to-day activity. However, as a result of her impairment she also finds it difficult to operate a computer keyboard and cannot use her PC to send emails or write letters. This is an adverse effect on a normal day-to-day activity.

> A man works in a warehouse, loading and unloading heavy stock. He develops heart problems and no longer has the ability to lift or move heavy items of stock at work. Lifting and moving such unusually heavy types of item is not a normal day-to-day activity. However, he is also unable to lift, carry or move moderately heavy everyday objects such as chairs, either at work or around the home. This is an adverse effect on a normal day-to-day activity.

> A man has had chronic fatigue syndrome for several years and although he has the physical capability to walk and to stand, he finds these very difficult to sustain for any length of time because of the overwhelming fatigue he experiences. As a consequence, he is restricted in his ability to take part in normal day-to-day activities such as travelling, so he avoids going out socially, and works from home several days a week. Therefore there is a substantial adverse effect on normal day-to-day activities.

Some cases under the pre-Equality Act 2010 law are included below by way of further illustration.

13.3.3.1 Pre-Equality Act 2010 case law

In *Paterson v Commissioner of Police of the Metropolis* [2007] IRLR 763, the EAT held, following an ECJ decision, that career exams and assessments could constitute normal day-to-day activities. In *Chief Constable of Lothian and Borders Police v Cumming* (UKEATS/0077/08), the EAT held that the claimant's minor eyesight impairment did not have a substantial adverse effect on normal day-to-day activities because making an application for a job was not a 'normal day-to-day activity'. In *Chief Constable of Dumfries and Galloway Constabulary v Mr C Adams* (UKEATS/0046/08), the EAT held that normal day-to-day activities, albeit carried out during the nightshift, fell within the definition of 'normal day-to-day activities'.

The EAT emphasised in *Goodwin v Patent Office* [1999] IRLR 4 that the DDA 1995 was not concerned with what a person *can* do. Neither was the 1995 Act concerned with whether the claimant had so modified his lifestyle that he might, in fact, manage reasonably well. It required tribunals to look, instead, at the person's ability to carry out daily activities. If the person managed reasonably well because he had adapted his lifestyle, he was still regarded as disabled if his ability to carry out one or more daily activities would clearly be regarded as adversely affected (*Vicary v BT plc* [1999] IRLR 680). On the facts of *Goodwin*, the EAT stated that the tribunal's error was that it had looked at the claimant's abilities to cope at home and come to a conclusion that he was not, therefore, disabled within the meaning of the Act. Instead, said the EAT, the tribunal should have looked at what the claimant could not do, eg carry on a normal conversation with work colleagues. The EAT concluded that the claimant was disabled.

In *Leonard v Southern Derbyshire Chamber of Commerce* [2001] IRLR 19, the issue for the EAT was whether the claimant's clinical depression had a substantial adverse effect on her ability to carry out normal day-to-day activities. The tribunal said she could catch a ball, and eat and drink, and weighed these against what she could not do, such as negotiate pavement edges safely. This, the EAT said, was inappropriate, since her ability to catch a ball did not diminish her inability to negotiate pavement edges safely. A tribunal should, the EAT repeated, concentrate on what claimants cannot do or only do with difficulty, rather than on things they can do.

13.3.4   The substantial condition

Section 212(1) of the Act defines 'substantial' to mean 'more than minor or trivial'. The Guidance states that this requirement:

> reflects the general understanding of 'disability' as a limitation going beyond the normal differences in ability which may exist among people.

The Guidance suggests a number of factors to consider, including the time taken to carry out an activity, the way in which an activity is carried out, the cumulative effects of an impairment, the effects of behaviour and the effects of the environment. In one case the EAT said, albeit *obiter*, that someone whose hearing impairment merely requires him to view the television with the volume up, and which results in occasional difficulty in hearing speech, may have difficulty in showing 'substantial adverse effect' (*London Underground Ltd v Bragg* (UKEAT/847/98)).

The Guidance states that the time taken by a person with an impairment to carry out a normal day-to-day activity should be considered when assessing whether the effect of that impairment is substantial. It should be compared with the time it might take a person who did not have the impairment to complete an activity. It gives the following example:

> A ten-year-old child has cerebral palsy. The effects include muscle stiffness, poor balance and uncoordinated movements. The child is still able to do most things for himself, but he gets tired very easily and it is harder for him to accomplish tasks like eating and drinking, washing, and getting dressed. Although he has the ability to carry out everyday activities such as these, everything takes longer compared to a child of a similar age who does not have cerebral palsy. This amounts to a substantial adverse effect.

The Guidance states that another factor to be considered when assessing whether the effect of an impairment is substantial is the way in which a person with that impairment carries out a normal day-to-day activity. The comparison should be with the way that the person might be expected to carry out the activity if he did not have the impairment. It gives the following example:

> A person who has obsessive compulsive disorder follows a complicated ritual of hand washing. When preparing a simple meal, he washes his hands carefully after handling each ingredient and each utensil. A person without the disorder might wash his or her hands at appropriate points in preparing

the meal, for example after handling raw meat, but would not normally do this after every stage in the process of preparation.

In relation to the cumulative effects of a condition the Guidance gives the following example:

> A man with depression experiences a range of symptoms that include a loss of energy and motivation that makes even the simplest of tasks or decisions seem quite difficult. For example, he finds it difficult to get up in the morning, get washed and dressed, and prepare breakfast. He is forgetful and cannot plan ahead. As a result he has often run out of food before he thinks of going shopping again. Household tasks are frequently left undone, or take much longer to complete than normal. Together, the effects amount to a substantial adverse effect.

In the Appendix to the Guidance, further illustrative and non-exhaustive examples are given of circumstances in which it would be reasonable to regard as substantial the adverse effect of the ability to carry out a normal day-to-day activity. In addition, illustrative and non-exhaustive examples are given of circumstances where it would not be reasonable to regard the effect as substantial. The EAT upheld the tribunal's decision in *Anwar v Tower Hamlets College* (UKEAT/0091/10) that the effect, although 'more than trivial', was still minor and therefore not substantial. It is hard to see how that interpretation can be correct – the test is whether the effect is more than minor *or* trivial.

If an impairment ceases to have a substantial adverse effect on a person's ability to carry out normal day-to-day activities, it is to be treated as continuing to have that effect if that effect is likely to recur (Sch 1, para 1).

Progressive conditions (eg rheumatoid arthritis) do not have to have a *substantial* adverse effect if the condition *is likely to* result in such an impairment (Sch 1, para 8). However, they need to have *some* effect. Therefore, once a person with a progressive condition experiences symptoms which have *any* effect on his normal day-to-day activities, he will fall within the definition of 'disability', so long as the effect of the impairment is likely to become substantial in the future (see *Mowat-Brown v University of Surrey* [2002] IRLR 235 and *Kirton v Tetrosyl Ltd* [2002] IRLR 840). (Note that the Act covers from the date of diagnosis people who have cancer, HIV/AIDS and multiple sclerosis – see **13.3.11**.)

An impairment which consists of a severe disfigurement is deemed to have a substantial effect on the ability of the person to carry out normal day-to-day activities (Sch 1, para 3). The Guidance indicates that assessing severity will be mainly a matter of the degree of the disfigurement. Examples of disfigurements include scars, birthmarks, limb or postural deformation, or diseases of the skin. The Equality Act 2010 (Disability) Regulations 2010 make clear (reg 5) that a severe disfigurement is not to be treated as having a substantial adverse effect on the ability of the person concerned to carry out normal day-to-day activities if it consists of either a tattoo (which has not been removed) or a piercing of the body for decorative or other non-medical purposes, including any object attached through the piercing for such purposes.

13.3.5 Medical evidence

Medical evidence has traditionally played an important role in disability discrimination cases. In *Kapadia v London Borough of Lambeth* [2000] IRLR 699, the tribunal discounted uncontested medical evidence and held that the claimant's medical condition did not have a substantial adverse effect on his ability to carry out day-to-day-activities. The Court of Appeal, agreeing with the EAT, held that the tribunal had erred in rejecting the medical evidence, and reversed the decision. Pill LJ said that uncontested medical evidence need not be accepted by the tribunal where the evidence, on the basis of which the doctor has formed an opinion, is rejected, or where the doctor has misunderstood the evidence he was invited to consider. Nevertheless, the Court of Appeal said the issue of whether an individual has a disability within the meaning of the DDA 1995 is a legal issue, and is one to be determined by the tribunal itself, in light of the medical evidence. In *Abadeh v British Telecommunications plc* [2001]

IRLR 23, the EAT held that the tribunal had erred in deciding that an employee was not disabled within the meaning of the DDA 1995 by, in effect, adopting the doctor's assessment as to whether the adverse effects of the impairment were substantial, instead of making its own assessment based on the medical evidence. In *McKechnie Plastic Components v Grant* (UKEAT/0284/08), the EAT held that the tribunal had been free to reach a finding of discrimination when an agreed expert's medical report did not support such a finding, except that it had failed to apply the correct test with respect to whether the impairment was long-term.

In *J v DLA Piper UK LLP* (see **13.3.2.1** above) the EAT remitted the case to the employment tribunal because the tribunal had wrongly declined to give effect to the evidence provided by the claimant's GP on the issues of impairment and 'deduced effect' (see **13.3.7**), having concluded that the GP was not a specialist.

Reference should be made to the EAT's judgment in *De Keyser v Wilson* [2001] IRLR 324 for guidance as to how expert evidence should be collected in employment tribunal cases.

13.3.6   The long-term condition

Under Sch 1, para 2, the effect of an impairment is long-term if it has lasted for at least 12 months, it is likely to last for at least 12 months, or it is likely to last for the rest of the life of the person affected.

In *SCA Packaging Ltd v Boyle* [2009] UKHL 37, the House of Lords held that the word 'likely' should be interpreted as meaning 'could well happen' rather than 'more likely than not'. Their Lordships rejected previous authority that 'likely' in the DDA 1995 was taken to mean a 51% chance, and applied a lower standard.

The Guidance states that 'likely' should be interpreted as meaning that it could well happen, rather than it is more probable than not that it will happen.

The Act states that if an impairment has had a substantial adverse effect on a person's ability to carry out normal day-to-day activities but that effect ceases, the substantial effect is treated as continuing if it is likely to recur. Conditions with effects which recur only sporadically or for short periods can still qualify as impairments for the purposes of the Act in respect of the meaning of 'long-term' (Sch 1, para 2(2)).

The Guidance gives as an example a person with rheumatoid arthritis, who may experience substantial adverse effects for a few weeks after the first occurrence and then have a period of remission. If the substantial adverse effects are likely to recur, the Guidance says they are to be treated as if they were continuing. If the effects are likely to recur beyond 12 months after the first occurrence, they are to be treated as long-term. It should be noted that some impairments with recurring or fluctuating effects may be less obvious in their impact on the individual concerned than is the case with other impairments where the effects are more constant. Likelihood of recurrence should be considered taking all the circumstances of the case into account. This should include what the person could reasonably be expected to do to prevent the recurrence.

The Act provides that a person who has had a disability within the definition is protected from some forms of discrimination even if he has since recovered or the effects have become less than substantial. In deciding whether a past condition was a disability, its effects count as long-term if they lasted 12 months or more after the first occurrence, or if a recurrence happened or continued until more than 12 months after the first occurrence (s 6(4) and Sch 2, para 2).

13.3.7   Examples of disabilities under the Act

The Explanatory Notes to the Act give the following examples:

- A man works in a warehouse, loading and unloading heavy stock. He develops a long-term heart condition and no longer has the ability to lift or move heavy items of stock at work. Lifting and moving such heavy items is not a normal day-to-day activity. However, he is also unable to lift, carry or move moderately heavy everyday objects such as chairs, at work or around the home. This is an adverse effect on a normal day-to-day activity. He is likely to be considered a disabled person for the purposes of the Act.

- A young woman has developed colitis, an inflammatory bowel disease. The condition is a chronic one which is subject to periods of remissions and flare-ups. During a flare-up she experiences severe abdominal pain and bouts of diarrhoea. This makes it very difficult for her to travel or go to work. This has a substantial adverse effect on her ability to carry out normal day-to-day activities. She is likely to be considered a disabled person for the purposes of the Act.

- A man with depression finds even the simplest of tasks or decisions difficult, for example getting up in the morning and getting washed and dressed. He is also forgetful and can't plan ahead. Together, these amount to a 'substantial adverse effect' on his ability to carry out normal day-to-day activities. The man has experienced a number of separate periods of this depression over a period of two years, which have been diagnosed as part of an underlying mental health condition. The impairment is therefore considered to be 'long-term' and he is a disabled person for the purposes of the Act.

13.3.8   The effect of medical treatment

Where measures are being taken to treat or correct an impairment that would be *likely* to have a substantial adverse effect on the ability of the person to carry out normal day-to-day activities but for the fact that measures are being taken to treat or correct the condition, the effects of treatment are disregarded and that impairment is still treated as amounting to a disability (save that spectacles and contact lenses are taken into account) (Sch 1, para 5). The Court of Appeal held in *Woodrup v London Borough of Southwark* [2003] IRLR 111 that clear medical evidence will be required in 'deduced effect' cases.

Further analysis of the statutory provisions relating to the effects of medical treatment under the old law may be found in *Abadeh v British Telecommunications plc* [2001] IRLR 23.

13.3.9   Perceived disabilities

The new definition in the Act is wide enough to include people who are discriminated against because they are perceived to be disabled, ie where the discriminator thinks that a person has a disability which he does not have, and discriminates against him for that reason. This is achieved by the use of the terms 'because of' (direct discrimination, s 13) and 'related to' (harassment, s 26) – see **13.5** below.

Two pre-Equality Act 2010 cases looked at the issue of perception discrimination – see *J v DLA Piper UK LLP* (UKEAT/0263/09) and *Aitken v Commissioner of Police of the Metropolis* (UKEAT/0226/09). Although in neither case was the issue properly before the EAT, it made clear its rejection of the claimants' arguments. One of the reasons given by the EAT in *J v DLA Piper* for rejecting perception discrimination was the conceptual difficulty in fitting it into the framework of the DDA 1995. In particular, how would a tribunal establish that what the employer 'perceives' actually amounts to a disability? The Foreword to IDS Brief 905 (July 2010) suggests that similar difficulties may apply under the 2010 Act, which retains the same definition of 'disability' as the DDA 1995:

> For example, suppose an employer suspected a job applicant to be emotionally unstable and refused a job on that basis. Could the applicant bring a claim on the basis that the employer had discriminated on the basis of a perceived disability, such as depression? Or would the employer easily defeat the claim on the basis that, while he perceived that the claimant was irrationally and unpredictably moody and so would be difficult to work with, he was perceiving something less than an actual disability? Adopting a broad and purposive approach, tribunals might consider it sufficient that an employer declines to employ because he perceives some adverse effect on the employee's ability to do the job in question. This could be evidence that he perceived the employee's 'condition' to be serious enough to qualify as a

disability. However, such an interpretation would deprive the word 'disability' of its specific, technical meaning. It would also potentially mean that any job applicant rejected because of the employer's perception that they would be difficult to work with would have an arguable claim.

It is not clear whether the employee must be perceived as having an impairment (that has a substantial and long-term adverse effect, etc) or whether having a noticeable impairment is sufficient.

13.3.10 Past disabilities

Past disabilities, for example a mental illness which is now cured, are protected under Sch 1, para 9 to the Act. It provides that:

(1)   A question as to whether a person had a disability at a particular time ('the relevant time') is to be determined, for the purposes of section 6, as if the provisions of, or made under, this Act were in force when the act complained of was done had been in force at the relevant time.

(2)   The relevant time may be a time before the coming into force of the provision of this Act to which the question relates.

13.3.11 Certain medical conditions

The Act covers from the time of diagnosis people who have cancer, HIV/AIDS and multiple sclerosis (Sch 1, para 6). This means that such people do not have to rely on the condition having 'some' effect as a progressive condition (see **13.3.4**). Otherwise, conditions which will develop into a disability in the future are not protected until the person develops some symptoms, but those symptoms do not have to have a substantial adverse effect if the condition is a progressive one (Sch 1, para 8).

13.3.12 Relationship between the disability and the allegedly discriminatory act

The EAT, in *Cruickshank v VAW Motorcast Ltd* [2002] IRLR 24, held that the tribunal must assess, on the basis of the evidence available at that time, whether the claimant had a disability *at the time of the alleged discriminatory act*, rather than at the time of the hearing. That approach was confirmed by the Court of Appeal in *Richmond Adult Community College v McDougall* [2007] IRLR 771 in the context of when to determine whether the effect of an impairment is likely to last for at least 12 months (see **13.3.6**). At the time the decision (not to employ) was taken, there was no evidence that the illness was likely to recur, and the tribunal held that it did not therefore have a long-term effect.

13.3.13 The definition of disability under the EC Equal Treatment Framework Directive

The EC Equal Treatment Framework Directive (2000/78) sets out a framework for eliminating employment and occupational discrimination in a number of areas, including disability. The concept of disability is not defined in the Directive. In *Chacon Navas v Eurest Colectividades SA* (Case C-13/05) [2006] IRLR 706, the ECJ had to decide if sickness was covered by the Directive, and in particular if an employee who was dismissed solely on the grounds of absence from work due to sickness was protected. The ECJ said he was not. The ECJ's approach to what amounted to a disability was broadly the same as that contained in the DDA 1995, although interestingly the Court focused on the effect of any impairment on the employee's *professional* life, in contrast to the Act's focus on the impact on 'normal day-to-day activities'. The ECJ's approach appears, therefore, to be more restrictive than UK law.

13.4 UNLAWFUL DISCRIMINATION IN EMPLOYMENT

13.4.1 Recruitment

Under s 39(1) of the Act, it is unlawful for an employer to discriminate against a disabled person:

(a)   in the arrangements which he makes for the purpose of determining to whom he should offer employment;

(b)   in the terms on which he offers that person employment; or

(c)   by refusing to offer or deliberately not offering him employment.

There is a new provision in the Act (s 60) which prevents a prospective employer asking an applicant for work about his health before work is offered or he has been included in a pool of successful candidates to be offered a job when a vacancy arises. This is not, however, a blanket ban on pre-employment health enquiries. There is a limited set of circumstances in which health-related inquiries can be made. For instance, s 60 does not apply to questions that are necessary to establish whether the applicant will be able to carry out a function intrinsic to the work concerned. Only the EHRC can enforce a breach of this provision, but where the employer asks such questions and rejects the applicant, if the applicant brings a claim of direct discrimination, it will be for the employer to show that he has not discriminated against the applicant.

Section 159 allows an employer to take disability into account when deciding whom to recruit, where disabled people are at a disadvantage or under-represented. This can be done only where candidates are equally qualified. This does not allow employers automatically to prefer disabled candidates. Each case must be considered on its merits, and any action must be a proportionate means of addressing such disadvantage or under-representation. It is not known when this section will be implemented.

13.4.2   Promotion and dismissal

Under s 39(2) of the Act, it is unlawful for an employer to discriminate against a disabled person whom he employs:

(a)   in the terms of employment which he affords him;

(b)   in the opportunities which he affords him for promotion, a transfer, training or receiving any other benefit;

(c)   by refusing to afford him, or deliberately not affording him, any such opportunity; or

(d)   by dismissing him, or subjecting him to any other detriment (dismissal, for the purposes of the Act, includes constructive dismissal (s 39(7)). Detriment does not include harassment (s 212).

Section 159 allows an employer to take disability into account when deciding whom to promote, where disabled people are at a disadvantage or under-represented. This can be done only where candidates are equally qualified. This does not allow employers automatically to prefer disabled employees. Each case must be considered on its merits, and any action must be a proportionate means of addressing such disadvantage or under-representation. It is not known when this section will be implemented.

13.4.3   Post-employment discrimination

Section 108 prohibits discrimination after relationships have ended. Where an employment relationship has come to an end, it is unlawful for the employer to discriminate against the former employee or harass the former employee where the discrimination arises out of and is closely connected to that former relationship. This means, for example, that former employees are protected from being discriminated against on grounds of disability so far as references are concerned, or in a post-dismissal appeal (see also 8.4.3).

Article 5 of the Equality Act 2010 (Consequential Amendments, Saving and Supplementary Provisions) Order 2010 made changes to s 108(4). The amendment was intended to ensure that the new provision replicated the 'old' law (ie, that even if a person becomes disabled after the relationship has ended, the duty to make a reasonable adjustment (see 13.5.2) still applies). The original provision could have been interpreted as meaning that the duty arose only if the person already had a disability at the time the relationship ended.

13.5   TYPES OF DISCRIMINATION

There are six ways in which an employer may discriminate against a disabled claimant, employee or former employee. Each will be considered in more detail below. As a matter of ease of approach, the various heads have been considered in this order: direct discrimination, failure to make reasonable adjustments, discrimination arising from disability, indirect discrimination, harassment and victimisation. This approach has been adopted because discrimination arising from disability and indirect discrimination may be justified.

13.5.1   Direct discrimination

Direct discrimination occurs where the reason for a person being treated less favourably than another is a protected characteristic listed in s 4. Direct discrimination occurs where someone is discriminated against *because* he is disabled.

Therefore an employer's treatment of a disabled person will amount to direct discrimination if:

(a)   the treatment is because of his disability;

(b)   the treatment is less favourable in comparison to the treatment of a person not having that protected characteristic is (or would be); and

(c)   the relevant circumstances, including the abilities, of the person with whom the comparison is made are the same as, or not materially different from, those of the disabled person.

Section 13 provides:

> (1)   A person (A) discriminates against another (B) if, because of a protected characteristic, A treats B less favourably than A treats or would treat others.
>
> ...
>
> (3)   If the protected characteristic is disability, and B is not a disabled person, A does not discriminate against B only because A treats or would treat disabled persons more favourably than A treats B.

The Code gives an example of treatment that might amount to direct discrimination:

> During an interview, a job applicant informs the employer that he has multiple sclerosis. The applicant is unsuccessful and the employer offers the job to someone who does not have a disability. In this case, it will be necessary to look at why the employer did not offer the job to the unsuccessful applicant with multiple sclerosis to determine whether the less favourable treatment was because of his disability.

Note that the tribunal case of *Attridge Law v Coleman* [2007] ICR 654 was referred to the ECJ for clarification as to whether the UK's then current discrimination legislation properly implemented the EC Equal Treatment Framework Directive. Mrs Coleman was not disabled, but her son was. She resigned after allegedly being refused flexible working. She claimed constructive unfair dismissal, direct discrimination and harassment related to disability under the DDA 1995. The ECJ ruled ([2008] IRLR 722) that the EC Framework Directive covers discrimination by association, and sent the case back to the tribunal to see if it could 'fit it into' the current UK law, ie whether the DDA 1995 could be construed to give effect to this interpretation (Case C-303/06). In *Coleman v EBR Attridge Law LLP and Another* (ET/2303745/2005) the tribunal held that the DDA 1995 was capable of an interpretation consistent with the Directive so as to include discrimination by association. The respondent appealed on the basis, inter alia, that the tribunal had 'distorted and rewritten' the DDA 1995. The EAT upheld the tribunal's decision (UKEAT/0071/09) and read words into the DDA 1995 to achieve 'the purpose and effect of the directive'.

The definition of direct discrimination in the Act now states that direct discrimination occurs where the reason for a person being treated less favourably than another is a protected characteristic listed in s 4, and the definition is broad enough to cover cases where the less favourable treatment is because of the victim's association with someone who is disabled, or because the victim is wrongly thought to have a disability. The definition in the Act also states that, in relation to disability, it is not discrimination to treat a disabled person more favourably than a person who is not disabled.

There is a new exception to what would otherwise be direct disability discrimination in Sch 9, para 1 ('work occupational requirements'). Where being disabled is an occupational requirement for work and a person does not meet that requirement, it will not be discriminatory to reject that person. The requirement must be a 'proportionate means of pursing a legitimate aim', and the burden of showing that rests on those seeking to rely on it. An example might be where an organisation advertises for a deaf person who uses British Sign Language (BSL) to work as a counsellor for other deaf people who use BSL.

The wording used for direct discrimination because of disability is now identical to the wording used in connection with other protected characteristics, and readers are referred to **Chapter 9** for more details about direct disability discrimination, including:

(a) association and perception (see **9.2.3**);

(b) the interpretation of the phrase 'because of' (see **9.2.4**);

(c) what amounts to 'less favourable treatment' (see **9.2.5**);

(d) the use of comparators (the treatment of the claimant must be compared with that of an actual or a hypothetical person – the comparator – who does not share the same protected characteristic as the claimant (or, in the case of dual discrimination, either of the protected characteristics in the combination) but who is (or is assumed to be) in not materially different circumstances from the claimant. The Code gives an example in a disability case:

> A disabled man with arthritis who can type at 30 words per minute applies for an administrative job which includes typing, but is rejected on the grounds that his typing is too slow. The correct comparator in a claim for direct discrimination would be a person without arthritis who has the same typing speed with the same accuracy rate. In this case, the disabled man is unable to lift heavy weights, but this is not a requirement of the job he applied for. As it is not relevant to the circumstances, there is no need for him to identify a comparator who cannot lift heavy weights.

See too *High Quality Lifestyles Ltd v Watts* (EAT/0671/05), the Court of Appeal's judgment in *Aylott v Stockton-on-Tees Borough Council* [2010] EWCA Civ 910 for useful guidance on how to construct the correct hypothetical comparator in a direct disability discrimination claim (see **9.2.5**) and, most recently, *Cordell v Foreign and Commonwealth Office* (UKEAT/0016/11). In *Aylott*, the Court of Appeal upheld the tribunal's decision that the proper hypothetical comparator was someone who did not have the claimant's disability but had a similar absence record; and

(e) motive (see **9.2.7**).

13.5.2 Failure to make reasonable adjustments

An employer also discriminates against a disabled person if he fails (without justification) to make reasonable adjustments.

Sections 20 and 21 of the Act provide as follows:

20   Duty to make adjustments

(1)   Where this Act imposes a duty to make reasonable adjustments on a person, this section, sections 21 and 22 and the applicable Schedule apply; and for those purposes, a person on whom the duty is imposed is referred to as A.

(2)   The duty comprises the following three requirements.

(3)   The first requirement is a requirement, where a provision, criterion or practice of A's puts a disabled person at a substantial disadvantage in relation to a relevant matter in comparison with persons who are not disabled, to take such steps as it is reasonable to have to take to avoid the disadvantage.

(4)   The second requirement is a requirement, where a physical feature puts a disabled person at a substantial disadvantage in relation to a relevant matter in comparison with persons who are not disabled, to take such steps as it is reasonable to have to take to avoid the disadvantage.

(5)   The third requirement is a requirement, where a disabled person would, but for the provision of an auxiliary aid, be put at a substantial disadvantage in relation to a relevant matter in comparison with persons who are not disabled, to take such steps as it is reasonable to have to take to provide the auxiliary aid.

(6)   Where the first or third requirement relates to the provision of information, the steps which it is reasonable for A to have to take include steps for ensuring that in the circumstances concerned the information is provided in an accessible format.

(7)   A person (A) who is subject to a duty to make reasonable adjustments is not (subject to express provision to the contrary) entitled to require a disabled person, in relation to whom A is required to comply with the duty, to pay to any extent A's costs of complying with the duty.

(8)   A reference in section 21 or 22 or an applicable Schedule to the first, second or third requirement is to be construed in accordance with this section.

(9)   In relation to the second requirement, a reference in this section or an applicable Schedule to avoiding a substantial disadvantage includes a reference to—

(a)   removing the physical feature in question,

(b)   altering it, or

(c)   providing a reasonable means of avoiding it.

(10)   A reference in this section, section 21 or 22 or an applicable Schedule (apart from paragraphs 2 to 4 of Schedule 4) to a physical feature is a reference to—

(a)   a feature arising from the design or construction of a building,

(b)   a feature of an approach to, exit from or access to a building,

(c)   a fixture or fitting, or furniture, furnishings, materials, equipment or other chattels, in or on premises, or

(d)   any other physical element or quality.

(11)   A reference in this section, section 21 or 22 or an applicable Schedule to an auxiliary aid includes a reference to an auxiliary service.

21   Failure to comply with duty

(1)   A failure to comply with the first, second or third requirement is a failure to comply with a duty to make reasonable adjustments.

(2)   A discriminates against a disabled person if A fails to comply with that duty in relation to that person.

13.5.2.1   Duty to adjust

Under ss 20 and 21 an employer can be liable for failing to take positive steps to help overcome the disadvantages resulting from disability. An employer is under a duty to make reasonable adjustments where a disabled person is placed at a substantial disadvantage in comparison with non-disabled people.

The first requirement (s 20(3)) covers changing the way things are done (such as changing a practice), the second (s 20(4)) covers making changes to the built environment (such as providing access to a building) and the third (s 20(5)) covers providing auxiliary aids and services (such as providing special computer software or providing a different service).

Where the first or third requirement involves the way in which information is provided, a reasonable step includes providing that information in an accessible format (s 20(6)). Under the second requirement, taking steps to avoid the disadvantage will include removing, altering or providing a reasonable means of avoiding the physical feature, where it would be reasonable to do so (s 20(9)). It also makes clear that, except where the Act states otherwise, it would never be reasonable for a person bound by the duty to pass on the costs of complying with it to an individual disabled person (s 20(7)).

The Court of Appeal in *Cave v Goodwin and Another* [2001] EWCA Civ 391 stressed that the duty does not arise where the disabled person is not placed at a substantial disadvantage. The Act defines substantial as more than minor or trivial (s 212).

The Code states that 'provisions, criteria and practices' should be construed widely and include formal and informal policies, rules, one-off decisions and actions etc. The duty to make reasonable adjustments will apply, for example, to selection and interview procedures as well as to job offers, contractual arrangements and working conditions.

Physical features, according to the Code, include, for example, steps, kerbs, parking areas, lighting, furniture etc. Auxiliary aids include, for example, specialist equipment, sign language interpreters and support workers.

The duty applies in recruitment and during all stages of employment, including dismissal (see *Aylott v Stockton-on-Tees Borough Council* [2010] EWCA Civ 910).

Section 21 makes clear that a failure to comply with any one of the reasonable adjustment requirements amounts to discrimination against a disabled person to whom the duty is owed. It also provides that, apart from under this Act, no other action can be taken for failure to comply with the duty.

13.5.2.2 Identifying the comparator

The s 20 duty arises when a provision, criterion or practice or physical feature or failure to provide an auxiliary aid places the disabled person at a substantial disadvantage when compared with the non-disabled. The House of Lords, in *Archibald v Fife Council* [2004] IRLR 651, identified how the non-disabled comparator should be identified. In that case, the employee had been a road sweeper with the Council. She had minor surgery which gave rise to complications, leaving her virtually unable to walk and therefore unable to do her job. The Council took various positive steps to seek to redeploy her, such as by retraining her and short-listing her for various posts for which she might be eligible. However, she was not appointed to an alternative post and was dismissed for failing to be able to carry out her job. She claimed that her employers had failed to make reasonable adjustments because she had still had to go through a competitive interview process. The House of Lords held that her dismissal was for a reason related to her disability, and the employers were not justified in dismissing her unless they had carried out all reasonable adjustments. In the course of his speech, Lord Rodger identified the comparator as being those employees who were not disabled, could carry out the functions of their job and therefore were not at risk of dismissal. In *Smith v Churchills Stairlifts plc* [2006] IRLR 41, the Court of Appeal considered the judgment in *Archibald* and concluded that 'the comparator is readily identified by the disadvantage caused by the relevant arrangements'. In *O'Hanlon v The Commissioners for HM Revenue & Customs* [2007] ICR 1359, the Court of Appeal upheld the EAT's decision that the comparators were those who were not disabled and did not as a consequence have illnesses of a length which meant their sick pay entitlement would be used up more quickly. The Code confirms this line of case law.

13.5.2.3 Has the employer made reasonable adjustments?

Once a comparison has identified a substantial disadvantage, the question will be whether the employer has made reasonable adjustments – the onus is on the employer to show this. This will depend on the circumstances of each case. That question has to be determined objectively. In the *Smith v Churchills Stairlifts* case (at **13.5.2.2** above), the position was summarised as follows (section numbers adjusted to reflect the amended legislation):

There is no doubt that the test required by [s 20] is an objective test. The employer must take 'such steps as it is reasonable, in all the circumstances of the case ...' The objective nature of the test is further illuminated by [the draft Code]. Thus, in determining whether it is reasonable for an employer to have to take a particular step, regard is to be had, amongst other things, to ... the financial and other costs which could be incurred by the employer in taking the step and the extent to which taking it would disrupt any of his activities.

It is significant that the concern is with the extent to which the step would disrupt any of his activities, not the extent to which the employer reasonably believes that such disruption would occur. The objective nature of this test is well established in the authorities: see *Collins v Royal National Theatre Board Ltd* [2004] EWCA Civ 144, [2004] IRLR 395 in which Sedley LJ said (at paragraph 20):

'The test of reasonableness under [s 20] ... must be objective. One notes in particular that [s 21] speaks of 'such steps as it is reasonable ... for him to have to take.'

A duty is imposed on the employer only to take such steps as are reasonable in all the circumstances of the case. The employer can therefore undertake a cost–benefit analysis when considering reasonable adjustments.

The Code provides that, in determining whether it is reasonable for an employer to have taken a particular step in order to comply with the duty, the following factors *might be taken into account*:

(a)   whether taking any particular steps would be effective in preventing the substantial disadvantage;

(b)   the practicability of the step;

(c)   the financial and other costs of making the adjustment and the extent of any disruption caused;

(d)   the extent of the employer's financial or other resources;

(e)   the availability to the employer of financial or other assistance to help make an adjustment (such as advice through Access to Work); and

(f)   the type and size of the employer.

In *British Gas Services Ltd v McCaull* [2001] IRLR 60, the EAT ruled that there was nothing in the Act which prevented an employer arguing at a tribunal that a particular step was not a reasonable one, even if it did not put its mind to the question of accommodation at the time. The obligation to make adjustments is an ongoing one (*Wilding v British Telecommunications plc* [2002] IRLR 524). For another decision on reasonable adjustments, see *Home Office v Collins* [2005] EWCA Civ 598.

The EAT in *Tameside Hospital NHS Foundation Trust v Mr Mylott* (UKEAT/0352/09) (a case decided under s 4A of the DDA 1995) held that the duty to make reasonable adjustments involves taking steps to enable the employee to stay in employment, not to compensate him for having to leave it – so in Mr Mylott's case, there was no duty to offer him ill-health retirement.

13.5.2.4   What adjustments might be made?

The following are examples of steps which an employer might take in relation to a disabled person in order to comply with the duty to adjust. The examples are from the Code:

- making adjustments to premises;
- providing information in accessible formats
- allocating some of the disabled person's duties to another worker;
- transferring him to fill an existing vacancy;
- altering his hours of working or training;
- assigning him to a different place of work or training or arranging home working;
- allowing him to be absent during working hours for rehabilitation, assessment or treatment;

- giving or arranging for training or mentoring (whether for the disabled person or any other person);
- acquiring or modifying equipment;
- modifying procedures for testing or assessment;
- providing a reader or interpreter;
- providing supervision or other support;
- allowing the person to take disability leave;
- employing a support worker;
- modifying disciplinary or grievance procedures;
- adjusting redundancy selection criteria;
- modifying performance-related pay arrangements.

The EAT held, in *Kenny v Hampshire Constabulary* [1999] IRLR 76, that the duty to adjust under the DDA 1995 was limited to job-related matters. So, in this case, the provision of a carer to assist a disabled person when using the toilet was not something the employer had to provide under the duty to adjust. However, the EAT thought that if the worker had his own personal carer then the employer would be expected to make physical arrangements to accommodate the carer at the workplace.

The House of Lords in *Archibald v Fife Council* (see **13.5.2.2**) considered whether the duty to make reasonable adjustments applied to the position of a disabled employee who became totally incapable of doing the job for which she was originally employed but who could do another job in the same organisation. Mrs Archibald was interviewed for a sedentary post, but a more qualified person was appointed and Mrs Archibald was dismissed. The House of Lords held that there was a positive duty to make reasonable adjustments. Unlike sex and race discrimination, an employer was obliged to discriminate positively in favour of disabled people. The House of Lords gave a very wide meaning to the concept of 'arrangements'. In this case, there was, it said, an 'arrangement' which placed Mrs Archibald at a substantial disadvantage, namely that if she was physically unable to work as a road sweeper, she was liable to be dismissed. The positive obligation to make reasonable adjustments potentially includes allowing disabled persons to 'trump' candidates for other jobs, even if the disabled employee is not the best candidate, if the disabled employee is suitable to do that work.

As Baroness Hale said:

> [In the cases of sex and race discrimination] men and women or black and white, as the case may be, are opposite sides of the same coin. Each is to be treated in the same way ... Pregnancy apart, the differences between the genders are generally regarded as irrelevant. The 1995 Act, however, does not regard the differences between disabled people and others as irrelevant. It does not expect each to be treated in the same way. It expects reasonable adjustments to be made to cater for the special needs of disabled people. It necessarily entails an element of more favourable treatment.

This decision made clear that employers needed to take proper medical advice and consult with the employee before making decisions about reasonable adjustments (see, eg, *Southampton City College v Randall* [2006] IRLR 24). It is also clear that the need to make reasonable adjustments continues throughout the employment on an ongoing basis. In *Rothwell v Pelikan Hardcopy Scotland* [2006] IRLR 24, the EAT held that the employer's failure to consult with the employee (after having accommodated his disability for many years) before dismissing him on grounds of ill-health was a failure to make reasonable adjustments. In *Greenhof v Barnsley Metropolitan Borough Council* [2006] IRLR 98, the EAT suggested that a serious failure to make a reasonable adjustment would almost inevitably amount to a breach of the implied term of trust and confidence, so entitling an employee to resign and claim constructive dismissal.

In *Environment Agency v Rowan* [2008] IRLR 20, the EAT held that a trial period (of home working on the facts) could not normally be a reasonable adjustment. The EAT said that a trial period would be a means of assessing whether a future adjustment was a reasonable adjustment, rather than the adjustment in itself.

In *Secretary of State for Work and Pensions (Job Centre Plus) and Others v Wilson* (UKEAT/0289/09), an agoraphobic employee requested to work from home. The EAT held that the tribunal had been wrong to focus on the employer's failure to accede to this request without first considering whether the adjustment would have been futile. The evidence showed that the work, which involved face-to-face interviews with the public and handling confidential files that others in the office needed to access, could not be done effectively from home. In addition, the employer had considered alternative work, at a more senior grade, which might not involve such responsibilities, but no such work was available.

In *Chief Constable of South Yorkshire Police v Jelic* [2010] EWCA Civ 744 the EAT held that reasonable adjustments may extend to swapping roles of employees within an organisation.

There have been conflicting decisions on whether an employer's failure to make an assessment of a disabled employee is of itself a failure to make a reasonable adjustment (see, eg, *Mid-Staffordshire General Hospitals NHS Trust v Cambridge* [2003] IRLR 566). However, in *Tarbuck v Sainsbury's Supermarkets Ltd* [2006] IRLR 664, the EAT said it was not. That approach was confirmed again by the EAT in *Spence v Intype Libra Ltd* (UKEAT/0617/06), where the claimant sought to argue on appeal that *Tarbuck* had been wrongly decided or could be distinguished on its facts. The EAT upheld the tribunal's decision. In *Scottish and Southern Energy plc v Mackay* (UKEAT/0075/06), the EAT said 'we follow the *Tarbuck* line'.

13.5.2.5   Knowledge of disability

Note that the duty in s 20 is not to make adjustments to facilitate the employment of disabled people generally. The duty arises only in relation to particular identifiable individuals. Schedule 8, Pt 3, para 20 states that an employer is not subject to a duty to make reasonable adjustments if the employer does not know, and could not reasonably be expected to know, that a person has (or has had) a disability and is likely to be placed at a substantial disadvantage. That language reflects wording that was used previously, where an employer was exempted from the duty to make reasonable adjustments if 'he did not know, and could not reasonably be expected to know, that someone was likely to be placed at a substantial disadvantage'. In *DWP v Alan* (UKEAT/0242/09) the EAT held that, to ascertain whether that exemption applies, two questions arise:

1. 'Did the employer know both that the employee was disabled and that his disability was liable to affect him in the manner set out in [s 20]'. If the answer is no, then the second question is:

2. 'Ought the employer to have known both that the employee was disabled and that his disability was liable to affect him in the manner set out in [s 20]'. If the answer to this question is also no, there is no duty to make reasonable adjustments.

In *Department of Work and Pensions v Hall* (IDS Brief 792/10), the employer was held to have constructive knowledge of an employee's disability because, inter alia, the employee's manager had seen her application for disabled person's tax credit.

The Code states that 'an employer must do all [it] can reasonably be expected to do to find out if a worker has a disability...[and this is] an objective assessment'.

13.5.2.6   Concluding remarks

Schedule 8 to the Act sets out further guidance in respect of reasonable adjustments. If two or more people have a duty to make reasonable adjustments for the same person, each of them must comply with the duty in so far as it is reasonable for each of them to do so.

The Explanatory Notes to the Act give the following examples of reasonable adjustments:

- A utility company knows that significant numbers of its customers have a sight impairment and will have difficulty reading invoices and other customer communications in standard print, so must consider how to make its communications more accessible. As a result, it might provide communications in large print to customers who require this.

- A bank is obliged to consider reasonable adjustments for a newly recruited financial adviser who is a wheelchair user and who would have difficulty negotiating her way around the customer area. In consultation with the new adviser, the bank rearranges the layout of furniture in the customer area and installs a new desk. These changes result in the new adviser being able to work alongside her colleagues.

- The organiser of a large public conference knows that hearing-impaired delegates are likely to attend. She must therefore consider how to make the conference accessible to them. Having asked delegates what adjustments they need, she decides to engage BSL/English interpreters, have a palantypist and an induction loop to make sure that the hearing-impaired delegates are not substantially disadvantaged.

- An employee develops carpal tunnel syndrome which makes it difficult for him to use a standard keyboard. The employer refuses to provide a modified keyboard or voice-activated software which would overcome the disadvantage. This could be an unlawful failure to make a reasonable adjustment which would constitute discrimination.

- A private club has a policy of refusing entry to male members not wearing a collar and tie for evening events. A member with psoriasis (a severe skin condition which can make the wearing of a collar and tie extremely painful) could bring a discrimination claim if the club refused to consider waiving this policy for him.

- A visually-impaired prospective tenant asks a letting agent to provide a copy of a tenancy agreement in large print. The agent refuses even though the document is held on computer and could easily be printed in a larger font. This is likely to be an unlawful failure to make a reasonable adjustment which would constitute discrimination.

13.5.3 Background to discrimination arising from disability and indirect discrimination – disability-related discrimination and the House of Lords decision in Malcolm

Under the DDA 1995, an employer discriminated against a disabled person if, for a reason relating to the person's disability, he treated him less favourably than a person to whom that reason did not apply and he could not show that the treatment was justified. The reason for the less favourable treatment only needed to be related to the person's disability, not necessarily on the grounds of it.

In *Clark v Novacold Ltd* [1999] IRLR 318, the employee was dismissed after a period of long-term absence by reason of ill health following a work accident. The Court of Appeal held that he had been dismissed for a reason relating to his disability, and gave the following further example:

> If no dogs are admitted to a café, the reason for denying access to refreshment in it by a blind person with his guide dog would be the fact that no dogs are admitted. That reason 'relates to' his disability. ...

The House of Lords, in *London Borough of Lewisham v Malcolm* [2008] IRLR 700, overruled that analysis. Their Lordships held that 'a reason which relates to a person's disability' has to be construed narrowly. *Malcolm* was not an employment case. Mr Malcolm was a tenant of the London Borough of Lewisham. He suffered from a form of chronic schizophrenia which had led to a number of hospital admissions, some of them involuntary. His illness was not disabling when controlled by appropriate medication; but when such medication was not taken, his ability to carry out normal day-to-day activities was substantially impaired. Contrary to Lewisham's rules, Mr Malcolm sublet his flat. Lewisham sought to obtain possession, and an issue arose as to whether in doing so it was discriminating against him (under what was then s 22(3)(c) of the DDA 1995, which stated that 'It is unlawful for a person managing any premises to discriminate against a disabled person occupying those premises ... by evicting the disabled person, or subjecting him to any other detriment'). Section 24(1) provided that, for the purposes of s 22, a person discriminated against a disabled person if:

(a)   for a reason which relates to the disabled person's disability, he treats him less favourably than he treats or would treat others to whom that reason does not or would not apply; and

(b)   he cannot show that the treatment in question is justified.

This wording was identical to the equivalent employment provision in s 3A(1) of the DDA 1995. So, although the case was a housing case, it had direct relevance to the employment context.

The House of Lords decided that Mr Malcolm was a disabled person but that the reason for Lewisham's treatment of him did *not* relate to Mr Malcolm's disability. The House of Lords said the real reason for the treatment was that Lewisham, as a social landlord with a limited stock of housing and a heavy demand from those on its waiting list, acted as it did because it was not prepared to allow tenancies to continue where the tenant was not living in the premises demised. Their Lordships went on to hold (with some reservations, as they felt that 'but for' his mental illness, Mr Malcolm would probably not have behaved so irresponsibly as to sublet his flat and move elsewhere) that Lewisham's reason for seeking possession – that Mr Malcolm had sublet the flat and gone to live elsewhere – was a pure housing management decision which had nothing whatever to do with his mental disability. Lord Bingham held that that the expression 'a reason which relates to the disabled person's disability' denoted 'some connection, not necessarily close, between the reason and the disability'. On the facts, there was no evidence that the Council was aware that Mr Malcolm suffered from a disability.

Lord Scott stated:

> If the physical or mental condition that constitutes the disability has played no motivating part in the decision of the alleged discriminator to inflict on the disabled person the treatment complained of, the alleged discriminator's reason for that treatment cannot ... relate to the disability.

His Lordship (using the 'no dogs' policy example given above) said that if a restaurant refuses to allow a blind person to bring his dog onto the premises, there is no discrimination in such a case because 'the problem is the dog', not the disability.

Importantly, however, Lord Scott did accept that in the *Clark* case the employer's reason for the dismissal was that the employee's injury was going to keep him off work for a year or so. This was plainly a reason that had been caused by, and, in that sense, *related* to the employee's disability.

Until the House of Lords decision in *Malcolm*, the correct comparator in these cases was said to be someone to whom that reason (for the treatment) did not or would not apply (*Clark v Novacold Ltd*). In *Clark*, the reason for the treatment was C's inability to do his job. Therefore, the correct comparator was someone who was able to perform the main functions of his job. Such a person would not have been dismissed, and therefore Mr Clark had been treated less favourably than someone to whom the reason for the treatment did not apply. In *Malcolm*, their Lordships, assuming (contrary to their actual conclusion) that the reason for the treatment related to Mr Malcolm's disability, went on to consider who the appropriate comparator should be in such a case. Referring to the 'care and detail' of Mummery LJ in *Clark v Novacold*, the House of Lords said the issue in Mr Malcolm's case was whether 'the others' with whose treatment the treatment of Mr Malcolm was to be compared were:

(a)   persons without a mental disability who have sublet a Lewisham flat and gone to live elsewhere, or

(b)   tenants of Lewisham flats who have not sublet or gone to live elsewhere, or

(c)   some other comparator group, and if so what?

Lord Bingham, with whom Lords Scott, Brown and Neuberger agreed, commented that, based on his understanding of the judgment in *Clark v Novacold*, the correct comparison would be with group (b). But, he went on to say, he found that decision 'difficult to accept' for the reason succinctly given by Toulson LJ in the Court of Appeal (at para 155):

> ... the complainant is logically bound to be able to satisfy the requirement of showing that his treatment is less favourable than would be accorded to others to whom the reason for his treatment did not apply. For without the reason there would not be the treatment.

Lord Bingham, finding that this would defeat Mr Malcolm's complaint of discrimination, went on to say that 'a more natural comparison, as it seems to me, is with group (a)'. On this analysis, the comparison would fall to be made on the bases rejected in *Clark v Novacold*, ie with a person who had a dog but no disability, or a diner who was a very untidy eater but had no disability-related reason for eating in that way. Looking a group (c) as a possibility, he said it would make it attractive, if possible, to identify an intermediate comparator group (c), as this 'would avoid absurdity and give fair effect to the statute. But I do not think that any such intermediate comparator group has been suggested, and none is identified by the statutory language'. On that basis, he said, 'I find it hard to accept that *Novacold* was rightly decided. I am in any event satisfied that a different principle must be applied in the present context.'

Lord Scott said that:

> The Lord Justice's [Mummery's] conclusion in *Clark* emasculates the statutory comparison. What is the point of asking whether a person has been treated 'less favourably than others' if the 'others' are those to whom the reason why the disabled person was subjected to the complained of treatment cannot apply?

He went on:

> Confusion regarding the blind man and his guide dog example has, I think, crept in because of the over-concentration on the refusal to admit entry to the dog. The dog is not a potential beneficiary of the 1995 Act. It is the blind man who is. If he is refused entry it is not because he is blind but because he is accompanied by a dog and is not prepared to leave his dog outside. Anyone, whether sighted or blind, who was accompanied by a dog would have been treated in the same way. The reason for the treatment would not have related to the blindness; it would have related to the dog.

Baroness Hale in her dissenting speech pointed out that Parliament introduced the new definition of direct discrimination on the assumption that *Clark* was properly decided.

The view of most commentators was that the effect of imposing a much stricter comparator test in these claims would be that claimants would rarely be able to clear the hurdle of showing less favourable treatment. The decision appeared to render the disability-related provisions of the DDA 1995 meaningless, and to make it extremely hard (if not impossible) for a claimant to succeed in a claim of disability-related discrimination which existed under the DDA 1995.

In late November 2008, the Government announced that it would be issuing a consultation document setting out its proposals for dealing with the problems posed by *Malcolm*. The Government published its response to the consultation in April 2009. In brief, it proposed removing disability-related discrimination as a concept, and replacing it with 'indirect' discrimination. The intention was that there would also be a provision requiring a duty-holder to fulfil the duty to make reasonable adjustments before he could seek objectively to justify indirect discrimination (see **13.5.5** below).

It is against this background that the measures in the 2010 Act relating to discrimination arising from disability and indirect discrimination have been introduced.

13.5.4 Discrimination arising from disability

Section 15 of the Act was enacted with the intention of rebalancing the situation, post-*Malcolm*, which it was felt had restricted the wider purpose of the DDA. Section 15 provides:

(1) A person (A) discriminates against a disabled person (B) if—

(a)   A treats B unfavourably because of something arising in consequence of B's disability, and

(b)   A cannot show that the treatment is a proportionate means of achieving a legitimate aim.

(2)   Subsection (1) does not apply if A shows that A did not know, and could not reasonably have been expected to know, that B had the disability.

The explanatory notes state that s 15 is aimed at 're-establishing an appropriate balance between enabling a disabled person to make out a case of experiencing a detriment which arises [from] his or her disability, and providing an opportunity for an employer or other person to defend the treatment'. It provides that it is discriminatory to treat a disabled person unfavourably not because of the person's disability itself, but because of something arising from, or in consequence of, his or her disability, such as the need to take a period of disability-related absence. It is, however, possible to justify such treatment if it can be shown to be a proportionate means of achieving a legitimate aim. There is no requirement for a comparator under s 15. It remains to be seen whether the phrase 'because of something arising ...' is given a wider interpretation than the predecessor wording of s 3A of the DDA (which stated, 'for a reason which relates to the disabled person's disability').

Discrimination arising from disability is different from direct discrimination in that the question is whether the person has been treated unfavourably *because of something arising in consequence* of his disability (cf direct discrimination which is less favourable treatment *because of the disability*). So, for example, this section may be relied on by persons who are dismissed while on long-term sick leave; if the absence is due to a disability, the dismissal would appear to be potentially unlawful discrimination arising from the person's disability.

The Code gives an example:

> An employer dismisses a worker because she has had three months' sick leave. The employer is aware that the worker has multiple sclerosis and most of her sick leave is disability-related. The employer's decision to dismiss is not because of the worker's disability itself. However, the worker has been treated unfavourably because of something arising in consequence of her disability (namely, the need to take a period of disability-related sick leave) ...

> It is irrelevant whether or not other workers would have been dismissed for having the same or similar length of absence. It is not necessary to compare the treatment of the disabled worker with that of her colleagues or any hypothetical comparator. The decision to dismiss her will be discrimination arising from disability if the employer cannot objectively justify it.

The Explanatory Notes give the following examples:

- An employee with a visual impairment is dismissed because he cannot do as much work as a non-disabled colleague. If the employer sought to justify the dismissal, he would need to show that it was a proportionate means of achieving a legitimate aim.

- The licensee of a pub refuses to serve a person who has cerebral palsy because she believes that he is drunk as he has slurred speech. However, the slurred speech is a consequence of his impairment. If the licensee is able to show that she did not know, and could not reasonably have been expected to know, that the customer was disabled, she has not subjected him to discrimination arising from his disability.

- However, in the example above, if a reasonable person would have known that the behaviour was due to a disability, the licensee would have subjected the customer to discrimination arising from his disability, unless she could show that ejecting him was a proportionate means of achieving a legitimate aim.

13.5.4.1   Objective justification

This is the same test that applies to indirect discrimination. See **13.5.5** below (and **Chapter 10**).

13.5.4.2 Knowledge of disability

For discrimination arising from a disability to occur, the employer or other person must know, or reasonably be expected to know, that the disabled person has a disability.

Section 15(2) states that 'subsection (1) does not apply if A shows that A did not know, and could not reasonably have been expected to know, that B had the disability'. That is the same wording used with regard to s 21, so readers should have regard to the interpretation given to the phrase in *DWP v Alan* (UKEAT/0242/09) (see **13.5.2.5**).

13.5.5 Indirect discrimination

Section 19 provides:

(1) A person (A) discriminates against another (B) if A applies to B a provision, criterion or practice which is discriminatory in relation to a relevant protected characteristic of B's.

(2) For the purposes of subsection (1), a provision, criterion or practice is discriminatory in relation to a relevant protected characteristic of B's if—

(a) A applies, or would apply, it to persons with whom B does not share the characteristic,

(b) it puts, or would put, persons with whom B shares the characteristic at a particular disadvantage when compared with persons with whom B does not share it,

(c) it puts, or would put, B at that disadvantage, and (d) A cannot show it to be a proportionate means of achieving a legitimate aim.

This is another new provision in relation to disability, which was introduced as a consequence of *Malcolm* (above) but it is a familiar concept in relation to discrimination on other grounds (see **Chapter 10**). Indirect discrimination occurs when a policy which applies in the same way to everybody has an effect which particularly disadvantages people with a protected characteristic. Where a particular group is disadvantaged in this way, a person in that group is indirectly discriminated against if he is put at that disadvantage, unless the person applying the policy can justify it. Unlike discrimination arising from disability, there is no requirement in s 19 that an employer need know about an employee's disability.

Indirect discrimination may also occur when a policy would put a person at a disadvantage if it were applied. This means, for example, that where a person is deterred from doing something, such as applying for a job or taking up an offer of service, because a policy which would be applied would result in his disadvantage, this may also be indirect discrimination.

In order objectively to justify indirect discrimination, the employer will need to show that there is a legitimate aim and that the provision, criterion or practice is a proportionate way of achieving that aim.

The definition and interpretation of indirect discrimination in this context are identical to those set out in the Equality Act 2010 for the other protected characteristics (see **Chapter 10**). However, the reference in s 19 to persons who share a protected characteristic is defined as a reference to persons who have the *same disability* (the guidance suggests that this is assessed in terms of symptoms – eg mobility impaired). Indirect discrimination may cause difficulties for a disabled person who has to show a group disadvantage under this section, and it may well be that this section will be little used, as in most cases a claimant will be able to rely on discrimination arising from disability and a failure to make reasonable adjustments.

Readers should refer to **Chapter 10** for more details.

13.5.6 Harassment (s 26)

The definition of 'harassment' is new for disability discrimination but is identical to that set out in the Act for the other protected characteristics. See **11.2** for more details.

The Code provides an example:

> A worker has a son with a severe disfigurement. His work colleagues make offensive remarks to him about his son's disability. The worker could have a claim for harassment related to disability.

Note that the Act prohibits harassment based on association and perception: the prohibition on harassment 'related to' disability can cover treatment of the employee based on the disability of a third party (see *Coleman v Attridge Law* at **13.5.1** above). The definition of 'harassment' may well also cover combined discrimination because the harassment 'relates' to each of the grounds (see the House of Lords debates on the Equality Bill, *Hansard HL*, cols 546–47, 13 January 2010). Harassment by an employer also covers harassment by a third party where the employer has failed to take such steps as are reasonably practicable to prevent the party from so acting. This will not apply unless the employer knows the employee has been harassed in his employment on at least two other occasions by a third party, although this does not have to be the same party on each occasion.

13.5.7 Victimisation (s 27)

There is a new definition of 'victimisation', but the definition and interpretation of victimisation are identical to those set out in the Act for the other protected characteristics. If a worker or employee is treated less favourably as a result of complaining about discrimination, or raising the issue or doing any other 'protected act', the claimant will be able to complain to the tribunal of unlawful victimisation. See **11.3** for more details.

13.6 BURDEN OF PROOF

The burden of proof is on the employer (s 136). The legislation provides that where a complainant can establish facts from which the tribunal could decide there has been direct discrimination, the tribunal *must* make a finding of unlawful discrimination *unless* the employer proves that there is a non-discriminatory explanation. This means that the complainant does have to establish some facts from which a tribunal could decide that there has been discrimination before looking to the employer for a non-discriminatory explanation. See **9.5.10.3** and **11.2** for more details.

13.7 VICARIOUS LIABILITY

An employer is vicariously liable for acts of discrimination by his employees during the course of their employment by virtue of s 109 of the Act (see **8.6** for more details).

13.8 ENFORCEMENT AND REMEDIES

The employment tribunal has exclusive jurisdiction to consider claims of disability discrimination in the field of employment. The complaint must be presented within three months beginning with the date of the act complained of, unless the tribunal considers that it is just and equitable in the circumstances to hear the claim outside that period. In *Matuszowicz v Kingston upon Hull City Council* [2009] EWCA Civ 22, the Court of Appeal held that the three-month period runs from the point at which the employer makes it clear that no adjustment or further adjustment can be made. In cases where the employer simply does nothing, time, said the Court, will run from when, if the employer had been acting reasonably, it would have made the adjustment. That will be an artificial date, and difficult to second-guess what the tribunal will conclude. It is unfortunate, in the authors' view, to impose a start date that the parties may not realise has begun. Of course, the employment tribunal retains a discretion to extend time if it considers it just and equitable to do so – where, for example, the employee did not realise time had begun to run.

Enforcement proceedings may be brought by an individual or by the EHRC. The EHRC has power to conduct formal investigations and serve non-discrimination notices, and to give assistance to an individual pursuing a claim. The same principles apply to those in relation to sex, race, etc discrimination. Compensation may be awarded for injury to feelings. The EAT held in *Instant Muscle Ltd v Khawaja* (UKEAT/216/03) that the guidance in *Vento* should be applied to awards for injury to feelings in a case under the DDA 1995. See **8.8** for more details.

SUMMARY

Provisions relating to disability in the Equality Act 2010 are in some ways very different from other discrimination legislation, such as that relating to sex, race, religion or belief, sexual orientation or age, where the emphasis is on treating all people the same. In disability discrimination, the opposite may be true – a person's individual circumstances must be considered, and such consideration is crucial to avoid discrimination (**13.1**).

A person has a disability if he has a physical or mental impairment which has a substantial and long-term adverse effect on his ability to carry out normal day-to-day activities (s 6(1)). A 'disabled person' means a person who has a disability (s 6(2)). It also covers, from the time of diagnosis, people who have cancer, HIV/AIDS and multiple sclerosis (**13.3**).

Under s 39(1) of the Equality Act 2010, discrimination is outlawed in the employment field against job applicants, employees and former employees. It is unlawful (s 39(2)) for an employer to discriminate against a disabled person whom he employs in terms of access to opportunities for promotion, transfer or training, or other benefits, facilities or services; or by dismissing him or subjecting him to any other detriment (**13.4**).

There are six ways in which an employer may discriminate against a disabled applicant, employee or former employee.

(a) Direct discrimination (s 13). This is where someone is discriminated against because he is disabled. Such discrimination cannot be justified (**13.5.1**).

(b) Failure to make reasonable adjustments (ss 20–22). An employer may be liable for failing to take positive steps to help overcome the disadvantages resulting from disability. The defence of justification is not relevant here (**13.5.2**).

(c) Disability arising from disability (s 15). An employer may discriminate against an individual if he treats that individual unfavourably because of circumstances arising out of his disability (**13.5.4**). An employer may justify such treatment if he can show that it was a proportionate way of achieving a legitimate aim.

(d) Indirect discrimination (s 19). This covers the application of a provision, criterion or practice which disadvantages a disabled person (**13.5.5**). An employer may justify such treatment if he can show that it was a proportionate way of achieving a legitimate aim.

(e) Harassment (s 26). The definition is the same as for sex, race, religion or belief, etc (**13.5.6**).

(f) Victimisation (s 55). The definition is the same as for sex, race, religion or belief, etc (**13.5.7**).

Remedies and enforcement are dealt with at **8.8**. A flowchart summarising disability discrimination is set out at **Figure 13.1** below.

Figure 13.1 Flowchart: Disability Discrimination

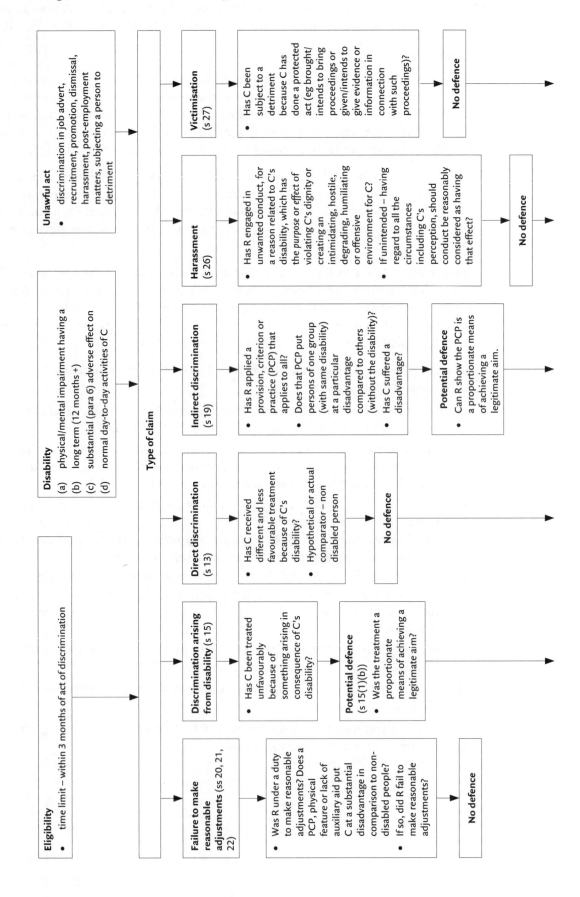

Vicarious liability

R will be vicariously liable for acts of employees committed in the course of employment (*Jones v Tower Boot Co/Chief Constable of Lincolnshire Police v Stubbs*) unless R took all reasonably practicable steps to stop/avoid the discrimination (s 109(4))

Remedies

- Declaration of employee's rights
- Recommendation that employer take action to alleviate or reduce the effect of the discrimination
- Order for compensation (no maximum)
  - pecuniary losses
  - aggravated damages if employer has behaved in a high-handed, malicious, insulting or aggressive manner
  - injury to feelings (*Vento/Da'Bell*)
  - psychiatric or physical injury
  - possibility of exemplary damages
  - increase or decrease if employer or employee unreasonably fails to comply with Acas 2009 Code

CHAPTER 14

MATERNITY AND OTHER FAMILY-FRIENDLY RIGHTS

> **LEARNING OUTCOMES**
>
> After reading this chapter you will be able to:
>
> - describe the special rights afforded to pregnant women and women on maternity leave
> - explain the differences between the ordinary and additional maternity leave regimes
> - understand the significance of automatically unfair dismissal under s 99 of the ERA 1996
> - list the other family-friendly rights.

14.1 INTRODUCTION

In this chapter we look briefly at some of the special rights afforded to pregnant women. The chapter also briefly considers the laws which create family-friendly rights such as adoption, paternity and parental leave, the right to request flexible working arrangements and to unpaid time off work to deal with emergencies at home. Only employees working under contracts of employment (see **1.3**) are entitled to these rights (but note that workers do have protection from discrimination (see **1.3.4.2**)).

The law concerning maternity and parental leave rights is contained in the ERA 1996, as amended. However, much of the detail in respect of maternity rights and parental leave, etc is contained in secondary legislation, the Maternity and Parental Leave etc Regulations 1999 (SI 1999/3312) (MPLR 1999), as amended by the Maternity and Parental Leave (Amendment) Regulations 2002 (SI 2002/2789) (MPL(A)R 2002) and the Maternity and Parental Leave etc and Paternity and Adoption Leave etc (Amendment) Regulations 2006 (SI 2006/2041) (MPLPAL(A)R 2006). Legislation relating to pay is contained principally in the Social Security Contributions and Benefits Act 1992, the Statutory Maternity Pay Regulations 1986 (SI 1986/1960) and the Statutory Paternity Pay and Statutory Adoption Pay Regulations 2002 (SIs 2002/2818, 2820 and 2822).

The detail about flexible working is contained in the Flexible Working (Eligibility, Complaints and Remedies) Regulations 2002 (SI 2002/3236) and the Flexible Working (Procedural Requirements) Regulations 2002 (SI 2002/3207).

The MPLPAL(A)R 2006 were made under the authority of the Work and Families Act 2006.

14.2 MATERNITY LEAVE

Only employees who work under contracts of employment are entitled to maternity leave. Workers who do not fit the definition of 'employee' set out in s 230(1) of the ERA 1996 (see **1.3**) do not qualify for the right to time off, but they do have protection from discrimination (see **1.3.4.2**, **Chapters 8** and **9** and **14.13**).

All pregnant women are entitled to up to 52 weeks' maternity leave. The first 26 weeks are known as 'ordinary maternity leave' (OML). The remaining period of up to 26 weeks is known as 'additional maternity leave' (AML), which commences on the day after the last day of a woman's OML. There are some differences between the two regimes which will be dealt with below. Statutory maternity pay (SMP) is currently payable for 39 weeks.

Mothers of children due on or after 3 April 2011 are able to transfer up to six months of their maternity leave to the father when they return to work (see **14.17**).

14.3 ORDINARY MATERNITY LEAVE (OML) (ERA 1996, s 71 AS AMENDED)

14.3.1 Notice provisions (MPLR 1999, reg 4(1))

No later than the end of the fifteenth week before the expected week of childbirth (EWC), or, where that is not practicable, as soon as reasonably practicable, a woman should notify her employer of:

(a)   her pregnancy;

(b)   the EWC;

(c)   the date on which she intends to start her maternity leave. This part of the notice must be in writing if the employer so requests;

and in addition, if the employer requests,

(d)   provide him with a certificate from a registered medical practitioner or registered midwife stating the EWC.

A woman who has given notice under reg 4 can revise the date by giving further notice. If she wants to postpone the start date, she must give at least 28 days' notice before the date previously notified. If she wants to start leave earlier, she must give at least 28 days' notice before the new start date, unless it is not reasonably practicable to do so (eg, if the baby is born early).

If the woman fails to serve the correct notices, she may not be able to start her leave on the intended date.

14.3.2   When can a woman start her maternity leave? (MPLR 1999, reg 4(2))

A woman cannot start her maternity leave period earlier than the eleventh week before the EWC, unless the baby is born before the eleventh week; and the maternity leave cannot start later than the birth of the baby.

Subject to the above, a woman can start her leave when she chooses. So, for example, she could take 11 weeks before the birth of the baby and the remainder after, or she could take six weeks before and the rest after, or work up to the birth and take all her maternity leave after.

However, if a woman is absent from work wholly or partly because of pregnancy in the four-week period before the EWC, she will have to start her leave on that date (reg 6(1)). The woman must notify her employer as soon as reasonably practicable that she is absent for a reason related to pregnancy (reg 4(3)). Additionally, maternity leave will be automatically triggered where childbirth occurs before the date she has notified, or, before she has notified a date. In that event, she must notify her employer as soon as reasonably practicable of the date of the birth (reg 4(4)).

14.3.2.1   Employer's notice

An employer who is notified of the date on which an employee's maternity leave will start or has started shall, within 28 days of notification, notify the employee of the date her AML will end (reg 7(6)).

14.3.3   Rights and obligations during OML period (s 71)

14.3.3.1   Rights

During the OML period, the woman's contract of employment continues. A woman is entitled to the benefit of all the terms and conditions of employment which would have applied to her had she not been absent during the OML period, including non-contractual benefits, except remuneration. The ECJ ruled, in *Gillespie v Northern Health* [1996] IRLR 214, that nothing in EC equal pay law requires that a woman or maternity leave should receive her normal full pay while on leave. The law only requires that the amount paid complies with the Pregnant Workers Directive and is adequate and not so low as to jeopardise the general purpose of maternity leave. Remuneration is defined as 'sums payable to the employee by way of wages or salary' (MPLR 1999, reg 9). Thus, a woman on OML is entitled to continue to receive benefits in kind, such as private medical insurance, the company car (if for company and personal use), club membership, subsidised loans, etc, and she will continue to accrue statutory and contractual holiday entitlement. In *Merino Gomez v Continental Industries del Caucho SA* [2004] IRLR 407 the ECJ suggests that if a woman were to lose her entitlement to statutory annual leave, this would amount to sex discrimination.

In *Hoyland v Asda Stores* [2006] IRLR 468, the Court of Session held that a claim for a bonus while an employee was absent on maternity leave was excluded by s 6(6) of the SDA 1975. It said claims of this type should be brought as equal pay claims under the EPA 1970. (Note that s 1(2)(e) of the EPA 1970 now implies an equality clause into a woman's contract of employment in respect of terms relating to bonus payments, the effect of which is that an employer can apportion a bonus to take account of ordinary and additional, but not any compulsory maternity leave.)

If the employer denies the woman such benefits, he will be acting in breach of contract, and such action will also be discriminatory if the denial is based essentially on the fact of pregnancy. Section 47C of the ERA 1996 also protects the woman from being subjected to any detriment short of dismissal because she took OML (see **14.8**).

Statutory and contractual holiday accrues during OML (and AML).

The woman who takes OML continues to be bound by any obligations arising out of her terms and conditions, for example the implied duty of good faith. The obligation does not extend to terms that are inconsistent with the right to OML, for example the obligation to turn up and work.

14.3.3.2   Working during maternity leave

Regulation 12A of the MPLR 1999 enables an employee on maternity leave to agree with her employer to work for up to 10 days during the statutory maternity leave period without bringing that period to an end as a result of carrying out the work. For the purposes of that provision, 'work' may include training or any other activity undertaken to assist the employee in keeping in touch with the workplace. The new provision also sets out that reasonable contact, which employers and employees are entitled to have with each other during the maternity leave period, does not bring that period to an end. Any such work must be by agreement between the parties and there is no right for an employer to demand that an employee undertake any such work, nor for an employee to do such work. The regulation also provides that any such days' work shall not have the effect of extending the maternity leave period.

14.3.4   Right to return to what?

A woman who takes only OML is entitled to return to the job in which she was employed before her absence with her seniority, pension rights and similar rights as they would have been had she not been absent, and terms and conditions no less favourable than they would have been had she not been absent. The OML period counts towards the woman's period of continuous employment for both statutory and contractual rights. 'Job' is defined in MPLR 1999, reg 2(1) and has the same meaning as that described below in relation to AML (see **14.5.3**).

14.4   COMPULSORY MATERNITY LEAVE (ERA 1996, s 72 AS AMENDED)

An employer must prohibit a woman from returning to work during a two-week period from the date of childbirth. To allow her to return in that period is a criminal offence and the employer will be liable, on conviction, to a fine not exceeding level 2 on the standard scale (currently £500). This applies to employees and workers.

This period counts as time worked for the purposes of a discretionary bonus.

14.5   ADDITIONAL MATERNITY LEAVE (AML) (ERA 1996, s 73 AS AMENDED)

Additional maternity leave (AML) will commence on the day after the last day of a woman's OML period (MPLR 1999, reg 6(3)) and continue for *up to* 26 weeks from the day it begins.

The woman does not have to tell her employer that it is her intention to take AML when she gives her initial maternity leave notice.

14.5.1   Rights during AML period (s 73(4), (5))

All women whose expected week of childbirth begins on or after 5 October 2008 are entitled to the same terms and conditions of employment as are enjoyed under OML. This means that women will continue to accrue contractual benefits, such as holiday entitlement, mobile phone use, medical cover and life insurance. It is also possible that women could claim entitlement to pension contribution, as a contractual benefit, once SMP runs out (ie weeks 39 to 52). Government guidance is that pensions are *not* intended to be caught in this way, but commmentators believe that pension contributions are covered.

Whilst it is not expressly stated that the contract of employment continues during the AML period, by virtue of the fact that the right conferred is a right to 'leave', and by providing that terms and conditions of employment continue to apply, the contract must continue during the AML period (SDA (Amendment) Regulations 2008). The Regulations were implemented in response to the High Court's ruling in *EOC v Secretary of State for Trade and Industry* (see **11.1.2.1**), that the previous situation did not comply with European law. One effect is to remove the distinction between OML and AML for the purposes of determining benefits while on maternity leave.

During AML, the woman is still not entitled to remuneration.

14.5.2   Working during AML

See **14.3.3.2** above for the provisions on working during maternity leave.

14.5.3   Returning to work (s 73)

The woman does not have to give any notice if she simply intends to return at the end of the AML period. However, if she intends to return earlier than the end of the AML period, she must give her employer eight weeks' notice of the date on which she intends to return (reg 11(1)). If she fails to do so, the employer is entitled to postpone her return to work to a date that will ensure he receives eight weeks' notice, unless the employer has failed to comply with his duty under reg 7(6), in which case the employer cannot prevent her from returning early (see **14.3.2.1**).

The statutory right is to return to the job in which she was employed before her absence, or, if not reasonably practicable for the employer to allow her to return to that job, for a reason other than redundancy, to a suitable and appropriate job:

(a)   on no less favourable terms and conditions as to remuneration than those which would have been applicable had she not been absent;

(b)   with seniority, pension and similar rights preserved as they would have been if the period of employment prior to AML were continuous with her employment following her return to work.

So, for example, if all employees of her grade received a pay rise during her leave, she will be entitled to this higher rate of pay on her return. The AML period will not count towards service related contractual benefits, but will be counted for the purpose of statutory rights that depend on length of service.

'Job', for the purposes of AML, is defined as the nature of the work which she is employed to do in accordance with her contract and the capacity and place in which she is employed (MPLR 1999, reg 2(1)). So, if for example her contract provides that she can be required to work in one of three departments (A, B and C), although she actually worked in Department A, she could be taken back in Department B or C.

In *Blundell v Governing Body of St Andrew's Catholic Primary School* [2007] IRLR 652, the EAT gave guidance on what the 'same job' is, saying that a returner should come back to a work situation as near as possible to that which she left, but held that a teacher could not insist on returning to teach the same class after her leave.

If it is not reasonably practicable *for a reason other than redundancy* for the employer to let the woman return to the job in which she was employed before her AML (eg due to a business reorganisation or some other substantial reason), the employer must allow her to return to another job which is both suitable for her and appropriate for her to do in the circumstances (MPLR 1999, reg 18(2)). The terms and conditions of the job offered must not be less favourable than those that applied (or would have applied) to the old job. The BIS guidance states that if the offer is suitable and the woman refuses the job, she will have 'effectively resigned'. This view has not been tested, and in the authors' view she is more likely to have been dismissed. Such dismissal will not be automatically unfair but may be 'ordinarily' unfair, depending on the facts. If the offer is not suitable, the woman can bring a complaint of unfair dismissal (and perhaps pregnancy/maternity discrimination/wrongful dismissal (see below)).

14.5.4   Returning on different terms and conditions

An employee may wish to return to work on different terms and conditions, for example part time or working different hours to fit in with her family responsibilities. She has no such right under the existing statutory provisions. She may, however, be able to allege indirect sex discrimination if the employer refuses, for example, to allow her to return on a part-time basis (see generally **Chapter 8** and *Sibley v The Girls Day School Trust, Norwich High School for Girls* (UKEAT/1368/01)). In addition, employees who are parents of young children have a right to request flexible working patterns (see **14.19**).

14.5.5   Failure to return at the end of AML

A failure to return at the end of AML will not of itself terminate the contract of employment. The court will look at the intention of the employee: if the employee intended her failure to return to end the contract then the court will interpret her act as terminating the contract. Failing any express intention, employers will need to take steps to discover the reason for any late return before deciding what action to take (eg whether to treat it as a disciplinary matter) (see *Rashid v Asian Community Care Services Ltd* (UKEAT/480/99). A failure to treat an AML late returner in the same way as any other late returner could also give rise to a potential discrimination claim under the general provisions of the SDA 1975 (see **14.13** and **Chapters 8 and 9** generally) or unfair dismissal (see **14.9**). Furthermore, if the employer has failed to specify the return date (see **14.3.2.1**) and the woman reasonably believed that her maternity leave had not ended, then any dismissal will be automatically unfair (see **14.9**).

14.6   SICKNESS AT THE END OF AML

Where a woman is unable to return to work at the end of her maternity leave, according to BIS guidance, the normal contractual arrangements for sickness will apply. She should be treated like any other sick employee. Generally, if an employee has a pregnancy-related sickness after the end of her maternity leave, she does not have *automatic* protection from sex discrimination (see **14.13**).

14.7   REDUNDANCY DURING OML OR AML PERIODS (ERA 1996, s 74 AS AMENDED)

If it is not practicable for the employer, by reason of redundancy, to continue to employ the woman under her existing contract of employment, she is entitled to be offered a suitable available vacancy before the contract ends, where there is a suitable vacancy (in priority to other employees). The new contract must be such that:

(a)   the kind of work to be done under it is both suitable in relation to the employee and appropriate for her to do in the circumstances; and

(b)   its provisions as to capacity and place in which she is employed, and as to other terms and conditions of her employment, are not substantially less favourable than her previous contractual terms and conditions (MPLR 1999, reg 10).

If the woman is dismissed by reason of redundancy and this provision is not complied with, the dismissal will be automatically unfair (MPLR 1999, reg 20, see **14.9**).

In *Simpson v Endsleigh Insurance Services Ltd* (UKEAT/0544/09) the EAT gave guidance on the right of employees facing redundancy while on maternity leave to be offered a 'suitable available vacancy'. The EAT held that the suitability of the vacancy is to be assessed by the employer, having regard to the employee's personal circumstances and work experience.

14.8 PROTECTION FROM DETRIMENT SHORT OF DISMISSAL (ERA 1996, s 47C)

The ERA 1996, s 47C contains special protection from acts short of dismissal for pregnant/maternity leave employees. The situations when that protection arises are set out in MPLR 1999, reg 19. They are similar to those set out in s 99 (see **14.9** below) relating to dismissal.

The woman can complain to the tribunal that she has been subjected to a detriment in contravention of s 47C under ERA 1996, s 48. Her remedies will be a declaration and/or compensation.

Note that no period of continuous employment is required to claim under the above provisions.

14.9 AUTOMATICALLY UNFAIR DISMISSAL (ERA 1996, s 99 AS AMENDED)

A woman who is dismissed is entitled, under s 99, to be regarded as unfairly dismissed if the reason or the principal reason is connected, inter alia, with:

(a)   the pregnancy of the employee (MPLR 1999, reg 20(3)(a));

(b)   the fact that she has given birth to a child and the dismissal ends the woman's OML or AML period (reg 20(3)(b));

(c)   the fact that she is on maternity suspension under ERA 1996, s 66 (reg 20(3)(c));

(d)   the fact that she took OML, or sought to take OML or availed herself of the benefits of any of the terms and conditions of her employment preserved by ERA 1996, s 71 (reg 20(3)(d));

(e)   the fact that she took AML or sought to do so (reg 20(3)(e));

(f)   a failure to return after AML in a case where the employer did not give her notice of the date on which the AML would end and she reasonably believed that that period had not ended; or the employer gave less than 28 days' notice of the end of AML and it was not reasonably practicable for her to return on that date (reg 20(3)(ee));

(g)   the fact that she undertook, considered undertaking or refused to undertake work in accordance with reg 12A (reg 20(3)(eee)).

If the dismissal is shown to be for any of the above reasons, then the tribunal does not have to go on and consider whether the dismissal was reasonable in accordance with ERA 1996, s 98(4).

The MPLR 1999, reg 20(3)(b) applies only where the dismissal ends the employee's OML or AML period (reg 20(4)). This means that a woman will not be protected under this provision from a childbirth-related dismissal that occurs after the end of her maternity leave. Most commentators therefore consider that a woman who is dismissed for an illness related to childbirth at the end of maternity leave cannot allege that her dismissal was automatically unfair under reg 20.

A dismissal is also automatically unfair under s 99 if the reason or principal reason for the dismissal is that the employee was redundant and that MPLR 1999, reg 10 has not been complied with (see above at **14.7**). In other words, she has not been offered suitable alternative employment before the end of her existing contract (where a vacancy exists) and the dismissal ends the woman's OML or AML period. The duty to offer a suitable alternative vacancy appears to be an absolute one; if a suitable vacancy exists, it must be offered to the woman on OML or AML in preference to any other affected employee.

If reg 10 has been complied with, the dismissal may still be automatically unfair, if the reason or principal reason for her dismissal is that the employee was redundant and it is shown that the circumstances constituting redundancy applied to other employees who held similar positions and the reason for which the woman was selected for redundancy was for a reason in reg 20(3) (see (a)–(f) above).

The employee is not required to prove that her dismissal was for one of the above reasons. She only has to adduce some evidence to create a presumption and, if the employer is arguing that the dismissal was for a reason other than pregnancy, the burden is on him to prove this. If it is found that the reason for dismissal fell within the above provisions, there is no scope for the employer to argue that it was nonetheless reasonable in all the circumstances. The dismissal is automatically unfair.

Note again that no period of continuous employment is required to claim automatically unfair dismissal under the above provision.

If the woman's dismissal is not automatically unfair under the above provisions, it may still be unfair under ERA 1996, s 98(4) (see **Chapter 5**). In *Visa International Service Association v Paul* [2004] IRLR 42, the EAT held that the employer's failure to keep the woman on leave informed of job opportunities in her department was a fundamental breach of contract entitling the woman to treat herself as constructively dismissed and that her dismissal was automatically unfair as it was for a reason related to maternity leave.

14.9.1 Exception to protection from automatically unfair dismissal

The automatic unfair dismissal protection does not apply where it is not reasonably practicable for a reason other than redundancy for the employer to allow the woman to return from OML or AML to a job which is suitable for the employee and appropriate for her to do in the circumstances, but an associated employer offers her a job of that kind and the employee accepts the job or unreasonably refuses that offer (MPLR 1999, reg 20(7)).

Of course, even where these exceptions apply, a woman could still claim that her dismissal was unfair under ERA 1996, s 98(4) (see **Chapter 5**).

14.9.2 Written reasons for dismissal (ERA 1996, s 92(4))

If a woman is dismissed while pregnant or during the OML/AML periods, she is entitled, without prior request, to a written statement giving the reason for her dismissal.

14.10 REMEDIES FOR UNFAIR DISMISSAL

A complaint must be brought within three months of the date of dismissal. If the complaint is upheld, the usual remedies are available. If reinstatement is ordered, it will be in the job to which the woman was allowed to return. If the dismissal occurred before the commencement of leave, the tribunal may include in the reinstatement order a declaration that all rights in connection with maternity leave are to be restored (see **Chapters 5** and **6**).

14.11 REDUNDANCY PAYMENTS

If no suitable alternative vacancy exists and the woman is genuinely redundant within the meaning of ERA 1996, s 139 (see **Chapter 4**), then, provided she is eligible, she will be entitled to a redundancy payment.

If a suitable alternative job is offered and she unreasonably refuses it, the right to a payment will be lost.

14.12 WRONGFUL DISMISSAL

If the woman is dismissed during pregnancy, OML or AML, or after she has returned from leave, she is entitled to receive proper notice, unless she has acted in repudiatory breach of contract. If the woman does not receive proper notice she will be able to claim wrongful dismissal. Even if she is on maternity leave, she is entitled to full pay if her notice period is the statutory period under s 86 (see s 87(4)).

14.13 PREGNANCY/MATERNITY DISCRIMINATION

In addition to the statutory right to leave described above and the right to pay described below, there is also protection from discrimination.

Section 18 of the Equality Act 2010 reads:

(1) This section has effect for the purposes of the application of Part 5 (work) to the protected characteristic of pregnancy and maternity.

(2) A person (A) discriminates against a woman if, in the protected period in relation to a pregnancy of hers, A treats her unfavourably—

    (a) because of the pregnancy, or

    (b) because of illness suffered by her as a result of it.

(3) A person (A) discriminates against a woman if A treats her unfavourably because she is on compulsory maternity leave.

(4) A person (A) discriminates against a woman if A treats her unfavourably because she is exercising or seeking to exercise, or has exercised or sought to exercise, the right to ordinary or additional maternity leave.

(5) For the purposes of subsection (2), if the treatment of a woman is in implementation of a decision taken in the protected period, the treatment is to be regarded as occurring in that period (even if the implementation is not until after the end of that period).

(6) The protected period, in relation to a woman's pregnancy, begins when the pregnancy begins, and ends—

    (a) if she has the right to ordinary and additional maternity leave, at the end of the additional maternity leave period or (if earlier) when she returns to work after the pregnancy;

    (b) if she does not have that right, at the end of the period of 2 weeks beginning with the end of the pregnancy.

(7) Section 13, so far as relating to sex discrimination, does not apply to treatment of a woman in so far as—

    (a) it is in the protected period in relation to her and is for a reason mentioned in paragraph (a) or (b) of subsection (2), or

    (b) it is for a reason mentioned in subsection (3) or (4).

Section 18 makes it unlawful during the protected period to treat a woman unfavourably on the ground of her pregnancy, or on the ground that she is exercising or seeking to exercise a statutory right to maternity leave. No comparator is needed and no justification defence is available. Pregnancy or maternity leave must be a substantial reason for the treatment (see *O'Neill v Governors of St Thomas More* [1996] IRLR 372). Once the protected period has ended, a comparator will be needed. Note that as the right to maternity leave is generally statutory (unless an employer has a contractual scheme), only employees have the right to maternity leave, and therefore workers are not protected under s 18 (other than during their pregnancy or for their two weeks' compulsory leave after giving birth (see **14.4**)). Section 18 also covers less favourable treatment as a result of pregnancy-related illness. However, where a woman falls ill with a pregnancy-related illness, such as post-natal depression, after she returns from maternity leave, that illness is not subject to any special protection.

The protected period referred to in s 18 above is defined (following *Brown v Rentokil* [1998] IRLR 445, ECJ) as beginning with pregnancy and ending at the end of the maternity leave period or, if the woman returns to work before then, when she returns to work.

14.14 OTHER RIGHTS

14.14.1 Suspension from work on maternity grounds

It may happen that a pregnant woman cannot safely continue with her existing job. Her employer cannot simply dismiss her without falling foul of ERA 1996, s 99. He could, however, suspend her under s 66. This will amount to a suspension on maternity grounds if it is due to:

(a)   any statutory requirement (eg Ionising Radiation Regulations 1985); or

(b)   any recommendation contained in a Code of Practice issued under the HSWA 1974.

If an employer has available suitable alternative employment (on terms and conditions not 'substantially less favourable'), he must offer the pregnant woman such work on full pay before suspending her on maternity grounds (see BA Ltd v Moore and Botterill [2000] IRLR 296). A failure to make such an offer may result in the woman bringing a complaint to the employment tribunal.

A woman who is suspended on maternity grounds is entitled to be paid in full (see Mahlburg v Land Mecklenburg-Vorpommern [2000] IRLR 276, ECJ).

As both men and women are entitled to parental, paternity and adoption leave, it is unlikely that either sex will have a claim for direct sex discrimination if dismissed, or if subjected to any other detriment in relation to taking time off. If, however, it is less acceptable in a particular workplace for a man rather than a woman to take parental, paternity or adoption leave, and as a result he is treated less favourably, this would be direct discrimination.

14.14.2 Health and safety risk assessments

Regulation 3(1) of the Management of Health and Safety at Work Regulations 1999 (SI 1999/3242) imposes a general duty on an employer to safeguard the health and safety of its employees by making a suitable and sufficient assessment of the risks to which they are exposed at work. A failure to carry out a risk assessment may amount to a detriment under s 26 of the Equality Act 2010, as well as unlawful discrimination under s 18 of that Act (see **14.13**) (see Day v T Pickles Farms Ltd [1999] IRLR 217 and Hardman v Mallon [2002] IRLR 516). If there is a causally linked dismissal, it will be automatically unfair under ERA 1996, s 99 or reg 20 of the MPLR 1999 (see **14.9**).

14.14.3 Maternity pay

The ECJ ruled in Gillespie v Northern Health and Social Services Board [1996] IRLR 214, that nothing in EC (now EU) equal pay law requires that a woman on maternity leave should receive her normal full pay while she is on leave. It requires only that she receives an amount that is adequate and not so low as to jeopardise the general purpose of maternity leave (see the Pregnant Worker Directive).

A woman on maternity leave may be entitled to receive statutory maternity pay (SMP). This is paid by the employer who recoups it from the State. It is paid for a maximum period of 39 weeks, which may begin at the start of the eleventh week before the expected week of confinement.

Statutory maternity pay is presently set at 90% of the woman's normal weekly earnings for the first six weeks, and for 33 weeks thereafter at £135.45 per week or 90% of the normal weekly earnings if this is less than £135.45 (for babies due on or after 3 April 2012).

14.14.4 Time off for ante-natal care (ERA 1996, s 55)

A pregnant woman has the right not to be unreasonably refused time off during her working hours to attend ante-natal appointments. She is entitled to be paid for such absence (ERA 1996, s 56).

The right is available only to employees. Case law suggests that tribunals are reluctant to find refusals reasonable where appointments have been made on proper medical advice. The employer may ask for evidence of the appointment, except in the case of the first appointment (ERA 1996, s 55(2) and (3)).

14.15 ADOPTION LEAVE

Since April 2003, employees have had the right to take time off work after adopting a child. The statutory right is set out in the ERA 1996, ss 75A–75D, and the detail is contained in the Paternity and Adoption Leave Regulations (PALR 2002) (SI 2002/2788). The law is very similar to the law which applies to women taking OML or AML. The summary below sets out in outline only the legal framework.

As a basic proposition all employees are entitled to take up to 52 weeks' adoption leave if they satisfy certain conditions.

Under PALR 2002, reg 17(1), an employee must tell his employer no later than seven days after the date the employee is told that he has been matched with a child for adoption (in writing if requested):

(a)   the date the child is expected to be placed;

(b)   the date the employee is going to start his adoption leave;

(c)   if requested, the employee must also give the employer evidence of his entitlement to adoption leave (from the adoption agency).

An employee who is entitled to OAL will also be entitled to 26 weeks' additional adoption leave (AAL), which will start on the day after the last day of the OAL period (reg 20). This is the same period as AML (**14.5**).

The employer must notify the employee of the date AAL will end, in the same way that an employer must tell a woman of the date her OML or AML will end (see **14.3.2.1**).

The terms and conditions of employment that apply during ordinary adoption leave (OAL) are exactly the same as those which apply to a woman during OML (see **14.3.3.1**).

The terms and conditions of employment which apply during AAL are exactly the same as those which apply during AML (see **14.5.1**)

Exactly the same rules that apply to women returning from OML or AML apply to employees returning from OAL or AAL (see **14.5.3**). In essence, eight weeks' notice must be given of any return to work if the employee intends to return earlier than the end of the AAL period (MPLPAL(A)R 2006, reg 15).

Returning employees are entitled to almost the same rights as those which apply to women returning from OML or AML (see **14.3.3**; **14.5.3**).

The rules which apply when a redundancy situation arises during an employee's OAL or AAL are the same as those which apply to redundancy situations which arise while a woman is on OML or AML (see **14.7**).

Employees who take or seek to take adoption leave are protected in the same way as women who take or seek to take maternity leave (see **14.8**; **14.9**) against detrimental treatment, and will be regarded as automatically unfairly dismissed if the reason for their dismissal was connected to the fact that they took or sought to take adoption leave.

Where a couple is notified of being matched with a child for adoption on or after 3 April 2011, additional paternity leave can be taken (Additional Paternity Leave Regulations 2010, reg 3(2)) – see **14.16** for more details.

As both men and women are entitled to parental, paternity and adoption leave, it is unlikely that either sex will have a claim for direct sex discrimination if dismissed, or if subjected to any other detriment in relation to taking time off. If, however, it is less acceptable in a particular workplace for a man rather than a woman to take parental, paternity or adoption leave, and as a result he is treated less favourably, this would be direct discrimination.

An employee who adopts a child and takes adoption leave may be entitled to statutory adoption pay (SAP). The qualifying conditions are set out in the Social Security Contributions and Benefits Act 1992 (as amended) and the Statutory Paternity Pay and Statutory Adoption Pay (General) Regulations 2002 (SI 2002/2822). Detail of the provisions are outside the scope of this book, but essentially an employee who is eligible for adoption leave and who takes that leave will normally be entitled to SAP.

Statutory adoption pay is paid for 39 weeks by the employer at a weekly rate of £135.45 (from April 2011) or 90% of the employee's normal weekly earnings, whichever is the lower.

The administrative requirements which pertain to SAP are extremely complex; the rules are contained in the Statutory Paternity Pay and Statutory Adoption Pay (Administration) Regulations 2002 (SI 2002/2802).

14.16 PATERNITY LEAVE

The Employment Act 2002 (EA 2002) introduced a new right for fathers and other partners to take up to two weeks' paid paternity leave (ordinary paternity leave: OPL). The EA 2002 introduced ss 80A–80D into the ERA 1996, which allows the Secretary of State to make Regulations governing the new right. Such Regulations have been made in the form of the PALR 2002, where the detail of how the right works is set out. The summary below sets out in outline only the legal framework.

Statutory paternity pay is currently £135.45 (from April 2012) a week or 90% of normal weekly earnings if less, and is payable for a maximum of 28 weeks.

Additional paternity leave for fathers and partners of mothers to children due on or after 3 April 2011 came into force on 6 April 2010 (Additional Paternity Leave Regulations 2010 (SI 2010/1055) (APLR 2010)). Mothers of children due on or after 3 April 2011 are able to transfer up to six months of their maternity leave to the father when they return to work. Additional leave can be taken once the mother has returned to work; there is no requirement that the leave must begin directly after the mother returns to work. The earliest that this leave may be taken is 20 weeks after the birth, and it must end 12 months after the birth. The maximum length of leave which may be taken is 26 weeks and the minimum two weeks. The leave must be taken in multiples of complete weeks and as one continuous period. Subject to qualifying conditions, fathers/partners of mothers may be able to receive statutory additional paternity pay for the remainder of the mother's maternity pay period. Equivalent rules apply to partners of adopters of children who are notified of the match on or after 3 April 2011. The two weeks' leave taken around the birth/adoption has been renamed 'ordinary' paternity leave.

The provisions and requirements that apply to employees taking paternity leave are exactly the same as those that apply to women taking OML (see **14.3**).

The Government has said that the APLR 2010 are only an interim measure, as it intends a more in-depth overhaul of all family-friendly provisions.

For a more detailed analysis of the APLR 2010 and a discussion of some of the potentially problematic areas, readers are referred to the IDS Employment Law Brief, *Focus on additional paternity leave and pay* (No 921, March 2011).

14.17 PARENTAL LEAVE

The European Parental Leave Directive was implemented by the ERA 1996 as amended by the EA 2002. The details of the rights are set out in supporting Regulations (the Maternity and Parental Leave etc Regulations 1999 (MPLR 1999) as amended by the Maternity and Parental Leave (Amendment) Regulations 2002 (SI 2002/2789) (MPL(A)R 2002) and the MPLPAL(A)R 2006).

The provisions and requirements which relate to the parental leave period are exactly the same as the terms and conditions that continue to apply to a woman during AML (see **14.5**).

14.18 RIGHT TO REQUEST FLEXIBLE WORKING

Qualifying parents have the right to request flexible working. Employers must consider such requests seriously, but they may refuse the request on certain grounds. The right to request flexible working applies to carers of adults and to parents of children under 16 (or disabled children under 18). This right extends to spouses, civil partners and near relatives, and also includes someone who lives at the same address as the adult in need of care.

A 2010 survey by Pricewaterhouse Coopers found that flexible working was the most valued benefit for employees. Of the 1,167 surveyed, 47% said it was their most important benefit (bonuses were second).

14.18.1 Changes to contract that may be requested

The statutory provisions relating to the new rights are set out in ERA 1996, ss 80F–80I and in the supporting Regulations (the Flexible Working (Eligibility, Complaints and Remedies) Regulations 2002 (SI 2002/3236), and the Flexible Working (Procedural Requirements) Regulations 2002 (SI 2002/3207)).

Under s 80F, an employee may ask his employer for a change in his terms and conditions of employment if the change requested relates to:

(a)   hours of work;

(b)   times of work;

(c)   where he works.

This means, for example, that an employee might ask to work from 10 am and through his lunch hour, rather than starting at 9 am, or to work from home one day per week. Acas envisages that a wide range of working patterns could be suggested.

14.18.2 Qualifications for the right to request flexible working

Although the right itself is set out in the ERA 1996, the eligibility criteria are set out in supporting Regulations: the Flexible Working (Eligibility, Complaints and Remedies) Regulations 2002 (the Eligibility etc Regulations). BIS has a useful interactive website which helps employers, employees and carers work out whether they are eligible to request flexible working.

The conditions of eligibility to make a request for flexible working are set out in reg 3. Section 80F(2) of the Act and reg 4 of the Eligibility etc Regulations set out the formal requirements for an application by an employee. The employer must follow the statutory procedure set out in the Flexible Working (Procedural Requirements) Regulations 2002 (Procedural Requirements Regulations). The chart below was taken from the BIS website (with the relevant regulations added).

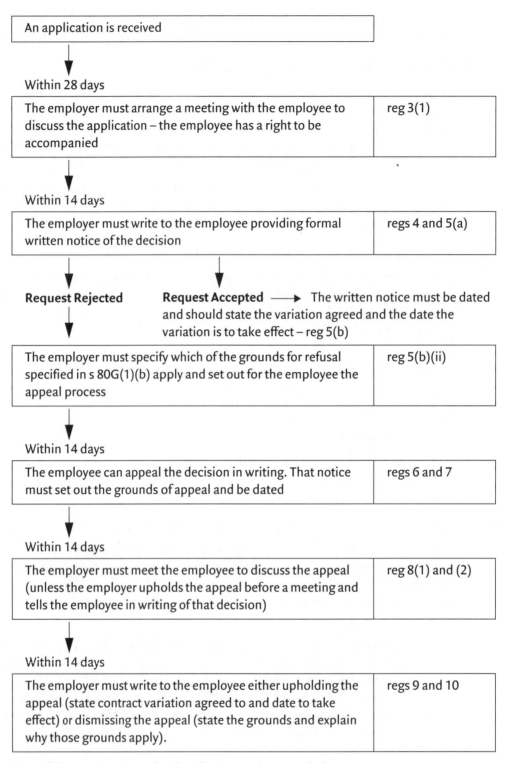

An application is received	

Within 28 days

The employer must arrange a meeting with the employee to discuss the application – the employee has a right to be accompanied	reg 3(1)

Within 14 days

The employer must write to the employee providing formal written notice of the decision	regs 4 and 5(a)

Request Rejected

Request Accepted ⟶ The written notice must be dated and should state the variation agreed and the date the variation is to take effect – reg 5(b)

The employer must specify which of the grounds for refusal specified in s 80G(1)(b) apply and set out for the employee the appeal process	reg 5(b)(ii)

Within 14 days

The employee can appeal the decision in writing. That notice must set out the grounds of appeal and be dated	regs 6 and 7

Within 14 days

The employer must meet the employee to discuss the appeal (unless the employer upholds the appeal before a meeting and tells the employee in writing of that decision)	reg 8(1) and (2)

Within 14 days

The employer must write to the employee either upholding the appeal (state contract variation agreed to and date to take effect) or dismissing the appeal (state the grounds and explain why those grounds apply).	regs 9 and 10

Note: If the parties agree, the time limits may be extended.

14.18.3 Right to be accompanied to meetings

Under reg 14 of the Procedural Requirements Regulations, an employee has the right to be accompanied to any meeting with the employer. The companion must be a fellow-worker employed by the same employer.

14.18.4 Grounds for refusal

An employer can refuse the employee's request for flexible working only where one or more of the grounds set out in ERA 1996, s 80G(1)(b) apply:

(a)   additional costs;

(b)   detrimental effect on ability to meet customer demand;

(c)   inability to reorganise work among existing staff;

(d)   inability to recruit additional staff;

(e)   detrimental impact on quality;

(f)   detrimental impact on performance;

(g)   insufficiency of work during the periods the employee wants to work;

(h)   planned structural changes.

The Regulations specify that the employer should state the grounds for refusal and give a sufficient explanation as to why those grounds apply (reg 5(b)(ii)).

The BIS guide gives useful examples of the sort of explanation that an employee can expect from the employer. For example:

Marie, an experienced hair stylist working in a small hairdressers, applies to reduce her full-time hours to working between 10.00 am–3.00 pm. In the letter refusing the request, the manager gives the business reason of detrimental effect on ability to meet customer demand as the basis of refusal, and explains that the salon does not have the spare capacity to manage the parent's (i.e. Marie's) customers in her absence:

> ... for the last six months all stylists have been fully booked up in advance on almost every day of the week, with the beginning and end of each day being particularly busy. As you are aware, you are highly regarded by our customers and the majority ask for you by name and would not accept a trainee stylist in your absence.
>
> I regret therefore that I am unable to cover your absence at present. Your absence would mean that we are unable to serve our usual number of customers. I would, however be happy to revisit your request in a year's time, when Sally, our trainee stylist, will have completed her training.

14.18.5   Complaining to the tribunal

There are only limited grounds on which an employee whose application to work flexibly is declined can complain to a tribunal (but see also **14.18.7** and **14.18.8** below). These are set out in ERA 1996, s 80H. The grounds are:

(a)   that the employer has not followed the proper procedure set out in the Regulations (s 80H(1)(a));

(b)   that the employer did not reject the employee's application on one of the listed grounds in s 80G(1)(b) (s 80H(1)(a));

(c)   that the employer made his decision based on incorrect facts.

Tribunals do not have the power to question the commercial validity of a decision to refuse a request for flexible working. The tribunal's role is essentially to ensure that the employer has taken the request seriously and followed the procedure.

Complaints must be brought within three months from the date on which the employee is notified of the decision on appeal or the date on which a breach of the regulations occurred. The tribunal may extend the period where it is satisfied that it was not reasonably practicable for the complaint to have been brought within the three-month period.

14.18.6   Remedies

Remedies are dealt with in s 80I and reg 7 of the Eligibility etc. Regulations. In addition to awarding compensation, the tribunal can make an order for reconsideration (see, eg, *Snelling v Tates Ltd t/a Spar* (ET/1502720/03)).

The maximum compensation that an employee can be awarded where the tribunal decides that the employee's complaint is made out is eight weeks' pay. The statutory maximum (£430 as at February 2012) applies when calculating a week's pay. The amount actually awarded will depend on what the tribunal considers just and equitable (see *BA plc v Starmer* [2005] IRLR 862 and *Coxon v Landesbank Baden-Wurttemberg* (ET/2203702/04) for two examples of this).

14.18.7 Detriment and automatic unfair dismissal (ERA 1996, ss 47E and ERA 1996, s 104C)

Employees who make an application to work flexibly, or who exercise their rights under the above provisions to work flexibly, are protected against detrimental treatment in the same way as women who take or seek to take maternity leave, and will be regarded as automatically unfairly dismissed if the reason for their dismissal was connected to the fact that they sought to work flexibly or exercised their rights under the above provisions. An employee who is dismissed because she tried to exercise the right to work flexibly may also bring a claim to have been dismissed for asserting a statutory right under s 104(1)(a) or (b) (see *Horn v Quinn Walker Securities* (ET/2505740/03) for an example).

So long as the employee has two years' service (or one if employed before 6 April 2012), she could also bring a normal unfair dismissal claim (see, for an example, *Superdrug Stores plc v Fannon* (UKEAT/1190/96)).

If an employer acts perversely or unreasonably in dealing with or refusing a request, an employee may be entitled to resign and claim constructive dismissal (see *Clarke v Telewest Communications plc* (ET/1301034/04)).

14.18.8 Overlap with sex discrimination law

Where a woman returning from maternity leave asks to work part-time, she may, if the employer refuses her request, have a claim of unlawful indirect sex discrimination. If she made the request under the above statutory provisions she may also, depending on the facts, have a complaint under s 80H of the ERA 1996, for unjustified refusal of a request for flexible working (see, for an example, *Girvin v Next Retail Ltd* (ET/1900767/05)). A man may also be able to bring a direct sex discrimination claim if he can show that a woman's request would have been treated more favourably.

14.18.9 Case example

In *Clarke v Telewest Communications* an employment tribunal highlighted a number of errors made by an employer when handling an application for flexible working. The claimant's hours were Monday to Friday, 10.00 am to 6.30 pm and she was obliged to work weekends. In July 2003, while on maternity leave, she requested to change her hours to 37.5 hours a week, Monday to Friday, 9.30 am to 5.00 pm. At a meeting, Telewest rejected the request. It offered a number of alternative patterns, but they all included weekends and evenings. The tribunal found that:

(a)   Telewest failed to reply promptly and in time to the original request or hold a meeting within 28 days of the original request.

(b)   The decision to refuse the request was made before the meeting and before proper consideration of its merits.

(c)   No adequate explanation of the refusal was given.

(d)   The written reasons for the refusal did not state which of the business grounds applied and this did not allow the employee a fair chance of appeal.

It can be important, therefore, to determine what heads of claim an employee has. The table at **14.19.3** below summarises the main differences between the various potential heads of claim.

The Government consulted on extending the right to flexible working to all employees in 2011, and said in October 2012 that new legislation will be announced soon.

14.19 TIME OFF TO CARE FOR DEPENDANTS

As a basic proposition, all employees are entitled to reasonable unpaid time off work to look after a dependant (dependant care leave) (ERA 1996, s 57A).

14.19.1 Entitlement to dependant care leave

Section 57A(1) of the ERA 1996 states that an employee is entitled to be permitted to take a reasonable amount of unpaid time off work in order to take action necessary:

(a)   to assist a dependant who is ill, has given birth, is injured or assaulted;

(b)   to arrange care for an ill or injured dependant;

(c)   as a result of the death of a dependant;

(d)   due to care arrangements being disrupted or ending;

(e)   to deal with an incident at the child's school.

The amount of time the employee can take off work to care for a dependant is a reasonable amount of time to take *necessary* action. In *Royal Bank of Scotland v Harrison* (UKEAT/0093/08) the EAT gave guidance on what was meant by 'necessary'. It said that there was no justification for inserting words such as 'sudden' or 'emergency' into s 57A(1)(d).

In order to be entitled to take time off to care for a dependant, the employee must tell his employer:

(a)   the reason for his absence as soon as reasonably practicable; and

(b)   How long he expects to be absent (s 57A(2)).

'Dependant' is defined in s 57A(3), (4) and (5) as follows:

(a)   The employee's spouse, civil partner, child, parent or person who lives in the same household (but not a tenant, lodger or boarder). The definition clearly extends to non-married partners.

(b)   'Dependant' also includes anybody who *reasonably relies upon* the employee for help when a person is ill or injured or assaulted or to make arrangements for care. The BIS guidance states that this may be where the employee is the primary carer for another person, or is the only person who can help in an emergency: for example, an elderly neighbour living alone who falls and breaks a leg, where the employee is closest at hand at the time of the fall.

14.19.2 Meaning of reasonable amount of time off

The decision in *Qua v John Ford Morrison Solicitors* [2003] IRLR 184 was the first reported appellate decision on the right to time off to care for dependants. Ms Qua was absent from work for 17 days (over a period of eight separate occasions) as a result of her young son's medical problems.

The EAT considered the meaning of 'reasonable amount of time off work' and stated that when determining what is a reasonable amount of time off work, a tribunal should always take into account the circumstances of that individual and should ignore any disruption to the employers' business. The EAT pointed out that an employee is entitled to be permitted to take a reasonable amount of time off work to take the action needed to deal with a sick child. But, as the EAT indicated, the section is dealing with the unforeseen. Once a parent knows that a child is suffering from an underlying medical condition which is likely to cause further relapses, such a situation no longer falls within the section. The employee would, in such a situation, be entitled to a reasonable period off work to make arrangements for longer-term care. Thus the advice to the employer in respect of an employee who wishes to take three weeks off work to care for her sick child is that the employee cannot do this. She is entitled to take time off to make arrangements for his care, but not to take the three weeks and care for him herself.

In *Royal Bank of Scotland Plc v Harrison* (UKEAT/0093/08) an employee learnt on 8 December that her childminder would be unavailable on 22 December and argued that the time she took off to look after her child was time off to care for a dependant under s 57A. The Bank argued that absence of anyone to care for her child was not unexpected and s 57A only applied to situations that arose suddenly or in an emergency. The EAT disagreed. It held that an event is 'unexpected' at the moment the employee learns of it. Once aware of it, he or she must try to make alternative arrangements, but if it is not possible to do so, it will become necessary for the employee to take time off under s 57A.

14.19.3 Potential heads of claim: the right to request flexible working and indirect discrimination

	Indirect sex discrimination	Indirect marital discrimination	Rights to request different working pattern
Qualifying period	None	None	26 weeks
Who can claim	Mother or female carers (depending on evidence)	Married person	Fathers as well as mothers, adopters, foster parents, guardians and partners (same or different sex) Employees caring for an adult in need of care
Employee or worker	Worker	Worker	Employee only
Age of child	No age limit, could apply, for example to elderly care as well	No age limit	Child under 16 If disabled under 18
When can request be made	Any time, eg before or after maternity leave or when applying for a job	As for indirect discrimination	Before the child's 16th birthday or 18th if disabled
Restriction on number of requests	None	None	Only one request can be made every year
Procedure	No set procedure	No set procedure	Prescribed procedure must be followed by employer and employee
On what basis can the employer refuse the request	Where it is objectively 'justifiable' to refuse	As for indirect sex discrimination	Where the employer decides to refuse on a specified ground
Time-limit for making claim	3 months less one day but may extend if just and equitable	As for indirect sex discrimination	3 months less one day, subject to reasonable practicable extension
Remedies on refusal	Declaration Recommendation Compensation (uncapped) including injury to feelings	As for indirect sex discrimination	8 weeks' pay subject to the statutory maximum of a week's pay

© Palmer Wade 2008

14.19.4 Detriment and automatic unfair dismissal (ERA 1996, s 99 and MPLR 1999, regs 19 and 20)

Employees who take or seek to take dependant care leave are protected in the same way as women who take or seek to take maternity leave against detrimental treatment, and will be regarded as automatically unfairly dismissed if the reason for their dismissal was connected to the fact that they took or sought to take dependency leave (MPLR 1999, regs 19 and 20(3)(e)(iii)). (See **14.8** and **14.9**.)

Similarly, an employee will be regarded as automatically unfairly dismissed if there was a redundancy situation and those circumstances (ie the redundancy situation) applied to other employees, and the reason the employee was selected for redundancy, was because he took or sought to take dependency leave (reg 20(2)).

14.19.5 Remedies

The remedies available to employees in relation to their right to take time off to care for a dependant are set out in s 57B of the ERA 1996. The time-limit for making a complaint is three months from the date of the refusal. If the tribunal decides that the complaint was well-founded, it may make a declaration and/or award compensation, of such amount as the tribunal considers to be just and equitable having regard to the employer's behaviour and any loss sustained by the employee.

14.20 FURTHER READING

Blackstone's Employment Law Practice (OUP, 2012).

Harvey, *Industrial Relations and Employment Law* (Butterworths), Vol 2, Div J.

SUMMARY

The provisions relating to maternity rights have been implemented as a result of the Equal Treatment Directive 1976 and the Pregnant Workers Directive 1992. The law is contained in the ERA 1996, as amended. However, much of the detail in respect of maternity rights and parental leave is contained in the Maternity and Parental Leave etc Regulations 1999 (as amended) (**14.1**). The following checklist summarises points of importance when considering maternity rights:

- Length of service.
- Detrimental treatment.
- Dismissal.
- Reason for dismissal – ERA 1996, s 99/other.
- If not s 99, eligibility/fairness of employer's actions under s 98(4).
- Whether entitled to a redundancy payment and/or to claim sex discrimination and/ or wrongful dismissal.

The main rights afforded to pregnant woman relate to the right to take maternity leave and to return to work after that leave expires. In most instances, some of that leave will be paid for. All pregnant women are entitled up to 52 weeks' maternity leave. The first 26 weeks are known as 'ordinary maternity leave' (OML) (**14.3**). The remaining period of up to 26 weeks is known as 'additional maternity leave' (AML) (**14.5**). There are some differences between the two regimes.

A woman who wants to take maternity leave must notify her employer of the fact of her pregnancy, the expected week of childbirth and the date she intends to start her maternity leave. There are rules about the time by which this must be done (**14.3.1**).

During OML, the woman's contract of employment continues. A woman is entitled to the benefit of all the terms and conditions of employment which would have applied to her had she not been absent during the OML period, including non-contractual benefits, except remuneration. A woman who takes OML is entitled to return to the job in which she was employed before her absence, with her seniority, pension rights and similar rights as they would have been had she not been absent, and on terms and conditions no less favourable than they would have been had she not been absent. The OML period counts towards the woman's period of continuous employment for both statutory and contractual rights (**14.3.3**).

An employee on maternity leave may agree with her employer to work for up to 10 days during her maternity leave without bringing that period to an end. 'Work' may include training or any other activity undertaken to assist the employee to keep in touch with the workplace.

During AML, the woman is not entitled to remuneration. The statutory right to return to a job after AML is more restricted than after OML. A woman on maternity leave may be entitled to receive statutory maternity pay (SMP), which is paid for a maximum period of 39 weeks (**14.5**).

Under ss 47C and 99 of the ERA 1996, pregnant/maternity leave employees have special protection from acts short of dismissal and/or dismissal (**14.8** and **14.9**). Section 18 of the Equality Act 2010 states that it will be sex discrimination where a woman is treated less favourably because she is pregnant or exercising or seeking to exercise, or has exercised her right to maternity leave (**14.13**).

Since April 2003, employees have the right to take time off work after adopting a child. The law is very similar to the law which applies to women taking OML or AML. An employee who adopts a child and takes adoption leave may be entitled to statutory adoption pay (SAP) (**14.15**).

The Employment Act 2002 (EA 2002) introduced a right for fathers and other partners to take up to two weeks' paid paternity leave. The Paternity and Adoption Leave Regulations 2002 set out the relevant details. Employees who take or seek to take paternity leave are protected against detrimental treatment in the same way as women who take or seek to take maternity leave, and will be regarded as automatically unfairly dismissed if the reason for their dismissal was connected to the fact that they took or sought to take paternity leave. An employee who takes paternity leave is entitled to statutory paternity pay (SPP) (**14.16**).

Under the Maternity and Parental Leave etc Regulations 1999 (as amended), an employee is entitled to take up to 13 weeks' unpaid parental leave (18 weeks for a disabled child). Employees who take or seek to take parental leave are protected against detrimental treatment in the same way as women who take or seek to take maternity leave, and will be regarded as automatically unfairly dismissed if the reason for their dismissal was connected to the fact that they took or sought to take parental leave (**14.17**).

The detail about flexible working is contained in the Flexible Working (Eligibility, Complaints and Remedies) and (Procedural Requirements) Regulations 2002. The right to request flexible working applies to carers of children and carers of adults (**14.18**).

Under the ERA 1996, s 57A, all employees are entitled to unpaid time off work to look after a dependant who is ill, has given birth, is injured or assaulted, or who has died, and to deal with an incident at a child's school. The amount of time the employee may take off work to care for a dependant is a reasonable amount of time to take necessary action (**14.19**).

Table 14.1 below summarises the main rights and remedies available with regard to maternity leave, parental leave, time off for dependants, paternity leave, adoption leave and requests for flexible working.

Table 14.1 Summary of main rights and remedies

The right (jurisdiction in brackets)	Main features	Who qualifies?
Rights and remedies covering maternity leave, parental leave, time off for dependants, paternity leave, adoption leave, requests for flexible working		
Pregnancy/maternity discrimination (Equality Act 2010, ss 18 and 39)	Unfavourable treatment because of pregnancy/maternity leave	All female workers who are pregnant, employees on maternity leave & workers for 2 weeks after the birth
Sex discrimination (direct and indirect) (Equality Act 2010, ss 13, 19 and 26) and harassment	Where there is less favourable treatment on grounds of sex/ marital status or unjustified PCP which disadvantages one sex	All workers, male and female
Automatic unfair dismissal (ERA s 99, MPL Regs 20, PAL Regs 29, ERA s 104C)	Automatic unfair dismissal if the only or principal reason is connected with a right to leave for family reasons	All employees regardless of length of service
Protection from detriment (ERA s 47C & 47E, MPL Regs 19, PAL Regs 28)	Covers leave for family and domestic reasons and in relation to flexible working	All employees regardless of length of service
'Ordinary' unfair dismissal (ERA s 98)	Where the dismissal is not fair. Note also the possibility of automatic unfair dismissal under ss 100 (H&S) and 104 ERA (asserting of a statutory right)	Employees with two years' service (for those who start work on or after 6 April 2012)
Written reasons for dismissal (ERA 1996 s 92(4) & (4A))	Applies if s/he is dismissed when pregnant or on maternity or adoption leave	All employees whether or not they have requested the reasons in writing, otherwise reasons must be requested in writing
Specific rights and remedies		
Time off for antenatal care (ERA ss 55–56)	Reasonable paid time off	All employees
Refusal of time off for antenatal care (ERA ss 57)	Specific remedy in addition to protection from dismissal, detriment and discrimination	
H&S protection (Management of Health and Safety at Work Regulations 1999 and ERA ss 66–69)	Protection from risks is the employer's responsibility culminating in suspension on full pay	All employees, must notify pregnancy in writing to benefit from alternative work & paid suspension
Breach of H&S provisions	Compensation (ERA s 70), automatic unfair dismissal in relation to suspension (MPL Regs 20(3)(c)), sex discrimination)	Note: a dismissed employee may have a claim under ERA s 100 and the employer is also liable to prosecution
Ordinary maternity leave (OML) (ERA s 71, MPL Regs 4–11)	26 weeks	All employees regardless of length of service
Additional maternity leave (AML) (ERA s 73, MPL Regs 5–12)	Starts when OML ends and runs for 26 weeks	All employees regardless of length of service
Refusal of maternity leave (ERA s 99 and 47C)	Automatic unfair dismissal or detriments	
Contractual rights during OML and AML (for births due on or after 5.10.08) (ERA s 71, Reg 9)	All rights set out in contract continue to accrue apart from remuneration	

The right (jurisdiction in brackets)	Main features	Who qualifies?
Redundancy during maternity or adoption leave (ERA ss 74 and 75C) MPL Reg 10, PAL Reg 23)	Right to be given first refusal of any suitable alternative job available	All employees on OML and AML and adoption leave
Return to work after OML (ERA s 71)	Right to return to the same job	
Return to work after AML (ERA s 73, MPL Reg 18)	Right to return to the same job. Only if that is not reasonably practicable may the employer offer a suitable alternative	All employees
Statutory Maternity Pay	90% of salary for 6 weeks, fixed rate (or 90%, whichever is the lower) for 33 weeks	All employees and other workers who have NI deducted at source and who have been employed for 26 weeks by the 15th week before the EWC & earn at least £95 a week
Failure to pay SMP, paternity and adoption pay	ERA Part II (see section 27(1)(c)); or The government pay	Note: the employer is also liable to prosecution
Maternity allowance	Fixed rate (or 90%, whichever is the lower) payable by the DSS for 39 weeks	Employed and self employed workers who work during their pregnancy but do not qualify for SMP
Incapacity benefit, means tested benefits	Support from the welfare benefits safety net via DWP for women who cannot claim SMP or MA	
Parental leave (ERA s 76, MPL Regs 13–18)	Thirteen weeks for each parent for each child under 5 years old (18 weeks if the child is disabled)	Employees with responsibility for a child who have been employed for one year
Parental leave: unreasonable postponement or refusal (ERA s 80)	Declaration and compensation under ERA s 80	
Time off for dependants (ERA s 57A)	Time off to care for dependant in an emergency	All employees
Refusal of time off for dependants (ERA s 57B)	Declaration and compensation under ERA s 57B	
Paternity leave (ERA s 80A, PAL Regs)	2 weeks' leave to be taken together	Employees with 26 weeks service by the 15th week before the EWC or the date of matching for adoption
Refusal of paternity leave (ERA s 99 & 47C)	Automatic unfair dismissal or detriment	
Statutory paternity pay	Fixed rate for 28 weeks	Average earnings must be £95 pw
Refusal of paternity pay	Unlawful deduction from wages (ERA s 27(1)(ca))	Refusal of adoption pay
Adoption leave (ERA s 75A, PAL Regs	52 weeks leave	Employees with 26 weeks service by the date of matching for adoption
Refusal of adoption leave (ERA s 99 and 47C)	Automatic unfair dismissal or detriment	
Statutory adoption pay	Fixed rate for 39 weeks	Average earnings must be £95 pw

The right (jurisdiction in brackets)	Main features	Who qualifies?
Refusal of adoption pay	Unlawful deduction from wages (ERA s 27(1)(cb))	
Flexible working (ERA s 80F, FW regs)	The right to ask for flexible working in respect of a child under 16 or an adult in need of care	Employees with 26 weeks' service.
Refusal of FW	ERA s 80H and indirect sex discrimination	

HUMAN RIGHTS, MONITORING AND DATA PROTECTION

LEARNING OUTCOMES

After reading this chapter you will be able to:

- understand how the Human Rights Act 1998 may influence UK law
- explain when Article 6 may impact upon internal disciplinary proceedings
- explain how Article 6 impacts upon employment tribunal hearings
- describe how Article 8 is relevant to employment tribunal claims
- describe the relevance of the Regulation of Investigatory Powers Act 2000 and of the Data Protection Act 1998.

15.1 HUMAN RIGHTS ACT 1998 – INTRODUCTION

The HRA 1998 came into force on 2 October 2000. It incorporates into domestic law the European Convention for the Protection of Human Rights and Fundamental Freedoms 1950 ('the Convention'). Although the UK was already a signatory to the Convention and was therefore bound by it as a matter of international law, until the HRA 1998 came into force the Convention was not directly part of UK domestic law and individuals could not enforce Convention rights in the domestic courts.

15.2 THE SCHEME OF THE HUMAN RIGHTS ACT 1998

Schedule 1 to the HRA 1998 sets out the relevant Convention rights which are protected under the Act. Section 3 states that 'so far as it is possible to do so' primary and secondary legislation must be read and given effect in a way which is compatible with the Convention rights; this includes (s 2) taking account of any judgments and decisions of the European Court of Human Rights (ECtHR).

In order to give effect the spirit of the Convention, UK courts and tribunals adopt a 'purposive' approach to the interpretation of such legislation. (This is an area with which the UK courts are reasonably familiar, albeit in a different context, as they have been applying a purposive approach to EC Regulations and Directives for some time. The House of Lords in *Litster v Forth Dry Dock and Engineering Co Ltd* [1989] IRLR 161 (see **7.3.2**) had to put a very strained interpretation on the Transfer of Undertakings (Protection of Employment) Regulations 1981 in order to make them comply with the (old) Acquired Rights Directive which they were intended to implement.) If any primary or subordinate legislation is found to be incompatible with a Convention right, the HRA 1998 provides that such legislation remains effective. In such a situation, certain courts (the High Court and named appellate courts, but not including employment tribunals or the EAT) can make (s 4) a 'declaration of incompatibility' in relation to that legislation, upon which Parliament may act if it wishes. (This allows for the sovereignty of Parliament to remain unchallenged.)

The HRA 1998 creates a new free-standing cause of action for the victims of unlawful acts by public authorities. (Victims are entitled to rely on their Convention rights in proceedings brought against them, or in conjunction with other existing causes of action – for example breach of contract or unfair dismissal claims.) Section 6 provides that it is unlawful for a public authority to act in a way which is incompatible with Convention rights. It allows 'victims' who claim that a public authority has acted (or proposes to act) unlawfully to bring proceedings in the 'appropriate court or tribunal'. It creates no new remedies (s 8).

The important Convention rights, from an employment perspective, are identified at **15.4**. Most of those rights are not absolute rights but are limited by counter-balances which permit legitimate interferences with those rights in certain situations. Most human rights cases are not about whether the right exists but whether there has been an interference with the right and whether that interference is legitimate and necessary. That will involve questions of proportionality and relevance being considered.

It has now been settled by two cases (R v Lambert [2002] 2 AC 505 and Pearce v Governing Body of Mayfield Secondary School [2001] IRLR 669) that the Act does not apply retrospectively to the acts of courts or tribunals that took place before the Act came into force.

15.3 KEY DEFINITIONS

The mainstay of the HRA 1998 is that it permits victims to sue public authorities.

15.3.1 Public authorities

The HRA 1998 does not define 'public authority', but it recognises three categories of legal persons for the purposes of the Act:

(a)   clear public authorities (eg central and local government, the police, HM Revenue and Customs, courts and tribunals);

(b)   mixed authorities (eg privatised utilities like Railtrack, which retain some public functions, or private companies which carry out some public duties, like G4S);

(c)   private persons.

The scope of the Act differs according to each category. Clear public authorities fall within the scope of s 6 (ie they have to act in a way which is compatible with the Convention rights) in relation to all their activities. Mixed authorities fall within the scope of s 6 in relation to only those acts they carry out which are of a public nature. Private persons are entirely outside the direct scope of s 6.

Defining what category a particular body falls within is a difficult area. As far as mixed authorities are concerned, determining whether acts are private acts or public acts is a distinction with which the UK courts are fairly familiar, not least in determining whether bodies are susceptible to judicial review. Current case law suggests that judicial review is not available merely where private contractual rights are involved (see, eg, R v East Berkshire Health Authority, ex p Walsh [1985] 1 QB 152; R v Hammersmith and Fulham London Borough Council, ex p Nalgo [1991] IRLR 249).

In a case involving a housing association in Poplar (Poplar Housing and Regeneration Community Association Ltd v Donoghue [2002] QB 48), the Court of Appeal held that housing associations were not to be regarded as public authorities for all purposes. The fact that the association was a charity motivated by the public interest did not point towards it being a public authority.

However, the Court said that an act which would otherwise be private, could become public if it had features that imposed a 'public stamp', and concluded that the role of the housing association was so 'closely assimilated' to that of the local authority that it should be regarded as a 'hybrid' public authority for the purposes of s 6. In a later decision (*R (Heather and Others) v Leonard Cheshire Foundation and Others* [2002] 2 All ER 936) the Court of Appeal decided that the Leonard Cheshire Foundation, which was a charitable voluntary organisation, was not performing a public function within the meaning of s 6(3) because the provision of care was not a 'public function'.

In *YL v Birmingham City Council* [2007] UKHL 27, the House of Lords held (3:2) that a private care home for the elderly under contract with a local authority was not exercising 'functions of a public nature'.

15.3.2 Victims

A victim is defined (s 7(7)) to include a person, non-governmental organisation or group of individuals. Thus, in addition to individuals, victims may include companies, political parties, professional bodies and trade unions. Victims must be 'directly affected' by the act complained of (or at risk of being so affected). But note that in some situations the ECtHR has allowed those 'indirectly affected' (eg relatives of a dead victim) to bring a complaint. The ECtHR has not allowed pressure group claims, and the scope for representative actions is limited.

A difficult issue arises with regard to employees. As far as pure public authorities are concerned, some commentators have queried whether the HRA 1998 gives any direct rights to such individuals (as opposed to, say, customers of such bodies). The same argument would apply to mixed authorities when they are carrying out any public functions. As far as mixed authorities in their private capacity and private persons are concerned, their employees have no direct claims under the HRA 1998 but may be able to rely on it indirectly to 'aid' existing causes of action such as unfair dismissal and breach of contract claims.

15.3.3 Reliance

Section 6 creates a free-standing cause of action for victims of unlawful acts done by public authorities (see **15.3.2** above). They do not need to 'hang' such a claim on any other existing cause of action. Such persons are therefore entitled to bring a claim under s 7 in the 'appropriate court or tribunal'. Employment tribunals and the EAT fall within that definition. They can adjudicate on free-standing claims under the HRA 1998, have to interpret any legislation in accordance with Convention rights (s 3) and, as they are themselves public authorities, are obliged to act in compliance with Convention rights in accordance with s 6.

Those persons who do not fall within the category of persons who may bring direct free-standing claims (eg private sector employees) will still be able to avail themselves of Convention rights but not as a free-standing claim. Because tribunals are themselves public authorities, and are obliged to act in compliance with Convention rights under s 6, and because they will have to interpret UK legislation in accordance with Convention rights under s 3, such other persons can rely on Convention rights to help in the interpretation and application of any existing causes of action (eg unfair dismissal or breach of contract claims).

15.4 RELEVANT CONVENTION RIGHTS

Identified briefly below are those Convention rights which may be of relevance to UK employment law. Reference is also made in other chapters, where appropriate, to specific employment law areas where the HRA 1998 may have application.

15.4.1 Article 6

This creates a right to a 'fair and public hearing within a reasonable time by an independent and impartial tribunal established by law'. There has been discussion about whether this applies to internal disciplinary procedures. *Tehrani v United Kingdom Central Council for Nursing, Midwifery and Health Visiting* [2001] IRLR 208 establishes that the position is different where there are disciplinary proceedings which may determine a right to practise a profession (see also *Preiss v General Dental Council* [2001] IRLR 696; *R v Securities and Investments Authority, ex p Fleurose* [2001] IRLR 764; *R (Puri) v Bradford Teaching Hospital* [2011] EWHC 970; and *Mattu v The University Hospitals of Coventry and Warwickshire NHS Trust* [2011] EWHC 2068). In *Kulkarni v Milton Keynes Hospital Trust* [2009] EWCA Civ 789, the Court of Appeal held that NHS doctors are entitled to legal representation if facing charges of misconduct or lack of capability, or where the charges would be of such gravity if proved that they might mean that someone was unable to work in the future. See though *Hameed v Central Manchester NHS Trust* [2010] EWHC 2009 (QB) (**5.4.2.2**).

In *R (G) v The Governors of X School* [2011] UKSC 30, the Supreme Court held (by a 4:1 majority) that a teaching assistant's rights under Article 6 of the European Convention on Human Rights had not been breached by the school's decision to prohibit legal representation at his internal disciplinary hearing.

The claimant was employed as a teaching assistant at a primary school. He was accused of kissing and having sexual contact with a 15-year old boy, who was undergoing a period of work experience at the school. As a result of the accusations the claimant was suspended and disciplinary proceedings were commenced. Criminal proceedings were not brought against the claimant. The claimant asked for legal representation at the disciplinary hearing, which was to take place before the school's governors. This request was refused as the school's disciplinary policy provided for accompaniment only by a work colleague or union representative. The disciplinary hearing resulted in a finding that the allegations were substantiated, and the claimant was summarily dismissed.

Statutory provisions obliged the school, when it made a serious finding of misconduct, to make a reference to what became the Independent Safeguarding Authority (ISA) (originally the Secretary of State) to consider whether the claimant should be should be placed on the 'children's barred list' and prevented from working with children in the future. Under this statutory framework, the claimant would have a right to legal representation before the ISA; and if dissatisfied with its decision, there was a right of appeal.

The claimant appealed the decision of the school's disciplinary committee to the appeal committee of the school's governors. He requested permission to be legally represented at this hearing, but this was refused. He brought judicial review proceedings, alleging that the disciplinary proceedings were unfair and constituted a breach of his rights to a fair hearing under Article 6 of the Convention. His appeal to the appeal committee of the school's governors was stayed, pending the outcome of the civil proceedings.

The High Court held that although the internal disciplinary proceedings involved the determination of a civil right (as opposed to a criminal charge), the claimant was still entitled to be legally represented. The Court of Appeal held that where the consequences of an internal disciplinary proceeding were sufficiently linked to the determination of an individual's civil right's to practise his chosen profession (in the sense of having a 'substantial influence or effect' on the outcome of a subsequent process which is determinative of civil rights (in this case the outcome of the ISA's process, which could have meant that the claimant's name was added to the register)), the school had to have regard to Article 6. Laws LJ said (para 47):

> It seems to me that there is every likelihood that the outcome of the disciplinary process in a case like this, where there has been a finding of abuse of trust by virtue of sexual misconduct, will have a profound influence on the decision-making procedures relating to the barred list …

Having concluded that Article 6 was 'engaged', the Court of Appeal decided that Article 6 required that the claimant should be allowed legal representation in the disciplinary proceedings.

The Supreme Court agreed with the Court of Appeal on the appropriate test to be applied in determining whether Article 6 is engaged in the course of an internal disciplinary procedure. The Supreme Court, by a majority, applying the 'substantial influence or effect' test, overruled the Court of Appeal's finding that Article 6 required that the claimant should be allowed legal representation in the disciplinary proceedings

In its view, the fact that the ISA was required by statutory provisions and published guidance to 'exercise its own independent judgment both in relation to finding facts and making an assessment of their gravity and significance', before forming a view as to whether G should be placed on the barred list, was significant. The Supreme Court considered that the governors' determination that G had been guilty of gross misconduct would *not* have a 'substantial influence or effect' on the ISA's decision-making process. It followed that G's Article 6 rights were not engaged at the internal disciplinary stage, but only at the subsequent ISA hearing.

In his dissenting judgment, Lord Kerr considered that the ISA's decision in the barring procedure would inevitably be affected by the governors' report on the allegations. Accordingly, in Lord Kerr's view, Article 6(1) required that G should have been permitted legal representation by the school governors at the internal disciplinary hearing.

Provided there is no contractual obligation to permit legal representation, it appears that, while employers should always consider in any particular case the gravity of the allegations and the possible implications of an adverse finding, the vast majority of employers will not need to be concerned by requests for legal representation at disciplinary hearings.

In *Mattu v The University Hospitals of Coventry and Warwickshire NHS Trust* [2012] IRLR 619, the Court of Appeal rejected the proposition that the fair trial guarantees contained in Article 6(1) were engaged at the stage of disciplinary proceedings brought by an employer that could lead to dismissal and career damage. This was a different situation from R *(G) v The Governors of X School* (above), as it was the effect of dismissal that could render the employee unemployable in the NHS thereafter. All three members of the Court of Appeal agreed that Article 6 would not be engaged by the decision to dismiss. It also said that dismissal was a contractual matter, not the determination of a civil right.

Article 6 does apply to employment tribunals and the EAT, although there is some suggestion in the Strasbourg jurisprudence that disputes relating to the employment rights of public officials are not 'civil rights and obligations' but are disputes about the rights of civil servants (see, eg, *Neigel v France* (2000) 30 EHRR 310 and *Balfour v UK* [1997] EHRLR 665). However, while the UK courts have to have regard to ECtHR case law, they are not obliged to follow it. Article 6 may be used to challenge areas such as:

(a)   access to the courts. In *Devlin v UK* [2002] IRLR 155, the ECtHR held that a total block on the applicant bringing proceedings for religious discrimination on grounds of national security, amounted to a disproportionate restriction on the applicant's right of access to a court and was therefore in breach of Article 6. By contrast, in *Fogarty v UK* [2002] IRLR 148, the same court held that excluding an employee of the US embassy from bringing discrimination proceedings did not breach Article 6 because there was a legitimate aim being pursued and the exclusion was proportionate, namely, the promotion of good relations between States through respect for State sovereignty;

(b)   limitation periods;

(c)   qualifying periods;

(d)   funding. In *Airey v Ireland* (1979) 2 EHRR 305, the ECtHR found a breach of Article 6 where legal aid was not available to assist a litigant who wished to apply for a judicial separation;

(e)   refusal to grant adjournments (see *Teinaz v London Borough of Wandsworth* [2002] IRLR 721 and *Andreou v Lord Chancellor's Department* [2002] IRLR 728). In *Robinson v Home Office* (UKEAT/0533/01) the EAT held that the employment tribunal acted arbitrarily when it refused to grant an adjournment without explaining why the claimant's medical evidence was unsatisfactory;

(f)   delays in hearings. For example, it may allow a challenge to the lengthy delays in equal pay cases. In *Somjee v UK* [2002] IRLR 886, the ECtHR held that the delays cause by the conduct of the employment tribunal and EAT amounted to a breach of Article 6. It took eight and seven years respectively for the applicant's claims to be disposed of, and despite the fact that some of the delays were caused by the applicant herself and that the proceedings were complex, because the employment tribunal and EAT had contributed to the delays, there was a breach of Article 6. In *Kwamin and Others v Abbey National plc and other cases* [2004] ICR 841, the EAT held that excessive delay between hearing and decision renders the decision unfair. The EAT said that Article 6 requires a fair hearing to be conducted within a reasonable period;

(g)   representation (see *R (G) v The Governors of X School* and *Kulkarni v Milton Keynes Hospital Trust* above);

(h)   closed proceedings, such as for reasons of national security. While a closed material procedure does not contravene Article 6, a claimant who is excluded from proceedings must be told the 'gist' of the closed material so as to enable him effectively to challenge it (see *Home Office v Tariq* [2010] EWCA Civ 462).

(i)   independence and impartiality. The House of Lords held in *Lawal v Northern Spirit Ltd* [2003] IRLR 538 that there is a real possibility of bias where counsel appears as representative in front of a division of the EAT where he has previously sat as part-time judge with one or both wing members. The House of Lords stated that '[they] consider that the present practice in the EAT tends to undermine public confidence in the system. It should be discontinued.' Part-time judges have now been phased out.

In *Breeze Benton Solicitors v Miss A Weddell* (UKEAT/0873/03), the appeal by the solicitors' firm was based on the refusal of the employment tribunal chairman to recuse himself following previous proceedings involving the same firm and the firm's complaint concerning the chairman's conduct. The EAT said with regard to the test of bias:

(i)   that the test properly applied requires the tribunal to recuse itself if there is a real possibility of bias. If such a risk is found, the tribunal is not entitled to balance against that risk considerations of prejudice to the other party resulting from delay,

(ii)   that if in any case there is a real ground for doubt, that doubt should be resolved in favour of recusal,

(iii)   that it is no answer to a recusal application to say that the chairman was only one of three members with an equal vote, given the important position of the legally qualified and presiding member of a tribunal of three members, and

(iv)   unless he admits to the possibility of bias, the claim of the person asked to recuse himself that he will not be or is not partial is of no weight because of 'the insidious nature' of bias.

Applying these principles to the facts, the EAT concluded that the fair-minded and informed observer, having considered all the facts, would decide that there was a real possibility of bias and that the chairman should thus have recused himself; and

(j)   fairness in terms of 'equality at arms' (eg the right of both parties to present their cases without being placed at a substantial disadvantage when compared to the means of and resources available to the other party).

In *Home Office v Tariq* [2011] UKSC 35, the Supreme Court held that the use of a closed material procedure in employment tribunal proceedings is compatible with Article 6 of the European Convention and EU law. Mr Tariq was suspended from his job as an immigration officer with the Home Office after the arrest of his brother and cousin as part of a major counter-terrorism investigation. There was no suggestion that Mr Tariq had been involved in any terrorism. He brought direct and indirect discrimination claims on the grounds of race and religion. The Home Office made an application for the use of a closed material procedure, on grounds of national security. The use of the procedure would mean that Mr Tariq and his representative would be excluded from certain aspects of the proceedings. His interests would be represented by the appointment of a special advocate, who is allowed to see the material but not to tell his client about it. The Court of Appeal dismissed Mr Tariq's appeal but held that Article 6 required Mr Tariq to be provided with the gist of the allegations made against him. The Home Office appealed against that decision and Mr Tariq cross-appealed against the conclusion that a closed material procedure could be used. The Supreme Court unanimously dismissed Mr Tariq's cross-appeal and by a majority of 8:1 allowed the Home Office's appeal. It held that ECtHR case law has established that national security may require the imposition of special systems whereby a party may not be permitted to know about secret material which is protected by national security. There were sufficient safeguards in the availability of special advocates. As far as the right to know the gist of the case was concerned, the Supreme Court said that ECtHR case law provides that where the liberty of the subject is involved, Article 6 requires the gist be provided, but this case did not involve the liberty of the subject.

15.4.2   Articles 8 and 10

This provision gives a right to respect for private and family life, home and correspondence. Article 8(2) permits 'interference' by a public authority which is in accordance with the law and is necessary in a democratic society in the interests of national security, public safety or the economic well-being of the country, for the prevention of disorder or crime, for the protection of health or morals, or for the protection of the rights and freedoms of others. It is unclear the extent to which this extends to an individual's 'work' life. In *Botta v Italy* (1998) 26 EHRR 241, at para 32, the ECtHR said:

> Private life, in the court's view, includes a person's physical and psychological integrity; the guarantee afforded by [Article 8] is primarily intended to ensure the development, without outside interference, of the personality of each individual in his relations with other human beings.

See also *Niemietz v Germany* (1992) 16 EHRR 97, *Bensaid v UK* (2001) EHRR 205 and *Pretty v UK* (2002) 35 EHRR 1.

Common law in the UK has been moving towards protecting privacy through the law of confidence (see, eg, *Douglas v Hello!* [2005] EWCA Civ 595; *McKennitt v Ash* [2006] EWHC 1996; and *Browne v Associated Newspapers Ltd* [2007] EWCA Civ 295), but there is still no free-standing tort of invasion of privacy. In the employment context, Article 8 is used to protect employees' privacy. It may allow employees to challenge over-intrusive policies by employers. For example, if the employer opens 'private and confidential' mail addressed to an employee, the employee may be able to bring a claim under Article 8. If the employee is a public sector employee, he may (see **15.3.2**) have a free-standing claim under Article 8. If the employee is a private sector employee, he may be able to rely indirectly on Article 8 in an unfair dismissal or breach of contract context.

Note that Article 8 has been specifically relied upon by the courts in cases involving disabled persons (see, eg, *Price v UK* (2001) 34 EHRR 1285; *JAB and Y v East Sussex CC* [2003] EWHC 167) to recognise that the concept embraced in 'physical and psychological integrity', protected by Article 8, is the right of the disabled to participate in the life of the community.

In *Halford v UK* [1997] IRLR 471, Alison Halford, an Assistant Chief Constable with the Merseyside Police, brought an allegation that private conversations from a phone she had been given expressly for her private use had been intercepted. It was an extreme case and the ECtHR had no difficulty in finding that her rights under Article 8 had been violated.

In *Copland v UK* [2007] ECHR 253, the ECtHR held that the collection and storage by an employer of information regarding an employee's telephone, e-mail and Internet use was, in the absence of any legal provision, unjustified (but see now the Telecommunications (Lawful

Business Practice) (Interception of Communications) Regulations 2000 (SI 2000/2699), made under Regulation of Investigatory Powers Act 2000 (see **15.5.1**), which allow monitoring subject to certain conditions).

If an employer insists on pre-employment screening or testing without proper justification (eg there will be some groups of workers where there is a genuine risk that they could infect others – such as surgeons), or, for example, asks questions about whether an applicant/employee is HIV-positive, that may itself give rise to an Article 8 complaint. Article 8 may also be relevant to the question of whether employers can search their employees or test them for drugs (see *O'Flynn v Airlinks Airport Coach Company Ltd* (UKEAT/0269/01).

In *Pay v Lancashire Probation Service* [2004] IRLR 129, the EAT agreed that s 98(4) of the ERA 1996 must be read in a way which is compatible with human rights. However, on the facts, the EAT decided that because the activities the applicant was involved in (performing in fetish clubs and merchandising of products connected with bondage, domination and sado masochism; photographs were also available on the Internet of him involved in these activities) were not private, and that the interference with freedom of expression was justified, there was no infringement of the applicant's rights under Article 8 or 10 (freedom of expression) of the Convention. Mr Pay was a probation officer who worked with sex offenders. The EAT said that the interference with Article 10 was justified on the facts because of the competing interests of the employer to protect their reputation and maintain public confidence. Dismissal was a proportionate response on the facts.

In *X v Y* [2004] IRLR 625, the Court of Appeal dealt with the question of whether tribunals must take account of Convention rights (in this case Article 8) when deciding unfair dismissal claims brought against private sector employers. Mr X was a charity worker and worked with young offenders. He was arrested after a 'passing' policeman discovered him and a man he did not know 'engaging in sexual activity' in the toilets of a transport café. Mr X accepted a caution, and his name was placed on the Sex Offenders Register. Subsequently, his employers, who worked closely with the Probation Service, discovered this and dismissed him on the grounds of gross misconduct. The tribunal found the dismissal was fair. The Court of Appeal had to decide whether a tribunal, when deciding whether a dismissal is fair or unfair, was bound to have regard to the right to respect for privacy in private life. The employer here, however, was a private sector employer. The EAT did not answer the question. It got round the point by holding that Article 8 was not engaged. The EAT considered that an act of 'gross indecency', committed in a public place, which attracted a caution, was a public matter not a private one. ('We are not persuaded that transitory sexual encounters between consenting male adults in public lavatories fall within the right to respect for private life enshrined in Article 8.')

The majority of the Court of Appeal (Mummery and Dyson LJJ) agreed with the EAT that Article 8 was not engaged. Brooke LJ doubted this (on the basis that acts in a secluded room in private could be private in nature), but thought that the acceptance of the caution by Mr X subsequently removed the private aspect of it. Mummery LJ went on to state that there should be no difference in approach whether the employer is private or public sector. He described the effect of the Convention as 'oblique', rather than horizontal. He said the HRA 1998 did not give an applicant any cause of action against a respondent that was not a public authority. In this sense, he said the HRA 1998 did not have full horizontal effect. However, he said the effect of s 6 in a case involving a claim against a private employer was to reinforce the strong interpretative obligation imposed on a tribunal by s 3. By a process of interpretation, the right to privacy was 'blended' with the law on unfair dismissal, but without creating new private law causes of action against private employers.

In *Whitfield v General Medical Council* [2003] IRLR 39, the Privy Council rejected a claim for breach of Article 8 where a doctor relied on the provision in an appeal against the GMC condition that he abstain from all alcohol and submit to random testing. The doctor argued this was a breach of his right to respect for private and family life as it deprived him of the enjoyment of social drinking on family occasions. The Privy Council said that there was nothing to stop him going out and drinking soft drinks, and, moreover, that the interference was justified on public safety grounds.

In *Jones v University of Warwick* [2003] 1 WLR 954, the Court of Appeal held that evidence gathered in breach of Article 8 (secret footage of the claimant filmed in her home) was admissible as it was relevant, and so it was in the interests of justice for it to be considered.

In *McGowan v Scottish Water* [2005] IRLR 167, the employee alleged a breach of Article 8. The claimant was dismissed following covert surveillance of his house which confirmed he was falsifying time sheets. The EAT said that covert surveillance of a home 'raises at least a strong presumption that the right to have one's private life respected is being invaded'. Nevertheless, on the facts the employer was justified in its actions because it was seeking to preserve its assets and investigating a crime.

In *Hanlon v Kirklees Council* (UKEAT/0119/04) the EAT upheld the decision of a tribunal to strike out the claimant's case because he refused to consent to the disclosure of his medical records under the Access to Medical Reports Act 1988. The claimant argued that it was a breach of his right to respect for private life to have to consent. The EAT pointed out that the right to respect for private life had to be balanced against a protection for the rights of others, and in litigation the right of the other party to a fair trial was important. Striking out the claimant's case did not offend against the claimant's right to respect for private life.

Article 8 has also been used to protect the interests of homosexuals serving in the armed forces. See *Lustig Prean v UK* [1999] IRLR 734, where the ECtHR held that the applicants' discharge from the armed forces as part of a blanket ban on homosexuals infringed their right to respect for their private life. The internal investigation which was carried out prior to their discharge was also found to be a breach of Article 8. The UK Government was unable to show that either breach was necessary in a democratic society.

The landmark decision of the ECtHR on the rights of transsexuals is *Goodwin v United Kingdom* [2002] IRLR 664. The Court held that the lack of recognition in the UK of a transsexual's new gender indentity for legal purposes was a breach of Article 8 (and Article 12 – right to marry).

The issues raised by Article 8 are also reflected in two other pieces of legislation – the Regulation of Investigatory Powers Act 2000 (RIPA 2000) and the Data Protection Act 1998 (DPA 1998) (see **15.5**).

15.4.3   Articles 9 and 10

Article 9 protects freedom of thought, conscience, and religion. Article 10 gives the right to freedom of expression. Both these provisions are subject to restrictions similar to those contained in Article 8. These Articles are most likely to be relevant to, for example, employees' attendance at religious ceremonies and employers' imposition of dress codes. In terms of the latter, there would be no need for a comparison between the sexes as, under the Equality Act 2010, the issue would be simply whether the interference with the freedom could be justified by the employer (eg on health and safety grounds – but what about enhancing the employer's business reputation?). To a large extent the protection offered by Article 10 is mirrored in the Public Interest Disclosure Act 1998. Article 10 may also impact on confidentiality clauses in contracts (see also **1.8.6**).

In *Copsey v WWB Devon Clays Ltd* [2005] IRLR 811 (a case decided before the Religion and Belief Regulations 2003 came into force), the Court of Appeal considered the issue of whether and when a refusal to work on a Sunday is unfair. The case looks at the impact of Article 9 on UK unfair dismissal law. For different reasons (there are three separate judgments) the Court of Appeal held that such a dismissal was not unfair. However, the decision makes clear that employers must try to minimise the impact of changes to working hours (for example by offering alternative jobs) where employees hold strong religious beliefs.

15.4.4 Article 11

Article 11 protects the right to freedom of association, including the right to form and join a trade union, and thus is outside the scope of this book.

15.4.5 Article 14

This prohibits discrimination, but only in the context of other Convention rights (see **8.13** for more detail).

15.5 MONITORING AND DATA PROTECTION IN THE WORKPLACE

What follows is a very brief introduction.

15.5.1 Regulation of Investigatory Powers Act 2000

The RIPA 2000 implements Article 5 of the Telecommunications Data Protection Directive (97/66). While most of the Act is aimed at the security services and the State, the provisions on the interception of communications sent and received on public and private telecommunication systems are of much more general application. As far as the interception of communications is concerned, unless there is (expressly or by implication) consent (by both parties to the communication) to the interception, a criminal offence may be committed. An employer can lawfully intercept communications without consent (from both parties to the communication) only if it complies with the provisions of the Telecommunications (Lawful Business Practice) (Interception of Communications) Regulations 2000 (SI 2000/2699). The Regulations create in effect a number of 'lawful purposes' whereby employers can monitor and record communications between parties without their consent, provided that the employer has made 'all reasonable efforts to inform' every person who uses the telecommunication system that their communications may be monitored and recorded. These lawful purposes include:

(a)   creating records in case a dispute arises;

(b)   ensuring compliance with regulatory or statutory rules;

(c)   customer care;

(d)   prevention of crime and security against hackers;

(e)   investigating the unauthorised use of the telecommunications system.

In practice, the RIPA 2000 appears to have caused few problems for employers – it permits most types of surveillance, provided they are for business-related reasons.

Readers should refer to the Act and Regulations for the detail.

15.5.2 Introduction to the Data Protection Act 1998

All Member States in the EU are obliged by the European Data Protection Directive (95/46/EC) to introduce local data protection laws which provide a minimum level of protection for an individual's data. The UK enacted the Data Protection Act 1998 to implement its obligations under the Directive.

Under the DPA 1998, employers must process their employees' personal data 'fairly and lawfully' (see Sch 2 and, for sensitive data, Sch 3). Protection covers both computer-processed personal data, if the data were retrieved 'by reference to an employee', and paper-based personal records stored in filing systems 'by reference to employees or criteria relating to them'. There are wide-ranging rights for employees to receive copies of their personal files, to ask for corrections or removal of inaccuracies, and to be told why personal information about them is being kept (see below). Employers should have an identified individual who has responsibility for ensuring that the company complies with data protection requirements.

The definition of 'personal data' appears to be wide enough to cover appraisals and assessments. (There is a specific exemption for confidential references.) The Information Commissioner's Office (ICO) has issued Data Protection Technical Guidance on what constitute personal data which includes many useful examples. Readers are advised to have regard to that guidance (see www.ico.gov.uk).

The DPA 1998 imposes obligations as regards the 'processing of the data' (including notification to the ICO). This covers most of the routine personnel tasks, from the creation of personnel information to its filing, retention and storage. The Act sets out, by way of stated 'data protection principles', some basic safeguards and controls about data processing. As far as employees are concerned, these safeguards and controls mean, among other things, that personal data must be obtained only for specific and lawful purposes, must be processed fairly and lawfully, and must be kept accurate and up to date. At least one of the Sch 2 conditions must be satisfied.

There are additional and more severe restrictions on the processing of 'sensitive' personal data – this includes data about an employee's racial or ethnic origins, political beliefs, physical or mental health, or sex life, and the commission of offences. Where sensitive data is involved, at least one of the Sch 3 conditions must be met, eg explicit consent.

Employees have the right, upon request (and payment of a fee up to £10), to be told (within 40 days) whether personal data about them are being processed and, if so, to be told what the specific data are, why they are being processed and to whom they are going. The request should be in writing. The DPA 1998 provides that, when requested, a copy of the data must be provided (there are some exemptions, eg confidential references given by the data controller but not received by the data controller). This is known as a 'Subject Access Request'. If personal data on one employee contain personal data on another, that employee's permission will be needed or details may be blanked out. Personal data may include copies of appraisals, disciplinary records, sickness/holiday forms, as well as informal notes/emails passing between managers about the employee.

The Information Commissioner (who is also responsible for freedom of information under the Freedom of Information Act 2000) has responsibility for the working and policing of the DPA 1998. The Commissioner's responsibilities include the publication of codes of practice to assist those who have control of personal data.

The Information Commissioner has published Employment Practices Data Protection Code (available at www.ico.gov.uk). The Code is a consolidation of a series of four smaller guides relating to recruitment and selection, employee records, monitoring at work and workers' health records. Although the Code contains guidance and is not legally binding, it provides the benchmarks that the Commissioner will use.

The Code is accompanied by supplementary guidance that provides explanatory notes, examples and frequently asked questions (FAQs) to help readers.

A summary guide, aimed specifically at small businesses, has also been published. This outlines the key points any business should consider in order to meet its obligations under the Act.

The Employment Records part of the Code sets out the procedures (and penalties) for storing personal data about employees and job applicants, and explains when employees (and unsuccessful job applicants) may insist on obtaining copies of those records (for a £10 fee). Most of the Code deals with data collection and storage procedures.

The Monitoring at Work part of the Code provides, for example, that it will normally be intrusive to monitor workers; employers should normally carry out an impact assessment before monitoring and should be sure that the monitoring is justified by real benefits; workers should normally be told if and why they are being monitored; employers should be careful when monitoring personal communications such as e-mails which are clearly personal; employers should not undertake covert monitoring except in the rarest circumstances where there are grounds for suspecting criminal activity, it has been authorised at the highest level of the business, and where there is a risk that notifying workers of the monitoring would prejudice the prevention or detection of that criminal activity. At the heart of the Code is proportionality. Of course, monitoring will also require employers to have regard to RIPA 2000 (at **15.5.1** above).

The Code explains how the Act applies to employee references. Due to an exemption in the Act, if employers are asked to provide a copy of a confidential reference they have written, they do not *have* to provide it but *may* do so if they wish. The position is different with regard to references received from someone else, which will be covered by the normal access provisions – if these contain confidential information, employers should check with the referee.

Readers should refer to the Act and the Code for the detail.

Readers should note that as a result of the Criminal Justice and Immigration Act 2008, the ICO was given the power to impose substantial fines on organisations breaching the DPA 1998. The maximum fine must not exceed £500,000.

SUMMARY

The Human Rights Act 1998 incorporates into domestic law the European Convention for the Protection of Human Rights and Fundamental Freedoms 1950 ('the Convention'). Although the UK was already a signatory to the Convention and was therefore bound by it as a matter of international law, until the HRA 1998 came into force the Convention was not directly part of UK domestic law and individuals could not enforce Convention rights in the domestic courts (**15.1**).

Schedule 1 to the HRA 1998 sets out the relevant Convention rights which are to be protected under the Act:

- Article 6 creates a right to 'a fair and public hearing within in a reasonable time by an independent and impartial tribunal established by law'.
- Article 8 gives a right to respect for private and family life and correspondence.
- Article 9 protects freedom of thought, conscience and religion.
- Article 10 gives the right to freedom of expression.
- Article 11 protects the right to freedom of association, including the right to form and join a trade union.
- Article 14 prohibits discrimination, but only in the context of other Convention rights (**15.2**).

The important Convention rights, from an employment perspective (eg Articles 6, 8, 9 and 10), are not absolute rights but are limited by counter-balances which permit legitimate interferences with those rights in certain situations. Most human rights cases are not about whether the right exists but whether there has been an interference with the right, and whether that interference is legitimate and necessary. That will involve questions of proportionality and relevance (**15.4**).

United Kingdom courts and tribunals must (s 3) adopt a 'purposive' approach to the interpretation of UK legislation. If primary legislation is found to be incompatible with a Convention right, the HRA 1998 provides that such primary legislation remains effective but permits certain courts (the High Court and named appellate courts, but not employment tribunals or the EAT) to make (s 4) a 'declaration of incompatibility' in relation to that primary legislation, upon which Parliament may act if it wishes (15.2). (This allows for the sovereignty of Parliament to remain unchallenged.) Secondary legislation may, however, be struck down.

The Regulation of Investigatory Powers Act 2000 (RIPA 2000) is intended to implement Article 5 of the Telecommunications Data Protection Directive (97/66). As far as the interception of internal communications is concerned, unless there is (expressly or by implication) consent (by both parties to the communication) to the interception, a criminal offence may be committed. An employer may lawfully intercept external communications without consent only if it complies with the provisions of the Telecommunications (Lawful Business Practice) (Interception of Communications) Regulations 2000. The Regulations create in effect a number of 'lawful purposes' whereby employers can monitor and record communications between parties without their consent, provided that the employer has made 'all reasonable efforts to inform' every person who uses the telecommunication system that their communication may be monitored. These lawful purposes include:

(a)   creating records in case a dispute arises;

(b)   ensuring compliance with regulatory or statutory rules;

(c)   customer care;

(d)   prevention of crime and security against hackers (**15.5.1**).

The Data Protection Act 1998 (DPA 1998) attaches rights of privacy to 'collected personal data'. Protection covers both computer-processed personal data, if the data are retrieved 'by reference to an employee', and paper-based personal records stored in filing systems 'by reference to employees or criteria relating to them'. The DPA 1998 applies to the 'processing of the data'. This covers most of the routine personnel tasks, from the creation of personnel information to its filing, retention and storage. Personal data must be obtained only for specific and lawful purposes, must be processed fairly and lawfully, and must be kept accurate and up to date. There are special restrictions on the processing of 'sensitive' personal data – these include data about an employee's racial or ethnic origins, political beliefs, physical or mental health or sex life, and the commission of offences (**15.5.2**).

Employees have the right, upon request (and payment of a fee up to £10), to be told (within 40 days) whether personal data about them are being processed and, if so, to be told what the data comprise, why they are being processed and to whom they are going.

The Information Commissioner has responsibility for the working and policing of the DPA 1998. The Information Commissioner has published an Employment Practices Code, relating to recruitment and selection, employee records, monitoring at work and workers' health. Although the Code contains guidance and is not legally binding, it provides the benchmarks the Commissioner will use.

Appendix 1
Statement of Terms and Service Contract Examples

Example of Statement of Terms under the Employment Rights Act 1996, s 1

[In this example the employer is a limited company. The employee is a clerk.]

From [Employer   ]
To   [Employee   ]

This statement sets out certain particulars, as at the date of the statement of the terms and conditions of your employment which are required to be given to you under s 1 of the Employment Rights Act 1996.

1. Your employment commenced on [   ]. No employment with a previous employer counts as part of your period of continuous employment.

2. The title of your job is [   ]. [The duties which this job entails are set out in the attached job description [   ] and in addition to those duties you may be required to undertake additional or other duties as necessary to meet the needs of the business.

3. Your place of work is [   ].

4. Your remuneration is [   ] per year, payable at [   ] intervals on [   ] directly into your bank account.

5. Your normal hours of work are from [   ] to [   ] Monday to Friday inclusive. A [   ] hour break may be taken for lunch.

6. You are entitled to [   ] days paid holiday in each calendar year to be taken at times convenient to us, in addition to public holidays. During holidays you will be entitled to your normal basic remuneration. On termination of your employment your entitlement to accrued holiday pay will be in direct proportion to the length of your service during the calendar year in which termination takes place. No holidays may be taken during a period of notice.

7. You will be paid your normal remuneration during absence through sickness or injury up to a maximum [   ] weeks in any period of 12 months, provided that you supply a medical certificate in the event of any such absence for seven or more consecutive days. Such remuneration will discharge our liability to pay you Statutory Sick Pay and you will be required to give credit for any other national insurance sickness benefits payable to you as a result of such absence.

8. [You are eligible to join the [   ] pension scheme. Full details can be found in the booklet entitled [   ], a copy of which can be obtained from [   ]. A contracting out certificate is [not] in force for the employment in respect of which this statement is given.] [No pension scheme is applicable to your employment, but we shall provide you with access to a designated stakeholder pension scheme. We do [not] make contributions.]

9.1 The disciplinary rules which will apply to you are set out in the booklet entitled [   ] [a copy of which can be obtained from   ]. The rules do not form part of your contract of employment.

9.2 If you are dissatisfied with any disciplinary decision relating to you, you may appeal to [   ] for the matter to be reconsidered.

9.3   If you have any grievance relating to your employment you may seek redress by applying to [   ]. The steps consequent upon an application of this kind are set out in the booklet entitled [   ] a copy of which can be obtained from [   ]. The rules do not form part of your contract of employment.

10.1   The length of notice which you are obliged to give to us to terminate your employment is [   ].

10.2   The length of notice you are entitled to receive from us to terminate your employment is (subject to 10.3):

10.2.1 One week's notice if your period of continuous employment is less than two years.

10.2.2 One week's notice for each year of continuous employment, if your period of continuous employment is two years or more, subject to a maximum of 12 weeks' notice after 12 years' continuous employment.

10.3   You may be dismissed without notice in the event of your committing an act of gross misconduct.

11.   There is no collective agreement in force which affects your terms and conditions of employment.

Dated [   ]

Signed Employee [   ]

For and on behalf of Employer [   ].

© The College of Law 2012

Example of Service Contract

[In this example the employer is a partnership. The employee is a member of the firm's middle management. In order to avoid the necessity of a separate statement of terms, the requirements of ERA 1996, s 1 have also been included.]

THIS AGREEMENT dated [   ] [*year*] is made BETWEEN:

(1)   [   ] ('the Employer')
(2)   [   ] ('the Employee')

1. Definitions

'Business' the business carried on from time to time by the Employer

'Confidential Information' includes any trade secrets, secret manufacturing processes, technical data, know-how and all information relating to the affairs and finances of the Employer (including business contacts)

'Employment' the Employee's employment under this agreement

'Incapacity' any illness accident or similar reason preventing the Employee from properly carrying out the Employment

'Partner' any partner in the firm [   ]

'Partners' the partners for the time being of the firm [   ]

2. Job title and length of employment

2.1   Subject to clause 18, the Employer agrees to employ the Employee as [   ] from (and including) [   ].

2.2   No employment with a previous employer counts as part of the Employee's period of continuous employment with the Employer.

3. Duties

3.1   The duties which this job entails are set out in [   ] and in addition to those duties the Employee may be required to undertake additional or other duties as necessary to meet the needs of the Business.

3.2   The Employee must:

3.2.1 perform to the best of his/her ability all the duties of the job,

3.2.2 do all in his/her power to promote, develop and extend the Business,

3.2.3 comply with the reasonable directions of the Partners.

4. Place of work

4.1   The Employee's usual place of work is [   ] but the Employee may be required to work in any place which the Partners may reasonably require.

4.2   The Employee may also be required to travel on the business of the Employer anywhere within the European Union.

5. To devote full time

5.1   The Employee's normal hours are [   ] to [   ], but he/she will be expected to work whatever other hours are necessary to meet the needs of the Business.

5.2   The Employee must (unless prevented by Incapacity) devote his/her whole time and attention to the Business.

5.3   The Employee must not without the prior written consent of the Partners:

(a)   take part in any other business or employment (of whatever nature), or

(b)   except where permitted by clause 5.4, have an interest in any other business which is similar to or competes with the Business.

5.4   The Employee may have an interest in shares or other securities which are quoted on a recognised stock exchange, so long as the interest does not extend to more than 2% of the total amount of the shares or securities of the company in question.

5.5   [Working time opt out if appropriate: see **1.11.3.4**.]

6. Remuneration

6.1   The Employer agrees to pay to the Employee a salary (accruing from day to day) at the rate of [£   ] per year payable in arrear by equal monthly instalments on the 5th day of each month directly into the Employee's bank account.

6.2   The Partners must review this salary annually and may increase the salary with effect from the review date.

6.3   [PILON if appropriate: see **2.3.3**.]

7. Expenses

7.1   Subject to 7.2, the Employer agrees to repay the Employee for all reasonable hotel and other expenses wholly and exclusively incurred by him/her in the performance of the Employment.

7.2   The Employee must give the Employer receipts or other evidence of these expenses.

8. Company car

8.1   The Employer agrees to provide a car for the Employee in accordance with the Firm's car policy as published and varied by the Employer from time to time.

8.2   The Employee must:

8.2.1 take good care of the car,

8.2.2 comply with the provisions of any insurance policy relating to it, and

8.2.3 return the car and its keys to the Employer at its principal place of business (or any other place the Employer may reasonably specify) immediately upon the ending of the Employment.

9. Holidays

9.1   The Employer's holiday year runs from 1st January to 31st December.

9.2   The Employee is entitled to [   ] working days' paid holiday in each holiday year (in addition to the usual public holidays) to be taken when convenient to the Employer.

9.3   The Employee may not without the consent of the Partners carry forward any unused part of his/her holiday to a subsequent holiday year.

9.4   On termination of this employment, the Employee's entitlement to accrued holiday pay will be in direct proportion to the length of service during the calendar year in which termination takes place.

9.5   The Employee will be required to repay to the Employer pay received for holiday taken in excess of basic holiday entitlement accrued at termination.

10. Private health and permanent sickness insurance

The Employer agrees to cover the cost of the Employee's membership of an appropriate permanent sickness insurance and private patients' medical plan with such reputable insurance schemes as the Employer may decide from time to time.

11. Pension

11.1 On completion of [   ] months' employment the Employee may join the [   ] pension scheme. Details are set out in the booklet [   ]. A copy can be obtained from any Partner.

11.2 A contracting-out certificate is [not] in force in respect of this employment.

12. Confidentiality during the Employment

12.1 The Employee is aware that in the course of the Employment he/she may be given or come across Confidential Information.

12.2 The Employee must not disclose or use any Confidential Information (except in the proper course of his/her duties).

12.3 The Employee must use his/her best endeavours to prevent the disclosure of any Confidential Information.

12.4 All notes of any Confidential Information which the Employee acquires or makes during the Employment belong to the Employer. When the Employment ends (or at any time during the Employment should any Partner so request) the Employee must hand over these notes to someone duly authorised by the Partners to receive them.

13. Confidentiality after the Employment ends

After the Employment ends, the Employee must not disclose or use any of the Firm's trade secrets or any other information which is of a sufficiently high degree of confidentiality as to amount to a trade secret.

14. Unfair competition after the Employment ends

14.1 The Employer is entitled to protect its Confidential Information, its goodwill and its trade connections from any unfair competition by the Employee.

14.2 Therefore

14.2.1 For [   ] months after the Employment ends, the Employee agrees not to seek business from any person, firm or company who at any time during the [   ] months immediately preceding the ending of the Employment has been a customer of the Employer, or done business with it and with whom the Employee has had personal contact.

14.2.2 For [   ] months after the ending of the Employment, the Employee agrees not to be associated with the business of [   ]

(a) within [   ] miles of the Employer's premises at [   ] or

(b) within [   ] miles of any other premises of the Employer where the Employee was employed for at least [   ] months in the last [   ] months of the Employment.

15. Incapacity

15.1 If the Employee cannot work because of Incapacity, he/she must immediately tell a Partner. The Employee must provide a medical certificate, specifying the nature of the Incapacity and its likely duration, within eight days of the start of his/her absence and then at weekly intervals.

15.2 The Employee will be paid during absence due to Incapacity (payment to be inclusive of statutory sick pay) for a total of up to [   ] weeks in any one calendar year of the Employment.

15.3 After that, the Employee will continue to be paid salary only at the discretion of the Employer.

15.4 The Employee must inform the Employer of the amount of any social security benefit he/she receives and the Employer may deduct this from the salary paid to him/her under this clause.

16. Grievance Procedure

A copy of the current edition of the Grievance Procedure is attached. The procedure is revised by the Firm from time to time and the Employee may apply to a Partner at any time to inspect the most recent copy.

17. Disciplinary Procedure

A copy of the current edition of the disciplinary procedure affecting the Employee is attached to this agreement, although it does not form part of this contract and will not have contractual effect. The procedure is revised by the Firm from time to time and the Employee may apply to a Partner at any time to inspect the most recent edition.

18. Collective Agreement

There is no collective agreement in force which affects your terms and conditions of employment.

19. Ending the Employment

The Employer may end the Employment without notice or pay in lieu of notice in the following circumstances:

19.1 If the Employee has committed a serious or repeated breach of any of his/her obligations under this agreement or the Employer has reasonable grounds for believing he/she has done so.

20. Notice of termination

20.1 The Employee is obliged to give the Employer [   ] weeks' notice in order to terminate this contract.

20.2 The Employee is entitled to receive [   ] weeks' notice from the Employer in order to terminate his/her contract (subject to clause 19.1).

21. Notices

21.1 Notices by the Employee must be by letter addressed to the Employer at its principal place of business. Notices by the Employer must be by letter addressed to the Employee at his/her last known address in Great Britain.

21.2 Any notice given by letter will be treated as being given at the time at which the letter would be delivered in the ordinary course of second class post. Any notice delivered by hand will be treated as being given upon delivery. In proving service by post it will be enough to prove that the notice was properly addressed and posted.

SIGNED by ....

In signing this, the Employee acknowledges and confirms that s/he agrees that these terms constitute his/her contract of employment with the Employer.

© The College of Law 2012

[Note: This is not an exhaustive list. Increasingly contracts may include clauses relating to e-mail and Internet use (in order to comply with the requirements of notice under the Telecommunications (Lawful Business Practice) (Interception and Communications) Regulations 2000), records and monitoring, garden leave, bonuses, whistleblowing, equal opportunities, health and safety, maternity, flexible working, etc. Consideration must be given as to whether such terms are to be contractual or not.]

Appendix 2
Case Study

Employment Tribunals Claim Form

This interactive form enables you to make a claim to an Employment Tribunal by completing and editing the form offline. You can save a part of fully completed form, email a saved form to another person to amend or for approval, and submit it securely online to the Employment Tribunals. Please make sure you have read the guidance notes on our website on how to make a claim before you fill in the form. We are unable to accept any attachments included or sent with this form.

Multiple Claims – If this claim is one of a number of claims arising out of the same or similar circumstances please fill in a claim form for the first claimant and then give the other claimants on the multiple form (maximum 28 claims). If more than 28 claims need to be submitted please create a multiple claims .csv file.
For guidelines please click here http://www.employmenttribunals.gov.uk/multiple/index.htm, enter the details in the correct column and attach the .csv file to this form below before submitting this claim form.

For Claimants in England and Wales - If someone is advising or representing you in relation to your claim, they must, unless they are a practising solicitor or barrister, be authorised to do so, wherever they are based (including Scotland, the Channel Islands and all of Europe). Trade Union officials, Citizens' Advice Bureau advisors or a personal friend helping you present your claim may be exempted from these requirements. However, to check your representatives status, and for more information, telephone 0845 450 6858 or go to www.claimsregulation.gov.uk

Select the type of claim you wish to make:

- ✔ I want to make a claim.
- ☐ I want to make a claim on behalf of more than one person.

Select the reason(s) for the claim:

- ✔ Unfair dismissal or constructive dismissal
- ☐ Discrimination
- ☐ Redundancy payments
- ☐ Other payments you are owed
- ☐ Other complaints

| Email to client | Save | Print | Clear | New | Start Claim ↑ |

Need Help?
If you require any help completing your form or have a general question about the tribunals process please contact the Employment Tribunals Enquiry Line on **08457 959 775** or minicom **08457 573 722** between 9am and 5pm Monday to Friday (closed on Bank Holidays).

If you require technical support please click below to email us.

Support Request

We regret we cannot provide any legal advice.

Please Note:
By law, your claim must be submitted using an approved form supplied by the Employment Tribunals (We are unable to accept any attachments included or sent with the form except for .csv file templates issued with multiple claims from our website), and you must provide the information marked with * and, if it is relevant, the information needed with (see' Information needed before a claim can be accepted')

General Information:
Once you have completed your form you can submit it securely on-line to the TS. On-line forms are processed faster than those sent by post.

1 Your details

1.1	Title:	Mr ✔	Mrs	Miss	Ms	Other

1.2* First name (or names): **James**

1.3* Surname or family name: **Gold**

1.4 Date of birth (date/month/year): **30/06/1956**   Are you: male? ✔ female?

1.5* Address:
- Number or Name: **12**
- Street: **Douglas Crescent**
- Town/City:
- County: **Guildshire**
- Postcode: **GU12**

1.6 Phone number including area code (where we can contact you in the day time): **01111 123456**

Mobile number (if different):

1.7 How would you prefer us to communicate with you? (Please tick only one box)   E-mail ✔   Post

E-mail address: **james.gold@hotmail123.com**

2 Respondent's details

2.1* Give the name of your employer or the organisation you are claiming against. **Car Parking PLC**

2.2* Address:
- Number or Name: **The Business Centre**
- Street:
- Town/City:
- County: **Guildshire**
- Postcode: **GU12**

Phone number: **020 8123 1234**

2.3● If you worked at a different address from the one you have given at 2.2, please give the full address and postcode.

Postcode

Phone number:

If there are other respondents please complete **Section 11.**

3 Employment details

3.1 Please give the following information if possible.

When did your employment start? `10/10/2009`

Is your employment continuing? Yes ☐ No ✔

If your employment has ceased, or you are in
a period of notice, when did it, or will it, end? `30/04/2011`

3.2 Please say what job you do or did.

Team Leader

4 Earnings and benefits

4.1 How many hours on average do, or did, you work each week? `40` hours each week

4.2 How much are, or were, you paid?

Pay before tax £ `1916` .00   Hourly ☐

Weekly ☐

Normal take-home pay (including £ `1482` .00   Monthly ✔
overtime, commission, bonuses and so on)

Yearly ☐

4.3 If your employment has ended, did you work
(or were you paid for) a period of notice?   Yes ✔   No ☐

If 'Yes', how many weeks' or months' notice
did you work, or were you paid for? `2` weeks ☐ months

4.4 Were you in your employer's pension scheme?   Yes ☐   No ✔

Please answer 4.5 to 4.9 if your claim, or part of it, is about unfair or constructive dismissal.

4.5 If you received any other benefits, e.g. company car, medical insurance, etc, from your
employer, please give details.

4.6 Since leaving your employment have you got another job?   Yes ☐   No ✔
If 'No', please now go straight to section 4.9.

4.7 Please say when you started (or will start) work.

4.8   Please say how much you are now earning (or will earn). £ ☐ .00 each ☐

4.9   Please tick the box to say what you want if your case is successful:

   a   To get your old job back and compensation (reinstatement) ☐

   b   To get another job with the same employer and compensation (re-engagement) ☐

   c   Compensation only ☐

5   Your claim

5.1* Please tick one or more of the boxes below. In the space provided, describe the event, or series of events, that have caused you to make this claim:

   a   I was unfairly dismissed (including constructive dismissal)   ✔

   b   I was discriminated against on the grounds of

   Sex (including equal pay) ☐   Race ☐

   Disability ☐   Religion or belief ☐

   Sexual orientation ☐   Age ☐

   c   I am claiming a redundancy payment ☐

   d   I am owed   notice pay ☐

                                         holiday pay ☐

                                         arrears of pay ☐

                                         other payments ☐

   e   Other complaints ☐

5.2* Please set out the background and details of your claim in the space below.
      The details of your claim should include **the date when the event(s) you are complaining about happened**; for example, if your claim relates to discrimination give the dates of all the incidents you are complaining about, or at least the date of the last incident. If your complaint is about payments you are owed please give the dates of the period covered. Please use the blank sheet at the end of the form if needed.

   Please see attached Statement of Case.

5.3 If your claim consists of, or includes, a claim that you are making a protected disclosure under the Employment Rights Act 1996 (otherwise known as a 'whistleblowing' claim), please tick the box below if you wish a copy of this form, or information from it, to be forwarded on your behalf to a relevant regulator (known as a 'prescribed person' under the relevant legislation) by the Tribunals Service.

6 What compensation or remedy are you seeking?

6.1 Completion of this section is optional, but may help if you state what compensation or remedy you are seeking from your employer as a result of this complaint. If you specify an amount, please explain how you have calculated that figure.

Compensation

7 Other information

7.1 Please do not send a covering letter with this form. You should add any extra information you want us to know here. Please use the blank sheet at the end of the form if needed.

8 Your representative

Please fill in this section only if you have appointed a representative. If you do fill in this section, we will in future only send correspondence to your representative and not to you.

8.1 Representative's name:	Fred Mclean
8.2 Name of the representative's organisation:	Collaws Solicitors LLP

8.3 Address:

Number or Name	20 The Street
Street	
+ Town/City	
County	Guildshire
Postcode	GU12

8.4 Phone number (including area code):	07777 123456
Mobile number (if different):	
8.5 Reference:	FM/JG

8.6 How would they prefer us to communicate with them?
(Please tick only one box)

E-mail ✔   Post ☐

E-mail address: fm@collaws.co.uk

9 Disability

9.1 Please tick this box if you consider you have a disability   Yes ☐
Please say what this disability is and tell us what assistance, if any, you will need as your claim progresses through the system, including for any hearings that may need to be held at Tribunal Service premises.

10 Multiple cases

10.1 To your knowledge, is your claim one of a number of claims against the same employer arising from the same, or similar, circumstances?   Yes ☐   No ✔

11 Details of Additional Respondents

- Name of your employer or the organisation you are claiming against.

- Address: Number or Name

 Street

 + Town/City

 County

 Postcode

 Phone number:

- Name of your employer or the organisation you are claiming against.

- Address: Number or Name

 Street

 + Town/City

 County

 Postcode

 Phone number:

- Name of your employer or the organisation you are claiming against.

- Address: Number or Name

 Street

 + Town/City

 County

 Postcode

 Phone number:

Please read the form and check you have entered all the relevant information. Once you are satisfied, please tick this box.

Data Protection Act 1998. We will send a copy of this form to the respondent(s) and Acas. We will, if your claim consists of, or includes, a claim that you have made a protected disclosure under the Employment Rights Act 1996 (and you have given your consent that we should do so) send a copy of the form, or extracts from it, to the relevant regulator. We will put the information you give us on this form onto a computer. This helps us to monitor progress and produce statistics. Information provided on this form is passed to the Department for Business, Innovation and Skills to assist research into the use and effectiveness of employment tribunals.

Additional information for sections 5.2 and 7.

Equal Opportunities Monitoring Form

You are not obliged to fill in this section but, if you do so, it will enable us to monitor our processes and ensure that we provide equality of opportunity to all. The information you give here will be treated in strict confidence and this page will not form part of your case. It will be used only for monitoring and research purposes without identifying you.

1. What is your country of birth?
- ✔ England
- Wales
- Scotland
- Northern Ireland
- Republic of Ireland
- Elsewhere, *please write in the present name of the country*

2. What is your ethnic group?
Choose ONE section from A to E, then ✓ the appropriate box to indicate your cultural background.

A White
- ✔ British
- Irish
- Any other White background *please write in*

B Mixed
- White and Black Caribbean
- White and Black African
- White and Asian
- Any other Mixed background *please write in*

C Asian or Asian British
- Indian
- Pakistani
- Bangladeshi
- Any other Asian background *please write in*

D: Black or Black British
- Caribbean
- African
- Any other Black background *please write in*

E Chinese or other ethnic group
- Chinese
- Any other, *please write in*

3. What is your religion?
✓ box only
- ✔ None
- Christian (including Church of England, Catholic, Protestant and all other Christian denominations)
- Buddhist
- Hindu
- Jewish
- Muslim
- Sikh
- Any other religion, *please write in*

4. Sexual orientation
Which of these best describes you?
✓ box only
- ✔ Heterosexual
- Gay or lesbian or homosexual
- Bisexual
- Other

5. Disability
Do you have any health problems or disabilities that you expect will last for more than a year?
✓ box only
- Yes
- ✔ No

Click Here to return to the Home page when you have finished completing the form

Copy 1

Employment Tribunals - Multiple Claim Form

Please use this form if you wish to present two or more claims which arise from the same set of facts. Use additional sheets if necessary.

The following claimants are represented by [＿＿＿＿＿＿] (if applicable) and the relevant required information for all the additional claimants is the same as stated in the main claim of

[＿＿＿＿＿＿＿＿＿＿＿＿＿＿＿＿＿＿＿＿＿＿] V

[＿＿＿＿＿＿＿＿＿＿＿＿＿＿＿＿＿＿＿＿＿＿＿]

[＿＿＿＿＿＿＿＿＿＿＿＿＿＿＿＿＿＿＿＿＿＿＿]

Title	
First name (or names)	
Surname or family name	
Date of birth	
Number or Name	
Street	
Town/City	
County	
Postcode	

Title	
First name (or names)	
Surname or family name	
Date of birth	
Number or Name	
Street	
Town/City	
County	
Postcode	

Title	
First name (or names)	
Surname or family name	
Date of birth	
Number or Name	
Street	
Town/City	
County	
Postcode	

IN THE Guildshire Employment Tribunal

Case Number XXXXXX/2011

Mr J Gold (Claimant)

v

Car Parking PLC (Respondent)

Originating Application – Statement of Case

1. The Claimant was employed by the respondent as a Team Leader based at the Guildshire car park.

2. He started working in this role in December 2009. He was dismissed on the grounds of redundancy on the 30th April 2011.

3. The Claimant does not accept that there was a genuine redundancy situation and understands that a new employee is currently employed in his role at the car park.

4. The Claimant further argues that the selection criteria were unfair in that his level of experience and expertise was underscored.

5. He appealed his dismissal but was unsuccessful in the appeal which was heard on the 20th April 2011. The Claimant only saw the scoring for the first time after the appeal so he didn't have an opportunity to contest the score before the appeal, or at the appeal. The scoring was only forwarded to him after the appeal hearing was adjourned. The Claimant expected to return to the appeal to raise his complaints but this didn't happen and he received a letter confirming his dismissal. The Claimant has worked previously for the respondent for a number of years and was Tupe'd out to a different employer. He has worked in this industry for approximately 4 years. He argues the procedure adopted was unfair and predetermined.

6. On viewing the score he was horrified to see he had been scored 1 for his skills for the current position and job. He had no performance issues and had a good appraisal. There was simply no justification to score him one meaning 'not acceptable'.

7. In conclusion the respondent did not allow the claimant the opportunity to contest his scores. They concluded the appeal then sent him his score, and when he saw his score he found that the score was unfair and didn't reflect his skills and ability. The Claimant had no performance issues and was never advised that his performance was below par. He would have expected to score 4 'good' and not 1.

8. His comparators in the pool were 3. The Claimant asked for an alternative role locally. He was aware that two members of staff in a more junior role were leaving. His request was ignored by the contractor manager. These jobs were given to two more junior staff with no rail experience at all; they were only used to off street car parks. The machinery and procedures are very different in the rail track contract sites. The Claimant could easily have done either role. The respondents offered a junior role miles from his home and on less pay.

EMPLOYMENT TRIBUNALS

To: Car Parking PLC

e-mail: GuildshireET@tribunals.gsi.gov.uk

Case Number: 123456/2011

Mr J Gold	Claimant

v

Car Parking PLC	Respondent

NOTICE OF A CLAIM

The Claim

The Employment Tribunal has accepted a claim for unfair dismissal against the above respondent. It has been given the above Case Number, which should be quoted in any communication relating to this case.

A copy of the claim is enclosed for the respondent.

The Response

To submit a response, a prescribed form must be used. Alternatively you may respond on-line at www.employmenttribunals.gov.uk. It must be received at this office by 26/07/2011. If a response is not received by then, and no extension of time has been applied for and given, the claim will proceed undefended, or a default judgment may be made.

Acas

Acas (whose services are free) may be able to help the parties resolve the matter at any time.

Representative

If you appoint a representative to act for you, please pass these documents to your representative as soon as possible. You remain responsible for ensuring that the representative deals with all matters promptly.

Enclosures

A copy of the claim

A prescribed response form

A copy of the booklet 'Responding to a claim' can be found on our website at www.employmenttribunals.gov.uk/Publications/publications.htm

If you do not have access to the internet, paper copies can be obtained by telephoning the tribunal office dealing with the claim

Signed *D Smith*

D SMITH

For the Secretary of Employment Tribunals

Guildshire ET

Dated: 28 June 2011

cc   Acas

RESPONSE TO AN EMPLOYMENT TRIBUNAL CLAIM

In the claim of:

Mr J Gold

-v-

Car Parking PLC

Case Number: 123456/2011
(please quote this in all correspondence)

This requires your immediate attention. If you want to resist the claim made against you, you must use the prescribed response form. Your completed form must reach the tribunal office within 28 days of the date of the attached Notice. If the form does not reach us by 26/07/2011 you will not be able to take part in the proceedings and a default judgment may be entered against you.

Please read the guidance notes and the notes on this page carefully **before** filling in this form.

By law, you **must** provide the information marked with ⋆ and, if it is relevant, the information marked with • (see guidance on Pre-acceptance procedure).

Please make sure that all the information you give is as accurate as possible.

Where there are tick boxes, please tick the one that applies.

If you fax the form, do not send a copy in the post.

You must return the full form, including this page, to the tribunal office.

ET3

Employment Tribunals Response Form

You can make a response to an Employment Tribunal by completing and editing the form offline. You can save a part or fully completed form, email a saved form to another person to amend or for approval, and submit it securely online to the Employment Tribunal Service.

Please make sure you have read the guidance notes on our website or in our booklet on how to make a response before you fill in the form.

In order to proceed you must enter the case number and names of the parties printed on the form and letter we sent you.

Case number   123456/2011

Names of parties   MR J GOLD
v   CAR PARKING PLC

Tribunal office dealing with claim   --please select--

Need Help?

If you require any help completing your form or have a general question about the tribunals process please contact the Employment Tribunals Enquiry Line on

0845 795 9775

minicom 08457 573 722

between 9 am and 5 pm Monday to Friday, our lines are closed on Bank Holidays.

If you require technical support please click below to email us.

Support Request

We regret we cannot provide any legal advice.

Please Note:

By law, your claim must be submitted using an approved form supplied by the Employment Tribunals Service, and you must provide the information marked with ★ and, if it is relevant, the information marked with ● (see 'Information needed before a claim can be accepted')

General Information:

Once you have completed your form you can submit it securely on-line to the ETS. On-line forms are processed faster than those sent by post.

Print   New   Continue ➔

POWERED by legatio

Version 7.4

Case number: 123456/2011

1 Claimant's name

1.1	Claimant's name:	J Gold

2 Respondent's details

2.1* Name of Individual, Company or Organisation — Car Parking PLC

Contact name: Ms J Price

2.2* Address:

Number or Name	
Street	The Business Centre
+ Town/City	
County	Guildshire
Postcode	GU12

2.3 Phone number including area code (**where we can contact you in the day time**): 01234 567789

Mobile number (**if different**):

2.4 How would you prefer us to communicate with you? (Please tick only one box)

E-mail ✔   Post

E-mail address: j.price@carparkingplc.co.uk

2.5 What does this organisation mainly make or do?

car parking

2.6 How many people does this organisation employ in Great Britain? 1500

2.7 Does this organisation have more than one site in Great Britain? Yes ✔   No

2.8 If 'Yes', how many people are employed at the place where the claimant worked? 8

3 Employment details

3.1 Are the dates of employment given by the claimant correct? Yes   No ✔
If 'Yes', please now go straight to section 3.3.

3.2 If 'No', please give dates and say why you disagree with the dates given by the claimant.

When their employment started	09-11-2009
When their employment ended or will end	30-04-2011

3   Employment details (continued)

Is their employment continuing?   Yes ☐   No ✔
I disagree with the dates for the following reasons.

Start date was incorrect

3.3   Is the claimant's description of their job or job title correct?   Yes ✔   No ☐
If 'Yes', please now go straight to section 4

3.4   If 'No', please give the details you believe to be correct below.

4   Earnings and benefits

4.1   Are the claimant's hours of work correct?   Yes ✔   No ☐

If 'No', please enter the details you believe to be correct.   ☐ hours each week

4.2   Are the earnings details given by the claimant correct?   Yes ✔   No ☐
If 'Yes', please now go straight to section 4.3

If 'No', please give the details you believe to be correct below.

		Hourly ☐
Pay before tax	£ _____ .00	Weekly ☐
Normal take-home pay (including overtime, commission, bonuses and so on)	£ _____ .00	Monthly ☐ Yearly ☐

4.3   Is the information given by the claimant correct about being   Yes ✔   No ☐
paid for, or working, a period of notice?
If 'Yes', please now go straight to section 4.4

If 'No', please give the details you believe to be correct below. If you gave them no notice
or didn't pay them instead of letting them work their notice, please explain what happened
and why.

4.4   Are the details about pension and other benefits,   Yes ✔   No ☐
e.g. company car, medical insurance, etc, given by the claimant correct?
If 'Yes', please now go straight to section 5.

If 'No', please give the details you believe to be correct below.

5 Response

5.1* Do you resist the claim?   Yes ✔   No ☐
   If 'No', please now go straight to section 6.

5.2● If 'Yes', please set out in full the grounds on which you resist the claim.

Please see additional notes page

6   Other information

6.1   Please do not send a covering letter with this form. You should add any extra information
you want us to know here.

7   Your representative   If you have a representative, please fill in the following.

7.1	Representative's name:	V Alavy
7.2	Name of the representative's organisation:	Swallows & Co LLP
7.3	Address: Number or Name	12 High Street
	Street	
	+ Town/City	
	County	Guildshire
	Postcode	GU12
7.4	Phone number:	01999 234567
7.5	Reference:	
7.6	How would you prefer us to communicate with them? (Please tick only one box)	E-mail ✔ Post
	E-mail address:	v.alavy@swallows.co.uk

**Please read the form and check you have entered all the relevant information.
Once you are satisfied, please tick this box.**   ✔

ET3 v03 004   ET3 v03 004

Additional space for notes.

Mr J Gold v Car Parks PLC
Case number: 123456/2011

Statement of response

The respondent is the UK's leading provider of 'off-street' parking services. It has approximately 1,500 employees. The claimant worked as a Team Leader at its car parks in Guildshire, where about 8 people work. The Claimant was employed from 9th November 2009 until 30th April 2011, when he was dismissed by reason of redundancy.

The Claimant's claims are denied in their entirety.

On 16th February 2011, the Claimant and his colleagues were invited to a meeting on 21st February 2011 about proposed changes to the workplace.

The Respondent operated what was known as the 'First Contract' at 3 railway stations. There were three Team Leaders, including the Claimant. In order to increase focus and accountability and to reduce the overhead cost, the business proposed to reduce the Team Leaders to two, who would be expected to cover the three stations. The three Team Leaders were told of the proposal and were informed that they were at risk of redundancy and would be consulted severally.

Martin Smith, the Contract Manager, and Jack Tawse, from the Human Resources department, conducted the first consultation with the Claimant on 23rd February 2011. The restructuring proposed was discussed, along with the process of consultation and selection. The Claimant was told that a process of selection would determine which one of the three Team Leaders would be at risk of redundancy. The Claimant had no question or comment.

A second consultative meeting took place with the Claimant on 7th March 2011. The Claimant was asked whether he had any questions or comments. He did not. He was given estimates of the payments that he would receive if he were made redundant. He was told about the internal vacancies. The Claimant had no questions outstanding.

A third meeting took place on 22nd March 2011. The Claimant again had no comments or questions.

So, on 22nd March 2011, Martin Smith undertook to score the Claimant and his two colleagues against the following criteria:

Skills for the current position/job
Performance
Skills for other positions/jobs with Car Parks PLC
Length of service
Disciplinary record

They were rated as follows:

Not acceptable/incomplete 1
Acceptable 2
Good 4
Exceptional 5

The Claimant scored 16.

The Claimant's colleagues scored 18 and 24

Unfortunately the Claimant's experience was at one of the three sites only. The other two Team Leaders had experience at the other sites.

At the next consultative meeting on 25th March 2011 the Claimant was told that, because he had recorded the lowest score, he was at risk of redundancy. He was served with the notice that his employment would be terminated on 30th April 2011, unless alternative employment could be found.

The Claimant was sent the company's weekly bulletin of internal vacancies and asked to indicate any that were of interest.

Additional space for notes.

This was confirmed to the Claimant in writing, including the Claimant's right of appeal, on 25th March 2011.

The Claimant was off sick from 1st April 2011.

The Claimant appealed by letters dated 5th April 2011 and 11th April 2011. He said that:

1 he had shown unquestionable loyalty
2 he carried out all instructions, often going beyond what was asked of him
3 he had built a strong team in the site where he worked
4 he had had to query why a number of his staff were not receiving their expenses, some of which were outstanding
5 he had supported the staff team at night and at weekends when proper cover could not be found
6 he had been working 'on-call' without receiving any payment
7 he had not been shown the scoring process
8 he thought that there would be more work not less, so could not understand the reduction in the staff.

Alan Savage, the Head of Operations, conducted the appeal hearing on 20th April 2011. Jack Tawse was present. The Claimant confirmed that he was satisfied with the process, but his main concern was not having received details of what he scored. These were given to him.

On appeal, the dismissal was upheld. Unfortunately, no alternative employment acceptable to the Claimant could be found.

Before the employment tribunal the Respondent will argue:

– that was a genuine reason for the redundancy
– that the selection process was fair
– that the dismissal of the Claimant by reason of redundancy was fair and reasonable in all the circumstances
– that, contrary to his assertion, the Claimant has not been 'replaced',

EMPLOYMENT TRIBUNALS

Case No. 123456/2011

Mr J Gold	**Claimant**
v	
Car Parking PLC	**Respondent**

ORDER FOR DIRECTIONS

An Employment Judge has directed that:

1   This case will be given a one day hearing.

1.1   The parties are required to prepare and present their cases to enable the Tribunal to deal with all the issues, and remedy if applicable, in that time.

1.2   You **must** inform the Tribunal **immediately** if you believe the hearing date, time or length is not appropriate and, if so, give detailed reasons why.

2   No later than **8 September 2011** the Claimant **must** send a **Schedule of Loss** to the Respondent and the Tribunal.

3   No later than **20 September 2011** each party **must** send to each other party a **copy of any document** it has relevant to the claims in the proceedings.

4   The parties **must** agree **a bundle** of **documents** for the tribunal hearing. The [First] Respondent **must** ensure that **six copies of the bundle** are available at the tribunal hearing.

5   <u>**No documents or copy correspondence should be sent to the Tribunal before the hearing date unless a party is required to do so.**</u>

6   Each party must prepare **six copies of a written witness statement** for each person who is to give evidence at the hearing. This includes the Claimant and any personal Respondent. The statements will normally be read aloud at the hearing and the person will then be questioned about the contents.

7   The statement shall contain **all** of that person's evidence. No person can give evidence without a statement unless the Tribunal agrees.

8   **Not later than 14 days before the hearing** there shall be simultaneous exchange of witness statements by each party providing to each other party one copy of each witness statement.

<u>**GUIDANCE ON THE ABOVE ORDERS IS GIVEN BELOW**</u>

GUIDANCE

Schedule of Loss

1   A Schedule of Loss **must** set out the money you want as compensation for each part of your claim and the way it has been calculated. You may find it helpful to use a spreadsheet program.

Documents

2   'Documents' includes letters, notes, emails, memos, diary entries, audio or visual recordings, text messages and any other legible records.

3   If extensive hand-written document/s are being relied on a typescript **must** be provided by the party relying on the document/s.

4   If a recording is being relied on a transcript **must** be prepared by the party relying on it. That typescript **must** be included in the bundle and sent to any other party, together with a copy of the recording.

Bundles of Documents

5   The bundle **must** contain a copy of any relevant document any party intends to use at the Tribunal hearing. Two-sided copying is encouraged.

6   The parties **must** agree on the inclusion of only relevant extracts of lengthy documents. A full copy of such a document should be brought to the Hearing.

7   All the documents **must** be in date order, with the oldest at the front.

8   Each page **must** be numbered.

9   The bundle **must** have an index showing the date, description and page number of each document.

10   The bundle **must** be held together so it opens flat.

11   Witness statements **must not** be included in a bundle.

Witness Statements

12   Each witness statement **must**:

12.1   have page numbers, be typed single-sided with double line spacing with at least 2.5cm page margins;

12.2   use a 'standard' (e.g. Arial, Times New Roman or similar) size 12 font;

12.3   contain **all** the evidence of the witness;

12.4   be laid out in short consecutively **numbered** paragraphs;

12.5   set out **in chronological order,** with dates, the facts which the witness can state;

12.6   not contain matters irrelevant to the issues;

12.7   refer **by page number in the bundle of documents** to any document mentioned in the statement;

12.8   be signed and dated;

12.9   not be contained in a bundle.

NOTES

1   Failure to comply with an Order for DISCOVERY/INSPECTION may result on summary conviction in a fine of up to £1,000 being imposed upon a person in default under section 7(4) of the Employment Tribunals Act 1996.

2   If a person does not comply with Orders made under the Employment Tribunals Rules of Procedure, rule 8 of the Employment Tribunals (Levy Appeals) Rules of Procedure or rule 7 of the Employment Tribunals (Health and Safety – Appeals against Improvement and Prohibition Notices) Rules of Procedure an Employment Judge or Tribunal may:

2.1   make an order in respect of costs or preparation time (if applicable) under rules 38 to 46; or

2.2   at a pre-hearing review or a Hearing make an order to strike out the whole or part of the claim or, as the case may be, the response and, where appropriate, order that a respondent be debarred from responding to the claim altogether.

3   The Tribunal may also make a further Order (an 'Unless Order') providing that unless it is complied with, the claim or, as the case may be, the response shall be struck out on the date of non-compliance without further consideration of the proceedings or the need to give notice under rule 19 or hold a pre-hearing review or a Hearing.

4   An Order may be varied or revoked upon application by a person affected by the Order or by an Employment Judge on his own initiative.

Dated: 18 August 2011

Employment Judge

ORDER SENT TO THE PARTIES ON

.......19 August 2011........

....

FOR THE SECRETARY OF EMPLOYMENT TRIBUNALS

[Guildshire Employment Tribunal]

To: Mr Fred Mclean
       Collaws Solicitors LLP
       20 The Street, Guildshire, GU12

       V Alavy
       Swallows & Co LLP
       12 High Street, Guildshire GU12

Cc: Acas

EMPLOYMENT TRIBUNALS

To: Mr Fred Mclean
Collaws Solicitors LLP
20 The Street, Guildshire, GU12

V Alavy
Swallows & Co LLP
12 High Street, Guildshire GU12

Case Number: 123456/2011

<table>
<tr><td align="center">**Mr J Gold**</td><td align="right">Claimant</td></tr>
<tr><td align="center">v</td><td></td></tr>
<tr><td align="center">**Car Parking PLC**</td><td align="right">Respondent</td></tr>
</table>

NOTICE OF HEARING
Employment Tribunals Rules of Procedure 2004

The claim will be heard by an Employment Tribunal at **Guildshire House, Guildshire,** on **Thursday, 27 October 2011** at **10:00 am** or as soon thereafter on that day as the Tribunal can hear it. The Tribunal may transfer your case at short notice to be heard at another hearing centre within the region.

The Hearing has been allocated **1 day** including remedy, if appropriate. If you think that is not long enough, you must give your reasons, in writing, and your time estimate within 14 days of this Notice.

Unless there are exceptional circumstances, no application for a postponement will be granted. Any such application must be in writing. The application should include any dates agreed for re-listing the case or should advise the Tribunal of your unavailable dates within two months of the original Hearing.

You may submit written representations for consideration at the hearing. If so, they must be sent to the tribunal and to all other parties not less than 7 days before the hearing. You will have the chance to put forward oral arguments in any case.

It is your responsibility to make sure that your witnesses come to the Hearing.

You must comply with any Case Management Order issued in relation to this case and refer to the guidance in the booklet 'The hearing'.

A copy of the booklet 'The hearing' and expenses leaflet can be found on our website at www.employmenttribunals.gov.uk/Publications/publications.htm

A location map for the office can be found at wwwv.employmenttribunals.gov.uk/ HearingCentres/hearingCentres.htm

If you do not have access to the Internet, paper copies can be obtained by telephoning the tribunal office dealing with the claim.

To   Mr Fred Mclean
      Collaws Solicitors LLP
      20 The Street, Guildshire, GU12

and

      V Alavy
      Swallows & Co LLP
      12 High Street, Guildshire GU12   Signed R Drummond
                                                  For the Secretary of Employment Tribunals

      Dated: 19 August 2011

cc   Acas

Mr J Gold v Car Parking PLC

Case number: 123456/2011

SCHEDULE OF DOCUMENTS

Page	Description	Number of sheets
	Tribunal Papers	
1–11	Claim	11
12–18	Response	7
19–21	Order for Directions	3
22–23	Notice of Hearing	2
	Documents	
24–26	Offer letter dated 6th November 2009	3
27	Letter to the Claimant dated 16th February 2011	1
28	Announcement	1
29	Letter to the Claimant dated 21st February 2011	1
30–33	Notes of first meeting dated 23rd February 2011	4
34	Letter to the Claimant dated 25th February 2011	1
35	Notes of second meeting dated 7th March 2011	1
36	Letter to the Claimant dated 17th March 2011	1
37	Notes of third meeting dated 22nd March 2011	1
38–39	Blank criteria for selection	2
40–42	Criteria for selection – the Claimant	3
43–46	Criteria for selection – others	4
47	Letter to the Claimant dated 23rd March 2011	1
48	Letter to the Claimant dated 25th March 2011	1
49	Letter to the Claimant dated 25th March 2011	1
50–51	Fit note dated 1st April 2011	2
52	Letter from the Claimant dated 5th April 2011	1
53	Letter to the Claimant dated 6th April 2011	1
54	Letter from the Claimant dated 11th April 2011	1
55	Letter to the Claimant dated 15th April 2011	1
56–57	Fit note dated 18th April 2011	2
58 – 61	Letter to the Claimant dated 20th April 2011	4
62–64	Document headed 'Monday to Friday 17.00–08,00 (if no team leader)'	3
	Remedy	
65	Schedule of loss	1
66–94	Evidence of job searching	29
95–112	Payslips	18

Guildshire Employment Tribunal

Case Number 123456/2011

Mr John Gold (Claimant)

v

Car Parking PLC (Respondent)

CLAIMANT'S WITNESS STATEMENT

1.   Prior to commencing employment with the respondent, I was in the army for 10 years. I was employed for 8 years of this in the transport section. I joined Car Parking PLC in March 2007 on the network rail contract; that contract covered 4 mainline stations and I was employed as a team leader managing 17 staff. I was transferred under the TUPE rules to a different employer in 2008. I remained in this role until I was made redundant in July 2009. This information is relevant because it shows I had previous service with the company with more responsibility and it also shows a degree of management experience and flexibility. I had 4 years experience managing staff in car parks.

2.   I started working for the respondents as a team leader at the Guildshire Car Park. Guildshire is an International Station and as such the role and nature of the duties differed to that of the normal shopping type car park. There are security issues because of customs and immigration, there are terrorist issues and there is liaison with lots of other agencies. I commenced my employment in November 2009. I refer to my contractual offer letter (p 24-26). This is not accurate. I received this document having already started work.

3.   The machinery and equipment differed, it was antiquated and prone to breakdowns, the staff were expected to provide more information to customers utilising the service, the staff had to be on the concourse near the car park machines to assist passengers to pay for their parking, car-parking could also be for longer periods than normal. There are two external car parks with 300 plus spaces. Then there is a six floors multi-storey car park with about 1200 spaces. The car parks are linked to the station. The car park is manned 24 hours a day all year round. There are two staff on days and two on nights. Other staff are on rest days and holidays. I covered a forty plus hours shift covering as and when required. I was on call when I was not working.

4.   I was in charge of 8 staff based at this large car park. The car park is very busy and I certainly considered that I was busy and that the role I performed did not cease or diminish.

5.   The normal car parks in Guildshire operate not on a 24 hour basis and they are closed in the evenings, they are primarily for shopping centre users and 9 to 5 staff working in the city centre.

6.   On 16th February I received a letter (p 27). The letter invited me to attend a briefing. At this briefing I would then refer to the announcement document and point out that in this document it states 'we will comply fully with all our obligations for consultation'. The document also says that they will answer **'any questions or challenges which you may have'**. On 21st February the 30 day consultation started. I now refer to the various notes regarding the meetings. You will note that I am not provided any great detail on why the business has decided to remove my post. I am aware that I am entering an assessment process. I now refer to the selection criteria for the surviving positions. I do not recall seeing the criteria at all during the process. Looking at the criteria now under skills for my current position I had been doing the same job since 2007 and in fact my previous role was more complex and I had more staff to manage. I also had extensive management experience and that can be seen throughout my level of experience. I would challenge anyone who suggests that I am not qualified to do the role I was employed to do.

7. In relation to performance I prided myself on running an efficient service, we had very few customer complaints, the staff worked well with me and I worked well with them. My attendance was excellent, my service although broken was linked and I think that my previous service should have been taken into account as it was not my fault I was transferred under the TUPE process. I had no disciplinary history.

8. I can only describe the consultation process as a tick box exercise. I had nothing to say because I did not know how I was being scored and who was in my pool for redundancy. I now refer you to the document that I only received after my appeal hearing had concluded and when I was advised that I had no further right of appeal. I refer the appeal outcome letter that clearly shows this was the case. It scores me under the skills section not acceptable. The criteria is training courses or from experience with CP PLC or elsewhere. I had a great deal of experience with CP PLC previously and elsewhere doing the identical job at a much higher level. I would say my score should have been exceptional. I would also point out that it lists my job as a customer service advisor; that really worries me I am a team leader not a customer service advisor. It is dated 22nd March yet it takes them until 20th April to send it to me. My last consultation meeting took place on the 22nd March. That is the date when apparently I was scored. The question is did the scoring take place before or after this meeting. Mr Smith provides no information to me at this meeting about my scores, he asks me no questions about my experience.

9. How can this process I say amount to meaningful consultation?

10. I was in a position where I was fighting in the dark. I had no idea what reason I was scored down on to cause me to be made redundant. I only obtained this information after my appeal. It was in my view that they were deliberately concealing my scores because they could not fairly justify them until I had had my appeal.

11. Since I now have had sight of the criteria and my scores and the apparent reasons for the scores I would make the following comments under each criteria head;

12. **Skills and Knowledge for the current Position/Job**

    I had several years experience in the role. So I clearly had the relevant skills to do the job I was employed to do at Guildshire. The criteria refer to experience with CP PLC or elsewhere. The criteria does not ask about performance in my role; it clearly excluded that the score should be based on the actual skills and experience in the role. I have skills and other positions that would cover knowledge of other systems in other sites (p 40). I refer to the reasons (p 41-42). I am scored down because of a perceived lack of knowledge on the different parking system at used at the other two stations. Firstly that was not the site I was employed at. If the other team leaders attended my site they couldn't operate the machines on my site easily either. The criteria are irrelevant to the job I was employed at. Secondly on the occasions I attended at these sites I gained a working knowledge of this system and familiarised myself with it. I just hadn't been formally trained on it because it was not my normal site. To score me at one was frankly an insult with my level of experience and cannot be justified according to the criteria. A fairer score would have been 4.

13. **Performance**

    The site ran efficiently. Problems were always solved at the site without the need for outside help. No examples are given of how I do not solve problems. This is simply rubbish and is not supported by proof. I am scored 2 and yet if you now look at my Comparators you will note that basically this is an assessment based purely on the perception of the person scoring. It is not based on any evidence. I was well respected, problems solved and I always met what was asked of me yet I only score 2? (p 43-46).

14. **Skills for other positions and jobs**

    I had done the job previously. I had helped set up the systems at one of the other stations and I was familiar with all necessary skills apart from being formally trained on the different parking system. Again a score of 4 would have been appropriate.

15. In my view the scorer didn't apply the criteria correctly or provide evidence to support his conclusions. The scores were in effect one person's preferences.

16. In relation to length of service they could for example have considered my previous service which was only broken because of Tupe. You will note that I am scored below Good on all aspects and only scored exceptional when all those comparators are scored the same.

17. In conclusion the consultation process was in my view a tick box process, I expected to be given at some point my scores and the criteria and an explanation with evidence of how my scores had been arrived at. This didn't happen. I had been through a similar process in the past and it had happened on that occasion. My second one to one dealt with internal vacancies, how to apply etc. At this point though I was at risk I didn't know I was selected so I had no real comments. My third one to one dealt with the criteria that was to be used but the scoring was not yet done. It was on 25th March I was told I was selected for redundancy and that I was dismissed. At no time during the consultation could I know of or discuss my actual scores. I was shocked that I had been selected and became ill with stress at work. I appealed verbally and confirmed it in writing. I also applied for the more junior role at Ashford. I was unsuccessful despite having managed staff which really was humiliating. I submitted details of my appeal. You will note that I specifically refer in my appeal to not being shown the scoring. At the time of preparing this statement the respondents have not produced the minutes of the appeal. In the appeal I clearly said that I had no opportunity to put my case and that I should have the scores. Despite making this clear in my appeal letter they still had not bothered to show me my scores. The whole process was unfair and predetermined. At the appeal I recall being told that the appeal would be adjourned so I could get my scores and then once I had them it would be reconvened so that I could put my points.

18. That's not what happened I get instead a decision with my scores and the letter makes it clear the process is over (p 58).

19. I consider that the process was completely unfair and that if a fair process had taken place I would not have been selected for redundancy. I consider that when I received my scores after the process concluded it showed me that this was simply Mr Smith taking a personal view on me and it had little or nothing to do with the evidence.

20. In relation to steps of mitigation I would say as follows. I was sick with work related stress for approximately 3 weeks after my dismissal. I then signed on for Job Seekers Allowance. I looked at various job agencies but I could find little to apply for so I decided to seek work via the Job Centre via newspapers and through online web sites.

21. As you will see I looked at a wage spectrum of jobs in the junior management level. I have also obtained job details via an ex forces agency. I have had five interviews to date. The first was in mid-April with a security firm. I was then interviewed on 14th July for the position of Department Manager at Parkhome Leisure.

22. The third was an interview for a company called Petrol Services as an account manager. The fourth was for the position of Facilities Manager at Dupont College Guildshire on the 3rd of August. I have also recently been interviewed on 20th September for the position of assistant Project Manager. I have been unsuccessful in all my interviews.

23. I have tried for jobs with salaries as low as 14,000 pounds.

24. I refer to the various positions I have applied for and the documents in support of the same.

25. In conclusion this Statement is true to the best of my knowledge and belief.

Mr J Gold v Car Parking PLC

Case number: 123456/2011

STATEMENT OF EVIDENCE OF MARTIN SMITH

My name is Martin Smith

1. I am employed by the Respondent as Contract Manager. I have worked in that capacity since November 2008. For 6 months prior to this I was acting as Duty Manager to become familiar with the role. At the time of the Claimant's dismissal I was responsible for the car parks attached to the 'First Contract' three rail stations. I have experience of the CP PLC dismissal procedures and have received a one day training course on the company dismissal procedures.

2. The claimant worked as a Team Leader at the CP PLC car parks in Guildshire International. The Claimant was employed from 9th November 2009 until 30th April 2011, when he was dismissed by reason of redundancy. His contract appears at page 24 to 26 of the bundle. The Claimant was always located at Guildshire International apart from when he was required to cover a Team Leader at one of the other sites. I am aware that the Claimant had previously worked for the Respondent but this was before my time.

3. On 16th February 2011, I invited the Claimant and his two colleagues to a meeting on 21st February 2011 about proposed changes to the workplace. My letter appears at page 27 of the bundle.

4. There were three Team Leaders, including the Claimant. In order to increase focus and accountability and to reduce the overhead cost, the business proposed to reduce the Team Leaders to two. The two would be expected to cover the three stations. The three Team Leaders were told of the proposal and were informed that they were at risk of redundancy and would be consulted individually. The announcement appears at page 28 of the bundle. I read this out to them when they were all together.

5. I, along with Jack Tawse, from the Human Resources department, conducted the first consultation with the Claimant on 23rd February 2011. My letter inviting the Claimant to that meeting appears at page 29 of the bundle.

6. The restructuring proposed was discussed, along with the process of consultation and selection. The Claimant was told that a process of selection would determine which one of the three Team Leaders would be at risk of redundancy. He was told the selection would be by way of a desk top exercise. In front of me during the meeting was the template criteria for selection for redundancy which appears at page 38-39 of the bundle. I explained the criteria that were to be used. The Claimant had no question or comment and in fact said he had been through the process four times before. To me that meant he was familiar with the process which is why he did not ask any questions. The notes of the meeting appear at page 30-33 of the bundle. I followed the same format for the other two Team Leaders who were at risk.

7. A second consultative meeting took place with the Claimant on 7th March 2011. My invitation to him appears at page 34 of the bundle. At this point I had not conducted the desk top selection exercise. But I went through with him other opportunities that were available in CP PLC. It followed the same process with all three of the Team leaders who were at risk. The Claimant was asked whether he had any questions or comments. He did not. He was given estimates of the payments that he would receive if he were made redundant. He was told about the internal vacancies. The Claimant had no questions outstanding. The notes of the meeting appear at page 35 of the bundle. At that meeting we did not discuss the selection process any further.

8. A third meeting took place on 22nd March 2011. The invitation appears at page 36 of the bundle. The Claimant again had no comments or questions. The notes of the meeting are at page 37 of the bundle. I confirmed to him and the other two Team Leaders that I would now conduct the desk top selection exercise.

9. So, on 22nd March 2011, I undertook to score the Claimant and his two colleagues against the following criteria:

    Skills for the current position/job

    Performance

    Skills for other positions/jobs with NCP

    Length of service

    Disciplinary record

    They were rated as follows:

Not acceptable/incomplete	1
Acceptable	2
Good	4
Exceptional	5

    The Claimant scored 16.

    The Claimant's colleagues scored 18 and 24.

    Whilst I was scoring the candidates I was looking at suitability for the job going forward. There was to be two team leaders covering the three sites. One of the requirements would be to produce compliance and audit documentation which unfortunately the Claimant did not do to the extent of the other Team Leaders. Unfortunately the Claimant's primary experience was at Ashford International only. The other two Team Leaders had experience at the other sites. In addition the Claimant had only be in post since November 2009.

    The scoring charts appear at pages 40-46 of the bundle.

10. Before I met with the three Team leaders again I sent the scoring assessment that I had done on each to Dave Hirst, Head of Operations to review what I had done. He confirmed to me that it was in order and I arranged to see the three Team Leaders to confirm the outcome.

11. At the next consultative meeting on 25th March 2011 I informed the Claimant that, because he had recorded the lowest score, he was at risk of redundancy. He was served with the notice that his employment would be terminated on 30th April 2011, unless alternative employment could be found. The letter inviting the Claimant to the meeting appears at page 47 of the bundle and the letters confirming that he was at risk of redundancy and giving notice of redundancy appears at page 48-49 of the bundle. I would have sent him both letters dated 25th March 2011. One confirms that the position of Team leader that he held was redundant and the other was a personal letter to the Claimant giving him notice of redundancy including details of his right of appeal.

12. At the meeting I told the Claimant he had been selected for redundancy. I had the scoring sheet in front of me. But unfortunately the Claimant said a few words and stood up and walked out of the office. I was unable to provide him with any more details of the scoring as he had left. Jack Tawse from Human Resources was also present during the meeting.

13. That was the last I heard until Dave Hirst asked me for the details of the scoring process and the consultation process. I gave Dave the relevant paperwork.

14. I understand that the Claimant has said that he was unable to challenge the scores that I gave him in the desk top selection exercise. Firstly I would say that the Claimant did not contribute to any of the meetings that I had with him. Secondly I would say that the scores would not have changed. His length of service is a fact. And it was a fact that he did not have certain skills required for the job going forward. So, even if he had raised an objection his scores would have remained the same.

15. This statement is true to the best of my knowledge and belief.

Signed   M Smith

Dated 27.10.11

Mr J Gold v Car Parking PLC

Case number: 123456/2011

STATEMENT OF EVIDENCE OF JACK TAWSE

My name is Jack Tawse

1. I am employed by the Respondent as Human Resources Business Partner. I have worked in that capacity for just over 16 months. I started with respondent around 2009 when I joined as Human Resources Policy Manager. As Human Resources Business Partner I provide HR support and advice to the managers in the area.

2. The Respondent does not have a Redundancy Policy. The approach adopted will depend upon the particular circumstances. We have been involved in situations which have required collective consultation as well as individual consultation in the past.

3. I provided Human Resources advice and assistance throughout the process of consultation, selection, dismissal and appeal in relation to the Claimant.

4. I am providing this evidence as the Employment Tribunal refused to postpone the hearing when it learnt that Dave Hirst, the manager hearing the appeal, was unavailable. I was present during the appeal hearing to provide HR advice to Dave Hirst.

5. I was involved in the first consultation meeting with the Claimant. I do recall Martin Smith going through the agenda items outlined at page 30 of the bundle. I also recall Martin Smith specifically explaining the desk top selection exercise to the Claimant and the other two Team Leaders. At that stage we were seeking comments from the Team Leaders about the proposal itself and selection methodology proposed. The Claimant had no comment to make.

6. I was also involved in the meeting on 25th March 2011 with the Claimant. Martin Smith confirmed that the Claimant had been selected for redundancy. The purpose of the meeting was to explain the selection process. But when the Claimant was informed that he had been selected, he said something along the lines of that he felt it had been a foregone conclusion and he left without Martin being able to explain his rationale and his scoring.

7. On 1st April 2011, after the Claimant received notification of his redundancy, he was off sick. The sick notes appear at pages 50-51of the bundle.

8. The Claimant appealed to Dave Hirst by letter dated 5th April 2011. It appears at page 52 of the bundle. In preparing for the Employment Tribunal proceedings I have discussed matters with Dave Hirst. After the Claimant appealed on 5th April 2011, he had been in touch with Dave Hirst and arranged to meet him informally. The Claimant was asking whether there were any openings in CP PLC in the south area. At that time all that Dave was aware of was a Mobile Support Officer. The Claimant said he would think about it and in the meantime confirmed that his letter of appeal dated 5th April 2011 should be ripped up. Dave Hirst became aware that the Claimant was not interested in the vacancy and wanted to pursue his appeal.

9. We then received the letter dated 11th April 2011. He said that:

    (a) he had shown unquestionable loyalty

    (b) he carried out all instructions, often going beyond what was asked of him

    (c) he had built a strong team in Ashford with limited support from Ebbsfleet

    (d) he had had to query why a number of his staff were not receiving their expenses, some of which were outstanding

    (e) he had supported the staff team at night and at weekends when proper cover could not be found

    (f) he had been working 'on-call' without receiving any payment

    (g) he had not been shown the scoring process

    (h) he thought that there would be more work not less, so could not understand the reduction in the staff.

The Claimant's letter appears at page 54 of the bundle.

10. Dave Hirst, the Head of Operations, conducted the appeal hearing on 20th April 2011. The invitation appears at page 55 of the bundle. I was present.

11. I accept that there are no notes of the appeal hearing. It was a quick meeting. During the appeal the Claimant confirmed that he was satisfied with the process, but his main concern was not having received details of what he scored. These were shown to him at the appeal hearing. But he said nothing. He said he did not have a copy so it was agreed a copy would be sent to him by post, which is what was done.

12. I recall however that Dave did take the opportunity to review the scores not least because he was surprised that it had been the Claimant who had had the lowest score. But when looking at the scores and the rationale that Martin Smith had given, Dave was satisfied that they had been correct.

13. So, on appeal, the dismissal was upheld. Unfortunately, no alternative employment acceptable to the Claimant could be found.

14. The outcome letter appears at page 58 of the bundle.

15. Overall, I would say that the Claimant was a good employee and had the business not been in a position where it needed to reduce numbers he would have still been employed. It had not been a foregone conclusion. It had been a fair process and each Team Leader was assessed objectively and fairly. It was unfortunate that the Claimant's score was the lowest.

16. This statement is true to the best of my knowledge and belief.

Signed J *Tawse*

Dated 27.10.11

EMPLOYMENT TRIBUNALS

Case No. 123456/2011

BETWEEN

Mr J Gold   Claimant

and

Car Parking PLC   Respondent

Held at Guildshire on   27 October 2011

Representation   **Claimant:**   Mr T Robinson, Non practising Barrister
                           Respondent: Ms R Bates, Counsel

Employment Judge   Smith-Jones

Members: Mr N Amin
                                          Mr D Forge

JUDGMENT

It was the unanimous decision of the Tribunal that the Claimant was unfairly dismissed by the Respondent.

REASONS

Introduction

1.   The Tribunal convened on 27 October 2011 to hear the Claimant's claim, as set out in his ET1 / Claim Form submitted on 22 June 2011 of unfair dismissal, namely that the Respondent had followed a flawed procedure when selecting him for redundancy, particularly with regard to the consultation and selection process adopted. The Respondent in its ET3 denied this claim. It submitted that the Claimant was dismissed for a fair reason, namely redundancy, following a reorganisation in response to a need to reduce operational costs. Further, it said that it acted reasonably within the meaning of section 98(4) ERA 1996. In particular, the Respondent said it carried out a fair consultation and selection procedure and explored options for alternative employment. There was no dispute that the Claimant had been dismissed. It was indicated at the commencement of the hearing by Mr Robinson that it was accepted that the dismissal was by reason of redundancy.

Issues

2.   The matter was listed before us as a full merits hearing. The principal issues for us to determine were whether, in accordance with the principles set out in *Polkey v AE Dayton Ltd* [1988] ICR 142, the Respondent had:
     (a)   Warned and consulted with the Claimant
     (b)   Adopted a fair basis for selection, fairly applied
     (c)   Taken such steps as may be reasonable to avoid or minimise redundancy

3.   If we found that there was an unfair dismissal, then it would be necessary to consider what remedy was appropriate.

Witnesses/evidence

4. The Claimant provided a witness statement, which was taken as read. The Respondent's representative had the opportunity to cross-examine him and the Tribunal was able to ask questions of its own. On behalf of the Respondent, witness statements were provided on behalf of Mr Martin Smith (Contract Manager) and Mr Jack Tawse (Human Resources Business Partner (South) who provided Human Resources advice and assistance to the Respondent with regard to the consultation, selection, dismissal and appeal of the Claimant). Both witness statements were taken as read by the Tribunal. The Claimant's representative had the opportunity to cross-examine them and the Tribunal was able to ask questions of its own.

5. The Tribunal also had an agreed paginated bundle of documents. Where a number appears in brackets in this Judgment [ ] that is a reference to a page in this bundle. There was also a separate bundle of additional documents provided relating to the Claimant's job search and the issue of mitigation.

6. Both representatives made short oral submissions at the close of the evidence. Both parties' submissions are summarised below. A brief oral judgment on liability and some matters of principle on remedy was given at the end of the hearing. This document formally records that judgment and gives the reasons for it. The parties subsequently agreed the remedy between themselves.

Brief Summary of Facts

7. Mr Gold was employed as a Team Leader at the Respondent's car park at Guildshire, with effect from 9th November 2009. The Claimant was primarily based at Guildshire but was one of three Team Leaders covering three stations. He was required to cover at the other sites from time to time. A different (and older) technology system was employed by CP PLC to manage the car parking at Guildshire than was used at the other two sites.

8. In early 2011, in order to increase focus and accountability and to reduce over head costs, a decision was taken by the Respondent to reduce the Team Leaders from three to two. On 16th February 2011, Mr Smith invited the Claimant and his two colleagues to a meeting on 21st February to discuss proposed changes to the workplace [27]. At that meeting, they were told of this proposal, informed that they were at risk and would be consulted individually [28]. The same procedure was followed with regard to each of the three Team Leaders.

9. On 23rd February, a first consultation meeting took place with the Claimant, conducted by Mr Smith, accompanied by Mr Tawse [29, 30–33]. At this meeting, the restructuring was discussed, along with the proposed process for consultation and selection. The Claimant was told what the selection criteria were [38–39]. These included skills for the current job, performance skills for other jobs within CP PLC, length of service and disciplinary record. The Claimant made no comment. A second consultation meeting with the Claimant took place on 7th March [34, 35]. Possible vacancies were discussed and the Claimant was given estimates of any payments he might receive were he to be made redundant.

10. A third consultation meeting took place on 22nd March [36, 37]. Following this meeting, Mr Smith conducted a selection procedure using the selection criteria referred to above. He carried out this exercise on his own using his personal knowledge and expertise of the three Team Leaders along with information from their personnel files. The Claimant was scored with the lowest mark of the three Team Leaders. Mr Smith's evidence was that while he was conducting the scoring he was looking at suitability going forward. There was not a revised job description for the new posts. Under the reorganised structure, it would however be necessary for a Team Leader to have responsibility for all three sites, and knowledge of and ability to use the system in place at the other two sites was deemed by Mr Smith to be essential. On any analysis. the Claimant had less experience of this system than the other two team leaders and would require training to operate it. Mr Smith thought such training might take a week and

approximately a month on the job to assimilate it. He did not discuss this with the Claimant. The Claimant was given lower marks than his colleagues on the skills for the current job, performance, and skills for other jobs criteria. He also had less continuous service than the other Team Leaders [40–46].

11. A further meeting was held with the Claimant on 25th March [27]. He was informed that he had received the lowest score and was therefore at risk of redundancy. He was subsequently sent letters confirming he was at risk of redundancy [48] and was given notice including his right of appeal [49]. The Claimant stood up and left the meeting shortly after being told he had received the lowest score. Mr Smith said he was ready to give the Claimant his score but was unable to because the Claimant left the meeting.

12. The Claimant was signed off sick shortly afterwards [80–81]. He appealed the decision to dismiss him by letter dated 5th April [52] and subsequently by letter dated 11 April [54]. In his letter of appeal, the Claimant said, amongst a number of points, that he had not been shown the scoring process.

13. An appeal hearing was conducted by Mr Hirst on 20th April [55]. There are no notes of this meeting. It was not disputed that the meeting did not last long. The Claimant was told his scores, and these were later sent to him by post. No alternative employment was available. The Claimant rejected a lower grade job and there were no other suitable internal vacancies.

Claimant's Submissions

14. Mr Robinson submitted that the Respondent had not followed a fair and objective selection procedure. He submitted there was an unfair assessment of the Claimant's capabilities, and also that the consultation exercise was inadequate because no opportunity was given to the Claimant to discuss or challenge his scores. On this basis, he said the Claimant's dismissal was unfair. He had no issue with the pool of the three team leaders but said that the criteria were not fairly applied to the Claimant. The three consultation meetings all predated the scoring exercise. The meeting after it had been completed was a fait accompli – the Claimant was told he was dismissed. There was no meaningful consultation after the decision to dismiss had been taken. The Claimant was not shown the notes of the selection at the appeal and there was no opportunity given to him to embark on any meaningful review at that stage. Further, the scoring adopted was very subjective and appeared to be based on penalising the Claimant for lacking future skills, although the first criteria was only about his current skills. Although the Claimant was offered an alternative job this was a demotion and he was not obliged to accept it in order to mitigate his position.

15. Mr Hughes referred the Tribunal to E-ZEC Medical Transport Services Ltd v Gregory (UKEAT/0192/08) (a case where the EAT upheld a finding by an employment tribunal that a subjective marking system without prior consultation had led to a finding of unfair dismissal; and where a tribunal had found on the facts that a meeting which had been described as a consultation meeting was in essence a meeting to impart the scores and not to review the process); and Budenberg Gauge Co Ltd v Griffiths (UKEAT/43/93 and 162/93) (an appeal against a tribunal finding of unfairness centering around the use of selection criteria used in a redundancy exercise, where the Claimant was not shown her scores and was therefore unable to comment on them).

Respondent's Submissions

16. Ms Bates on behalf of the Respondent submitted that the Claimant was dismissed for a fair reason relating to redundancy. There was an economic / operational need to reduce the number of Team leaders from 3 to 2. The job had not changed but the individuals doing it needed to be more diverse. It was about capability going forwards. There was a group notification, followed by three separate consultation meetings. The selection criteria were put to Mr Gold and he raised no objection to them. They were objective. Mr Smith was the best placed manager to carry out the selection process. Unfortunately because the Claimant lacked experience of the newer parking system and he had less service, he was scored lower. Lack of experience on that system was a fair criteria for

him to use. He had given Mr Gold proper credit for his previous experience. Because Mr Gold walked out of the meeting telling him about this, there was no opportunity to give him his scores. The issue was revisited on appeal but the decision was upheld by Mr Hirst. She submitted that there was a fair and reasonable procedure and proper consultation and full discussion about all relevant matters. There were no other suitable equivalent vacancies but the Claimant had been offered employment, albeit of a lower status, but he had not wanted to take it. Ms Bates referred the Tribunal to the cases of *Buchanon v Tilcon* [1983] IRLR 417 and *British Airways v Greene*.

The law

Unfair dismissal – reason

17. Where there is a dismissal, an employer has to prove, in the sense that the burden of proof is on it, that the reason for the dismissal falls within one of the potentially fair categories listed in section 98 ERA 1996. These include redundancy. Where there is a potentially fair reason for dismissal, a tribunal must decide whether the employer acted reasonably or unreasonably in treating that as a sufficient reason for dismissal.

18. So far as material, section 98 ERA 1996 provides:

>   98   '(1)   In determining for the purposes of this Part whether the dismissal of an employee is fair or unfair, it is for the employer to show–
>
>   (a)   the reason (or, if more than one, the principal reason) for the dismissal, and
>
>   (b)   that it is either a reason failing within subsection (2) ...
>
>   (2)   A reason falls within this subsection if it ...
>
>   (c)   is that the employee is redundant, ...'

19. It was said by Cairns LJ in *Abernethy v Mott Hay & Anderson* [1974] IRLR 213, at 215 that,

>   'A reason for the dismissal of an employee is a set of facts known to the employer, or it may be a set of beliefs held by him, which cause him to dismiss the employee.'

It is not for the employment tribunal to consider the substance of the employer's reasons at the section 98(1)(b) stage (provided they are more than '*whimsical or capricious*' [*Harper v National Coal Board* [1998] IRLR 260 at para 8, referred to in *Scott v Richardson* at paragraph 17]). As Griffiths LJ observed in *Kent County Council v Gilham* [1985] ICR 233, if on the face of it the employer's reason could justify the dismissal, then it passes as a reason and the enquiry moves on to section 98(4) and the question of reasonableness.

20. The definition of redundancy is set out at section 139 ERA. This provides, as far as relevant:

>   '(1)   For the purposes of this Act an employee who is dismissed shall be taken to be dismissed by reason of redundancy if the dismissal is wholly or mainly attributable to–
>
>   (a)   the fact that his employer has ceased or intends to cease–
>
>   (i)   to carry on the business for the purposes of which the employee was employed by him, or
>
>   (ii)   to carry on that business in the place where the employee was so employed, or
>
>   (b)   the fact that the requirements of that business–
>
>   (i)   for employees to carry out work of a particular kind, or
>
>   (ii)   for employees to carry out work of a particular kind in the place where the employee was employed by the employer,
>
>   have ceased or diminished or are expected to cease or diminish'.

Unfair dismissal – reasonableness

21. Where there is a potentially fair reason for dismissal, a tribunal must then go on to decide whether the employer acted reasonably or unreasonably in treating that potentially fair reason as a sufficient reason for dismissal of the employee. The material statutory provisions are set out in section 98(4) Employment Rights Act 1996, which, so far as relevant, are as follows:

'(4)   Where the employer has fulfilled the requirements of subsection (1), the determination of the question whether the dismissal is fair or unfair (having regard to the reason shown by the employer)–

(a)   depends on whether in the circumstances (including the size and administrative resources of the employer's undertaking) the employer acted reasonably or unreasonably in treating it as a sufficient reason for dismissing the employee, and

(b)   shall be determined in accordance with equity and the substantial merits of the case.'

22.   *Iceland Frozen Foods v Jones* [1982] IRLR 439 (as confirmed by the Court of Appeal in the joined cases of *HSBC (formerly Midland Bank) v Madden and Post Office v Foley* [2000] IRLR 827), sets out that 'a decision to dismiss must be within the band of reasonable responses which a reasonable employer might have adopted'. Tribunals should not, when considering these matters, look at what they would have done but should judge, on the basis of the range of reasonable responses test, what the employers actually did. The appropriate test is whether the dismissal of the Claimant lay within the range of conduct that a reasonable employer could have adopted. The EAT, in *Sheffield Health and Social Care NHS Foundation Trust v Crabtree* (UKEAT/0331/09), reminded Employment Tribunals that the burden of proof under s 98 (4) is neutral.

Unfair dismissal – procedural fairness in a redundancy situation

23.   In a redundancy case, the procedural circumstances identified in numerous cases including *Williams v Compair Maxam* [1982] IRLR 83, *Polkey v A E Dayton Services Ltd* [1987] IRLR 503 and as emphasised by the EAT in *Mugford v Midland Bank plc* [1997] IRLR 208, need to be considered. The principles which were put forward in *Williams* as generally accepted principles (where employees are represented by an independent union but have since been recognised as having more general application – see for example *Freud v Bentalls* [1982] IRLR 443 where it was held that the same principles would apply to a workplace where there was no trade union) were –

'1.   The employer will seek to give as much warning as possible of impending redundancies so as to enable the union and employees who may be affected to take early steps to inform themselves of the relevant facts, consider possible alternative solutions and, if necessary, find alternative employment in the undertaking or elsewhere.

2.   The employer will consult the union as to the best means by which the desired management result can be achieved fairly and with as little hardship to the employees as possible. In particular, the employer will seek to agree with the union the criteria to be applied in selecting the employees to be made redundant. When a selection has been made, the employer will consider with the union whether the selection has been made in accordance with those criteria.

3.   Whether or not an agreement as to the criteria to be adopted has been agreed with the union, the employer will seek to establish criteria for selection which so far as possible do not depend solely upon the opinion of the person making the selection but can be objectively checked against such things as attendance record, efficiency at the job, experience, or length of service.

4.   The employer will seek to ensure that the selection is made fairly in accordance with these criteria and will consider any representations the union may make as to such selection.

5.   The employer will seek to see whether instead of dismissing an employee he could offer him alternative employment.'

24.   In particular, the appropriate test of fairness under s 98(4) ERA 1996 in a redundancy situation was that an employer would be expected to (i) sufficiently warn and consult affected employees (unless the tribunal finds that the employer acted reasonably in taking the view that, in the exceptional circumstances of the case, consultation or warning would be 'utterly useless'); (ii) adopted a fair (objective) basis on which to select for redundancy; and (iii) take such steps as may be reasonable to avoid or minimise redundancy by redeployment within its own organisation. A failure to act in accordance with one of these does not necessarily mean a dismissal is unfair: the

tribunal must consider this in the light of the circumstances known to the employer at the time he dismissed the employee. Issues of fairness and reasonableness need to be judged by reference to the 'range of reasonable responses' test (see *Beddell v West Ferry Printers* [2000] ICR 1263).

25. Warning and consultation. Consultation should be 'genuine and meaningful'. Case law has established that, for redundancy dismissals to be fair, the employer must usually warn employees of the possibility of redundancy and then consult individually with them before reaching any conclusion regarding their dismissal. This rule is not absolute, and the courts have repeatedly stressed that a procedural failure does not inevitably lead to a finding of unfair dismissal. Rather, tribunals must focus on the overall picture when determining whether, in the particular case, the employer has acted reasonably in dismissing.

26. It is unclear on the authorities as to whether there are separate obligations of warning and consultation. In *Rowell v Hubbard Group Services Ltd* [1995] IRLR 195, the EAT said there were separate obligations to warn and consult. However, in *Coney Island Ltd v Eikouil* [2002] IRLR 174, the EAT, which was referred to *Rowell* as well as to *Compair Maxam* and *Polkey*, held that there is no separate duty to warn and that warning and consultation are part and parcel of one single process of consultation which begins with the employee being given notice that he is at risk. On either analysis, whether these are separate duties or combined, it is clear that a tribunal should look at whether, in all the circumstances, adequate and reasonable warning of impending redundancy has been given and should consider whether there has been fair and adequate consultation.

27. Consultation involves giving the person consulted a fair and proper opportunity to understand fully the matters about which he is being consulted, and to express their views on those subjects, with the consultor thereafter considering those views properly and genuinely. It would appear that employees themselves may sometimes have a responsibility to ensure the effectiveness of such consultation as does take place.

28. Criteria for selection. In *Drake International Systems Ltd v O'Hare* (UKEAT/0384103), the EAT emphasised that tribunals should not impose their own views as to the reasonableness of the selection criteria or the implementation of the criteria: the correct question was whether the selection was one that a reasonable employer acting reasonably could have made.

29. One distinction which case law has determined since *Williams* is that there is a distinction between an exercise which is selecting for redundancy from within an existing group – ie is looking solely at reducing numbers and an exercise which is seeking to achieve that by selecting for a new role. Where an employer has to decide which employees from a pool of existing employees are to be made redundant, the criteria will reflect a known job, performed by known employees over a period. Where, however, an employer has to appoint to new roles after a re-organisation, the employer's decision must of necessity be forward-looking. It is likely to centre upon an assessment of the ability of the individual to perform in the new role. In *Akzo Coatings v Thompson* (EAT/117/94) His Honour Judge Peter Clark said:

> 'There is, in our judgment, a world of difference between the way in which an employer approaches selection for dismissal in a redundancy pool where some will be retained and others dismissed. It is to that exercise which points 2-4 in the *Williams* guidelines are directed. These observations have no application when considering whether the employer has taken reasonable steps to look for alternative employment.'

30. In *Ball v Balfour Kilpatrick Ltd* (EAT/823/95) His Honour Judge Smith said that there is no rule of law that selection criteria must be exclusively objective. He went on to say:

> 'It is clear on the authority of *Akzo Coatings Plc v Thompson and Others* [1996] EAT (unreported) that the touchstone in such a situation is reasonableness rather than the application of either agreed selection criteria for redundancy or the application of objective criteria.'

31. In *Darlington Memorial Hospital NHS Trust v Edwards and Vincent* (EAT/678/95) His Honour Judge Hull said:

'If these are new posts with a different job description from anything which the various Applicants brought to them, then it seems to us that the employer is most certainly not under a duty to carry out something very like the exercise which he has to carry out in deciding who to select for redundancy. On the contrary, if he is to be allowed to manage his business, he must select as he thinks right. If he tells the employees that they will be allowed to apply for new jobs, as was manifestly the case here, then of course he will be required to carry out the exercise in good faith. If they are to be allowed to apply their applications must be considered properly. If the criteria are different from the old jobs so be it, that was part of the original occasion of redundancy, it was as much reorganisation as redundancy, although redundancy was the result. But to say that they are the same process and that it must be based on similar principles is quite simply, in our view, wrong. It may be, we are not going to decide this, that the duty goes beyond faith, and it may be said that there is some sort of duty of care, but there it is, it is something which the employer has said he will do and he must do it. He must consider the applicants.'

32. Another difficult question for tribunals is to decide the extent to which they should examine the marking that has been applied in a selection exercise. The EAT and the courts have considered on a number of occasions the principles that pertain to the investigation of marking and scores in a redundancy exercise and have made clear that close scrutiny is inappropriate. What is in issue is the question of fairness of the selection procedure and marking should only be investigated where there are exceptional circumstances such as bias or obvious mistake: see *Eaton v King* [1995] IRLR 75 (subsequently upheld by the Court of Session). Lord Coulsfield observed at paragraph 11 that:

'every redundancy situation is one of distress for employees who are affected: and every redundancy situation is one in which hard decisions have to be made. It is, however, essential to remember that what is required of the employer is that he should act reasonably'

33. Further guidance is to be found in *British Aerospace plc v Green* [1995] IRLR 433:

'13.   The whole tenor of the authorities to which I have already referred is to show, in both England and Scotland, the courts and tribunals (with substantial contribution from the lay membership of the latter) moving towards a clear recognition that if a graded assessment system is to achieve its purpose it must not be subjected to an over-minute analysis. That applies both at the stage when the system is being actually applied, and also at any later stage when its operation is being called into question before an industrial tribunal. To allow otherwise would involve a serious risk that the system itself would lose the respect with which it is at present regarded on both sides of industry, and that tribunal hearings would become hopelessly protracted.'

34. The judgment of Lord Johnston in relation to the issue of fair consultation (again in the context of a trade union consultation) in *John Brown Engineering v Brown Ltd* [1997] IRLR 90 is frequently cited. He started by referring to the judgment of Glidewell LJ in *R v British Coal Corporation, ex Parte Price and Others* [1994] IRLR 72:

'Fair consultation means:

(a)   consultation when the proposals are still at a formative stage;

(b)   adequate information on which to respond;

(c)   adequate time in which to respond;

(d)   conscientious consideration by an authority of a response to consultation.

Another way of putting the point more shortly is that fair consultation involves giving the body consulted a fair and proper opportunity to understand fully the matters about which it is being consulted, and to express its views on those subjects, with the consultor thereafter considering those views properly and genuinely.'

35. Case law suggests that one of the requirements for fair consultation in a redundancy exercise involves giving an employee sufficient information about and explanation for his scoring so he understands it and has a meaningful chance to comment on and challenge it. See, for example, the two cases referred to by Mr Hughes (*E-ZEC Medical Transport Services Ltd v Gregory* (UKEAT/0192/08) and *Budenberg Gauge Co Ltd v Griffiths* (UKEAT/43/93 and 162/93). This was emphasised recently by the Court of Appeal in *Pinewood Repro Limited t/a County Print (County Print) v Page* (EAT/0028/10). In that case, the

employer agreed the selection criteria (attendance, quality, productivity, abilities, skills, experience, disciplinary record and flexibility) with the trade union, ensured that the scoring was carried out by two senior managers and gave the employee a right to appeal his selection for redundancy, but did not explain to Mr Page why he had received lower scores than the two other people in the selection pool. Mr Page was provided with a copy of his scores; he queried why he had been marked down for 'abilities, skills and experience' given his level of qualifications and 27 years experience. He also queried why he had been marked down for flexibility as he was 'as flexible as the next man.' He was given no explanation as to how the scores had been arrived at, being told only that 'we believe that the scores given by the assessors are responsible and appropriate'. On appeal, he was told that the employers were 'satisfied that the scoring was factual and correct'. A tribunal found that Mr Page had been unfairly dismissed. The EAT upheld their decision and took the opportunity to review the relevant authorities and, whilst cautioning against an impermissible 'microscopic analysis' of scoring by tribunals, indicated that, particularly with subjective criteria, employees should have sufficient information to understand their scores and an opportunity to challenge them. In *Dabson v David Cover & Sons*, (EAT/0374/2011), the EAT emphasised that when assessing the fairness of selection for redundancy, the marks awarded in the selection exercise should only be investigated in exceptional circumstances such as bias or obvious mistake.

36.   Alternative employment. Following the principle in *Polkey*, dismissal will not normally be regarded as a reasonable step on the employer's part unless he takes such steps as would be reasonable to avoid or minimise redundancy by way of redeployment within his organisation. In *Thomas & Betts Manufacturing Ltd v Harding* [1980] IRLR 255, the Court of Appeal ruled that an employer should do what he can so far as is reasonable to seek alternative work. This does not mean, as the EAT pointed out in *MDFI Ltd v Sussex* [1986] IRLR 126, that an employer is obliged by law to enquire about job opportunities elsewhere, and a failure will not necessarily render a dismissal unfair. It is all a question of what is reasonable in the context. It was established in *Williams* that as a matter of good industrial practice, managers should make reasonable efforts to look for alternative employment for employees before making them redundant. The NIRC in *Vokes Ltd v Bear* [1973] IRLR 353, said that an employer who had failed to investigate whether there were job vacancies within the group which might have been offered to an employee as an alternative to making him redundant, had behaved unfairly:

> 'The employer had not yet done that which in all fairness and reason he should do, namely to make the obvious attempt to see if Mr Bear could be placed somewhere else in this large group'.

37.   None of the cases go so far as to amount to a proposition that there was a duty to find alternative employment (see *Brush Electrical Machines Ltd v Guest* (1976) EAT 382/76). The duty under s 98(4) is to take reasonable steps to try and find alternative employment.

Conclusions

38.   The Claimant's claim was that he had been unfairly dismissed contrary to ss 94 and 98 of the Employment Rights Act 1996. There was no issue about the dismissal. We were satisfied that the exercise was genuinely implemented in an honest belief that it was the sensible way forward in order to achieve efficiencies and cost savings and was based on genuine commercial and operational reasons. We were satisfied that the definition of redundancy as per the three stage test identified particularly by the House of Lords in *Murray and another v Foyle Meats Limited* [1999] IRLR 562 was met. The Claimant did not, before the Tribunal, dispute the existence of a potential redundancy situation.

39.   We then moved on to look at fairness in three main areas, consultation, selection and the adequacy of searches with regard to alternatives to redundancy. We looked at the overall picture up to the date of termination to ascertain whether the employer has or has not acted reasonably in dismissing the employee on the grounds of redundancy.

40.   With regard to the consultation, and subject to what we have to say below on the selection scoring, our view was that what the Respondent did here was reasonable. Overall, we were satisfied that the efforts the Respondent made did fall within the range

of reasonable responses. There was, we felt, adequate warning, consultation about the impending redundancy situation, why it had arisen and how the Respondent was intending to deal with it and the opportunity was given to the Claimant to discuss these issues. There were several meetings about the redundancy situation with the Claimant. What was done, which is what we have to look at as far as the law is concerned, was not so inadequate in our judgment as to fall outside the range of reasonable responses test. So we did not feel that the consultation process per se was such as to give rise to unfair dismissal.

41.   We then moved on to consider the selection process. It is not for us, when we apply the range of reasonable responses test, to say what we would have done. We must look at what the Respondent actually did. In our view, the failure by the Respondent to give the Claimant his scores and to allow him an adequate opportunity to discuss them before indicating the finality of the decision that he was the one to be dismissed was unreasonable and fell outside the range of reasonable responses test. We bore in mind the Claimant's reaction to the meeting after the selection process had been concluded but we nonetheless felt that this meeting was not designed to be a meeting to discuss the scores as opposed to a meeting to tell the Claimant he had been selected and would be dismissed. This was borne out by the letters of 25th March [48, 49] – for example 'This desktop exercise has now been completed and unfortunately you have been selected for redundancy'. The Respondent could for example, have written to the Claimant after this meeting enclosing his scores and giving him an opportunity to discuss them before sending the letter of dismissal. We felt the lack of opportunity allowed to the Claimant to have a meaningful opportunity to contest his selection was not remedied by the appeal process, which still failed to allow the Claimant to engage in the process. Lack of consultation implies a loss of opportunity, not that the opportunity, if given, would have made necessarily any difference. We have not engaged in a remarking process but it was also in our judgment unfair that, in the circumstances in this case, Mr Smith applied criteria relating to what he regarded as future skills needed, when these were not on the face of it one of the criteria he was selecting under, so no-one was aware this was a relevant criteria and therefore did not have the opportunity to engage or challenge or discuss it; and further (as indicated from the analysis of the cases above), while there is nothing wrong in using future skills as a criteria where a new job is being proposed in this case, here there was no new job just the same job going forward. This could put another way be said to be a failure of the consultation process, in that consultation involves giving the person consulted a fair and proper opportunity to understand fully the matters about which he is being consulted, and to express their views on those subjects, with the consultor thereafter considering those views properly and genuinely. This did not happen in this case.

42.   In our assessment, what was done here was we felt sufficiently inadequate as to fall outside the range of reasonable responses test.

43.   On the third and final area, ie whether consideration was given to seeing if there was an alternative to making the Claimant redundant, on the facts, we were satisfied that the Claimant was provided with a list of vacancies and that neither he nor the Respondent identified any that might amount to suitable alternative employment opportunities within the Respondent. The opportunity offered was a clear demotion and could not be said to be a suitable alternative; we were satisfied that the vacancies mentioned by the Claimant were not available as at the date of his dismissal. We were satisfied that what was done was reasonable in the circumstances and fell within the range of reasonable responses test.

44.   Having looked at all these matters in the round, as well individually, on balance we were satisfied that the Respondent's failings in the areas identified above were such as to give rise to an unfair dismissal. On that basis, our overall finding was that this was an unfair dismissal on the grounds of redundancy.

45.   We went on to consider whether there should be any sort of *Polkey* deduction, on the basis of considering whether there was a chance that even had a fair procedure been

followed, the Claimant would still have been dismissed. This is always to some extent going to be a hypothetical exercise. However, we bore in mind that any unfairness that we have identified above with regard to the approach to and application of the selection criteria and discussion thereon may have resulted in different marks being applied to the others in the pool. Further, there were only three in the pool and one had to go. In addition, Mr Smith sent his scoring assessment to a third party, who was standing in for Dave Hirst, to review. He raised no concerns. Further, Mr Hirst had reviewed it and had identified no concerns such as to overturn it. On balance, we felt taking these matters into account there was still a chance that the Claimant might have been dismissed. We assessed that risk at 25%.

46. In the light of the findings indicated above, the parties subsequently reached an agreement between themselves as to the appropriate remedy. It was agreed that the proceedings would be stayed for a period of 14 days with liberty to restore if necessary. The Recoupment Regulations do not therefore arise for consideration.

Employment Judge Smith-Jones

Judgment and Reasons sent to the parties on 24 November 2011 and entered in the Register.

.... for Secretary of the Tribunals

EMPLOYMENT TRIBUNALS

To: Mr Fred Mclean
        Collaws Solicitors LLP
        20 The Street, Guildshire, GU12

        V Alavy
        Swallows & Co LLP
        12 High Street, Guildshire GU12

Date: 24 November 2011

Case Number: 123456/2011

<table>
<tr><td></td><td align="center">**Mr J Gold**</td><td align="right">**Claimant**</td></tr>
<tr><td></td><td align="center">v</td><td></td></tr>
<tr><td></td><td align="center">**Car Parking PLC**</td><td align="right">**Respondent**</td></tr>
</table>

EMPLOYMENT TRIBUNAL JUDGMENT

A copy of the Employment Tribunal's judgment is enclosed. There is important information in the booklet 'The Judgment' which you should read. The booklet can be found on our website at www.employmenttribunals,gov.uk/Publications/publications.htm. If you do not have access to the internet, paper copies can be obtained by telephoning the tribunal office dealing with the claim.

The Judgment booklet explains that you may request the employment tribunal to <u>review</u> a judgment or a decision. It also explains the <u>appeal</u> process to the Employment Appeal Tribunal including the strict 42 day time limit. These processes are quite different, and you will need to decide whether to follow either or both. Both are **subject to strict time** limits. <u>An application to *review* must be made within 14 days of the date the decision was sent to you. An application to *appeal* must generally be made within 42 days of the date the decision was sent to you; but there are exceptions: see the booklet.</u>

The booklet also explains about asking for written reasons for the judgment (if they are not included with the judgment). These will almost always be necessary if you wish to appeal. You must apply for reasons (if not included with the judgment) within 14 days of the date on which the judgment was sent. If you do so, the 42 day time limit for appeal runs from when these reasons were sent to you. Otherwise time runs from the date the judgment was sent to you or your representative.

For further information, it is important that you read the Judgment booklet. You may find further information about the EAT at www.employmentappeals.gov.uk. An appeal form can be obtained from the Employment Appeal Tribunal at: Audit House, 58 Victoria Embankment, London EC4Y ODS or in Scotland at 52 Melville Street, Edinburgh EH3 7HS.

Yours faithfully,

....

MISS R SMITH

For the Secretary of Employment Tribunals

INTEREST ON TRIBUNAL AWARDS

GUIDANCE NOTE

1. This guidance note should be read in conjunction with the booklet, which you received with your copy of the Tribunal's judgment.

2. The Employment Tribunals (Interest) Order 1990 provides for interest to be paid on employment tribunal awards (excluding discrimination or equal pay awards* or sums representing costs or expenses) if they remain wholly or partly unpaid after 42 days.

3. The 42 days run from the date on which the Tribunal's judgment is recorded as having been sent to the parties and is known as 'the relevant judgment day'. The date from which interest starts to accrue is the day immediately following the expiry of the 42 days period called 'the calculation day'. The dates of both the relevant judgment day and the calculation day that apply in your case are recorded on the Notice attached to the judgment. If you have received a judgment and subsequently request a reasons (see 'The Judgment' booklet) the date of the relevant judgment day will remain unchanged.

4. 'Interest' means simple interest accruing from day to day on such part of the sum of money awarded by the tribunal for the time being remaining unpaid. Interest does not accrue on deductions such as Tax and/or National Insurance Contributions that are to be paid to the appropriate authorities. Neither does interest accrue on any sums which the Secretary of State has claimed in a recoupment notice (see 'The Judgment' booklet).

5. Where the sum awarded is varied upon a review of the judgment by the Employment Tribunal or upon appeal to the Employment Appeal Tribunal or a higher appellate court, then interest will accrue in the same way (from 'the calculation day'), but on the award as varied by the higher court and not on the sum originally awarded by the Tribunal.

6. The Judgment booklet explains how employment tribunal awards are enforced. The interest element of an award is enforced in the same way.

---

* The Employment Tribunals (Interest on Awards in Discrimination Cases) Regulations 1996 prescribes the provisions for interest on awards made in discrimination and equal pay cases.

NOTICE

THE EMPLOYMENT TRIBUNALS (INTEREST) ORDER 1990

Tribunal case number(s): 123456/2011

Name of case(s): Mr J Gold v Car Parking PLC

The Employment Tribunals (Interest) Order 1990 provides that sums of money payable as a result of a judgment of an Employment Tribunal (excluding discrimination or equal pay awards or sums representing costs or expenses), shall carry interest where the sum remains unpaid on a day ('*the calculation day*') 42 days after the day ('*the relevant judgment day*') that the document containing the tribunal's judgment is recorded as having been sent to the parties.

The rate of interest payable is that specified in section 17 of the Judgments Act 1838 on the relevant judgment day. This is known as 'the stipulated rate of interest' and the rate applicable in your case is set out below.

The following information in respect of this case is provided by the Secretary of the Tribunals in accordance with the requirements of Article 12 of the Order-

'the relevant judgment day' is: 24 November 2011

'the calculation day' is: 5 January 2012

'the stipulated rate of interest' is: 8%

....

MISS R SMITH

For and on Behalf of the Secretary of the Tribunals

Appendix 3

Example Agenda for Case Management Discussion

Case No: **Target hearing date:**

AGENDA FOR
CASE MANAGEMENT DISCUSSION

Rules 10-13, 17 and 28
Employment Tribunals Rules of Procedure 2004

It will assist the conduct of the Case Management Discussion if each party or representative could complete this agenda, as far as possible and as relevant to the case. Send a completed copy to each other party and to the Tribunal in good time before the Case Management Discussion. An agreed agenda is particularly helpful.

1. Parties

1.1	Are the names of the parties correct?	
1.2	Should any person be joined as a respondent or party?	
1.3	Should any respondent be dismissed from the proceedings?	
1.4	Is this claim part of a multiple claim?	
1.5	Are there any claims that should be considered together or separately?	

2. The claim and response

2.1	What are the complaints or jurisdictions raised in the claim?	
2.2	Is there any application to amend the claim?	
2.3	Is there any application to amend the response?	
2.4	Is there any request for additional information?	
2.5	Has a statutory questionnaire been served and/or replied to (discrimination cases only)? Is leave to serve a statutory questionnaire sought? Why?	

Case No: **Target hearing date:**

3.   Remedy

3.1	If successful, what does the claimant seek by way of remedy?	
3.2	What is the value of the claim?	
3.3	Has a schedule of loss been prepared? Date for service?	
3.4	What mitigation of loss has occurred?	

4.   The issues

4.1	What are the issues or questions for the Tribunal to decide?	
4.2	Are there any preliminary issues or jurisdictional issues?	
4.3	Are there any issues under the Human Rights Act or EU Law?	
4.4	Should the parties or their representatives prepare a schedule of issues (to be approved by the Tribunal)? Dates?	

Case No: **Target hearing date:**

5.   Preliminary hearings

5.1	Is a further case management discussion required? What agenda? Time allocation? Dates?	
5.2	Is a pre-hearing review required? What applications or issues? Time allocation? Dates?	
5.3	Is any other type of interim or preliminary hearing required? What applications or issues? Time allocation? Dates?	

6.   Documents and expert evidence

6.1	Have lists of documents been exchanged? Date for mutual exchange of lists?	
6.2	Have documents been inspected or copies exchanged? Date for inspection or mutual exchange of copies? • for a preliminary hearing • for the Hearing	
6.3	Who will be responsible for preparing • draft index of documents? • the hearing bundles? Date for completion of this task?	
6.4	Is this a case in which medical evidence is required? Dates for • disclosure of medical records • agreeing any joint expert • agreeing any joint instructions • instructing any joint expert • any medical examination • producing any report • asking questions of any expert • making any concessions	
6.5	Is this a case in which any other expert evidence is required? Relevant dates?	
6.6	Are there any other disclosure requirements?	

Case No: **Target hearing date:**

7.   Witnesses

7.1	How many witnesses will each party call? Who are those witnesses? What is the relevance of their evidence?	
7.2	Are any witness orders required? Who are those witnesses? What is the relevance of their evidence?	
7.3	Should witness statements be prepared? Should exchange be on the same date? Dates for exchange? • for a preliminary hearing • for the Hearing	

8.   The hearing(s)

8.1	Time estimate for: • case management discussion • pre-hearing review • other preliminary hearing • Hearing	
8.2	Dates to avoid (with reasons)	
8.3	Hearing dates for: • case management discussion • pre-hearing review • other preliminary hearing • Hearing	
8.4	Is there an application for a private hearing (rule 16)? Why?	
8.5	Is there an application for a hearing (or part of one) via electronic communications (rule 15)? Why?	
8.6	Is a restricting reporting order (rule 50) or register deletion order (rule 49) required? Why?	

4

Case No: **Target hearing date:**

9.   Other preparation

9.1	Should there be admissions? Dates?	
9.2	Should there be agreed facts? Dates?	
9.3	Should there be a chronology? Dates?	
9.4	Should there be any other agreed document to aid the Tribunal? What? Dates?	
9.5	Should there be written submissions or skeleton arguments? Dates?	
9.6	Is reading time for the Tribunal required? Why?	
9.7	Does a party require further guidance on any matter of preparation?	
9.8	Are any reasonable adjustments required?	

10.   Judicial mediation

10.1	Is this a case that might be suitable for judicial mediation?	
10.2	Are the parties interested in the possibility of judicial mediation?	
10.3	JUDICIAL USE ONLY	If relevant, Judge to consider whether criteria for judicial mediation apply and then raise with the parties and record response. If necessary, give a direction for a response. Refer to REJ, if appropriate

11.   Any other matters

5

Index

ν